American Art Song and American Poetry

Second Edition

Ruth C. Friedberg
Robin Fisher

THE SCARECROW PRESS, INC.
Lanham • Toronto • Plymouth, UK
2012

Published by Scarecrow Press, Inc.
A wholly owned subsidiary of The Rowman & Littlefield Publishing Group, Inc.
4501 Forbes Boulevard, Suite 200, Lanham, Maryland 20706
www.rowman.com

Estover Road, Plymouth PL6 7PY, United Kingdom

British Library Cataloguing in Publication Information Available

Library of Congress Cataloging-in-Publication Data
Friedberg, Ruth C., 1928– author.
  American art song and American poetry / Ruth C. Friedberg, Robin Fisher. — Second edition.
     pages ; cm
  Includes bibliographical references and index.
  ISBN 978-0-8108-8174-7 (cloth : alk. paper)
  1. Songs—United States—History and criticism. I. Fisher, Robin, 1960– author. II. Title.
  ML2811.F75 2012
  782.421680973—dc23
                              2011052517

⊖™ The paper used in this publication meets the minimum requirements of American National Standard for Information Sciences—Permanence of Paper for Printed Library Materials, ANSI/NISO Z39.48-1992.

Printed in the United States of America

Contents

From the Authors

When the original three volumes of this work began to be published in the 1980s, little had been written about the American art song and even less about settings of American poetry. As a partial remedy, a study was undertaken that would treat American songs from MacDowell to the present with the intended focus on the interrelationships between the composer and the poet and the ways in which these had influenced the completed song. Pieces selected for inclusion had a dual function of being important contributions to the performing literature as well as illuminating some phase of America's cultural past.

In the second and third volumes of the first edition, it became possible to contact directly a number of living composers. In an effort to gain firsthand knowledge of their views on American art songs, many personal and telephone interviews were conducted, and letters and e-mails exchanged. These sources are all annotated in the notes following each chapter.

In the past twenty years, a hope expressed in the first edition that out-of-print songs might again become available, has been at least partially fulfilled. Almost all of the out-of-print songs of John Duke have been re-issued by Carl Fischer, G. Schirmer, and Boosey & Hawkes, and four volumes of his songs that were still in manuscript have been published by Southern Music of San Antonio. New editions of out-of-print songs by Edward MacDowell, Charles Griffes, and Charles Martin Loeffler have also appeared.

On the other hand, songs by publishers such as General Music, Weintraub, and Boston Music Company, which have now closed their doors, may be difficult to find. The Library of Congress and the New York Public Library at Lincoln Center are always primary resources for out-of-print material, and the reader is also referred to the website www.worldcat.org which will provide access to a host of other libraries with song holdings worldwide.

The new edition has been revised to update virtually all of the original material, and ten composers have been added together with the poets of the selected song texts. The term "art song" continues to be used to refer only to settings of already existent poetry, thus excluding folk songs. Moreover, the word "song" is still used only in the sense of solo song with piano accompaniment, so that compositions for more than one voice or for voice and chamber group are not discussed.

We continue to maintain our expectation that although our primary audience will be musicians, readers may also include lovers of poetry and many of those engaged in the study of various facets of American civilization.

Ruth C. Friedberg
Robin Fisher
December 2011

Foreword

Song is a metaphor of the imagination; it is poetic thought encapsulated in music. Poetry, while having many forms, is driven by the basic instinct to tell the story of existence.

The American poetic tradition is a particularly rich narration of both being a people and becoming a culture; a culture chiseled out of a fierce independence of mind and heart and soul forever grounded in the very myriad of racial histories from which it emanates.

The nation "America" has always meant different things to different people and the place we call the New World is no less profound or real than the image of that New World. So many poems and so much music has been inspired by the journey inward and outward to a land where things could be thought anew, in that emerging nation founded on the promise of "Life, Liberty and the Pursuit of Happiness." And, while perhaps now in the twenty-first century we speak of "American poetry and music," the real story is to be found when we speak of poetry and music *in* America.

The exploration of poetry and song in America invites one into the psyche of the "New World" as do few other disciplines. Poets and composers in America have always been as preoccupied with the contemplation of their existence as artists as with their own unique artistic effort in America. This self-examination is indicative of the far greater collective experience we call the "American Experience," i.e., the passion for self realization; the challenge of existence of the one among the many; the tolerance of the specific in the context of the greater good; the obsessive love/hate dialogue with form, whether political, social, religious or musical; the confusing preoccupation with "art" vs. "popular" as concepts; and certainly, above all, the persistent longing to define "American." Following the threads of their own national identity, laced with the European origins from which most sprang, American composers have created a distinctive and vibrant musical tradition in song, which has shaped our culture, contributed to the development of the intrinsically American forms of folk, jazz, and musical theater, and, during the last century, increasingly achieved distinction and identity from international musicians and audiences.

It was the great philosopher, poet and orator Ralph Waldo Emerson, who—challenging the poet and seer to reconstruct the original self from whence "sprang the sun and the moon" and to see the body as the "circumference of the soul"—so inspired Walt Whitman to burst forth in a totally new, vibrant, and fiercely egalitarian voice. "The United States are themselves the greatest poem," he says echoing Emerson as he further exhorted that "poets and not presidents are the common referees" of a nation. It is they who will absorb the traditions of the past (of all the pasts of all the peoples) and turn them into something new and distinctly native. This will be found in what Whitman called a language recognized by its "sonorous strength, breadth and openness."

Alexis de Tocqueville heard this sonority when he with foresight recognized that "poets living in democratic times will prefer the delineation of ideas and passions to that of persons and achievements. . . . This forces the poet below the surface of the external . . . palpable to the senses . . . in order to read the inner soul." It was he who recognized this "man alone" separated from the massive structures—both physical and mental—of Europe, gazing at a vast richness and terrifying absence that was the New World to be envisioned, created and realized.

The "Birth of the Modern," as the historian Paul Johnson so aptly describes the age ushered in by Beaumarchais, Wordsworth, Byron, Heine and Baudelaire, found a resonance of personal determination in the distant voices of William Cullen Bryant, Emerson, Whitman, Poe, Longfellow, Dickinson, Thoreau, and Melville. This intense personal identity that erupted into the twentieth century, destroying and rebuilding countries and art forms alike, has always had a spiritual even metaphysical insistence about it, often conveyed through what seems to be sentiment and melodrama, but is in fact the simple yet profound risk of embracing the subjective narrative.

Poets of the twentieth century such as T. S. Eliot, Wallace Stevens, Langston Hughes, W. H. Auden, Theodore Roethke, or Paul Goodman, hearkening to the challenge of Whitman, have embraced their "traditions," redefined their "native" and excavated below the surface recognizing, as Wallace Stevens puts it, that "the first idea was not our own." These ideas, now thoughts and words of a new world, have been a great creative impulse for the composers of the last 150 years; music *in* America reflecting the best of what is spontaneous and by definition eclectic in the arts. In this sense, our songs in America and of America have become a kind of diary of the American experience.

This "diary" began with Francis Hopkinson, a signer of the Declaration of Independence, who is credited with composing the first American art song, "My days have been so wondrous free," dated 1759. Hopkinson recognized his unique place in American music when in a volume of keyboard works and songs, he wrote in his dedication to General George Washington, "However small the Reputation may be that I shall derive from this Work, I cannot, I believe, be refused the Credit of being the first Native of the United States who has produced a Musical Composition." And he continues, most prophetically: "If this attempt should not be too severely treated, others may be encouraged to venture in a path, yet untrodden in America, and the Arts in succession will take root and flourish amongst us."

Like a direct descendant, at least in spirit, at the beginning of the twentieth century, Arthur Farwell, the great champion pedagogue, composer and missionary of all things to root or flourish in musical America, declared in a textbook for the study of American Music:

> Prophecy, not history, is the most truly important concern of music in America. What a new world, with new processes and new ideals, will do with the tractable and still unformed art of music; what will arise from the contact of this art with our unprecedented democracy—these are the questions of deepest import in our musical life in the United States.

And as if to preempt the argument of "popular" versus "art," he further admonishes: "Too many persons are ready to suppose that the issues of music in America lie wholly within the scope of purely musical considerations, and that they do not depend, as is actually the case in certain important respects, upon the nature of the national ideals and tendencies."

The genius of Charles Ives' truculent and impatient resistance to art for art's sake gives further thought to the song as the "diary" of American Culture when he writes,

> The fabric of existence weaves itself whole. You cannot set an art off in the corner and hope for it to have vitality, reality and substance. There can be nothing "exclusive" about a substantial art. It comes directly out of the heart of experience of life and thinking about life and living life.

And so we tumbled into the modern age, where, at one time encumbered with the forms of past sentiments, we now strive at all costs and risks for the artful expression of life's realizations. Fiercely fending off the supposition of superficiality and publicly embracing the eclectic of American Arts and Humanities, we were surprised that the following statement could be made—only shortly after Ives' declaration—by William Treat Upton, in his ground breaking survey, *Art-Song in America*. He registers the significant evolution in the development of the song:

> It is coming to be more and more recognized that modern song can no longer be regarded as merely text plus music or music plus text; it is rather text multiplied by music, music multiplied by text, text so reacting upon music, music so reacting upon text, that the two elements become indissolubly merged into one another, the one really incomplete without the other. In fact, it seems to me that this might well be our test of the modern song.

It is precisely this test of the modern song—the modern articulation of the individual in poetry and music—that we explore and come to know as our own in the much expanded, revised book *American Art Song and American Poetry* by Ruth C. Friedberg and Robin Fisher. This language of heart and mind says everything about the culture that created it through the ever-present eyes of our poets and the ears of our composers chronicling the "now" of life both seen and intuited. The wealth of considerations about our language, our ideals, our very attempts to express what is our "now" in word and tone—and those considerations in larger contexts of specific generations—are treated in depth and detail that invigorate both listener and performer alike. And when we then sing our own songs, those who hear us will have experienced the best of what freedom of thought and our "pursuit" can achieve in the creation of great art.

This seems to me the very heartbeat of song: the ability to suspend life's successive moments and pulses for the expanded reflection of a greater present, allowing for the individual to find his innermost self.

Thomas Hampson
2011

Introduction

At the conclusion of his illuminating article "Problems of a Song Writer," Mario Castelnuovo-Tedesco made the following generous and provocative statement in 1944: "let me express a hope that English-speaking people (Americans especially) find in their admirable poetry—which has given so much joy to me, an Italian, a rich source of inspiration for their song literature, towards the furthering of happiness and fraternity among men, as their great poet, Walt Whitman, would have wished."[1]

Leaving aside this composer's noble but perhaps unrealistic trust in the salvation of humankind through the art song, we may still find in his statement three suggestions of the greatest importance to the present study. The first, which is not new but which receives expressive emphasis here, is the widespread ardor of Western civilization for English-language poetry. The second is the crucial distinction that is made between American poetry and that of other English-speaking peoples. The third is the implication, fortunately less common today than it was sixty-five years ago, that Americans have indeed not already produced a large body of song literature based on this very source of inspiration.

The American art song has, in fact, profited greatly from the general explosion of interest in American music that was attendant on the Bicentennial celebrations of 1976. The decade of the 1970s brought forth a plethora of recordings, books, articles, bibliographies, and performances centering on the existent literature, as well as a number of commissions and incentives for new compositions in this genre. Although only relatively recently beginning to be afforded full recognition, the American art song is not a new phenomenon, having developed over the last hundred and fifty years with literature worthy of note in all periods of its chronology. One of its problems, which can also be seen as a source of strength, has been America's possession of a common language with another civilization—admittedly an ancestor of our own, but a civilization that no longer entirely represents us. This situation has in the past produced the kind of cultural schizophrenia that characterized much of American artistic thinking: the need to escape from, to rebel against, to go beyond or outside of the British and European heritage, mingled strongly with the desire to learn from, to emulate, and to draw the water of life out of this same fountainhead. "We are transposed Europeans," said Paul Nordoff, "and have been robbed of our heritage."[2] Vincent Persichetti, on the other hand, saw in the American nature the well-developed and desirable talent of "taking a little from everyone" to create a sort of "one-world" synthesis.[3]

Regardless of one's stance toward the relationship of America's culture and particularly of its language to the countries of origin, our situation vis-à-vis the art song remains unique. Whereas one is confronted with the proper and satisfying spectacle of German composers setting German poets and French composers setting French poets (among the rare exceptions are Hugo Wolf's Italian and Spanish songbooks), the American composer seeking a text has always had the problem of choosing between William Blake or Walt Whitman, A. E. Housman or Emily Dickinson, W. B. Yeats or Robert Frost, and an infinite number of similar British or American possibilities. The writers maintain that a particular aesthetic strength emerges from the cultural reinforcement of American composers setting the works of American poets, and it is to the consideration of selected examples of such collaborations that this study is dedicated.

Our intent will be to unravel the threads that have been subsumed into the richly textured tapestry of American song as it continues to be interwoven with its close companion, American poetry. It will be the renewed task of this study to examine the details of its color and design, and to come to a more intimate knowledge of its weavers, as the millennium advances.

Historical Survey

A brief consideration of the roots of American poetry and song seems in order here. In her excellent treatment of the ancestors of American art song, Yerbury confesses, "All my life I wished to find America original in the arts. I know now she has not been."[4] Given America's beginning as a colony, an initially derivative culture would hardly seem surprising. Indeed, "influences" on creative artists have often proved to be enriching contributions to their personal stylistic syntheses. The great J. S. Bach himself is generally recognized as having combined German, French, and Italian elements in his ultimately universal style. It is nevertheless the authors' contention that America does eventually find her own voice both in poetry and in song and that this finding has its beginning in the nineteenth century and its flowering in the twentieth and twenty-first. Nor are we lacking in "breakthrough" figures, artists who do not merely reflect their age but who create a new one through basic changes in the language of their art form. Few would deny that Walt Whitman and Emily Dickinson hold such a place in literature, as does Charles Ives in music.

In order to trace the rise of any song tradition, we must begin with the poetry, for it is a fact well known to music historians that the great ages of song composition in all countries always follow, with a variable time lag, the great periods of lyric poetry. The golden age of German lieder trails on the heels of Germany's poetic outpourings of early Romanticism. French song comes into its own in the late nineteenth century upon inspiration from Verlaine and the Symbolists. In America, the sequence of events is the same, but her poetry develops very slowly in colonial times. The earliest forms are funeral verses and religious meditations, for the Puritans allowed little range to the arts except where they might directly serve the sober purposes of life in this world and contemplation of the world to come. Interestingly enough, this metaphysical stance, this search for personal meaning in a world full of darkness and evil, becomes one of, if not the dominating theme of the entire history of American poetry.

With the passing of Puritanism, the coming of the Enlightenment and all the upheavals attendant on the American Revolution eventually produced the new social, political, and cultural climate of the early nineteenth century. The times were now ripening for America's authentic literary voice to emerge. Longfellow, Whittier, Bryant, Lowell, and Holmes are the first to consider themselves "poets" by principal profession,[5] thus publicly declaring the importance to our civilization of the poetic art, but their writings are still largely derivative. It remains for Walt Whitman at mid-century to strike out in new directions and draw universal attention to the now fully matured artistic creativity of America.

*   *   *

The early history of song and singing in this country begins, as we would expect, in the same place as its poetry, with the liturgical needs of the Puritans, Moravians, Hermits of Wissahickon,[6] and other persuasions. At the same time, a strong secular tradition produces battle and marching songs and, particularly in the eighteenth century, many ballad operas and various "parody" forms, all of which are based on British or continental models.

In the first half of the nineteenth century, American song is dominated by the sentimental ballad, also an English derivation, which in time shows variation in form, melody, and harmony stemming from French and Italian sources.[7] Born half a century later than the "Longfellow school" of poets, Edward MacDowell stands in an analogous position to them in music, as the first to achieve recognition as a valid American composer, although his language never really breaks away from his German training. He will be discussed along with Loeffler and Griffes, as they set the largely Romantic poetry of nineteenth-century America in an amalgam of German and French musical styles. Then we shall see Charles Ives, the iconoclast, setting eleven American poets and using his songs as a medium in which to develop the new modes of musical expression that were his continuing concern. And, as the new century unfolds, we shall encounter a group of composers, setting poetry from Emily Dickinson to Theodore Roethke, who became firmly established in the judgment of the world community as "American" and who labored consciously to express their native culture in a musical language that derived from it, in both character and content.

The composers born in the first quarter of the twentieth century will show the profound effect of two major events. One is World War I, and the other, the beginning of the American poetic renaissance.[8] War in Europe meant that the obligatory pilgrimage to German conservatories was no longer possible, and once the pattern had been broken, it was never reinstated. In actuality, the necessity for foreign training no longer existed, for American conservatories and university departments of music, often staffed by European born and/or trained faculty, were growing in numbers, size, and quality.

As a result, we will find that Mary Howe and John Duke chose, from their mid-Atlantic origins, to study at the Peabody Conservatory; Ross Lee Finney stayed in Minnesota for undergraduate training at the state university and Carleton College; Virgil Thomson came east to Harvard from St. Louis; Charles Naginski, Sergius Kagen, and Paul Nordoff congregated at the recently established Juilliard School in New York; while Samuel Barber was among the first to enroll at the new Curtis Institute in Philadelphia. It is, of course, likewise true that a number of American composers, including Thomson, Duke, and Finney, took their newly acquired technical competence to Paris for periods of study with Nadia Boulanger, who not only passed on to them the twentieth-century French traditions (including Stravinsky's neoclassicism) but also encouraged their own experimentation in the search for the unique creative self. None, however, with the exception of Virgil Thomson, stayed in Paris, and there emerged no colony of American musical expatriates to parallel the "lost" literary generation.

One very plausible explanation for this may be that despite the many economic upheavals of the period, there was considerable musical excitement to be found at home. The twenties and thirties saw not only the rise of the conservatories and university departments, but also a centering of musical energy around summer activities at the MacDowell, Yaddo, and Seagle colonies and the festivals which they generated. Aaron Copland and Roger Sessions carried their championship of American music into a series of New York concerts, and Sessions became the mentor of a number of younger composers seeking to extend their grasp of avant-garde technique.

Beside and beyond all this, and of prime importance to the song composer, was the flood of poetry that began to pour from American writers in the early twentieth century. This phenomenon, since termed the American poetic renaissance (see n8), was certainly equal in size and quality to the products of German Romanticism and the French Symbolists. In similar fashion, it provided the inspiration for the large body of American art song which followed, and which, in fact, is still being written today.

Much of the vitality of this poetic movement will be seen to originate from the attempt to infuse new forms and philosophies into the calcified traditions of the Victorians. E. A. Robinson makes a beginning with his dramatic, regional portraits of New Englanders, and this initiation is extended by Robert Frost whose "plain speech" is still contained within familiar poetic structures. Carl Sandburg goes still further and adapts Whitman's free verse to the harsh, urban world of the twentieth century, while Amy Lowell and Marianne Moore flirt with the Imagist emphasis on objective reality.

Another spring feeding into this poetic river is the major contribution made by women writers who find poetry an important medium of expression of the early impulses toward "liberation." With the Equal Rights Ammendment, and even women's suffrage in the historical future, Sara Teasdale struggles to integrate her artistic life with her perceptions of the female role in society, while Adelaide Crapsey easily wins academic and literary stature, only to fall prey to her own mortality. Edna St. Vincent Millay and Elinor Wylie break free of convention but find that freedom carries burdens, as it does to their male counterparts; Millay's poetry records the painful knowledge, and Wylie's, her attempt to master it.

A major force that emerges in support of this burst of poetic activity proves to be the "little magazines," those periodicals aimed at a small group of discriminating readers whose ancestor was *The Dial* of 1840–1844, edited by Ralph Waldo Emerson and Margaret Fuller. It is undoubtedly true that "writers were never before received and encouraged to continue as they have been in the little magazines of our century."[9] This study will refer many times over to Harriet Monroe's Chicago-based *Poetry*, founded in 1912, which fought for and free verse in their early days, and presented some of the first published work of Frost, Sandburg, Moore, Millay, and Wylie. *The Mirror* of St. Louis will appear in connection with publications of Teasdale and Millay, and *The Egoist* of London with Imagist writers of the 'teens.

Almost inseparable from American artistic history of the twenties is *The Dial* reconstituted in 1921 by Scofield Thayer and Sibley-Watson, and destined to prominence as the birthplace of the "new" literary criticism, as a source of encouragement for the experimental in all forms of art, and as the yearly purveyor of *The Dial* award for significant literary contribution. Many connections to *The Dial* will be forthcoming among the writers and composers of this period, for Marianne Moore was its editor from 1925 to 1929, e.e. cummings and Conrad Aiken frequent contributors of poetry and reviews, and Virgil Thomson a sought-after but unwilling addition to its staff of writers.

By the middle of the third decade, a significant musical journal joined their ranks. *Modern Music*, edited by Minna Lederman, provided a unique and invaluable forum for twentieth-century music, and during the twenty-two years of its existence (1924–1946) gave rise to the tradition of the composer-journalist. Pioneers in this new "criticism by creators" had been Aaron Copland, Roger Sessions, and Virgil Thomson. In the latter years of the magazine, Paul Bowles had become a frequent contributor, and Israel Citkowitz (teacher of Richard Hundley–see Chapter 11) had written an article, crucial to the future of American song, in which he decried the notion of separating voice from text and using it "as pure tonal instrument."[10]

As the century progressed, the phenomenon of the American composer-journalist would become even more firmly established. Among the composers included in this volume, Hugo Weisgall, Norman Dello Joio, Vincent Persichetti, and William Flanagan will all be seen as valued contributors to newspapers and magazines, and Persichetti will produce an important book called *Twentieth Century Harmony*. Ned Rorem will explode into literature as the author of autobiographical diaries and collections of critical articles. And Paul Bowles will abandon music altogether in deference to his greater recognition as a novelist.

*   *   *

An important stylistic trend in American art song which also manifests in the crucial third decade is the abandonment of what Frank Rossiter describes as the "genteel tradition" of the late nineteenth and early twentieth centuries, i.e., a reverence for European Romanticism coupled with a disdain for the culture of the American masses.[11] Breaking free had opened the door to important new influences that now begin to manifest in the work of song composers. Echoes of the modernist revolt against the German Romantic tradition will be found in the catalogs of such composers as Hugo Weisgall, Vincent Persichetti, Jack Beeson, and Richard Owen. New sounds and moods from America's mass culture will creep into the folk-like ballads of Paul Bowles, and the Broadway-tinged settings of William Flanagan, Richard Cumming, and Richard Hundley. Even the remaining strains of Romanticism purveyed by Samuel Barber, John Duke, and Norman Dello Joio will strike a different note that will embody the individual's search for a new order in a new world.

American poetry, following the enormous vitality of the "poetic renaissance," had gone into an initial period of retrenchment. Edwin Seaver, editor of *Cross-Section*, a yearly collection of new American writing published from 1945 to 1948, remarked in his introduction to the final publication, "the literary revolution that began in the second decade . . . and flourished in the twenties and thirties is at an end. Today," he continued, "we seem hell-bent for conformity,"[12] and in the years following his assessment, this cultural trend was to be intensified by the political climate of fifties McCarthyism. Experiment broke loose once again, however, as the forces gathered which would produce the sixties' counterculture, and it took the forms of concrete poetry, the "beat" influence, and the poetry/jazz movement.

Throughout this period, the "little magazines" had continued to proliferate. One of the most long-lasting, the *Partisan Review*, severed its Marxist ties of the thirties to become an independent journal dividing its pages between creative work and the growing emphasis on criticism. William Phillips, its editor since 1934, made an insightful comment on the late twentieth-century state of literature, writing in 1978 in *The Little Magazine in America*. "The dominant mood," says Phillips, "is one of confusion. Even though a good deal of serious poetry, fiction, and criticism is being written, an air of uncertainty about our relation to the modernist tradition and to the mass culture hangs over us."[13]

The vicissitudes of literary movements notwithstanding, American composers have continued to search for and discover the poetic texts that suit their expressive needs. Many of them will be seen setting the newer poets of the twentieth century's middle decades. Among these are Frederic Prokosch, Paul Goodman, Theodore Roethke, Peter Viereck, Kenneth Patchen, and Howard Moss, all of whom were publishing regularly in *Poetry*, the enduring Grande Dame of "little magazines," as well as in volumes of their own. Other composers will pull back to the slightly earlier generation represented by e.e. cummings, Wallace Stevens, and William Carlos Williams, or further into the literary past to set such transitional pre-"renaissance" figures as Adelaide Crapsey, Sara Teasdale, and the enigmatic Stephen Crane.

Nineteenth-century poets, in the persons of Walt Whitman, Herman Melville, and Emily Dickinson, will also continue to speak meaningfully to twentieth and twenty-first century composers who set them with unabating enthusiasm. A whole new category of textual sources will be seen to arise as some composers begin to work extensively in musical theater and to elicit poetic texts from dramatists (Tennessee Williams, Edward Albee, Philip Minor, William Hoffman) whose literary voices they have come to know and trust. And in the most recent decades, composers will depart even further from traditional poetic sources, some, such as Ricky Ian Gordon, composing their own "lyrics" for Broadway-like settings, and others, such as Libby Larsen, adapting texts from novels and short stories with their own additions.

With the historical clock now over a decade into the new century, recent trends among American art song composers have emerged. First of all, we see a gradual increase in the number of women who are making important contributions to this literature. Secondly, there are more composers (Jake Heggie, Lori Laitman, Ricky Ian Gordon) whose catalogs concentrate, unabashedly, on vocal music of various categories. And thirdly, the practice begun by Flanagan, Cumming, and Hundley of incorporating harmonies and rhythms of the jazz and musical theater scene into their art song compositional language has become almost universal.

The American Approach to Word Setting

Robert Schumann described the desirable relationship between text and setting in these words: "The poem should lie like a bride in the minstrel's arm, free, happy, and entire."[14] American composers of today have felt the same passion for the poetry they set. "I love our language," Paul Nordoff said, "and it's very good for poetry. This is because the large number of one syllable words make it flexible and adaptable to many rhythms, and also because of the great number of similar words which have slightly different meanings."[15] Vincent Persichetti read a great deal of poetry and preferred it to newspapers or novels. He often realized only after considerable passage of time that he wanted to set a particular poem to music.[16]

Several of our song composers, notably Edward MacDowell and Charles Ives, have been sufficiently moved by the poetic impulse to set their own texts. Indeed, MacDowell was convinced that language and music could be most effectively combined only if the same person had written both. Ned Rorem takes strong exception to this point of view. "The most important thing," he maintains, "is that what a composer sets is good poetry. I don't set my own poetry because I don't think it's good literature." He also feels that attempts at writing poetry with the avowed purpose of setting it to music are doomed to failure.[17]

In the face of so much devotion professed by composers to the art of poetry, it is curious to observe Calvin S. Brown's statement in *Music and Literature* that "remarkably little attention has been given to the relationship between text and music."[18] Perhaps if comparison is made with the total weight of musical aesthetic studies in existence, this charge may prove well founded, but it is also true that for the past hundred years a considerable body of writing on this very relationship has emerged from the composers, poets, critics, and aestheticians of this country. There are three main areas into which most of the problems of word setting seem to fall in these discussions. The first has to do with prosody, and all rhythmic aspects of the poetry and musical setting, both separately and together. The second involves tone color—the "pure sound" component, we might say—which also has an ostensibly different meaning in verse than it has in music. The third area, the most difficult in some ways, is that of word meaning. Here the battle continues between those who believe, as did Stravinsky, that music, unlike words, cannot "express" anything, and those who attempt to prove, often by involved systematic analysis, that it can and does.

A composer beginning to deal with the first problem area, that of the rhythmic scheme for a setting, is at once faced with the necessity of deciding whether or not to employ what Donald Ivey, in his illuminating study on *Song*, calls a "literal transfer of poetic meter to musical."[19] An example of this from the American song repertoire would be John Duke's setting of e.e. cummings's "The Mountains Are Dancing," that begins:

> When / fa - ces called / flow - ers float / out of the / ground
> And / breath - ing is / wish - ing and / wish - ing is / having

Duke exactly paralleled the strong dactylic pattern with a 3/8 meter that has a corresponding "swing" and accent distribution.

When fa - ces called flow-ers float out of the ground, and breathing is wish-ing, and wish-ing is hav-ing

Example A, mm. 8–16

If the composer decides against the literal transfer, he or she is then free to choose a rhythmic scheme that stems from widely varying factors of word sound or meaning. Aaron Copland, for instance, in "The Chariot" (the last of his *Twelve Poems of Emily Dickinson*) was setting a clear iambic meter:

> Be - cause / I would / not stop / for Death
> He kind / - ly stopped/ for me.
> The car - / riage held / but just / our - selves
> And Im - / mor - tal / - i - ty.

Sensing no doubt that a literal transfer was not appropriate here, the composer instead chose a subtle rhythmic scheme in which the dotted patterns suggest the motion of the carriage, and the long-held tones, the pause in the rush of living imposed by Death's visit.

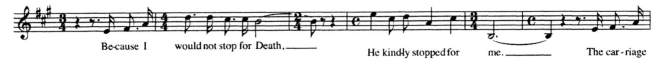

Be-cause I   would not stop for Death,_____   He kindly stopped for   me._____   The car-riage

Example B, mm. 6–11

When the process of transfer just described is treated by critics and scholars, one finds, perhaps not too surprisingly, that while some are prone to stress the differences between musical and poetic rhythm, others go to considerable lengths to stress their similarity. In an intriguing little book called *The Science of English Verse,* the poet Sidney Lanier, who often brought his years as a professional musician to bear on his creation of and theorizing about poetry, presents the following notion:

> The English habit of uttering words, prose or verse, is to give each sound of each word a duration which is either equal or simply proportionate to the duration of each other sound; and since these simple proportions enable the ear to make those exact coordinations of duration which result in the perception of primary rhythm, we may say that all English word-sounds are primarily rhythmical, and therefore that the signs of these sounds . . . are in reality also signs of primary rhythm; so that we may say further, written or printed English words constitute a sort of system of notation for primary rhythm.[20]

He goes on to derive secondary rhythms, which approximate grouping of verse sounds into bars and accents.

Although Lanier's attempt to equate exactly the poetic foot with the musical measure may seem a bit simplistic (Calvin S. Brown discusses at some length the reasons for the greater complexity of musical rhythm),[21] the impulse stems from the constant pursuit of a kind of rhythmic osmosis between words and music that composers and often poets, too, seem to long for. John Duke described his own version of the pursuit in this way:

> I now make a regular practice of making a "rhythmic sketch" or planning out of the time values of a melody in accordance with my feeling for the natural rhythmic utterance of the words before I attempt to conceive the melody as definite pitch variations. Of course, this is no good if it does not become part of a really good melody but (assuming that the melody is good) it does make sure that the words will reinforce and become part of the whole melodic conception rather than seem to run counter to the melody as I think they often do in unconvincing songs.[22]

All aspects of rhythm in word setting must of course finally come under the larger heading of poetic form. One problem that every composer must face is that repetition is almost a basic principle of musical form, whereas it is frequently destructive in the poetic context. Ivey discusses instances of text repetition at length, pointing out that deletion (of entire stanzas or words within a stanza) can be equally mutilating.[23] Interestingly, Edward MacDowell, despite his strong poetic bent and his expressed belief that "song-writing should follow declamation,"[24] was known on occasion not only to sacrifice natural word accent to melodic design, but to give way (if indeed it is a capitulation) to both word repetition and stanza deletion in the Howells settings we shall discuss in chapter 1.

In the final analysis, it becomes clear that no matter how careful the composer's attention to prosody and poetic form, the musical rhythm will either swallow the poetic feet and stanzas whole or digest them into a new synthesis. The reader should be forewarned that this idea of synthesis will return like a principal theme as we examine the other two problem areas of word setting.

"Tone color," unlike rhythm, is a term that is traditionally familiar in its musical applications but much less so in its poetic meanings. Lawrence Perrins, in *Literature—Structure, Sound, and Sense,* points out that poets achieve musical quality by two principal means. One is the arrangement of accents and the other is the choice and arrangement of sounds,[25] that, reduced to the terminology here being employed, would read "rhythm" and "tone color." He goes on to indicate that an important factor in sound arrangement is repetition—not repetition of words, which, as already pointed out, must be limited in poetry, but repetition of *word components,* such as initial consonants (alliteration), final consonants (consonance), vowel sounds (assonance), and combinations of these that can result in rhyme. Poets may use these sound repetitions to create an emphasis (just as they may use the metrical pattern), which leads in turn to the vast possibilities of sound suggesting meaning (onomatopoeia and related usages).

This attribution of the "music" of poetry to the sound arrangements of its syllables and letters appears quite logical. Once again however, in treating tone color, Sidney Lanier would have us believe that poetry and music present differences in degree rather than in kind, that indeed there are "tunes" in English verse (i.e., organized melodies of the speaking voice) and that words themselves are musical sounds produced by a reed instrument (the human voice). He goes on to postulate that every vowel, consonant, and combination of letters is a change of tone color and that written letters are therefore a system of notation for tone color (the corollary of his theory of English words as a notational system for rhythm). Finally, he brings in the idea of "scale," which in music represents only selected tones, whereas the scale of verse embraces all possible tones within limits of the human voice.[26]

In looking for the roots of Lanier's remarkable theories, it is not difficult to find them in the writings of Edgar Allan Poe, the idol of his early years. Both men were concerned with the effects of sound and with theories of prosody, and both were interested in the physics of music (Helmholtz in particular influenced Lanier) as well as poetry. In his treatise *The Poetic Principle,* Poe gives literary expression to these practical concerns. "Music in its various modes of metre, rhythm and rhyme," he says, "is of so vast a moment in Poetry as never to be wisely rejected. . . . It is in music, perhaps, that the soul most nearly attains the great end for which, when inspired by the Poetic Sentiment, it struggles—the creation of Supernal Beauty."[27] The word "rhyme," it seems clear, was used by Poe to refer to all those aspects of tone color in poetry that we have been discussing.

The question now must arise as to whether these subtle verbal tone colorings of poetry are not also swallowed in song by the more flamboyant timbres of the singing voice and the piano. Certainly, as Donald Ivey points out, composers do on occasion underline poetic alliteration by the use of other musical elements.[28] A good example of this is the following passage from Samuel Barber's "Sure on This Shining Night":

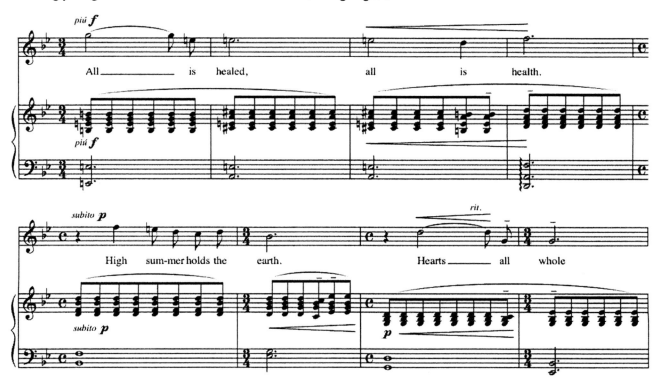

Example C, mm. 13–20

The initial "h" sounds here are emphasized by both the metrical accent and contour of the melodic line. But in general it certainly seems true that color factors of poetry, such as alliteration, assonance, and even rhyme, become less important in their own right when absorbed in song and that the concept of a compromise or synthesis of timbres is again useful.

Before we leave our explorations of rhythm and tone color in verse and music, further speculation suggests itself. Some critics seem to feel that the theoretical attempts of Poe and Lanier to equate the music of poetry with the music of music were invalidated by the former's creation of such works as "The Raven" which were experiments in sound but incorporated little meaning or real poetic value and by the latter's poem "The Symphony" in which he fails in his seeming attempt to suggest verbally the sound of orchestral instruments. It is the opinion of these writers that these admittedly flawed creative products do not negate the possible worth of their creators' theories.

Side by side with the suggestions of Poe and Lanier, let us examine the fascinating idea presented by Ned Rorem[29] that not only do the contours of vocal music depend on the language being set, but that instrumental music as well takes its shape from a nation's speech (and thereby, in a further extension of the hypothesis, resembles the people). If this were true, would it not validate Lanier's notion about the "tunes" of speech and make it likely that these formulations might subliminally be taken into a composer's palette of available sounds? Might it not also explain why the "tunes" and rhythms of American speech and poetry are different not only from German and French but also from British speech and poetry, and why the most convincing artistic products arise when the poetry and music of a song have the same national origins?

Although the scope of the subject is too great for the present volume, the authors strongly support for future inquiry the possibility that rhythmic patterns, tone color, melodic interval choice, and perhaps even harmonic structure in the American art song may indeed be linked to American speech and thereby have a common source that contributes to an American style.

Finally, as we approach consideration of the meaning of words as one of the most important aspects of their musical setting, we find that as great a poet as T. S. Eliot insists on the total integration in poetry of meaning with sound elements. In his treatise *The Music of Poetry* (originally a lecture delivered at the University of Glasgow), he maintains that "the music of poetry is not something which exists apart from the meaning" and furthermore that "a musical poem is a poem which has a musical pattern of sound and a musical pattern of the secondary meaning of the words which compose it, and that these two patterns are indissoluble and one."[30]

However one feels about meaning in its relation to "music" in poetry, there is no doubt that the meaning does exist—that words have associations that have nothing or at least very little to do with their physical sound components. Opinion is not nearly as unanimous on the question of meaning in music. Calvin S. Brown holds that music differs from poetry in that there is no counterpart in music to the associative meanings of words.[31] Others disagree. Donald Ferguson and Deryck Cooke have written books called *Music as Metaphor*[32] and *The Language of Music*,[33] respectively. Edward MacDowell delivered a lecture called "Suggestion in Music"[34] (now published with others in book form) while teaching at Columbia University. All of these[35] attempt to show at some length and with numerous examples how specific musical elements, such as pitch, rhythm, volume, or harmony, have been traditionally used by composers in an activity often termed "word painting" to portray not only emotional states but also such specific concepts as direction, types of motion, light and darkness, water, and many others.

In the opinion of the authors, this metaphoric musical language not only has a very definite existence but also figures strongly in what we have come to be familiar with as the art song style of word setting, no matter what the language of the poetry. It is, in fact, a very important factor in our perception of the composer's choices as appropriate or inappropriate and thereby in our judgment of the song as a success or failure. The only area of art song in which this would perhaps not be true are some contemporary examples in which the words are used purely as sound elements without associative meaning, the question then arising as to whether these compositions still belong to the category of art song or should rather be considered chamber music with the voice as a participating instrument.

By threading our way through what we have now seen to be a considerable body, indeed, of principally American writings on the relationship of text and music, we have arrived at two summarizing, and analogous, concepts: the "music" of poetry and the "meaning" of music. Granting that the two art forms do have many elements in common, what do we find happening to the integrity of each in their coming together? The aesthetician Susanne K. Langer has formulated "the principle of assimilation," in which she describes the process of writing a good song as a transformation of all verbal material (both sound and meaning) into musical elements.[36] Perhaps it is this view, which suggests the poetry disappearing into the music, that has led many poets of the past to reject even the greatest settings of their works, believing that they had been not only "assimilated" but destroyed.

Donald Ivey points the way to a resolution of the words/music dichotomy with a concept of equal function. Song, he suggests, "is a true hybrid in which both art forms relinquish some but not all of their individual characteristics. Even though the poem may lose its original poetic form when taken into a song, the words do not lose their function as language." He also points out that although the form and content of the poetry and that of the music exist independently, they nevertheless *function* concurrently, and that "if the emotion aroused by the music is compatible with the emotion aroused by the poetry, the images have synthesized and the expressive experience is complete."[37]

American poets have, on many occasions, appeared to welcome song composers rather than to resent them. e.e. cummings expressed admiration for Nordoff's settings of his poems[38] as did Wallace Stevens for Vincent Persichetti's *Harmonium*. Stevens, in fact, felt that Persichetti's cyclical treatment in this work illuminated some aspects of the poetry in a way that was only possible in music.[39] Paul Goodman also described himself as deeply moved by Ned Rorem's settings, and there are a number of American poets today who are interested in writing poetry for the express purpose of having it set to music.[40] Perhaps these writers have come to believe, as do the authors, that the best songs are a true union between the individual characteristics of poetry and music, in which, as in all loving unions, neither is lost but each is fully realized in the other.

Notes

1. Mario Castelnuovo-Tedesco, "Music and Poetry: Problems of a Songwriter," in *Reflections on Art*, ed. Susanne Langer (Baltimore: Johns Hopkins University Press, 1958), 310. This article originally appeared in *The Musical Quarterly* 30, no.1 (1944): 102–11.

2. Interview with R. Friedberg at the home of Mrs. Curtis Bok, Philadelphia, Pennsylvania, 5 February 1975.

3. Interview with R. Friedberg at Theodore Presser Co., Bryn Mawr, Pennsylvania, 3 February 1975.

4. Grace D. Yerbury, *Song in America from Early Times to About 1850* (Metuchen, N.J.: Scarecrow Press, 1971), iv.

5. Hyatt H. Waggoner, *American Poets from the Puritans to the Present* (New York: Dell, 1968), 34.

6. The Hermits of Wissahickon, a little-known mystic sect of German origin, is described by Yerbury, *Song in America*, 37.

7. This statement summarizes the detailed and thorough treatment of the early nineteenth-century ballad found in Yerbury, *Song in America,* Part II.

8. For a detailed discussion of the "poetic renaissance," its forerunners, and descendants see: Horace Gregory and Marya Zaturenska, *A History of American Poetry: 1900–1940* (New York: Harcourt, Brace, 1942).

9. Hoffman, Allen, and Ulrich, *The Little Magazine* (Princeton, N.J.: Princeton University Press, 1947), 229.

10. Israel Citkowitz, "Abstract Methods and the Voice," *Modern Music* 20, no.3 (March–April 1943).

11. Frank Rossiter, "The Genteel Tradition in American Music," *Journal of American Culture* 4 (Winter 1981): 107–15.

12. Edwin Seaver, ed. *Cross Section*, 1948 (Nendeln, Liechtenstein: Kraus Reprint, 1969), ix.

13. William Phillips, "On Partisan Review," *The Little Magazine in America*, edited by Elliot Anderson and Mary Kinzie (Yonkers, N.Y.: Pushcart Press, 1978), 140.

14. Susanne K. Langer, *Feeling and Form* (New York: Scribner's, 1953), 154. The source of the original quotation also appears here.

15. Interview, 5 February 1975.

16. Interview, 3 February 1975.

17. Interview with R. Friedberg at his home, New York City, 16 April 1975.

18. Calvin S. Brown, *Music and Literature* (Athens: University of Georgia Press, 1948), 46.

19. Donald Ivey, *Song: Anatomy, Imagery, and Styles* (New York: Free Press, 1970), 5.

20. Sidney Lanier, *The Science of English Verse* (New York: Scribner's, 1893), 73 ff.

21. Brown, *Music and Literature*, 20.

22. Letter to R. Friedberg, 18 June 1961.

23. Ivey, *Song*, 78 ff.

24. Lawrence Gilman, *Edward MacDowell: A Study* (New York: Da Capo Press, 1969), 163. This book, in the Da Capo Reprint Series, was originally published in 1908.

25. Laurence Perrins, *Literature—Structure, Sound, and Sense* (New York: Harcourt, Brace and World, 1970), 689 ff.

26. Lanier, *The Science of English Verse*, 47 ff.

27. Edgar Allan Poe "The Poetic Principle," in *American Poetry and Poetics*, edited by Daniel G. Hoffman (Garden City, N.Y.: Doubleday, 1962), 305.

28. Ivey, *Song*, 82 ff.

29. Ned Rorem, *Music from Inside Out* (New York: Braziller, 1967), 59.

30. T. S. Eliot, *The Music of Poetry* (Glasgow: Jackson, Son and Co., 1942), 18–19.

31. Brown, *Music and Literature*, 14.

32. Donald Ferguson, *Music as Metaphor* (Minneapolis: University of Minnesota Press, 1960).

33. Deryck Cooke, *The Language of Music* (London: Oxford University Press, 1959).

34. Edward MacDowell, "Suggestion in Music," in *Critical and Historical Essays*, ed. W. J. Baltzell (Boston: Stanhope Press, 1912).

35. Ivey also has many examples of the use of melody, harmony, and rhythm to articulate the text. See *Song,* chapters 5–7.

36. Langer, *Feeling and Form,* 150.

37. Ivey, *Song,* 95–96.

38. Interview, 5 February 1975.

39. Interview, 3 February 1975.

40. Interview, 16 April 1975.

Chapter 1

A Nation Finds Its Voice

MacDowell, Loeffler, and Griffes were all born in the second half of the nineteenth century, when the aesthetic of German Romanticism and the mystique of German musical training still retained a firm grip on the musical thinking of Western Europe and America. All three of these composers received an important part of their preparation in Germany, and their songs for the most part reflect the lied tradition in poetic atmosphere and musical language.

Some intimations of a newly emerging synthesis can be sensed, however, as each composer infuses the existent tradition with his unique contributions. MacDowell draws on his Celtic ancestry and sense of dramatic simplicity. Loeffler demonstrates an uncanny rapport with the burning lyricism of Poe and the ability to translate it into musical terms. Griffes adds the colors of French Impressionism to his expanding palette and also experiments with an austerity of style that, in its response to the starkness of John Tabb's verses, seems like an early stirring of twentieth-century neoclassicism The winds of change, then, are already rising as the old century ushers in the new.

Edward MacDowell (1861–1908)

Although Edward MacDowell maintains his historical position as the first American composer to achieve an international reputation, critical judgment of his music has fluctuated widely during the last seventy-five years from adulatory[1] to patronizing[2] and contemptuous,[3] with a balanced synthesis only recently beginning to emerge.[4] His songs have had a similar fate, for although Finck, during MacDowell's lifetime, named him as one of the two greatest living song writers (Grieg was the other),[5] the ensuing decades of the twentieth century brought little but neglect. Eventually, the impetus of the bicentennial celebration brought about a reissuing of five opus numbers (including the Howells settings) in the *Earlier American Music* series[6] and the recording of several MacDowell songs.[7]

That his solo songs comprise ten opus numbers out of his published fifty-four attests to the importance of song writing to this composer. Yet these songs did not come to him in an easy, natural, Schubertian flow, but were instead the products of long and tortured analysis of the relationship between words and music. Despite—or perhaps as a result of—his being a sometime poet, MacDowell was convinced that "language and music have nothing in common," although he had "made many experiments for finding their affinity."[8] This conviction led him, interestingly, not to abandon the song medium, but to attempt to reduce its disabilities in two principal ways: first, by writing many texts himself, since he was able to find very little poetry that to him seemed suitable for setting, and second, by making the accompaniment "merely a background for the words," so that "the attention of the bearer should be fixed upon the central point of declamation."[9] The latter goal, that of concentrating on literary values, is well served by the basic song style that MacDowell evolved: a well-conceived vocal line of relative simplicity supported by the sustained chord type of accompaniment in which characteristic motifs are rarely if ever employed. It is less well served by the composer's strong tendency toward word repetition and distortion of syllabic accent. One wonders, on comparing MacDowell's songs with those of later American composers, whether it was the rigidity of much tradition-bound nineteenth-century poetry that led him to despair of any true correspondence between music and poetry or whether it was rather an innate lack of the ability, so essential to a song composer, to assimilate or blend their disparate elements into a new and meaningful whole.

William Dean Howells (1837–1920)

In the settings of William Dean Howells's poetry that occur among the eight songs of opus 47, we find some of MacDowell's most successful instances of musical correspondence to poetic ideas, despite his avowed aim being more likely the suppression of musical factors than their directed employment. His choice of Howells as a poet is interesting in itself, since this "dean" of nineteenth-century American letters made his creative reputation primarily as a writer of novels and essays. At the same time, he was also occupied successively as editor of the *Atlantic Monthly*, *Harper's*, and *Cosmopolitan*, and it was undoubtedly while living in Boston in association with the first of these positions that his contacts with MacDowell were formed.[10] Howells began his literary career as a poet, and while his early attempts in this medium tend to be weakened by formal clichés and Victorian sentimentality, the author's return to poetry in later life evidenced a considerable growth in originality and depth of feeling.

This growth is clearly demonstrated in the three poems that MacDowell set in opus 47. "Through the Meadow" and "Gone" (MacDowell changes the latter's title to "Folksong") both appear in an early collection published in 1873, when Howells was thirty-seven. Although MacDowell uses only fourteen lines of the original twenty-two in "Through the Meadow," the omission is not enough to mitigate the cloying nature of the poetry, which the composer's pleasant but undistinguished melodic line does not disguise. "Folksong" is a somewhat stronger poem and a better setting, for the change of title indicates that MacDowell had caught the elemental, folk flavor of the girl and her departing lover. The composer's penchant for uncluttered melody and chordal accompaniment reinforce this flavor, as do the ABA form, the minor key, and the rhythmic reference to Celtic folk song in the "Scotch-snap" at the beginning of measure five:

Example 1.1, mm. 4–5

A rare example of word painting for this composer occurs in the B section of "Folksong," in which the text describes the fading sound of the lover's horse and his disappearance from sight. MacDowell repeats "grow faint" and "has passed" two times each, over indicated diminuendos, in an obvious musical imitation of the diminishing sound and view of the rider. At the same time, the melodic line, which opens with a trumpet-call reference, is reharmonized on its repetition to create greater pathos through increased chromaticism, ending with a diminished chord on the word "sight."

Example 1.2, mm. 10–17

In the final stanza of this poem, Howells loses the strong simplicity of the other two in overblown language and an antiquated syllabic separation:

> She presses her tremulous fingers tight
> Against her closéd eyes,
> And on the lonesome threshold there,
> She cowers down and cries.

MacDowell cannot overcome this, but he lightens the onus by raising a minor third to a major at the beginning and end of this section (on "presses" and on the final word "cries"), which has the effect of lessening the personal involvement and opening out to a more universalized feeling, perhaps through our sublimated recognition of the Baroque "Picardy third" convention.[11]

"The Sea" is a later poem, and with it Howells has come into his own. The language is concise and forthright, there is not a trace of sentimentality, and the poetic form is an unusual one in which the last stanza effectively adds an extra poetic foot to the first line. MacDowell's setting matches the quality of the poetry. Folk elements are again utilized to some extent for this age-old subject of a lover lost at sea. The 6/8 meter and opening dotted rhythmic pattern suggest a swinging sea-chanty; the Scotch-snap recurs in the grace notes of the melody;[12] the repetition of the simple ABA form is again the structural choice. But combined with these folk-like elements are the more sophisticated ones that give this song its unique character. The melodic line begins with the stepwise, narrow-range patterns typical of MacDowell but lunges into three full-octave leaps at the words "On the sullen water dies," while at the same time the diatonic harmony of the opening pulls to a tortuous chromatic bass line and chord structures.

Example 1.3, mm. 7–10

The accompaniment, unlike the other Howells settings, uses widely spaced chords with many octave doublings in the bass, all of which lend the larger dimension of an orchestral sonority. The key is surprisingly major (the usual choice for a sad folktale would be the minor mode), and in the coda that results from a text repetition of the last two lines plus the final word once again, MacDowell effectively underlines the tragedy of the lover's death with a melodic lowered sixth on "coral" and a poignant secondary dominant chord just before the last "asleep."

Example 1.4, mm. 29–35

Charles Martin Loeffler (1861–1935)

Born in Alsace, Charles Martin Loeffler was an American by adoption. Loeffler, who was one of Joachim's[13] favorite pupils, studied the violin in Russia and France and played professionally in a private European chamber orchestra before he came to this country at the age of twenty. It is true that he was then to spend his remaining fifty-four years in America, until 1903 as first-desk player with the Boston Symphony, and thereafter as composer and recluse on his Massachusetts farm. Yet it is not the overwhelming proportion of American years to European years that merits Loeffler's position in this study. It is rather his remarkable affinity for the poetry of the pivotal and enigmatic Edgar Allan Poe and the resultant power of the two Poe settings that appeared in Loeffler's *Four Poems Set to Music* of 1906.[14]

Edgar Allan Poe (1809–1849)

Regarding the details of their lives, these two artists were far apart, indeed. The composer had a stable home life and a long, successful career as an orchestral musician, and died, probably in his bed, at a ripe old age. The poet battled poverty and personal tragedy all of his life and died under mysterious circumstances in a Baltimore hospital at forty. Nevertheless, a study of their creative influences, goals, and methods reveals a surprising number of connections. France is perhaps the first and most obvious link. Loeffler who studied with Debussy's teacher, Ernest Guirand, at the Paris Conservatory and maintained a lifelong friendship with Fauré, certainly derived a great deal stylistically from the Impressionistic palette. Moreover, as a devotee of French literature,[15] he set the poetry of Verlaine and Baudelaire and based a symphonic poem on a work of Maeterlinck. It is not surprising that he would be drawn to Edgar Allan Poe, whose writings influenced Debussy and Maeterlinck profoundly, and who, as the following quotation indicates, has been awarded by literary historians a seminal role in the Symbolist movement: "French Symbolism, with its desire to gain the suggestiveness of music, began at the moment when Baudelaire recognized in Poe's logical formulas for a poem his own half-developed thoughts combined to perfection."[16]

French civilization is a strong connection between the two men, but there are others. Although Poe's life span falls well within the flush of early Romanticism and Loeffler's certainly does not, both men show a deep involvement with the nineteenth-century predilections for "olden times" (Loeffler was a medievalist), exotic settings, fantasy, and the macabre. As counterparts to Poe's "Annabel Lee," "The Raven," "Masque of the Red Death," and "Fall of the House of Usher," Loeffler's creative catalog includes *The Fantastic Concerto* for cello and orchestra; *La Villanelle du Diable* (the devil's villanelle), an orchestral work; a symphony called *Hora Mystica* showing strong plainchant influence; and *Pagan Poem* for chamber group based on Virgil's *Eighth Eclogue*, in which a girl attempts sorcery to bring her lover back.[17] This tendency toward highly imaginative and often demonic fantasy coupled with the sensuous appeal of Loeffler's lush harmonies and Poe's onomatopoetic syllables brought similar critical salvos: Loeffler was called a "decadent" by Philip Hale (who later decided that his decadence was irrelevant[18]), and Poe was excoriated by his own literary executor, the Reverend Rufus Griswold, as a veritable monster who showed "scarcely any virtue in his life or writings."[19] With the passage of time, the qualities that were little understood by their contemporaries have emerged as the particular artistic strength of these men, that is, the ability to combine a free-flowing Romantic sweep of ideas with the tightest technical control over all aspects of the material.

In considering any settings of Edgar Allan Poe, one's first thought might be whether or not his poetry, which is so rich in verbal music, will lend itself to song, or whether the composer will indeed find nothing to add to the mellifluous sounds and well-developed imagery. Further reflection, however, leads one to the realization that the poems Loeffler has chosen—"A Dream Within a Dream" and "To Helen"—are among Poe's tersest lyrics, which, by virtue of short lines and thoughts suggested rather than fully stated, provide considerable scope for musical amplification. Loeffler, unlike MacDowell, does not repeat even one word of the poetry; the verses appear to the syllable as Poe wrote them. Also unlike MacDowell, Loeffler chooses to embed the text in a decorative and often polyphonic instrumental texture that, particularly in "A Dream Within a Dream," is reminiscent of the sweeping arpeggios and broad melodic lines in octaves that occur in the piano part of his *Two Rhapsodies for oboe, viola and piano*.[20]

"A Dream Within a Dream," written when Poe was only eighteen, is a tight, powerful poetic statement of an already full-blown existential despair over human destiny: total extinction after a life that has much suffering but little more reality or purpose than a dream. Loeffler opens his setting with a pianistic figure repeated several times in rising sequence, which by virtue of its rhythmic repetition suggests an almost hypnotic, dreamlike atmosphere, but whose offbeat accents in the bass line lend a feeling of uneasiness.

Example 1.5, mm. 1–3

The overall rhythmic scheme of 12/8 (occasionally changing to 9, 8, or 6 beats per measure) proves a very flexible vehicle for the interesting and irregular poetic meter. Rhythm is also used to convey the poet's growing anxiety as the eighth notes break up into wildly rushing sixteenths.

Increasing harmonic instability reinforces the rhythmic push. A relatively diatonic opening in D-flat major moves to traditional cadences in the keys of the dominant and subdominant, which become heavily decorated with nonchord tones. The tension continues to mount with enharmonic modulations and increased chromaticism, which culminates in the piano interlude following "can I not save one from the pitiless wave?"

Example 1.6, mm. 37–38

At the same time, the vocal line has shown growing contrapuntal interaction with the piano, and the pianistic melody has swelled from an opening narrow-range chant to a broad, fortissimo series of octaves. All of this tension finds musical release in the postlude following the final refrain ("Is all that we see or seem/But a dream within a dream?") with a return to the rocking pattern of the opening, which seems to suggest a retreat from anguished cerebration to a dreamlike state.

"To Helen," which dates from 1831, when Poe was twenty-two years old, is one of his finest lyrics. With surprising compression and great elegance of choice in poetic meter, rhyme scheme, and imagery, the Romantic artist's concept of Woman as a refuge from the storms of life and as an inspiration toward the noblest impulses of his own intellect and emotions[21] is set forth with great power. Loeffler utilizes his exquisite sense of harmonic appropriateness and considerable skill in motivic manipulation to create a seemingly "inevitable" setting.

One of the composer's effective devices is to lengthen the time value of the last syllable of each line. This affords the opportunity for the pianistic counterpoint to grow into lush melodic lines, which often derive from previous vocal or instrumental material. The romantic excitement of the poem is underlined by what we have come to recognize, perhaps only subliminally at times, as typical nineteenth-century harmonic procedures: modulation to the mediant (F major going to A major before the first piano interlude), the sudden introduction of a lowered-sixth chord after a *rallentando* for textual emphasis

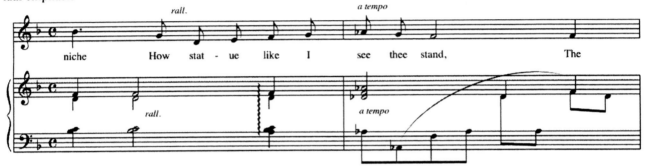

Example 1.7, mm. 33–34

and the climactic treatment of the final poetic line. This treatment includes a fortissimo accompaniment in octave triplets and a chromatic rising vocal curve that diminuendos to an unexpected thirteenth chord.

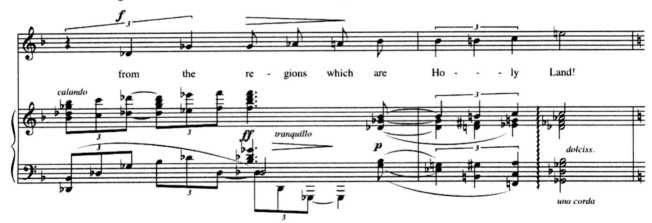

Example 1.8, mm. 39–40

Loeffler now writes another postlude, which this time takes the form of a long winding-down after a burst of melody, in a manner reminiscent of Duparc's "Phidylé." Like the best of the Schumann postludes, this one has the effect of reinforcing the emotional content of the song at least partially through the return of motivic material.

Finally, it should be said that the principal motivic material, just referred to for the second time, consists of a descending chromatic line,

Example 1.9, mm. 4–5

and a rising series that combines whole- and half-steps:

To   his   own   na - - - tive   shore._____

Example 1.10, mm. 12–13

Both of these reappear at many pitch levels, in varying rhythmic contexts, and with changing harmonic backgrounds, and it is impossible to miss the yearning quality imparted by the sliding chromatics, particularly when incorporated in the rising line.

Charles Griffes (1884–1920)

Although his tragically short life cut off the promise of still further development, Charles Griffes nevertheless created during his thirty-six years a body of compositions that marks him as one of the major American composers of the early twentieth century. No lesser authority than Gilbert Chase, the elder statesman of American musical historians, puts the case succinctly in these terms: "[Griffes's] major works are American classics; his songs are among the best we have."[22]

It must also be said, to the credit of the musical public that the well-deserved reputation of Griffes's songs seems never to have been in dispute. William Treat Upton writing in *Art Song in America*, which was published only ten years after the composer's death, presented a treatment of his style that is remarkable for its thoroughness and insight into Griffes's great strengths as a song composer.[23] Performances of the songs, however, which proliferated during the composer's lifetime,[24] diminished thereafter except for the anthologized "By a Lonely Forest Pathway"[25] and "The Lament of Ian the Proud."[26] In 1966, recordings began to appear,[27] and three scholarly studies that involve Griffes songs have now been written: a descriptive catalog of all the Griffes works, a master's thesis on the songs alone, and a biography of the composer.[28] As a result of this renewed interest and attention, in 1987 G. Schirmer published all its Griffes song holdings in two volumes, for high and medium voice.[29]

Charles Griffes, according to all we know of his life and interests, was an artist who was open to not only the new musical trends of his time as represented by Debussy, Scriabin, Stravinsky, Schoenberg, and Varèse, but also to influences from Asian and European cultures. In addition, he showed considerable skill in sketching and photography. It is particularly interesting in the context of this wide-ranging sensibility to note the American poets that Griffes chose for setting and to speculate on their attraction for him. His early biographer, Maisel, mentions that Griffes "was much interested in the new American poetry movement,"[30] but the evidence consists of only a single song: Sara Teasdale's "Pierrot" (unpublished), written in 1912,[31] which is a light-textured, serenade-type setting somewhat reminiscent of Debussy's "Mandoline" but less harmonically subtle—in all, a work of some charm but little depth, like the poem. This, then, was Griffes's only venture into the American poetry of his contemporaries, and apparently he found it an unfruitful field for his own inspiration. His other American settings, all of which date from 1911 and 1912, consist of one poem by Sidney Lanier and five by John Tabb, both of who were born approximately forty years before the composer.

The songs that we shall examine of this group are three that were refused publication by G. Schirmer in 1912 (along with "Pierrot") but were finally published by the same company in 1941 and reprinted in 1989 (see n29): "Evening Song," the Lanier poem, and "The Half-Ring Moon" and "The First Snowfall," two poems by John Tabb. Two other Tabb settings, called "Phantoms" and "The Water-Lily,"[32] show instances of Griffes's skill as a sensitive harmonic colorist but suffer from the weakness of the poems. These are overblown, conventional apostrophes to falling snow and a flower, respectively, whose Victorian language is at war with the Impressionistic chord structures of the settings. Indeed, in most of the songs circa 1912, Griffes was turning away from the Brahms-Strauss influence of his 1901 *Five German Poems* and absorbing into his style many of the new French elements then making their way across the Atlantic.

John Tabb (1845–1909)

John Tabb is a little-known American poet, native to Virginia, who was born an Episcopalian but after years of soul-searching converted to Catholicism. Ordained as a priest, he nevertheless held no parish, and taught English literature all his life. While serving as a blockade-runner in the Civil War, he was captured and sent to Point Lookout, where he met a fellow prisoner, Sidney Lanier. The two became lifelong friends, and Tabb helped to direct Lanier toward his eventual

adoption of a serious career as a poet. Another coincidence meaningful to this study is the strong absorption of both men in music, for Tabb would have become a professional musician had his eyes not been weak from an early age, and La-nier played almost all instruments as a child and served as first flautist in the Peabody Orchestra of Baltimore in the early 1870s. Similarities end, however, in the area of poetic style and artistic goals, and the differences we shall find clearly delineated in the three posthumous songs of 1941.

Standing quite apart from the diffuse style of most of his contemporaries, and particularly those of the South, John Tabb worked throughout his life in the direction of poetic clarity and concision. "His ability to say much in little, to sug-gest profound thought by a single word, has been recognized by all critics," says Francis Litz, Tabb's editor.[33] This seeming simplicity, together with a polished technique and a tendency toward religious overtones in concept and image-ry, is strongly reminiscent of Emily Dickinson, whose works might well have been known by Tabb in his maturity, since he was forty-five at the time of the first publication of her poetry (1890).

The settings of "The Half-Ring Moon" and "The First Snowfall" are as concise as the poetry: for each eight-line po-em Griffes has composed two pages of music, running twenty measures in each case. "The Half-Ring Moon" is a fairly early poem (1884), which in its few short lines tells a story of a lover who comes no more over the sea, but whose pledge of love, the half of a golden ring, can be seen hanging in the sky. On hearing this setting, one is struck by the fact that the accompaniment figure seems to hark back to Griffes's German songs in its Brahmsian wide-spaced chords and two-against-three rhythmic patterns. It is perhaps a bit heavy for the folkish character of the poem, but the song is redeemed by its considerable harmonic interest. A constant wavering between major and minor colorings and a prolonged empha-sis on the VI chord before the final introduction of the E minor tonic lend an archaic flavor that matches the poetic at-mosphere of such lines as "My love he is gone to a far countrie." Also the enormous skill as a writer of counter-melodies in the piano part, which Griffes shares equally with Loeffler, is used for dramatic effect in underlining the pathos of the climactic line "He comes no more from the far countrie":

Example 1.11, mm. 11–14

"The First Snowfall" shows John Tabb at his best in a laconic, Dickinson-like observation that the same snowfall is at once life-giving to the fir tree and a messenger of death to the last falling leaf. Griffes's setting, which Hans Nathan found to have several "intriguing aspects,"[34] is as austere as the poem and creates most of its effect through the harmonic means of Impressionism. These include non-resolving chord tones added for coloristic effect, pedal points to contribute a tonal orientation, and Griffes's own instruction that the piano part is to be "veiled through a constant use of both pedals" (*una corda* and damper). The last few measures of the piece are illustrative of most of these elements, as well as of the relatively simple and diatonic melodic line, which mirrors the leanness of the text.

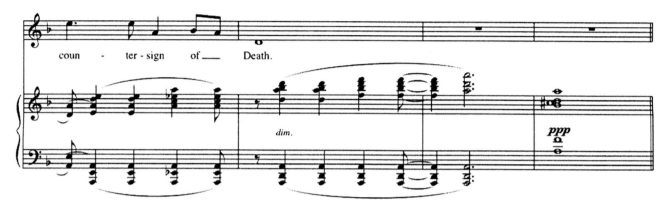

Example 1.12, mm. 17–20

Sidney Lanier (1842–1881)

For Sidney Lanier's "Evening Song," Griffes returns to the full, chordal accompaniment of his "German period" and adopts many of the lush, nineteenth-century harmonic procedures that Loeffler utilized in setting Lanier's poetic counterpart, Edgar Allan Poe. The altered chords, the chromatic sideslips to foreign keys, modulations to the third, and frustrated harmonic goals of motion all intensify the rush of emotion in this "spontaneous yet controlled" lyric, in which Lanier finally found the perfect expression he had been seeking of his feeling for his wife.[35] In truth, this powerful setting, which Griffes's unerring color sense placed in the key of C-sharp minor so that its many sharps might impart a quality of ecstatic brightness, is a perfect representation of all the characteristics of the composer's style that lend it to greatness. These include the inherent beauty and textual appropriateness of the melodic and harmonic choices, and his seemingly effortless ability to adapt poetic meter to musical structure (there are no word repetitions and no important deletions in any of these songs). Still another strength is his fine instinct for form, which here involves a much-modified ABA structure for the three stanzas of verse and also includes an effective repetition of the introductory material transposed before verse three.

Lanier has been denigrated by critics through the years for his tendency to sentimentality and lack of intellectual control. There is, however, little question that he, like Poe, made his very considerable poetic contributions through his great sensitivity to patterns of sound, and his ability to communicate "the excitement of music to verse."[36] In "Evening Song,"[37] Griffes reconverts this excitement into actual musical terms. One example is the tentative opening figure, in which the tonic chord in its major and minor form alternates with tension-producing dissonant neighboring chords:

Example 1.13, mm. 1–3

Another is the chromatic sidestep to a B-flat chord on the word "sun," which in its creation of a sense of wonder through a sudden move to a foreign harmony is very evocative of Schumann's *Dichterliebe*.

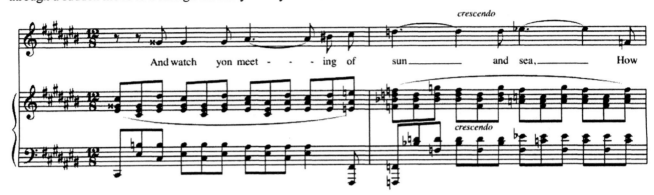

Example 1.14, mm. 7–8

A third is the setting of "Cleopatra night drinks all. 'Tis done," in which the moment of suspense before the sun drops into the sea is given exquisite musical expression. Griffes delays the expected resolution of the V chord by the interruption of an altered VI with an appoggiatura, before it returns to the tonic (Verse two is cadencing at this point in E major):

Example 1.15, mm. 17–21

Finally, the postlude begins its passionate outburst with a pianistic appoggiatura similar to the one just quoted, which musically unites that former moment of deep emotion with the final prayerful exhortation:

O night! divorce our sun and sky apart,
Never our lips, our hands.

Example 1.16, mm. 35–36

Notes

1. Lawrence Gilman, *Edward MacDowell: A Study* (New York: DaCapo Press, 1969), Chapter 3, "His Art and Its Methods."

2. Daniel Gregory Mason in *Contemporary Composers* (New York: Macmillan, 1918), 276: "His range of expression . . . is not wide, and within it he frequently cloys by an oversweet sentimentalism. But MacDowell is sincere and he is always himself. . . . His style is very narrow but it is his own."

3. Paul Rosenfeld in his chapter on MacDowell found in *An Hour with American Music* (Philadelphia: Lippincott, 1929), 143: "Where his great Romantic brethren, Brahms, Wagner, and Debussy, are direct and sensitive, clearly and tellingly expressive, MacDowell minces and simpers, maidenly and ruffled. He is nothing if not a daughter of the American Revolution."

4. John Tasker Howard in *Our American Music* (New York: Crowell, 1965), 325: "MacDowell is probably the first of our creative musicians for whom we need make no allowances for lack of early training. None of his limitations was caused by his being an American. . . . And after we have put him under the magnifying glass, stripped him of . . . idealization . . . he will emerge with several of his banners still flying."

5. Henry T. Finck, *Songs and Song Writers* (New York: Scribner's, 1900), 240.

6. H. Wiley Hitchcock ed., *Earlier American Music* 7 (New York: DaCapo Press, 1972).

7. See CD recording by John K. Hanks and Ruth C. Friedberg, *Art Song in America* (Durham, N.C.: Duke University Press, 1997). Contains "Thy Beaming Eyes," "Long Ago, Sweetheart Mine," and "The Sea." See also Edward MacDowell, *Complete Songs*, Steven Tharp, tenor, and James Barbagallo, piano (Naxos American Classics, 1996).

8. An interview with the composer is quoted in Gilman, *Edward MacDowell,* 164.

9. Gilman, *Edward MacDowell,* 163.

10. Howells was in Boston from 1865 to 1891, and MacDowell from 1888 to 1896. These terms of residence coincide from 1888 to 1891, and the Howells settings were published in 1893, hence the authors' hypothesis.

11. The common Baroque practice of ending a work in the minor mode with a major chord or phrase.

12. The recurrence of this rhythmic motif recalls MacDowell's Celtic ancestry.

13. Joseph Joachim (1831–1907) was a German violinist and teacher of great renown.

14. Charles Martin Loeffler, *Four Songs, Opus 15* (Huntsville, TX: Recital Publications, 1983). "A Dream Within a Dream" is recorded in Hanks and Friedberg (see n7). "To Helen" is included in the Thomas Hampson CD *I Hear America Singing* (2006), available at ArkivMusic.com.

15. Edwin Burlingame Hill, "Charles Martin Loeffler," *Modern Music* 13 (November–December 1935): 26–31.

16. Robert E. Spiller, Willard Thorpe, Thomas J. Johnson, Henry Seidel Canby, and Richard M. Ludwig eds., *Literary History of the United States* (New York: Macmillan, 1963), 340.

17. For a fuller description of Loeffler's works, see Howard, *Our American Music,* 349–51.

18. Philip Hale's critical comments are discussed in Carl Engel, "Charles Martin Loeffler," *Musical Quarterly* 2, no. 3 (July 1925): 320.

19. Spiller, et al., *Literary History,* 321.

20. Charles Martin Loeffler, *Two Rhapsodies for oboe, viola, and piano* (out of print).

21. For a different interpretation of this poem, which suggests the egocentricity of its message, see Hyatt H. Waggoner, *American Poets from the Puritans to the Present* (New York: Da Capo, 1968), 141.

22. Gilbert Chase, *America's Music* (New York: McGraw-Hill, 1966), 522.

23. William Treat Upton, *Art Song in America* (New York: Ditson, 1930; reprinted 1969, Johnson Reprint Corp.), 265–66.

24. Considerable information on early performances of Griffes's songs can be found in the following references: (a) Edward M. Maisel, *Charles T. Griffes* (New York: Knopf, 1943); (b) Marion Bauer, "Charles Griffes as I Remember Him," *Musical Quarterly* 29 (July 1943): 355–80; (c) Donna K. Anderson, *Charles T. Griffes: An Annotated Bibliograph-Discography* (Detroit: College Music Society, 1977).

25. This song appears in *50 Art Songs from the Modern Repertoire* (Milwaukee: Hal Leonard Corp., 1986).

26. This is in the collection called *Songs by Twenty-two Americans*, compiled by Bernard Taylor (Milwaukee: Hal Leonard Corp., 1986) and in the Paul Sperry collection of 1989 (see n29).

27. See Anderson, *Charles T. Griffes*, n24c.

28. (a) Anderson, *Charles T. Griffes*, n24c; (b) Carolyn Lambeth Livingston, *The Songs of Charles T. Griffes* (Chapel Hill: University of North Carolina Master's Thesis, 1947); (c) Donna K. Anderson, *Charles T. Griffes: A Life in Music* (Washington, D.C.: Smithsonian Institution Press, 1993).

29. Paul Sperry, ed., *The Songs of Charles Griffes* (Milwaukee: Hal Leonard Corp., 1989). Contains "Evening Song," "The First Snowfall," "The Half-Ring Moon," and "Phantoms" (in its first publication).

30. Maisel, *Charles T. Griffes,* 111.

31. Manuscript in the Library of Congress.

32. The manuscript of "The Water Lily" is in the Library of Congress. The ms. of still another Tabb setting, "Cleopatra and the Asp," has been lost.

33. Francis A. Litz, ed., *The Poetry of Father Tabb* (New York: Dodd, Mead, 1928), vii.

34. Hans Nathan, "The Modern Period—United States of America," *A History of Song*, ed. Denis Stevens (New York: Norton, 1960), 428.

35. Charles R. Anderson, ed., *Sidney Lanier, Poems and Poem Outlines* (Baltimore: Johns Hopkins Press, 1945), iii.

36. Spiller et al., *Literary History,* 907.

37. A recording of "Evening Song" is included in *I Hear America Singing* (see n14).

Chapter 2

Charles Ives (1874–1954)

Charles Ives stands alone. He belongs to no historical "group," and indeed he resisted all influences except the "still, small voice" within that drove him to a secret life of innovative creativity that has become legend. The songs of Charles Ives represent his stylistic development in microcosm. They begin with traditional German and French settings during the 1890s and grow increasingly "American" in their orientation as well as increasingly experimental in all elements of musical style.

Ives's songs, like the rest of his compositions, were conceived in isolation and born into a hostile world. Nevertheless, since their original printing these songs have become a valued part of America's national heritage. They were heralded in 1934 by Aaron Copland in an article that was to prove an important opening wedge in the recognition of Ives's work.[1] They have been explored since in varying degrees by all the major Ives scholars and chroniclers.[2] As yet unexplored, however, are the relationships between Ives and those leading American poets of the nineteenth and early twentieth centuries whose texts he had begun to set soon after graduation from Yale, under the growing conviction of having, in Emerson's words, "listened too long to the courtly muses of Europe."[3]

Ralph Waldo Emerson was already well established as one of Ives's heroes when as an undergraduate Ives listened to Horatio Parker[4] expound on the philosophy of the "sage of Concord." Ives even went so far as to submit a paper on Emerson to a campus literary publication; in ironic prophecy of disappointments to come, it was rejected. Emerson, in his writings on "Self Reliance" and "The American Scholar," sought to arouse courage and authenticity of thinking in his countrymen. Those qualities were early established in the young Ives by a father who encouraged musical experimentation and originality. In another pivotal essay, "The Poet," Emerson called for a new voice to express the soul of America, and Walt Whitman seemed to him to be the fulfillment of that prophecy. In Charles Ives's work, we find not only a continuation of the search to express America, but something that would have pleased Emerson equally: a translation into musical terms of Transcendentalism, his religio-philosophic system based on the oneness of nature, humanity, and God.[5]

The all-inclusiveness of this philosophy, which was deeply ingrained in Ives, accounts for both the coexistence (either successively or simultaneously) of very disparate elements in individual songs, and for the enormous range of style, mood, and text in the songs as a whole. Both of these types of diversity will be encountered in the following list of twelve songs to be discussed in this chapter. This list is given in chronological order of composition and indicates those instances (numbers 3 through 7) in which the original scoring was other than for voice and piano:

	Song	Poet	Original	Rescoring
1.	"The Children's Hour"	Longfellow	1901 voice/piano	–
2.	"The Light That Is Felt"	Whittier	1904 voice/piano	–
3.	"Serenity"	Whittier	1909 chorus/orch.	1921 voice/piano
4.	"The Last Reader"	O. W. Holmes	1911 voice/chmbr. group	1921 voice/piano
5.	"The Indians"	Chas. Sprague	1912 voice/chmbr. group	1921 voice/piano
6.	"Duty"	Emerson	1911/12/13(?) chorus/orch.	1921 voice/piano

7.	"Walt Whitman"	Whitman	1913 chorus/orch.	1921 voice/piano
8.	"General Wm. Booth	V. Lindsay	1914 voice/piano	–
	Enters Into Heaven"			
9.	"Thoreau"	Thoreau	1915 voice/piano	–
10.	"The Swimmers"	L. Untermeyer	1915–1921 voice/piano	–
11.	"Afterglow"	J. F. Cooper Jr.	1919 voice/piano	–
12.	"Maple Leaves"	T. B. Aldrich	1920 voice/piano	–

Although these twelve songs represent a span of twenty years, two important characteristics prevail throughout the list. The first is what might be termed a nonobservance of poetic integrity, which includes using fragments of larger poems, word repetition and omission, changes in word order or in the words themselves, and occasional retitling of the original poem. These practices by no means originated with Ives, and it is not surprising that a man who also set texts written by himself, his wife, newspaper journalists, and indeed anything that seemed appropriate to the overall goal of his broadened concept of musical expression, would approach the poetry of the masters in a similar context of "means toward an end." Set over against this, however, is the other characteristic of these songs, which is a careful and effective attention to the details of word setting that is in the finest tradition of art song composition and belies any suspicion of randomness that might arise from the poetic fragmentation.

Henry Wadsworth Longfellow (1807–1882)

"The Children's Hour" was written in 1901, when Ives was three years out of Yale, living in New York as a bachelor insurance clerk and spending his "spare" time as church organist, choirmaster, and composer. This song, by virtue of its relatively few performance difficulties and the aptness and elegance of its construction, has become one of the most popular of the "114."[6] However, like many another great poetic setting, Ives's "Children's Hour" is quite different from Longfellow's.

Henry Wadsworth Longfellow, along with Bryant, Lowell, Holmes, and Whittier, falls into a group of nineteenth-century writers who were our first actual American "poets," i.e., men who were accepted as such both at home and abroad. They are quite generally conceded to have been minor figures, and their styles leaned heavily on models, but each was to write a few poems that would become landmarks for nineteenth-century America. Longfellow was born in Portland, Maine, the son of an attorney and member of Congress, and was educated at Bowdoin College. He had a seemingly peaceful and rewarding life as a man of letters and held professorships of modern languages successively at Bowdoin and at Harvard University before retiring in 1854 to devote himself exclusively to writing. But personal tragedy did not spare the gentle scholar despite his reputation and affluence. In 1831, his first wife died in childbirth. Thirty years later, his second wife burned to death in their home when her dress accidentally caught fire, and he was left with five growing children, three of whom appear in this poem.[7]

The inconsistencies that marked his life are not absent from the poetry. Although in much of his work he seems, in Walt Whitman's words, to be the poet of "sympathetic gentleness" and "of the mellow twilight of the past," lurking just below the surface is the melancholy sense of "time as inherently and inevitably man's enemy, bringing only loss and nothingness."[8] Even the "mellow twilight" glow of "The Children's Hour," with its golden merry little girls, is eventually dispelled as the poet gives way to a rather coy self-pity ("such an old mustache as I am") and a despairing resolve to cling to the memory of this moment:

> In the round-tower of my heart . . .
> Till the walls shall crumble to ruin
> And moulder in dust away.

Not surprisingly, Ives, in the full flush of his early transcendental optimism, chose to set the delightful, living moment and to omit all mention of its threatened dissolution. Out of an original ten stanzas, he sets only three, and closes with a shortened version of stanza one. This verbal repetition coincides with an ABA musical structure (the return to A is also shortened), which Ives was to use rarely, particularly in his later songs. There are other early style characteristics evident here also, such as the diatonic harmony, lyricism and chordal leaps of the melodic line, and conventional metric schemes with much repetition of rhythmic patterns. There is, in fact, a rhythmic ostinato used throughout the first A section, whose softly hypnotic insistence provides an initial sense of the hush and quiet of twilight in the days before electricity.

Adagio sostenuto

Example 2.1, mm. 1–2

This ostinato also serves a melodic function and at the same time a harmonic one, as with the change of a very few notes, chordal meanings are subtly shifted.

Example 2.2, mm. 8–10

Also notice in Example 2.2 how Ives provides, as a mirror of the text, a 2 1/2-beat "pause" on the word "hour" before continuing. As he enters the B section, the ostinato disappears and a new triplet figure increases the urgency of the *più moto* indication as the text becomes alive with "the patter of little feet" and the sound of voices and doors being opened.

Example 2.3, mm. 11–12

Stanza 3, still musically in the B section, moves to a 6/8 rhythm, which provides an opportunity for interesting cross-accents between voice and piano (see Ex. 2.4). The section climaxes with an unexpected key shift from D major to A-flat major that lends a fresh sound to the use of the rapid sixteenth-note triplet on the word "laughing."

Example 2.4, mm. 15–19

The return of the section-A ostinato has the satisfying effect of rounding off the picture that has been created and fixing it in place. Ives's understated polytonal implication of overlapping G and A triads in the final measure creates an unresolved musical atmosphere that suggests not the nostalgia of memory but the permeation of the present moment by eternity.

Example 2.5, mm. 25–27

John Greenleaf Whittier (1807–1892)

John Greenleaf Whittier, who had been a friend of Ives's father-in-law, also shared a New England heritage with the composer, as did almost all the leading American poets Ives was to set. He was born in Haverhill, Massachusetts, but into much less auspicious circumstances than was Longfellow, and as a consequence led a far different kind of life. Whittier, the son of a Quaker farmer, was largely self-educated. When his literary talents began to be evident, he plunged into a successful career as a newspaper editor and politician. He was an active abolitionist and a founder of the Republican Party. In 1865, he served as a presidential elector. After the Civil War, however, his life became more that of the cloistered poet. At the age of seventy, he finally received recognition from the academic world as a man of letters in the form of honorary degrees from Haverford College and Harvard University.

Whittier's most successful poems are generally conceded to be those that reflect the life of the mid-nineteenth-century New England farmer. He is particularly effective when dealing with nature, childhood, and his deeply felt, relatively orthodox religious perceptions. All three of these categories, but principally the last, are represented in varying combinations in the two texts of his that Ives chose for setting. It is worthy of note that Whittier is the only leading American poet that Ives set more than once.

Religion was as strong an element in Ives's life as it was in Whittier's, not only as a focus of such activities as revival meetings, church organist positions, and the like, but also as a shaping force in all his thinking about human nature and destiny. Interestingly, in setting these two texts, both of which deal in direct, simple terms with the place of God in human life, Ives employs two completely different styles. These are like an example in microcosm of the change that was to take place in his writing around 1907.

"The Light That Is Felt" dates from 1904,[9] relatively the same period in Ives's life and composition as "The Children's Hour." It, too, is diatonic and in general falls into the category of Ives's "household songs," which H. Wiley Hitchcock describes as "pleasant to perform and to hear, and not too demanding technically."[10] But this song is deceptive and in the same manner as the much later "Two Little Flowers" (1921), in that it also contains details of style that prove quite surprising in this context. The first surprise occurs in measure 4 in the form of a quite shocking chromatic alteration of the tonic B to B-sharp. This creates an unexpected dissonance in both verses of the strophic setting with no seeming textual origin.

Example 2.6, mm. 4–7

The next striking feature of the setting is its rhythmic organization. Ives has used the first two out of the three stanzas in the original poem. He has translated the somewhat unusual five-line verse form into a standard 2/4 meter, but with an asymmetrical and arresting overall phrase structure, which has the following measure grouping:

Verse I: 5, 5, 2
Verse II: 5, 5, 3

The asymmetry is further emphasized by the fact that the inner vocal phrases do not coincide with those of the arpeggiated accompaniment, the latter beginning frequently on weak beats with a syncopated effect that is a direct parallel to the piano part of "Two Little Flowers."

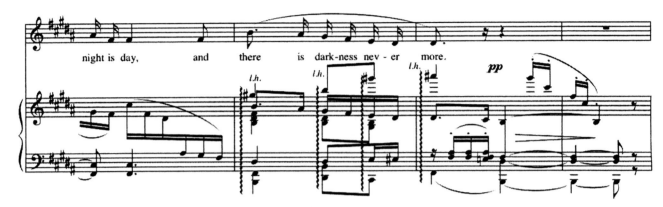

Example 2.7, mm. 19–25

Finally, Ives's small but cogent alterations in the text of this poem must be noted. In each verse, Ives repeats a short but emotionally climactic phrase (verse I: "O, mother, take my hand"; verse II: "The night is day") and begins the repetition with a striking octave leap upward. In the second verse, Ives adds the word "then" rather than land on the upper octave with an unsuitable "the." Further, just before the repetition in verse II, Ives changes the text from

> and only when our hands we lay
> Dear Lord, in thine, the night is day

to the way it appears in Example 2.7, substituting "Oh, God" for the weaker "Dear Lord," and shifting the word order for even stronger musical effect.

The years 1907 and 1908 were pivotal ones for Charles Ives. In 1907, he started his own insurance agency with Julian Myrick, and in 1908, after an impatient courtship, married Harmony Twichell. The liberating effects of being in business for himself and having a mate who was constantly encouraging of his creative originality combined to make the next decade his most experimental and prolific. Performances of his works by the outside world, however, were very rare in this period, and in despair of finding singers who were able or willing to sing difficult intervals, Ives turned to setting texts for unison chorus and orchestra, or for voice and chamber group with the voice part sometimes being taken by an instrument (despite the notated text).

Songs 3 through 7 on the list originated in this fashion between 1909 and 1913 and will be discussed in order of their original composition, although they were not arranged for voice and piano until Ives gathered his *114 Songs* for publication in 1921. "Serenity" began, in Ives subtitle, as a "unison chant"—a Whitman-like concept, no doubt, of a people's chorus, for Ives was to believe in the fundamental goodness of the majority until the debacle of World War I and his physical collapse in 1918. In its solo form, it becomes a very intimate, meditative distillation of the soul yearning for inward peace: a transmutation of the Gregorian spirit into a twentieth-century frame of reference.

"Serenity" is Ives's title, not Whittier's, and no doubt derives from a hymn tune of the same name (based on another Whittier text), which Ives quotes at the end of both musical stanzas.[11] The text of Ives's song is two verses only out of seventeen that the poet had called "The Brewing of Soma." The poem describes the use through the ages of "brews," drugs, and many other forms of artificial stimulation to achieve mystic union with God. It closes with an affirmation of inner tranquility as the only truly receptive state for spiritual grace, and it is from this conclusion that Ives extracted the idea of "Serenity" that was to form his title and the all-pervading mood of the song. The chant-like atmosphere that Ives deemed appropriate to this mood is achieved by a combination of carefully controlled musical details. One is the stepwise melodic line with many repeated notes and subtle combinations of duple, triple, and syncopated rhythms (see Ex. 2.8). Another is the shifting of melodic centers from G to F and back to G again, a process very reminiscent of liturgical chant despite the fact that the context is tonal rather than modal. The spare accompaniment figure of two repeating bell-like chords in the upper register reinforces the repetitive, hypnotic nature of the chant, and this pattern is interrupted only twice by the hymn quotation ending in a plagal cadence that occurs before each caesura (see Ex. 2.8, last measure).

Example 2.8, mm. 7–12

One final detail in the exquisite craftsmanship of this song is the introduction of an extra accompaniment chord in measure 19, which shifts the direction of the harmonic movement and causes a lifting effect that is exactly appropriate to the poetic phrase.

Example 2.9, mm. 17–20

Oliver Wendell Holmes (1809–1894)

The setting of Oliver Wendell Holmes' "The Last Reader" originated as one of the "sets" (Ives's term for his songs with chamber orchestra); this 1911 version called for two flutes, cornet, violas, and organ. The poem is an interesting choice from several points of view, and the setting illustrates many aspects of Ives's style in this increasingly experimental period.

Oliver Wendell Holmes was Cambridge born and reared and Harvard educated. His life presents an interesting parallel to the composer's, in that he earned his living as a doctor and professor at Harvard Medical School while leading a second life as a writer of poetry and prose. Holmes' work, however, unlike Ives's, found no obstacle to publication in his lifetime, and he was widely esteemed for his poetry, essays, and lectures. There were many scientific papers as well, and it is perhaps not surprising that with the passage of time, Holmes turned increasingly to lighter subjects for his verse. His writing career, however, was of great importance to him, as is clear in the following statement from his essay collection *The Poet at the Breakfast Table*: "I should like to be remembered as having said something worth lasting, well enough to last."

In "The Last Reader," Holmes voices the disquieting possibility that oblivion might indeed fall on his "neglected songs" but is soothed by the thought that they will still have meaning to him as memories of his youth and "thoughts that once were mine." The title of the poem emerges from the last two lines:

> And give the worm my little store
> When the last reader reads no more.

Despite the growing disillusion caused by the world's neglect, Ives once again, in 1911, chose only the most positive parts of this poem for setting (verses I and III out of a total of eight). He used the stanzas that describe how the poet's own verses bring him joy and even assuage the pain of old age, and discarded the somewhat morbid musings on death and oblivion. The last two lines (quoted previously) do not appear in the song, which makes the title difficult to comprehend and causes some question as to why Ives did not change it, as he did so many others.

In the setting for voice and piano (number 3 in the *114 Songs*), Ives indicates two quotations in the vocal line: one by Spohr, which opens the piece (see Ex. 2.11), and one in the third score, by Haydn. Ives's use of quotations had, of course, become an integral part of his mature writing, and in typical fashion, he quotes the melodies first in simple diatonic form and then proceeds to introduce chromatic alterations and dissonant chordal backgrounds.

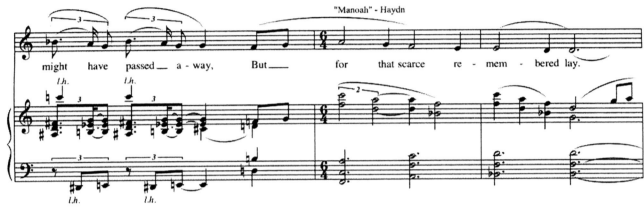

Example 2.10a, mm. 7–9

Example 2.10b, mm. 17–19

The psychological genesis of the use of quotations here seems to be the poem's references to times past and "scarce remembered lays," and Ives's interest in the past is well known. It is also easy to see how he could have identified at this period of his public neglect with Holmes' opening lines:

> I sometimes sit beneath a tree
> And read my own sweet songs;
> Though naught they may to others be . . .

Whatever the sources of the poem's appeal, one finds Ives involved in fascinating complexities in its setting. The rhythmic structure at times mirrors the poetic feet with a 6/4 meter that imitates the iambic pattern, but as often departs into a 3/4 or 4/4 meter that completely transforms the original poetic accents and line arrangement.

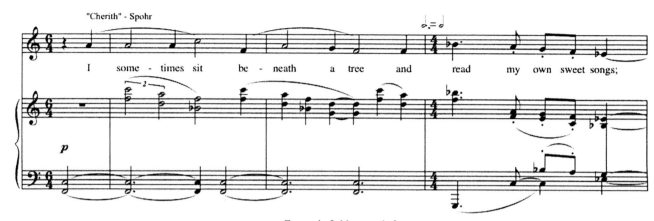

Example 2.11, mm. 1–3

In the beginning of verse III ("As on a father's careworn cheek") rhythmic groupings in the piano's left hand are orga-nized to present a misty, uneven background flow behind the more steadily moving voice line: an effective device but one that is considerably challenging to the performers (see Ex. 2.12).

Harmonic aspects of this song are equally interesting, revealing an essentially diatonic vocal melody that embodies a few surprising chromatic alterations in pursuit of subsequent key shifts, such as the change from a G center to B-flat in measures 11 to 14 (Ex. 2.12). Also notice in measure 11, Example 2.12, that the B-flat triad is already being expressed in the bass clef while the uppermost voice suggests a G harmony and the middle voices, a gratuitous C minor chord.

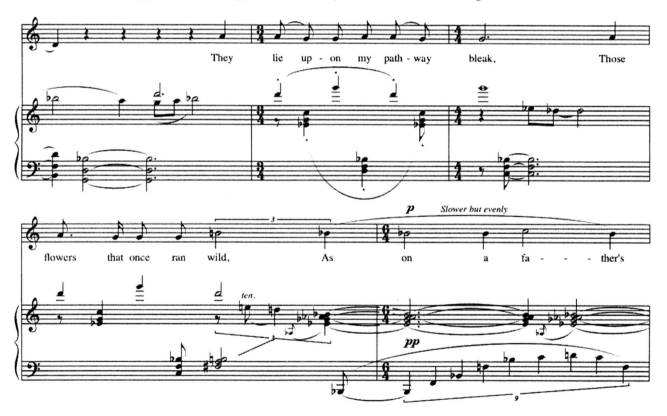

Example 2.12, mm. 10–14

Ives's harmonic vocabulary in the accompaniment includes milder augmented chords and more dissonant minor ninths but all are muted by the *piano* dynamic context. The open fifths of the piano's right hand that begin the song as consonances close its final measures as further soft dissonances. These fifths very likely stem from the original string writing, and their vague, cloudy sound reinforces the poetic portrait of the past seen through the veil of memory.

Charles Sprague (1791–1875)

Charles Sprague was born in Boston only fifteen years after the founding of the United States, and his family was closely tied to the early history of the nation. His father, Samuel Sprague, was present at the Boston Tea Party. His mother, Joanna Thayer, was a descendant of Peregrine White, the first child to be born to the Mayflower group on this continent. From this illustrious background evolved quite naturally his long, respected career as a Boston banker, while from an early devotion to literature arose his lifelong avocation as a poet. Sprague was evidently a man of some reserve, and the majority of his poems were written not to express personal feelings but to commemorate various public events. Among these were *Prologues* celebrating the opening of theaters in New York (1821) and Philadelphia (1822), which won the offered prizes and gained him national recognition. Similar occasions and prizes followed, and in 1830 he produced the "Centennial Ode" for the hundredth-anniversary celebration of the settlement of Boston. It is from this tribute to the Pilgrims and to the indigenous peoples they found here that Ives took his text for "The Indians."

Charles Sprague's moving requiem for the natives of America was, in 1830, prophetic of the sufferings they were to endure during the rest of the nineteenth century. When Charles Ives encountered it almost a hundred years later, the subject obviously made a considerable appeal to his strong sense of social justice and his immersion in America's past. He orchestrated it first in 1912 for voice, trumpet, bassoon, piano, Indian drum, and strings, and arranged it in 1921 for voice and piano. In this remarkable song, Ives intended to create a dirge for a lost race, as is clearly indicated by the slow tempo, narrow-range melody, and repetition in both voice and piano parts. Ignoring the damage to the original rhyme scheme, which is no longer pertinent to his musical assimilation of the poetry, Ives omits lines 2, 7, and 8 of this ten-line poem and repeats the key phrase "No more" in measure 7. From the impetus of this repetition, the vocal line begins a keening incantation, which mounts in intensity through carefully placed accents and increased tempo and dynamic levels (see Ex. 2.13).

Throughout this chant (as in the entire song) measure signatures are constantly changing, syncopations abound, and there are many instances of the kind of misplaced accents on unimportant words that were later to characterize Stravinsky's English-language settings (see Ex. 2.14). The dirge-like character of this modified ABA form is also underlined by a repeated chordal pattern in the accompaniment, which is stated alone in the first two measures and many times thereafter behind the voice (primarily in the A section). These chords, which give the effect of melancholy strumming on an ancient folk instrument, also participate in the voice's melodic material. In a very rare instance in his work, Ives repeats the top line of the chordal sequence in canonic imitation for the vocal setting of the last phrase: "Their children go to die." Notice that the chords that accompany this phrase are a stripped down, barer version of the original sequence that reappears in mm. 18–19 exactly as in mm. 1–2 (see Ex. 2.15).

Example 2.13, mm. 5–8

Example 2.14, mm. 11–13

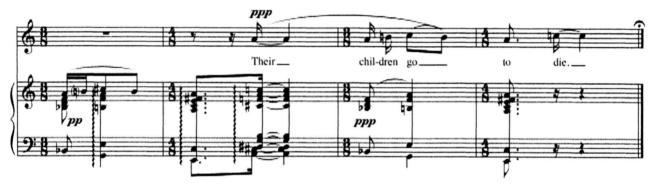

Example 2.15, mm. 18–21

Ralph Waldo Emerson (1803–1882)

Ralph Waldo Emerson, perhaps the greatest of all nineteenth-century American men of letters, led a life filled with paradox. He was a mediocre student at Harvard and a minister who left the calling, yet his writing and religious thought were to influence many generations. He knew the darkness of youthful poverty and the deaths of two brothers, his first wife, and young son, yet went on to establish the Concord Transcendentalists, whose belief rested in essential goodness. Finally, although his literary reputation was for many years founded primarily on his essays and the lectures on which they were based, critics are now coming to believe that Emerson's poetry and its influence on the major American poets who followed have both been grossly underrated.[12]

Despite Emerson's vast importance to the creative life and thought of Charles Ives, it was not primarily as a poet that the composer valued him. In the opening sentence of "Emerson" (number two of the *Essays Before a Sonata*[13]), Ives writes, "It has seemed to the writer that Emerson is greater . . . in the realms of revelation—natural disclosure—than in those of poetry, philosophy or prophecy. Though a great poet and prophet he is greater, possibly, as an invader of the unknown—America's deepest explorer of the spiritual immensities."

Interestingly, it is this very aspect of Emerson as spiritual explorer that places him in the forefront of a characteristically American tradition of poetry. In H. H. Waggoner's words, "American poetry has tended . . . strongly toward the metaphysical" and "at its best . . . has generally centered its attention on searching out the possibilities of discovering ultimate meaning in individual experience."[14] It is perhaps impossible and certainly unnecessary for our purposes to delineate the boundary between Emerson the poet and Emerson the mystic. It is sufficient to observe that the total impact of the man on Charles Ives is magnificently revealed in the "Emerson" movement from the monumental *Concord Sonata* and the essay that precedes it. The song setting called "Duty" is a tiny fragment by comparison, but an interesting one.

"Duty" was originally composed for male chorus with orchestra, somewhere between 1911 and 1913, and rescored for voice and piano in 1921. It forms a pair with a setting of a Latin text by Manlius called "Vita" (or "Life"). Ives's original subtitle—"Two slants, or, Christian and Pagan"—refers to a church sermon heard in Redding, Connecticut, which was the inspiration for these two songs. The Emerson fragment says simply:

> So nigh is grandeur to our Dust
> So near is God to man,
> When Duty whispers low 'Thou must,'
> The youth replies 'I can.'

The Manlius quotation is a single line stating that we are born to die and our end is implicit in our beginning.

It is easy to see why this sermon would have had meaning to the optimist and activist Ives, who believed in religion as a foundation from which every human being might rise to life's challenges. The source of the Emerson verse is section III of a poem called "Voluntaries" (a voluntary being a musical prelude). These particular preludes are trumpet calls to war (in this case the Civil War), for the first two sections mourn the plight of the black in America while the last three importune the youth of the country to heroic action in the slave's behalf.

The setting of "Duty" is the first one of this list to have no meter signature, although all seven measures except the first are in a clear 4/4 or 5/4 grouping. It is also the first to show no repetition in its formal structure, and indeed almost all the songs remaining to be considered will be through-composed. The piano writing incorporates the huge handfuls of dissonant chords covering several octaves that are typical of Ives's orchestral reductions. Frequently these chords are made up of several separate triadic elements, such as the one that occurs on the first syllable of "grandeur" and includes E-flat minor in the bass clef topped by an F major seventh and an open fifth on C-sharp (see Ex. 2.16).

Even in this short space of seven measures, Ives incorporates many details of word painting in setting the text, which help to make this brief musical moment into a complete dramatic experience. Notice the upward sweep of the melodic line over the word "grandeur" and the literal use of the closest chromatic interval, the half-step, to set "near."

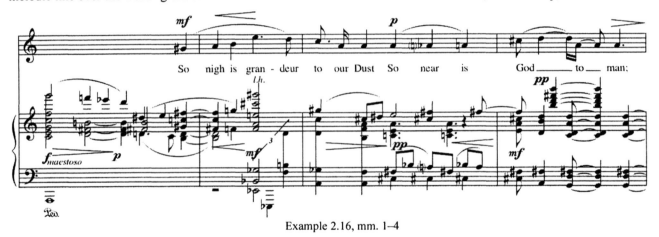

Example 2.16, mm. 1–4

In the second score, Duty's whispering is suggested by very soft portamentos, and the Youth's bold reply is a loud straightforward diatonic cadence, which seems doubly strong after the harmonic and rhythmic confusion that precedes it.

Walt Whitman (1819–1892)

Walt Whitman was not New England born nor was he a product of its historical and intellectual tradition. His father was a Quaker farmer and carpenter, and the family moved to Brooklyn from a Long Island farm when Walt was five years old. Whitman's only formal education was in the Brooklyn public schools, but he read widely on his own and absorbed a great deal from the opera, theaters, and immigrant cultures of New York City. In contrast to those writers who looked toward Europe and were tied to America's past, Whitman's gaze was westward. He was an expansionist in matters geographical, political, and personal, and to express these widened horizons he invented a new poetic language.

This language had its source in the Old Testament of his childhood and in the Shakespearean and operatic cadences that became so familiar to him as a young man. It was to find its chief object in the glorification of the common people—whom Emerson and Transcendentalism had philosophically applauded but never artistically portrayed.

Whitman's debt to Emerson was great, and its true extent is only beginning to be understood.[15] It was no doubt Emerson's concept of a spiritually based, free, original American poet that enabled Whitman to grow into that image. It follows with equal logic that Ives, who shunned the preciousness of the "Rollos"[16] of the world and who described his own spiritual and artistic quest in terms of the aggressive, the masculine, and the homespun, would be drawn to the poetry of Walt Whitman.

Yet although Whitman was indeed one of his favorite poets, Ives set him only once. The song called "Walt Whitman" was originally scored, in 1913, for chorus and orchestra, but the orchestration was vague and sketchy, with the instrumentation indicated toward the end by marginal notes only. In 1921, he rescored it for voice and piano along with a number of others as previously discussed. Given that Ives was to compose only one Whitman setting, this choice of text seems exactly appropriate. It is a pithy, five-line extract from the twentieth section of the most important poem in Whitman's monumental *Leaves of Grass*. "Walt Whitman" is actually an earlier title of "Song of Myself," which many critics consider to be Whitman's greatest poem. Indeed, this poem is central to Whitman's celebration of his own mind and body and that of his fellow human beings.

Although there is no formal repetition in this setting, two types of alternating material appear that seem to grow out of the text. The opening challenge of the question and the all-inclusiveness of the answering description is set in a broad, sweeping style whose chromatic melody, big polytonal chords, and nonmetric rhythm create an appropriate sense of freedom and abandon (see Ex. 2.17). The next four measures move to a 4/4 meter with a square, almost martial rhythm and simple, diatonic triads using open fifths in the piano's treble clef. One sees this as probably a musical representation of strength, both that specifically referred to in the text and the strength that Ives felt pervaded Whitman's life and art.

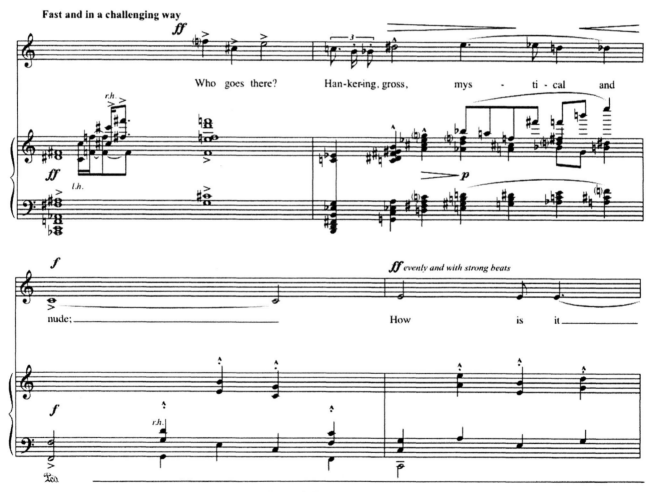

Example 2.17, mm. 1–4

Ives makes two small textual omissions from the line that follows, quoted here in the original (italicized words omitted):

> What is *a* man anyhow? What am I? *and* what are you?

In setting these three questions, he now combines the two former styles, retaining the heavily accented rhythm but breaking it down into faster-moving eighth notes, whose urgency increases with the returning chromaticism. Then the quarter-note rhythm comes back, along with the diatonic harmony, now expressed in full four-voiced accompanying chords. In the extremely interesting final measures, Ives goes from diatonicism to chromaticism to whole-tone scales in an increasingly ambiguous harmonic coloration (see Ex. 2.18).

It has been pointed out that the tendency to ambiguous endings in Ives's work relates to Realism, a literary movement of the late nineteenth century that attempted to imitate life.[17] The lifelike suggestion here is that the song has simply stopped, not ended, and it is reinforced by the fact that the dynamic level remains fortissimo, even as the tempo increases to a sudden and unexpected cutoff:

Example 2.18, mm. 12–17

Vachel Lindsay (1879–1931)

Vachel Lindsay is the only poet of this group who was of midwestern origin. He was born in Springfield, Illinois, and turned an early desire to be a missionary into a lifelong crusade for the arts in America. Like William Blake, he was an artist as well as a poet, and in his early poetry shows the influence as well of Poe, Lanier, and Swinburne. But it is the later Lindsay whom we consider typical: the Lindsay who traveled the country reading such hypnotic verses as "The Congo" and "General Booth" to excited crowds who joined in the chants and perhaps provided the indicated instrumental accompaniments.

Walt Whitman had begun to speak for the common people; Vachel Lindsay brings whole groups of common people before us in living color and action. Although he acknowledged Emerson and Whitman in his "Litany of Heroes," it is not known exactly how well Lindsay was acquainted with their writings. The vigorous grass-roots attitude clearly derives from Whitman, while the style does not. When an uneven poetic inspiration began to fail him totally, Lindsay tragically ended his own life by drinking poison at the age of fifty-two. (For additional biographical material on Vachel Lindsay, see chapter 12.)

"General William Booth Enters into Heaven" was one of the twenty-odd poems using the four-stress line that Vachel Lindsay read with great effect to college crowds and other groups throughout the United States. He had been moved by Booth's story, as it appeared in the death notices, to create this poem in the rhythm of a Salvation Army hymn.[18] In similar fashion Charles Ives was moved to set it after reading a few selected lines reprinted in a local newspaper's bookreview section in 1914. This is certainly one of Ives's best-known, most extensive, and dramatically effective songs, and some of its aspects have been discussed at length in the Ives literature.[19]

This song is a representation in microcosm of all Ives's major philosophical and musical preoccupations. Here we find again the Realist's imitation of life, this time through the inclusion of a multiplicity of sound materials (instrumental imitations, hymn and song quotations, shouts and screeches), which add up to the evangelist's aural chaos. We also find the various levels of Ives's religious experience and concern, which ranged from revivalism itself to the Transcendental belief in the primacy of the common.

Musically, the Ives trademarks are many, now fully developed and at the same time totally subservient to dramatic ends. Here is the additive structure of one unlike section following another, unified by frequent interpolations of the hymn-tune quotation, which comes into full flower at the end. Here are Ives's dissonant cluster chords utilizing their percussive effect in imitation of Booth's "big bass drum" (see Ex. 2.19), and here are the declamatory vocal passages employing many repeated or adjacent tones, which Ives often used to suggest the speech-like quality of his text (see Ex. 2.20).

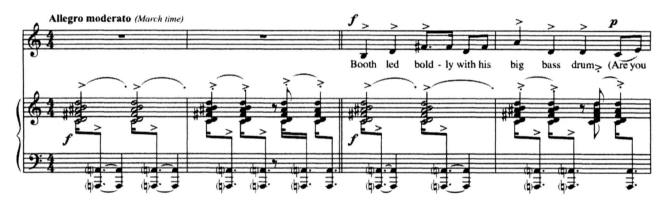

Example 2.19, mm. 1–4

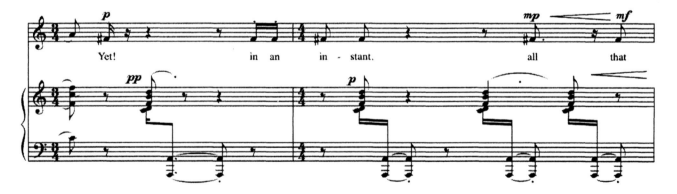

Example 2.20, mm. 91–92

Ives's well-known complexity of rhythmic organization is strongly in evidence throughout this song. One form it assumes is unusual meter signatures and/or unlike adjacent meters (see Ex. 2.21). Another form is that of a complex relationship within a measure between notes and accompaniment (see Ex. 2.20).

Example 2.21, mm. 61–65

One of the most effective aspects of Ives's setting of "General Booth" arises from his well-developed ability to sense what he needed from a poem and how he must adapt it for his purposes. In this instance, Ives uses thirty-one lines out of fifty-six, or three sections out of seven (sections here being defined as separated by instrumental indications). From the lines chosen, he omits only two words ("the" before "saints" in measure 13 and "there" before "round" in measure 87); he adds only two ("Hallelujah" in measure 10 and "Lord" in mm. 62 and 63); and changes only one ("Then" becomes "yet" in measure 91). But it is his constant use of text *repetition* throughout the setting that in large measure creates the hysterical crescendo of emotion that is the prevailing climate of revivalism. Almost every poetic statement of the refrain "Are you washed in the blood of the lamb?" is repeated by Ives as a whole or in multiple parts (see Ex. 2.22).

Example 2.22, mm. 75–80

The phrase "round and round" is repeated four times in a narrow-range vocal chant that becomes increasingly hypnotic:

Example 2.23, mm. 88–90

Finally, Ives expands a single "Hallelujah" in the second section to a veritable litany of five "Hallelujahs" and two "Lords" in a frenzy of evangelical ecstasy that is reinforced by the tumbling syncopation and uneven measures (see Ex. 2.21).

Henry David Thoreau (1817–1862)

Thoreau was another of Ives's New England philosophical mentors of the transcendental persuasion. Like Emerson, he was an indifferent scholar at Harvard while receiving a sound classical education there, and he refused Harvard's diploma, claiming that he had "better use for five dollars." During his working lifetime, he was variously engaged as a schoolmaster, manager of his father's pencil factory, and handyman and disciple in the home of Emerson. The years 1845 and 1847 were spent in the well-known sojourn by Walden Pond, where his true vocations of naturalist and essayist received free rein.

The principal sources of Thoreau's writing were the journals that he kept from 1834 to his untimely death from tuberculosis in 1862. In the early 1840s, he gave up poetry, which had never been a congenial medium, for prose, which was, in his hands, a poetic form. Indeed, the text of "Thoreau " is a quotation adapted and rearranged from the essay in *Walden* entitled "Sounds," yet the writers find the inclusion of this song with other settings of American poetry totally appropriate.

The song bears the date of 1915 and comes at the end of Ives's long years of work on the *Concord Sonata* (1909–1915).[20] Like many of his other songs that were to emerge from instrumental works, this one was adapted from the material of the last movement of the sonata, which was also titled "Thoreau." Both the piano piece and the song are representative of what Hans Nathan calls Ives's "Thoreauesque communion with Nature." This is a theme that runs through much of his music, and by which he is inspired "in particular by the chance simultaneity of heard and seen phenomena such as rustling trees, echoes, mist, and their variegated intensities."[21]

The text is actually divided into two sections, the first of which is printed with the obvious intention of being read aloud by the singer, although it is unfortunately omitted in some performances. These lines are a perfect example of the "simultaneity of heard and seen phenomena" mentioned above, and describe the effect of distance on Thoreau's perceptions at Walden of the Concord bell and of a far-off azure-tinted ridge of earth. For the music played by the piano as background to the reading, Ives draws from the second score of page 63 of the *Concord Sonata*.[22] He uses chordal material which he first presents as a harp-like sweep up the keyboard (suggested by the text), then as an alternation of hazy chordal configurations and bell-like tones. This material, like all the rest in this adaptation, is transposed up for the song setting, and in this case is a whole-tone higher than in the sonata.

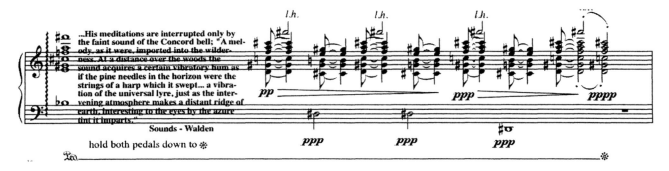

Example 2.24

The rest of the text, which is sung by the voice, describes Thoreau lost in his reveries at Walden, and here Ives has added to the original material a vocal line that is largely chant-like with many single-note repetitions. He superimposes this line on material that is drawn from page 66, third score, in the sonata (transposed up a half-tone) followed by page 65, third and fourth scores (transposed up a whole-step).

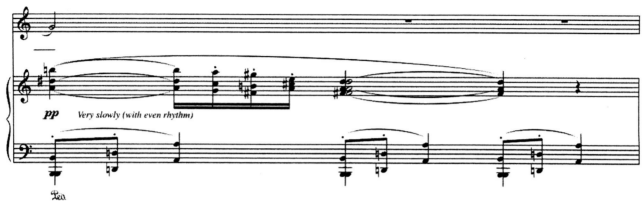

Example 2.25

All these elements come together to produce a remarkable effect despite the brevity of this setting. The sense of concentrated, meditative stillness is achieved by the soft dynamic level, the vocal repetition and the ostinato figure in the bass, which perfectly sustains the mood if performed according to Ives's directions ("very slowly and with even rhythm;" see Ex. 2.25). As a final crowning touch, Ives sets the last syllable of the word "solitude" as a unison between the voice and piano, which creates a very "solitary" effect indeed coming after the preceding mass of blurred, unresolved dissonances.

Example 2.26

Louis Untermeyer (1885–1978)

Louis Untermeyer was a New York poet who led a long and distinguished career in American literature. Besides his volumes of original poetry, he also published translations, paraphrases, and witty imitations of other poets, and is perhaps best known in his capacity as editor of such critical anthologies as *Modern American Poetry*.[23]

Much of his original poetry is distinguished by an expansive, Romantic quality that is certainly apparent in "The Swimmers," a poem that captured Ives's attention when it appeared in the *Yale Review* of July 1915. Here again, Ives uses only an eleven-line fragment of the original fifty-eight, but his setting maintains the vigorous, life-intoxicated atmosphere of this moment, when a young man pits his strength against the sea.

This song, like "Thoreau," is composed essentially without bar-lines. Although some sections do have a clear metric organization, the overall effect is that of a free ranging rhythm in constant response to the ebb and flow of the text. The accompaniment is among Ives's most pianistic and technically demanding. Shades of Chopin are evoked in his opening indication of "Slowly (as a Barcarolle)" and by virtuoso passages of rapid scales and arpeggios, full and broken-chord figures, etc. We know, however, that we are in Ives's world, not Chopin's, not only by the dissonance but also from the

Ivesian footnotes. These inform the pianist to play a phrase not precisely the number of times written, or to add an extra player in a very heavily scored section, or to make the suggested variations of the most difficult figurations.

In this type of footnote (similar to those that appear in the song "Charlie Rutlage" and other of his compositions), Ives makes it clear that the precise musical details are less important to him than their contribution to the overall effect. And a highly dramatic effect it is indeed, as the piano imitates the surge and swell of the water, at the same time forming the background and also a kind of adversary to the vocal line, which expresses the poet's struggle to master the sea's natural force.

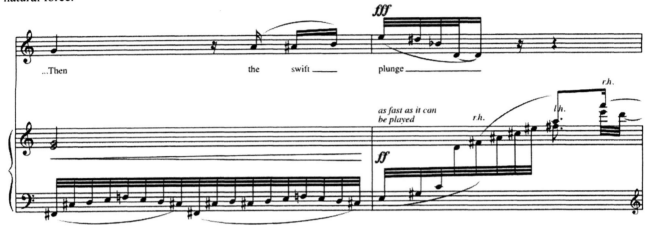

Example 2.27

Against the unconventional aspects of this setting, Ives here again juxtaposes time-honored techniques of word painting in the vocal line. "The swift plunge" is portrayed by a rapid downward rush of three increasingly large intervals (see Ex. 2.27). "Swiftly I rose" is an upward chromatic line with a tempo marking of "gradually faster."

Example 2.28

"Turbulent strife" and "the feverish intensity of life" are also set with rapidly moving notes and the harmonic urgency of chromatic intervals (see Ex. 2.29).

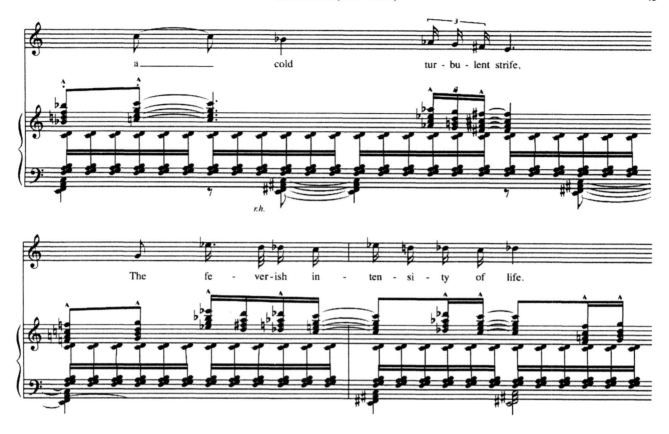

Example 2.29

The vocal setting of "I lurched and rode the wave" forms an actual picture of the text in its melodic movement of a large leap followed by a gently rocking alternation of whole-steps up and down.

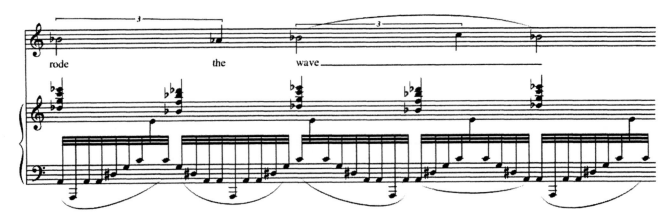

Example 2.30

"Swimming hand over hand" is another pictorial suggestion, which is heightened by Ives's repetition of "over hand" (see Ex. 2.31).

In the final line, the "sea's vain pounding" is suggested by an alternating pattern of accented chords in the accompaniment, as the piano continues to represent the water to the end of the song. Interestingly, the word "master," which connotes the strength and resolution of man triumphing over nature, is set here with a simple D major diatonic triad: the only one of its kind in the entire song. This is reminiscent of the similar diatonic ending of "Duty" on the words "I can," and seems to give the lie to a notion expressed by some writers that Ives always equated strength with difficulty and complexity in his music (see Ex. 2.32).

Example 2.31

Example 2.32

James Fenimore Cooper (1892–1918)

World War I was a shock from which Charles Ives and his faith in human progress never recovered. In 1918, he had a serious illness that left him with permanent damage to his heart, and from 1919 to 1921 his composition was limited to the solo-song arrangements from former choral or instrumental works, and a few new songs. After 1921, there were no further completed works, although Ives lived on until 1954.

The Charles Ives of "Afterglow" (1919) and "Maple Leaves" (1920) is a different man from the Ives of the earlier songs. Gone is the social libertarian's faith in the common people and their destiny, and gone is the joyful Transcendental immersion in the eternal oneness of nature and God. What is left, as expressed in these texts, seems to be an autumnal resignation to the transitory nature of the good and beautiful things of life.

James Fenimore Cooper Jr., who was born in Albany, New York, was a great-grandson of the novelist,[24] but was unlike his famous forebear in two important ways. Whereas the elder Cooper had been expelled from Yale after two years, the younger not only graduated Phi Beta Kappa from the same institution but received other literary and scholarly honors, and was class secretary as well. Further, where the great-grandfather's early experiments in poetry had revealed his incapacity for the art, the great-grandson showed considerable promise as a poet, a promise that was cut off by his early death.

After leaving Yale, James Fenimore Cooper spent several years traveling in Europe and the western United States, and made an unsuccessful attempt to study law at Harvard. He had about decided to settle at Cooperstown, New York (founded by the novelist's father), and pursue a writing career, when World War I drew him into the start of what seemed to be a promising career in the military. However, he caught pneumonia and died at Camp Dix, New Jersey, and the only published collection of his verse appeared in 1918 as a memorial volume.

A few of the poems in this volume (of which "Afterglow" is the frontispiece) had already appeared in the Yale literary magazine, so it is possible that Ives had already known of the young poet's work before the posthumous publication. It is interesting that for both of these late songs Ives chooses very short poems ("Afterglow" is eight lines, "Maple Leaves" four) and sets them just as they are, with no deletions, additions, repetitions, or changes. The style of "Afterglow" is much like that of "Thoreau," with an absence of bar-lines, many widely spaced accompaniment chords made up of superimposed harmonies, and a narrow-range melody of largely stepwise motion. At various points in this stepwise motion, Ives employs two of his favorite nondiatonic forms of organization: the whole-tone scale for the opening phase and the chromatic scale to set "Lingers still the afterglow."

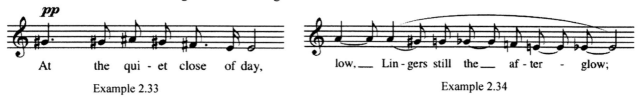

Example 2.33   Example 2.34

The song as a whole seems to center around E and its stepwise neighbors (E-flat, D, F, F-sharp) in a technique reminiscent of one Stravinsky was to use heavily in his neoclassic period.[25] The two vocal fragments just quoted center on E and E-flat, respectively, and the close of the song approaches E by the Phrygian lowered second step.

Example 2.35

Other melodic goals of the vocal line are F and F-sharp, while the piano has many reiterations of E-flat as a low pedal tone.

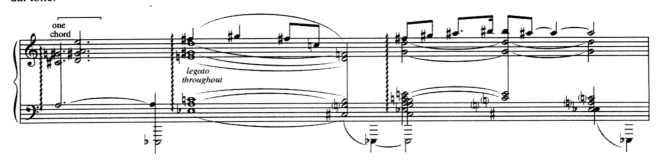

Example 2.36

Word-painting does not occur in this song, although the entire setting is a musical expression of such words as "quiet" and "gently," which occur in the first two poetic lines. Ives's footnote, which says "The piano part should be played as indistinctly as possible and both pedals used almost constantly," suggests the hazy, almost inaudible aura of sound he wishes to establish. The mood that emerges represents the psychological hush that occurs as the dying of the light reaches its final moments. In Griffes's setting of Lanier's "Evening Song," this same moment is one of love's joyous confirmation. By contrast, the dying of the light in "Afterglow" seems attended by uncertainty and regret.

Thomas Bailey Aldrich (1836–1907)

Thomas Bailey Aldrich, born in Portsmouth, New Hampshire, became a well-known novelist and poet despite the fact that his father's death prevented him from attending Harvard as he had planned. He began his career, as did so many nineteenth-century writers, as a newspaper editor, and also served as correspondent in the Civil War. In 1865, he moved to Boston, and in 1881 took over the editorship of the *Atlantic Monthly* from William Dean Howells. After 1891, he retired from the *Atlantic* and devoted his remaining years to writing.

Aldrich's position in literary history is as one of a group of conservatives who, from the Civil War to the turn of the century, tried to hold the line against the materialism of the age and against Realism in literature. His poetry surpassed his prose, and he was a superb craftsman in the poetic art. The "quatrains," or four-line poems, are generally conceded to be among his best poetic statements, and "Maple Leaves" is one of these.

Ives's craftsmanship in this setting is in every way equal to the poet's, and the result is a tiny jewel of a song almost glittering in the brilliant perfection of its eleven measures. The composer now returns to the world of bar-lines, and the beats add up to 4/4 throughout, although there is no meter signature. Syncopations and unusual accents in the text setting and accompaniment, however, belie the seeming simplicity of the rhythmic organization.

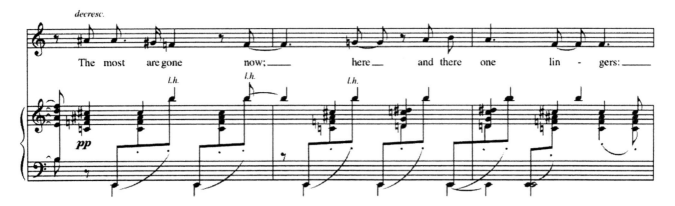

Example 2.37, mm. 4–6

The harmony proves deceptive, also, and a simple opening in G major soon begins to "turn" just like the maple leaves. Increasing chromatic additions to voice and piano parts culminate in a most unexpected D-sharp on "gold," and the foreign quality of the harmony portrays the shock of the color transformation.

Example 2.38, mm. 1–3

With the second score, a note of the inevitability of loss begins to sound, and Ives matches the text with his melancholy descending vocal line ("The most are gone now"),[26] cloudy harmonies, and faintly insistent repetition of the high B in the piano score (see Ex. 2.37).

In measure 7, we realize that this small song is actually a modified ABA form, and it is interesting to note that Ives comes back to the more traditional modes of rhythm and structure in this very late composition. With the return to material like the opening, Ives now expands the chromatic milieu of mm. 2 and 3 (Ex. 2.38). The voice part, as it describes the leaves slipping from the twigs, is a group of short, uneasy half- and whole-step phrases, and in a final portamento series of disappearing half-steps, the leaves cling desperately but vainly to the tree, just as the dying miser tries to hold on to his coins. This is musical pictorialism of great subtlety and power, the more effective in its seeming simplicity.

Notes

1. This article, called "The Ives Case," was first published in *Modern Music* in 1934. In 1940, a few revisions were made and it was republished in Aaron Copland's *The New Music* (New York: Norton, 1968).

2. For general discussions of Ives's songs, see: (a) Hans Nathan, "The Modern Period—United States of America," *A History of Song*, ed. Denis Stevens (New York: Norton, 1960), 431–37; (b) Henry and Sidney Cowell, *Charles Ives and His Music* (New York: Oxford University Press, 1969), 182–91 and scattered references throughout the text; (c) H. Wiley Hitchcock, *Music in the United States: A Historical Introduction* (Englewood Cliffs, N.J.: Prentice-Hall, 1969), 155–62; (d) John Kirkpatrick, *Charles E. Ives—Memos* (New York: Norton, 1972), complete listing of all published songs and their reprints to date of publication, 167–77; (e) Rosalie Sandra Perry, *Charles Ives and the American Mind* (Kent, Ohio: Kent State University Press, 1974), scattered references; (f) H. Wiley Hitchcock, *Ives* (New York: Oxford University Press, 1977), 9–27.

3. The quotation is from Emerson's essay "The American Scholar."

4. Horatio Parker (1863–1919) was an American composer and educator who chaired the Yale Music Department for twenty-five years. For a discussion of his influence on Charles Ives, see Perry, *C. Ives and the American Mind*, 9.

5. Perry, *C. Ives and the American Mind*, Chapter 2, "Ives and the Transcendental Tradition."

6. In 1922, Charles Ives had issued a privately printed collection that he called *114 Songs*. Although smaller numbers of these were subsequently reprinted, the collection as a whole went out of print and was finally reissued in 1975 by Peer International Corp., New York. All the songs discussed in this chapter may be found in the *114 Songs* except "General William Booth Enters Into Heaven" which is available in Ives's *19 Songs* published by Theodore Presser. See also the following critical edition: H. Wiley Hitchcock, ed., *Charles Ives: 129 Songs* (Middleton, Wisc.: A-R Editions, 2004),

and for a description of the problems encountered in its preparation, see H. Wiley Hitchcock, "Editing Ives's *129 Songs*" in *Ives Studies,* ed. Philip Lambert (New York: Cambridge University Press, 1997).

7. By an interesting coincidence, the last of the three girls who appear in stanza 3 ("Grave Alice and laughing Allegra and Edith with golden hair") bore the same name as Charles Ives's adopted daughter.

8. Hyatt H. Waggoner, *American Poets from the Puritans to the Present* (New York: Dell, 1968), 42.

9. There is an earlier anthem version of "The Light That Is Felt" of uncertain date (1895–1902). See Appendix 2, 148, and Appendix 4, 172, in John Kirkpatrick, ed., *Charles E. Ives: Memos* (New York: Norton, 1972).

10. Hitchcock, *Ives*, 9.

11. For a further discussion of this hymn and its textual associations, see Hitchcock, *Ives*, 99 ff.

12. See Waggoner, *American Poets*, chapter on Emerson, 90 ff.

13. *The Essays Before a Sonata* were originally designed to accompany the second piano sonata (or *Concord Sonata*) but were finally printed separately because of their considerable length. For an extensive treatment of these essays, see Cowell, *Charles Ives and His Music*, 81 ff.

14. Waggoner, *American Poets,* 94.

15. Waggoner, *American Poets,* 150 ff.

16. "Rollo" was Ives's personification of what he conceived to be a weak, unadventurous, overly traditional approach to the art of music. As an example, see Ives's remarks concerning "Rollo" Henderson (a *New York Times* music critic) quoted in Kirkpatrick, *Memos*, 30 ff.

17. For a discussion of the influence of Realism on Ives's work, see Perry, *C. Ives and the American Mind,* 56 ff.

18. General William Booth was the founder of the Salvation Army.

19. Particularly recommended are the treatments in the Hitchcock references listed in n2. For speculations on the chronology of existing instrumental sketches, see Kirkpatrick, *Memos*, 162 and 176.

20. The text of the song "Thoreau " was originally embedded in the final chapter of *Essays Before a Sonata.* Ives printed a small portion of this chapter at the beginning of the "Thoreau" movement of the *Concord Sonata.* Its use as the song text was, therefore, its third appearance.

21. Nathan, "The Modern Period," 436 ff.

22. The page and score numbers given here derive from the Associated Music Publishers' edition of the *Concord Sonata.* As there are very few bar lines in the work, measure numbers cannot be supplied.

23. A conversation between Charles Ives and Louis Untermeyer took place in 1943 or 1944 and is described by Untermeyer in Vivian Perlis, *Charles Ives Remembered* (New Haven, Conn.: Yale University Press, 1974), 211–13. Especially interesting are Untermeyer's speculations as to why Ives set so little contemporary poetry.

24. In 1905, Harmony Twichell (a graduate nurse since 1900) made a trip to Europe as companion to Mrs. Dean Sage of Albany. By coincidence, the trip was made in company with J. F. Cooper, the novelist's son, and his son Jimmie, later to become the author of "Afterglow."

25. Ives's structures in this song resemble the technique (called "pan-diatonicism") in his use of stepwise adjacent tonal centers. Ives's language, however, is chromatic, whereas Stravinsky's, in this context, was primarily diatonic.

26. For a revealing anecdote told by John Kirkpatrick about Ives's notation of this vocal fragment, see Perlis, *Charles Ives Remembered*, 220–21.

Chapter 3

Settings by Six "Americanists"

The first two decades of the twentieth century saw the American art song enriched by two diverse strains. On the one hand, there were composers, such as Charles Griffes, whose works incorporated the most sophisticated of foreign influences. On the other, there was Charles Ives, whose secret flowering of astonishingly original songs was largely rooted in native soil. During these twenty years, a new group of composers was developing. Many of these would follow Ives's lead in turning away from European artistic domination[1] and would become "Americanists," in Gilbert Chase's terminology.[2] They would explore and incorporate into their serious composition such indigenous American elements as minstrelsy, ragtime and blues, jazz, Negro spirituals, and Anglo-American folk music.[3]

With the passage of almost a century, it has become clear that the impulse toward "Americanism" was to a large extent the artistic counterpart of post World War I isolationism in the political sphere. In truth, half of the six "Americanists" whose songs are about to be discussed did hone their creativity in Europe with Nadia Boulanger. Several of them also experimented at some point with the atonality and serial techniques that were gaining strength as the new European musical language. But the urge to define what was "American" in musical terms was a powerful one to all of them. As the Depression brought the needs of the common people into sharp relief, and the developing mass media made it possible to reach them, these composers labored to find a form of expression that would have meaning to the vast, emerging American musical public.

The songs about to be discussed are by Douglas Moore, Ernst Bacon, William Grant Still, Florence Price, Roy Harris, and Aaron Copland. Their dates of composition range from the 1920s to 1950. The texts are similar in that they are all by American poets, but they differ inasmuch as these American poets include male and female, white and black, and personalities ranging from intellectual recluse to self-educated man of the people. The musical settings are as varied as their poetic origins, yet each is a unique embodiment of the "American" in music: an artistic representation, as it were, of one of the many faces of America.

Douglas Moore (1893–1969)

Few, if any, American composers have equaled Douglas Moore in number of generations of ancestors in this country. His father's forebears emigrated from England before 1640 to establish the oldest English-speaking settlement in New York State at Southold Town on Long Island. His mother traced her family tree back to Miles Standish and John Alden, and Moore's elder daughter reinforced the Puritan strain by marrying a descendant of Governor Bradford.

The composer himself was born in Cutchogue, Long Island, and while preparing at Hotchkiss for Yale he met Archibald MacLeish, a classmate. MacLeish was the first American poet of the several with whom Douglas Moore was to establish fruitful collaborations. At Yale, he studied, as had Charles Ives, with Horatio Parker, and spent two years beyond the Bachelor of Arts taking a second undergraduate degree in music. During one of his summer vacations, he wrote a number of songs while living at the MacDowell Colony, which was a summer retreat for creative artists in New

Hampshire and an enterprise to which his family had made financial contributions. A stint in the U.S. Navy during World War I led to collaboration with John Jacob Niles on an amusing volume called *Songs My Mother Never Taught Me*. When the war was over, Moore resisted pressure to enter the family publishing business and went off to Paris to study. Here he worked with Vincent D'Indy and also with Nadia Boulanger, the gifted teacher who helped so many Americans find their own unique styles of composition.

In Paris, he met Stephen Vincent Benét, who became his second major American literary source. Through the years, Moore set many of his poems, both for solo voice and choral groups. Their association culminated when Benét's short story "The Devil and Daniel Webster" became Douglas Moore's opera of the same name in 1939. Vachel Lindsay, the third major American poetic force in the composer's life, appeared by chance one day in the library of the Cleveland Museum of Art when Moore was employed there as Curator of Music in the early 1920s. Lindsay was the person who opened his perceptions to the beauty and flavor of American life. Indeed, it was this encounter that inspired an orchestral work called "The Pageant of P. T. Barnum"—the first in Moore's long line of compositions based on American themes.

Douglas Moore was woven even more firmly into the fabric of American musical life by means of his long teaching career at Columbia University. Having joined the music faculty in 1926, he held the position of executive director of the department from 1940 to 1962. From this vantage point, he exerted considerable influence on large numbers of teachers, composers, and performers who received their training at Barnard College or Columbia University (including R. Friedberg). For a number of years, his course in twentieth-century music was a highlight of the Columbia undergraduate curriculum offerings. He distilled the essence of his classroom lectures into two volumes published ten years apart: *Listening to Music* (1932)[4] and *From Madrigal to Modern Music* (1942).[5]

It is easy to see, therefore, how Gilbert Chase's designation of Moore as an "Americanist" came about. It derived first of all from his choices of subject matter in all musical forms. These included the symphonic poem he programmatically titled "Moby Dick," a setting of Benét's "Ballad of William Sycamore" for voice and chamber orchestra, and most characteristic of all in contemporary minds, *The Ballad of Baby Doe*—that highly successful opera, produced in 1955, that dealt with the era of silver mining in the West. Reinforcing the literary and historical allusions, moreover, is the musical language developed by the composer, which Aaron Copland found to be highly "evocative of the homely virtues of rural America." This language, in its "simplicity and unadorned charm" bore no similarity to anything in serious European music, and was the musical counterpart of a regionalism that had found expression somewhat earlier in American literature and painting.[6]

Moore himself delineated his own artistic goals in much the same terms. "The particular ideal which I have been striving to attain," he said, "is to write music which . . . will reflect the exciting quality of life, traditions and country which I feel all about me. . . . If we . . . feel romantically inclined, if we like a good tune now and then, is it not well for us to admit the fact and try to produce something which we like ourselves?"[7] The great extent to which he succeeded in these aims is noted by all who have studied and written about his music. It has been perhaps most cogently expressed by the conductor Thomas Scherman, who had been his student at Columbia University. "What I . . . have . . . come to appreciate," writes Scherman, "is Moore's very personal melodic drive, the inherent dramatic variety and contrast in his music, and above all the ingenuous and intoxicating exuberance it exudes."[8]

Stephen Vincent Benét (1898–1943)

Stephen Vincent Benét, who wrote the text of the first song to be considered, was, like Douglas Moore, an Easterner, and was born in Bethlehem, Pennsylvania. There is no record of their meeting before Paris, but one is drawn to speculate on how closely their paths might have crossed during the two undergraduate years when they were both at Yale. (Moore graduated in 1917 and Benét in 1919.) Although he died at the early age of 45, Benét contributed during that short span to many literary forms as poet, playwright, radio dramatist, and short-story writer. Not only was *his* life devoted to writing, but other family members as well rose to literary prominence. His brother, William Rose Benét, and sister-in-law, Elinor Wylie, were both well-known poets, and his wife, Rosemary, to whom he dedicated some of his most sensitive verses, collaborated with him on a number of occasions.

Stephen Vincent Benét's imagination, again like Douglas Moore's, was fired by American heroes and history. His epic poem *John Brown's Body* won him a Pulitzer Prize in 1928. It quickly became an American classic for its sympathetic portrayal of the ordinary individuals involved in the Civil War. *Western Star* (1943), which dramatized the journey of the Pilgrims, was the first part of another American epic unfortunately left unfinished at his death. While much of his poetry, particularly the historical portraits, exhibits a sweeping Romanticism,[9] the flavor of "Adam Was My Grandfather,"[10] which Douglas Moore set in 1938, is somewhat different.

The original title of the poem was "For All Blasphemers." In it, the speaker boasts of his kinship with Adam's disobedience and Noah's drunkenness, and his attraction to the charms of Lilith. He also knows that his certain destiny will be "gaudy Hell" and the ministrations of "His Worship" (the Devil). The four swaggering verses are full of a kind of frontier irreverence, which acknowledges a strong faith in the Bible but is nevertheless willing to take on the consequences of sin in exchange for present pleasure.

Moore has made only two small alterations in the poem for purposes of his setting. In the second verse, he changes "Past Hell's most shrinking star" to "Beyond a shrinking star," and in the final stanza, "when His Worship takes me up" becomes "then His Worship." The latter is likely a printer's error, since the original is both sensible and grammatical whereas the change is neither.

The rollicking, lusty tone of the poem is perfectly captured by the strongly accented accompaniment of the song, with its overlay in the voice part of heavy syncopation.

Example 3.1, mm. 9–14

The Lilith verse changes to *dolce*, which mood is fostered by legato arpeggios in the accompaniment and a melodic line of melting contours.

Example 3.2, mm. 59–65

The harmonic style is for the most part simplistically diatonic, but contrast is created by the fact that verses 1 and 4 are in F minor, while 2 and 3 move to C and D-flat major, respectively. There is an interesting chromatic sidestep near the end to B major through its dominant seventh of F-sharp. This seems designed to represent "gaudy Hell" by means of harmonic color.

Example 3.3, mm. 92–96

Theodore Roethke (1908–1963)

The second setting by Douglas Moore to be treated here is somewhat similar in musical language but quite different in mood and atmosphere. "Old Song"[11] was written a dozen years later than "Adam" and uses a text by Theodore Roethke.

Roethke published his remarkable first collection of poetry, *Open House*, in 1941, and in the ensuing decades came to be regarded as one of our leading twentieth-century American poets. He was born in Saginaw, Michigan, and his childhood impressions were much influenced by his experiences in the greenhouses of his father, who was a flower-grower by profession. In maturity, his poetic style ranged widely between strict and free forms, the lyric and the dramatic, the rational and irrational, the natural and the mystical. Although Roethke's language remains simple,[12] the thought often leans toward the metaphysical. Some of our finest critics have for this reason placed him in our major poetic tradition as defined by Emerson, Whitman, and Dickinson.[13] Theodore Roethke affirms this metaphysical stance by his own characterization of a poem as "part of a hunt, a drive toward God; an effort to break through the barrier of rational experience."[14]

In "Old Song," the sophisticated simplicity of Moore's style is a perfect foil for the economy of Roethke's language, as the poet recounts how he "came to the willow alone" and waited for his true love by the river until "at last the whole dark came down." The poet and the composer seem, as the title suggests, to have created a folk ballad in which the age-old situation of lost love is lamented strophically in direct, uncomplicated terms. The regular rhythmic patterns and mostly diatonic harmonies reinforce this folk-like atmosphere, while the occasional melodic alterations to a lowered third, sixth, or seventh scale degree give it an almost Elizabethan or at least Appalachian flavor. Subtle details, however, reveal the hand of the art song composer, such as the canonic treatment of voice and piano,

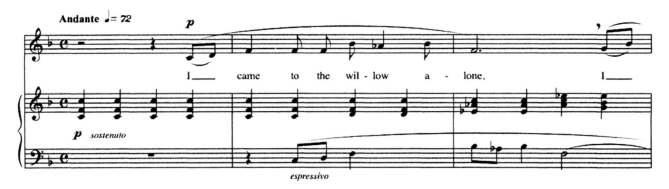

Example 3.4, mm. 1–3

the pathos of the large melodic leaps,

Example 3.5, mm. 9–13

the pictorial suggestion of flowing water in the left hand of the accompaniment,

Example 3.6, mm. 24–25

and the ending that trails off into uncertainty on the dominant with an unresolved circling figure below.

Example 3.7, mm. 39–43

Still another level of meaning appears to the writers as inherent in this poem and its setting. It is underlined by the fact that Moore keeps the mode primarily major and the nature imagery, such as a pianistic birdcall, joyfully pastoral,[15] so that the overall mood of the song is peace, rather than pain. Is there then, one wonders, no specific love, and is the poet rather indulging the favorite fantasy of youth in a beautiful natural setting? Or even further, is this Roethke, the metaphysician telling us that what he is really "waiting" for is that sense of unity with the material and spiritual world that he has elsewhere expressed in these terms: "I lose and find myself in the long water."[16] Many levels of love, it seems, may be suggested here, and the song retains its power on all of them.

William Grant Still (1895–1978)

In typical American fashion, William Grant Still possessed a mixed racial heritage, which included Indian, Negro, and European strains. His parents were both college-trained teachers, but his father, who had taught music at the Agricultural and Mechanical College of Alabama, died in his son's infancy. After this, his mother moved from Woodville, Mississippi, to Little Rock, Arkansas, where she joined the English faculty of a local high school. Young William's developing musicality continued to be fostered by a grandmother who sang the traditional Negro spirituals and hymns around the house, and a step-father who bought him the early Red Seal operatic recordings and took him to concerts and musical shows.

William's mother, like so many other parents of artistic children, would have preferred the more "respectable" profession of medicine for him, but his growing interest in music drew him to Oberlin, where a scholarship in composition was specially created for him. Similar grants allowed him to study with George Chadwick at the New England Conservatory and Edgard Varèse in New York. Through these studies, he became well grounded in the European modes of composition that prevailed in the first quarter of the century in the Eastern cultural centers. It is also interesting to note that Still gained experience playing orchestral instruments and orchestrating for people like W. C. Handy, Sophie Tucker, and Paul Whiteman between the Oberlin and New England Conservatory years. This gave him the considerable advantage of being able to think orchestrally in his composition and at the same time makes all the more remarkable his sensitive piano writing in the songs, since his keyboard skills were not very highly developed.

In the article "My Arkansas Boyhood," the composer relates that although his works in Varèse's dissonant idiom brought him critical acclaim, he felt that they did not truly represent his own musical individuality and decided to adopt a racial form of expression "I then made an effort," he wrote, "to elevate the folk idiom . . . though rarely making use of actual folk themes. For the most part, I was developing my own themes in the style of the folk."[17] The song that he composed in 1927 called "Winter's Approach"[18] is representative of this period.

Paul Laurence Dunbar (1872–1906)

The text of the song is by Paul Laurence Dunbar, a late-nineteenth-century poet born in Ohio, where his parents had settled after escaping slavery in Kentucky. While in high school in Dayton, Dunbar was already writing for student publications. Upon graduation, lacking funds to go on to law school as he wished, he took a job as an elevator operator. In 1893, he published one volume of poetry at his own expense (raising funds by selling copies on the elevator) and was then aided by friends in the publication of a second. One of these friends was William Dean Howells, who in 1896 gave him a full-page review in *Harper's Weekly*, and also wrote a highly laudatory preface to Dunbar's *Lyrics of Lowly Life*. In this preface, Howells has particular praise for the poems in Negro dialect, which he found to be quite unique "divinations and reports of what passes in the hearts and minds of a . . . people whose poetry had hitherto been inarticulately expressed in music but now finds, for the first time in our tongue, literary interpretation of a very artistic completeness."[19]

"Winter's Approach," a poem from the collection *Lyrics of Sunshine and Shadow*, tells how "Ol' Brer Rabbit be a-layin' low," knowing "dat de wintah time a-comin'" and that "de huntah man" and his dog are waiting for him while the hunter's wife gets the skillet ready. The Brer Rabbit tales are an old tradition in American black folklore and were originally told in the Gullah dialect of the blacks who still inhabit the isolated islands off the South Carolina coast. As Dunbar writes the poem, it is a skillful crystallization of dialect and rhythmic patterns into an evocative folk ballad, which draws sympathy for the crafty but beleaguered rabbit while it understands the realities of the society that threatens him.

It was quite natural that Still would turn to a Dunbar dialect poem during the period when he was trying to make a racial statement by means of "elevating the folk idiom." He uses the three swinging verses of the poem exactly as they were written, except that instead of the indicated repetitions of the line "He know dat de wintah time a-comin'," which follow each couplet, the composer substitutes a knowing little five-note humming pattern.

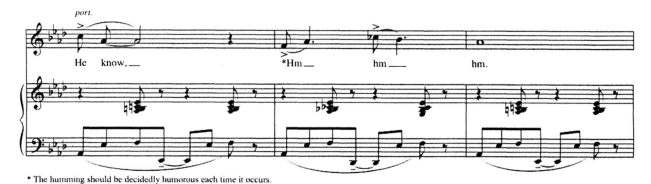

* The humming should be decidedly humorous each time it occurs.

Example 3.8, mm. 15–17

This humming refrain and the instruction that it "should be decidedly humorous each time it occurs" recalls the "walk-around" of black minstrelsy, and indeed this derivation is reinforced by the suggestion of a strummed banjo in the accompaniment figure of the last verse.

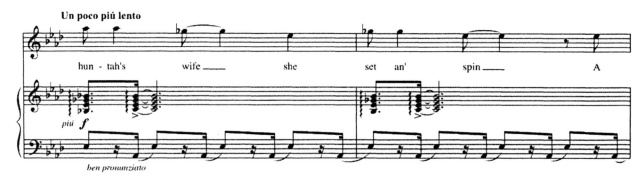

Example 3.9, mm. 35–36

Most of the stylistic features, however, derive from ragtime, including the syncopated accents, repeated outlining of simple harmonies in the left hand, and coloristic "blue" notes in both the offbeat chords and melodic line.

Example 3.10, mm. 12–14

Langston Hughes (1902–1967)

William Grant Still's other song of 1927, "The Breath of a Rose,"[20] is very different from "Winter's Approach." In it, he forsakes all folk influences and employs the more "universal idiom" that he was now to turn toward, as he said, in the search for "my own individuality as a composer."[21] The text is by Langston Hughes, one of the major black literary figures of the twentieth century. In the two earliest poems to bring him public notice—"The Negro Speaks of Rivers"[22]

(1923) and "The Weary Blues" (1925)—Hughes was already indicating the preoccupation with the sorrows of his race and the literary transmutation of their speech and song that was to characterize much of his work.

In "The Breath of a Rose," however, Hughes, like Still, writes not as a black but simply as an American finding his artistic voice. It is a delicate lyric yet full of repressed emotion, comparing the evanescence of love to the perfume of a rose and to other beautiful things in nature that quickly fade or disappear. Literary historians date the poem to Hughes's 1923 interlude in Paris after serving for six months as a crewman on the *S.S. Malone*. In this city, he quickly became part of the black expatriate community, and was inspired to write the poem by a brief relationship with a young black English woman named Ann Marie Cousey.

Perhaps the most striking element in this setting is its musical color, or timbre. The harmonic structure, which uses chords with many augmented fourths, fifths, and sixths over pedal points drawn from the basic key of B-flat major, is one of the prime contributors to this color. Another is the alternately sonorous and hazily veiled palette of pianistic effects.

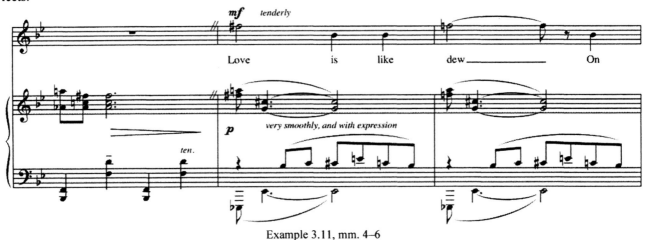

Example 3.11, mm. 4–6

Over this background, a soprano voice has its gentle, repetitive phrases, which become almost rhythmically hypnotic, only to be interrupted by strange little chant-like recitative figures.

Example 3.12, mm. 10–12

The influence of Debussy, and the Impressionistic use of aural color to portray the visual aspects of natural scenes, certainly comes to mind in this song, but the composer's specific application of the technique is quite fresh, and the result is a uniquely appropriate setting of this text.

Almost twenty years were now to intervene before William Grant Still, in 1945, would compose *Songs of Separation*,[23] a remarkable cycle that sets the works of five black poets. During these intervening years, Still wrote operas, symphonies, and choral compositions in his new stylistic synthesis but with subjects often linked to the black experience in the New World. These brought him widespread recognition. Besides a long list of commissions, fellowships, and honorary degrees, he received the additional distinction of being the first black to conduct a major symphony orchestra in the United States and to have an opera produced by a leading company. Howard Hanson, an important patron of the rising composer, presented many of his new works at the annual Eastman festival. Still's second marriage, to Verna Arvey, a fine pianist and writer, proved nourishing to both the personal and artistic aspects of his life.

Songs of Separation is a finely structured cycle of five songs recounting stages and emotions connected with "separation"—not that of a black from white society, but rather of a man from the beloved woman who has rejected him. To create this cycle, the composer made selections from the poetry of Arna Bontemps, Philippe de Marcelin, Countee Cullen, and again, as in 1927, Dunbar and Hughes. He then placed these in a dramatic sequence so that together they formed an effective unit in which the protagonist moves through irony, bitterness, and despair to a restorative search for a new love.

Arna Bontemps (1902–1973)

Number one, "Idolatry," sets a poem by Arna Bontemps, who was born in Alexandria, Louisiana, and who became a central figure in black literary circles of the mid-twentieth century as a writer, teacher, and editor. Together with Countee Cullen, he worked on the dramatization of the musical *St. Louis Woman*, which was produced in New York in 1946. He also collaborated with Langston Hughes on the volumes *The Poetry of the Negro* (1949) and the *Book of Negro Folklore* (1958). In "Idolatry," the poet tells his lost love that he will set a statue in a shrine to the memory of what they once shared, so that he can journey there and "set an old bell tolling." The vocal style of this song is based on an arioso-type melodic line that varies from expansive contours to narrow-range recitative. It sets the tone of the entire cycle, which as a whole shows some operatic influence, as befits its dramatic orientation, but nevertheless retains the compression and intimacy of the art song.

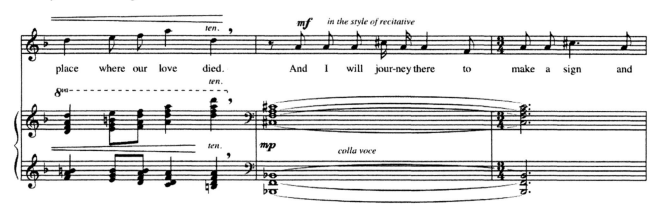

Example 3.13, mm. 15–17

"Poème," the second song, is in French and sets the work of de Marcelin, a Haitian composer, so on both counts will not be treated here, as it is outside the scope of this study. Number three is "Parted," a setting of one of Paul Laurence Dunbar's poems in literary English. It may well have been inspired by his own marriage to Alice Ruth Moore, a beautiful, well-educated mulatto from New Orleans whom Dunbar courted largely through letters over a period of several years. The union ended shortly after it began and recent scholarship documents considerable spousal abuse on Dunbar's part[24] which was not uncommon in the social mores of the time. The poet, however, immortalizes his own version of the marital dissolution with an ironic closing comment on human self-deception.

> Tho' I'll confess that I'm no saint,
> I'll swear that she's no martyr.

William Grant Still sets these crisp and biting verses with a declamatory, frequently chromatic vocal line and spare, punctuating chords in the accompaniment.

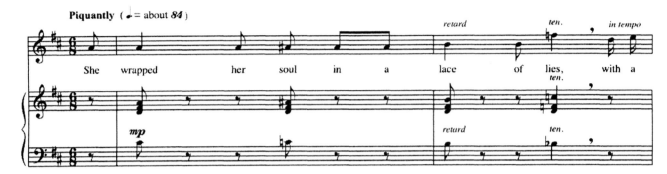

Example 3.14, mm. 1–2

This song, which occupies the middle position in the cycle, provides necessary contrast to legato, lyric settings on either side of it.

Countee Cullen (1903–1946)

The fourth poem, "If You Should Go," is by Countee Cullen, who was born in New York City in 1903. This was only one year after Arna Bontemps's birth, and both men were part of the Harlem Renaissance in the 1920s, which saw a flowering of talent among black artists. Cullen was a highly educated, scholarly man who was elected to Phi Beta Kappa while at New York University and who received his M.A. from Harvard in 1926. Although he preferred not to be known as a black poet, but simply as a poet, many of his themes are racial, and he published a great deal in the black journals *Crisis* and *Opportunity*. Cullen's poetry has been compared to Keats's by virtue of its lyrical quality, and "If You Should Go" certainly demonstrates this in its tenderly expressed request that his love depart as quietly as "the gently passing day" or a vanished dream.

The composer rises to equal heights of lyricism in this short but exquisite setting. The melodic contour builds inevitably to its climax on "Go quietly."

Example 3.15, mm. 6–8

The hazily subdued, repeating chordal patterns that characterize the piano part prepare the appropriate atmosphere for the line "a dream, when done, should leave no trace."

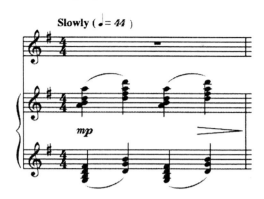

Example 3.16, m. 1

And as final elegant details, Still uses a musical caesura to underline the afterthought quality of the final phrase, and a melodic supertonic degree on the last note to blur the harmonic and emotional image.

Example 3.17, mm. 11–13

For the last song, "A Black Pierrot," the composer returns to the poetry of Langston Hughes. This time, unlike in "The Breath of a Rose," Hughes is very aware of his color, and in the only "black-oriented" poem of the cycle, he sees himself as a clown with a "once gay colored soul" creeping away into the night, which is also black. The poem and the cycle do not end on this despairing note, however. In this only instance of poetic repetition in the *Songs of Separation*, Still builds a crescendo of hope on the last two lines by repeating the second one twice and the first four times over a rising melodic sequence.

> I went forth in the morning
> To seek a new brown love,

This builds to a dramatic peak at the end, with the added lift of the ascending form of the melodic minor scale.

Example 3.18, mm. 40–43

Florence Price (1888–1953)

Florence Smith Price and William Grant Still, the two leading African American composers of the twentieth century, were born just eight years apart, and exhibit many parallels in the details of their early lives. Both had college-trained parents who fostered their artistic development (Price's mother was her first music teacher); both were educated as children in the black schools of Little Rock, Arkansas; and both studied composition with George Chadwick at the New England Conservatory.

In 1906, Florence Smith graduated from the Conservatory with degrees in piano pedagogy and organ performance. After holding several lesser teaching positions, she was impressively launched on an academic career as head of the music department at Atlanta's Clark University, but gave it up in 1912 to marry Thomas J. Price, a rising young Little Rock attorney. Three children were born of this marriage: two daughters, and a son who died in infancy. Florence Price taught and composed throughout their childhood, and her works were beginning to gain the attention of the musical world.

In 1927, Little Rock's deteriorating racial climate, climaxed by a lynching in a black middle-class neighborhood, persuaded the family to move and settle in Chicago. In this major artistic center, Price's gifts came into full flower. She continued to study composition at the Chicago Musical College, American Conservatory, and the University of Chicago. She also continued to perform on the piano and organ, and to compose for these instruments. Teaching remained another important area of her interest, and her most successful student was Margaret Bonds, another leading African American composer of the mid-twentieth century Chicago group.

By 1928, G. Schirmer had begun to publish Price's compositions, and in the 1930s her reputation grew rapidly after she won first prize in the Wanamaker competition for her Symphony in E Minor. As she began to add songs to her catalog of works, the composer came to the attention of several prominent black singers. Marian Anderson was especially fond of her arrangement of the spiritual "My Soul's Been Anchored in the Lord" as well as of her setting of the Langston Hughes poem "Song to the Dark Virgin." Although she continued to compose in all genres until her death in 1953, Price's full historical assessment was hampered by the fact that many of her manuscripts remained unpublished and a number of the larger works had been lost. Until the early 1970s, she was virtually unknown outside of Chicago.[25]

With the publication in the 1980s of Willis C. Patterson's first collection of *Art Songs by Black American Composers*,[26] Price's stature as a song composer was revealed to the musical public by the inclusion of her settings of "Night" (text by Louise Wallace) and "Song to a Dark Virgin," mentioned above. About a decade later, an important dissertation on Price's unpublished songs by Lisa Lee Sawyer[27] came to the attention of R. Friedberg and this led to the publication of six more Price settings: two of Dunbar's dialect poetry ("Dreamin' Town" and "What's the Use?"); two spiritual arrangements ("Go Down, Moses" and "My Little Soul's Goin' to Shine"); and two quasi-spirituals with texts by Langston Hughes and Price herself ("Feet o' Jesus" and "Trouble Done Come My Way").[28]

When we attempt to gain an overall perspective on Florence Price's body of song, her poetic choices seem to indicate that Price, like William Grant Still, exhibits the creative split of many twentieth century black artists. This dichotomy manifests as the desire, on the one hand, to artistically represent their racial heritage, and on the other hand, to ignore it and blend in with the overall stylistic trends of America's white European heritage.

Paul Laurence Dunbar (1872–1906)

For two songs written in the early nineteen twenties, Price turned to Dunbar's dialect poetry, which, as discussed previously in the William Grant Still material, had gained great critical praise. What is less generally known is that, although dialect poems, following the successful work of James Whitcomb Riley, were quite popular in that era with both white and black audiences, Dunbar himself seemed to have considered it an inferior medium, in which he continued to write largely for the fees that resulted from sales and readings. That said, it is nevertheless true that Dunbar's poetic skill imbued these poems with qualities of tenderness and ironic humor that are seldom to be found in dialect poetry.[29]

"Dreamin' Town" and "What's the Use?" both set poems from *Lyrics of Sunshine and Shadow.* In the first, Price responds to the poetic warmth by creating a tender folk-ballad that she dedicates "to Florence, my daughter." With repetitious piano figures suggestive of a strummed instrument and a rocking melodic treatment of the delights of dreamland,

Example 3.19, mm. 3–7

Price begins the setting as a simple lullaby, but creates an art song with unexpected chromatic interpolations (see Ex. 3.20) and extensions of the vocal tessitura (see Ex. 3.21).

Example 3.20, mm. 42–46

Example 3.21, mm. 54–58

"What's the Use?" employs a syncopated, ragtime piano accompaniment to match the ironic monologue which makes light of the black man's plight for the entertainment of white audiences.

Example 3.22, mm. 4–7

The most poignant line, "What's the use o' even weepin'" is underlined by Price's fermata and a piano "riff" as the poet assumes the "smile" of black minstrelsy.

Example 3.23, mm. 24–26

Langston Hughes (1902–1967)

Dunbar is now considered to have been an important precursor of the Harlem Renaissance of the 1920s when a strong group of black writers emerged onto the American literary scene. Twenty years after Dunbar's death, Langston Hughes becomes the first writer to unashamedly celebrate blackness and to record the glories and struggles of his race. Florence Price's settings of two of his earliest poems create an interesting contrast in literary and musical style. "Feet o' Jesus" from *Fine Clothes to the Jew* (1927) is a powerful mixture of the language of the black spiritual with an unexpectedly poetic simile such as "sorrow like a sea."

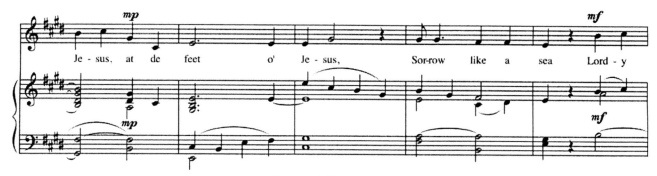

Example 3.24, mm. 6–10

Price begins her setting with the voice in a medium range and the piano supporting with a simple chordal background. Then, as in "Dreamin' Town," she amplifies the vocal range, melodic contour, and instrumental complexity to create a powerful art song.

Example 3.25, mm. 42–49

With "Song to a Dark Virgin," from *The Weary Blues* (1926), Hughes not only exchanges "folk" for literary style, but reverts to nineteenth century poetic use of "thy" and "thou." It is as though the poet's intent is to place his dark-skinned, virginal heroine on an equal footing with all the pale, white virgins of European and American literary history.

The poem has an interesting verse structure, calibrated to increasing intensity of emotion, which Florence Price plays out for us in musical terms. In the first stanza, the poet is worshipful, and Price places a fermata on "feet" to allow contemplation of the beloved object, surrounded by fragments of jewels.

Example 3.26, mm. 4–6

The second stanza is longer, and as the poet imagines enfolding her like a garment, "hold" and "hide" are elongated in anticipation of ecstatic touch.

Example 3.27, mm. 13–14

The last verse is the shortest, poetically and musically, as passion finds its climax.

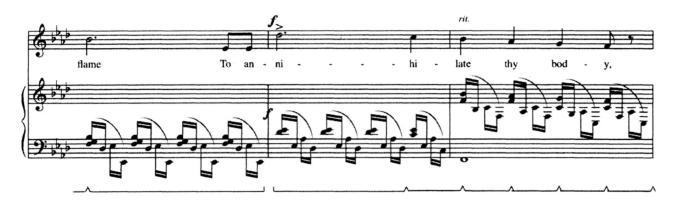

Example 3.28, mm. 22–24

For all of this, Price's harmonic language is straightforwardly diatonic with the addition of colorful ninth chords for textual extensions (see Ex. 3.27). Diatonicism with chromatic coloration is also found in the Patterson collection's exquisite chordal setting of "Night," text by the as-yet unidentified poet, Louise Wallace. Finally, it should be noted that

"Trouble Done Come My Way," the spiritual with words and music by Price herself, is dedicated to her most notable, long-time advocate, Marian Anderson.

Ernst Bacon (1898–1990)

Ernst Bacon's roots were in the urban Midwest. He was born in Chicago in 1898, did undergraduate work at the University of Chicago, then followed the proverbial "Go West" dictum by taking an M.A. at the University of California. His musical path eventually led back to Rochester, New York, where after studying with Ernest Bloch and the conductor Eugene Goossens, Bacon won the post of assistant conductor of the Rochester Opera Company. Like Douglas Moore, he also became strongly involved with American university education, by serving initially as a teacher of piano and theory and later as director of the School of Music of Syracuse University.

When he was only nineteen, Ernst Bacon had published the brochure "Our Musical Idiom,"[30] which discussed the newer harmonic language of the day. His own compositional idiom developed as an individual style that was based on the European traditions as well as more current developments. In the 1940s, Bacon grew interested in American themes and composed, among other larger works, an orchestral suite called *From Emily's Diary* to words by Emily Dickinson: a poet whom he was to set often in the art song context as well. The Anglo-American folk-song heritage also attracted him very strongly, and in 1941 (the same year as the publication of the songs we are about to consider), he arranged some of these in the collection *Along Unpaved Roads*.

Ernst Bacon's abiding interest and keen insights into the state of vocal music in this country are evidenced in the chapter called "The Singer," which appeared in his *Words on Music* of 1960.[31] While deploring the decline of the solo song recital and particularly the neglect of our own language in favor of European settings, he nevertheless maintained that "it is quite possible that some of the best musical writing in America has taken the form of song."[32] He went on to say that "in America we have a wealth of lyric poetry calling for song, particularly the contributions of the women, beginning with Emily Dickinson."[33]

Emily Dickinson (1830–1886)

It is certainly true that the poems of Emily Dickinson have been exerting an ever-growing fascination on American composers, especially since the publication of the increasingly authentic editions. The romantic life story of the recluse dressed in white, who for twenty years collected her small packets of verse in the seclusion of her Amherst home, would draw our attention even without the towering genius of the poetry. Her gifts, however, are tellingly described by H. H. Waggoner: "If one were forced to choose just one poet to illuminate the nature and quality of American poetry as a whole, to define its . . . preoccupations, its characteristic themes and images, its diction and style . . . one ought to choose Dickinson."[34]

Emily Dickinson, like Douglas Moore, was descended from many generations of American ancestors. The first of these sailed to the New World in 1630 and established the town of Hadley, Massachusetts. Later descendants crossed the Connecticut River to found the city of Amherst, where Emily was born in 1830. Her father was a prominent lawyer and legislator, and her girlhood and youth were actively occupied with education and the society of siblings and friends. Trips to Worcester and Boston were common, and she visited Washington in 1854 during her father's Congressional term.

The first of the two Bacon songs to be discussed, "It's all I have to bring,"[35] sets a fairly early poem written in 1858, when the joy of living was still strong in the writer's consciousness and before coming tragedies had begun to cast their shadows. The text of this song is drawn from the 1929 collection *Further Poems*, edited by Emily's niece, Martha Dickinson Bianchi, who had also issued another collection *The Single Hound*, in 1914. These two editions contained very few alterations, but some misreadings. On the other hand, the approximately five hundred Dickinson poems previously published in the 1890s as transcribed by Mabel Loomis Todd (wife of an Amherst professor) had been "corrected" by Thomas Wentworth Higginson, the editor who had given Dickinson encouragement but little comprehension through the years of her writing. Even the Bianchi versions, however, were to be superseded by Thomas H. Johnson's first actual scholarly edition of all the poetry in an unreconstructed text published by Harvard University in 1955. In this last edition of "It's all I have to bring," a change of a single letter alters the meaning of the sixth line. In the Bacon song, it reads "Someone the su*n* could tell" whereas in the original, as edited by Johnson, it is "Someone the su*m* could tell."

In either case, the basic feeling of the poem remains the same. The atmosphere is clearly pastoral and filled with the images of fields, meadows, bees, and clover. The mood remains "sunny" even with the loss of the actual word in the definitive edition. The B-flat major key establishes all this, as do the essentially diatonic harmonies, broken only by the accidentals that pictorially surround the word "bees." The melodic line participates in establishing the atmosphere by means of long, smooth legato phrases, punctuated by occasional joyous leaps.

Example 3.29, mm. 22–25

The "common meter" of Emily Dickinson's verses, which she adapted from hymns because she felt its simplicity suggested life rather than "Literature," is transformed here into a straightforward 2/4 time signature. The addition of an occasional 3/4 bar, however, lends a subtle touch to the musical rhythm, which hints at the tremendous sophistication underlying the apparent simplicity of all Dickinson's poetry.

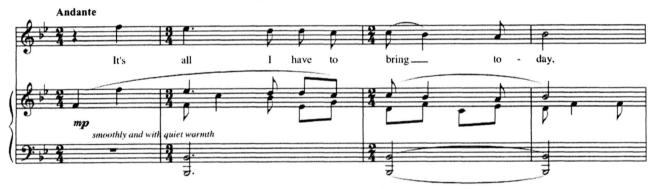

Example 3.30, mm. 1–4

One is, in fact, led to speculate as to whether an urge toward simplicity is not perhaps a characteristic trait of American art in all forms, as a reaction, possibly, against the increasing complexities with which Europe had come to express its older and less vigorous cultures. Holding this thought in abeyance until a later time, we come now to the second Bacon song called "And this of all my hopes,"[36] which sets a poem dating from 1864. By this time, personal crises and the loss of probably the greatest love object of Emily Dickinson's life, the mysterious Reverend Wadsworth, had begun to be reflected in her poetry, which speaks increasingly of pain and limitation. Pulling away from her early Emersonian belief in transcendental goodness, she began to find "God faceless and nature silent."[37] The poem, then, describes the "silent end" of hope and the early decline of the "bountiful colored morning" of her life.

Its contrasting setting employs a minor key and more dissonant harmonies. The narrower melodic line takes on a crawling, chromatic contour to portray the "confident worm" boring at the roots of her being. The dotted rhythms and little running groups of sixteenth notes contribute a nervous, unsettling quality, and all elements join in a telling musical portrait of gentle despair.

Example 3.31, mm. 17–20

Roy Harris (1898–1979)

The legendary quality of Roy Harris's "Americanism" began with his birth in a log cabin in Lincoln County, Oklahoma. Although his parents, who were of Irish and Scottish descent, had been early settlers in that state, in 1903 they succumbed to the lure of the golden Pacific coast and moved to California. Harris attended the University of California in 1919 and 1920 as a special student in philosophy and economics, but his musical studies were conducted privately. An important influence in later musical directions was his first major composition teacher, Arthur Farwell, who had been an early champion of new American music and had founded the Wa-Wan Press in 1901.

After Harris's work attracted the attention of Howard Hanson at Eastman, the young composer made the reverse geographical pilgrimage and spent the late twenties absorbing Eastern influences. After working for a time at the MacDowell Colony, he was able, with the aid of several fellowships, to go to Paris, where Nadia Boulanger sharpened and refined his as-yet-undisciplined talent. Back in the United States, he began a long, fruitful career as composer-in-residence and teacher at colleges and universities in many areas of the country.

Roy Harris was very articulate about his aims as a composer and tried to establish verbal equations between the American character and American music. In an essay published in 1933, he developed the theory that Americans have different rhythmic impulses than Europeans, that they lean toward modality to avoid the clichés of major and minor, and that they avoid cadential definition because of an aversion to anything final.[38] All of these elements are brought into play in the song we shall examine, as well as the melodic gift that Aaron Copland found to be Harris's most striking characteristic. Regarding Harris's overall style, Copland felt "its American quality strongly." He perceived it as "music of real sweep and breadth with power and emotional depth such as only a generously built country could produce."[39]

Interestingly enough, whereas Harris was a prolific composer of instrumental works, he wrote no operas and very few songs. The combining of music with words seemed to have little appeal for him, although he did compose a number of choral works based on the poetry of Walt Whitman, whom he looked upon as a kindred spirit. He felt, in fact, that he had tried to do for music what Whitman had done in poetry. It was therefore not surprising that for the text of the one important art song that Harris contributed to the American repertoire he turned to a poem by Carl Sandburg, who more than any other writer had taken on the stylistic and conceptual heritage of Whitman.

Carl Sandburg (1878–1967)

This heritage is aptly described by Babette Deutsch who characterizes Sandburg's contribution to American poetry as "a renewed awareness of ordinary life as of ordinary language, including slang as poetic diction of a fresh sort."[40] Born in Galesburg, Illinois, to poor Swedish immigrants—his mother was a chambermaid and his father a blacksmith who could not write—Carl Sandburg was well equipped to be the poet of the common people. His lifelong sympathy for the oppressed and exploited was expressed politically by his populism and his labors on behalf of social reform. His artistic need to express the American experience took many forms, which included performing and collecting folk songs all over the country, and literary triumphs ranging from the prose of the famous Lincoln biography to the many rich collections of poetry.

Despite the fact that he spent the last twenty-two years of his life in Flat Rock, North Carolina, it is essential to remember that Sandburg experienced his formative years in the Midwest with such great creative contemporaries as Theodore Dreiser, Sinclair Lewis, and Sherwood Anderson. This enormous Midwestern vitality dominated the American literary scene between the two World Wars, after which it passed on to the South. Sandburg was already becoming a part of this scene by virtue of his writing for newspapers in Milwaukee and Chicago, when in 1916 his reputation was firmly established with the publication of *Chicago Poems*.

"Fog,"[41] that forms the text of Roy Harris's song, is perhaps the most famous poem of that collection. It has often been cited as a prime example of the "Imagist" approach to poetry, since its brief six lines personify the fog creeping over the city as a silent animal that comes and goes on "little cat feet." Although short, the poem embodies Sandburg's basically unmetered, unrhymed, "nonpoetic" style derived from common speech. Its similarly nonpoetic content, which paints a rather dreary urban scene, reminds us that Sandburg was a contemporary of the "Ashcan" school of American painters.

Harris opens the song with a five-measure piano introduction in which Impressionistic use of the soft pedal for color and the sostenuto to sustain a D-flat pedal point immediately create the desired "misty" effect.

Example 3.32, mm. 1–2

The composer's penchant for polytonality comes to the fore in his superimposition of D-flat major and D minor harmonies, and his modal tendencies are reflected in the melodic setting of "It sits looking over harbor," which also pulls into a pictorial rising curve.

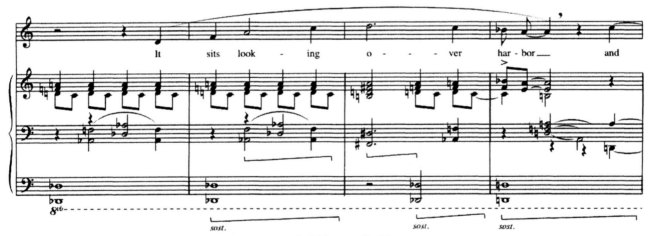

Example 3.33, mm. 12–15

Both the modality and polytonality, expressed as they are at a very soft dynamic level, contribute to a harmonic blur. This lack of aural definition is reinforced rhythmically by the subtle, shifting quality lent by the interpolated 5/4 measures embedded in a basically 4/4 meter (see Ex. 3.32). The end of the song, which is suspended on the uncertain sixth degree of the scalar harmony, is a perfect example of Harris's theory of American avoidance of the final. In his portrait, the fog drifts slowly away, as gradually and silently as it had come.

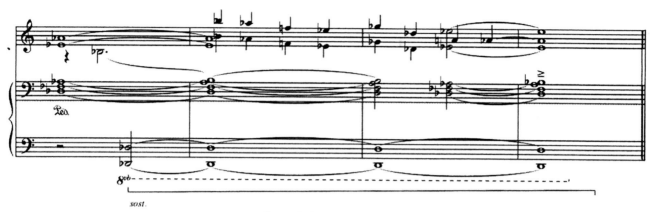

Example 3.34, mm. 24–27

Aaron Copland (1900–1990)

Having been drawn increasingly westward by the origins of Still, Bacon, and Harris, we return, with our final "Americanist," to the New York area. *Unlike* Douglas Moore, with his seventeenth-century ancestors, however, Aaron Copland was born in Brooklyn to parents who were Russian Jewish immigrants. Having discovered the art of music on his own, the young Copland studied harmony with Rubin Goldmark, who was also George Gershwin's teacher. After high school, he decided to concentrate totally on music rather than seek a college education and in 1921 enrolled at the Fontainebleau school as the first of the many Americans to study composition with Nadia Boulanger. Here he would shortly meet Douglas Moore, as later in the decade he was to encounter Roy Harris at the MacDowell Colony; and here his personal style would begin to crystallize by exposure to what Copland saw as Boulanger's "critical perspicacity, encyclopedic knowledge of music and ability to inspire the pupil with confidence in his own creative powers."[42]

Copland had early been drawn to Debussy and Ravel, and continued while in Paris to expand this creative affinity for the French tradition through his studies of Stravinsky, the Gallicized Russian. In 1971, in conversation with Edward Cone, he expressed his admiration of Fauré and revealed that he had never been comfortable with German chromaticism, even in serial form.[43] By the time he left Paris, however, a preoccupation with seeking an *American* musical identity was already growing among the Boulanger students. "We wanted," said Copland, "to find a music that would speak of universal things in the vernacular of American speech rhythms . . . music with a largeness of utterance wholly representative of the country that Whitman had envisaged."[44]

Copland, from the early days of his career, thus became not only one of his country's finest composers, but also, in Irving Lowens's words, "one of our most lucid thinkers and writers about the art"[45] and a great interpreter and champion of the works of others. He had been a moving spirit and organizer of many groups that promoted new American music, such as the Copland-Sessions concerts of 1928 to 1931, the first American Festival of Contemporary Music at Yaddo (1932), and the American Composers' Alliance. It was, in fact, at the Yaddo Festival that the famous performance of seven songs by Charles Ives occurred, which together with Copland's article on the *114 Songs* proved to be the opening wedge in public recognition of Ives's genius.[46]

During the thirties and forties, Copland was much occupied with reaching as broad an American public as possible through the new media of radio, cinema, and phonograph. This was the era of the "big ballets" and a style that eschews former complexities in favor of folk-influenced melodies and rhythms. By 1950, however, the year during which he labored over the monumental *Twelve Poems of Emily Dickinson*,[47] a new synthesis had already emerged. In it were incorporated the jagged, leaping melodic lines, diatonic dissonances, and rhythmic ingenuity that had become the distillation of Copland's search for an American musical aesthetic.

Since it was such a major addition to the American art song literature, and by a composer who had previously been known mostly for his instrumental works, the cycle attracted a great deal of comment in print during the dozen years that followed its publication. Critical barbs, such as Hans Nathan's judgment of unconvincing text interpretation[48] and Joseph Kerman's dissatisfaction with some of the chord construction,[49] were the exceptions. The overwhelming majority opinion, including that of these writers, aligned itself with William Flanagan's citing of the work as "probably the most important single contribution toward an American art song literature that we have to date." With a composer's intimate appreciation of another's genius, Flanagan, who himself wrote many fine songs before his tragic death, praised its surpassing originality, varied emotional range, and a "vocal- instrumental fusion which . . . is one of the most satisfactory in any contemporary music."[50]

Emily Dickinson (1830–1886)

The poems chosen by Copland for these settings cover a twenty-five-year span of Emily Dickinson's life, the earliest dating from 1858 and the latest from 1883. The composer tells us in a brief foreword that they all treat subject matter particularly close to the poet ("nature, death, life, eternity") and that he has attempted to give to the collection the aspect of a song cycle, a musical counterpart of Dickinson's personality. The texts are all drawn from the *Collected Poems*, which had been edited in 1937 by Bianchi and Hampson.[51] As mentioned above, that some of them were corrupt versions became evident in 1955 with Johnson's scholarly edition, but this fact has had very little effect, if any, on the overall impact of the work.

Copland, himself, related that "The Chariot," which became the final song, was the first Dickinson poem that he was inspired to set. Having first been captured by the visual image it evokes of Dickinson as the bride and Death as the groom, he was then drawn to one after another of her poems, until finally there were a dozen settings. Interestingly, "The Chariot" was the only song of the twelve to which Copland gave his own title, choosing an evocative word that does not appear in the poem itself. For the rest, he, like Ernst Bacon, simply used the first lines of the poems, since the author had never seen fit to lay the burdensome dignity of titles on her verses.

The composer had read and thought a great deal about the introverted and intellectual aspects of Emily Dickinson's nature and admitted his fascination with the notion that one day she simply "went upstairs and never came down." He saw the cycle as needing to be performed by a woman, and the poems interpreted as she would have interpreted them, "with a twinkle in the eye" and a very knowing manner. He considered a mezzo-soprano voice to be the most appropriate and preferred one that was capable of great drama, although through much of the cycle he thought of the singer as "talking the poetry."[52]

The first song is a setting of "Nature, the gentlest mother," a fairly early poem (1863), in which Nature is seen as a mother patiently and tenderly caring for her creatures, overseeing their prayers and silencing the earth while they sleep. In one of the final lines, the use of the seldom-seen comparative "infiniter" lends a retrospectively childlike quality to the whole poem.

> With infinite affection
> And infiniter care

This sophisticated innocence is one of Emily Dickinson's aspects that Copland emphasizes throughout the cycle by his poetic choices and musical treatments.

In this setting, he has used a careful definition of the vocal and pianistic material to delineate his characters and allow for a wonderful interplay between them. While the vocal line carries the warm, smooth, slower-moving contours of Mother Nature, the pianistic counterpoint uses rapid, pictorial figures to suggest the birds, squirrels, and crickets of her domain.

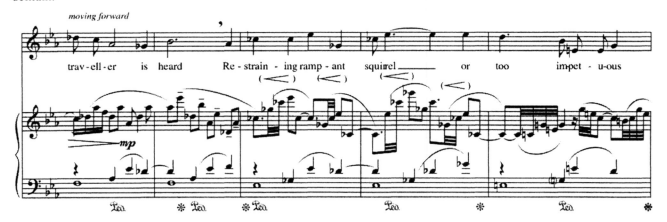

Example 3.35, mm. 22–26

The sundown prayers of her children grow to a crescendo of humming crickets and bee-laden flowers

Example 3.36, mm. 40–44

before silence is imposed. Copland's thickly sprinkled instructions for alterations in tempo, which appear throughout the cycle, indicate his sensitivity to the changing mood of the text and take full advantage of the greater flexibility of musical rhythm over its poetic counterpart.

Number two, "There came a wind like a bugle," presents a total contrast to the opening mood. This frightening picture of a violent storm was written in 1883, only three years before the poet's death, and the presence of such words as "chill," "doom," and "ghost" may well indicate a subconscious connection in her mind between the menacing storm and approaching, implacable death. Copland's musical imagery here, beginning with a percussive pianistic upward sweep of a scale in parallel sevenths, employs the resources of polytonality, dissonant harmonies, and angular vocal leaps to create a sense of turmoil and terror. Even more specific images include the piano trill that imitates the buzz of the "electric moccasin";

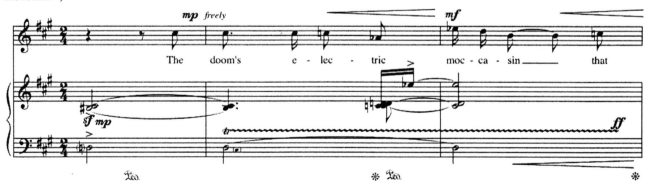

Example 3.37, mm. 22–24

the rapid, blurred fourths reminiscent of Schubertian "river" figures;

Example 3.38, mm. 34–36

and the steeple bell that tolls in both hands of the accompaniment.

Example 3.39, mm. 40–42

Vocal color also contributes a great deal, as the many low chest tones called for suggest the brooding "doom" of the poem.

In the third song, "Why do they shut me out of Heaven?," we find the only instance in the cycle of prolonged use of recitative-type setting. By this device, Copland indicates that, in the opening and closing lines, he is emphasizing the sense of the poetry being spoken. In the authors' opinion, Copland's music serves in this setting not only to enhance but to add meaning. The text of the 1861 poem is a rather wistful plea to the angels not to shut the door of Heaven because of the clamor of the poet's praises. Copland, however, repeats the lines "Don't shut the door" and "Could I forbid?" and, furthermore, brings back the opening two at the end of the song:

> Why do they shut me out of Heaven?
> Did I sing too loud?

This has the effect of creating an agitated, importuning atmosphere that almost makes one sympathize with the forbidding angels. Further, the setting of "Did I sing too loud?" with its double *forte* dynamic and large upward leaps (the second time to an unexpected dissonance) reinforces the suggestion of the speaker as a naughty, irreverent child, and attests to Copland's skill in the area of musical humor.

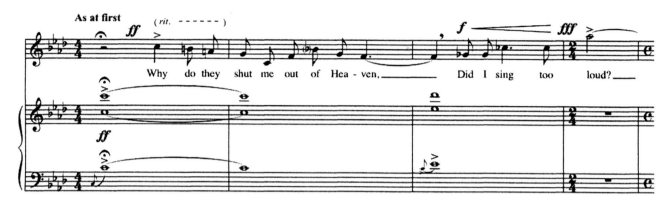

Example 3.40, mm. 27–30

"The world feels dusty," number four, is an inspired musical conception of a poem that states briefly and beautifully that love eases the moment of dying. Copland has here used a simple rhythmic piano motif (a quarter note followed by a half note), expressed in changing harmonies and dynamics and repeated throughout the song. The repetition provides both a feeling of the inevitability of death and of the sinking of the dying consciousness into a trance-like state. Over this, a finely contoured, lyric vocal line expresses the caring and compassion of the loving observer.

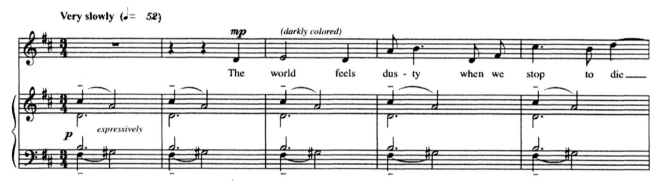

Example 3.41, mm. 1–5

The text of number five, "Heart, we will forget him," comes from one of the earliest poems of the set (1858). It is the only "love" poem of the cycle, and Copland no doubt chose it to exemplify the part of Emily Dickinson's nature that had been deeply drawn to a man whom she felt she must put out of her thoughts. There are many who agree with the anonymous British critic in *Music Review* who wrote that "this song is as exquisitely touching as any that has come out of America. Indeed," he continued, "I have a feeling that it may be the most affecting song written since Mahler's death."[53]

Example 3.42, mm. 1–6

In the two brief verses, the poet exhorts her heart to join her in forgetting "his" warmth and light, and to hurry, lest in the meantime she become swept by memory. The two elements that make Copland's setting so moving are first, the pathos of the melodic intervals, and secondly the use of constantly changing tempi to indicate the speaker's ambivalence. With the first marking ("very slowly—dragging"), the composer suggests that she is really loath to forget him (see Ex. 3.42), but is trying to act determined ("moving forward").

In the subsequent monologue, a sense of growing desperation is achieved by an accelerando,

Example 3.43, mm. 24–27

after which a flood of memory slows the musical motion to a halt. This is further emphasized by the caesura before "him."

Example 3.44, mm. 32–36

"Dear March, come in" (1874) follows with an animated treatment of Dickinson's whimsical conversation with the personified month. The effect of lively chatter is created by the tempo, 6/8 meter, and juxtaposition of a duple rhythm over the basic quarter-note/eighth-note, quarter-note/eighth-note pattern. The changes of key are integral in portraying the various stages of the visit, the first one mirroring a change of place ("come right upstairs") as the melodic line pictorially ascends.

Example 3.45, mm. 32–35

The second key change marks the arrival of April, whose knock is also heard in the left hand of the piano part.

Example 3.46, mm. 76–81

The final return to the opening F-sharp major brings back the initial joy of March's arrival.

"Sleep is supposed to be," number seven, begins with the opening motive of "The Chariot." Since the latter was Copland's first setting, the motive's appearance here in number seven is actually the quotation, rather than vice versa, and lets us know that this song also is about death (which is called "sleep" by "souls of sanity"). Emily Dickinson's "morning" in this metaphor stands for Resurrection, and Copland clothes this idea with a "wake-the-dead" phrase—the highest and loudest of the entire cycle. Reinforcing the vocal line is a polytonal harmonic construction that suggests the all-inclusiveness of "Eternity."

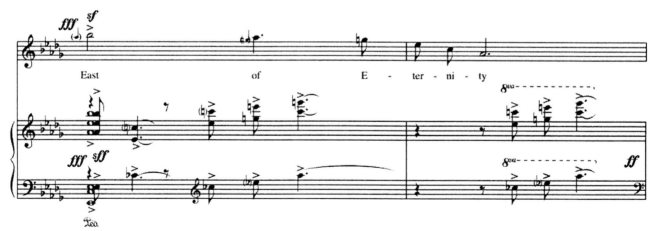

Example 3.47, mm. 31–32

In many respects, the next song, "When they come back," typifies the entire work. Inspired by the conciseness and precision of language with which Emily Dickinson has stated the ancient fear that spring might not return, Copland has brought to bear the spareness and linear clarity that are hallmarks of his style on one of the cycle's most outstanding settings. Although the composer saw the performing style of number eight as "musing" and displaying "little emotion as though there were no audience,"[54] the tempo indication ("gradually faster") seems to suggest a rising tide of anxiety.

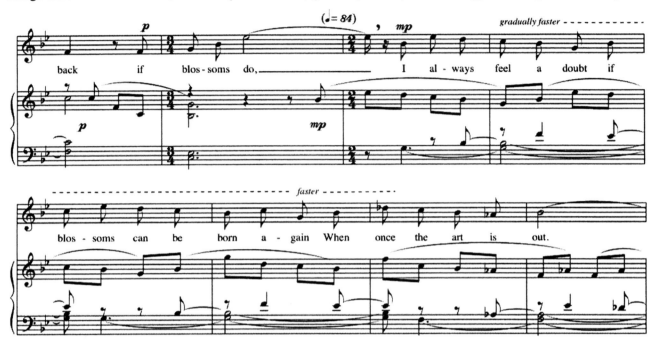

Example 3.48, mm. 5–12

This breathless quality is intensified by the closeness of the canonic imitation that occurs off and on throughout the song, always beginning in the piano part and followed by the voice at the interval of only a single quarter note (see beginning of Ex. 3.48).

"I felt a funeral in my brain," which is perhaps the most dramatic setting of the twelve, is the second instance in the cycle of the composer electing to repeat parts of the text for added emphasis. In this frightening description of the poet imagining her own funeral, Copland adds an extra "treading" (see Ex. 3.49) and an extra "beating" (see Ex. 3.50) to increase the hypnotic terror of the vision.

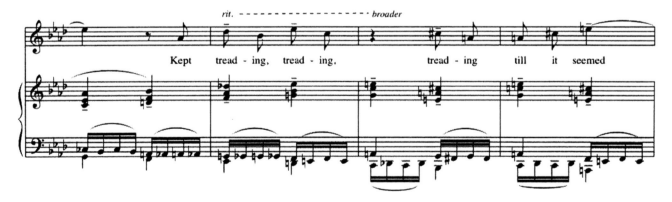

Example 3.49, mm. 10–13

Example 3.50, mm. 23–25

An apt evocation of the musical macabre, vaguely reminiscent of Berlioz's "March to the Scaffold" in *Symphonie Fantastique*, is produced by the inexorable polytonal marching figures of the opening

Example 3.51, mm. 1–3

and the thudding drum imitations in the pianist's left hand, as the "service" begins.

Example 3.52, mm. 18–22

After the "tolling of space" is portrayed, once again, by a piano figure, the eerie ending softens and slows down as though to express the emotion of a final verse that appears in the Thomas H. Johnson version but not in the 1937 one that Copland had available:

> And then a Plank in Reason broke
> And I dropped down and down—
> And hit a World at every plunge,
> And Finished Knowing then—

Number ten, "I've heard an organ talk sometimes," gives Copland another opportunity to exercise his musical irony, as the poet speaks of the unconscious influences that were brought to bear on her by the church services of her girlhood. In this setting, the harmonies and voicing of the piano part are like a parody of musically unsophisticated church music, and the final vocal phrase, which Copland wanted to have a "fat" sound,[55] recalls the fundamentalist fervor that Ives builds to dizzying heights in "General William Booth Enters into Heaven."

Example 3.53, mm. 31–35

The poem "Going to Heaven" was written in 1859, a year before "I've heard an organ talk sometimes." Here again, we see Emily Dickinson struggling with the realization that most of the tenets of her early religious teachings are no longer acceptable to her mind. This time, the tone is again a mocking one, and Copland makes this clear with his playful vocal repetitions of the phrase "Going to Heaven," which occurs only twice in the poem as opposed to seven times in the setting.

Example 3.54, mm. 1–8

The tongue-in-cheek atmosphere that Copland intended[56] is induced by various pianistic comments, such as rapid imitative figures, rhythmic hemiolas, and gently tittering staccato passages. In the final verse of the poem, Dickinson confesses that although she herself doesn't believe in Heaven, she's glad that her two loved ones now dead had had their belief for consolation. Copland sets these more serious statements with an augmentation of the vocal rhythm to dotted quarter notes, but cannot resist a final snickering reference to the "Going to Heaven" theme, which is briefly and softly quoted by the piano.

Example 3.55, mm. 123–126

Last of the twelve is "The Chariot ," which, as we have seen, was the original, motivating creative impulse from which the others grew. The opening tempo indication "With quiet grace," captures the tone of mid-Victorian politeness in which Dickinson unfolds the tale of Death stopping for her in his chariot and driving her past the receding material world to the "swelling of the ground" (i.e., the grave) and thereby, eternity. This whole setting is based on the dotted rhythmic figures, which represent the motion of the horse-drawn chariot. Copland even makes the vocal rhythm conform to this, against the natural word accent, as if to attest to the invincible power of Death.

Example 3.56, mm. 4–7

As the soul widens out in Death to join with the universal, so does the melodic contour extend to the octave leap of "We passed" and the harmony broaden to a warm B major color for "the setting sun."

Example 3.57, mm. 30–36

The dotted-note rhythm begins to slow, then stops altogether. Now only brief quotations of the figure bring memories of the passage into the new state, which took place "centuries" ago.

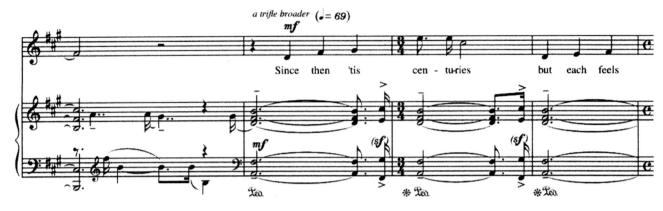

Example 3.58, mm. 44–47

"Toward eternity" is again set vocally in a dotted figure but this time in augmentation. The slower vocal motion suggests that the chariot ride of death (recalled by a piano quotation of the opening motive) was a temporary passage to the calm of the everlasting.

Example 3.59, mm. 52–56

In the Brooklyn College address mentioned above (see n45), Aaron Copland stressed that it is up to the artist to affirm the importance of the individual and to express the essence of the age in permanent form. He could have chosen no better candidate to aid him in the affirmation of the individual than the Amherst recluse, who, like Charles Ives, gained expressive strength through artistic isolation. The essence of our age and of our country as well may also be sensed as Emily Dickinson speaks through Aaron Copland's music. Clarity, simplicity, humor, a keen nose for fakery, and a deep spiritual commitment—these quintessentially American traits have been crystallized for all time in the *Twelve Poems of Emily Dickinson.*[57]

Notes

1. It must, of course, be remembered that Ives's work did not begin to be recognized until the 1930s. This group of composers, therefore, was for a time unaware that they were following in his footsteps.

2. See Chapter 24, "The Americanists," in Gilbert Chase, *America's Music* (New York: McGraw-Hill, 1966).

3. Chase, *America's Music,* 490.

4. Douglas Moore, *Listening to Music* (New York: Norton, 1932).

5. Douglas Moore, *From Madrigal to Modern Music* (New York: Norton, 1942).

6. Aaron Copland, "Musical Imagination in the Americas," in *Music and Imagination* (Cambridge, Mass.: Harvard University Press, 1966), 94.

7. This quotation appears in Madeline Goss, *Modern Music Makers* (New York: Dutton, 1952), 162.

8. Thomas Scherman, "Douglas Moore, The Optimistic Conservative," *Music Journal* 27 (October 1969): 25.

9. For a similar characterization of Benét's poetic style see Babette Deutsch, *Poetry in Our Time* (Garden City, N.Y.: Doubleday, 1963), 47.

10. Douglas Moore, "Adam Was My Grandfather" (Boston: E.C. Schirmer Publishing, 1938).

11. This song appears in *Contemporary Songs in English*, edited by Bernard Taylor (New York: Carl Fischer, 1956).

12. Deutsch, *Poetry in Our Time*, 200.

13. Waggoner, *American Poets from the Puritans to the Present* (New York: Dell, 1968), 564.

14. Waggoner, *American Poets*, 568.

15. For an interesting formulation of Roethke's "positive and negative imagery," see Ralph J. Mills Jr., *Theodore Roethke* (Minneapolis: University of Minnesota Press, 1963), 42.

16. Waggoner, *American Poets*, 569.

17. (a) William Grant Still, "My Arkansas Boyhood," *Arkansas Historical Quarterly* (Autumn 1967): 80–81. This article was reprinted in Robert Bartlett Haas, ed., *William Grant Still and the Fusion of Cultures in American Music* (Los Angeles: Black Sparrow Press, 1972). (b) For further biographical material see Verna Arvey, *In One Lifetime* (Fayetteville: The University of Arkansas Press, 1984). (c) See also Dabrishus-Quin-Still, *William Grant Still: A Bio-Bibliography* (Santa Barbara, Calif.: Greenwood Press, 1996).

18. William Grant Still, "Winter's Approach" in *Romantic American Art Songs* (Milwaukee: distr. by Hal Leonard, 1990).

19. *Complete Poems of Paul Laurence Dunbar with the Introduction to "Lyrics of Lowly Life"* by W. D. Howells (New York: Dodd, Mead, 1970), x.

20. William Grant Still, "The Breath of a Rose" in *The G. Schirmer Collection of American Art Song: 50 Songs by 29 Composers* (Milwaukee: Hal Leonard, 2007).

21. Still, "My Arkansas Boyhood."

22. The Howard Swanson setting of "The Negro Speaks of Rivers" has been published in the collection *Anthology of Art Songs by Black American Composers*, vol. 1 (New York: Edward B. Marks Music, 1977).

23. William Grant Still, *Songs of Separation* (Flagstaff, Ariz.: William Grant Still Music, 1998). This company is under the direction of Judith Ann Still, the daughter of William Grant Still and Verna Arvey.

24. Eleanor Alexander, *Lyrics of Sunshine and Shadow (The Tragic Courtship and Marriage of Paul Laurence Dunbar and Alice Ruth Moore: A History of Love and Violence among the African American Elite)* (New York: New York University Press, 2001).

25. For a complete biography and extensive bibliography on Florence Price, see R. Friedberg's article in *American National Biography* 17 (New York: Oxford University Press, 1999), 858–59.

26. See n22.

27. Lisa Lee Sawyer, *Unpublished Songs of Florence Price* (Kansas City: University of Missouri dissertation, 1990).

28. (a) Florence Price, *Two Songs* (San Antonio, Tex.: Southern Music Co., 1994); includes "Feet o' Jesus" and "Trouble Done Come My Way." Also *Four Songs* (San Antonio, Tex.: Southern Music Co., 2000); includes "Dreamin' Town," "What's the Use?" "Go Down, Moses," and "My Little Soul's Goin' to Shine." Both of these publications were collected and edited by R. Friedberg. (b) The most recent collection of Price songs: Florence Price, *Five Art Songs* (Classical Vocal Reprints, 2011), ed. Rae Linda Brown; includes two more settings of Langston Hughes's poetry ("Hold Fast to Dreams" and "Fantasy in Purple") and one of Paul Laurence Dunbar's ("Sympathy").

29. The information in the previous paragraph is derived from Peter Revell, *Paul Laurence Dunbar* (Boston: Twayne Publishers, 1979).

30. Ernst Bacon, *Our Musical Idiom* (Chicago: Open Court, 1917); reprinted from *The Monist*, October 1917.

31. Ernst Bacon, *Words on Music* (Syracuse, N.Y.: Syracuse University Press, 1960). This is a collection of addresses, essays, and lectures.

32. Bacon, *Words on Music*, 37.

33. Bacon, *Words on Music*, 38.

34. Waggoner, *American Poets*, 212–13.

35. Ernst Bacon, "It's all I have to bring" most recently published in *Romantic American Art Songs* (see n18).

36. Ernst Bacon, "And this of all my hopes" (see n35). These two songs by Bacon appear in the recorded anthology *Art Song in America* (Hanks/Friedberg), cited in Chapter 1, n7.

37. Waggoner, *American Poets*, 206.

38. Roy Harris, "Problems of American Composers," in *American Composers on American Music*, edited by Henry Cowell (Stanford, Calif.: Stanford University Press, 1933), 506.

39. Aaron Copland, "Roy Harris" in *The New Music, 1900–1906* (New York: Norton, 1968), 120.

40. Deutsch, *Poetry in Our Time*, 56.

41. This song is published in the Bernard Taylor collection cited in n11. It also appears in the recording cited in n36.

42. Copland, *The New Music*, 155.

43. Edward T. Cone, "Conversation with Aaron Copland," in *Perspectives on American Composers* (New York: Norton, 1971).

44. Hitchcock, *Music in the United States*, 179.

45. Irving Lowens, from a tribute to Aaron Copland on the occasion of his receiving an honorary degree from Brooklyn College (June 5, 1975). Lowens's and Copland's remarks were reprinted in the newsletter of the institute for *Studies in American Music*, vol. 5, no. 1 (November 1975).

46. See Chapter 2, n1.

47. Aaron Copland, *Twelve Poems of Emily Dickinson* (New York: Boosey & Hawkes, 1951).

48. Hans Nathan, "The Modern Period—United States of America," in *A History of Song*, edited by Denis Stevens (New York: Norton, 1960), 448.

49. Joseph Kerman, "American Music: The Columbia Series (II)." *The Hudson Review* 13 (1961): 408 ff.

50. William Flanagan, "American Songs: A Thin Crop," in *Musical America* 72 (February 1952), 23.

51. Martha Dickinson Bianchi and Alfred Leete Hampson, eds., *The Poems of Emily Dickinson* (Boston: Little, Brown, 1937).

52. The information in the preceding two paragraphs derives from an interview by R. Friedberg on 14 January 1978 with Carol Mayo, who was at that time professor of voice at Baylor University. Mayo had just been involved in a performance of the full cycle with Copland as accompanist. The concert was given to the Van Cliburn Society in Fort Worth, Texas, on January 12, 1978.

53. *Music Review* 14 (August 1953): 249. The reviewer is not identified.

54. Mayo interview.

55. Mayo interview.

56. Mayo interview.

57. In 1970, Copland completed the orchestration of eight of the Dickinson songs. The earliest recordings of the cycle for voice and piano were by Martha Lipton (1957) and Adele Addison (1967). Newer recordings of both piano and orchestral versions include performances by Jan de Gaetani, Roberta Alexander, Barbara Bonney, Marni Nixon, Helene Schneiderman, and Barbara Hendricks.

Chapter 4

Two American Originals

Mary Howe and Virgil Thomson were both born in the waning decades of the nineteenth century. Despite this fact they did not "sum up" the creative achievements of the preceding age but, on the contrary, were both in the vanguard of new waves that, in the twentieth century, were to flood the American musical scene with fresh life.

One of Howe's principal biographers, Madeleine Goss, states that, "chronologically Mary Howe belongs to the earlier group of American composers; but her work actually places her in a later period, for it is definitely modern in style."[1] This is especially evident in Howe's songs, in which her fresh harmonic language and rhythmic treatments combine with a discriminating ear for the finest poetry of the new American lyricists. Her status as an "original" must also be partly attributed to the fact that, while leading a rich family life, she managed to cultivate her own creative gifts with energy and devotion many years before the emergence of the historical phenomenon known as the "woman's liberation movement."

Virgil Thomson, another unique figure, embodies the surprising evolution of the son of a Kansas City post office clerk into a focal member of the most sophisticated Parisian artistic circles of the twenties and thirties. Eventually he was also to become an arbiter of musical taste in the United States, at the same time revolutionizing American vocal music with a totally new approach to the setting of English language texts.

Howe and Thomson had each studied for a time in Paris with Nadia Boulanger, the gifted nurturer of compositional originality, yet their musical styles were light years apart. The poets that drew them are equally different, and the settings that resulted are a part of the magnificent diversity that became American song by the twentieth century.

Mary Howe (1882–1964)

Mary Howe was a resident of Washington, D.C., throughout her life, although she had been born in her maternal grandmother's house in Richmond, Virginia. Her father, Calderon Carlisle, was an international lawyer of Scottish descent, her mother's ancestry was Welsh, and a touch of Spanish blood entered the family through the marriage of a great-aunt on the paternal side. Like many well-bred young women of her time, Mary Howe was educated totally at home, and one of her most important early influences was a Frenchwoman named Mlle. Seron who was her music instructor.[2]

As a girl she made frequent trips to Europe, and during one of these she studied the piano in Dresden with Richard Burmeister. Somewhat later she worked with Ernest Hutcheson and Harold Randolph at the Peabody Institute in Baltimore. In 1912 she married Walter Bruce Howe, a Washington lawyer like her father, who "knew very little about music but was totally supportive of his wife's musical activities."[3] Interestingly, it was three years after her marriage that she made her professional debut playing as half of a two-piano team. The other member of the duo was Anne Hull, who died in 1984 at the age of 96. The two women soloed with several leading orchestras, including the Cleveland, Baltimore, and National Symphonies, and when Mary Howe began to compose, music for two pianos was to be one of her favorite genres.

Madeleine Goss gives a detailed and absorbing account of the years during which Howe juggled the care of home and three young children with work toward her diploma in composition under Peabody's Gustav Strube.[4] Since her early education had been entirely at home, the final examination which she took for this diploma was the first she had ever experienced.[5] She passed this hurdle in 1922 and found herself, at the age of forty, beginning the productive part of her life as a creative artist.

During the next three decades Mary Howe composed an impressive catalog of vocal works, both solo and choral, and instrumental works for solo piano, two pianos, various chamber groups, and orchestra.[6] Her first public notice occurred at the Worcester Music Festival in 1925 with the performance of "Chain Gang Song." This was a choral piece inspired by the sight of a group of black prisoners that Howe had encountered many years earlier while riding horseback in the North Carolina mountains. Her reputation continued to grow through the performance of many of her orchestral compositions by symphonies of the stature of the New York Philharmonic, Chicago, Philadelphia, and BBC. Dr. Hans Kindler of the National Symphony, who was especially interested in programming contemporary American composers, premièred a number of Howe's works.

All the while, her catalog of songs was growing steadily. Mary Howe was a voracious reader and owned many volumes of poetry.[7] Her affinity to words included German and French poetry as well as English, as is demonstrated by the contents of her major publication of forty-nine songs in seven volumes:[8]

Volume I	*Seven Goethe Songs* (German)
Volume II	*English Songs: Part One*
Volume III	*Baritone Songs* (English)
Volume IV	*French Songs*
Volume V	*German Songs*
Volume VI	*English Songs: Part Two*
Volume VII	*English Songs: Part Three*

Each of these seven volumes contains seven songs, and the poetic choices range through four centuries. Shakespeare, Goethe, Tennyson, Victor Hugo, Baudelaire, and Rilke are among those represented, as well as Mary Howe herself in one setting, and Wylie and Lowell in six of the songs we shall examine.

Elinor Wylie (1885–1928)

Howe and Elinor Wylie were born only three years apart, and the poet's family had moved to Washington, D.C. from Philadelphia when she was twelve. Mary Howe knew her during these years of their girlhood and in later years, as a connoisseur of poetry, was attracted by the quality of Wylie's work and by its adaptability to musical setting. The MacDowell colony was another likely connection between Mary Howe, Elinor Wylie, and Amy Lowell as well. Howe, as an active musical philanthropist, was on the board of directors of the MacDowell Association and did much of her composing at the Colony in the summertime. Elinor Wylie also spent several summers there writing both prose and poetry in the seclusion that the Colony offered. Both Wylie and Lowell gave readings of their poetry at the MacDowell Club in New York to benefit the Colony[9] and it is not unlikely that the three women crossed paths in the course of their activities supporting this enterprise.

Elinor Wylie's background was very similar to Mary Howe's. She had distinguished Philadelphia ancestry on both sides of the family, and her father, Henry Martyn Hoyt, was to become solicitor general of the United States. When Elinor was two years old, the Hoyts moved to Rosemont, an affluent "Main Line" suburb of Philadelphia, and enrolled her in private school in Bryn Mawr. This type of education continued during her Washington years, and when she was eighteen, her grandfather took her and her sister Constance for a season in Paris and London.

Here the similarity to Mary Howe ends. In direct contrast to the composer's long, stable marriage, Elinor Wylie's personal life was stormy and highly unconventional for her time, causing her to live for many years as an outcast from the social milieu into which she had been born. At the age of twenty she had been prodded into marrying Philip Hichborn, a wealthy young Washingtonian who proved to be mentally unstable. They had one son who was to be reared by Hichborn's family, for in 1910 the poet eloped with Horace Wylie who was married and fifteen years her senior. The couple lived in England in virtual isolation under an assumed name until 1915. During this time, Horace Wylie opened the world of literature, history, and philosophy to Elinor, and created a life in which she could have been relatively happy had it not been for the snubs of English "society,"[10] Horace's ambivalence about his wife and children,[11] and the disquieting news, in 1912, of Hichborn's suicide.

World War I forced the couple to return to America, where Horace's wife finally agreed to a divorce and enabled them to marry. Still unacceptable to her former circle in Washington, Elinor Wylie gradually became a darling of the New York literary scene, as her writing, her beauty, and her dramatic personality began to be known. In 1921 she divorced Horace Wylie, and in 1923 married the poet William Rose Benét, who was a widower with three children. They had a few years of domestic life in Connecticut and New York City during which her restlessness and severe headaches, caused by chronic high blood pressure, continued unabated. After this she was drawn increasingly back to England and to a new romantic relationship that was cut short by her untimely death from the third of a series of strokes.

Mary Colum describes the moving occasion of the private funeral in William Rose Benét's apartment, with Elinor Wylie laid out in a favorite silver dress that still provided striking contrast to her flaming red hair. Present were not only the mother who had never entirely approved of her famous daughter and the son whom she had rarely seen since his infancy, but also such other creative artists of her circle as Douglas Moore and Edna St. Vincent Millay.[12] It was an appropriately dramatic farewell for this woman whose turbulent life had made inroads on her health and nervous stability but had left intact her remarkable courage, intellect, and artistry.

All of Elinor Wylie's major poetry (four volumes) was produced during the final eight years of her life. A book entitled *Collected Poems*, published in 1931, contained this work plus a group of "Hitherto Uncollected Poems" and an introductory memoir by William Rose Benét. The decade that followed saw a steady stream of Mary Howe's settings of these poems, two of which were written for chorus in 1936: "Spring Pastoral" for women's voices with piano (later transcribed for orchestra) and "Robin Hood's Heart" for men's voices with piano.[13]

The three Wylie settings for solo voice from the middle thirties—"Little Elegy" (1934), "Let Us Walk in the White Snow" (1935), and "When I Died in Berners Street" (1936)[14]—are among Mary Howe's finest works and demonstrate that unmistakable affinity of composer for poet which is all too rarely encountered in the song medium. All three of these poems show the typical Wylie preference for short lines and compact verse forms which served to "compress and intensify expression."[15] In the opinion of these writers, it is this very compression that has made Elinor Wylie's poetry (like Emily Dickinson's) so appropriate for musical setting, since the verbal tautness allows and invites musical amplification by the composer.

"Little Elegy" comes from Wylie's last volume of verse, *Angels and Earthly Creatures*, that was published posthumously in 1929. It was from this collection that the poet, newly returned to America, read to a group of close friends two nights before her death, confiding to Mary Colum that a developing relationship with a man in England had inspired many of the poems. "Little Elegy," an extremely concise yet moving tribute to this relationship, contains only ten lines of very regular iambic dimeter. In the opening lines

Withouten you
No rose can grow

Wylie chooses to use the Middle English form of "without" which serves a double purpose of filling out the poetic foot while it establishes an atmosphere of ancient and universal meaning.

The fact that Mary Howe made alternate settings of this text with piano and with string quartet[16] suggests its basically linear conception and the close interweaving of vocal and instrumental lines. Howe's lyrical gift and sensitivity to the poetic phrase is demonstrated by the individual contour of these lines. Form is imposed on this lyricism partially through a four note opening phrase ("Withouten you") announced by voice and piano.

Example 4.1, mm 1–5

This phrase recurs several times throughout the song (once in inversion) and has its last statement in augmentation in the piano part, serving to emphasize the final word, "nowhere" (see Ex. 4.2).

In examining rhythmic aspects of this song, we find that Mary Howe's setting has completely swallowed or "assimilated"[17] the original poetic form. The iambic dimeter has disappeared by virtue of the longer note values assigned to words at the end of each poetic line (see Ex. 4.1). Even the overall structure of the ten-line verse form has disappeared because of musical repetitions such as the following:

Example 4.2, mm. 21–28

However, the aesthetic result of these changes, as in all successful settings, is not a sense of loss, but rather one of "synthesis," to use Donald Ivey's term.[18] One senses that the condensed emotion of the poem has been musically released and amplified, much in the manner of Robert Schumann's handling of the similarly terse Heine texts.

Finally, two harmonic devices serve to further strengthen this setting. The first is the composer's use of chordal appogiaturas just before the pianistic interludes to build tension behind climactic words such as "sing."

Example 4.3, mm. 15–17

The second is the surprising enharmonic change from G-sharp to A-flat that occurs on the first "nowhere," marked *misterioso* to underline the strangeness of the sound and the poetic idea. In repetition, "nowhere" is set with a lowered second degree, whose nearness to the tonic suggests the meagerness of life without the subject of the "elegy" (see Ex. 4.2).

"Let Us Walk in the White Snow" is the first line of "Velvet Shoes," perhaps Elinor Wylie's best-known poem, and is also the title that Mary Howe assigned to her setting of it, written in 1935. Here again, Howe composed accompaniments for piano or string quartet[19] and indeed, much of the keyboard writing is in a spare, four part, non-pianistic style which could well relate to a prospective string adaptation. "Velvet Shoes" contains slightly longer lines than "Little Elegy" and there are four stanzas of five lines each that Mary Howe sets word for word without omissions, additions, or repetitions.

In this, Wylie's "virtuoso piece," the "relatively unobtrusive . . . prosodic effects" are indeed impressive as she slows down her basic, quickly moving, anapestic meter with extra unaccented and heavily accented syllables.[20] Mary Howe achieves this same plastic flow in musical terms by employing a flexible 5/8 rhythm that frequently alternates with 2/8, 4/8, etc. This allows for an extremely wide range of possibilities in shortening and lengthening syllables based on eighth-note increments.

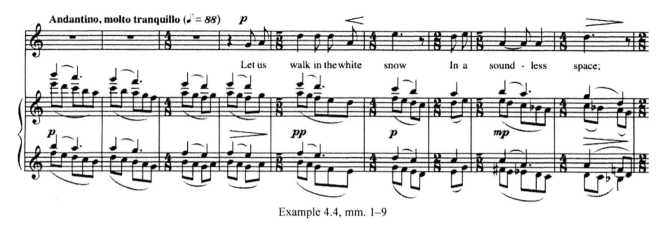

Example 4.4, mm. 1–9

This type of rhythmic organization is interrupted only by the setting of

Silence will fall like dews
On white white silence below.

Here the composer applies musical word painting to the concept of "silence" by achieving a falling off of sound both pitch-wise, through the descent of an octave, and dynamically through the decrescendo. Note that the effect is reinforced by its repetition with the second appearance of the word "silence." It is also intensified by the longer note lengths of this passage that trail off to nothing, and by the diminished participation of the piano.

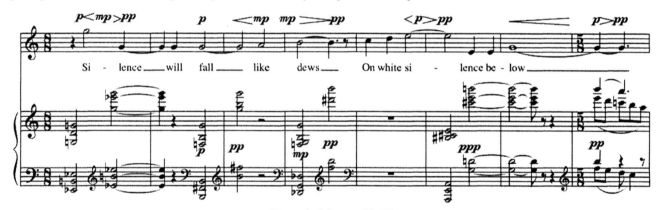

Example 4.5, mm. 59–66

Harmonic imagery also plays an important part in Howe's setting of this poem. Appropriately, she chooses the "whitest" of keys, C major, but with the opening measures she has already begun to add the diatonic and eventually chromatic nonchord tones that prevail throughout the song (see Ex. 4.4). Interestingly, the aural effect of this harmonic cloudiness seems not to endanger the "whiteness" of the setting, but rather to add a softness analogous to the textures of "velvet," "silk," and "wool" and a wandering quality which suggests the aimlessness of snow-impeded walking.

The third of these three poems displays still another aspect of Wylie's writing to place alongside the constricted emotional fervor of "Little Elegy" and the virtuosic, word-intoxicated tribute to austerity of sensation that is "Velvet Shoes." The occasional obscurity of meaning in her poetry, despite the unfailing clarity of her language, is attributed by Mary Colum to the fact that Elinor Wylie always wrote out of highly complex thought processes.[21] "When I Died in Berners Street" is the setting of such a poem, and its original poetic title of "A Strange Story" gives one the clue that some effort will have to be applied by the reader in order to penetrate its strangeness. The poem has six stanzas that Howe sets unchanged, except for the omission of the word "but" at the beginning of verses two and five. Each of the stanzas describes an imagined death in one of six different places. The missing piece of the puzzle is that all these places are various sections of London, a city that the poet knew well, both from the years of her exile with Horace Wylie, and from her frequent trips to England during the final years of her life.

The poem is a masterful portrait, again with unobtrusive but skillful metric control, of not one character, but six, whose lives are swiftly and colorfully evoked by the scenes of their passing. In one of the most dramatic settings of the twentieth century, Mary Howe selects a straightforward 4/4 meter and F minor tonality for a series of variations that employ all musical style characteristics in a most successful correspondence to the verbal structures. The death in Berners Street, a gloomy but respectable professional and residential section, is portrayed by broad, accented vocal lines, and a nervous, menacing accompaniment in staccato chords.

Example 4.6, mm. 5–8

The gruesome, poverty-stricken Houndsditch death in which

There came to lay me out
A washerwoman and a witch

receives an increasingly chromatic harmonic treatment, climaxing in loud, percussive, keyboard dissonances.

Example 4.7, mm. 27–30

Holborn, a residential area embodying faded wealth and position, is musically suggested in pompous, legato vocal phrases, emphasized by the accompaniment's octave doublings, all in a *meno mosso* tempo. The solitary Marylebone episode, one of the most chilling, prefigures the terrifying dirge in Benjamin Britten's *Serenade* for tenor and horn. In a funeral march tempo, with low, underlying dissonances in the piano part, the vocal line rises from a portentous Phrygian second step to a horror-stricken climax an octave above. Notice that the dramatic emotion is intensified by the indicated decrescendo on the word "alone" in which a shriek is transformed into a whisper.

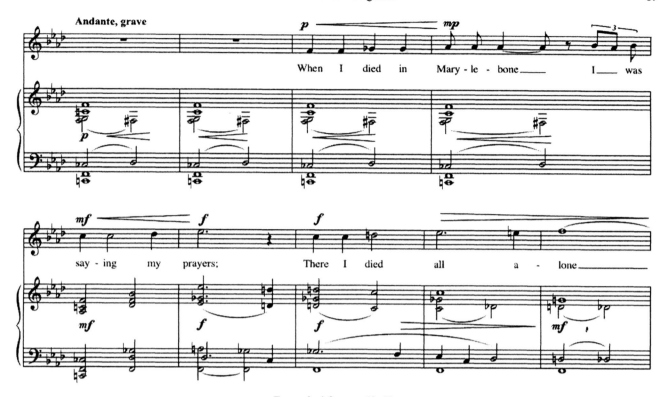

Example 4.8, mm. 49–57

Death near Lincoln's Inn, surrounded by acquisitive relatives, takes on a *vivace* tempo as their chattering occasions a rapidly repeating pianistic figure. In the final stanza, Elinor Wylie describes what one senses as her ideal death, in Bloomsbury: a pleasant area of late eighteenth-century houses near the British museum that was a literary district during the nineteenth and twentieth centuries. Mary Howe invests this death, occurring peacefully and beautifully "in the bend of your arm," with a turn to the parallel major key, diatonic harmony, and a flowing melodic line. The musical-theater flavor of the non-chord tones introduced in the final cadence aptly suggests the warmth of the surroundings, while the voice trails off on the dominant as though on an arrested breath.

Example 4.9, mm. 97–108

"A Strange Story" appeared in *Trivial Breath,* a collection of poetry published in 1928, the last year of Elinor Wylie's life. It is not beyond the realm of possibility that the writer, with an impending sense of her own end and increasing personal ties to England, morbidly imagined possible death scenes in the great city of London. Sadly, Destiny did not cooperate, and she died in a New York City apartment, far from Bloomsbury and the beloved presence.

Two more Howe-Wylie songs worthy of note appear in the Galaxy publications of 1959. The first, "Fair Annet's Song," is in Volume II (*English Songs: Part 1*). It sets a poem by the same name from *Angels and Earthly Creatures* (1929) which is a brief, poignant, eight-line statement of the impermanence of beauty and the consequent need to live in the present moment. Mary Howe's increasingly rich harmonic palette underlines the ambivalent, barely repressed anxiety of the text, and the attenuated note values intensify the final rise to a despairing vocal climax.

"Prinkin' Leddie,"[22] from Volume VII (*English Songs: Part 3*), also keeps the same title as the 1921 poem from *Nets to Catch the Wind.* In this song, Mary Howe, whose ancestry was part Scottish, was not surprisingly drawn to set verses in which Elinor Wylie imitated the Scottish ballads that she had loved in childhood. There are many folk-derived elements in this vigorous setting: the accented 6/8 meter, the dotted note patterns, and the rapid thirty-second note keyboard figures which imitate a strummed instrument. The poetic theme, expressed by the "primping lady" (as the title translates), is the need for visual beauty to sustain us in the storms of life, and is no doubt one which had a strong appeal to the artist and the homemaker as well in both Mary Howe and Elinor Wylie.

Amy Lowell (1874–1925)

Amy Lowell was born into a family of illustrious Boston Brahmins descended from Percival Lowell, who had come to Newburyport in 1637. James Russell Lowell, the witty New England poet and first editor of the *Atlantic Monthly,* was her grandfather's cousin. Her brother Percival, an astronomer, proved the existence of the planet Pluto, and postulated the Martian "canals." Another brother, Abbot Lawrence Lowell, was president of Harvard, although he admitted to understanding little of his sister's poetry.

The poet was to express regret in subsequent years that she had received the private education of a young lady of fashion instead of being sent to a college or university like the male Lowells. It is perhaps true, as some critics have suggested, that her lack of academic training is apparent in her major critical studies such as the two volume biography of Keats published in the last year of her life.[23] The precocious talent, however, was probably nurtured, as was Mary Howe's, by the lack of imposed scholastic structure, for at the early age of thirteen she contributed to a book (mostly written by her mother and older sister) which was published under the title *Dream Drops or Stories from Fairy Land.*

During her teens, Amy Lowell, who had fine features and an almost transparent skin, considered turning her talents toward the theater, but abandoned her hopes of being an actress when a glandular disturbance caused her to gain weight excessively. She then tried writing for the stage, and when this failed also, she decided to be a poet. This long pilgrimage toward her most natural mode of expression explains why Amy Lowell's first book of poetry, *A Dome of Many Coloured Glass,* was published in 1912 when she was already thirty-eight years old.

Having now turned her not inconsiderable energy and devotion to the poetic art, Lowellspent the next thirteen years of her life not only writing many volumes of her own poetry, but also engaging single-handedly in a massive public relations campaign in behalf of other writers. She wrote articles, books, reviews, and lectures on American poetry and helped start a series of anthologies that introduced Frost, Lindsay, Sandburg, Teasdale, Robinson, and Aiken to the public. She was also a staunch champion of new movements in poetic technique, and in 1913 went to England and took by storm the Imagist group of Lawrence, Pound, Fletcher, and H.D. When, on returning to America, she proceeded to publish *Some Imagist Poets* in three volumes that contained her own works as well, she was denounced as a usurper by Ezra Pound, who threatened suit.[24]

Indeed, an aura of controversy was never far from Amy Lowell, who was a central figure in the exciting meetings of the Poetry Society of America, founded in New York circa 1915. Colum describes her at the meetings as she "presented herself like a whirlwind and harangued the audience,"[25] and also recalls a lively incident at the MacDowell Club, when the poet, who had insisted on reading last (after Elinor Wylie and a number of others), was then highly offended by the sparseness of the remaining audience.[26]

Amy Lowell's colorful legend was fostered by her cigar-smoking, her pet English sheepdogs, her luxurious Boston mansion called Sevenels (for seven Lowells), and the strange work schedule by which she rose at 3 P.M., dined at 8, and wrote from midnight to 6 A.M. Those who knew her were also quick to point out her kind heart and willingness to do battle for an artistic cause. One senses from the Herculean labors that probably shortened her life, a desperate need for accomplishment, perhaps as a substitute for the relationships largely denied her by her physical form. From the elegance and passion of her poetry, one gleans, also, a sense of an inner world far different from the aggressive coarseness of manner which she assumed, and behind which she hid her disappointments.

The "Three Hokku" [27] which appear in Mary Howe's *English Songs: Part 2* (Volume VI of the Galaxy series) are settings drawn from Lowell's poetry collection *What's O'clock?* This collection, published in 1925, won the Pulitzer Prize posthumously, in 1926, and concludes with "Lilacs," probably Amy Lowell's best-known poem and her favorite of all her own lyrics. The three brief verses are numbers I, XIII, and XXII from "Twenty-Four Hokku on a Modern Theme" and have been set exactly as written, except for omission of capitals beginning the second poetic line in numbers two and three. Amy Lowell's strong interest in Asian poetry, much in vogue during her working years, had already been demonstrated by *Fir Flower Tablets* (1921), a volume of poetry she had translated and adapted from the Chinese, together with Florence Ayscough. In "Twenty-Four Hokku" she essayed the compressed Japanese poetic form which has become, in this century, such an appealing medium to Western poets practicing verbal condensation, and to composers inspired by the musical challenge. We find Mary Howe responding to this challenge as she submits her naturally more expansive style to the discipline of compression (each song is one page long).

The "modern theme" of Amy Lowell's title is clearly the death of love, and the twenty-four verses suggest the poet purging her grief by writing through the night. With the dawn she sees her garden and looks for comfort from the "cold-coloured flowers." Each of the verses Mary Howe chose to set centers around one of these flower images, and each contrasts human emotion with the appearance of nature: a time-honored poetic stance that is as familiar in the German lied as in the much earlier Oriental lyrics. In number one, a statement of gratitude for the unchanging beauty of the larkspur in a world of shifting relationships, Howe uses harmonic means to portray the text. A basic E-flat tonality takes on "uncertainty" through chromatic neighbors and passing tones in the piano introduction.

Example 4.10, mm. 1–7

The vocal line enters on E-flat scale tones and flowers to a lyrical climax on "heavenly blue," supported by clear E-flat harmonies. Thereafter, a hint of the opening chromaticism begins to return, and pervades the quiet, closing piano chords, revealing that the promise of the larkspur is not quite enough to dispel the muted anguish of loss.

Example 4.11, mm. 15–21

Number two asks the question "How am I worthy?" in comparison with the grace and delicacy of the blooming iris. The pleasure that the poet feels in contemplating the iris turns to pain with the realization that her own outward form has been found wanting. Mary Howe finds the perfect musical counterpart for the poetic idea in the harmonic device of pandiatonicism.[28] She begins the song by clearly establishing the key of D minor, but, even before the voice enters, has already begun to bring in elements of D-flat major which is the key of the entire vocal line.

Example 4.12, mm. 1–6

The accompaniment continues to express elements of both D and D-flat to the end of the song, in a dualism that mirrors the conflicting emotions of the text.

In number three, the poet, blinded by a "night of labour" described in the previous verse, sees a vision in the garden which could be either "a cloud of lilies" or the form of the lost love. Once again, chordal treatment, combined this time with pianistic timbre, is the element that creates a coloristic correspondence to the pallid images of the poetry. An Impressionistic pedal point on F, with changing harmonies above, produces a blur of sound, like the blurred vision of the poet. The pedal point also lends an obsessive quality to the setting (see Ex. 4.13), while reminiscences of the pandiatonic D and D-flat link it musically to the former one. It is as though love has produced a dizzying of the senses.

Beside the richness of Mary Howe's harmonic scheme in these songs, other stylistic elements remain relatively unobtrusive. Dynamics are subdued, the vocal lines stay mostly within the range of a fourth or fifth, and the metric schemes are regular and inflexible throughout. Only the colors, it seems, are allowed to blend and mingle. Finally, it should be noted that these remarkable songs bear a dedication to Adele Addison, the soprano who figured in performances of many important twentieth-century works such as Copland's Emily Dickinson songs and Lukas Foss's *Time Cycle*.

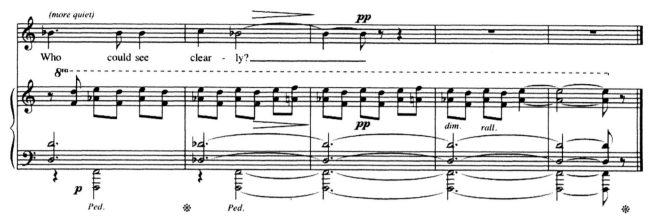

Example 4.13, mm. 15–19

Virgil Thomson (1896–1989)

The birthplace of Virgil Thomson was Kansas City, Missouri that, in 1896, was a city having a rich cultural life, yet with sufficient rural atmosphere to provide a pleasant, "neighborhood" setting for a growing child. The young Thomson started musical studies at five, and early began performing on piano and organ to the encouragement of a large, family audience despite his father's total lack of musical endowment. The composer expressed pride in his Southern forbears and in the fact that "the loyalties formed in my preadolescent years . . . are to music, companionship, and hospitality. The hospitality," he said, "stems from central Missouri that was my father's home, and from northern Kentucky, my mother's. Also from a legendary Virginia, as known through my grandmother and her brothers.[29] From this classical mid-South, seemingly so gentle, came my arrogance and my unhesitating disobedience."[30]

His developing skills and the assertive self-confidence whose genesis Thomson so aptly described, led him to a church organist position at the age of twelve, the same year in which he was to compose his first songs. A literary talent surfaced early as well, and while attending Kansas City Junior College, the composer founded a magazine and formed a literary society. His education was interrupted by World War I, in which he served as a radio engineer appointed to the school of Military Aeronautics at the University of Texas at Austin. The war ended, he completed Kansas City Junior College and departed for Harvard University.

Not surprisingly, Virgil Thomson was quickly integrated into the musical life of Harvard, both as an undergraduate member of the glee club, concertizing in Europe in the summer of 1921, and eventually as an instructor, after graduating in 1923. Nevertheless, the Northeast was an alien environment to him, and he never felt at home in Boston where "no one expands; the inhabitants seem rather to aim at compressing one another" by means of "wary eyes and necks that never turned around."[31]

Although uneasy in the environment, Virgil Thomson continued his musical enfolding at Harvard as he studied organ with Wallace Goodrich[32] and formed a deep appreciation of French music in courses with Edward Burlingame Hill. Sensing his imminent need of the language, he tutored with a cultured Parisian settled in Boston in return for piano lessons, so that he could "learn to speak French impeccably."[33] Following the Harvard Glee Club tour of 1921, he was able to remain in Paris for a year's study with Nadia Boulanger, as a result of a fellowship grant. On returning to the United States, he completed his Bachelor's degree and spent a post-graduate year instructing at Harvard and writing articles on music for *Vanity Fair*. With the five hundred dollars saved from the year's work, he set sail once again for his beloved France, to launch his life as a composer.

As Thomson himself described it, when he left America in 1925, he abandoned blooming careers as an organist, teacher, and conductor. Nor was he ever again to write for *Vanity Fair*, *The New Republic*, or *American Mercury*, though all wanted pieces from him, as did *The Dial*'s new editor, Marianne Moore.[34] In Paris, he could single-mindedly devote himself to composing, nurtured by the Gallic understanding of the necessity for involving all the faculties in the creative process. From ancestors who were mostly farmers, rather than shopkeepers or bankers, Thomson had apparently inherited the fortitude needed to depend on Providence in lieu of financial planning, and for the next eight years he lived on the support of patrons and an occasional fee or commission for music. The lively artistic life of Paris in the twenties proved to be an entirely natural milieu for his talent, urbanity, and gregariousness. Drawn quickly into the inner circles inhabited by Satie and "Les Six" (Picasso, Gide, Cocteau, Hemingway, Fitzgerald, and Gertrude Stein), Virgil Thomson settled down in 1927 at "numéro 17 quai Voltaire" and remained there until World War II.

While living in Paris in the thirties, Thomson's literary leanings had resurfaced and he had become a correspondent for *Modern Music* (the journal of the New York League of Composers). During this period, he also wrote articles and a book called *The State of Music* which was published in 1939 and reissued in 1962.[35] It was not surprising, then, that on his return to America he succeeded Lawrence Gilman as music critic for the *New York Herald Tribune*, holding the post until 1954. Many of his reviews, particularly from the period 1944–1947, were collected in *The Art of Judging Music*[36] and a number of these pieces are relevant to this study. Of particular interest are programs and reviews of New York voice recitals[37] and articles entitled "Singing Today" and "The American Song." In the sixties, Virgil Thomson rejoined the academic world as visiting professor at the University of Buffalo and Andrew Mellon professor at Carnegie Tech, also publishing his memoirs in 1967.[38] He continued to live in the Chelsea hotel overlooking southern New York City which had been his American home since 1940, and a television interview in the fall of 1980 showed views of this apartment as well as of 17 quai Voltaire in Paris. With eighty-four years behind him, most of them spent in the forefront of the musical world on two continents, Virgil Thomson affirmed to the viewing audience that he didn't believe in regretting things. "The outcome of anything or the way it happened," said he, "is the story of your life."

A year later, in October of 1981, R. Friedberg met Mr. Thomson while he was attending a performance of *The Mother of Us All* in San Antonio, Texas. Although somewhat hard of hearing on that occasion, Thomson retained his lifelong elegance, wit, and keen-edged intelligence, together with a lack of pretentiousness that made him prefer to be addressed as "Mister" despite his admittedly numerous honorary doctoral degrees. In discussing the various forms of his vocal writing, he expressed the opinion that one "works out difficulties in small pieces," i.e., songs, so that in the writing of "big pieces" (operas) one doesn't have to worry about technique, but he stressed that he had found each form to be uniquely challenging.

This devotion of Virgil Thomson to the vocal forms of composition is demonstrated by the fact that he began his composing career while still at Harvard with a choral piece, *De Profundis*, and a song called "Vernal Equinox" to an Amy Lowell text. (Thomson as an undergraduate was evidently in touch with the most recent directions in American poetry, for Lowell's work had begun to be published only a few years before he entered Harvard.) As time went on, he became increasingly committed to solving the problems of musical declamation in the English language that he felt had hardly been addressed. His collaborations with Gertrude Stein in the operas *Four Saints in Three Acts* and *The Mother of Us All* were particularly pertinent to this purpose, and critical estimation of his success is aptly voiced by Victor Yellin: "Virgil Thomson's main contribution to American music is his blending of the musical elements of melody, harmony, and rhythm into a musical style proper to American speech."[39]

Marianne Moore (1887–1972)

Thomson's place as a major contributor to and spokesman for twentieth-century American music is undisputed. Marianne Moore holds a similar position in her art form, and had become a revered "high priestess" of American poetry some thirty years before her death at the age of eighty-five. She was born in a suburb of St. Louis, Missouri, that was the home of her grandfather, the Reverend John R. Warner. Her mother had returned there from Massachusetts after her husband, a construction engineer, suffered a mental breakdown from which he never recovered. Marianne Moore never knew her father, but had an older brother who was later to enter the ministry, and the two children remained very close to each other and to their mother, Mary Warner Moore, all their lives. Mrs. Moore was an English teacher who imposed the strictest standards of behavior on herself and her children. The poet acknowledged the profound influence of this early training while admitting that she had experienced it as overly rigorous.

When Moore was seven years old her grandfather died, and the family moved to Carlisle, Pennsylvania, where she attended the Metzger Elementary School and the Metzger Institute, a secondary school for girls. In 1905 she entered Bryn Mawr College, and these formative undergraduate years were to provide both discouragement and support to the fledgling writer. The often-quoted English composition teacher's criticism, "I presume you had an idea, if one could find out what it is," drove her for a time into science courses where she developed precision of thinking and economy of expression. These qualities served her well on her return to literature, and she began to publish poems in *Tipyn O'Bob*, the campus magazine, and in the *Lantern* (Bryn Mawr's alumnae monthly) after her graduation in 1909.

In 1911, Marianne Moore began a five year stint on the faculty of the United States Indian School in Carlisle. Then she and her mother moved to Chatham, New Jersey, to be with her brother who had been made pastor of Ogden Memorial Church. The next move, two years later, was to Greenwich Village. Here she became a leading figure in a lively literary circle that included Wallace Stevens and William Carlos Williams. The poet, with her mother, left the Village in 1929 (the year of *The Dial*'s demise) for Brooklyn, where her brother was serving as chaplain at the Navy Yard. She returned to Greenwich Village thirty-six years later by herself (her mother having died in 1947) because of Brooklyn's rising crime rate, and it was to be her last move.

During the half century of Marianne Moore's life in the New York area, she supported herself in a number of ways that included private school teaching, working in the New York Public Library system, editing *The Dial* (1926–1929), acting as poet-in-residence at colleges such as Bryn Mawr (1953) and Barnard (late fifties),[40] and eventually receiving numerous prizes and fellowships as well as royalties on her many published volumes of poetry, essays, and translations. Her influence on her poetic contemporaries during the formative decade of the twenties was profound, as is evidenced by William Carlos Williams's description of her in his autobiography: "a rafter holding up the superstructure of our uncompleted building, a caryatid, her red hair plaited and wound twice about the fine skull . . . one of the main supports of the new order."[41] As time went on, the adulation of critics and other colleagues such as T. S. Eliot, Louis Untermeyer, and John Ashberry continued to proliferate, and by the end of her life she had received honorary degrees from nine colleges and universities, including N.Y.U. and Harvard, as well as Bryn Mawr's M. Carey Thomas award.

Marianne Moore felt a lasting debt of gratitude to Imagists such as T. S. Eliot and Ezra Pound who had had some of her early work published by the Egoist Press in London. Her own connection to Imagism has been alternately maintained and denied by critics. Most of them now agree that while her early poems follow the Imagist dictum of concentrating on objective data drawn from the natural environment, the later works increasingly incorporate Moore's affectionate but strongly ethical and value-oriented view of the world. Her poetic language that most commonly employs a syllabic form derived from French versification (in which accent plays little part), has been praised for its clarity and concision and, on occasion, damned for its awkwardness and obscurity.[42] A British critic, with the perspective of distance, has provided one of the most perceptive assessments of her work: "Unmistakably modern, she has no modern formlessness. . . . Her style, for all its asymmetry, is rapid, clear, unself-concerned, flexible, and accurate, and her work gradually discloses her exceptional sanity, intelligence, and imaginative depth."[43]

Virgil Thomson's connections with Marianne Moore had already begun when she had unsuccessfully solicited articles for *The Dial* from him in the mid-twenties. He was shortly thereafter to have considerable contact with her poetry through an interesting coincidence. In 1928, Thomson left Paris for a visit to the United States and stayed for a time in Massachusetts with Jessie Lasell, a woman who enjoyed reading aloud from the works of Marianne Moore, among others of her favorite poets. It might also be mentioned that Mrs. Lasell's son-in-law was J. Sibley Watson who had revived *The Dial* as a literary monthly together with Scofield Thayer,[44] and who had held the managing editorship just before Marianne Moore.[45] In later years, the independently wealthy Watson and his wife, Hildegarde, were to include Ms. Moore in a group of occasionally impoverished literary friends to whom they served as benefactors.[46]

It seems not at all surprising that Thomson would have, in time, been drawn to musical setting of some of Moore's texts, considering their mutually strong endowments in the areas of humor, sophistication, fondness for verbal sound manipulation, and preference for apparent simplicity over deliberate complexity. (Thomson had come to this preference in the process of turning away from "self-indulgent" German music[47] toward the restraint of the French, while with Moore it was the "modernist" reaction against nineteenth-century poetic Romanticism.) Interestingly, however, it was at the suggestion of Marianne Moore that Thomson wrote "English Usage" and "My Crow Pluto"[48] and she herself who chose for setting these two poems which had originally borne the titles "I've Been Thinking" and "To Victor Hugo of My Crow Pluto."[49]

Mr. Thomson described the incident in these terms: "I knew Marianne Moore for twenty or thirty years, and although she never had anyone over, she would come to my place now and then for lunch. On one occasion, she brought along these two poems and said 'I thought you might like to set these to music.' I replied 'They're very difficult—I think I will.'" Thomson added that he was referring not to a difficulty of meaning but of prosody, and that he felt impelled to rise to the challenge.[50]

It is indeed true that most of Marianne Moore's poetry consists of lines with varying numbers of syllables and accents, very infrequent rhymes, and a highly flexible, non-prosodic flow. It is a style that has apparently proved forbidding to song composers who, despite Moore's towering reputation, have, to this date, set little of her poetry. The two poems that she selected for Virgil Thomson, however, are somewhat different. They are both written in short-line couplets that mostly rhyme in "I've Been Thinking," and terminate in complementary "o" or "oo" vowel sounds throughout in "To Victor Hugo." Verbal accent patterns are fairly regular, also, and it is possible to see why these tighter structures were judged by the poet to be more appropriate to the musical medium, while still presenting as "difficult" to the composer in their distortions of the traditional rhythms of American speech.

"I've Been Thinking" appears in Moore's *Complete Poems* (published in 1967, her eightieth year) under the section heading "Hitherto Uncollected." Three small but interesting changes in the poem are to be found in Thomson's setting. In the seventeenth couplet he adds "eh?" after "I've escaped?" to make the question more emphatic. In couplet twenty-one he uses "Afric" instead of "capric," a change so major that one must assume the original as printed had been an error, now restored according to the poet's intent. Thirdly, the song carries a period rather than a colon after the line "I'm sure of this," which serves to link it to the former idea ("Not verse/Of course") rather than to the following one ("Nothing mundane is divine;/Nothing divine is mundane.") In this case, since the colon carries forward the poem's train of thought and the period does not, it seems likely that the period was an error in the music printing (see Ex. 4.16).

As already indicated, the title, too, has been changed from the ambiguous "I've Been Thinking" to the particular "English Usage." Actually, it is a very specific type of English usage that Moore satirizes and repudiates in this poem: the affected, upper class, pseudo-British speech that she possibly first encountered at Bryn Mawr College,[51] which typically overuses such epithets as "divine," "frightful," "perfectly mah-velous" and the like. With characteristic intellectual honesty, however, the poet admits that the whimsical couplets in which she has expressed her contempt, are themselves a form of the very same "word diseases" as the affected speech syndrome. Having confessed this, she plays with the sound of words, parodying her own verse form ("Attic/Afric-Alcaic"), then ends the frivolity as becomes her, with a moral statement indicating the real reason for her objection to at least one of the above epithets (i.e., "Nothing mundane is divine;").

So great is Virgil Thomson's mastery of musical declamation and the rhythm of language that he had frequently been known to improvise settings at the piano following the text on his music rack.[52] "English Usage" has some of that spontaneous quality, and the vocal line is primary throughout, with the piano supplying a supportive background of punctuating parallel chords. The most striking rhythmic aspect of this setting is the fact that Thomson has, in effect, destroyed the prosody of Moore's verse as written and has, instead, gone back to the more natural accent pattern of the lines as they would sound if spoken. In so doing, he has achieved the "solution," as it were, to the prosodic difficulties that he perceived as the original challenge.

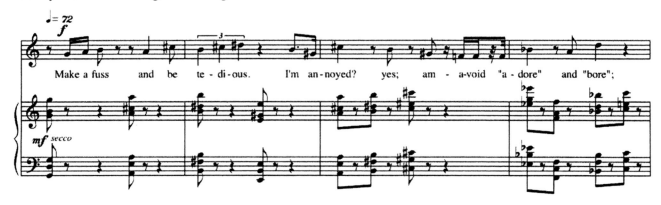

Example 4.14, mm. 1–4

The vocal line is non-lyric, and the many chordal leaps seem appropriate to the rapid and capricious leaping about from one verbal idea to another that occurs in the poem. The vocal line also shows a clear allegiance to the key of G major, with only occasional chromatic alterations. However, the accompanying chords, always in the cheerful major mode, seem to be applied vertically to the needs of the individual melody notes, rather than being governed by the horizontal demands of harmonic necessity. This serves to reinforce the disjointed, leaping melodic contour mentioned above.

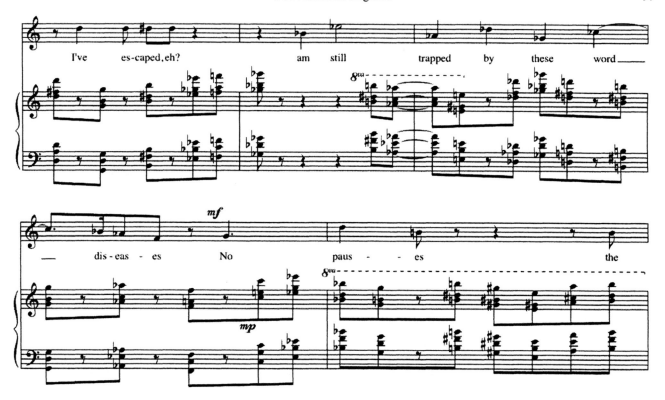

Example 4.15, mm. 24–28

To underline Marianne Moore's closing defense of divinity, Thomson provides a piano interlude of mock portent, and changes to a broad triplet pattern observed by both voice and piano. Because of the similar rhythmic movement, a polytonal feeling is created by the juxtaposition of the G major vocal line and the accompanying B-flat and A major elements. The effect of these musical devices is to suggest that a basically serious statement is being held up to good-humored self-parody.

Example 4.16, mm. 34–41

The poem "To Victor Hugo of My Crow Pluto," together with an explanatory essay ("My Crow Pluto—a Fantasy"), was published in 1966 in the collection *Tell Me, Tell Me,*[53] but had originally appeared in *Harper's Bazaar* of October 1961. Ironically, *Tell Me, Tell Me* also contained an essay called "A Burning Desire to Be Explicit" in which Moore decries the charge of obscurity which clings to her despite her constant efforts at clarity: a charge that has certainly been leveled, in some circles, at the "Pluto" writings.[54]

Part of the problem turns on the poet's erudition that Babette Deutsch describes in these terms: ". . . the mental acquisitiveness that furnishes her verse with some of its most remarkable details, sometimes turns it into a bibliographical curiosity."[55] Moore's dedication of this poem to Victor Hugo that formed part of the original title, is fairly easily understood; in couplets five through eight she agrees with the Hugo quotation set above the poem (and the song) which suggests that the winged spirit of her crow is indeed apparent, "even when the bird is walking." Thereafter, however, the need for explanatory notes increases, as Moore begins to feed in snatches of what she calls a "pseudo esperanto," and which she translates at the end of her poem, as the song's publishers unfortunately do not. The story of her relationship with the crow who adopted her is clearly set forth in the essay that, in our opinion, should also have been printed with the song, in the fashion of some of the notes and quotations attendant on Charles Ives's song publications. Plato, we discover in the essay, was a verbal variant of her name for him, as well as a judgment of his qualities. "Lucro è peso morto" ("Profit is a dead weight") is an Italian phrase found in the poem's eighteenth couplet, and is also the title of another of Moore's essays. Her strong conviction on this point, she tells us, made her uneasy with the spoils of the crow's skillful thievery. The end of the story that is clear from the poem as well as the essay was her return of the bird to natural woodland, not without regret for the loss of a handsome and large-spirited companion.

Perhaps the reason that Virgil Thomson was not concerned about detailed explanations of this somewhat puzzling verbal material is to be found in his own statement concerning English musical declamation. It was made in regard to his collaborations with Gertrude Stein, but is directly appropriate to this situation as well. "My theory was," he says, "that if a text is set correctly for the sound of it, the meaning will take care of itself. . . . With meanings . . . abstracted, or absent, or so multiplied that choice among them is impossible, there is no temptation toward tonal illustration, say of birdie babbling by the brook or heavy hangs my heart."[56] In these terms, Thomson underlines his fundamental opposition to the musically descriptive German lied approach to vocal writing, and indeed, the Moore settings seem rather to derive from the composer's lifelong Gallic devotion. They not only express an insouciance reminiscent of his (by then) forty-year-old Dadaist connection, but are also dedicated to the memory of Francis Poulenc, a leading member of "Les Six" who had died in 1962, just one year before these songs were written.

There are two levels, then, of meaning in this song, and interestingly, the setting works on both of them. On the first level, we find a structure in which merely the sound of the words has been joined to accompaniment so as to create a musically satisfying experience. The piano writing is much more linear here than in "English Usage," and the legato lines of the keyboard mirror the liquid sound of all the "o" and "oo" rhymes as well as the Italianate flow of the "esperanto madinusa" (made in U.S.A.) as Moore calls it.

Example 4.17, mm. 1–7

Supporting rhythmic patterns are grouped into a skillful three-part form, in which the piano at first mimics the voice's quarter- and eighth-note narrative (see Ex. 4.17), then breaks up into the greater urgency of sixteenth-note arpeggios,

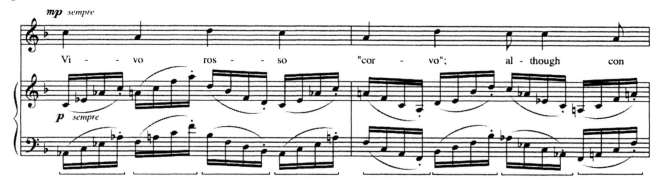

Example 4.18, mm. 15–16

and ends with staccato and syncopated eighths and quarters in a continuing crescendo of rhythmic excitement.

Example 4.19, mm. 36–38

Adding to the build-up of musical tension is the gradually increasing dynamic level that opens at a modest piano and ends fortissimo with the steepest ascent in the last section (see Ex. 4.19).

On the second level, with our informed understanding of the dramatic elements of the text, we can begin to view the soft, legato opening with accompaniment doubling the voice line, as a thoughtful and wryly affectionate reminiscence (see Ex. 4.17). Agitation mounts in section two as the poet brings the relationship more vividly to mind, recalling their private language and the looting that enforced their separation. Section three is now seen as an exaggerated tribute to the wild beauty and nobility of the bird, with the final "addio" backed by a rush of ascending whole-tone scales in a parodied wail of grief.

Example 4.20, mm. 42–47

Notes

1. Madeleine Goss, *Modern Music Makers* (New York: E. Dutton, 1952), 71.

2. Interview with Calderon Howe, M.D. (Mary Howe's son) by R. Friedberg, 24 May 1981.

3. See n2. Dr. Howe added that his mother's only conflict between her work and family life had arisen in the thirties, when Mary Howe's mother's protracted illness made the composer reluctant to fulfill her out-of-town commitments.

4. Goss, *Modern Music Makers*, 71–72.

5. As a further sidelight on her academic career, it should be noted that Mary Howe received an honorary degree from George Washington University in 1961.

6. Goss includes a fairly complete catalog of Howe's works up to 1950 (*Modern Music Makers*). The principal compositions beyond that date are the seven volumes of songs (see n8).

7. Interview, 24 May 1981.

8. New York: Galaxy Music Corporation, 1959.

9. Mary Colum, *Life and the Dream* (Garden City, N.Y.: Doubleday, 1947), 338. The MacDowell Club readings are one among many invaluable pieces of information in this book relating to American literary life ca. 1914–1940. Mary

Colum, herein writing her memoirs, was the wife of Padraic Colum, the Irish author, and an editor and literary critic in her own right.

10. Colum describes an agonizing occasion at an English country house when a fellow guest recognized Elinor and Horace and reported on the scandal surrounding them to the hostess (*Life and the Dream,* 337). Commenting on the poet's lifelong praise of Horace Wylie's personal qualities, Colum says "a man who could throw his life away for love, flinging prudence to the wind, is rare anywhere, and almost impossible in that period in America, so I am inclined to credit Elinor's vision of him." (*Life and the Dream,* 341).

11. Stanley Olson, *Elinor Wylie, A Life Apart* (New York: Dial, 1979). Olson takes a different view of Wylie. He sees him as a charming but rather weak man, with an impetuous and changeable nature.

12. For further material on Douglas Moore see Chapter 3. Edna St. Vincent Millay is discussed in Chapter 5.

13. Mary Howe, "Spring Pastoral" (New York: G. Schirmer, 1936). The manuscript of the orchestral version is in the New York Public Library at Lincoln Center. Mary Howe, "Robin Hood's Heart" (unpublished).

14. Mary Howe, "Little Elegy" (San Antonio, Tex.: Southern Music Co., 1995); "When I Died in Berners Street" (San Antonio, Tex.: Southern Music, 1995); "Let Us Walk in the White Snow" (New York: Carl Fischer, 1948); "Let Us Walk in the White Snow" has been reprinted in *Contemporary Songs in English* edited by Bernard Taylor (New York: Carl Fischer, 1956).

15. Thomas A. Gray, *Elinor Wylie* (New York: Twayne, 1969), 49.

16. The string quartet setting is available on rental from G. Schirmer, Inc.

17. See Introduction.

18. See Introduction.

19. This string quartet setting is available on rental from Carl Fischer, Inc. The manuscript is held by the Library of Congress, Washington, D.C., and the New York Public Library has a photostat.

20. Gray, *Elinor Wylie,* 50.

21. Colum, *Life and the Dream,* 364.

22. "Fair Annet's Song" and "Prinkin' Leddie" are both for medium high voice.

23. Colum, *Life and the Dream,* 252.

24. The major source of the foregoing biographical material is Louis Untermeyer's introduction to Amy Lowell, *The Complete Poetical Works* (Boston: Houghton Mifflin, 1955), xxi–xxix.

25. Colum, *Life and the Dream,* 251.

26. Colum, *Life and the Dream,* 338.

27. Medium high voice.

28. Pandiatonicism is the use of step-wise, adjacent tonal centers. It was a harmonic device frequently employed by Igor Stravinsky. For Ives's usage of a similar device, see Chapter 2, n25.

29. One of Virgil Thomson's ancestors had helped to found the colony of Jamestown, Virginia.

30. Thomson, *Virgil Thomson* (New York: Knopf, 1967), 18.

31. Thomson, *Virgil Thomson,* 48.

32. Wallace Goodrich or "Goody," as he was affectionately known to many Harvard and Radcliffe undergraduates, had a long, fruitful teaching career in mid-twentieth century. R. Friedberg remembers, in her own undergraduate days at Bryn Mawr College, "Goody" coming along with the Harvard Glee Club on their trip to Bryn Mawr for a joint concert in 1946.

33. Kathleen Hoover and John Cage, *Virgil Thomson, His Life and Music* (Freeport, N.Y.: Books for Libraries Press, 1959), 34.

34. Thomson, *Virgil Thomson,* 73.

35. Published by Henry Holt and Co.

36. Published by Alfred A. Knopf, 1948.

37. A review entitled "Pretty Singing" (V. Thomson, *The Art of Judging Music,* 83) prints the program of a recital by Muriel Rahn. Included are two songs by William Grant Still, "Winter's Approach" and "Breath of a Rose," both of which are discussed in Chapter 3.

38. See n30.

39. Victor Yellin, "The Operas of Virgil Thomson," *American Music Since 1910,* edited by Virgil Thomson (New York: Holt, Rinehart and Winston, 1971), 91. In this same collection, there is a very interesting essay by Thomson himself called "American Musical Traits" which traces the ethnic derivations of style characteristics such as melody, rhythm, and dynamics.

40. Ms. Natalie Beller, of San Antonio and Santa Fe, who received her B.A. from Barnard College in 1959, has vivid recollections of Marianne Moore's warmth and energy during the poetry readings she held on campus. Personal recollections of Ms. Moore at a slightly earlier period (i.e., in the thirties and forties) are presented at some length in the following memoir: Elizabeth Bishop, "Efforts of Affection," *Vanity Fair* 46, no. 4 (June 1983): 44–61.

41. William Carlos Williams, *Autobiography* (New York: Random House, 1951), 146.

42. Some of the outstanding critical studies on Marianne Moore: (a) Bernard F. Engel, *Marianne Moore* (New York: Twayne, 1964); (b) George Nitchie, *Moore: An Introduction to the Poetry* (New York: Columbia University Press, 1969); (c) Pamela White Hadas, *Moore: Poet of Affection* (Syracuse, N.Y.: Syracuse University Press, 1977).

43. M. J. Alexander, "Marianne Moore," *Great Writers of the English Language—Poets*, ed. James Vinson (New York: St. Martin's, 1979), 710.

44. Mary Colum has much to say concerning Scofield Thayer's nobility of character, coupled with a nervous instability that led eventually to a breakdown. One moving passage (*Life and the Dream*, 384) describes his generous handling of a desperate request for funds sent by James Joyce to the Colums after the start of World War I.

45. Most of the foregoing information in this paragraph comes from Thomson, *Virgil Thomson*, Chapter 13, ("American Interlude").

46. Interview with R. Friedberg, 4 October 1981. He added that Marianne Moore, "an odd woman," was not as poor as she seemed, and at her death surprised everyone by leaving a sizable sum of money to her nephew.

47. Thomson, *Virgil Thomson,* 117.

48. Virgil Thomson, "English Usage" in *Contemporary Art Songs: 28 Songs by American and British Composers* (Milwaukee: distr. by Hal Leonard Corp., 1970); "My Crow Pluto" in *Twentieth Century Art Songs* (Milwaukee: distr. by Hal Leonard Corp., 1997). Both of these songs were recorded by Meriel and Peter Dickinson, British singer and pianist. The recording, titled *An American Anthology*, was issued under the Unicorn label.

49. The information contained in the foregoing sentence comes from a personal letter by Virgil Thomson to R. Friedberg, 30 September 1980.

50. Interview, 4 October 1981.

51. Forty years later, during R. Friedberg's years at Bryn Mawr College (see n32), this type of speech affectation was still widely encountered.

52. Yellin, "The Operas," 95.

53. Published by Viking Press.

54. Nitchie, *Marianne Moore,* 150.

55. Babette Deutsch, *Poetry in Our Time* (Garden City, N.Y.: Doubleday, 1963), 229.

56. Thomson, *Virgil Thomson*, 90.

Chapter 5

John Duke (1899–1984)

"Fifty years from now, John Duke is going to be known as the representative figure of his era in American song-writing." This statement was made in 1982 to R. Friedberg by John Seagle[1] who, as director since 1947 of the Seagle summer vocal colony[2] at Schroon Lake, New York, had at that time been actively involved with American singers and composers of vocal literature for almost forty years. An equally impressive accolade came from the pen of the redoubtable Virgil Thomson. After lamenting the generally sorry state of the American art song in a 1947 critical essay,[3] Mr. Thomson ended his review of a Povla Frisch recital the following year by remarking that "John Duke's 'Bells in the Rain' was the only song that stood up as workmanship beside the Poulenc pieces."[4]

There is no doubt that John Duke made one of the major contributions of the twentieth century to the growing body of American art songs. His total catalog (published and unpublished) reached the impressive number of two hundred and fifty-two settings,[5] which covered an extremely wide range of poetic subject matter and musical treatment. Yet a paradox always surrounded this man who devoted a long, vigorous lifetime to the art of setting poetry to music, and it stemmed from the fact that it was not exactly what he had had in mind. "I am still amazed," he wrote in 1981, "at the way my musical career has turned out. In my early days, my ambition was to be a great pianist, and I could not have believed anyone who told me I was destined to be a song composer."[6]

John Duke made his home in Northampton, Massachusetts, for well over half a century. From 1964, until his death twenty years later, his home was a sunny, two-story, white frame house of comfortable proportions on tree-shaded Harrison Avenue.[7] However, despite this typical New England setting in which he became totally at home, Duke's origins were Southern, and a family legend claimed that his paternal grandfather left Columbia, South Carolina, on the last train before Sherman burned the city. His father, Harry K. Duke, spent his youth in Charles Town, West Virginia, then moved to Cumberland, Maryland, where he engaged in various business ventures, including a bookstore. John Duke was born in Cumberland, and recalled "an almost ideal family life"[8] as the eldest of six children. His father had a strong interest in literature, and one of the composer's earliest memories was of hearing him read aloud famous passages from Shakespearean plays. Duke's mother, Matilda Hoffman, was a singer of some accomplishment, and an old photograph shows her playing the guitar, her preferred accompanying instrument. It was a household devoted to both words and music: the ideal nurturing ground for a song composer.

After learning to read music under his mother's instruction, John Duke began his formal study of the piano at the age of eleven, with a woman named Beatrice Holmes. He evidently made rapid progress, as a year later he was already playing the piano and organ in local church services. His most intensive training began when at sixteen he won a scholarship at the Peabody Conservatory in Baltimore. Here he was to remain for three years, climaxing his studies with a performance of the Saint-Saëns G minor concerto accompanied by the Conservatory orchestra.[9]

Peabody had been patterned by its founder after European models, and Duke's teachers were solidly grounded in nineteenth-century traditions. John Duke studied the piano with Harold Randolph who had himself been trained at Peabody by pupils of von Bülow, Clara Schumann, and Liszt. Randolph, a member of one of the "first families of Virginia" which had been impoverished by the Civil War, was a fine solo and ensemble pianist. He was also an able administrator, and built the Conservatory into an outstanding music school during his years as director. John Duke's mentor in composition was Gustav Strube, the "grand old man" of post–World War I music in Baltimore, who had been born in the Hartz mountains in Germany and had studied at the Leipzig Conservatory with Karl Reinecke before coming to this country.[10] Strube had also been Mary Howe's professor of composition,[11] but although she had taken her degree in 1922, just four years after Duke's graduation, their paths did not cross. "I don't remember ever meeting Mary Howe," wrote John Duke, "although I was very well acquainted with her friend, Anne Hull, with whom she often gave two-piano recitals."[12]

A period of volunteer service in the army during which he was stationed with the SATC at Columbia University brought the young musician to New York City. When World War I ended, he remained there to study the piano with Franklin Cannon (a Leschetizsky pupil) and composition under Howard Brockway and Bernard Wagenaar. Both of these composers possessed an active vocal orientation which no doubt strengthened the student's inclinations. Brockway, who had taught at Peabody before settling in New York, published two albums of Kentucky folk song settings in 1916 and 1920, which was in line with the growing interest of the era in indigenous musical material. Wagenaar, a native of Holland and only five years older than Duke, was also making a significant contribution to the art song at this time. In 1925 and 1928 (several years after Duke's period of study), he wrote song cycles to the poetry of Edna St. Vincent Millay, thus placing himself among the pioneers in the setting of contemporary American poetry, and prefiguring John Duke's Millay settings which began in 1935.

Between 1922 and 1923, Duke was employed in editing pianola rolls for the Ampico recording laboratories. It was while working on Artur Schnabel's recordings that a friendship was formed that later took him to Berlin to study with the world-famous pianist. Just before Christmas 1922, John Duke married Dorothy Macon of Falls Church, Virginia, whose father was Capt. Edward N. Macon of the U.S. Army and whose brother, General Robert C. Macon, played a leading role in the final European campaign of World War II. This was the beginning of a long and devoted relationship[13] that was to become a professional partnership as well, for Mrs. Duke had reacted strongly against her military background when she found herself increasingly drawn toward literature and the arts. As a writer, she shared her husband's deep interest in poetry,[14] and in the course of time served as his librettist on several occasions.[15]

The year 1923 was an important one for John Duke, as it marked the beginning of a long teaching career at Smith College during which he was to become Henry Dike Sleeper Professor of Music. The same year also saw the first appearance of his compositions in print, with G. Schirmer's publication of a piano work ("The Fairy Glen") and two songs ("I've Dreamed of Sunsets" and "Lullaby") which had been written in 1920 and 1921 respectively.[16] Now thoroughly settled in the academic way of life, Duke spent his first sabbatical leave (1929–1930) in the European musical capitals of Berlin and Paris where he studied the piano with Schnabel and compositional analysis with Nadia Boulanger. The latter experience was to have an immediate, discernible effect on his composition, and many of his songs written in the 1930's show the combination of French and avant-garde influences together with a reaching out toward a unique personal style that was this creative teacher's legacy to all her students.

From 1930 until his retirement from Smith College in 1967 as professor emeritus, John Duke divided his activities into three principal categories: teaching, performing, and composing. Some of the highlights of his teaching career were a course on the "History of Technical Theory in Piano Playing" given for the University Extension in Springfield and Amherst; a series of lectures on "The Arts Today" in association with Oliver Larkin, given at the Smith Summer Session of 1944; and an address to the December 1954 National Association of Teachers of Singing Convention in Chattanooga on the subject "A Composer Looks at Contemporary Song Literature," after which a program of his works was presented.

Also in 1954, Duke began his long and fruitful involvement with the Seagle Music Colony[17] where he continued each summer to preside over master classes in the performance of his works. Author R. Friedberg was fortunate enough to attend one of these sessions, held on July 31, 1982, the day after John Duke's eighty-third birthday.[18] In the rustic but acoustically grateful wooden theater overlooking a hazy Schroon Lake, sixteen young singers performed Duke songs old and new, several of which were first performances. To each, the composer (who always knew all the poetry he had set by heart and quoted it readily) stressed the importance of a meaningful reading of the poem as a prelude to successful interpretation of the song, and made other comments on tempi or rhythmic inaccuracies that most often related to verbal and poetic elements.

As a further result of this professional and personal association between Duke and the Seagle Music Colony, the composer arranged to spend his sabbatical year of 1955–1956 as a visiting professor of piano at Trinity University in San Antonio, Texas, where John Seagle was professor of voice from 1947 to 1980. This appointment was in the nature of a homecoming for Mrs. Duke, who, because of her military background had from her girlhood various ties to Fort Sam Houston.

.

In the capacity of performing pianist, John Duke presented innumerable concerts throughout his career. These indicated a freely ranging musical curiosity and a particular interest in the American scene that began with his programming of MacDowell's *Keltic Sonata* on a number of recitals in the early twenties. For several summers he appeared as piano soloist and chamber player at the Yaddo summer colony of creative artists in Saratoga Springs, and in 1936, as executive chairman of the concert committee, was able to organize as well as participate in programs of contemporary American music. The Yaddo experience brought him into contact with other American musicians and writers such as Roy Harris, Ralph Kirkpatrick, and John Cheever, for that valuable cross-fertilization of ideas which is a principal "raison d'être" of the summer artists' colony.[19]

John Duke also gave many first performances of works by well-known American composers in New York, Boston, and Princeton as well as Saratoga Springs. One of these was the Roger Sessions *Piano Sonata #1* which he premiered at one of the historic Copland-Sessions concerts of contemporary music in New York.[20] Others included works by Walter Piston, Bernard Wagenaar (his former teacher), and the *Piano Sonata #3* by Ross Lee Finney who was a colleague of Duke's at Smith College before his move to a position at the University of Michigan. By way of combining his interests in teaching and performing American piano literature, Duke presented numerous lecture-recitals through the years on the works of Louis Moreau Gottschalk.[21] In this undertaking he had the assistance of Dorothy Duke, who was also interested in the career of this colorful musician, and who collected material on Gottschalk for inclusion in a book which was completed, but not published.

A chronological survey of John Duke's compositional output shows a meaningful and increasing pull toward vocal forms. During the 1930s and 40s he produced nine major instrumental works, of which two were orchestral and seven for various chamber groups. Among performances of these, the following were notable: the *String Quartet* played by the Walden and N.B.C. quartets; the *Concerto for Piano and Strings* performed over New York's WQXR in 1945; the *String Trio* played at a Yaddo festival; and the *Carnival Overture* performed by the Boston Pops Orchestra and the National Orchestra Association of New York.

In the 1950s, Duke developed an "increasing interest in opera,"[22] partly, no doubt, because of the performance opportunities provided by his newly formed association with the Seagle Music Colony. In the summer of 1953, his first opera, *Captain Lovelock*, was performed at Schroon Lake. For this work, John Duke prepared his own libretto, which he adapted from a Danish play. In his second opera, *The Sire de Maletroit's Door* (1958), taken from a Robert Louis Stevenson story, he had the collaboration of Dorothy Duke as librettist. She had also filled a similar role in the composition of the 1944 *Musical Fantasy for Children* which was based on a Rudyard Kipling story, "The Cat That Walked by Himself."

The middle of the same decade (1955) saw the publication by G. Schirmer of "O, Sing Unto the Lord" for women's voices and string orchestra or organ, and Duke has also written five other choral works. But the overwhelming body of his composition, which he produced copiously during the decades of his involvement with other forms, and almost exclusively during the last twenty years of his life was songs. Partly, perhaps, in the effort to explicate the power of his attraction toward this medium, and partly because the increased leisure afforded him the opportunity to write as well as compose, John Duke, after his retirement published two articles which rank as classics in the literature on song writing: "Some Reflections on the Art Song in English"[23] and "The Significance of Song."[24] Also, in retirement, Duke continued to be involved throughout the country in recitals of his songs in which he served as accompanist. R. Friedberg took part in one such occasion at Duke University in the 1960s when she moderated a panel discussion titled "Words and Music" which preceded a concert of Duke songs for soprano, baritone, and tenor.[25]

By the 1980s, John Duke had become a celebrated name in the American vocal scene. In the spring of 1983, Margarita Evans spearheaded a large Duke festival at Wheaton College, Illinois, to initiate the Society of the Friends of John Duke. This group would begin publication of his unpublished songs with Southern Music Company of San Antonio, an ongoing project which presently numbers four volumes.[26] In 1984, the last year of his life, Duke participated in Glenda Maurice's Delaware Vocal Arts Festival, and voice therapist Oren Brown's yearly seminar in Amherst. Another outstanding event was a concert he attended in Northampton in which the prominent soprano, Wilhelmina Fernandez, included a group of the composer's songs in her program.

During the last quarter of the twentieth century, John Duke's songs were much recorded, first on long-playing records and then with the newly available CD technology. The composer was represented in the 1977 anthology, New World Records, with three of his Edwin Arlington Robinson settings (see n62). In the same decade, two complete recordings of his songs were issued presenting John Duke himself at the piano: the first with Donald Boothman, baritone, in 1977[27] and the second with Carole Bogard, soprano, in 1979.[28] The anthology called *Art Song in America* which contained eight John Duke songs was reissued as a CD in 1997.[29] In this recording, R. Friedberg was the pianist and author of the liner notes, and the singer was tenor John Hanks, who headed the Duke University voice department from 1954 to

1987. Hanks was closely associated with the composer during his six years on the faculty of Smith College before coming to North Carolina, and remained one of John Duke's leading interpreters until his death in 2002.

Twenty-first century singers and recording artists continue to be drawn to the works of John Duke. Complete CDs of Duke songs were issued in 2001 by Lauralyn Kolb, soprano,[30] and in 2002 by the tenor, James Taylor.[31] And ironically, given John Duke's unsuccessful attempts to encourage this during his lifetime, all of his major publishers have, since his death, reprinted their John Duke song holdings in impressive collections: G. Schirmer in 1990, Boosey & Hawkes in 1998, and Carl Fischer in 2002.

*   *   *

John Duke often expressed his gratitude for the advantages of an academic environment in the fostering of his creative development. One of these advantages was the opportunity to nurture "a lively interest in philosophy and aesthetics. At one time," said Duke, "I read extensively in the philosophy of Bergson, mainly, I think, because it dealt so brilliantly with the problem of the discursive intellect when faced with the mysteries of the creative instinct. As time went on I became more and more of an *anti-intellectual*, especially so far as music is concerned, and more and more conscious of the limits of discursive language in trying to probe its depths."[32]

Despite these reservations, however, John Duke continued, throughout his career, to employ his own discursive intellect and impressive verbal skills in the writing of letters and articles. He did this in the attempt to understand and delineate his passion for vocal melody, his innately powerful response to lyric poetry, and his lifelong involvement with song, the form which combines them. In 1961, Duke explained his growing disinterest in instrumental composition in these terms:

> My early training was concentrated almost exclusively on the piano and ever since I have had a most intense interest in piano playing. . . . Why then have I written so little for the piano and why am I now writing exclusively for the voice?
>
> I think it is because of my belief that vocal utterance is at the basis of music's mystery. The thing that makes melody a concrete expression of feeling and not just a horizontal design in tones is its power to symbolize the pull, the tension of our feeling of duration. In this view, all music, no matter how complex in texture, is an extension of our urge to sing,—to go beyond speech in intensity and beauty of form. . . . I had gradually come to feel that using words as musical material seemed to give my songs a quality that my instrumental music lacked. The words and their associations with concrete situations and feelings seemed to give my melodies a form and "authenticity" that I could not get without them. . . . It may be that someday I shall go back to writing instrumental music. But at present I feel that the twentieth century experiments in instrumental music have tended to take the concreteness, the humanity out of melody, and I want to be among those who are trying to bring back this quality.[33]

Having, therefore, become committed to the use of "words as musical material," Duke gradually developed a technique for finding the ones he needed. He described the process thus:

> In the course of reading literally thousands of poems in English in my quest for song texts, I have developed an ability to sense quickly, usually after a single reading, the possibilities of a poem as musical material, at least as far as my own musical sensibilities are concerned. What do I look for? Lines which immediately suggest a "singable" phrase; stanzas which offer contrast in mood and suggest varieties of musical treatment; open vowels at climactic points; variety and subtlety in the spoken rhythms. . . . But the most important thing of all is the ability to sense the possibility of assimilating all of the material that the poem offers into a strong and concise musical form.[34]

John Duke here alluded to the concept of word-setting as "assimilation," a process in which the music swallows all elements of the poetry to become a special (but in no way "impure") kind of music.[35] The composer came upon the formulation of this principle while studying the works of Susanne Langer,[36] an aesthetician whose writings he describes as "aesthetics at its best" and as "a good example of using art to describe art."[37] In applying the assimilative principle, Duke has been constantly "devoted to trying to realize in English the ideal of the German lied, i.e., the same intimate and inseparable relationship between the text and music."[38]

The meticulous craftsmanship that supported this philosophical concept is revealed in John Duke's description of his working methods:

> I now make a regular practice of making a "rhythmic sketch" or planning out of the time values of a melody in accordance with my feeling for the natural rhythmic utterance of the words, before I attempt to conceive the melody as definite pitch variations. Of course, this is no good if it does not become part of a really good melody but (as-

suming that the melody is good) it does make sure that the words will reinforce and become part of the whole melodic conception rather than seem to run counter to the melody as I think they often do in unconvincing songs.[39]

In 1981, John Duke contributed what he described as "his final word on the subject of song" to be published as the
lead article in Volume I/1 of *Ars Lyrica*: the journal of the newly established Lyrica Society for Word-Music Relationships. This article, entitled "The Significance of Song" and mentioned above, was characterized by Mark Van Doren, a
long-time friend of the composer's, as "not a definition but rather a summoning of the subject, so that while one reads
one hears— . . . a priceless experience."[40] What is indeed "heard" in this remarkable summation is a spiritual perspective
on the meaning of song in human life. "The mystery of melody," Duke wrote, "seems to reside in its creation of an experience in which time loses the character of successive moments and becomes an ever expanding present."[41] To reinforce
this idea, he turned to Henri Bergson, mentor of a lifetime, and his concept of "the continuous melody of our inner
life."[42] (Although she is not mentioned here, it is certainly worthy of note that Susanne Langer makes the directly pertinent observation in her discussion of poetry that "the whole creation in a lyric is an awareness of a subjective experience,
and the tense of subjectivity is the 'timeless' present."[43])

Interestingly, Duke then quoted the poem "What Are Years?" by Marianne Moore, who was considered by many to
be the most prosaic of poets (see Chapter 4), and whom John Duke had never set. A powerful image toward the end of
the poem, however, served him well:

. . . The very bird
grown taller as he sings, steels
his form straight up.

From this, Duke derived that "by its very nature, song cannot be used to express a denial of life." On the contrary,
he tells us, "all song . . . is saying in effect 'I am alive and I affirm the value of living.'"[44]

*   *   *

In a song catalog of Schubertian proportions, which was almost entirely based on English language poetry, John Duke
devoted fully 75 percent of his settings to the work of American poets. According to the composer, this did not result
from a conscious exclusion, but rather from years of combing anthologies, "always thinking of the poem as I would
speak it . . . and how I would transfer or transfigure the spoken word into music."[45] By indirection, then, we perceive that
it was the cadence of American speech and American poetry that had the most power to draw him and to suggest musical
form.

Nine of the American poets represented in Duke's catalog will be discussed in this chapter, and the order of their
treatment will be based not on the chronology of their birth but on the historical position of the specific settings in the
composer's list of works. Thus we begin with Adelaide Crapsey, born in 1878, whose "Rapunzel" was published by
Duke in 1935, and conclude with *Six Poems by Emily Dickinson*, the earliest of the nine, who was born in 1830, but
whose settings Duke published over three decades later, in 1968.

Adelaide Crapsey (1878–1914)

Adelaide Crapsey was born in Brooklyn Heights, but her family moved to Rochester, New York, one year later, and she
attended public schools there until 1893. Although her father was an Episcopalian minister, conservative thinking was
hardly her heritage. Reverend Crapsey was deposed from the ministry after being tried for heresy in 1905, and her mother, Adelaide Trowbridge, of an equally unorthodox turn of mind, fostered extreme intellectual independence in each of
her nine children. Despite their strength of intellect and conviction, however, the family members were marked for tragedy. Sister Ruth (age eleven) died of undulant fever in 1898, sister Emily (age twenty-four) of appendicitis in 1901, and
brother Philip (age thirty-one) of the aftereffects of malaria in 1907. Adelaide herself was doomed to end a promising
academic career and artistically creative life by dying of tuberculosis at the age of thirty-six.

The poet prepared for college at Kemper Hall in Kenosha, Wisconsin, and entered Vassar in 1897. Her literary preoccupations already strengthening as an undergraduate, Crapsey became class poet and editor of the yearbook, besides
appearing in several plays and belonging to the debating team. She graduated with honors and was elected to Phi Beta
Kappa in 1901, then returned to Kemper Hall as a teacher of history and literature.

For the next decade, Adelaide Crapsey alternated trips to Europe for the purpose of study and travel with several
teaching positions in the United States, the last and most prestigious of these being an instructorship in poetics at Smith
College which she held from 1911 to 1913. Her principal area of scholarly investigation was English metrics, and she

did intensive research in 1911 at the London museum for an exhaustive technical thesis entitled *Analysis of English Metrics* that was to remain only two-thirds completed at her death.

Although Crapsey apparently saw herself primarily as a scholar, not a poet, her study of English prosody led to a fascination with Asian verse forms that preceded Ezra Pound's by several years. Inspired by Japanese Hokku and Tanka poetry, she created the five-line "cinquain" containing fixed numbers of syllables that reduced the verbal material to its most economical terms, and wrote in this form from 1911 to 1913. By this time, an increasing physical exhaustion of ten years' duration had developed into her terminal illness, and Adelaide Crapsey spent her last months writing much of her finest poetry while knowingly awaiting death in a sanatorium at Saranac Lake, New York.

A slim volume of Crapsey's poetry appeared posthumously in 1915, entitled simply *Verse*. Seven poems were added to the 1922 edition, and twenty more to the one published in 1934. In these volumes are printed a few poems from 1905, the "cinquains" of 1911–1913, and the rest from 1909 on. While the earlier work treats predominantly romantic subjects in the restricted terms available to a woman of her era, the later poems become increasingly reminiscent of Emily Dickinson in their brevity, directness, obsessive preoccupation with death, and penchant for unusual punctuation (Crapsey using multiple dots in place of the Dickinson dashes).

The poem "Rapunzel" (grouped under Part II of the 1922 edition, but undated) has been given a most remarkable setting by John Duke,[46] who was strongly conscious of his Smith College faculty kinship with the ill-fated poet. He, in fact, lived just across the street from her closest friend for many years and learned a great deal about her. "Judging by her photographs," Duke wrote, "she was a really beautiful woman."[47] "Rapunzel" consists of three short stanzas of four lines each. It begins in a regular iambic meter that is soon broken by the powerful thrust of the question which closes each of the three verses: "Ah, who is there?" Much of the strength of the poem comes from the dramatic immediacy of using Rapunzel herself as the speaker, as she loosens her hair and waits for the unknown. Although various interpretations of Crapsey's meaning are possible, depending on the date of the writing (which is, unfortunately, unknown) John Duke's conception of it is quite clear. "The poem," he said, "seems rather cryptic until we realize that the author was waiting for *death*, symbolized by the *witch*."[48]

The composer wrote this song in 1935 as one of a group of settings that, as previously suggested, had been influenced by his studies with Boulanger, and by his subsequent exploration of the newer compositional trends. Duke's primarily linear thinking in this period is evidenced by his suite for viola alone composed in 1933, while the songs of 1934 and 1935 are oriented toward two voice counterpoint and have a sparseness of texture which places them completely apart from all the Duke settings that preceded or followed. The piano part of "Rapunzel" is actually a single line doubled at the octave and scored for two hands. Above this, the brief, punctuated vocal phrases are set in a declamatory style, in which stepwise motion is used to create a trancelike atmosphere in the narrative (see Ex. 5.1), and increasingly wide leaps to underline the speaker's mounting dread (see Ex. 5.2).

Example 5.1, mm. 30–37

Very few Duke songs of this period carry key signatures and this one is no exception, but it would not in any case, since it opens and closes in the natural form of A minor, or the Aeolian mode. Modal elements, in fact, predominate in both vocal and instrumental lines, and they lend an appropriate color to the retelling of the ancient fairy tale. The almost unremitting eighth-note motion is a commonly encountered rhythmic innovation in the American art song of the thirties[49] and serves the dramatic purpose of suggesting Rapunzel's restless agitation. Another and very effective twentieth-century device is the polytonal source of the final dissonance, as the singer holds an anguished high A from the tonic chord over a piano figure which mercilessly repeats the hammered suspense of the dominant.

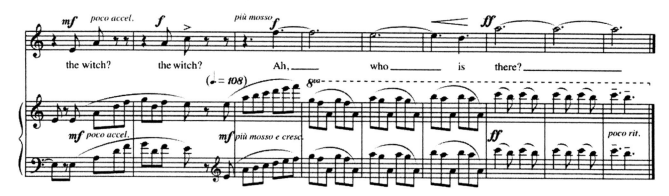

Example 5.2, mm. 60–68

It should be mentioned here that all verbal repetitions in this song are from the original poem. John Duke, unlike a great many song composers, remained meticulously faithful to the text in the vast majority of his settings. On occasion, he omitted a verse or two in order to create a more compact and manageable musical form, but even this was rare in his catalog. Interestingly, however, the composer eventually began to place musical form above poetic integrity as his primary artistic goal in song writing. "If you get the form just right, it has great power,"[50] said Duke toward the end of his life, adding that he was now more willing to change or leave out parts of poems to serve this end.

Edna St. Vincent Millay (1892–1950)

The year 1892 saw the birth of another woman poet whose childhood heritage of independent thinking was to be imprinted with the form and polish of a Vassar education. Breaking away from established patterns began for Edna Millay with the middle name chosen by her parents for their first-born child. St. Vincent's was a hospital in her home state of Maine where her sailor uncle had received excellent care after a shipwreck, and this eldest daughter of three was to be called "Vincent" by family and intimates throughout her life. Cora Buzzelle Millay, an even more strong-minded and unconventional woman than Adelaide Trowbridge Crapsey, divorced Edna's father when the girl was eight—a daring move in 1900. Her modest, intermittent salary as a practical nurse and frequent absences from home developed an admirable independence of spirit and indifference to material comforts in the three girls, especially Vincent as the oldest. But a far greater gift was her mother's fostering of her literary and musical talents which early began to bear fruit amid the nurturing mountains and seashore of Penobscot County, Maine.

Millay had an inborn knack for musical composition, and studied the piano quite seriously in her teens. She abandoned hopes of a concert career when her hands were pronounced too small, but for the rest of her life was to find "comfort as well as pleasure in playing and listening to music."[51] In high school, her theatrical gifts for both play-writing and acting also surfaced, but her principal vocation as poet became clearly established with the acceptance, in 1912, of "Renascence" by an American poetical anthology called *The Lyric Year*. The enormous outcry over her poem having failed to win a prize brought her instant literary notoriety, as well as the attention of Caroline P. Dow who arranged funding so that she might enroll in Vassar College for the academic training which her talent and intellect warranted.

A semester of pre-Vassar preparation at Barnard College in the spring of 1913 enabled Millay to sample the artistic climate of New York City at the moment in time when modern poetry was just beginning to challenge traditional forms on the American scene. (An analogous development in the world of visual art was the legendary "armory show,"—the International Art Exhibit which the young woman attended in March.) The literary world was eager to meet her, and during a memorable party hosted by Jessie Rittenhouse, then secretary to the Poetry Society of America, the poet was introduced to some of its leading figures, including Sara Teasdale and Witter Bynner. The latter had written an admiring note to Millay concerning "Renascence" at the time of its publication, together with another poet, Arthur Davison Ficke, who would become one of the most beloved persons in her life.

The rules and regulations of Vassar proved trying to the poet's nature, but its literary offerings nourished her mind, and its strong interests in drama and singing gave her further creative outlets. In 1917, her senior year, Millay responded to Sara Teasdale's request to reprint her poem, "Ashes of Life," in *The Answering Voice*, Teasdale's anthology of love poetry by women. In a sprightly letter, the young poet teased the experienced one, only a few years married to Ernst

Filsinger, saying "Whadda you mean having husbands and anthologies at the same time?"[52] One wonders if this flippant reference to a marriage already going sour, coupled with Teasdale's distrust of Millay's unconventional approach to life may have been among the factors that militated against the growth of a friendship between them. It is nevertheless true that just before her suicide in 1933, Sara Teasdale wrote to Edna Millay of her early admiration, which had apparently survived the passage of the years. "I like to think," she said, "that when I first read you long ago, I knew you and named a star."[53]

Following graduation came the famous Greenwich Village years that saw Millay's association with the Provincetown Players as actress, playwright, and director, and publications in *Vanity Fair*, *The Dial*, Harriet Monroe's *Poetry* and *The Mirror*, a St. Louis journal edited by W. M. Reedy. Her poetry collection, *A Few Figs from Thistles*, appeared in 1920, and the couplet beginning "My candle burns at both ends" was seized upon, somewhat to the poet's later dismay, as the motto of a generation eager to throw off the shackles of Victorian propriety. The Edna St. Vincent Millay of this period possessed a compelling beauty and personality that drew her into relationships with a number of men of her literary circle. Among them were the playwright Floyd Dell, Edmund Wilson, and Witter Bynner, all of whom unsuccessfully proposed marriage. Ironically, Arthur Davison Ficke, whom she loved deeply all her life after their meeting and affair in 1918, did not ask her to be his wife, even when his first marriage dissolved.

The poems of *Second April*, published in 1921, include a number of sonnets written in the lonely aftermath of the Ficke encounter. The sonnet was to become one of her most characteristic and successful forms as she poured the new wine of contemporary speech into the old bottles of the prescribed metric and rhyme schemes. Returning home in ill health from a European writing stint for *Vanity Fair*, Millay was married in 1923 to Eugen Boissevain, a businessman with a deep admiration for the arts. He was twelve years older than the poet and this fact, coupled with his devotion to her talent, gave her the sense of the fatherly care she had never experienced, as well as the assurance that she would not have to bury her Muse in domesticity. The decade of the twenties also saw the development of a strong friendship with Elinor Wylie whose *Nets to Catch the Wind* had been given a glowing review by Millay in the *New York Evening Post* of January 1922. When the League of American Penwomen snubbed Wylie because of her personal life, Edna Millay refused their proffered honors in a scathing letter, and she poured her grief over the tragic early death of Elinor Wylie into a number of poems which were published in *Huntsman What Quarry?* (1939).

By 1935, Millay had reached the peak of her career, with her writing much in demand and requests increasing for her highly dramatic readings of her own poetry. A strong social conscience which had involved her in the Sacco-Vanzetti case and the post–World War I pacifist movement, now impelled her toward the Spanish Loyalist cause, and a heavy investment of time and effort in propaganda for the Allied effort in World War II. Increasing physical problems caused a breakdown when the war ended, and she was just beginning to respond to her husband's dedicated care when he died following surgery in 1949. After a single year of reclusive, grief-stricken life, the poet had a heart attack on the stairs at "Steepletop," their home in the Berkshires since 1925, and joined him in death.

The twelve love sonnets of Millay's *Second April* are followed by an eight-line poem called "Wild Swans" which concludes the volume. Its brevity and irregular lines sprinkled with bold metric choices are in direct contrast to the preceding sonnets, as is the force of its compressed emotion. In it, Millay, who all her life had a passionate attachment to wild birds and natural beauty, finds release in the flight of the swans from her "tiresome heart, forever living and dying." She leaves her "house without air" and exhorts the swans to fly "over the town again" with a cry that seems to celebrate their unsullied freedom while it carries an echo of human pain.

John Duke chose this poem for setting in 1935,[54] the same year as "Rapunzel," but in this song, contours of the severe linear approach have been somewhat softened as chordal elements return and the piano has two hands independently occupied. Duke now begins to exhibit a style that is typical of many of his finest songs. In a process very close to that of instrumental chamber music, voice and piano each carry their own motivic material, the two lines for the most part unrelated, yet indissolubly meshed. Thus, we find the accompaniment motif expressed in the piano prelude (see. Ex. 5.3), and reentering around the vocal line at another pitch level (see Ex. 5.4).

Example 5.3, mm. 1–4

Example 5.4, mm. 29–32

A possible connection between the two emerges near the end of the song as the voice picks up the large interval leaps from the piano motif.

Example 5.5, mm. 50–53

These large intervals which are for the most part intensified by leaping from a short note to a longer one, create an aural context of desperate "abandon," the quality called for in the composer's marking (see Ex. 5.3). The longing implicit in the poem is perfectly translated by John Duke into suspended dissonances such as the first right hand piano note of measures one and two respectively, and the vocal pitches of E natural and E-flat in Example 5.5. The characteristic leaps and suspensions receive their final statement in the piano postlude that loses energy in the diminishing dynamic level but retains much unresolved emotion in the extended minor ninth that ends the song.

The fluid metric scheme of continuous eighth-note motion with varying numbers of beats per measure is carried on here from "Rapunzel," and becomes a perfect foil for the unpredictable poetic feet of Millay's poem. A key signature is still absent, but tonal areas are clear, with D minor the principal key. Two interesting chromatic modulations are dictated by the text, both moving upward tonally to parallel images of flight. The first begins as follows and ends with Example 5.4, and the second has been cited in Example 5.5.

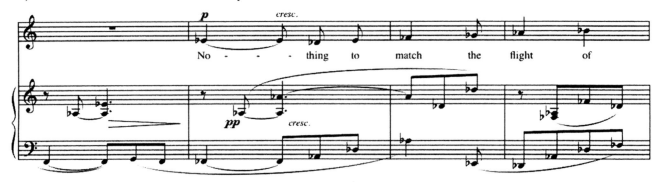

Example 5.6, mm. 25–28

Edwin Arlington Robinson (1869–1935)

E. A. Robinson's life, one totally devoted to the writing of poetry, was almost equally divided between the nineteenth and twentieth centuries, and he is generally recognized as the most important poet writing in America in 1900. He had grown up in Gardiner, Maine, as the virtually ignored youngest son of Edward and Mary Palmer Robinson who had desperately wanted their third child to be a daughter. Most of the parental attention, therefore, turned to Dean, the intellectual, who became a physician and eventually a drug addict, and to Herman, the handsome extrovert, who ruined the family business and sought refuge in alcohol. Edwin entered Harvard in 1891, but had to leave a year later when his father died, a death that was followed with tragic haste by his mother's in 1896 and brother Dean's in 1899.

Having no recourse to family support after his mother died and with his work as yet unrecognized, the poet was forced to hold a number of non-literary jobs for short periods of time. These varied from administrative assistant to Harvard's President Eliot, to time-checker for the construction of the first New York subway. His reluctance to continue to do anything that took him from his writing and his scorn for the prevailing materialism of society was evidenced in a letter of this period to Harry deForest Smith. "This diabolical, dirty race that men are running after (dollars) disgusts me. . . . Business be damned," said Robinson.[55]

In 1905, Theodore Roosevelt was so impressed by a reading of his poetry collection *Children of the Night* that he wrote a critical review of it in *The Outlook* and had Robinson appointed to a position in the New York Collector of Customs' office that he held until 1909. In that year, brother Herman died and Robinson returned to Gardiner in the hope of reestablishing a relationship with Herman's widow, Emma Shepherd Robinson, whom he had loved since high school. This failing, he devoted the rest of his life to producing a prodigious number of volumes of poetry which at last began to bring him fame and a modest living.

By 1913, Robinson was publishing in *Harper's* and the *Atlantic Monthly*; in 1921 he received the first of three Pulitzer Prizes to be given him in six years' time; and in 1922 he was awarded honorary doctorates by Yale University and Bowdoin College. The last twenty-four summers of his life were spent at the MacDowell Colony in Peterborough, New Hampshire (see chapter 4) and there are many accounts of meetings with him there during those years. Mary Colum relates an exchange in the dining room of the Colony when the poet, with his "dry Yankee humor," told Harriet Monroe of *Poetry* magazine that he was unable to work, and was having to take a course in poetry from Colum to awaken his mind.[56] John Duke also remembered meeting Robinson during a visit to the Colony and shaking hands with him. "He was," said the composer, "MacDowell's 'prize catch'—a strange, withdrawn creature, but in my opinion, one of our greatest poets."[57]

Robinson's historical position as a straddler of two centuries and their prevailing systems of thought, accounts for the major sources of tension which fed his poetic gift. Torn all his life between Emersonian Idealism and the newer scientific philosophy of Naturalism, he shared also in the dilemma of those poets who rejected the free verse *structures* of the modern poetry movement but incorporated a new freedom of *content* in their work. "The Imagists," he told Amy

Lowell, "seem to me rather too self-conscious and exclusive to stand the test of time" but added "I don't care a pinfeather what form a poem is written in so long as it makes me sit up."[58]

What did not make Robinson sit up were the celebrations of nature that had been the preoccupation of his Romantic forbears. He turned instead in his own poetry to an emphasis on people with the avowed purpose of showing "that men and women are individuals."[59] His particular combination of compassion and irony became a legacy for many of the twentieth-century poets who followed, as did his willingness to introduce comic elements into serious poetry.[60] One characteristic that Robinson shared with many of his fellow poets, past and future, was a responsiveness to music that had begun in Gardiner with a limited study of both violin and clarinet. In time he came to feel that music and poetry were closely allied as forms of artistic expression, "music being poetry and poetry being music," as he wrote to a friend.[61]

Robinson's prolific output includes more narrative than lyrical poetry, and all of it demonstrates an impressive variety of verse forms. His reputation today is based largely on his early work, the short character sketches of people who live in a place called Tilbury Town. This city is generally accepted to be a poetic representation of Gardiner, Maine, and the eccentric misfits and failures of Robinson's portraits to derive, at least in part, from the poet's view of himself and his brothers. In 1945, John Duke set three of these short narratives:[62] "Richard Cory" and "Luke Havergal" from *Children of the Night* (1897) and "Miniver Cheevy" from *The Town Down the River* (1910). Written ten years after "Rapunzel" and "Wild Swans" (with only half a dozen songs between), these three, in accordance with the totally different needs of the Robinson texts, exhibit a broad, dynamic, vigorous style with an expansive "pianism" that Duke is employing for the first time.

The sixteen lines of the poem "Richard Cory" present a well-drawn sketch of a rich and elegant man who "glittered when he walked" as perceived by his envious fellows. In a surprise ending involving only the final couplet, Richard Cory goes home "one calm summer night" to "put a bullet through his head." It has been suggested that Cory is a thinly disguised Herman Robinson, whose personal qualities showed such promise, but who destroyed himself slowly with alcohol after his disastrous investments of 1893. Herman did not actually die until 1909, twelve years after the publication of *Children of the Night*, but the contrast between his charming exterior and inward despair may well have been apparent to his brother during the period when those poems were being written (1890–1897).

Duke's rhythmic scheme in the setting of "Richard Cory" is one of its most interesting aspects, as he translates the unwavering iambic pentameter of the text into not one but two different metric patterns. While the lilting, sophisticated 6/8 accompaniment figures present Cory's musical portrait, the voice of the narrator sings in the blunt, square 2/4 of the less privileged townspeople.

Example 5.7, mm. 17–20

The steady, pianistic motion of six eighth notes to the bar comes to seem like the very thread of the protagonist's life and indeed it stops only in the measure in which the bullet ends it.[63]

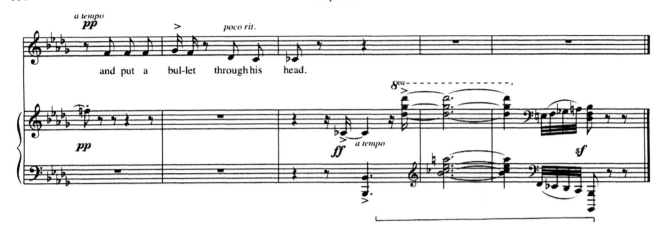

Example 5.8, mm. 89–93

In the songs of the forties, John Duke returns to notated key signatures, and "Richard Cory" has three tonal areas: a lightly scored B-flat major opening which sets the stage (see Ex. 5.7), a modulating bridge passage between verses three and four which moves through A major, and a third section in D-flat major. This final key has a more heavily scored piano part, whose pitch and dynamic levels rise with the growing envy of the townfolk (see Ex. 5.9).

Example 5.9, mm. 69–73

Musical word-painting is also an effective device in this setting, as a tremulous accompaniment figure suggests "fluttering pulses"

Example 5.10, mm. 46–48

and multiple grace notes at brilliant pitch levels approach an aural equivalent of "glitter."

Example 5.11, mm. 49–52

Robinson's obsessive feelings for the beautiful Emma Shepherd, who became his sister-in-law, gave rise to many poems about love unfulfilled or lost forever. "Luke Havergal," characterized by the poet as his "uncomfortable abstraction,"[64] is one of the most haunting of these, despite a certain ambiguity which led Theodore Roosevelt to write that he liked the poem, but was not sure he understood it. In these verses, Luke Havergal, apparently mourning a dead love, is never described but is rather addressed, in a monologue by a ghostly messenger "out of a grave" who points to "the western gate" as "the one way to where she is." This theme of lovers being reunited in death provided the occasion for Duke's composition of one of his finest Romantic ballads which offers a gratifying vehicle to singer and pianist at the same time that it captures the brooding passion of the text.

Robinson's "Luke Havergal" has four verses, but this is one of the rare instances mentioned above in which John Duke omits part of the poem in his setting. In a tight, workable ABA structure, he sets the first and last stanzas which deal with the "western gate"[65] in the key of E-flat major (see Ex. 5.12a), and creates an eerie G-sharp minor contrasting section for the third verse in which the messenger describes his other-worldly origins (see Ex. 5.12b).

Example 5.12a, mm. 9–12

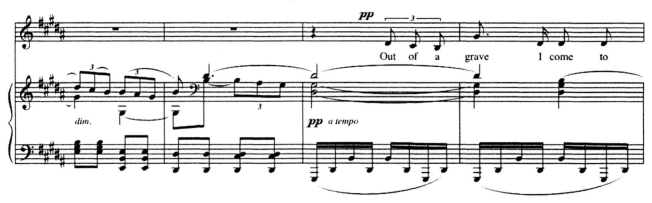

Example 5.12b, mm. 47–50

This three-part form necessitates the omission of stanza two, and one line of the fourth stanza is also omitted to impel the musical/dramatic climax. In all other ways Duke remains faithful to the text, including the verbal repetitions that close each verse.

Example 5.13, mm. 37–41

John Duke's writing for the piano in "Luke Havergal" begins to exhibit the neo-Romantic idiom in the figurations which is typical of this period. Passages in parallel thirds and octaves, and widely spread broken chord patterns build an enveloping world of sound around Havergal's mystical ecstasy. The melodic contour of the entire song is one of Duke's most lyrical inventions, and takes on quasi-operatic dimensions in the climactic line that rises an octave and a fourth in a shattering crescendo.

Example 5.14, mm. 104–106

One of the strongest portraits among the citizens of Tilbury Town is "Miniver Cheevy" who has been aptly termed the "archetypal frustrated romantic idealist."[66] It is easy to credit a not uncommon opinion among literary critics that Miniver, a "child of scorn" who "had reasons" to regret "that he was ever born" is Robinson himself: an unwanted son to whom life had brought considerably more pain than happiness. The poet too, like Miniver, had been drawn to the glories of past ages, had mourned the low status of "Romance" and "Art" in the present, and had "scorned the gold he sought" in a lifelong conflict between the struggle to live decently and a revulsion toward the materialism of society. In the last two stanzas of eight, Miniver is revealed as a dreamer lost in thought and the consolations of alcohol, but the prevailing tone of the poem is ironic rather than tragic, and the writer's compassion for his antihero is evident.

John Duke's setting of "Miniver Cheevy" is an admirably crafted set of variations based on a theme which both outlines the contours of the vocal line, and establishes the harmonic background in passacaglia style (see Ex. 5.15). The nine variations that follow account for the eight verses of the poem plus an epilogue, and in them the composer employs all the traditional musical devices of variation in the service of the text.

Example 5.15, mm. 1–8

"The days of old . . . when steeds were prancing" is set with an accompaniment figure whose meter and rhythmic pattern is clearly suggestive of horses' hooves (see Ex. 5.16).

Example 5.16, mm. 17–18

The third and fourth verses in which Miniver sighs for past glories and mourns over the prosaic present call for slow tempi and the "dolorous" key of G minor. In contrast, Variation V portrays his identification with the nobility of the Medici in terms of G major, a faster tempo and a majestic piano figure which covers the keyboard in broad, sweeping gestures.

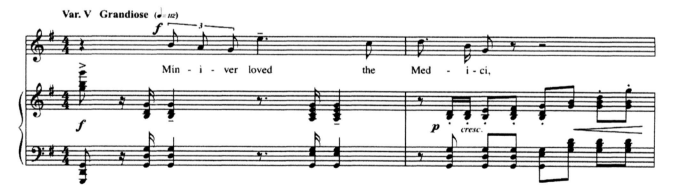

Example 5.17, mm. 41–42

Example 5.18, mm. 69–72

As evidenced from Examples 5.16 and 5.17, John Duke has preceded the tempo marking of each variation with an adjective that indicates the mood to be established by the performers. For Variation VIII he chooses "tipsy," and the piano writing now takes on a lurching quality, which culminates in the rapidly descending arpeggio of measure 72, suggestive of a drunken fall (see Ex. 5.18). The musical humor is deftly amplified in the epilogue, with minimal textual additions by the composer that are rare for Duke. Miniver, now obviously intoxicated, tries to imitate the piano's melodic fragments in canonic style. He begins boldly on "ah," but his imitations become softer and more grunt-like, then fail to find the correct pitch, and eventually trail off into merciful oblivion (see Ex. 5.19).

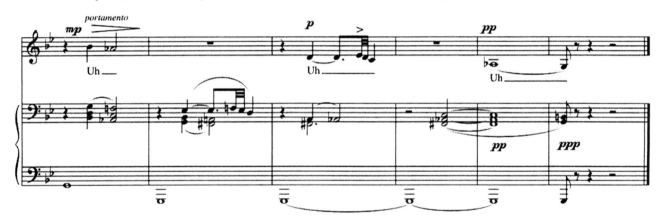

Example 5.19, mm. 78–83

Elinor Wylie (1885–1928)

The life of Elinor Wylie has been discussed at some length in Chapter 4 along with Mary Howe's settings of her poetry. John Duke had met this writer "in the late twenties, just before she died, at an evening of poetry and music in the home of Grace Hazard Conkling, professor of English at Smith and a poet herself. Elinor read one of her longer poems" continued Duke. "She was rather gaunt and ill-looking at the time, having lost most of her extraordinary beauty. It was not until some years after that I began to set her poems."[67] John Duke's first Wylie setting, written in 1946, was "Bells in the Rain."[68] It met with almost instant success, being performed just two years later by Povla Frisch in a New York recital.[69] The poem bearing the same title appeared in *Nets to Catch the Wind*, the volume which in 1921 established the previously unknown writer as a major talent on the American literary scene. In this collection, Wylie issued Athena-like from Zeus' forehead, as it were, with fully developed control over her "craftsman's concern for phrasing, and for the sensuous qualities of words."[70]

"Bells in the Rain" again demonstrates the Wylie predilection for compression, and consists of three four-line stanzas of iambic tetrameter punctuated by an occasional dactyl. In it, the "limpid drops of rain" falling on the town bring peaceful sleep which is "unheeded [by] the dead" but welcomed "most tenderly" by the living. Sensuous, indeed, in verbal components and visual images is the opening of verse two: "the bright drops ring like bells of glass,"—and it is this phrase which provides John Duke with the most important musical element of his setting. Beginning in the introduction and continuing throughout the song there is a pianistic figure of quietly insistent sixteenth notes placed high on the keyboard. The brilliant overtones of the pitches create a cross-sensory suggestion of glass, while the many intervals of fourths and fifths take on the melodic configurations of bells.

Example 5.20, mm. 1–4

Against this steady accompaniment of the bell-like rain drops, the vocal line is principally structured to suggest the peaceful descent of sleep. Sharing in this musical effect are the falling pitch levels and sustained length of "sleep falls" and the pianissimo dynamic level that dominates most of the song.

Example 5.21, mm. 9–10

Harmonic contexts involving both voice and piano combine in two of the most telling moments of the setting. For "The bright drops ring like bells of glass," Duke moves from his E minor tonality through the subdominant to an altered chord on the sub-mediant. The resulting brightness of the C-sharp major touch lends the required brilliance in a device that is very reminiscent of Griffes's procedures in "Evening Song."[71]

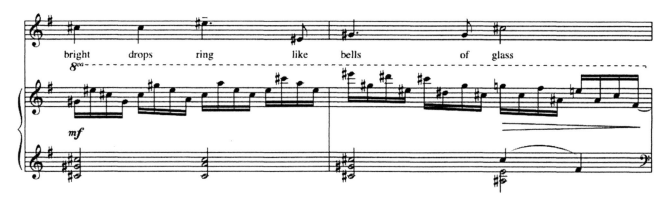

Example 5.22, mm. 15–16

In the final line of the song, the pivotal word "tenderly" is highlighted not only by its subito *pianissimo* following a surprising octave leap, but also by the change in its chordal meaning from root position in a G major triad, to a softer and more ambiguous situation as the seventh of the supertonic (see Ex. 5.23).

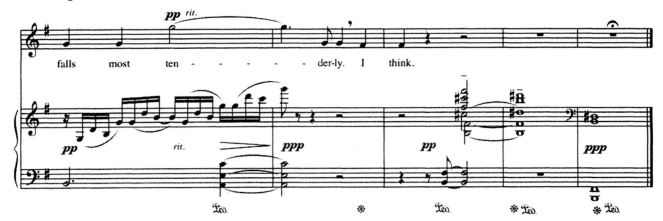

Example 5.23, mm. 33–37

"Little Elegy" had already been set by Mary Howe in 1934 (see chapter 4), and it is extremely interesting to compare hers with Duke's equally successful but quite different treatment composed twelve years later.[72] Both are in minor keys, considered appropriate by both composers for this tribute to a lost love.[73] Both are lyrical settings, with carefully molded and effective vocal contours. Howe's setting, however, puts much more emphasis on the piano with a more elaborate accompaniment throughout whereas Duke's piano writing is quiet and chordal, with some motivic imitation of the voice. Each gives particular harmonic attention to the line "If never seen Your sweetest face" and Duke travels all the way from his one flat tonic (D minor) to the six sharps of F-sharp major.

Example 5.24, mm. 11–16

For the climactic lines "No bird have grace / Or pow'r to sing / Or anything / Be kind or fair," Howe chooses to let the piano complete the emotional expression with two more measures of pianistic crescendo. John Duke, however, has it happen primarily in the vocal line, with several leaps to high sustained pitches while accompanied by unobtrusive rising chordal sequences.

Example 5.25, mm. 17–26

Finally, it should be noted that Mary Howe's setting repeats the final phrase "And you / Nowhere," while John Duke's, in characteristic faithfulness to the original text, does not.

"The Bird" was printed in Wylie's posthumous *Collected Poems* of 1932 as one of those grouped in the "Hitherto Uncollected" section. Of these poems, some had previously appeared in periodicals and others had never been published. In the first of these two contrasting short stanzas the bird is exhorted to "sing again" by the poet who is listening to the rain fall "through the long night." In the second, the bird has returned, and his "clearest voice" makes the "rain sing / And the dark rejoice." John Duke had his setting of this poem printed together with "Little Elegy," "The Bird," dedicated to the Brazilian soprano Bidú Sayão, is one of his most frequently performed songs.[74]

The chordal nature of the accompaniment seems to relate to "Little Elegy" but this is a much more passionate statement, as Duke uses the poetic repetition to build crescendos of pitch and dynamics.

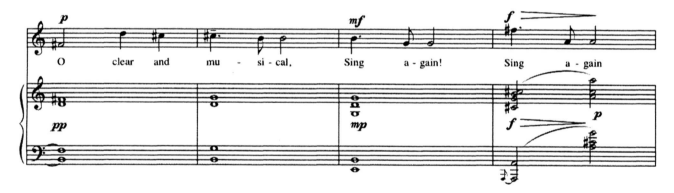

Example 5.26, mm. 5–8

A new element entering the accompaniment is the pianistic imitation of bird-song that the composer effectively employs in the formal structure as prelude, interlude between the two verses, and postlude.

Example 5.27, mm. 1–4

Key change is the device that most clearly embodies the contrast between the stanzas. The opening in B minor suggests the poet's longing for the absent singer (see Ex. 5.26 and Ex. 5.27). A turn to F major after the interlude brings with it a surge of hope

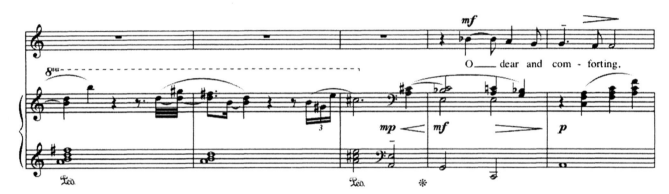

Example 5.28, mm. 18–22

and leads to the triumphant establishment of D major that holds through the quietly joyful conclusion.

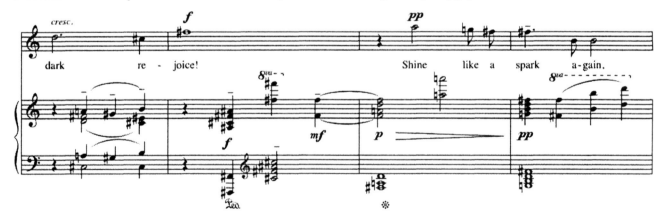

Example 5.29, mm. 27–30

Also among the "Hitherto Uncollected" poems of 1932, but far different in mood and statement, is "Viennese Waltz." This poem is characteristic of the many in which Wylie expressed a sense of impending disaster: not surprising in an artist whose life had encompassed divorce, social ostracism, miscarriage, the suicide of relatives, and a constant struggle against the pain of chronic illness. In "Viennese Waltz," the speaker addresses a partner whose "face is like a mournful pearl" in the hopes that the dancing will assuage their sadness and enable a momentary escape from "the tiger-snarling" in the night.

John Duke's setting of "Viennese Waltz "[75] which he composed in 1948 is conceived on a grand scale with a dramatic vocal line and demanding piano part. The original metric scheme of the four-verse poem has five accents per line, but this has been completely swallowed by Duke's 3/4 time. This transformation he achieves quite convincingly through a lengthening of certain vocal syllables and the imposition of a pianistic waltz background.

Example 5.30, mm. 7–12

Throughout the song, the voice moves in fairly broad patterns of quarter and half notes suggesting the helplessness of the doomed couple (see Ex. 5.30) while the accompaniment soon begins to break up into eighth notes and triplets as the gyrations of the dancing become more frenetic.

Example 5.30 also illustrates the composer's skillful use of delayed resolution of dissonance, as the tied-over A-flat on the word "tired" establishes the mood of disillusioned but yearning desire for peace and happiness that pervades the song. The chromaticism of the piano's introductory sequences is continued in all the instrumental interludes that are appropriately more reminiscent of the brooding brilliance of Chopin than of Johann Strauss's mindless Vienna.

Example 5.31, mm. 39–45

In the last two lines of the poem, the dancers seem to be choosing to confront their doom in a dream-like state that will mitigate its harshness:

Come, let us dream the little death that hovers
Pensive as heaven in a cloudy veil.

John Duke's musical clothing of this verbal withdrawal of energy takes the form of soft, sustained, high-pitched vocal sounds over equally quiet, "cloudy" altered chords that eventually retard to motionlessness. The dancers' world has ended: "not with a bang but a whimper."

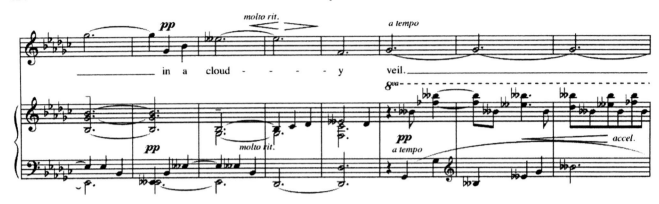

Example 5.32, mm. 166–73

Sara Teasdale (1884–1933)

Sara Teasdale and Elinor Wylie were born just one year apart and their formative years were similar in one important respect. Each had a dominant, controlling mother, who by example and conviction upheld the ideal of a narrowly conventional life for women. Sara Teasdale's birthplace was St. Louis, which in the 1880s was a large, commercial city of vigorous culture but an atmosphere of increasing conservatism.[76] She was the child of aging parents (born sixteen years after her nearest sibling), and soon demonstrated a proclivity toward ill health that resulted in part from their overanxious attention. Her father, a gentle, prosperous businessman, was descended from a dissenting Baptist who had left England in 1792 for New Jersey. Her mother traced her American ancestors back to Captain Simon Willard, who helped to found Concord, Massachusetts, in 1635. Sara felt a strong connection to this Puritan heritage, although her maternal grandmother had turned away from it, and like the Teasdales, had become a Baptist.

John Warren Teasdale provided his family with an elegant upper-middle-class home where Mrs. Teasdale paid homage to the traditional Victorian modes of behavior with all the strident force of her vigorous personality. Her daughter, as a result, was to be torn for many years between a desire for the life of artistic achievement promised by her developing talent, and a fear that its pursuit would deprive her of the loving fulfillments of womanhood. Many aspects of this struggle, particularly her search for the love that would justify the giving up of the separate self, became the themes of her poetry. (*Love Songs*, published in 1917, is one of her best-known volumes.) Another of its emotional by-products, resentment toward the mother's imposition of her own restricted pattern, no doubt helped contribute to the habitual eruption of mild but disabling illnesses which developed as a dutiful daughter's only acceptable form of protest.

There had been much idealistic ferment over education in the city of St. Louis during the second half of the nineteenth century, and some excellent schools had been the result. Teasdale attended two of these: the Mary School, which had been founded by T. S. Eliot's father, and Hosmer Hall, where she graduated in 1903 after a solid grounding in a college preparatory curriculum administered by a largely Eastern-trained faculty. For the next ten years, the young woman traveled in this country and abroad, made contacts with other writers and editors who encouraged her, and began to publish her work. Her first pieces appeared in *The Mirror*, and in 1907 her parents underwrote the publication of her first volume of poetry: *Sonnets to Duse and Other Poems*. In 1910, a second volume called *Helen of Troy* was accepted by Putnam's, and the poet's growing reputation produced an invitation to join the Poetry Society of America.

During her twenties, Teasdale carried on correspondences with John Myers O'Hara and John Hall Wheelock, two young poets who lived in New York City. Teasdale's shyness made written communication appealing, but subsequent meetings with each proved her hopes for a romantic attachment ill-founded. O'Hara was unsuitable, and Wheelock did not reciprocate her strong attraction although they remained lifelong friends. Returning from Europe in the summer of 1912, a relationship was formed on shipboard with an Englishman, Stafford Hatfield, which also did not mature into the desired commitment, and sent Teasdale home to St. Louis in a temporary state of physical and emotional collapse. When the poet was almost thirty, two ardent suitors finally appeared. One was Vachel Lindsay, who had met her through Harriet Monroe, the moving spirit of the Chicago literary group (mentioned above as the editor of *Poetry* magazine). The other was Ernst Filsinger, a St. Louis businessman like her father, who seemed to offer the peace and security that the impoverished, labile Lindsay could not. Teasdale married Filsinger in 1914, and the marriage survived fifteen years of Sara's illnesses and Ernst's increasingly lengthy business trips. In 1929, she traveled to Reno and divorced him while he was out of the country.

Marriage, then, had proved more draining than supportive to the material and emotional life of the poet. Motherhood, too, a cherished goal of her youth, in time became threatening to Teasdale's artistic career in view of her limited strength. In 1917, after much soul-searching, she had an abortion. Not surprisingly, perhaps, the closest relationship of the last few years of her life was with a young woman named Margaret Conklin who became her literary executor, and whom Teasdale referred to as "the daughter I never had."[77] But even this tie of affection proved insufficient to maintain her in an existence increasingly beset by financial worries and the imagined threat of incapacitating illness. In 1933, just over a year after Vachel Lindsay's suicide, Sara Teasdale took an overdose of sleeping pills and ended the long struggle to create an equilibrium between the opposing tensions of her life.

Some of the contradictions of Teasdale's thinking and emotional processes emerge in the history of her relations with and comments on the other major poets of her time. Edna St. Vincent Millay was invited to tea and dinner after their meeting in 1913, but a friendship failed to develop despite an exciting ride that the two women shared atop a New York City double-decker bus. Elinor Wylie's rapid rise to literary and social prominence received the following characterization: "(She) continues to climb the slopes of Parnassus before a dazzled multitude. Her work becomes more cryptic, crabbed and queer every week. . . . She is undoubtedly an attractive and clever person—but a great spirit? I wonder."[78] Robert Frost, too, is taken to task in another of Teasdale's letters for his "ill-temper under criticism,"[79] yet she wrote warm praise to the controversial and abrasive Amy Lowell for her *Pictures of a Floating World*, and went out of her way to arrange "audiences" at the two Lowell strongholds of Sevenels in Brookline, and New York's St. Regis hotel. Interestingly, although Amy Lowell (together with Vachel Lindsay and Edward Markham) accepted an honorary Doctor of Letters degree from Baylor University in 1920, Sara Teasdale declined, calling the process of academic investiture "flapdoodle."[80] She responded willingly, however, to another aspect of university life when she agreed to judge the Witter Bynner Undergraduate Poetry Contest of 1925. In a selection that is now part of literary history, Sara Teasdale awarded first place to a New York University student by the name of Countee Cullen.[81]

C. Day Lewis, in his Norton lectures of 1965–1966 on *The Lyric Impulse,* has pointed out that "one effect of the liberation of poetry from music is, paradoxically, a nostalgic yearning for the partner it has lost."[82] Sara Teasdale was strongly drawn to German lieder during her days at Hosmer Hall, and, in fact, referred to her poetry as "my songs" throughout her life. In another curious correspondence to Lewis who claimed that "melody—a singing line—has always been essential to the lyrical poem,"[83] Teasdale defended traditional lyric poetry against the rising tide of Imagism and free verse by insisting that poetry traditionally needed "melody" as a means of making itself easy to remember and of communicating emotions.[84] To Louis Untermeyer's complaint that her poems did not show her intellect, she replied "my heart makes my songs, not I" and added "my mind is proud and strong enough to be silent."[85] It was a curious characterization of poetry as a catharsis of the emotions that enabled the self's higher consciousness to remain aloof and contained.

It is true that Teasdale's choice of poetic language is simple and direct and that her verses eschew the convoluted thought processes of Wylie and occasionally obscure allusions of Marianne Moore. In spite of her own beliefs, however, one senses Sara Teasdale's intellect strongly at work in the assimilation of knowledge gained through reading and experience, and its transmutation into a poetic form of considerable refinement. A case in point is her poem "There Will Be Stars," published as the title piece of the opening section in *Dark of the Moon*, which appeared in 1926 and contains some of her most mature work. Astronomy had been one of Teasdale's favorite academic disciplines since her girlhood, and she returned to it eagerly during a stay in Santa Barbara in 1919. It is painfully clear from her letters of this period that the stars both attracted and repelled her. "It is all . . . seemingly so uselessly big" she wrote, and at the same time, "if I ever started a religion it would be star-worship."[86] As symbols of permanence in a changing universe, yet a cold mockery of human mortality, star images haunt and pervade her writing. Even her collection for children of formerly published work, the last publication during her lifetime, is titled *Stars Tonight*. One of the inclusions is "There Will Be Stars," illustrated with Dorothy P. Lathrop's delicate ink drawing of two glowing, angelic creatures gazing toward earth from their contiguous position in the heavens.

This poem very succinctly presents a distillate of Teasdale's experience and conviction. In it, two stars come together at the yearly equinox and shine on a particular earthly place throughout eternity, although all trace of the lovers who once inhabited it have long gone. It is a powerful poem, and John Duke, who considers Sara Teasdale to be "the most 'settable' of American poets"[87] chose to make a song of it in 1951.[88] Although the entire poem is only eight lines long, it contains three repetitions of the phrase "There will be stars." Duke emphasizes this phrase by beginning it each time on a weak beat and then moving, by means of a large vocal leap, to a strong beat and lengthened note value on the word "stars" (see Ex. 5.33a and Ex. 5.33b).

Example 5.33a, mm. 1–3

By choosing this metrical scheme, Duke has completely changed the original rhythmic structure of the poem, which incorporates a masterful variety of poetic feet, into a basic three stress line. But the elongated, high-pitched open vowel sound on the word "stars" with the leap that precedes it, creates a sense of distance coupled with desperate longing that is exactly analogous to the poetic thought. This is the very process of "assimilation" described by Langer in which "a song conceived poetically sounds not as the poem sounds, but as the poem *feels*."[89]

"Poised on the peak of midnight" leaps to a high G, pauses momentarily, and then descends in running stepwise motion. Throughout the song, but most insistently at the climactic moment, Duke employs a broken arpeggio figure traveling up the keyboard which he has used elsewhere as a symbol of light but nowhere to greater effect (see Ex. 5.33b).

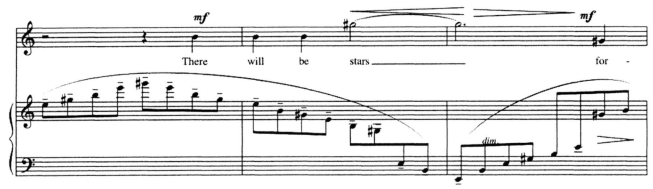

Example 5.33b, mm. 28–30

The texture of Duke's accompaniment remains thin throughout, never expanding to more than one or two voices except for a few chordal structures to open and close the sections of the modified ABA form. The voice, thereby, retains prominence, but its occasional silences are woven through with melodic snatches from the piano's upper voice in a tight, contrapuntal framework.

Example 5.34, mm. 7–9

Use of word-painting is appropriate and skillful. The phrase "earth circles her orbit" turns in on itself in both the vocal line and accompaniment.

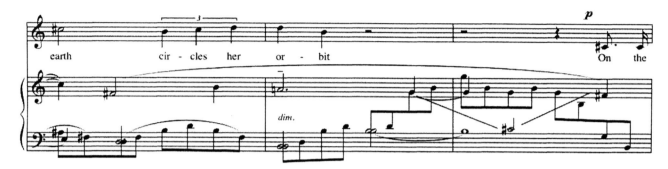

Example 5.35, mm. 10–12

Most of the writing in this setting is diatonic but there are moments of chromatic surprise. Two of these are the side-step to an altered C-sharp chord on "reach their zenith" and the raised fourth of the broken chord behind "while we sleep": a constricted harmony of Death. Duke, however, does not leave it there. As the voice sustains "sleep," the piano resolves to an E major triad that in this context is at once both peaceful and suspended, like Eternity itself (see Ex. 5.36).

Example 5.36, mm. 31–36

Robert Frost (1874–1963)

The life of Robert Frost is a study in paradox. Ignored for the first half of his more than four score years, he became, during the second half of his life, a world-renowned patriarch of the American literary scene. Recognized everywhere as the most characteristic of New England poets, he actually lived the first eleven years of his life in San Francisco. Even his pervading image as a blunt, plain-spoken man of the earth must be set off against the facts that he was an indifferent and not very successful farmer, who had spent three years studying the classics at Dartmouth and Harvard, and who had a long career himself as a university professor.

William Prescott Frost Jr., the poet's father, had taken the opposite road in adopted regionalism. Born in New Hampshire, he had married Isabel Moodie, a teacher and sometime poet, and moved to San Francisco where he became editor of *The Bulletin*. Despite his origins, he was a strong Southern sympathizer in the Civil War, and named his son Robert Lee Frost. William Frost was a man of unstable personality, given to excessive drinking and attendant violence. Robert Frost's sister inherited his mental instability and the poet himself engaged in a lifelong struggle to control his own explosive temper.

When his father died in 1885, Robert Frost's life as a New Englander began. The Frost family moved to Lawrence, Massachusetts, to make their home with Robert's paternal grandfather who tried to help the young man find himself after his graduation from high school as co-valedictorian (Elinor White, who shared the honors, later became his wife). For the next eight years, his grandfather supported him during his attendance at Dartmouth and later Harvard, helped him find jobs in between, and finally in 1900 bought him a farm in New Hampshire with the understanding that he was to live there at least ten years. By this time Robert Frost was married, and beginning to write poetry for which he could find no publisher. While struggling with this discouragement and the hardships of trying to make a living from the farm, the poet also suffered the loss of a son at the age of four, and a daughter who died at birth. Indeed, of the six children born to the Frosts between 1896 and 1907, only two survived their father, as daughter Marjorie died of tuberculosis in 1934 and son Carol committed suicide in 1940.

The gloomy, difficult years came to an end when Frost sold the farm in 1912, took his family to England and at last found the recognition for his work that his own country had refused him. In London, he met all the leading poets of the times and in 1913 was able to arrange the publication of *A Boy's Will*, his first volume of verse. Harriet Monroe and the rest of America now discovered him, and his poems were soon offered publication on his own side of the Atlantic. In 1915, the year of his return, Henry Holt published *North of Boston* and a new edition of *A Boy's Will*, closely followed by *Mountain Interval* in 1916. Now in demand as a teacher, Frost began the career which included three different periods of residence at Amherst College, and lectureships of varying lengths at Dartmouth College, the University of Michigan, Yale, Harvard, and Wesleyan universities. In 1920, he became a co-founder of the Bread Loaf School of English at Middlebury College, Vermont, and spent his summers there for many years. Among the numerous honors which came to him through the passage of time were four Pulitzer prizes, the gold medal of the Poetry Society of America, and honorary doctorates from both Oxford and Cambridge universities, which he received during a trip to England in 1957. The last years of his life introduced a final paradox when Frost, who had been a staunch conservative all his life, became the "poet laureate" of the liberal Kennedy administration and gave a moving reading of his poem, "The Gift Outright" during the inaugural ceremonies of 1961.

Like many great creative figures in the arts, Robert Frost has frustrated critics and eluded categorization. His connections to Thoreau and Emerson, he himself readily acknowledged, but the frequently mentioned kinship to E. A. Robinson is more problematic. Though the two are linked in their portrayal of New England and the peculiarities of the region, Frost strikes out on his own path to introduce new dimensions of non-literary language and, although he would certainly have protested this,[90] becomes akin to Carl Sandburg in his attempt to capture the true sound of his own corner of America. The consummate craftsmanship with which he embedded this new language into a variety of carefully controlled poetic structures is nowhere in dispute. The "meaning" of the poetry, always of prime importance to Frost, is also now approaching consensus, as he begins to be seen as an existentialist grounded in an inscrutable God, who must summon his courage, humor, and loving ties to men and nature in order to survive the dark trials of life in this world.

John Duke recalled meeting Robert Frost in Amherst, "on which occasion a mezzo from Smith sang my settings of 'To the Thawing Wind' and 'Acquainted with the Night.' He was very polite," said Duke, "but I could see that he had little understanding of what the art song really is. In fact, I do not blame poets," he continued, "if they object to the composers taking their verses and using them for their own purposes, sometimes with little regard for the original form of the poem."[91] One is, in fact, reminded of Goethe, and his legendary resentment of the Schubert settings, but it is also possible that Frost may have considered the addition of music to his poetry to be superfluous rather than invasive. As early as 1915 he had expressed a conviction that the tones of actual speech are themselves musical[92] and that speech could be converted into a poetic idiom by developing "the sound of sense."[93] It is interesting that the latter concept is extremely close to ideas expressed in 1942 by T. S. Eliot,[94] for many years Frost's arch rival, as leader of the "modernist" camp, and as winner of the Nobel prize, which Frost coveted but never received.

"To the Thawing Wind" appeared in *A Boy's Will*, Frost's first published collection. It is written in couplets, one of the poet's favorite structures, with a rhyming line added to the last couplet, making a total of fifteen lines. There are traces of literary language, such as the contractions "o'er" and "e'er," but the blunt, compact energy of Frost is already evident in this swinging trochaic invocation to a storm. Robert Frost's concept of poetry as metaphor (to which he often referred) serves him here as the speaker is revealed to be a poet working in his "narrow stall" who should be turned "out of door": a Thoreau-esque suggestion of the need for man to become involved in nature with his senses rather than with just his intellect.

John Duke's setting of "To the Thawing Wind," written in 1951,[95] seems to bear out Philip Gerber's observation that Frost equates water with fertility and vigor in his poetry.[96] From the opening measures, the song plunges into an extremely vigorous torrent of life-giving wind and rain, embodied in an accompaniment which employs the full span of the keyboard and many of its resources of dynamics and figuration. As the storm gathers outside, the repeated broken chord structures come in rising and falling waves of sound punctuated by scale and arpeggio figures in the vocal rests.

Example 5.37, mm. 5–6

With the poet's exhortation to the storm to enter his room, the pattern changes, as the words "Burst" and "Swing" are set with asymmetric accents on the weak second beat, and further dramatized by the swooping arpeggios of the accompaniment.

Example 5.38, mm. 25–26

The climax of the song, "Turn the poet out of door," begins with a sustained fortissimo high G, and this exciting moment is skillfully prepared by the composer. The setting of the preceding lines ("Run the rattling pages o'er / Scatter poems on the floor") introduces a counter-melody in the piano's upper voice, which flowers during an instrumental interlude into an imitation of the opening vocal line. It is as though the storm had become the singer, and nature and poet were one.

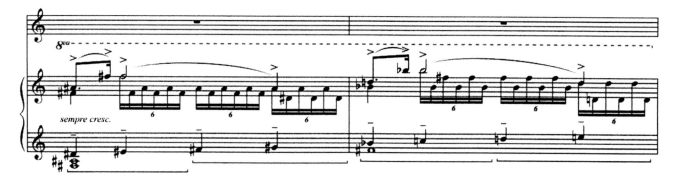

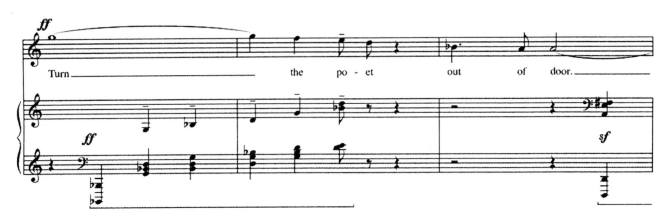

Example 5.39, mm. 35–39

In 1950, one year earlier, John Duke had set "Acquainted with the Night,"[97] Frost's enormously successful essay of the difficult "terza rima" form. This poem, appearing in the 1928 publication called *West-Running Brook*, also seems to exist on two levels of meaning. One is the common human experience of lonely, sleepless wandering through a deserted city, while the other is well described in Babette Deutsch's suggestion of a night "which is real enough but also figurative" and a city which "seems to represent some more significant, if less actual locale."[98]

Like many of the Duke songs of this period, this one also presents a characteristic accompaniment figure. In "Acquainted with the Night" it is a group of 3, 4, or 5 grace notes preceding a longer note value: a musical suggestion of walking, in which the grace notes represent the rise of the foot, and the more sustained following note, its fall to the ground.

Example 5.40, mm. 25–28

The key of the song is the appropriately dark G minor, which is clear enough although not delineated by a key signature. Considerable chromaticism in the time-honored "anguish" context of the Baroque period, creates an underlying current of anxiety, which is intensified by the altered chords and suspensions of the final phrase and piano postlude.

Example 5.41, mm. 48–55

In seemingly similar fashion to the song previously discussed, John Duke begins to weave a pianistic counterpoint to the vocal line near the end of the song.

Example 5.42, mm. 39–41

This, however, does not blossom into a transcendental moment as does its counterpart in "To the Thawing Wind." Rather, it falls back to a reminiscence of the opening walking figure, as the poet and composer quietly and wearily restate, "I have been one acquainted with the night" (see Ex. 5.41).

"The Last Word of a Bluebird,"[99] written in 1955, is Duke's last published Robert Frost setting. The poem comes from *Mountain Interval*, which appeared shortly after the poet's return to America. In it, Frost demonstrates one of his most appealing tones, falling "somewhere between the quizzical and the tender,"[100] as he treats a subject which, though originally "a commonplace of the countryside now becomes illuminated by . . . particularity."[101] The bluebird's last word before flying south is reported in simple, direct speech by a crow, who has been entrusted with a "goodbye" message for "Lesley": Robert Frost's daughter born in 1899, who was probably in her early teens at the time of writing. In a rare glimpse of the poet as affectionate father, the lines caution the child "to be good" and keep busy while awaiting the bird's return with the spring.

The vocal line of Duke's setting, which is dedicated to Louis Nicholas,[102] is distinguished by repetition, a mostly narrow contour, and short separated phrases in declamatory style, suggestive of crow-like squawkings. Behind this, staccato chords and rapid sixteenth notes in a moving tempo create a light, teasing atmosphere (see Ex. 5.43). As the song progresses, the bird's lurching, awkward speech becomes more and more fixed in the triplet figures which correspond to the poem's original anapestic feet (see Ex. 5.44) while the piano brings in an occasional reminiscence of the lovely trilling of the bluebird (see Ex. 5.45).

Example 5.43, mm. 4–9

Example 5.44, mm. 10–12

Example 5.45, mm. 22–24

Eventually, the staccato accompaniment chords give way to more urgent figures that imitate the vocal triplets. With rising excitement, almost like an incantation, the child's winter tasks are set forth.

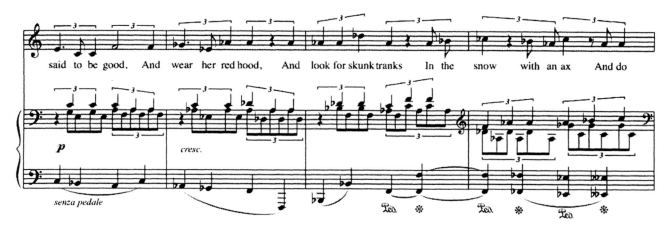

said to be good,   And   wear her red hood,   And   look for skunk tranks   In the   snow   with an ax   And do

Example 5.46, mm. 31–34

And finally the composer achieves what the poet, with only words at his disposal, is unable to do. He opens his melodic line to a lyrical curve and lets the crow, for a brief, glorious moment, also become a singing bird.

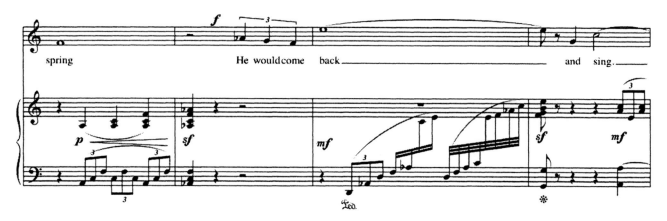

spring   He would come   back_____   and   sing._____

Example 5.47, mm. 35–38

e.e. cummings* (1894–1962)
*The lower case spelling used in this volume was the one preferred by the poet.

It would have been surprising if e.e. cummings had not become a poet. His Cambridge childhood was spent in a big comfortable house surrounded by rose gardens and populated by loving relatives who were his playfellows and artistic companions. His father, an amateur painter, had taught sociology at Harvard before becoming a prominent Unitarian minister in Boston. (Since the elder Cummings's first name was also Edward, e.e. was known to the family by his middle name, Estlin.) His mother's love for poetry and music was absorbed by her son so quickly that at the age of three he had written his first poem, which already demonstrated in embryo cummings's new visual and aural directions.[103]

Rebecca Cummings had selected Cambridge as the place to raise Estlin and daughter Elizabeth because she felt its ambient consciousness lay between Boston's intellectual sophistication and Concord's spirituality. Nor was she mistaken, for cummings's writing career was to be equally founded in the thorough education he received at the Boston Latin School and Harvard University, and in his absorption of the Transcendental world view. It is, of course, not unlikely that cummings's rather diffident personality was another result of his excessively protected and indulged formative years, but having raised her son to be a poet, Rebecca Cummings never withdrew her support from that enterprise. She gave him

Joy Farm, the family summer retreat in New Hampshire, paid for the printing of *No Thanks* (1935) when publishers re-fused the collection, and sent him money every month during the leanest times of the Depression.

It was during his Harvard years of 1911 to 1916, which culminated in a Master of Arts degree, that e.e. cummings turned away from the literary and artistic traditions he had been absorbing since birth. With growing excitement, he now began to explore recent European movements in painting, music, and poetry, and delivered a commencement address on "The New Art" which discussed the work of Cézanne, Matisse, Stravinsky, Schoenberg, Amy Lowell, and Gertrude Stein, among others. His mentors in this vital aspect of his education had not been his professors. Rather, they were classmates such as S. Foster Damon, editor of the *Harvard Music Review*, who taught cummings to play the piano and compose (he already played ragtime by ear); Scofield Thayer, who introduced him to Joyce and Eliot; and Sibley Wat-son, his closest lifelong friend, who brought the poetry of Verlaine and Rimbaud to his attention.

After leaving Harvard, cummings began to consolidate the poetic style that was to be characteristic of his future work as he experimented with the integration of visual images and sound patterns. He had just moved into a pleasant Greenwich Village studio that also enabled him to develop his talents as a painter, when he was drawn into World War I. Waiting for assignment in Paris was the only pleasant part of the experience. In this city, he felt that he "participated in an actual marriage of material and unmaterial things,"[104] and he was to return there for artistic sustenance many times during his life.

In 1919, the historic first issue of *The Dial* appeared in New York with Sibley Watson as publisher, Scofield Thayer as editor-in-chief, and Stewart Mitchell, another Harvard classmate, as managing editor. cummings was among the members of the old *Harvard Monthly* group from whom the editors solicited contributions, and several of his critical pieces appeared early on as did five of his "spring" poems in May 1920. He continued to write for *The Dial*, and other "little magazines" through the twenties, a decade that also saw the publication of *Tulips and Chimneys* (collected verse) and a dramatic collaboration with the Provincetown Players. cummings's personal life in these years was traumatic: his marriage to Elaine, the divorced wife of Scofield Thayer, ended in failure, and a daughter who never learned until adult-hood that cummings was her father. A second marriage, to Anne Barton, failed also, but by the early thirties he had come together with Marian Morehouse, an elegant fashion model and photographer, who remained a devoted wife, companion, and nurturer until his death.

In the late thirties, cummings finally gained the recognition of the literary world with the publication of *Collected Poems*. Awards followed, as did requests for him to read at various colleges, and in 1952–1953, he held the Norton Pro-fessorship of Poetry at Harvard. cummings, who had become increasingly reactionary and reclusive after his anti-Soviet travelogue *Eimi* was published in 1933, consistently refused to have a radio or television set, and would have nothing to do with World War II. Despite unrelenting economic pressures and failing health, however, he continued to write poetry of remarkable vigor and freshness, even up to the last few years of his life. Having finally, in 1962, persuaded Marian to publish a volume of her photographs, he did not live to see it, but died of a cerebral hemorrhage at Joy Farm.

e.e. cummings brought a whole new battle plan to the American Revolution in poetic language which had been started by Whitman and Dickinson and carried forward in his own century by Frost and Sandburg. Now the target was no longer merely traditional literary usage, but the conventional appearance and function of words themselves. Spurred on by Dadaist scorn of pomposity and a feeling of kinship with the "little" man,[105] he adopted the lower case "i" and began to distort punctuation and syntax in an imitation of the writing style of Sam Ward, the hired man at Joy Farm. At the same time, he applied the European techniques of the Cubist painters and Webern's reductionist "Klangfarbenmelo-die"[106] to a breaking apart of the formal lyric into new visual patterns. cummings's painter's eye was a vital element in the new arrangements, but his musician's ear was equally important in the free, rhythmic flow of sound sequences they embodied.

From the vantage point of the twenty-first century, it now begins to appear that e.e. cummings's message was slight-ly ahead of its historical time. His most perceptive critics have recognized the mystical implications of his poetry, and have traced the "cosmic" vocabulary with which he describes the "transcendent sphere of spiritual fulfillment central to (his) conceptual world."[107] In truth, cummings had gone beyond the twentieth century updating of Transcendentalism which was suggested by his "habit of associating love with the landscapes, the seasons, the time of day, and with time and death."[108] With pre-Hiroshima insight, he had always distrusted the goals of science, and as time went on he became more convinced that man's intellect was the breeding ground of fear and the enemy of love. In retrospect, his cause was that of the advancing Aquarian Age whose heralds were particularly vocal in America: a rebirth into a New World which is to be reached, not in the manner of our founding fathers, but by a voyage within.

The title of *Tulips and Chimneys*, which in 1937 was finally issued in the entirety of its original manuscript, seems to refer to a stylistic distinction. The "tulips," as "natural" structures, are mostly in free verse while the "chimneys" are sonnets, representing "artificial" structures.[109] "[I]n just-spring" is a "tulip"—one of five "Chansons Innocentes" which are all about children—and this is where cummings begins his experimentation with unconventional spacing and group-ing of lines into stanzas. A technique that the poet would develop later—the transformation of parts of speech—is used only once here, as an adjective becomes an adverb in the sentence "the little / lame balloonman / whistles far and wee."

The childhood that cummings celebrated in this poem was his own. On the Cambridge street where the big house stood, spring thaws always filled a low spot with a huge "mud-luscious" puddle and the "balloonman" blowing his whis-tle was the sure sign of the advent of the gentler season. When "eddieandbill come running from marbles and piracies" and "bettyandisbel come dancing" it is Edward Estlin himself and his sister Elizabeth who, with their companions, have been released by spring into the out-of-doors. "Just-Spring"[110] was John Duke's first e.e. cummings setting (written in 1949), and it contains musical elements which serve to capture in a remarkable fashion not only the mood of the poem but the very look and spacing of the words on the page.

The sound and "feel" of children playing in the streets is immediately established in the introduction by a "taunt" melody that runs in and out of the modulating accompaniment.

Example 5.48, mm. 1–3

It frequently breaks up into smaller melodic components that skip around the keyboard in gleeful abandon,

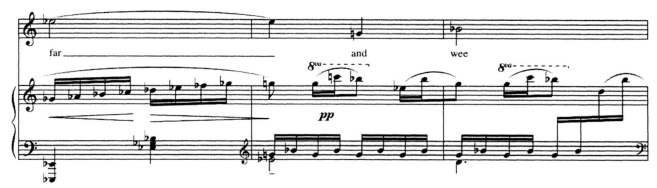

Example 5.49, mm. 51–53

Over this background, Duke has worked out a rhythmic scheme for the vocal line which applies sustained notes to the words which are alone on their poetic lines or separated by extended spacing, and short, run-together note values for those words which are placed close to each other. Thus

        in Just-
        Spring

becomes this as shown in Example 5.50:

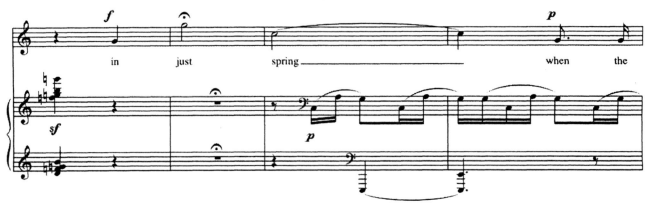

Example 5.50, mm. 10–13

While

    and bettyandisbel come dancing

takes this form in Example 5.51.

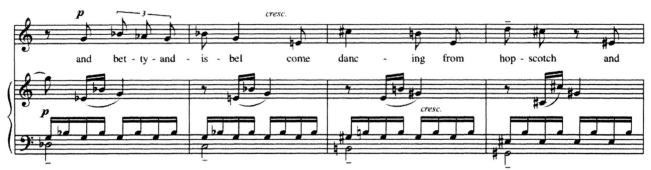

Example 5.51, mm. 54–57

The setting of the

      far
      and
      wee

whistling of the balloon man takes on the further aspect of musical word-painting through pitch (this is one of the "far"thest pitches called for in a Duke song), while the dynamic indications suggest his "goat-footed" retreat down the city-street, and into the haze of his mythical origins.

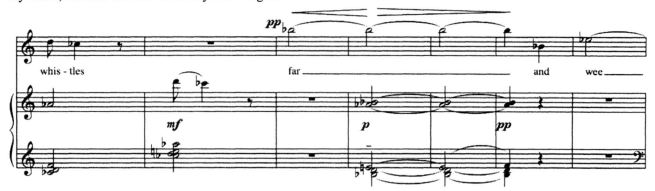

Example 5.52, mm. 68–74

"The Mountains are Dancing" [111] is from *XAIPE*, a poetry collection published in 1950 when cummings was fifty-six. Now plagued intermittently by back pain, depressive episodes, and an increasing sense of isolation from society, he nevertheless gave the book a Greek title which translated means "rejoice." The collection is dedicated to Hildegarde Watson, who was Sibley's wife and a devoted friend to many poets.[112] It contains the full flowering of his artistry and thought, with many of the poems structured in almost conventional forms, except for the absence of capitals and some punctuation. "The Mountains are Dancing" is one of these, written in three seven-line stanzas, which incorporate skillful variations of meaning and sound as well as two evolving refrains that tie the verses together.

The Duke setting of the poem[113] (1955) is mentioned in the Introduction as an example of an exact rhythmic correspondence between the dactyllic poetic feet and the 3/8 musical meter which breaks the steady eighth note movement of the vocal line only at the refrains (see Ex. 5.53). The poem is a joyous celebration of love in the human and natural worlds, and validates "wishing, having and giving" while it negates the "unworld" of "keeping and doubting." Duke appropriately makes of it a rollicking dance with breathless, though lightly textured, accented, pianistic arpeggios propelling the motion (see Ex. 5.54).

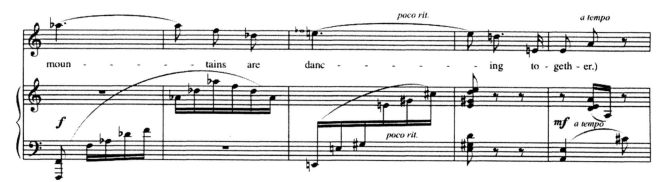

Example 5.53, mm. 43–47

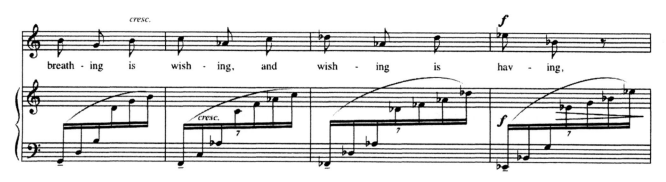

Example 5.54, mm. 13–16

The verbal variation is matched by musical changes in the keys and vocal contours of each verse. The final refrain returns to the opening key of G major with a jubilant, sustained A on "dancing" that holds while the dance expends its final burst of energy.

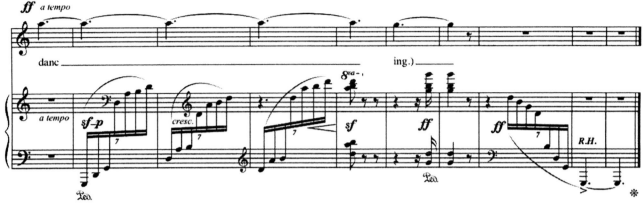

Example 5.55, mm. 139–48

Notice also that Duke pictorializes the "unworld" with a descending line that derives from the word "downward,"

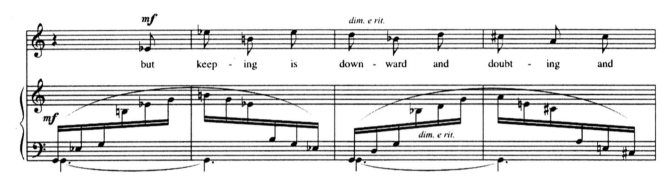

Example 5.56, mm. 17–20

while "breathing, wishing and having" always take on a rising sequence (see Ex. 5.54).

Eight years after *XAIPE*, cummings published *95 Poems*. Fifteen of them are love poems, and they have received the highest critical acclaim. "The force, the depth, and the intensity of the emotions in these poems" says Norman Friedman, "are unmatched in all of modern poetry."[114] Number 92 of the group is the sonnet "i carry your heart": a full, mature expression of the poet's belief in love as a transforming and transfiguring force in the natural world ("and it's you are whatever a moon has always meant"). "The deepest secret" and "the wonder" to which he alludes in the third stanza refer to his further conviction that the living world of the spirit needs the material world in order to transcend it.[115]

For this, the last of his cummings settings, composed in 1960,[116] John Duke has restructured the sonnet's original groupings of five-stress lines which cut across and into verbal meanings. cummings's

> i carry your heart with me (i carry it in
> my heart) i am never without it (anywhere

becomes as shown in Example 5.57.

Example 5.57, mm. 5–11

By the third stanza, cummings's lines and meaning have grown together, but he does choose to visually separate the final line into a refrain position. This gives Duke the opportunity to compose a coda which contains reminiscences of both the principal vocal motif and recurring pianistic figurations.

Example 5.58, mm. 59–66

As can be seen from this coda, "i carry your heart" contains some of Duke's most lyrical writing for both voice and piano, full of melting melodic contours and warm instrumental passages of consecutive thirds. The exciting crescendo which precedes the coda is built on a series of rising chromatic sequences that culminate in the same climactic pitch (G-sharp) as in his setting of Teasdale's "There Will Be Stars." However, cummings's affirmation of the power of love is many universes away from Teasdale's despair, and Duke's musical context makes this unerringly clear.

Example 5.59, mm. 52–58

Mark Van Doren (1894–1972)

"The world, I am certain," wrote Mark Van Doren in his autobiography, "is a terrible place, but I am just as certain that I love it."[117] "By some odd chance," he added, "and for no good reason, I am happy."[118] The ability to make these statements in 1958, despite the trials and terrors of life in the twentieth century would seem in itself a remarkable accomplishment. Nor were the words those of a recluse who had retained his equilibrium through isolation and withdrawal. Rather, they came from a man who had been constantly engaged with life and people, as teacher, editor, writer, and loving member of a large family.

His earliest memories were of the Van Doren farm in Hope, Illinois, where he was "an affectionate child in an affectionate family."[119] His father was a country doctor, and his mother an intelligent woman, devoted equally to each of her five sons, who taught Mark to read at the age of four. The house was filled with books and it was not surprising that Mark and his older brother Carl both chose to spend their lives with literature.

The family moved to Urbana when Van Doren was six, and remained there, so the choice of the University of Illinois for undergraduate studies was a natural one. By his senior year, he was editor of the *Illinois Magazine*, which also published his essays, one story, and a few poems. One more year of study there produced a master's degree and a thesis on Thoreau which soon found its way to publication by Houghton Mifflin, who had published the writings of Thoreau himself.

In 1915, Mark followed Carl's path to Columbia University, and began writing his doctoral dissertation on the works of Dryden—a subject also suggested by his brother. The choice was never to be regretted, for Van Doren not only came to "admire (Dryden's) music" but to believe that music to have been "the chief determining factor upon the poems

I myself would write."[120] He went on to say that he would never forget the feeling for melodic structure which Dryden had given him. It is interesting to observe how often Mark Van Doren, who had studied the piano as a child and played at his brother Guy's wedding in 1910, would, along with so many other poets, describe poetry (his own and others') in terms of music.

Drafted into the infantry in World War I, he eventually received officer's training, and was so haunted by the richness of his army experiences that on his return to New York he was forced to exorcise them in a manner which became his habit: by writing an account of them. After a year of a traveling fellowship in Europe that he spent in company with his lifelong friend, Joseph Wood Krutch, he settled down in New York City and began a teaching career at Columbia that was to continue for more than thirty years.

Thomas Merton, who became a contemplative monk as well as writer, was only one of the many students whose minds flowered in the "sanity and wisdom"[121] of Mark Van Doren's classes. In his own autobiographical writing, Merton praises the simplicity and sincerity with which the professor encountered generation after generation of students, and describes the inspired questions with which he led his pupils to say "excellent things" that they did not know they knew and "had not, in fact, known before."[122] In truth, it was more than literature that was being taught, for in Van Doren's famous Shakespeare course, the discussion was really about "the deepest springs of human desire and hope and fear, . . . precisely in (Shakespeare's) own terms."[123]

Teaching was not all of Van Doren's life during the Columbia years. In 1921, he married Dorothy Graffe, who was also a writer and editor. In time they had two sons, moved into a house on Bleecker Street in New York's Greenwich Village, and also bought a country place in Connecticut that was to be the setting for several fruitful sabbatical years. City and country equally enriched the spirit of this man who claimed that books and studies had never completely filled his world and that he had "loved as many things outside as in."[124] The city, to him, was "a drama, as without words or music, the country is a lyric," and at the same time he perceived New York to be "a quiet place. For many," he explained, "it is not quiet, but they have not penetrated to that mysterious part of it where multiplicity, pleased with itself, lies down and dreams that it is one thing after all."[125]

Mark succeeded Carl as literary editor of *The Nation* (1924–1928) and served the publication for three years in the middle thirties as film critic. His editing talents were also put to use in a number of anthologies, notably the *Oxford Book of American Prose* and the *Anthology of World Poetry*. The latter is an impressive collection of fine translations chosen by a discerning ear which had been honed not only by long devotion to reading and teaching poetry, but by writing vast amounts of his own. In a letter to John Duke, written in 1971, one year before his death, Van Doren describes himself as still pursuing his favorite occupation of "reading several anthologies of English poems. . . . When I do that," he tells the composer, "certain lyrics sing out. They are more than words; they are music. Not music with notes—or yes, with notes, and the notes are the words."[126]

There are many parallels between the lives of John Duke and Mark Van Doren. Both had long rewarding teaching careers at major Eastern centers of higher education; both had stable marriages to women named Dorothy who were writers; and both used the relative protection of the academic environment to permit an enormous flowering of lifelong creativity. It was predictable that a warm friendship would result when the Van Dorens called on the Dukes, the morning after Mark Van Doren had given a lecture on Shakespeare at Smith College. "It was a most memorable visit," wrote Duke. "He was most enthusiastic about my settings of his poetry and from then on we kept up quite a frequent correspondence. . . . I have always regretted that I never got around to accepting his urgent invitation to visit him at his home in Falls Village, Connecticut. For he was one of the most charming personalities I have ever encountered."[127]

The first collection of the hundreds of poems Mark Van Doren was to write, appeared in 1924 under the title of its opening lyric: *Spring Thunder*. Critics called them "country poems" and aligned him with Robert Frost.[128] As Van Doren pointed out in his autobiography, "country poems" were certainly a category that he had never ceased to write, but that it had been only one among many. "Spring Thunder" is a powerful treatment, in three, short four-line stanzas, of the moment just before a thunderstorm breaks on a warm night in the awakening season. John Duke's song by the same name,[129] written in 1960, is an equally terse two-page setting which allows very little in the way of sustained notes or piano interludes to interrupt the headlong moment of the storm's approach.

Written in the midst of a period of songs with relatively quiet, chordal accompaniments, this song brings back more elaborate pianistic figures: rising arpeggios which suggest the sky's eerie, ascending glow of warmth and light (see Ex. 5.60a), and the pounding broken octaves of nature's menace (see Ex. 5.60b).

Example 5.60a, mm. 9–12

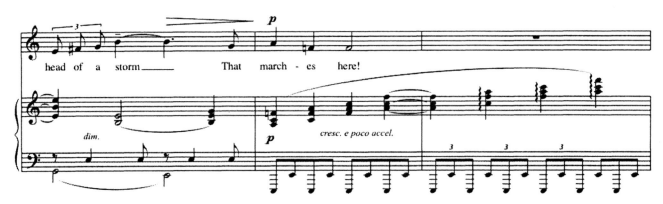

Example 5.60b, mm. 16–18

Diminished chords predominate in the accompaniment harmonies and are outlined in the vocal line, creating a sense of unease throughout. By contrast, the major triads that do occur have a comforting aural effect appropriate to the setting of such phrases as "it is warm,"—the verbal acknowledgment of fierce winter's slackening (see Ex. 5.60a). The final line of the song is a masterful instrumental representation of the barely audible moment in which the "edge of winter" begins to "crumble." This is followed by a whispered vocal speculation on the event, whose echo of the foregoing diminished chord carries a suggestion of doubtful hope.

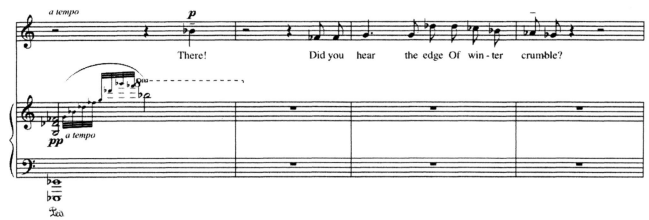

Example 5.61, mm. 23–26

Through the years when Mark Van Doren was in demand on the lecture circuit, he managed to schedule many side trips back to Urbana, usually by train. The poems he wrote while riding these trains became the group called "In that Far Land," which were published in the collection *Spring Birth* (1953). The distance separating him from that land was not geographical. Rather, it was far off in time: the world of the poet's childhood, and the poem "Only for Me" recreated one of its most poignant memories. Beth Knowlton, a girl who had captured Mark's twelve-year old heart, had been reported by brother Frank to have been seen with another boy. Van Doren crystallized the unforgettably painful jealousy he experienced in a poem called "Only for Me," which changed the sufferer into a girl named Linda Jane who wept and died for him in a youthful dream.

The song, "Only for Me,"[130] written in 1954, was actually John Duke's first Van Doren setting. In it, the composer's fluidity of harmonic rhythm suggests the emotional liability of the adolescent protagonist, while the high tessitura and leaping contour of the vocal line adds the breathless awkwardness of the age.

Example 5.62, mm. 11–16

The truly magical moment of this setting derives from the last line of verse two: "Weeping everywhere like rain." The voice having made a stifled, wondering leap of an octave, the piano then takes over in a spilling torrent of tears (see Ex. 5.63). The memory of this emotion, symbolized by the piano figures of broken sixteenth notes, continues behind the "sunrise," and the "growing up" as a dream lingers into waking. It stops, musically as well, only with "the forgetting" (see Ex. 5.64).

Example 5.63, mm. 35–41

Example 5.64, mm. 48–50

In *New Poems* (1948), there is a group which Van Doren called "Words for Music, More or Less." Of these, the poet wrote "a number of poems in the section were subsequently set to music as I had hoped they would be. . . . Nothing pleases me more than that."[131] Among this group is "One Red Rose," a celebration of a long lasting love "that lives / When nothing else does any longer." The poet's tribute to his life's companion became the composer's as well with John Duke's setting written in 1964,[132] the forty-second anniversary year of a marriage that was to end only with Mrs. Duke's death in 1977. Again, as in the cummings love song, "i carry your heart," a sweepingly lyrical vocal line is emphasized. Surrounding, supporting and entwining with this line is a lush, melodic counterpoint in the piano.

Example 5.65, mm. 34–39

For the final phrases of the song, the counter-melody ceases, so as to concentrate attention on the vocal suspensions that highlight the words "loving" and "true."

Example 5.66, mm. 61–68

Joseph Wood Krutch was of the opinion that all Van Doren's poems are love poems. These writers agree, and find, furthermore, that the passion of the poet increases and the expression of it gains compression and force in the late poetry as mortality threatens an end to feeling and perception. "O, World," the first of the *Late Poems* published in 1963 contains two verses whose lines lack Van Doren's usual regularity of length and meter as though emotion had shattered form. John Duke, in his 1965 setting of "O, World,"[133] translated this loosening of constraint into great keyboard-spanning instrumental figurations.

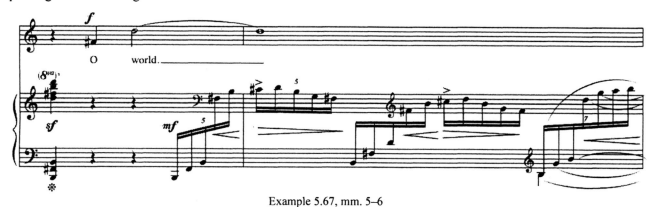

Example 5.67, mm. 5–6

The passion ebbs and flows at rising and falling pitch levels with varied rhythmic groupings of notes per beat. "O Stillness" takes on an element of mystery by virtue of its enharmonic vocal derivation, while the contrasting, and final, "O great sky," has dramatically expansive cluster chords, and a sustained fortissimo vocal tone that suggests the reaches of the universe and the human heart (see Ex. 5.68).

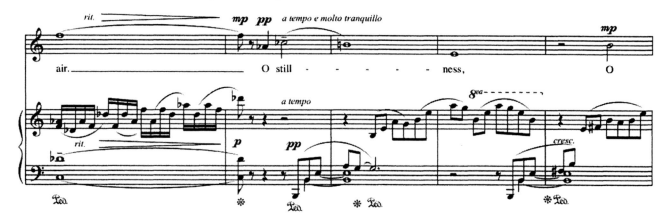

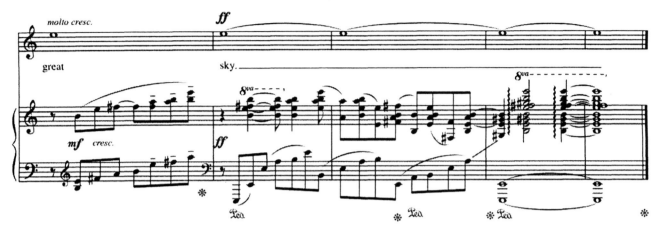

Example 5.68, mm. 47–56

Three more masterful Van Doren settings, entitled "Slowly, Slowly Wisdom Gathers," "So Simple," and "Dunce's Song," were composed by John Duke between 1966 and 1969 and were published by Smith College's New Valley Music Press in 1982, in time to celebrate the composer's eighty-third birthday.[134] The text for "Dunce's Song" came from *New Poems* of 1948 but the other two were published by Van Doren in the last decade of his life: "So Simple" in the *Late Poems* of 1963 and "Slowly, Slowly Wisdom Gathers" as the lead poem of a slim volume called *That Shining Place* that appeared in 1969, three years before his death. All three settings are a reflection on and a celebration of human existence and John Duke described them in a letter as being especially close to his heart. "As I grow older," he added, "I am more and more impressed with what Emily Dickinson called 'the mere fact of being alive' which is what these poems are really about. The urge to somehow penetrate to the final meaning of this mysterious, beautiful (and terrible) universe is, in some ways, man's greatest experience, even though from this point of view we are all 'Dunces' as in the last of the three songs."[135]

"So Simple" is a short, eight-line poetic statement that praises "singing" as the poet's only remaining delight "in times so curst". It receives an equally brief setting by the composer, but these are two pages of Duke's most meltingly lyrical writing, with the piano contributing an exquisite pianissimo pictorialization of "the length of day-dream." Songs one and three are more dramatic, with grateful and convincing melodic shapes and a more flamboyant use of the keyboard. Particularly effective are the broken chords which sweep up and down the keyboard in "Dunce's Song"—a musical equivalent for the all-pervading and mysterious wind of the text that "sees" but "cannot be seen."[136]

Emily Dickinson (1830–1886)

The reader is referred to Chapter 3 for material on Emily Dickinson in connection with settings of her poetry by Ernst Bacon and Aaron Copland. Curiously enough, it was not until 1968, that John Duke chose to deal with her work in the *Six Poems by Emily Dickinson for Soprano,*[137] by which time 143 of his songs had preceded them. This fact is surprising, at least partly because of Northampton's close proximity to Amherst, which contains the Dickinson family home and Amherst College, the latter founded largely through the efforts of Emily's grandfather at a ruinous cost to his own fortunes. Eventually, however, Duke did become involved with this nerve-center of the Dickinson legend, and he describes a meeting with Martha Dickinson Bianchi, the poet's niece, that occurred when he played the organ for a service in the Congregational Church just down the street from Emily's house. It might also be noted that the cover of John Duke's recording with Carole Bogard, soprano (which contains a sensitive performance of the *Six Poems*) displays a photograph of the singer and composer with the imposing Dickinson Homestead (as it was called) in the background (see n28).

Having come to this poetry late in his composing career, Duke had the advantage of the complete Thomas H. Johnson edition, which had been unavailable to Bacon and Copland and other composers setting her work before the edition's appearance in 1955. Duke studied these volumes as well as a whole shelf of critical and biographical works on Emily Dickinson that he kept in his upstairs study. He spoke of "the controversy over her poetry" and the fact that "some of it is hard to decipher (since) parts of the Johnson collection are only scraps,"[138] but professed great admiration for many of the verses, particularly the ones he had set.

Mid-twentieth century scholarship, notably that of Richard B. Sewall,[139] drew together the extensive Dickinson research of the preceding several decades into a newly comprehensive synthesis. The picture that now emerges is no longer that of a reclusive martyr to an early episode of unrequited love. Indeed there is considerable evidence pointing to the poet's deep emotional involvement with both Samuel Bowles, editor of the *Springfield Republican*, and Judge Otis Lord of Salem, in the years following her conjectural attachment to the Rev. Charles Wadsworth which has never received documentary support. Many other devotions of the heart, to friends and family members, to Amherst and her family home, are also now clearly seen to have loomed large in her existence, but the principal counter-subject to love in Dickinson's life seems, constantly and tragically, to have been loss. With many girlhood friends and with Susan Gilbert, her brother's wife, the loss appears in the form of rejection by those whose spirits were not equal to the floodtides of the poet's affections. With the men to whom she gave her passion, all married and therefore unattainable, the loss was implicit at the outset. But the supreme agent of loss, and the enemy who most engaged her, was Death, whose strokes separated her throughout her life from many she held dear including her beloved nephew, Gilbert, who died at the tender age of nine.

Gradually, as the losses accumulated, and as Dickinson began to realize how removed she was, intellectually and spiritually, from the simplistic pietism and the literary traditions of her environment, it became easier to live in her own world, inside the home that she always perceived as a haven of peace and beauty. The *Six Poems* that John Duke set have been given dates by Johnson which place them between 1858 and 1865: years of great upheaval in Dickinson's life, during which these patterns of withdrawal were being set in motion. This was the period of Samuel Bowles' visits to the Dickinson home, and of his departure for Europe. It was also a time of anxiety over her mother's health, her brother's marriage, her sister's ill-fated love affair, and her own threatened loss of sight; all of which were compounded by the failure to evoke understanding of her work from Higginson, the short-sighted editor of the *Atlantic Monthly*, whose advice she had sought. Of the six poems, three clearly stem from the sorrows of her life and her ambivalent feelings about Death, while the other three arise out of her strong ties to Nature, always one of her greatest comforters.

The contrast in the poetry occasions equal contrast in the settings, which are, in general, quite different in style from the musical expansiveness of the Duke songs that immediately preceded them.[140] Most of the writing is fairly thin in texture and mirrors the qualities of intimacy and simplicity with which Emily cut through the lush posturing of the Romantic age. The first poem, "Good morning, Midnight" (1862), is a delicately restrained lament by the writer over her need to remain in the figurative darkness of midnight, since she has been rejected by "day" and "sunshine" and all the brightness of life. The setting is quite transparent, with an uncluttered piano part that affords prominence to the vocal line. The latter is divided into short, broken-up phrases that seem to derive from the last couplet

But-please take a little Girl—
He turned away!

and lend a child-like atmosphere to the song.

Example 5.69, mm. 24–27

Number two, "Heart! We will forget him!" (written in 1858) presents a very different concept of this poem from the familiar Copland setting, and also employs the more authentic Johnson version of the poetry, which changes the sixth line from

That I my thoughts may dim

to

That I may straight begin

Unlike the nostalgic reminiscence of the earlier setting, John Duke's is rooted in agitation and anguish. The rushing pianistic triplets and an opening vocal leap of an octave clearly portray the active pain that belies the poet's exhortation to forget.

Example 5.70, mm. 1–2

The third song, "Let down the bars, Oh Death," is a quiet pause between the storms of two and four. The 1865 poem portrays Death as a haven of release for "the tired flocks . . . whose wandering is done"—an idea which Emily Dickinson struggled all her life to accept with varying success. Duke suggests this procession of weary souls with a tranquillo tempo, ceremonial 5/4 meter, and a succession of widely spaced piano chords in C-sharp minor.

Example 5.71, mm. 1–3

This is followed by a keyboard interlude whose pianissimo dynamic level and turn to the major mode establish the second verse's view of Death as a quiet, welcome comforter (see Ex. 5.72). The vocal leap to a soft, high, sustained tone on "tender," is the emotional climax of the song, and a perfect musical counterpart of the poet's notion of something that (if true) is too precious "to be told" (see Ex. 5.73).

Example 5.72, mm. 10–15

Example 5.73, mm. 20–22

"An awful Tempest mashed the air" is from 1860, and in this poem, Dickinson sees her beloved Nature briefly inhabited by demonic "creatures" who "chuckled on the Roofs . . . and swung their frenzied hair." The tempest, one feels, may well be symbolic of an inner storm, but by the end of verse three, "peace" like "Paradise" has returned to the inner and outer atmosphere. This is the most dynamic setting of the six, with its agitato piano prelude and interludes, and the unusual 5/8 4/8 meter creating a sense of the storm's uneven gusting.

Example 5.74, mm. 1–6

The final verse, when calm returns with morning, receives a lento setting, and bears some similarity to the tolling of the morning bells in the final section of Hugo Wolf's "In der Frühe."

The fifth poem, "Nobody knows this little Rose," carries the date of 1858 (actually the earliest year assigned by Johnson to any in the collection) and shows Dickinson, from the outset, giving literary form to her obsession with the impermanence of life and beauty. Here the subject is a flower, observed no doubt in her garden, which was one of Dickinson's chief sources of pleasure throughout her life. "Only a breeze" she says "will sigh" at the death of this little rose, and the reader assumes an intimated analogy to the scarcely marked passing from the physical world of all individual forms of life. John Duke's setting of the poem is the most lyrical of the six, and shows the heavy employment of consecutive thirds in the piano writing that the composer usually reserves for love songs in the conventional sense (see Ex. 5.75). The flexible harmonic movement with which Duke typically alights in a rapid succession of tonal areas is especially appropriate here in its suggestion of the busy movements of "bee," "bird," and "butterfly." The poignancy of the final couplet "Ah, Little Rose—how easy / For such as thee to die!" derives, in the setting, largely from the pianistic melody, with its grieving chordal appogiaturas, that fills in the vocal hold on "thee," and then repeats softly in augmentation in the brief postlude (see Ex. 5.76).

Example 5.75, mm. 4–6

Example 5.76, mm. 27–34

The final song sets "Bee! I'm expecting you!," a three verse poem of great charm from 1865, written in the form of a letter signed "Yours, Fly," which describes the busy springtime activities of all natural creation. Duke's setting is a masterpiece of musical word-painting in which small darting and buzzing creatures of the insect world are suggested in the piano by staccato tones and rapid, chromatic scale figures blurred by the pedal.

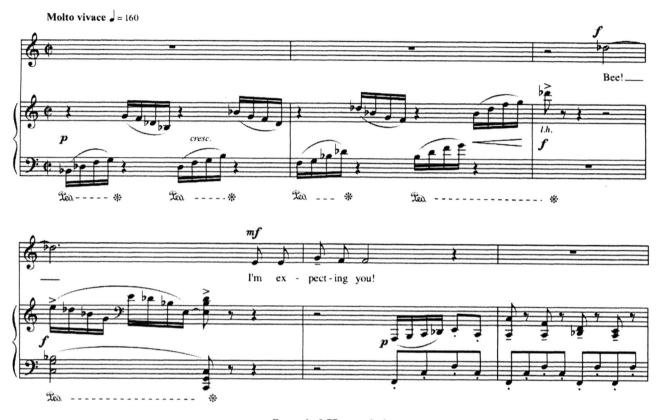

Example 5.77, mm. 1–6

Between these figures lie short, disconnected vocal phrases—the excited gasps of the fly as he alights for brief, breathless moments.

Example 5.78, mm. 31–36

Notes

1. The American baritone, John Seagle, interview at his home, San Antonio, Texas, 17 May 1982.

2. The Seagle Music Colony was started in 1916 by Oscar Seagle (John Seagle's father) who was also a leading American baritone and teacher. The colony, founded on a 100-acre tract of land on Schroon Lake in upper New York State, continues to train young singers in vocal technique and performance.

3. Virgil Thomson, "The American Song," *The Art of Judging Music* (New York: Knopf, 1948).

4. Virgil Thomson, "The Concert Song," *The Art of Judging Music*, 88.

5. Two complete catalogs of John Duke songs (chronological and alphabetical listings which include poets, voice type, and publishers) can be found in Ruth C. Friedberg and Robin Fisher, eds. *The Selected Writings of John Duke: 1917–1984* (Lanham, Md.: Scarecrow Press, 2007).

6. Personal letter to R. Friedberg, 5 July 1981. All letters from Duke cited in this chapter are reprinted in their entirety in *The Selected Writings of John Duke: 1917–1984,* eds. Ruth C. Friedberg and Robin Fisher (Lanham, MD: Scarecrow Press, 2007).

7. R. Friedberg's visit in John Duke's home, 28–30 July 1982, produced impressions of an unpretentious but inviting setting for an artist. The furnishings of a large downstairs living room included a Chinese rug, Breughel print, and a grand piano piled high with publications and manuscripts. One of the upstairs bedrooms had become a study and contained an upright piano, books on many subjects, and a collection of photographs, scrapbooks, and mementos.

8. Personal letter to R. Friedberg, 13 June 1982. The majority of the biographical data on John Duke was provided to R. Friedberg by the composer. Information on the Seagle Music Colony was drawn from the Seagle interview (see n1) and Friedberg's visit to the colony (30 July –2 August 1982).

9. In 1969, John Duke received the Peabody Alumni Association Award for distinguished service to music.

10. Gustav Klemm, "Gustav Strube: The Man and the Musician," *Musical Quarterly* 28 (July, 1942), 288–301.

11. See Chapter 4.

12. The Duke quotation is from a personal letter to R. Friedberg, 19 December 1981.

13. John and Dorothy Duke had a son, Jay Macon, and a daughter, Karen. Duke's song, "To Karen Singing," written in 1944, is the only instance of the composer setting his own text. Karen carried on the musical and theatrical traditions of the family and also wrote mystery novels on these themes under her married name of Karen Sturges until her death in 2002. Like her paternal grandmother, Karen sang and played the guitar as does her daughter, Morgan, and the two frequently performed together during Karen's lifetime.

14. For many years, while living in Northampton, Dorothy Duke wrote a poetry column for an area newspaper.

15. Dorothy Duke wrote the book and lyrics for John Duke's musical shows *The Yankee Pedlar* and *The Cat That Walked By Himself.* She also served as his opera librettist on the occasions indicated in the text.

16. All three of these compositions are out of print.

17. John Duke was introduced to the Seagle Music Colony through his daughter, Karen, who was enrolled there as a voice student for several summers in the early fifties. Also, John Seagle had come to know Duke's songs through his coach-accompanist, Nathan Price, and had performed a group of them at a New York recital in 1952.

18. The fact of Duke's birthday having belatedly come to light, it was celebrated on August 1. Helen Seagle, John's efficient and hospitable wife, arranged birthday cake and ice cream for the entire school following dinner in "the white house," as the colony's central structure is called.

19. Interview with R. Friedberg, 28 July 1982, in which Duke recalled the atmosphere at the Yaddo estate as an uncomfortable one, created by enormous and newly acquired wealth. One bedroom, he recalled, was larger than his present generously proportioned living room.

20. Interview with R. Friedberg, 2 August 1982, in which Duke mentioned in regard to this première that Sessions wrote very slowly and only had the first two movements of the sonata completed for the occasion. "Later," Duke said, "I played the whole thing at Smith, and then again in New York."

21. Interview with R. Friedberg, May 1982, in which John Seagle described a colorful Gottschalk evening which occurred during Duke's sabbatical year at Trinity University. In connection with a series of fund-raising dinners called "Texas Under Six Flags," John Duke was persuaded to impersonate the nineteenth-century composer in old fashioned evening clothes and cape, under the supposition that the Louisiana-born Gottschalk might well have concertized in the Republic of Texas.

22. Personal letter to R. Friedberg, 18 June 1961.

23. John Duke, "Some Reflections on the Art Song in English," *The American Music Teacher* 25, no. 4 (1976): 26.

24. John Duke, "The Significance of Song," *Ars Lyrica* I (1981), 11–21.

25. Participants in this panel discussion were John Duke, British composer Iain Hamilton who was at that time Mary Duke Biddle Professor of Music, and Professor Bernard Duffey, an American poetry scholar from Duke University's Department of English. The singers who performed with Duke in the recital of his songs were Claudia Bray, soprano; John Hanks, tenor (Duke University professor of voice); and Richard Rivers, bass-baritone (professor of voice at Converse College).

26. John Duke, *Songs, Volume 1 for High Voice* (1985); *Songs, Volume 2 for Medium Voice* (1985); *Songs, Volume 3* (1987); *Songs, Volume 4*, Ruth Friedberg, ed. (2001). All four volumes are published by Southern Music Co. of San Antonio.

27. Donald Boothman and John Duke, *Seventeen Songs by John Duke* (Washington, D.C.: Golden Age Recordings, 1977).

28. Carole Bogard and John Duke, *Songs by John Duke* (Framingham, Mass.: Cambridge Records, 1979).

29. John K. Hanks and Ruth C. Friedberg, *Art Song in America* (Durham, North Carolina: Duke University Press, 1997).

30. Lauralyn Kolb and Tina Toglia, *Just-Spring, Art Songs of John Duke* (New York: New World Records, 2001).

31. James Taylor and Donald Sulzen, *John Woods Duke Lieder* (Munich: Orfeo, 2002).

32. The foregoing paragraph and quotations are drawn from: personal letter to Louis Auld, 2 September 1979, founder of the periodical *Ars Lyrica* and a former colleague of John Duke's on the Smith College faculty. The reader should be advised that the italicized emphasis in this and all Duke quotations is the composer's.

33. Personal letter to R. Friedberg, 18 June 1961.

34. Duke, "Some Reflections on the Art Song in English." In a personal letter to R. Friedberg, 29 December 1980, John Duke commented "as a corollary to this, I have *rejected thousands* of poems because I have found them, either as a whole or in part, *un*assimilable."

35. See Introduction.

36. Suzanne K. Langer, *Feeling and Form* (New York: Scribner's, 1953), Chapter 9. The reader is also referred to two other works by Langer that contain illuminating treatments of both poetry and song: *Philosophy in a New Key* (Cambridge: Harvard University Press, 1951); and *Problems of Art* (New York: Charles Scribner's Sons, 1957).

37. Letter to Auld, 1979. One might speculate as to whether Langer's "artistic" approach to the arts was related to the fact that she herself was an amateur cellist of some accomplishment. Professor Gerard Jaffe of Incarnate Word College in San Antonio, Texas, recalled playing string quartets with her ca. 1960 when he was on the music faculty of Wesleyan University and Langer taught at the nearby Connecticut College for Women. He remembered her as a strong personality and an enthusiastic player who had a fondness for the literature that afforded notable cello solos.

38. Duke, "Some Reflections on the Art Song in English."

39. Letter to R. Friedberg, 18 June 1961.

40. Letter from Mark Van Doren to John Duke, 11 February 1971, held in the Smith College Archives, John Duke Papers, Box 29.

41. Duke, "The Significance of Song," 14.

42. Duke, "The Significance of Song," 14.

43. Langer, *Feeling and Form*, 268.

44. Duke, "The Significance of Song," 17.

45. Interview with R. Friedberg, 29 July 1982.

46. John Duke, "Rapunzel" (San Antonio, Tex.: Southern Music Co., 2001). Soprano. Range: e^1 to a^2.

47. Letter to R. Friedberg, 22 October 1981.

48. Letter to R. Friedberg, 22 October 1981.

49. William Treat Upton, *Supplement to Art Song in America* (Philadelphia: Oliver Ditson, 1938).

50. Interview with R. Friedberg, 31 July 1982. In discussing the importance of form, Duke also expressed his belief that "a song must end, not just stop. One must feel that everything has been said that needs to be."

51. Jean Gould, *The Poet and Her Book* (New York: Dodd, Mead, 1969), 49.

52. Norman A. Brittin, *Edna St. Vincent Millay* (New York: Twayne, 1967), 31.

53. Gould, *The Poet and Her Book*, 46.

54. John Duke, "Wild Swans" (San Antonio, Tex.: Southern Music Co., 2001). Medium voice. Range: d^1 to a^2.

55. Hoyt C. Franchere, *Edwin Arlington Robinson* (New York: Twayne, 1968), 22.

56. Mary Colum, *Life and the Dream* (Garden City, N.Y.: Doubleday, 1947), 374–76.

57. Letter to R. Friedberg, October 1981.

58. Franchere, *Edwin Arlington Robinson*, 25.

59. W. R. Robinson, *Edwin Arlington Robinson: A Poetry of the Act* (Cleveland, Ohio: The Press of Western Reserve University, 1967), 51.

60. Nancy Joyner, "Edwin Arlington Robinson," *Great Writers of the English Language—Poetry*, edited by James Vinson (New York: St. Martin's, 1979), 826.

61. Letter to Arthur Nevin, quoted in Franchere, *Edwin Arlington Robinson*, 29.

62. John Duke, "Richard Cory" (New York: Carl Fischer, 1948). Baritone. Range: a to e^2. John Duke, "Luke Havergal" (New York: Carl Fischer, 1948). Baritone. Range: b to f^2. John Duke, "Miniver Cheevy" (New York: Carl Fischer, 1948). Baritone. Range: g to f^2. All three of these songs are performed by Donald Gramm and Donald Hasard on the recording *But Yesterday Is Not Today*, issued in 1977 by New World Records and mentioned above in the text. "Luke Havergal" is included in the Thomas Hampson CD *Song of America* (2005) available at ArkivMusic.com.

63. John Duke's original choice for the final voice note was an appropriately dissonant C-flat. He later revised it to a more consonant B-flat for greater performance ease, but the C-flat was fortunately restored in Carl Fischer's posthumous Duke song collection.

64. Franchere, *Edwin Arlington Robinson*, 103.

65. An alternate interpretation to "the western gate" as a symbol for death was suggested to Friedberg by William Walker, a leading Metropolitan Opera baritone of the mid-twentieth century. In his view, "the western gate" was the overseas passage from England to the New World, which Luke Havergal had to undertake to find his beloved, already departed on that journey.

66. Hyatt H. Waggoner, *American Poets from the Puritans to the Present* (New York: Dell, 1968), 282.

67. Letter to R. Friedberg, 22 October 1981.

68. John Duke, "Bells in the Rain" (New York: Carl Fischer, 1948). High voice. Range e^1 to g^2.

69. See n4.

70. Babette Deutsch, *Poetry in Our Time* (Garden City, N.Y.: Doubleday, 1963), 252.

71. See Chapter 1.

72. John Duke, "Little Elegy" and "The Bird" (New York: G. Schirmer, 1949). Soprano. Range: f^1 to a^2.

73. Stanley Olson in his biography called *Elinor Wylie: A Life Apart* (New York: Dial, 1947) treats the poet's final passion for Henry Clifford Woodhouse as largely a creation of her imagination. Little evidence, in truth, is extant in regard to the exact nature of the relationship

74. Duke, "Little Elegy" and "The Bird."

75. John Duke, "Viennese Waltz" (Boston: R. D. Row Music, 1950). Selling agent: Carl Fischer. Medium high voice. Range e^1 to a flat^2.

76. The source of the following biographical material is Williams Drake, *Sara Teasdale, Woman and Poet* (San Francisco: Harper and Row, 1979). This is the first work on Teasdale to make use of hitherto unavailable materials that have now been released by Margaret Conklin, her literary executor.

77. Marya Zaturenska, "Foreword—The Strange Victory of Sara Teasdale," *Collected Poems of Sara Teasdale* (New York: Macmillan, 1971), xxxi.

78. Letter to Jessie Rittenhouse, Teasdale's friend. Quoted in Drake, *Sara Teasdale*, 214.

79. Letter to J. Rittenhouse in Drake, *Sara Teasdale*, 201.

80. Letter to J. Rittenhouse in Drake, *Sara Teasdale*, 194.

81. See Chapter 3 for material on Countee Cullen.

82. C. Day Lewis, *The Lyric Impulse* (Cambridge, Mass.: Harvard University Press, 1965), 18.

83. C. Day Lewis, *The Lyric Impulse*, 19.

84. Drake, *Sara Teasdale*, 158.

85. Drake, *Sara Teasdale*, 185.

86. Drake, *Sara Teasdale*, 222.

87. Personal letter to R. Friedberg, 25 June 1982.

88. John Duke, "There Will Be Stars" (New York: Boosey & Hawkes, 1953). Medium high voice. Range: b to G sharp^2.

89. Langer, *Feeling and Form*, 159.

90. As clearly revealed by his disparaging comments in the published letters, Frost was jealous of Carl Sandburg and looked upon him as a rival.

91. Personal letter to R. Friedberg, 22 October 1981.

92. See Introduction for a discussion of Sidney Lanier's quite similar theories.

93. Lawrence B. Holland, "Robert Frost," in *The Norton Anthology of American Literature,* vol. 2 (New York:

W. W. Norton, 1979), 1101.

94. See Introduction for a discussion of T. S. Eliot's *The Music of Poetry.*

95. John Duke, "To the Thawing Wind" (New York: Southern Music Publishing, 1964). Medium voice. Range: e[1] to g[2].

96. Philip L. Gerber, *Robert Frost* (Boston: Twayne, 1966), 160.

97. John Duke, "Acquainted with the Night" (New York: Southern Music Publishing, 1964). Medium voice. Range: b to f[2].

98. Deutsch, *Poetry in Our Time,* 80.

99. John Duke, "The Last Word of a Bluebird" (New York: G. Schirmer, 1949). Medium voice. Range: a to f[2].

100. Deutsch, *Poetry in Our Time,* 83.

101. Deutsch, *Poetry in Our Time,* 67.

102. Louis Nicholas had a long career as professor of voice at George Peabody College for Teachers in Nashville, Tennessee (now merged with Vanderbilt University). He also held prominent positions with the National Association of Teachers of Singing, including the chairmanship of the editorial board of the *NATS Bulletin.*

103. The poem was as follows:

> O, the pretty birdie, O
> With his little toe, toe, toe!

104. Charles Norman, *e.e. cummings: The Magic-Maker* (New York: Duell, Sloan and Pearce, 1964), 63.

105. Richard S. Kennedy, *Dreams in the Mirror* (New York: Liveright, 1980), 110. Kennedy points out that e.e. cummings, being small compared to his father, probably identified with the less powerful of the world.

106. "Klangfarbenmelodie" is literally "tone-color melody." It refers to Webern's technique of distributing small sections of a melodic line to a number of different orchestral instruments.

107. Norman Friedman, *e.e. cummings, The Art of His Poetry* (Baltimore: Johns Hopkins University Press, 1960), 67.

108. Friedman, *e.e. cummings,* 28.

109. Norman Friedman, *e.e. cummings, The Growth of a Writer* (Carbondale, IL: Southern Illinois University Press, 1964), 38.

110. John Duke, "Just-Spring" (New York: Carl Fischer, 1954). High voice. Range: d[1] to b flat[2].

111. The poem itself is untitled, marked only by the number 67—a frequent practice of cummings. "The Mountains Are Dancing" is actually John Duke's title.

112. See chapter 4.

113. John Duke, "The Mountains Are Dancing" (New York: Carl Fischer, 1956). High voice. Range: d[1] to a[2].

114. Friedman, *The Growth of a Writer,* 170.

115. Friedman, *The Growth of a Writer,* 7.

116. John Duke, "i carry your heart" (New York: G. Schirmer, 1962). Medium-high voice. Range: e[1] to g sharp[2].

117. Mark Van Doren, *The Autobiography of Mark Van Doren* (New York: Harcourt, Brace, 1958), 348.

118. Van Doren, *Autobiography,* 351.

119. Van Doren, *Autobiography,* 3.

120. Van Doren, *Autobiography,* 99.

121. Thomas Merton, *The Seven Storey Mountain* (New York: Harcourt, Brace, 1948), 179.

122. Merton, *Mountain,* 139.

123. Merton, *Mountain,* 180.

124. Van Doren, *Autobiography,* 61.

125. Van Doren, *Autobiography,* 174.

126. Personal letter to Duke from Mark Van Doren, 11 February 1971, held in the John Duke Papers, Box 29, Smith College Archives.

127. Letter to R. Friedberg, 22 October 1981.

128. This comparison was probably unwelcome to Van Doren who on p. 170 of his autobiography describes Frost's cynical and "devastating sentiments about the profession we shared" (i.e., teaching).

129. John Duke, "Spring Thunder" (New York: Carl Fischer, 1968). High voice. Range: e flat[1] to g[2].

130. John Duke, "Only for Me" (New York: Boosey Hawkes, 1955). Medium voice. Range: e[1] to g[2].

131. Van Doren, *Autobiography,* 290.

132. John Duke, "One Red Rose" (New York: Carl Fischer, 1970). Medium voice. Range: b flat to f^2.

133. John Duke "O World" (New York: Carl Fischer, 1970). Medium voice. Range: d^1 to f^2.

134. Reprinted as "Three Poems by Mark Van Doren" in *Songs of John Duke,* Vol. 4 (San Antonio, Tex.: Southern Music Co., 2001). Medium voice. Range: a to f^2.

135. Personal letter to R. Friedberg, 15 September 1982.

136. Parts of the preceding discussion are taken from R. Friedberg's review of the *Three Poems by Mark Van Doren* that appeared in the *NATS Bulletin* 39, no. 3 (1983): 36–37.

137. John Duke, *Six Poems by Emily Dickinson* (New York: Southern Music Publishing, 1968). Soprano. Range: e^1 to a^2.

138. Interview with R. Friedberg, 30 July 1982.

139. Richard B. Sewall, ed., *Emily Dickinson: A Collection of Critical Essays* (Englewood Cliffs, N.J.: Prentice-Hall, 1963); *The Lyman Letters—New Light on Emily Dickinson and Her Family* (Amherst: University of Massachusetts Press, 1965); *The Life of Emily Dickinson* (New York: Farrar, Straus and Giroux, 1974).

140. Parts of the following discussion are taken from Friedberg's review of the *Six Poems* that appeared in the *NATS Bulletin* 35, no. 3 (Jan/Feb. 1979): 38–39.

Chapter 6

Into the New Century

The six composers whose works will be discussed in this chapter were all born during the first decade of the twentieth century. Not surprisingly, their paths on occasion crossed or formed parallels during their musical training and careers; three of them, in fact, were students together at Juilliard in the early thirties. Further, the names of Rubin Goldmark, Nadia Boulanger, and Roger Sessions will be seen to recur in their various biographies as favored teachers of composition, and several of the six will, in time, themselves become teachers to the next generation.

There are, however, marked differences among them in regard to the position of songs in their body of composition, ranging from Ross Lee Finney whose solo songs represent relatively few opus numbers in a catalog heavy with instrumental and choral works, to Sergius Kagen who wrote nothing but songs and operas. The origins of these men also demonstrate a variety befitting the American melting pot. Nordoff, Barber and Bowles are born in the mid-Atlantic states, and Finney, half a country away in Minnesota. Kagen and Naginski are actually natives of Europe but adapt so quickly to the culture of the "new world" that there remains no question of their status as American composers.

Finally, one might observe the uneven workings of destiny in the varying lengths of their careers. Ross Lee Finney and Paul Bowles continued to lead creative lives into their ninth decade; Sergius Kagen, Paul Nordoff, and Samuel Barber died of natural causes at the ages of fifty-five, sixty-seven, and seventy-one respectively; while the ill-fated Charles Naginski was killed in a tragic accident at thirty-one, in the early flowering of his impressive talent.

Ross Lee Finney (1906–1997)

Ross Lee Finney was born in Wells, Minnesota, and as a boy studied both the cello and the piano. By the age of twelve he was proficient enough to perform as cellist with a piano trio in various small Midwestern communities. Entering the University of Minnesota in 1924, he continued to study the cello, and began composition lessons as well, with Donald Ferguson as his first instructor. Finney completed his bachelor of arts degree at Carleton College between 1925 and 1927, and remained there for a short time teaching cello and music history. Then a Johanson Fellowship made possible a year of study in Paris with Nadia Boulanger, after which he spent 1928 and 1929 at Harvard University taking the classes of Edward Burlingame Hill.

In the fall of 1929, Finney began his long, illustrious career of teaching in the colleges and universities of the United States. He taught at Smith College from 1929 to 1947, and during his tenure, founded the Smith College Music Archives and the Valley Music Press. Remarkably, he also found the time to serve concurrently on the faculties of nearby Mt. Holyoke College (1938–1940), Hartt School of Music (1941–1942), and Amherst College (1946–1947). World War II took him away from the campus from 1943 to 1945 for service with the Office of Strategic Services in Paris, during which time he was injured near the front and received the Purple Heart and Certificate of Merit. Thereafter reestablished at Smith College, he was, in 1948, appointed composer-in-residence and subsequently chairman of the Department of Composition at the University of Michigan in Ann Arbor, where he in time created an electronic music laboratory. His teaching career, which touched the lives of many younger composers, performers, and professors all over the country, had been interrupted by his own studies with Alban Berg[1] in Vienna (1931) and Francesco Malipiero in Venice (1937). During the thirties and forties, he had also worked with Roger Sessions on contemporary techniques that assumed increasing importance in his composition.

Another important association begun in the thirties was Finney's relationship with the American poet Archibald MacLeish. The composer's interest in English language text setting is traceable to this point in his career, and by 1960 he had set the poetry of MacLeish in five works: *Poems by Archibald MacLeish* (1935) for solo voice, *Bleheris* (1937) for tenor and orchestra, and the choral pieces *Pole Star for This Year* (1939), *Words to Be Spoken* (1946), and *Edge of Shadow* (1959).

Finney's Venetian studies in 1937 had been facilitated by a Guggenheim fellowship and a Pulitzer traveling fellowship. In 1947, he spent another year as a Guggenheim fellow composing in Claremont, California, so that Mrs. Finney, who was an authority in certain aspects of seventeenth-century literature and musicology, could use the Huntington library. During that year, Ross Lee Finney endeared himself to the Scripps College community by playing in amateur chamber music sessions, singing his folk-ballad repertoire to his own guitar accompaniment, and addressing a Scripps Convocation on "Music and the Human Need." Claremont, then, was a natural choice for Finney's return in the late fifties, on leave from the University of Michigan, to compose a symphony commissioned by the Koussevitzky Music Foundation. Once again he delivered an address at Scripps College, this time on "Analysis and the Creative Process," an illuminating explication of the composer's working methods that was thereafter published in the College Bulletin. Said Finney on this occasion,

> My own music seems to start with a sense of gesture that must be translated at some moment into musical notes before the creative process begins. . . . I would have to define a gesture as being movement, up or down, within time and conveying some expressive idea. . . .While I must agree that leaving my desk is usually an escape from work, sometimes in the course of the excitement that forces me to move around in my studio, a sense of gesture is born.[2]

Ross Lee Finney, as just demonstrated, was a gifted writer like his erstwhile Smith College colleague, John Duke (see Chapter 5). In numerous journal articles such as "Composer in Residence"[3] and "The Composer in Academia,"[4] he appeared as spokesman for those musicians who were pursuing combined careers as creators and instructors. In another, titled "Employ the Composer," he argued for the uniqueness of the composer's contribution to the college musical curriculum since "the composer does more than clarify musical practice; he evolves it."[5] He stated his further belief "that the function of the composer in education (is) to upset the apple cart . . . (a function) that should be valued and not feared, for the natural direction of the *status quo* . . . is down."[6] "Theory in a Period of Change" found him encouraging teachers of this discipline not to "accept the negative position of the reactionary or the advance guard" which would have the effect of turning the student "back into the museum or . . . loose without understanding in a chaotic world. He (the student) deserves," said Finney, "a positive pedagogy, one that will establish his position in the chain of history and at the same time develop his creative imagination for the possibilities of the future."[7]

In Finney's own composition, the "possibilities of the future" came to mean a turn toward serial techniques. No doubt as a partial result of his studies with Boulanger, Berg, and Sessions and coinciding with his appointment at the University of Michigan, he began to explore the idea of reconciling tone-rows with larger designs of organization, while maintaining an "essential lyricism that is a constant (even) in the 12-tone compositions."[8] Paradoxically, his path toward dodecaphony had begun with links to the "chain of history" that extended well back into the past of Western music in general, and American music in particular. A strong interest in seventeenth-century music during the 1930s had produced *Three Seventeenth Century Lyrics*[9] for voice and piano, and the Finney family's custom of singing folk songs not only gave the composer his life-long avocation, but had direct influence on a number of works in his catalog.[10] His creative curiosity also excited by the musical heritage of the New England colonies, Finney composed an orchestral piece in 1943 called *Hymn, Fuguing and Holiday* based on a hymn tune by William Billings,[11] and a choral work in 1945, *Pilgrim's Psalms*, which drew on melodies from the Ainsworth Psalter of the Puritans.[12]

Benjamin Franklin (1706–1790)[13]

The stage, then, had been appropriately set for the appearance in 1946 of *Poor Richard*,[14] Ross Lee Finney's masterful cycle based on texts by Benjamin Franklin. Immersed as he was at that time in colonial life of the eighteenth century, it is not surprising that the composer was captivated by the mind and writings of one of America's greatest geniuses, whose birth coincidentally preceded Finney's by exactly two hundred years. Born in Boston and destined to staggering achievements in the arts, sciences, and world of diplomacy, the young Franklin had begun his writing career at the age of seven, with ballads which were ridiculed by his father. Josiah Franklin, a candle maker by trade, wanted his sons to prosper in the world, and marking the impoverished condition of many educated men, set about discouraging Ben's intellectual proclivities, decided against sending him to college, and apprenticed him to his brother as a printer when he was twelve years old.

During the next five years, Franklin not only learned the printer's trade well enough to retire on its profits in 1748, but also occupied every leisure moment in a remarkably effective self-education. By the age of sixteen, he had polished his manners and his writing style and began to have accepted for publication letters that he had submitted to the New England *Courant* (his brother's periodical) under the pen name of Silence Dogood. The hoax eventually revealed, it became apparent that Ben's abilities needed more space in which to develop. He left Boston and his indentureship to settle, after arduous travels, into a printing job in Philadelphia, a city that reflects his influence in its intellectual life and political institutions to this day.

Franklin's next appearance as a writer occurred in London, where he had arrived in 1724 only to find himself stranded by unfulfilled promises of support from the governor of Pennsylvania. Once again he found work as a printer, and began to attract some notice in that sophisticated city with the *Dissertation on Liberty and Necessity* that he wrote, printed, and published. Back in Philadelphia in 1726, he was soon in business for himself, and the next year organized a group of young, poor, and enterprising Philadelphians in a society known as the Junto. This group's aims included both conviviality and philosophy, required the members to produce essays four times a year, and occasioned the writing of some of Franklin's liveliest drinking songs during its thirty-year existence.

The next few years were ones of remarkable achievement for a young man in his mid-twenties. In 1729, Franklin founded the *Pennsylvania Gazette*, which he served in the capacities of both writer and printer. In 1730, he became the official printer for the state of Pennsylvania, and in the same year began his long, rewarding marriage to Deborah Read, a stabilizing force in the life of this man whose only passion not entirely under rationalistic control was his strong attraction to women. The year 1733 was one of the most meaningful in Franklin's career, for it saw the first publication in the *Poor Richard*'s almanac series—a venture which was to bring him fame and fortune (by 1748 it was selling 10,000 copies annually) and provide the perfect medium for his simultaneous functions as philosopher, journalist, and (particularly germane to our purposes) balladeer and poet.

Although there had been several models for the name and format of his almanac, the humorous, homely essence of *Poor Richard* was Franklin's invention. In his early, livelier years, *Poor Richard* was by no means always on the side of prudence and calculation and spoke often of women with alternating cynicism and tenderness. The sources of his wit and wisdom were lodged in many literary masters and popular adages, and in numerous languages as well, for Franklin had, beginning in 1732, acquired a reading knowledge of French, Italian, Spanish, and German as well as his Latin of earlier acquisition. All the rich store of the author's literary acquaintance and incisive thinking was combed and adapted to suit his purpose and audience which in eighteenth century Philadelphia consisted mostly of immigrants looking for miracles and sudden riches. *Poor Richard* with "much wit and charm" educated them to the realization that "they must work to be happy, and save to be secure" and that "industry and frugality were the simple, natural roads to freedom."[15]

Says Ross Lee Finney of his Franklin settings, "*Poor Richard* reflects my love of early Americana. They were influenced by Francis Hopkinson[16] (especially the drinking song) and by the ballad songs of the 18th century."[17] In truth, it seems highly appropriate to set these texts in a style reminiscent of the period in which they were written since Franklin himself was a man strongly connected to the music of his time having learned to play the harp, guitar, and violin, as well as the glass harmonica (an instrument which he substantially improved in 1762). At meetings of the Junto, he had often taken his turn in singing, on some of these occasions writing words for already familiar airs. It is also more than likely that he composed a number of his own tunes, quite possibly for some of the texts that appear in this cycle.

Of the seven songs in Finney's *Poor Richard*, only three (numbers three, five, and six) actually employ texts drawn from the almanac. Number one, called "Epitaph," establishes the tone of the cycle both philosophically and musically as it sets the most famous of American epitaphs that Ben Franklin composed for himself in 1728. Humorously employing the language of his trade, the author states his belief that "the body of B. Franklin, printer," though presently "Food for Worms," will eventually appear "In a new and more elegant Edition / Revised and corrected, / By the Author." The vigorous, optimistic Deism of the writer is well matched by a musical style that has been aptly characterized as "forceful (and) masculine . . . in a music distinctly tonal, rhythmically energetic, and neoclassic in formal principle."[18] This style pervades the cycle, and the "Epitaph" performs a unifying function by stating the rising and falling groups of scale tones that will recur as a motto throughout the work.

Example 6.1, mm. 1–4

The key of this opening song is E minor, which Finney first employs in its natural form, giving the beginning phrases an ambiguous modal atmosphere (see Ex. 6.1). Soon, he moves through the melodic minor and further tonal alterations to a cadence on D major, in an expanded pandiatonicism (see Chapter 4, n28). This procedure together with the many dissonant non-chord tones (found throughout the cycle) are strongly reminiscent of Stravinsky in his neoclassic period.

Example 6.2, mm. 15–25

A fanciful interlude in the primarily syllabic vocal setting is the "elegant" melisma, which Finney assigns to that word in the text. A recognizable link in the musical "chain of history," it seems to look both in a backward direction toward the virtuosic embellishments of Baroque opera, as well as forward (from the eighteenth century) to Bellini's fioratura.

Example 6.3, mm. 41–45

The second setting, "Here Skugg Lies," is of another epitaph. This one was written forty-four years later during the period when Franklin, now wealthy and retired from business, served the colonies as diplomatic representative to England, the mother country whose apron strings he would soon help to untie. In 1772, the date of this writing, Franklin was a frequent visitor at Twyford, the home of Jonathan Shipley, the Bishop of Asaph. The Bishop had a son and five daughters and Franklin, a favorite with them all, had imported a grey squirrel from Philadelphia as a present for the girls. Skugg (which was a common English pet name for squirrels) had gotten out of his cage and been killed by dogs. The grieving children asked their benefactor to write an epitaph for Skugg's grave in the garden, and Franklin complied with an elaborate one that parodied the pompous style of contemporary graveyards. He then reduced it to four of the shortest and best known lines in the American tradition: "Here Skugg / Lies snug / As a bug / In a rug."

Given the brevity of the text, its repetition in the setting is not surprising. In "parlando," separated tones which suggest the staccato chattering of the squirrel, the voice has two statements of "Here Skugg / Lies snug," then finishes the text in a whispered pianissimo seemingly related to his diminutive size. The piano provides a scampering accompaniment that serves as prelude and interlude but gradually slows to a halt at the end of the one page song in imitation of Skugg's stillness in death.

Example 6.4, mm. 10–19

Number three, "Wedlock as old men note," is the first of these texts actually drawn from the almanac, and appeared as the poetic entry for May 1734. In these compact eight lines, skillfully constructed as to meter and rhyme scheme, Franklin sets forth the cynic's view of marriage, incorporating the familiar warning that "Married in haste, we oft repent at leisure." The final couplet, in a surprise ending, reminds us that the opposite is true, and that even those "married at leisure" may well "repent in haste." Interestingly, in a seeming effort to mitigate these harsh predictions by applying them to unions based on practicality rather than affection, Franklin immediately follows the poem with this adage: "Where there is marriage without love, there will be love without marriage."

Finney has employed his musical craft on the challenging poetic pentameter to recreate the rollicking 6/8 meter of the first song, which alternates the running eighth note scale steps of the motto with dotted half notes held into the next measure as if to slyly underscore a point.

Example 6.5, mm. 7–11

Most fittingly for a text written in 1734, the style of the composition is late Baroque counterpoint and indeed the opening lines are set in a canon at the unison, with the upper line of the accompaniment following the voice at the interval of a measure and a half (see Ex. 6.5). The sevenths and ninths, that, in the pianistic introduction, immediately invade the harmony make it clear, however, that this is still the eighteenth century as viewed from the twentieth.

Example 6.6, mm. 1–6

The recurring key contrast, which moves from an opening E major to several measures of C-sharp major at the vocal entry (see Ex. 6.5 and Ex. 6.6), creates a harmonic surprise forecasting the textual one that ends the poem. As a postlude, Finney cleverly restates the introduction up to the beginning of this modulation, as though to suggest the never-ending circles of human folly.

Example 6.7, mm. 54–60

The text of "Drinking Song," which follows as number four, stems from the 1740s, when Franklin was able to turn from his prospering business to the scientific and mathematical studies which interested him. At this time, he is characterized by Carl Van Doren as "something of a man of pleasure in sober Philadelphia. Comfortable at home, he was convivial in taverns, where he drank rum and Madeira, sang songs, and wrote some."[19] "Fair Venus Calls," Finney's choice, was among these—certainly an admirable example of an eighteenth-century sophisticate's drinking song. In the course of four verses, it praises love, money, and power while recognizing the essential vanity of them all, and predicting an early grave for convivial drinkers in a recurring chorus ("Friends and a bottle still bear the bell"). Notice that the composer makes one of his rare textual changes in this chorus, by omitting the word "still," which scarcely changes the sense of the line, but propels the vocal flow of the 3/2 measure which Finney interpolates into his 4/4 scheme like the sudden, unexpected lurch of a man in his cups.

Example 6.8, mm. 55–58

The composer's professed influence in this song by "Hopkinson . . . and the eighteenth century ballad songs" is readily seen in the sturdily accented rhythmic patterns, and stolid repeated tones and chordal leaps of the melodic line.

Example 6.9, mm. 6–9

The vocal contours, however, are considerably more elaborate than the earlier models (one might, for example, compare Hopkinson's "A Toast" written in honor of George Washington).[20] Further, a brief but arresting modulation from A major to D flat major which lends an invigorating change of harmonic color at the end of verses two and four, is Finney's comment on the drinking party, as an observer from the future.

The cycle having reached its dramatic climax with songs three and four, "When Mars and Venus" offers a reflective change of pace as number five. This rhymed two-line adage appeared in the 1735 edition of *Poor Richard*. Using the almanac symbols for Mars and Venus, it advised maidens to deny whatever their suitors might ask of them, in a season made astrologically dangerous by the collaboration of the deities of love and warfare. Finney now returns to the thoughtful andante of the opening song, and also employs the 6/8 meter and motto quotations of numbers one and three.

Example 6.10, mm. 1–5

These elements will return again in number seven to complete the cyclical connections. Also notable in this setting are the frequent absences of chordal thirds, which lack creates empty archaic sounding harmonies (see Ex. 6.10, mm. 1–2) and the subito pianissimo at the end of the song on the word "deny" which increases the threat in the moralist's mock warning.

Example 6.11, mm. 18–24

Number 6, "Epitaph on a Talkative Old Maid," uses the last of the *Poor Richard* texts. This one is Franklin's poetic offering for June, 1738. In his setting, Finney omits the word "her" before "cradle" in line three so that a rhythmic suspension may prepare the effect of the descriptive melisma on "talked."

Example 6.12, mm. 13–16

This song is made one of the most amusing of the seven by the employment of a Baroque-type perpetual motion figure in the piano which ebbs and flows in dynamics and degree of staccato in imitation of the lady's varied but unending conversational flow.

Example 6.13, mm. 9–12

In an artfully contrived ending, Finney has increasing numbers of rests begin to appear in the sixteenth-note groups which also get softer but do not slow down, like a machine that is beginning to fail, but is, nevertheless, loath to stop.

Example 6.14, mm. 53–57

The text of "In Praise of Wives," the closing song of the cycle, is another of Franklin's well-made ballads, this one dedicated to his faithful wife Deborah and written in 1742, the twelfth year of their marriage. It was occasioned by a remark made at "a supper of the Junto or some other convivial club . . . that they were all married men and yet singing the praise of poet's mistresses."[21] The following morning at breakfast, John Bard, who was one of the better singers among the club members, received the four verses of this song, asking him to be ready to perform it at the next meeting. The quotation of the ballad in the literary sources indicates a refrain between the verses, beginning "My dear friends, etc."[22] Finney has omitted this, but otherwise set the text verbatim, in a style that, as mentioned earlier, recalls the metric and motivic structures of all the odd numbers of the cycle.

In the course of the song, Franklin describes his wife as "my plain country Joan" and insists that virtue is more to be prized than beauty. One can only speculate as to Mrs. Franklin's reception of this aspect of his tribute. He does make it clear, however, that her many sterling qualities have made her "the joy of (his) life," and Finney matches this with vocal contours that are the most lyrical and expressive of any in the set.

Example 6.15, mm. 11–16

In fact, the high A quoted in the foregoing example is the highest point of the vocal range of *Poor Richard*. As this song, like three and four, is a strophic setting, the timbre of the cycle's close gains warmth and brilliance through the four-verse repetition of this phrase.

Charles Naginski (1909–1940)

An item in the *New York Times* of Sunday, September 8, 1940, reported the performance at Yaddo of a work by Charles Naginski: "a thirty-one year old composer who was drowned in Stockbridge Bowl in the Berkshires last month. His sinfonietta" it continued, "was performed by [the] chamber orchestra under the direction of Richard Donovan as a tribute to the gifted young composer who came to an untimely end." Indeed, the musical world had good cause to mourn its loss, for not since the death of Griffes in 1920 at the age of thirty-six had so much creative promise been cut off at such an early stage of its development.

The composer's parents were Abraham Naginski, a musician in the Russian army, and Natasha Mofshowitz whose Russian-Jewish family originated from Navharudok (now Belarus). Charles Naginski was born in Egypt, where his father had been invited to fill a position in Cairo as court musician to the Sultan. Abraham Naginski was his son's first piano teacher, and the growing boy soon began to evidence considerable talent in composition. When Charles Naginski, now eighteen years old, emigrated with his family to the United States, he soon was awarded a fellowship to study with Rubin Goldmark at Juilliard.

Goldmark, who headed the Juilliard composition department from 1924 until his death in 1936, was involved in the training of a number of promising young American composers, among them Copland, Gershwin, Giannini, Wagenaar, Kagen, and Nordoff. Goldmark was the nephew of Karl Goldmark, the Austrian composer, and although Rubin was born in New York City, he finished the training begun at City College in the country of his forbears, at the Vienna Conservatory. Never achieving great reputation himself as a composer, Rubin Goldmark nevertheless exerted a strong influence on twentieth-century American composition, and before taking up his prestigious post at Juilliard, had already left his mark on the Southwest by founding the Colorado College Conservatory in 1894.

Charles Naginski stayed at Juilliard from 1928 to 1933, the years that spanned the Institute's removal to Claremont Avenue in 1931. Before the move, it was housed in the old Vanderbilt mansion on East 52nd Street that offered too few practice rooms and eventually proved unworkable. An exciting group of students had come together at Juilliard during the period of Naginski's fellowship. It included Paul Nordoff and Sergius Kagen as well as a young singer named George Newton who retired in Indianapolis after a long performing and teaching career and died there in 1993. "Also at the Juilliard then," wrote Newton, "were Celius Dougherty and Vittorio Giannini, but I didn't know them well. They were older and buried in their work. Charles Naginski I did know fairly well," he continued. "He spoke five languages including English, all equally badly (I'm told). The Dean thought he needed help so he got us together and we traded lessons in English grammar for accompanying. He was an excellent pianist and it was a good trade for both of us. Nice fellow—tragic end."[23]

During the thirties, Naginski studied with Roger Sessions and encountered the familiar struggles of a young, unfunded composer trying to make his way in the world. Eventually, on the recommendation of Serge Koussevitsky, he was awarded a Prix de Rome in 1938 and was also in correspondence with the conductor for several years over the never-fulfilled possibility of having his music played by the Boston Symphony. He was studying with Paul Hindemith at Tanglewood during the summer session of 1940 when the tragic accident occurred in August.

At the time of his death, he had completed two symphonies, a poem and a suite for orchestra, a ballet called *The Minotaur*, several works for chamber groups and chamber orchestra, and a number of remarkable songs. What was remarkable about them was not only the innate gifts of arresting harmonic, melodic, and structural invention which they demonstrated. Even more surprising, in a man who was not native born and spoke so many languages, was the depth of his understanding of and response to American poetry, and the force and precision with which he was able to interpret it in musical terms.

Walt Whitman (1819–1892)

Chapter 2 treats Walt Whitman in connection with a Charles Ives setting. Ives may very possibly have been the first American composer to set to music the seemingly problematical verse of Whitman, but many followed in his footsteps in the course of the twentieth century. One might, in fact, conjecture that Charles Naginski could have become acquainted with the Ives songs when they were first introduced to the public by Aaron Copland at a Yaddo festival in the mid-1930s. Whether or not this was the initiating course of events, we find Naginski composing two powerful Whitman settings, both of which were published posthumously by G. Schirmer in 1942.[24]

The titles of the songs and the poems were the same: "Look down, fair moon" and "The Ship Starting," and both poems were included in the collection called *Drum Taps* which Whitman published in 1865. The decade preceding had been a momentous time for the poet, as it encompassed the first three editions of *Leaves of Grass* (1855, 1856, 1860) and several years of dedicated service to the wounded soldiers in the field and army hospitals of the Civil War. In an essay called "The Last of the War Cases"[25] Whitman portrays the terrible plight of these men, who were more often dying of starvation or diseases contracted in the hospitals than of their battle wounds. So great is his compassion for them, and so deep his horror of their fate that one is brought to remember that Elias Hicks, the fiery dissenting Quaker preacher, had been a strong influence on the poet's parents and the subject of an essay by Whitman himself.[26] The truth is that Walt Whitman, although drawn to the "inner light" doctrines of the Quakers, was not a pacifist. He, in fact, believed strongly in the Union cause, and had begun his hospital visits solely as a result of seeking out his brother George who had been reported wounded on the Virginia front.

"Look down, fair moon" is a four-line poetic summary of the horrors of war, as it exhorts the moonlight, usually the accompaniment of love scenes, to pour its "nimbus floods" on the ghastly faces of dead men "on their backs with arms tossed wide." Naginski's setting is short (two pages) and structured in a tight, almost ceremonial ABA form that seems to relate to man's effort to bear the agonies of the human condition by providing them with an artistic shape. As a part of this formal emphasis the composer chooses to repeat the poem's first line ("Look down, fair moon, and bathe this scene") at the end of the song, and it might also be noted that the original poem had read "*their* arms tossed wide," while the italicized word was deleted from the 1881 edition. The two A sections of the form—the piano introduction and postlude—are highly chromatic with clashing polytonal elements in the broken chords. The slow tempo and very soft, dynamic level of this keyboard dissonance gives it an ominous and chilling coloristic effect.

Example 6.16, mm. 1–3

In sharp contrast, the B section, which contains the text, is completely diatonic, based on the Aeolian mode. This harmonic context, along with the narrow range and repetitions of the vocal line, provides a reference to the Gregorian style which augments the ceremonial aspect of the song suggested earlier.

Example 6.17, mm. 4–6

Set against the liturgical suggestion, however, are the regularly metric, and therefore un-chant-like, hypnotic octaves of the accompaniment's bass line (see Ex. 6.17). These prepare a climactic leap of an octave to a mezzo forte outcry: a dramatic moment of protest at the fate of these dead, made the more appalling by its juxtaposition with the appellation "*Sacred* moon."

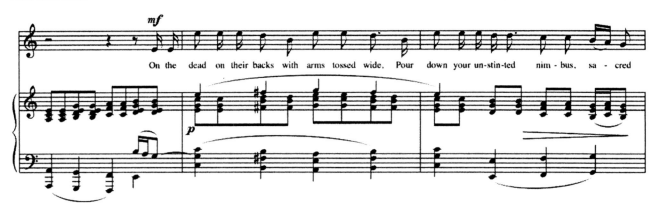

Example 6.18, mm. 10–12

Notice that the piano introduction concludes with superimposed chords of the tonic and dominant that prepare the vocal entrance in A minor (Example 6.17, m. 5). The second A section, however, takes a different harmonic turn to conclude with a series of diminished chords that trail off into the silence of the unspeakable.

Despite its title, the collection *Drum Taps* was, from the outset, not limited to war poems. "The Ship Starting" is among those based on other subjects. In the 1881 edition of *Leaves of Grass*, it was published in the section called "Inscriptions," which had become the title for the opening group of poems. The sea, ships, and journeys over water had long fascinated Whitman, and in these four lines he evokes "the unbounded sea" and the visual splendor of the vessel beginning to move across it with sails and pennant flying. One of the elements that Naginski uses to produce the effect of the ship's initial lumbering and lurching is a cross-rhythmic pattern which is duple in the voice line and triple in the accompaniment:

Example 6.19, mm. 1–2

As it begins to "speed so stately," the "emulous waves" are heard in the swooping scales of the piano part that are reminiscent of keyboard figures used by Ives in "The Swimmers" (see chapter 2).

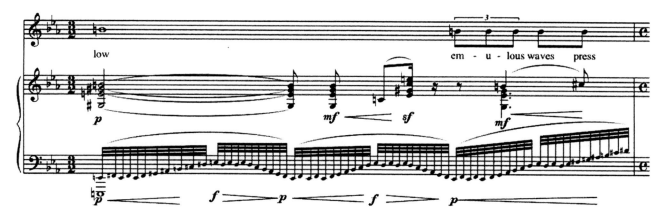

Example 6.20, m. 11

Over this instrumental turbulence, the vocal writing remains quite declamatory with much stepwise motion and repetition, either of single notes, or, as in the opening, of the interval of a fifth (see Ex. 6.19). Also in Example 6.19 may be seen the characteristic accented sevenths and ninths of the accompaniment that imitate the clashing noises of the launching. In this song, Naginski eschews a piano introduction and plunges into the song with the force of sudden movement, but he allows the rolling cascades of scales to continue at the end, while the vocal line dives into the foaming waters.

Example 6.21, mm. 16–17

Carl Sandburg (1878–1967)

The initial treatment of Carl Sandburg occurs in chapter 3, where his literary ties to Walt Whitman are discussed. It is also true that there are strong parallels in the life experiences of Whitman and Sandburg. Each had haphazard early schooling, held jobs of all descriptions including manual labor, and engaged primarily in newspaper work to support their early poetic efforts. Even more coincidentally, each was thirty-six years old at the time of his first major publication: Whitman's *Leaves of Grass* which appeared in 1855, and Sandburg's first group of verse, published in a 1914 issue of *Poetry* magazine. Two years later, this group was expanded into the now famous *Chicago Poems*, the source of the text for Naginski's only published Sandburg setting.[27]

"Under the harvest moon" is not typical of the *Chicago Poems* in which Carl Sandburg celebrated the world and speech of the American workingman with the attendant coarseness and ugliness of his twentieth-century environment. Rather, it seems to be a forerunner of some of the more sensitive lyrics of *Cornhuskers* (1918), characterized by one critic as "delicate perceptions of beauty (in which) raw violence is restrained to the point of half-withheld mysticism."[28] The poem is in two contrasting stanzas which portray the natural world's embodiment of life's mysteries: the "soft silver" of the harvest moon whispering of Death "as a beautiful friend," and the "flagrant crimson" of summer roses posing the "unanswerable questions" of love.

There are two main stresses in each of Sandburg's lines but the language has a free, speech-like prosodic flow, against which such highly poetic images as "Death, the gray mocker," and "the dusk of the wild, red leaves," take on a heightened intensity. Naginski clothes this poetic rhythm in flexible, changing vocal patterns that include many triplets and pairs of sixteenth notes (see "shimmering" in m. 4):

Example 6.22, mm. 1–6

The seemingly free flow is unified within an overall 4/4 meter with only one two-measure interpolation of 3/2. The latter occurs with Naginski's inspired characterization of Death, which takes the form of a long, mystical cantillation on the piano, sensuously unraveling as the vocal contour dreamily settles on the dominant harmony.

Example 6.23, mm. 9–10

This cantillation recurs at the end of the song where it expands by means of strummed piano chords. The expansion is needed to accommodate Sandburg's additional concluding line of verse two—a verbal lingering over the "thousand memories" of love, and their attendant questions.

Example 6.24, mm. 21–27

The suggested sound of an exotic folk instrument is implicit in the broken chordal effects and rapid, running passages of the two preceding examples. This atmosphere is deepened by the harmonic and melodic employment of the raised fourth degree of the scale, which is a derivation from the Lydian mode common in Slavic folk song (see the G-sharps of Ex. 6.22). Here, then, is an instance of American art song, originally heavily dependent on British and later German musical models, widening its circle of incoming influences to include Eastern Europe, for further enrichment.

Sara Teasdale (1884–1933)

An interesting corollary to this song is an extremely effective setting by Naginski of "Night Song at Amalfi." [29] This poem comes from Sara Teasdale's *Riders to the Sea*, a collection she published in 1915, just before her anthology of women's love poetry (see chapter 5). In this, probably one of Teasdale's best known lyrics, the poet asks the stars and the sea "what I should give my love" and is answered, to her dismay, by silence. Naginski's musical treatment is triggered by the word "song" in the title, a choice that attests to the manner in which Sara Teasdale usually thought of her poetry, as discussed in chapter 5. In a flexible rhythmic pattern of varying meters, he creates an improvisatory vocal line whose contours are very similar to the instrumental cantillations quoted here. This melodic construction also draws on the raised Lydian fourth, as well as the augmented seventh degree of the harmonic minor scale—an interval which contributes heavily to the poignancy of Eastern European folk music. The piano writing consists of only a few soft, punctuating chords, many of which are bare open fifths. The effect is simply, but brilliantly calculated to suggest a native singer, engaging in a gentle lament to his strummed instrument, the phrases of which fade in and out of a surrounding and threatening "silence."

Sergius Kagen (1908–1964)

No one in the United States who has been seriously involved with vocal literature during the past fifty years is unfamiliar with the name of Sergius Kagen. Yet, despite his formidable reputation as a coach, accompanist, teacher, and editor, there are relatively few people who know that he was also the composer of a substantial catalog of vocal works, which includes forty-eight songs, three cycles, and two operas. [30]

The Russian Revolution is responsible for the rich contributions of Sergius Kagen to the American musical scene. His father, Isaiah Kagen, was a Lithuanian Jew who had come to the university in St. Petersburg, and remained there as a reporter on and later owner of the *Petersburg Leaf*. Vera Lipshitz, his mother, was Russian-born, and a brilliant student of languages and literature at the university when she and Kagen met and they married. Isaiah's devoutly Jewish parents never accepted Vera, a self-styled atheist and soon-to-be active member of the Communist Party, but the Kagens prospered financially, and had three sons: Mark, Boris, and Sergius. All were flourishing in the atmosphere of a loving, affluent, intellectual home, complete with summers in a pleasant villa on the River Luga, when the Revolution irrevocably altered the peaceful fabric of their lives. Mark, the eldest son, who had been a promising young pianist, was killed in 1917 fighting the White Russians, and Vera, who perhaps blamed his death on her own political involvement, did not leave her room for an entire year. Onto Sergius's nine-year-old shoulders now fell the task of trying to replace his talented older brother and, his parents having enrolled him in the Petersburg Conservatory under Glazunov's personal supervision, he undertook it with great energy.

The famine and destruction attendant on the Revolution decimated the Petersburg population and two of Sergius' aunts together with their families did not survive the cataclysm. By 1920, the Isaiah Kagens were forced to seek an uncertain sanctuary in Berlin, which they reached with great hardship after traveling for several months in cattle cars. Sergius, still only twelve, had already experienced an emotional and historical lifetime. He emerged from it, and from his mother's intellectual fostering, with a drive toward artistic excellence and the capacity to endure the discomfort of unrelenting hard work. Another formative influence had been Vera's fears and superstitions that had caused the boy while still in Russia to be educated at home under a "nanny's" supervision. Sergius developed, as a result of the isolation, a somewhat shy and retiring personality that precluded easy intimacy, but at the same time were planted the seeds of stubborn, independent thinking. Later they would blossom into a remarkable career.

In Berlin, Sergius enrolled at the Hochschule für Musik to study piano with Leonid Kreutzer, while his father became a partner in a loan corporation. The business failed to prosper in an economy still weak from the effects of World War I, and increasingly hostile to both Jews and Russians. By 1922, the Isaiah Kagens began to emigrate, one at a time, to the United States, leaving the fifteen-year-old Sergius alone in Germany for a period of time. Finally settled in New York City, the young man undertook a routine of keeping house for his working parents, and practicing the piano, but even in that musical center found no one who drew him as a teacher until he heard the playing of Carl Friedberg,[31] in the late twenties. Friedberg taught at Juilliard, which was heavily endowed and therefore free to those passing the entrance examinations. In an audition now become legendary, Kagen began to play through the entire forty-eight preludes and fugues of Bach's *Well Tempered Clavier*, and was accepted when his intention and ability to execute it became clear to the judges.

Kagen's experience as a Juilliard student during the years 1930–1934 was, like all of his previous life to that point, a mixture of trauma and inspiration. The centrally important relationship with Carl Friedberg, his teacher, proceeded well on a personal level, but proved musically disappointing. Kagen, whose technique had been largely self-taught according to the traditions of the Petersburg Conservatory through Leschetizsky, had difficulty assimilating the technical instructions of his teacher. This was because Friedberg himself did not play as he taught, but based his extraordinary pianistic communication on the ability to form a clear mental image of the composition and on a total intellectual grasp of the score, which enabled the free operation of musical instinct in performance.[32] These principles later became cornerstones of Kagen's own teaching but while he was in the process of formulating them, he was sufficiently discouraged by the problems with his professor, and by his lack of perfect pitch among a group of students who mostly possessed it, to contemplate abandoning music as a career.

Kagen's highly developed critical faculties and independent thinking led him, in fact, to a clash with Frank Damrosch in a conducting class, which was nearly disastrous. Damrosch was the director of the Institute, and expelled Kagen after a heated exchange of insults in German, whereupon Carl Friedberg arranged for him to be admitted to the Juilliard Graduate School to complete his diploma in piano. Over and against these struggles, however, were the two very rewarding experiences of the composer's student days. One was friendship with fellow students, and among the most important of these friends was Charles Naginski, foreign-born like himself, and struggling to gain a foothold in American music. Naginski was the witness at his wedding to Genevieve Greer in 1937, and one can well imagine the depth of Kagen's grief at the loss of his young friend just three years later.

The other great light, which not only illuminated Kagen's life as a student but determined the direction of his unique career and contributions to music, was Marcella Sembrich, the brilliant recital and opera singer who was seventy-four at the time of their meeting. At the suggestion of Naginski, who could not work with her, Kagen tried out, successfully, as an accompanist for her Juilliard students, and the two worked closely together until her death in 1935. Their European backgrounds gave them a common experience and Sembrich could speak to the young man both in German and in her native Polish which was enough like Russian for him to understand it. Marcella Sembrich became probably his most important teacher and from her he learned the vocal literature and how it should be performed. At her death, he became the purveyor of the rich tradition, and the career of Sergius Kagen as professional accompanist, coach, and teacher began to flourish. Genevieve Greer, who became Mrs. Kagen,[33] had been a Sembrich student, and many of her other students whom Kagen had accompanied in her New York studio and Lake George summer home, continued working with him at her passing. Several were Metropolitan Opera stars, and there was scarcely a well-known singer in the thirties and forties whom Kagen did not accompany in Town Hall recitals or on short tours out of New York.

His teaching connections with Juilliard grew from part-time to full faculty status in 1940 and his areas of pedagogy continued to increase. Beginning as a vocal coach and instructor of a lieder class for singers, he eventually became a member of the voice faculty and also developed a training program for accompanists,[34] which has since been emulated by any number of graduate music departments around the country. John Hanks, professor of voice at Duke University (see chapter 5), was profoundly influenced by Sergius Kagen's vocal literature classes at Juilliard, of which he was a member both before and after his service in World War II (1941 and 1946).[35] These highly organized, demanding classes for which each student had to prepare five or six songs twice a week, became the model for a similar course at Duke in the mid-1960s in which R. Friedberg participated as accompanist and teacher of student accompanists. Professor Hanks remembered Kagen as a man who spoke English with a slight accent, and, in the European fashion, was impersonal and rarely complimentary in class. His criticisms of the performances included matters vocal and interpretative. Always, he stressed communication of the text, and his command of European languages was of great help in training these American singers to be expressive in the foreign bodies of literature.

By the end of the forties, Kagen began assembling in book form the gleanings of his fantastically wide experience as teacher and performer. In close succession, he published *Music for the Voice*[36] his descriptive list of concert and teaching material; *On Studying Singing*,[37] a distillation of his basic philosophy which he planned for many years and wrote in three weeks; and the opening collections in the International Publishing Company's series of song and aria editions which would eventually number thirty-nine volumes. His life as a performer was still active, and from 1940 to 1950, he was a member and unofficial director of the original Bach Aria Group, whose singers were drawn from his students. The fifties also saw a memorable recital collaboration with the American baritone, Mack Harrell,[38] who was a colleague of Kagen's on the Juilliard faculty, as well as the writing of many articles for the *Juilliard Review*. All of this frenetic, "in season" activity, was counterbalanced by soul-restoring summers in Vermont, where the Kagens rented peaceful but spartan quarters for many years. Money was always tight, for the brilliant musician was an indifferent businessman, and depended on his wife to manage most of the affairs of daily living, including driving the family car. For the last four years of his life, Sergius Kagen finally owned a summer home with some of the creature comforts such as electricity and a screened porch. The couple planned to retire there, but in March 1964, Kagen woke with a scream seemingly from one of the occasional nightmares that had plagued him all his life. In reality, it was the final episode of a heart condition he had had for a number of years. His labors at an end, Kagen was buried in his beloved Vermont.

In an article titled "The American Concert Song," Sergius Kagen expressed in 1954 his long-held conviction that "the concert song is a stepchild of contemporary American music."[39] He deplored the dearth of "musically fine songs in English" which could serve as models for young composers, and categorized the available, but undesirable American songs as either light-weight "salon" types in the Chaminade style or "wild" songs with tormented and unsingable vocal lines.[40] According to Professor Hanks, Kagen's vocal literature classes in the forties indeed contained no American songs, as though he considered none worthy of attention. Interestingly, however, at the end of the 1954 article Kagen expressed his optimism about the future "for in the last few years," he stated, "a number of startlingly good songs has appeared in America."[41] In 1949, in response to his wife's challenge, Sergius Kagen had begun to write his own songs, and this, the most creative of all his varied enterprises, brought him the greatest satisfaction during the last fifteen years of his life.

After having played all the finest songs of the Western vocal tradition in superlative fashion for two decades, Kagen's aim in starting to compose his own was twofold. He wanted to help develop a literature of "serious" but vocally grateful songs in English, and he also wanted to be among those involved in creating a recognizably American style in the art song. Like many of the foreign-born, Sergius Kagen had deep emotional ties to the adopted country that had tried and tested, but also nurtured him. His wife, Genevieve, had been born in Davis, Oklahoma, and her family background was partly American Indian: a heritage as close to the ethnic roots of the New World as it was possible to come. Kagen was drawn to this, and to the literary heritage of America as well. Almost 75 percent of his songs are based on American texts, and they are, for the most part, settings of poems that he had known well and loved for a good many years. They include the works of a healthy cross section of American poetry, ranging from Whitman and Dickinson in the nineteenth century, through Sandburg, Teasdale, cummings, and MacLeish, to Langston Hughes and James Agee, his close contemporaries in the twentieth century. The poems that he chose for setting, with the exception of the *Three Satires* cycle, were for the most part somber, reflective, or dramatic in tone. Kagen, in his rejection of the "salon" style that he also characterized as "encore" songs, was clearly determined to avoid the frivolous in his own work. Another overall aspect of his songwriting is interesting to observe at the outset. In direct contrast to the songs of John Duke that frequently display an elaborate pianism, Sergius Kagen's place all emphasis on the text and vocal line. The man who spent his life giving inconspicuous but invaluable support to singers continued this position in writing accompaniments which are sparse enough to highlight the voice, but which unfailingly outline the singer's notes.

Walt Whitman (1819–1892)

The five settings of Whitman, Sandburg, and Teasdale about to be discussed were all written during the flood-tide years of 1949 and 1950 that produced a total of forty-one songs. The Whitman fragment, "I Think I Could Turn . . ."[42] is the only instance of Kagen setting this poet, and the lines are taken from "Song of Myself," the central poem of *Leaves of Grass*.[43] In them, Whitman turns from his celebration of himself and his fellow men to extol the virtues of animals who, "placid and self-contained . . . do not whine about their condition (nor) weep for their sins," and are nowhere "respectable or unhappy over the whole earth." The poet continues to marvel that "not one is demented with the mania of owning things" nor do they "make me sick discussing their duty to God." It is easy to see why these iconoclastic sentiments, striking at America's prevailing materialism and pietism, would have had great appeal to Kagen whose family had suffered much from humanity's religious and political devotions, and who had chosen a life of artistic excellence over financial comfort.

The setting is a prime example of the careful prosody that characterizes all of the composer's word setting. The vocal line is declamatory, with many repeated notes, and a flexible use of meter and rhythms within measures to conform to Whitman's free flow of American speech patterns.

Example 6.25, mm. 15–17

The song is unified by a tonal, but chromatic walking bass pattern which seems to suggest the measured placidity of the animal world and which is repeated at different pitch levels. These sequences take on a rising curve as the fortissimo climax expresses the madness of those obsessed by possessions (see Ex. 6.25). Kagen repeats the opening two lines of the poem to create an ABA form and as the vocal line returns from storming protest to philosophic musing, the walking bass trails off on a scalar descent in the Phrygian mode, but stops a frustrated half step from musical and emotional completion.

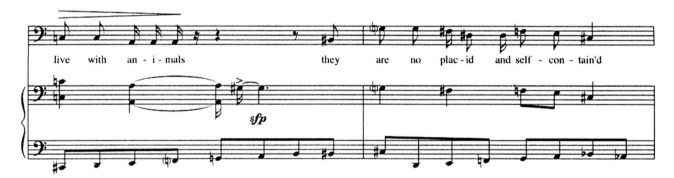

Example 6.26, mm. 26–30

Carl Sandburg (1878–1967)

Kagen's harmonic style throughout his song catalog which is heavily chromatic, often atonal, and at times serial, indicates that he was in touch with twentieth-century trends of the musical avant-garde that had grown out of Richard Strauss and Scriabin toward Schoenberg and his school. He was equally aware of developments in contemporary poetry, and became an early fan of Carl Sandburg. The poet's "plain speech" and sympathy for the common man touched a responsive chord in this highly cultivated musician whose life had been ruled by economic and historic forces beyond his control. "Mag"[44] is a moving dramatic monologue from Sandburg's *Chicago Poems*: the lament of a man who has been brought, by the grinding daily struggle of poverty, to wish that he had never married, and that "the kids had never come." The desperate outpouring is powerfully set by Kagen in a series of rising waves, with vocal contours that arch over every "wish" and settle back in discouragement on the minor triads of E-flat, B-flat and F-sharp.

Example 6.27, mm. 1–8

The portrayal of the speaker's mental anguish is intensified by the clashing, polytonal underpinning of an ostinato figure in the pianist's left hand, which begins as octaves (see Ex. 6.27) but changes to dissonant major sevenths behind his peaks of desperation.

Example 6.28, mm. 25–28

Sandburg ends the poem with his litany-like refrain, "I wish to God I never saw you, Mag. / I wish to God the kids had never come." Kagen lets this die away dynamically as though through the speaker's exhaustion, but saves a complex of clashing seconds and ninths in the accompaniment and a vocal leap of an augmented fourth for the final measures. The effect is that of a mind tormented beyond further protest or endurance, and trying to slip into oblivion.

Example 6.29, mm. 36–39

Sandburg's *Chicago Poems* had been the occasion of critical derision at their publication in 1916. By the appearance of the *Good Morning, America* collection in 1928, Carl Sandburg had been accepted into the mainstream of American literature, and indeed its title poem was read at a Harvard Phi Beta Kappa investiture. Kagen's setting of "Maybe"[45] from this collection is his shortest song (one page) and a contrast in every way to "Mag." This poem is also a monologue, but the speaker here is a young girl, rather coyly speculating on whether or not her suitor will propose, and what her answer will be. This is a totally diatonic setting without a single chromatic alteration. The resulting modal melodic structures lend an Elizabethan/Appalachian flavor of ancient innocence to the song, as do the "Scotch-snap" rhythmic figures (sixteenth followed by dotted eighth), which intensify the suggestion of British folk origins.

Example 6.30, mm. 1–5

The accompaniment, however, employs soft dissonant intervals and superimposed chordal elements to establish the twentieth century, and the uncertainty of the speaker's manipulative state of mind (see Ex. 6.30). Meter changes are again characteristically frequent, and the vocal line moves in appropriately melting, legato dotted note and triplet rhythmic patterns. A lone measure of pianistic melody echoes and telescopes the preceding vocal phrase and seems, by its poignant pleading, to prepare the decision to "say yes."

Example 6.31, mm. 10–14

Sara Teasdale (1884–1933)

The two poems by Sara Teasdale that Kagen chose for setting stem from an inner environment of delicate perceptions that is a far cry from Whitman's and Sandburg's world of strong, primary colors and basic, everyday reality. Both of the poems, however, are founded in regret, and the certain knowledge of the impermanence of natural beauty and human emotion. Interestingly, "A June Day"[46] is a setting of a short lyric from the collection *Stars Tonite* of 1930 that was subtitled *Verses for Boys and Girls* (see chapter 5). The poem is, basically, an exquisite verbal description of the sights and sounds "Down where the river sleeps in the reeds," during the passage from morning to "blue night" of an early summer day. The only jarring note in this peace and beauty occurs in the final couplet where "the day was ended / That never will come again," and it is worthy of note that Teasdale does not spare her young audience this disquieting thought.

Kagen's setting takes off from the opening line, "I heard a red-winged blackbird singing," and creates a background of pianistic bird-song that weaves in and out behind the voice and also provides the instrumental introduction and postlude.

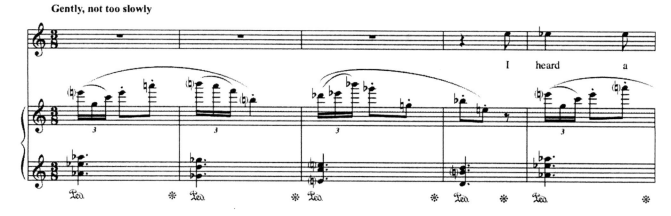

Example 6.32, mm. 1–5

The high tessitura of the vocal line and accompaniment (all above middle C) approach the vibratory range of the black-bird's singing while the rapid rhythmic patterns in short, disjointed, often leaping groups of notes, suggest his darting and hopping.

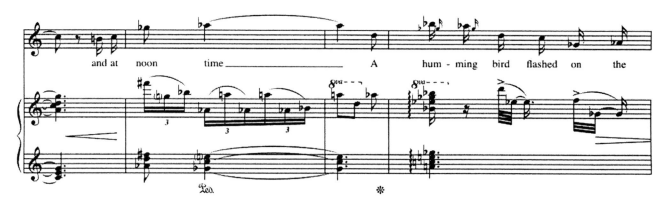

Example 6.33, mm. 16–19

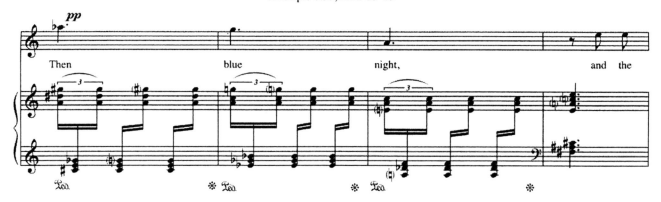

Example 6.34, mm. 30–33

A lyrical melodic curve descends with the fall of "blue night," (see Ex. 6.34) and the returning bird-song of the postlude consigns the day to memory. All of the foregoing is saved from triteness or banality by Kagen's harmonic skill in ma-nipulating the polytonality that pervades this setting. For the most part, the left hand of the accompaniment and the vocal line derive from the same chordal formations, while the right hand superimposes highly clashing structures often a minor ninth apart (see Ex. 6.32, m. 5). The result is a suspended, objective, and universal quality in the setting that throws the lush images of Teasdale's poem into sharp relief, as the more romantic treatments often afforded her poetry frequently fail to do.

"Let It Be Forgotten"[47] sets another eight-line poem, this time from Teasdale's *Flame and Shadow*, a collection published in 1920, at the height of her popularity. In this gently enigmatic lyric, the poet never states just what is to be forgotten "as a fire that once was singing gold." One can easily imagine, however, that with the passage of six years since the beginning of her disappointing marriage, Teasdale had long given up her early dream of a fulfilling love relationship. In one of her most telling lines, which ends verse one, she in fact states the credo of her remaining years: "Time is a kind friend, he will make us old."

The apparent simplicity of Kagen's setting of this poetry is the source of its artistic force. The dynamic level is mostly quiet, and the voice line moves over a fairly narrow range in quasi-recitative fashion as the piano strikes soft, intermittent chords. Kagen's command of his free-flowing prosody suggests an intimate acquaintance with Monteverdi, for he has succeeded in adapting the expressive plasticity of the *stile recitativo* to the aesthetic climate of the mid-twentieth century. Quartal[48] harmonies are prevalent in the chordal constructions and their empty ambivalence supports the poet's withdrawal of psychic energy.

Example 6.35, mm. 1–4

The end of the song decreases the movement of the already slow tempo by augmenting the length of the vocal notes, as the half-note triplet on "hushed foot-fall" almost drags to a halt.

Example 6.36, mm. 23–27

The three final bi-tonal piano chords unify the song as they recall the opening sequence at a lower pitch, and their wispy evanescence seems to complete the process of forgetting.

Paul Nordoff (1909–1977)

Paul Nordoff was born in Philadelphia and was largely raised by his grandmother who was from upstate Pennsylvania. One of his strongest childhood memories was of her standing at the foot of his bed and reciting poetry to him before saying goodnight.[49] Poetry, then, was an early and familiar friend, and, as a consequence, the medium of song became a highly congenial one to the composer.

Nordoff, whose musical talents were developing rapidly, entered the Philadelphia Conservatory of Music at the age of fourteen to study piano with Olga Samaroff, the great American pianist and teacher who had been born under the name of Hickenlooper in San Antonio, Texas. In 1929, Nordoff joined Charles Naginski as a fellowship student in composition of Rubin Goldmark's at Juilliard, having been brought to Goldmark's attention on the strength of his settings of German and French poetry. George Newton remembered Nordoff as well as Naginski and Kagen, and recalled that he "tried to get him to write some music that a basso could sing." Apparently, Paul Nordoff's talents as a song composer had already been recognized by faculty and fellow students alike.

In 1932, Nordoff completed his master of music degree at Juilliard and on the basis of Guggenheim fellowships awarded him in 1933 and 1935, was able to travel and compose in Europe. Germany seemed an initially hospitable environment. He concertized with a Munich singer and became friendly with the last grand Duke of Hesse. By 1937, however, with Hitler's political ambitions becoming ominously clear, Nordoff left Germany, after arranging for the publication of twelve of his songs by Schott and Company. Back in America, he was appointed, at the age of twenty-nine, to head the composition department of the Philadelphia Conservatory, where fifteen years earlier he had entered as an aspiring student. Nordoff held this position for five years and resigned in 1943. The year 1945 saw him entering the world of university music as assistant professor at Michigan State College; it was also the year of his marriage to Sabina Zay, a union which produced three children.[50] His second and last university-level appointment was as professor of music at Bard College, a small, well-endowed liberal arts school at Annandale-on-Hudson, and he served in this capacity from 1948 to 1959. No doubt on sabbatical from the college, he was one of the first composers to take advantage of the Mac-Dowell Colony's new winter facilities, and his residence there of several months was reported by the *Musical Courier* of January 15, 1956.

The rise of Nordoff's teaching career was paralleled by his growing reputation as a composer. During the forties and fifties, he was commissioned to write ballets for both Martha Graham and Agnes de Mille, an opera for Columbia University, and orchestral works for the Louisville and New Orleans symphonies.[51] There were also several chamber works composed during this period, as well as some piano pieces and a large number of songs. But paralleling Nordoff's success as a conventional composer in those years was his growing interest in the spiritual teachings of Rudolph Steiner's Anthroposophy,[52] and their practical applications to the education of handicapped children. Having been led further in this direction by information concerning the central nervous system's strong response to music in children with cerebral palsy, Paul Nordoff enrolled in the Combs College of Music in Philadelphia, and in 1960 emerged with a bachelor's degree in music therapy, and a new life. The years that remained to him were spent working with severely handicapped children in many institutions in the United States and Europe. Together with his collaborator, Clive Robbins, he wrote a number of articles and books describing the work,[53] as well as several musical plays and many play-songs designed for use in the therapeutic situation.[54]

Nordoff's drastic change of his musical focus evoked very mixed reactions from his friends and artistic colleagues. e.e. cummings, with whom he had had a close relationship for fifteen years and who adored the Nordoff settings of his poetry,[55] never came to understand the seeming desertion. On the other hand, Mrs. Nellie Lee (Curtis) Bok,[56] who was, in mid-century, a leading Philadelphia patron of the arts, described her longtime friend as a self-sacrificing and saintly man[57] and opened her home to him whenever he returned to Philadelphia. It was on such an occasion (February 5, 1975)[58] that R. Friedberg had the privilege of meeting Paul Nordoff, who was at that time under treatment at the University of Pennsylvania Hospital for the malignancy which took his life two years later. The interior of the narrow, redbrick Philadelphia townhouse was dark with faded opulence and the composer a gaunt shadow of the person shown in earlier photographs, but he spoke of writing songs with great warmth and played his own on an ancient, mellow Steinway. In studying many songs, Nordoff said, he had realized that "a composer tells you something about himself when he chooses a poem; he says 'this means something to me.' Debussy's (choices) tell us much about his humour and loneliness and great spirit." He went on to observe that he had continued to write songs all his life (two more e.e. cummings settings were completed even during his years as a therapist) despite the fact that "publishers ignore them because they don't sell. They should publish them anyway," said Nordoff, with heated emphasis.

The composer's expressed frustration was easy to understand. Of the dozens of Nordoff songs listed in his ASCAP catalog, only twenty, plus the ten of *Anthony's Song Book* (see n50), have ever been published. A recent effort in England to bring a number of the e.e. cummings settings to publication seems as yet unfruitful. Of the published songs, three are to texts by Conrad Aiken, whose early poetry, suffused as it was with verbal musical images, seemed to evoke the desire in the young composer to clothe it in actual music.

Conrad Aiken (1889–1973)

The life of Conrad Aiken was a strange mixture of conservative academic and literary events set over against bizarre personal incident. He was born in Savannah to parents who were transplanted New Englanders: a brilliant physician father, and an attractive mother who was the daughter of a Massachusetts Congregational minister. Conrad was the eldest of three sons and his mother's favorite. One can well imagine the effect on the boy, then eleven-and-a-half years old, of discovering his parents dead after the father had committed murder followed by suicide. The two younger brothers having been adopted by a Philadelphia family, Conrad now reclaimed his New England heritage and went to live with a great, great aunt in New Bedford, Massachusetts.

In 1907, he entered Harvard with an illustrious class that included Heywood Broun, Walter Lippmann, and John Reed. Having discovered his literary talents when he composed a poem at nine, Aiken now developed them with extensive contributions to the *Harvard Advocate* and *Monthly*. Placed on probation during his senior year for cutting classes to complete a poetic undertaking, Aiken resigned in protest, spent six months traveling in Europe, and returned to complete his Harvard degree in 1912. A few days after graduation, he married Jessie McDonald who, as the first of the poet's three wives, would also become the mother of his three children.

Conrad Aiken, throughout his career, had what is only dreamt of by most men of literature—a small independent income that made it possible for him to develop a richly varied career without the usual strains of financial necessity. Poetry was his earliest medium and one to which he would return throughout his life. In 1914, just as America's poetic renaissance was dawning, he published *Earth Triumphant*, and by 1920, there were five more collections of his verse in print. Briefly attracted to the Imagist movement, he moved, in 1915, from Cambridge to Boston to be near John Gould Fletcher, and for the next half-dozen years developed acquaintanceships with Pound, Eliot, Lowell, and others involved in the "new" poetry. In 1922, he took his family for a three-year stay in England and returned there in the thirties with his third wife, Mary Hoover (an artist), to conduct the Jeake's House Summer School for a small number of writers and painters. World War II forced the removal of this school to South Dennis, Cape Cod. Ironically, the second major war of the century had caught up with the man who had been exempted from service in the first on the grounds of his claim that poetry was "an essential industry."

Other than the summer school, Aiken's only formal teaching position was a year spent as an English instructor at Harvard in 1927–1928. This left his energies free to be invested in the many volumes of poetry and fiction he produced, as well as in extensive activities as editor and critic. From 1916 to 1919, he was a contributing editor to *The Dial*; during the twenties and thirties, he served as American or London correspondent to various periodicals on either side of the Atlantic; and between all of his own writing tasks, he found time to edit anthologies of American and English poetry. Although critical approbation was a long time coming to Conrad Aiken, by the age of sixty the literary world had begun to recognize his considerable achievements. He served as Consultant in Poetry to the Library of Congress from 1950 to 1952, and during the following two decades received many awards, such as the Bollingen Prize (1956), Academy of American Poets Fellowship (1957), and National Medal for Literature (1969).

From our present vantage point, it becomes easy to see that Conrad Aiken's early neglect was largely due to the initially overshadowing reputations of his contemporaries such as Ezra Pound and T. S. Eliot, and to the fact that he "refused to yield to the temptation to become fashionable."[59] Extraordinarily gifted as to the technique of his craft, Aiken also brought a deep interest in psychoanalytical theory (likely stemming from his childhood trauma) to bear on the poetic writings with the result that "no one has so exhaustively . . . explored the problems of the modern consciousness."[60] However, in the early poetry, from which the Nordoff settings are drawn, Aiken was still involved in the attempt to "formulate independent modes and philosophies."[61] Since childhood, he had been "passionately fond of music,"[62] and at thirteen had come under the influence of Edgar Allan Poe, a poet whose obsession with the "music" of words is discussed in the Introduction. It is not surprising then, that Conrad Aiken should attempt to infuse many parallels from the art of music—its forms, thematic structures, rhythmic patterns and tone-colors—into the poetic language and constructions of his early collections. He made his intentions clear by the inclusion of such words as "nocturne," "symphony" and "prelude" in his poetic titles, and suggested further musical allusions by the use of sectional repetition and a heavy reliance on mnemonic values.

In 1942, Paul Nordoff published "White Nocturne,"[63] one of his finest songs, to a poetic text from Aiken's volume called *Nocturne of Remembered Spring and Other Poems* (1917). The title of the poem indicates the writer's intention to combine the musical suggestion of a subdued, melancholy "night-piece" and visual, coloristic elements with his verbal material. The color effects, all overwhelmingly "white," are created by images of falling snow, pale hands, and the petals of white flowers, while the subdued tone of melancholy derives from the dramatic portrait which unfolds of a man and woman saddened by their knowledge of change and time passing. Nordoff has actually set only the twelve lines of section four, out of a poem that in its entirety runs to six sections and 143 lines. By this choice, he achieved a text which was the perfect length for a song, and which became a brief lyric expressing the memory of an exquisite moment, without the "sense of terror, and of death"[64] that is always strong in Aiken and that pervades the rest of the poem.

Section four, which begins "I would like to touch this snow with the wind of a dream," is, like the rest of "White Nocturne," made up of five-stress lines which employ varying rhyme schemes occasionally and inconsistently. In the original printing, line two read "With a sudden warmth of music and turn it all" but by the time it was reprinted in collections, Aiken had shortened it to "And turn it all." Nordoff went farther with the tightening process, omitting "that" in line three, and "floating in water" in line five. Now with a text shaped to his design, the composer was faced with the problem of finding a musical style appropriate to this very sensuous verse, which already possessed "a subaqueous music, strangely like the magic of Debussy."[65] It may indeed have been this very quality in the poetry which attracted Nordoff, who had always been a great admirer of French song in general and Debussy in particular. For his setting, then, he drew heavily on the hazy world of impressionistic harmony, and placed an exquisitely contoured, delicate vocal line against a wash of parallel fifths, octaves, and non-resolving cluster chords.

Example 6.37, mm. 4–10

The formal structure is simply but perfectly adapted to the text. It repeats the music of Example 6.37 behind the two poetic repetitions of "I would like to touch this snow," etc., but increases the dynamic level each time to accommodate to the emotion suggested by the changing second line of each couplet.

Example 6.38, mm. 34–44

The effect is of a gradually gathering crescendo of longing, which the poet, lacking the greater variety of musical device, had attempted to suggest by altering the punctuation marks that follow repetitions of the refrain:

    a) I would like to touch this snow with the wind of a dream,
    b) I would like to touch this snow with the wind of a dream;
    c) I would like to touch this snow with the wind of a dream:

    Also woven into the form is a recurrent rhythmic figure of a tied over half note followed by three eighths which first appears in the piano introduction

Example 6.39, mm. 1–3

and undergoes metamorphosis and expansion into a full-blown instrumental counterpoint.

Example 6.40, mm. 11–13

There is only one instance of word-painting in this setting which for the most part is designed to suggest the atmosphere of the text rather than specific images: the section which deals with walking "through snow" and "among the hills immortally white" pulls into a regular 3/4 rhythm and a *più mosso* tempo, suggesting a measured and purposeful stride. The harmonic mode also becomes major at this point, but soon begins to lose its accidentals and fade back to the softness of the minor for the setting of "Golden by noon and blue by night." Notice also in Example 6.38 that the major/minor ambiguity that characterizes the three repeated phrases becomes even more dreamlike and inconclusive with the descent of the brief postlude's pianistic melody to the lowered (Phrygian) second step of the E tonality (mm. 43–44).

Nordoff's two other Aiken settings both appeared in the Schott publications of 1938, which were originally issued through the Mainz office and later reprinted many times by Schott and Co. in London. "Music I heard with you"[66] sets one of Aiken's best known poems, which had originally been published in *Turns and Movies* (1917), his third collection of verse. As the first of a group titled "Discordants," this poem establishes the tone of the rest, in its lament over the loss of love and of its power to transfigure the physical world ("bread I broke with you was more than bread"). In this lyric, one can observe many of the poet's literary preoccupations: not only the threat of time, but the images of hands, fingers, and of course, music, begin to be seen as typical of this period. Nordoff's writing also relates to the later "White Nocturne" which it prefigures, in the use of a recurrent pianistic pattern, this time a rising and falling curve of eighth notes in the left hand.

Example 6.41, mm. 3–5

In all other respects, however, this is a very different setting from "White Nocturne," and the arching eighth notes release floods of pain, in a world of color and sensation far removed from the other's dreamy pallor.

Nordoff makes no changes at all in this poem and adapts Aiken's pentameter (a favorite poetic meter in his early work) to an unbroken 4/4 musical meter by setting one or two words in each line to a longer note value, such as a dotted quarter (see Ex. 6.41). Harmony is once again a prime ally of the composer's, and one of the most poignant musical moments of the setting occurs with the placing of a soft pianistic appoggiatura over the voice's F-sharp on the word "dead." This is immediately followed by an unexpected sequential repetition that begins to pull toward a wistful G major and the memory of the beloved touch on familiar objects.

Example 6.42, mm. 8–11

In 1922, Aiken published *Priapus and the Pool*, a collection of twenty-five lyrics, several of which have been called "as skillful as those of any contemporary American singer."[67] One of these is titled "This is the shape of the leaf," and it contains six masterfully constructed verses with an intricate metric scheme and mellifluous flow of language that are reminiscent of Swinburne in an earlier century. The tree on which the "leaf" grows is "In a land we never shall see": seemingly a mystical paradise inhabited in the evening by "three beautiful pilgrims" who wait for a bird's "clear phrase in the twilight / To fill the blue bell of the world." From the hindsight of familiarity with Nordoff's attraction in later years to the spiritual worlds described in Rudolph Steiner's Anthroposophy, the young composer's identification with this poem is readily understandable. His setting[68] is atypical but extremely interesting, its salient feature being a narrow-range, chant-like vocal line, frequently doubled by the piano at the interval of a fifth.

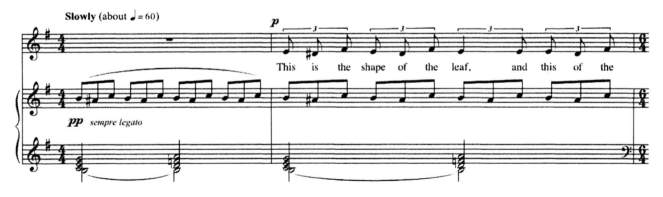

Example 6.43, mm. 1–2

The meditative, hypnotic effect of this circular motion is heightened by the Gregorian suggestion of the empty fifths, and the flexible meter that alternates between 6/4 and 4/4. In an inspired gesture, Nordoff provides contrast to the step-wise motion with his setting of the moment when the silence is ended by the bird's singing. Here the vocal line introduces the excitement of leaping intervals up to an octave, while the piano plays superimposed chords whose sonorities continue to increase as the song of the bird gradually fills "the blue bell of the world."

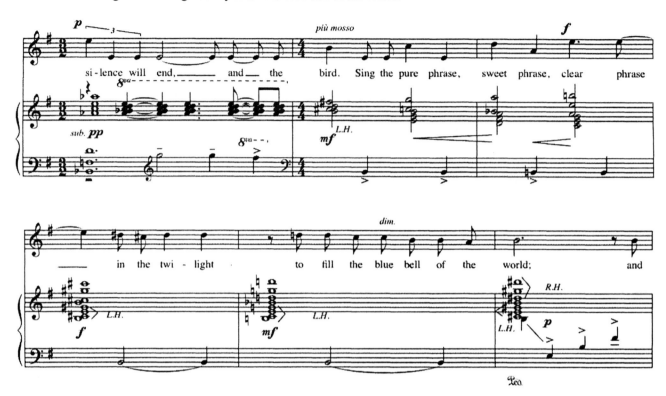

Examples 6.44, mm. 27–32

Elinor Wylie (1885–1928)

The other settings in Nordoff's 1938 Schott publications derive from a mixture of English and American poetic texts. One of these is Elinor Wylie's "Fair Annette's Song,"[69] which was set by Mary Howe some twenty years later (see chapter 4). The poem, in eight lines beginning "One thing comes and another thing goes," creates the atmosphere of a folk song by the simplicity of the language and universality of the recorded experience ("It is sad to remember and sorrowful to pray"). Mary Howe's setting embedded this text in jewel-like fashion within a harmonically and pianistically sophisticated accompaniment, and contributed a vocal line equally elaborate in its rhythmic variation, leaping contour, and extended range. The effect of this is to expose the intricate psychological levels that underlie the apparent simplicity of the statements.

Nordoff's setting takes the opposite course. His song, which is two pages long instead of Howe's five, completely avoids instrumental or vocal elaboration. With a diatonic voice line that is all stepwise motion and chordal leaps, he emphasizes the innocent grace of the poetry,

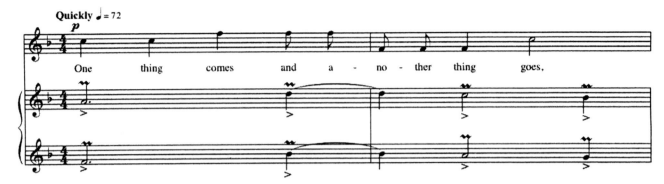

Example 6.45, mm. 1–2

and by turning from F major to the Aeolian mode of this tonal center, he lends a late-medieval atmosphere to the Ophelia-like poignancy of the words (see Ex. 6.46). Notice the added measure of 6/4 in Example 6.46. This is the only change in the otherwise strophic treatment of the second four-line verse, and its rhythmic extension and crescendo followed by a subito piano suggest "Fair Annette's" suppressed dismay over the fleeting loveliness of spring.

Example 6.46, mm. 12–16

A final point of interest in Example 6.46 is the capital "M" on the word "May" which occurs in the Nordoff setting. In Wylie's poem, the "m" is lower case, and the writer is clearly employing the word to mean "hawthorne," according to the British usage. Mary Howe's setting adheres to the lower case, leaving us to wonder whether Nordoff's embodies his own misconception, or a printer's error.

Samuel Barber (1910–1981)

The lyric genius of Samuel Barber was a gift of grace that occurs only once or twice in a generation. This gift had the further advantage of being nurtured from early childhood by Barber's father, a non-musical but supportive Westchester physician, and his mother, who came from a large family of gifted musicians. Indeed, one of Barber's earliest memories is of being "six [years old] and entranced"[70] at his first Metropolitan opera performance where his maternal aunt, Louise Homer, was singing Amneris in *Aida*. Although his parents did try to encourage other activities as well, it soon became apparent that young Sam, as he wrote in a note to his mother at the age of eight, "was meant to be a composer."[71] He had started writing music at seven, composed his first opera at nine, and by the time he was twelve showed so much promise that his uncle, Sidney Homer, himself a skilled writer of songs, began wholeheartedly to encourage the boy's creative goals.

The resources of Westchester, Pennsylvania, a solid Quaker town with a rich cultural life, proved adequate to begin the development of the performing skills that Barber also manifested at an early age. In 1916, he began to study the piano with William Hatton Green, a Leschetizky pupil, and six years later, was hired as organist by the Westminster Presbyterian Church. His refusal to allow unmusical distortions in the hymn-singing resulted in his resignation the following year. By 1924, his growing professionalism was recognized in an audition with Harold Randolph,[72] director of Peabody Conservatory, who advised him to leave school and devote himself to studies in piano and composition.

Following a modified version of this advice, Barber remained in high school but enrolled as one of the first students in the newly opened Curtis Institute of Music in Philadelphia. As president of the Westchester school board, Dr. Barber effected passage of a rule which enabled his son to spend Fridays in Philadelphia attending symphony concerts at the Academy of Music and classes at Curtis. The Institute had been handsomely endowed by Mary Curtis Bok,[73] a daughter of the well-known publishing family, and the finest teachers were available there in all areas of music.[74] Barber absorbed the Romantic tradition in his composition studies with Rosario Scalero, who had worked in Vienna with Eusebius Mandycewski, a close friend of Brahms. Pianistically, he flourished under the guidance of Isabelle Vengerova, also a Leschetizky pupil, who had taught at the Petersburg Conservatory. And in his third year of study, he was allowed to begin formal training of his pleasing baritone voice with Emilio de Gogorza, thus becoming the Institute's first triple major.

Barber had a natural flair for languages, and his studies in French, German, and Italian at Curtis strengthened the European influences purveyed by the faculty. At Philadelphia Orchestra concerts, Stokowski's interest in contemporary programming enabled Barber to hear the newest creative products of Europe (and of America as well). It was a stimulating environment for the young composer, and in 1928 his fluency in French caused him to befriend a Curtis student composer newly arrived from Milan who spoke no English. This friendship with Gian Carlo Menotti would become a personal and professional association of many years' duration, and just before the première of *Vanessa*, Barber would recall with gentle irony how the two, in their student days, had "signed a sort of blood pact never to write an opera."[75]

The year 1928 also brought Columbia University's award of the Bearns prize which supported the first of Barber's many trips to Europe. He visited with Scalero in the Italian Alps, paid his respects to Mandycewski in the Viennese countryside, and reacted unfavorably to a performance of *Parsifal* in Munich during which he "choked in a maddening melee of sickly chromaticism."[76] Through inclination and training, Barber's loyalties in the historic Brahms/Wagner controversy had already been clearly established.

Menotti's family in Italy also played host to Samuel Barber on many occasions during these early years, and after graduating from Curtis in 1933, the two young composers wintered in Vienna where Barber studied voice with John Braun, an American teacher. He made his debut there singing German lieder and several of his own songs. Another important vocal recital took place in 1934 near Mrs. Bok's estate in Maine where Barber had been invited to spend the summer. The following October, Mary Bok arranged for a private hearing of Barber's compositions with Carl Engel, president of G. Schirmer's, which resulted in the publication of three vocal works written while he was still at Curtis ("The Daisies," "With Rue My Heart Is Laden," and "Dover Beach") plus "Bessie Bobtail,"[77] composed during the previous summer in Maine.

The next decade was one of struggle and eventually of recognition for Samuel Barber. After having been once refused, he received the Prix de Rome in 1935, and was also awarded two traveling Pulitzer fellowships in the mid-thirties. From 1939 to 1942 he taught orchestration and trained the chorus at Curtis, but looked forward to a time when he could give up professional singing and teaching and be totally free to compose. Barber and his music took a sudden leap into world prominence with Toscanini's performance of his *Adagio for Strings* and *Essay for Orchestra* in 1938, and by the time he was inducted into Special Services in World War II, his reputation was such that he was encouraged to compose by the armed forces. Mustered out in 1945, he repaired to Capricorn, the comfortable house near Mt. Kisco, New York, which he had purchased with Menotti in 1943. The growing success of his music had brought him the long-coveted time and space for creative work—a way of life which was to last nearly thirty years, until increasing financial problems and waning emotional ties brought about the sale of the property.[78]

By 1981, the year of his death in New York City, Samuel Barber had published just under forty songs, most of which had been available for several decades in G. Schirmer's familiar gray volumes.[79] It was not a large output for "America's foremost lyricist,"[80] but it was consistently of extremely high quality. The *Hermit Songs* had become widely recognized, together with Copland's Emily Dickinson settings, as one of the two most important American song cycles of the century, while the James Joyce group[81] and the single settings were firmly ensconced in the teaching and concert repertoires of singers throughout the country. Interestingly, the large preponderance of poetry chosen by Barber for these settings is European in origin, with English, Irish, and French poets (some in translation) holding the clear majority. As suggested previously, Barber's mentors at Curtis, his command of foreign languages, and his friendship with Menotti had all contributed to a strongly European orientation in his creative life. One finds, indeed, only a single American in the following list of the composer's favorite authors which was reported by Nathan Broder in 1954: Stendhal, Dante, Goethe, Joyce, Proust, and Melville. Even this one American preference takes on cloudy origins with the realization that Barber's deep attraction to Melville and his never fulfilled desire to base a musical work on his writing began on the occasion of his reading *Moby Dick* in an Italian translation!

James Agee (1909–1955)

There were, however, two twentieth-century American poets whose texts the composer set in 1938 and 1940 with the fully developed force of his lyrical powers. The first of these was James Agee. By 1938, Barber had been successfully setting poetry for over a decade, and in all these early songs had exhibited the free-flowing Romanticism of the late nineteenth-century tradition to a degree that at once appalled and delighted the avant-garde saturated audiences of the 1930s. Not surprising, then, is the strong artistic affinity which Barber developed for Agee, whose literary style also carried Romantic overtones, and whose life, as well, embodied the passion, conflict, and self-destructiveness of the archetypical Romantic hero.

Agee was born in Knoxville, Tennessee, which is not an immense geographic distance from Westchester, Pennsylvania, but his life experiences were to be psychological light-years apart from those of Samuel Barber. Whereas the composer had a loving, stable childhood and followed a clear, well-disciplined progression toward recognition in his creative career, the writer's youth was torn by grief, and his energies sapped in adulthood by depression, self-doubt, and to some degree a wasteful scattering of his talent.

Agee's father was descended from Matthieu Agee, a Huguenot who had come to Virginia at the beginning of the Colonial period. The family had later migrated west to Tennessee and each generation continued to produce several farmers, such as the writer's grandfather whose farm was at La Follette, near Knoxville. The Tylers, Agee's maternal grandparents, before settling in Tennessee had moved to Michigan from the East Coast, and both had attended the University of Michigan (his grandmother becoming the first woman university graduate in America). It is easy to understand why James Agee saw himself as the product of a twofold and conflicting heritage, with his mother representing bourgeois refinement, the academic and artistic life, and conventional religion, while his father stood for the rugged, violent, and sensuous world of the proud, isolated "hills people" of the Tennessee mountains.

These opposing strains were not yet a problem in the early childhood of Agee for "the open, celebrative manner of Jay Agee [his father] was complemented by the retiring spirituality of his wife,"[82] and the resulting atmosphere produced a sense of "mysterious happiness"[83] in the boy. It was this pleasant, dreamlike ambiance, underlain with a growing anxiety, that Agee was to celebrate in *Knoxville, Summer of 1915*, the haunting fragment of poetic prose which Samuel Barber would set so movingly for soprano and orchestra as his Opus 24.[84] Tragically, the child's anxiety proved only too well-founded. When he was six years old, his father died in an auto accident, and James Agee's life turned upside down, never to be wholly righted again.

From 1919 to 1925, Mrs. Agee, who was a devout Episcopalian, had her son enrolled at St. Andrew's, a school run by the Anglican priests primarily for the nearby Tennessee farmers' sons. Agee flourished here intellectually from his extensive library privileges, free use of the piano for which he was showing considerable talent, and the relationship now beginning with his teacher, Father Flye,[85] who would become a lifelong friend. His personal life, however, held elements of painful loss, for he often stood longingly outside the house of his mother whom he was allowed to visit only once a week, and who was remarried in 1925 to the Reverend Erskine Wright, a choice which must have seemed a cruel rejection of his father's memory.

In the summer of 1925, Father Flye, who had found Agee an able student of the French language, took him on what was to be the only European tour of his life. After his return, the youth's ties to Tennessee were effectively broken. He spent the next three years at Exeter and the succeeding four at Harvard, increasingly involved in the Eastern literary world, while also developing a reputation as a non-conformist given to nocturnal wanderings, eccentric dress, and turbulent relationships. During this period he began to publish his writing and was also demonstrating sufficient fluency and improvisatory skill at the piano to suggest the possibility of a musical career.[86] He rejected the latter, sensing that he lacked sufficient self-discipline, but music remained a strong force in his life, and in the fall of 1930 he decided to become a writer, hoping "eventually to write works inspired by music—literary symphonies in which . . . the verbal orchestration he was after would enable him to imitate not only the sonorities of music but also its structure."[87]

It was a noble aim, and a volume of his poetry called *Permit Me Voyage*, published in 1934 by Yale University Press in their Younger Poets series, seemed to be fulfilling that promise. But the era was Depression and there were no family funds to provide a cocoon for creative activity. Agee was forced to depend on his facile pen that made him valuable to the Luce publications, *Fortune* and *Time*, as a writer of articles and reviews from 1932 to 1948. This was a period, too, of increasing dependence on alcohol and of severe depression, as he admitted in a revealing letter to the devoted Father Flye. "I realize," said Agee "that I have an enormously strong drive . . . toward self-destruction; and that I know little if anything about its sources or control."[88]

Agee's strong dramatic and visual sensibilities proved further distractions in his attempts at artistic focus. The medium of film increasingly absorbed him, both as reviewer and as scriptwriter, while in 1941 he collaborated with the photographer Walker Evans on *Let Us Now Praise Famous Men*, a stunning portrayal of the lives of Alabama sharecroppers (blood brothers in his mind, no doubt, to the "hills people" of his youth). Beset throughout his life by a strong and possibly, in light of early experience, insatiable need for love, companionship, and continuity, Agee married three times and fathered four children. The first ceremony of marriage (to Via Saunders, the cultivated daughter of a Hamilton College professor) had been performed within the Episcopal church. By the second, to Alma Mailman, a professional violinist, and the third, to Mia Fritsch, a fellow worker for *Fortune* magazine, his conventional religious ties had been severed. Yet in the deepest sense, his whole life was a spiritual struggle between the consciousness of sin formed in childhood and a maturing mystical experience of oneness in the subjects of his artistic scrutiny.

Superstitiously, Agee prepared for death in 1945, believing that he would die in his thirty-sixth year, as his father had. He did not, but a series of cardiac difficulties began in 1951, brought on by years of overwork, drinking to relieve the stress, and the more recent strain of maintaining the Hollywood pace during his West Coast film assignments. Ironically, Destiny did repeat itself, but ten years later than it had been expected. On May 16, 1955, the anniversary of his father's death, James Agee suffered a fatal heart attack and died as his father had done, in an automobile—in this case a New York taxicab.

As is so often the case, Agee's life and literary career began to receive much attention after his death which "evoked the image of a young genius cruelly brought to an end before his time"[89] and of a talent laid waste by contemporary America's failure to support the creative imagination. As the decade turned over into the sixties, Agee became a legend and model to his generation, and the embodiment of a magnificent dream "of a world from which all sterility would be banished."[90] His film scripts were posthumously published, as was *A Death in the Family* (see n84), and in 1968, the *Collected Poems* and *Collected Short Prose* appeared with Robert Fitzgerald, a longtime friend, as editor.

The *Collected Poems* leave no doubt that Agee's poetic muse declined in later years with his pull toward other and longer literary forms, and the consequent investing of his prose with "the poet's eye for detail [and] the poet's ear for phrasing."[91] But the youthful *Permit Me Voyage* (the only poetry ever published by the writer himself) contains many treasures among its lyrics and sonnets, in which Archibald MacLeish's foreword noted "a mature and in some cases a masterly control of rhythm" and "a vocabulary at once personal to the poet and appropriate to the intention."[92] The riches of this collection, whose title was borrowed from Hart Crane's *Voyages* and whose style elicited critical comparisons to the English poetic traditions and America's Whitman, created little stir in an era when much of the literary world was experimenting with a breakdown in poetic form. It remained for Samuel Barber, whose own romantic traditionalism was equally out of step with the musical times, to lift one of these lyrics from obscurity. His setting of it became number three in the four songs of Opus 13, that recognized masterpiece of American song literature, "Sure on this shining night."[93]

The world of this poem seems closely related to Agee's world of *Knoxville, Summer of 1915*.[94] Here it is also "high summer" with "hearts all whole," and the poet "weeps for wonder" at the mysterious beauty of the "star-made shadows." The hints of coming dissolution in the phrases "wandering far alone" and "kindness must watch for me" only increase the poignancy of the moment of perfection. The strong appeal of this text to Samuel Barber would have existed on several levels. He was an inveterate walker and lover of nature who had tramped the countryside of America and Europe on many sunny days and "shining nights." The poem (set without change or deletion) offered short lines embodying much compressed emotion that invited musical amplification. And the words themselves exhibited a great deal of sensuous alliteration in their repeated "sh" and "h" sounds,[95] as well as many vocally grateful vowels which could gain artistic reinforcement in a musical setting.

The visual appearance of the poem gives us two verses of four short lines followed by a very long ninth line ("Sure on this shining night I weep for wonder wandering far alone") and a much shorter tenth. Barber's setting in effect creates three equal stanzas, which translate to an exquisitely crafted three-part form. The contrapuntal mastery derived from Rosario Scalero's thorough training in this discipline is apparent as he adapts a two-part canon at the interval of a third to the needs of the text. It begins in quiet description in the first stanza with the piano following the voice by a measure. As the vocal contour rises to the joyous affirmation of the long vowels ("All is healed / all is health"), and the emotive climax of the piece is reached, the piano's canonic imitation stops, as though to allow momentary prominence to vocal and verbal values.

Example 6.47, mm. 12–17

The voice line having descended to a position of rest on the poetic summation, "Hearts all whole," the piano now takes over the canonic melody in a gorgeous burst of sound that prepares the vocal restatement.

Example 6.48, mm. 18–24

Though the harmonic scheme of this song is in no way unique, it becomes fresh and meaningful in the hands of a youthful master. The opening B flat major pulls to the relative minor through the subdominant chord for the somberness of "This side the ground." It affirms D minor through the authentic cadence which supports the crescendo, then moves suddenly, with a dynamic drop, back to B-flat major—the hushed realization of a wondrous wholeness, whose spiritual origins are subliminally suggested by the plagal cadence of the pianistic takeover (see Ex. 6.47 and Ex. 6.48).

Although at this stage in his writing Barber is still using meter signatures, his frequent variants of two- and four-beat measures from the basic three demonstrate a natural sensitivity to the prosodic flow, and lend a rhythmic fluidity to the lyrical outline. Finally, the evidence of a meticulous craftsman's orientation toward the microcosm of musical structure is to be found in the accent lines which the composer places in the pianistic conclusion over the interval of a minor third, one of the most prominent components of the canonic melody.

Example 6.49, mm. 30–34

James Agee had spent the summer of 1930 working at odd jobs around the country, and his short story "They that Sow in Sorrow Shall Reap," grew out of this experience. The following quotation from the work is a revealing indication of Agee's general concept of music as an analog to life, and seems also to serve in particular as a characterization of the remarkable "Sure on this shining night:"

> As a rule, experience is broken upon innumerable sharp irrelevancies, [yet at times the mind may become aware] of a definite form and rhythm and melody of existence: . . . out of long contrapuntal passages of tantalizing . . . elements there emerges sometimes an enormous clear chord. And at that moment . . . the whole commonplace of existence is transfigured, becomes monstrously powerful, and beautiful, and significant.[96]

Frederic Prokosch (1908–1989)

The second American poet whom Barber chose to set in his op. 13 songs was Frederic Prokosch. Born in Madison, Wisconsin, in a year variously recorded by biographers as 1906 and 1908, Prokosch was a second-generation American whose ties to Europe exerted strong influences throughout his life. His Austrian-born father, Eduard, came to the United States in 1898 and attended the National German-American Teachers' Seminary in Milwaukee. Here he met and married the director's daughter, Mathilde Dapprich, a well-known pianist who had been born in Baltimore. After earning a doctorate in linguistics and philology from Leipzig in 1905, Eduard held teaching positions at the University of Wisconsin, and at the University of Texas at Austin. He was dismissed from the latter in 1919 in the wave of anti-German sentiment that followed World War I, but in a year's time resumed an illustrious teaching career that was to last for two more decades and include prestigious appointments at Bryn Mawr College, Yale, and New York University.

As evidenced in his later writing, Frederic Prokosch was to regard the Wisconsin years as a time of innocent childhood, and the Texas experiences (1913–1919) as a period of lost innocence and maturation.[97] A formative year just after the family's move to Austin was spent by young Frederic attending school in Austria and Germany, and on his return to America in 1915, his spoken German was better than his English. As might have been expected, the boy had inherited both his father's scholarly aptitude for languages and literature and his mother's artistic endowment. The creativity started to surface during his high school years at Bryn Mawr where he put on a number of puppet shows, and after entering Haverford College in 1922, he became increasingly committed to the writing of poetry.

Prokosch's first published poem was printed in the *Virginia Quarterly Review* of July 1927, alongside a contribution by Allen Tate, one of the earliest participants in the barely emerging Southern literary renaissance. Thereafter, his poems appeared in many American and British magazines and in 1936 he published his first volume of verse that he titled *The Assassins*. During this same period Prokosch had taken graduate degrees at Haverford, Cambridge, and Yale, and had followed in his father's footsteps with teaching positions at Yale and New York University. There was yet a third side to the colorful personality of this artist-scholar whose sociability had emerged as an undergraduate along with considerable athletic prowess as a tennis and squash player. The Yale instructorship was to produce a reputation for dramatic teaching, as well as for a rather dashing lifestyle, which included a yellow convertible and a large German shepherd.

By 1937, having published two novels and won the Guggenheim Award and Harper Prize, Prokosch abandoned teaching and began to travel abroad. His second volume of poetry, *Carnival*, was published in 1938, and a third, *Death at Sea*, in 1940. Both received a rather cool critical reception, and Prokosch wrote little new poetry after that time, the *Chosen Poems* of 1948 being a selection from the earlier volumes. Concurrently with and subsequent to the poetry, Prokosch remained active as a novelist, and his next work in this medium was *America, My Wilderness* in 1972. The publication of *Voices: A Memoir* in 1981 that described the author's encounters with many prominent literary figures of the twentieth century, returned him to the limelight. His novels *The Asiatics* and *Seven Who Fled* were then reissued to much public acclaim.

After the death of his father in 1938, Prokosch lived in France for over fifty years and died there in 1989. He returned to America only for a brief period in 1942 to work for the Office of War information, and for a short stay in 1953–1954. Living in Lisbon in 1940 after the fall of France, he was surrounded by flocks of political agents and desperate refugees, and much of his writing around that time reflected the growing conflagration that was gradually engulfing Europe and that was on its way to becoming World War II. The poetry of *Carnival* also shares in this environment of impending war, while it continues to exhibit the two principal characteristics of *The Assassins*: a strong orientation toward places and journeys, and a richly musical style which suggests the influence of Yeats.

One of *Carnival*'s most striking poems is "Nocturne," whose effortless lyricism receives a tight metric structure in five verses of extremely regular four-stress lines. In adapting the poem for his purposes as number 4 of the Opus 13 songs,[98] Barber first chose to omit the third verse, which begins "Condors of the future rise / Through the stupor overheard." This had the effect of mitigating the looming historical disaster and of concentrating the poem's focus on love, with all its falsehood and frailties, as a refuge from the pain and hopelessness of the human experience. Next the composer decided to impede the flow of trochees with a recurrent vocal rhythmic figure of dotted quarter notes. This allowed time for the development of an agitated pianistic embroidery of broken arpeggios in the right hand and a rocking figure in the left, which suggests a lullaby behind "Close my darling both your eyes."

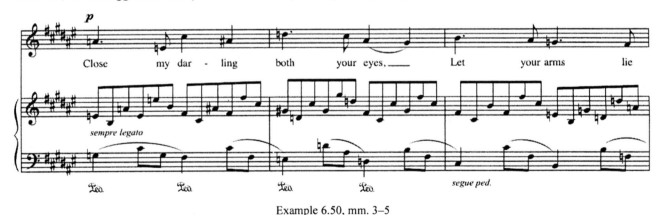

Example 6.50, mm. 3–5

The leaping contour of the opening vocal line is maintained and intensified throughout the setting, as the tumult of emotion rises. In a moment of exquisite musical correspondence, Barber then has the singer descend via chordal skips over a distance of an octave and a third in representation of grateful release, which is heightened by the suspended 5/4 meter resolving to the lesser tension of 4/4.

Example 6.51, mm. 18–24

Quiet, two-measure interludes, in which the piano imitates the preceding vocal lines, follow the conclusions of verse one ("And the wind of lust has passed") and verse two (see Ex. 6.51, mm. 20–23). From this point on, there is no pause in the dynamic and expressive crescendo that Barber derives from such incendiary phrases as "Blaze with such a longing now" and "Northward flames Orion's horn." Propulsive chords become the dominating accompaniment figure for verse three, and the shattering climax of the song is achieved with the addition of portentous dotted note figures in octaves to the returning broken chords, while the voice holds a defiantly ecstatic A-flat.

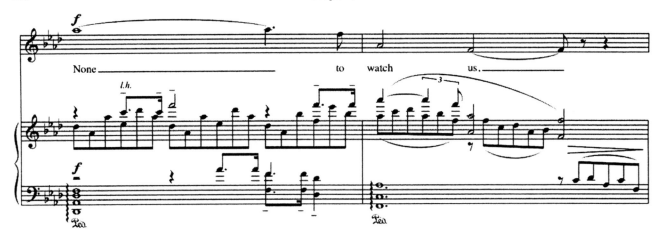

Example 6.52, mm. 38–39

This climax is also impelled harmonically by an enharmonic movement through an altered A sharp chord to one on B flat which introduces the most expansively diatonic phrase of the setting, an island of certainty in the surrounding sea of shifting chromaticism.

Example 6.53, mm. 34–37

Paul Frederic Bowles (1910–1999)

Paul Bowles began his life in a New York City brownstone where the family lived in an apartment above his father's dental office. To all outward appearances, it was a privileged, nurturing environment for a growing child, but the strain of its emotional climate engendered withdrawal mechanisms that Bowles would cultivate out of a healthy instinct for self-preservation.[99] In his autobiography, written after sixty years filled with artistic friends and a long marriage, the composer revealingly concludes that "Relationships with other people are at best nebulous; their presence keeps us from being aware of the problem of giving form to our life."[100]

Restrained by parental veto from a hoped-for career as concert violinist, Bowles's dentist father was a man given to raging outbursts over minor domestic details. Often, they were directed at this son whom he could not forgive for having diverted his wife's attention from himself. The boy's mother gave Paul what support she could in their uneasy household, and from her he learned the useful technique of "making his mind a blank and holding it," a skill he later credited for developing "whatever powers of self-discipline I have now."[101]

Bowles's most pleasant childhood memories were of visits to the maternal grandparents at Happy Hollow Farm in Massachusetts. In strong contrast was the gloomy Elmira home of his father's parents: two somber intellectuals who spent most of their time reading. His paternal grandmother was a Theosophist and two of her siblings were also devoted to yoga and various occult sciences. Bowles came naturally, then, to several instances of precognitive dreaming and "out-of-body" experiences during his childhood and adolescence. These predisposed him to a strong interest in exotic mysticism as an adult, and also fostered the sense of detachment from the physical universe that enabled him to psychically survive the definitive skirmish with his father at the age of nineteen. Having on this occasion declared "It's not my fault I'm alive, I didn't ask to be born" and having angrily hurled a meat knife, Bowles was convinced that he must leave home for the sake of all concerned, while "as usual [reminding himself] that since nothing was real it did not matter too much."[102]

The bizarre aspects of his childhood having made a "loner" of Paul Bowles, he was drawn at an early age to creative expression in the arts of music and literature. At eight he began piano lessons, also studying theory and solfège so that he could record his own musical ideas. A cracked sounding board in the piano caused a cessation in music lessons and Bowles turned to writing, thus laying the foundation for his second creative career. In junior high school, the piano lessons resumed, using an old Chickering sent by his grandmother from Elmira. By the time of his high school graduation, he had served as humor and poetry editors of the school magazine, become an avid buyer of books, and was in regular attendance at Carnegie Hall for the Saturday Philharmonic concerts.

College seemed a logical place to further his training, but the atmosphere at the University of Virginia proved too "country club" for his level of hard-won maturity. Bowles enjoyed tramping the countryside around Charlottesville, and was grateful for the introduction to T. S. Eliot, Gregorian Chant, and Prokofiev. Nevertheless, early in the spring semester he packed his belongings and left for Europe, impelled by what he had come to regard as his "other self," which had, on a previous occasion, functioned independently of his physical body.

During the next decade, Paul Bowles was in and out of Paris, Berlin, America, Morocco, and Mexico, having begun his lifetime pattern as a world traveler. This was also the period of his development as a serious composer, which was strongly influenced by his studies with Aaron Copland and his many contacts with Virgil Thomson. In the early thirties, six of his songs received an excellent reception when presented at the Yaddo summer festival, and he formed his own company called *Éditions de la Vipère*[103] to publish his songs and piano pieces, as well as works by David Diamond and Satie. Money was always a problem and a succession of odd jobs supported him, together with a small legacy from an aunt, once he had turned twenty-one.

There were two other important influences on Paul Bowles during these formative years. One was Gertrude Stein, who, obviously fond of the young man, declared him more of a "Freddy" than a "Paul," and whose texts he set on several occasions including a personal note which became "Letter to Freddy."[104] The other was his first experiences with Morocco, a country which he found languorous, violent, and totally magical, with an appeal so strong that it would eventually draw him back as a permanent resident. Toward the end of the thirties he traveled to Mexico and met Revueltas, Moncayo, Galindo, and others of the group of young composers who were revitalizing their country's music.

In 1937, just before her twenty-first birthday, Bowles married Jane Auer, a vivacious and talented young woman who would eventually publish a small but notable body of writing. Having gotten his first theatrical commissions two years earlier with the help of Virgil Thomson, the composer now began to be in demand as a writer of scores for Broadway plays, and enjoyed fruitful collaborations with William Saroyan,[105] and with Tennessee Williams, who had introduced himself to Bowles when both were staying in Acapulco in 1939.[106] This period of the composer's life also resulted in the writing of a number of his finest songs, including most of the Tennessee Williams settings. In 1945, Peggy Glanville-Hicks, the British composer and critic, stressed the importance of Bowles's work in this genre. "His contribution to the modern song repertory," she said, "is one of the most exceptional in recent years. [The songs] are spontaneous and fresh, they have a great vitality and a most original melodic form and colour."[107] In the same *Music and Letters* article, Glanville-Hicks also commented on Bowles's overall musical characteristics of a "neatness of execution, contrapuntal linear outlook, and fastidiousness of expression."[108] These she felt to be tendencies of the French school, transmitted to Bowles through Copland and Thomson, who had both been pupils of Boulanger. Copland himself, writing in *Modern Music* in 1936, had called attention to the young composer's work, and three years later had added "a talent as fresh as that of Bowles is not often found."[109]

Still another aspect of his musical career unfolded for Bowles when he began to write music criticism for *Modern Music* around 1940, and was shortly thereafter persuaded, again by Virgil Thomson, to join the daily reviewing staff of the *New York Herald Tribune*. He stayed at the *Tribune* until 1945, at which time he began to have recurrent dreams of a "magic city." Realizing at last that it was Tangier, he returned there to live, and to begin a new creative life as a writer of fiction and of travel pieces based on his perceptive explorations of Asia and Africa. A novel published in 1950 which Bowles titled *The Sheltering Sky* would become his best known literary work, a reputation further enhanced through its success as a film directed by Bernardo Bertolucci in 1990.

After moving back to Tangier, he continued to produce some theatrical scores, principally for Tennessee Williams, but his involvement with serious concert music gradually ended as critics and performers seemed to have lost interest in that aspect of his composition. His personal life, too, encompassed loss. Paul and Jane Bowles had for twenty years been the "golden couple" of a circle of friends, which included Bernstein, Barber, Menotti, Gore Vidal, Truman Capote, and many other composers and writers. In 1957, Jane suffered a slight stroke that left her with some aphasia and visual disturbance. As her husband was later to write, "the good years were over."[110] Her health and powers continued to decline until her death in 1973, after which Bowles, always ill-at-ease with the brashness and superficiality of much of American culture, chose to remain cradled in the reserved mystery of Tangier where "all around in the night sorcery (was) burrowing its invisible tunnels."[111] After his death there in 1999, his writing attracted increasingly favorable critical attention and in 2002, the Library of America issued a two-volume edition of his works. His music had also enjoyed a renaissance during the last decade of his life. In 1995, a New York festival took place featuring Bowles compositions, followed by the issuing of several CDs and a documentary film called *Night Waltz* in 1997.

Over the years, Bowles had assumed the task of familiarizing the Western world with the riches of Moroccan culture through his collections of native music, and translations of Moroccan literature. He also introduced many of his friends to the beauties of his adopted country and among these was Tennessee Williams who made several visits there beginning in 1949. That Williams had indeed become a friend as well as a professional associate is evidenced by his letters to Bowles of the late fifties following Jane's stroke, in which he expresses his concern for both of them and his high regard for Jane's worth as a person and an artist.[112]

Tennessee Williams (1911–1983)

Tennessee Williams's forbears had included Sidney Lanier, several Indian fighters, and a brother of St. Francis Xavier. It was a fitting ancestry for a man with a poetic ear and a propensity toward strong drink, who was to become the American theater's "laureate of the outcast."[113] Williams's early childhood was spent in the peaceful, pleasant towns of Mississippi which, after a family move to St. Louis in 1919,[114] would come to represent the lost Eden of his mythic Southern birthright. His boisterous, extroverted father was a traveling salesman who spent most of his time away from home. As a result, Williams developed a strong attachment to his mother, fostered by two years of recuperation at home from diphtheria. When he was eleven, his mother bought a typewriter for this son who was too shy to speak in class, and by the age of fourteen he had already dedicated his life to writing.

His literary efforts began to be recognized at the University of Missouri, where he enrolled in 1929, only to be removed by his father for failing ROTC. He returned to college in 1936 when his grandmother financed a year at Washington University; here he was not only introduced to the poetry of Rilke and Hart Crane but also had three plays produced by Willard Holland's little theater group. Williams's bachelor of arts degree was finally earned at the University of Iowa in 1937—the same year that his beloved sister Rose underwent a pre-frontal lobotomy.

The next six years were a time of writing, wandering, and financial struggle. In 1943, Audrey Woods, Williams's able agent, arranged a six-month contract with Metro Goldwyn Mayer. Ironically, MGM rejected all the scripts he produced including *The Glass Menagerie* that would shortly establish the author as one of America's major dramatists. In 1944, between the Chicago and New York productions of the play, Williams's poetry appeared in a volume called *Five*

Young American Poets. Most of these poems, some in revised form, would be republished in *In the Winter of Cities* (1956), and a few would reappear in his poetry collection of 1977 called *Androgyne, Mon Amour.*

The Glass Menagerie was presented with a background musical score by Paul Bowles. Over the next two decades Bowles, now living abroad, made return trips to New York to write scores for Williams's other important plays such as *Summer and Smoke* (1948), *Sweet Bird of Youth* (1959), and *The Milk Train Doesn't Stop Here Anymore* (1963). During the remaining years of his life, Williams suffered from intermittent depression and "the attrition of dramatic power that affects most playwrights after the age of 50."[115] The panic and sense of isolation attendant on this depression are movingly portrayed in his poem called "Tangier: The Speechless Summer," which is in the collection *Androgyne, Mon Amour.* Both Jane and Paul Bowles appear in this poem, and it is clear from the following lines that Williams's pain over his "speechlessness," which may be in part a symbol of failing creativity, also extends to the difficulty of communicating his despair to these dearest of friends:

> I love Paul, but once he said to me: "I've never had
> a neurosis."
>
> Jane, I said to you: "Jane, I can't talk anymore."
> and you said to me: "Tennessee, you were
> never much of a talker."

In the title poem of the earlier collection, *In the Winter of Cities*, Williams had already begun to record his own haunting fears that the vital, creative years of his life were over:

> Those who ignore the appropriate time of their going
> are the most valiant explorers,
> going into a country that no one is meant to go into,
> the time coming after that isn't meant to come after.

From the acknowledgment of this bitter insight, in the mid-fifties, to the end of his life, was a tormented span of nearly thirty years. In 1983, he died, like James Agee, in the same setting as his father had—in this case a lonely hotel room, where he choked on the swallowed cap of a medicine bottle. It was a death scene which Tennessee Williams himself might have written. The "laureate" had become one with the "outcast."

Williams's poetry then, like his plays, not infrequently bore a close connection to his own experience. As regards its position in his total literary output, critics for the most part are in agreement with Felicia Londré's estimate that "despite the fact that he has written some of the most poetic lines spoken on the American stage . . . [Williams's] poetry, as such, is extremely uneven."[116] Some of the most successful verses in the collections are the compact, unpretentious folk-like ballads often written in rhymed couplets, which employ Williams's genius for dramatic portrayal of both comic and tragic figures, and his unfailing ear for idiomatic language. The source of the folk idiom is primarily the writer's memories of the years of his rural, Southern childhood, and the literary world evoked by these ties is full of a healthy and unsophisticated tenderness, even toward its failures, that is a far cry from the violence and emotional excess of so much of his other writing.

The texts of the Bowles-Williams settings to be discussed next are all drawn from this world. Despite his highly cultivated and urbane intellect, Paul Bowles has always been quite at home, musically, in the folk milieu, and the "new simplicity"[117] of his style, praised by the critics of the forties, found a counterpart in this poetry. Bowles describes the selection process, saying "There's not much I can tell you about the text sources for the Tennessee Williams songs. In each case Mr. Williams handed me typed pages with the lyrics, saying that I might find them suitable for setting to music. There were other lyrics, but I chose the ones that appealed to me."[118]

"Blue Mountain" of the *Blue Mountain Ballads*[119] (1946) is a mythical town in Mississippi that represents Camden and/or Clarksdale where Williams had lived happily with his grandparents as a boy. In a number of Williams's plays set in the south, there are recurring references to towns such as Blue Mountain or Glorious Hill, Mississippi; in the early one-act play *At Liberty*, for instance, Gloria Greene, a former road show dancer, is back home in Blue Mountain, suffering from a chronic chest ailment. All four texts of the *Ballads* have four-stress lines with poetic feet of varying meters. All are in rhymed couplets, with the exception of "Lonesome Man" which is in triplets, the third line in each case being a slightly varied echo of the second. Three of the four—"Heavenly Grass," "Sugar in the Cane," and "Lonesome Man"—are dramatic monologues written in the first person, while "Cabin," the fourth, is a narrative, but paints an extremely vivid picture of human character and the events of its creation.

"Cabin" is a morality tale of a seduction, drawn with simple but powerful imagery, in which the sunny, flower-trimmed cabin seems to stand for the woman's innocence, and the winter storm that now sweeps it, for the passion that destroyed them both. Bowles's opening tempo suggestion is "Like a ballad," and the introduction establishes this ambiance with the warmth of its flowing, diatonic thirds in the right hand, and the suggestion of a plucked folk instrument in the spacing of the left hand's broken chords.

Example 6.54, mm. 1–4

The body of the song has an ABA form and harmonic scheme, with the A sections in F sharp minor. The B section, which incorporates the line "where they kissed and sinned," moves to the modal form of A, which forms a somber contrast to the bright expectations promised by the A major of the introduction. The contour of the vocal line is folk-song-like in its emphasis on chordal leaps and stepwise motion but the dissonant ninths in the accompanying chords add both a suggestion of menace, and a contemporary perspective on a timeless tragedy.

Example 6.55, mm. 5–7

Notice that by lengthening the second and fourth poetic foot in each line (Example 6.55), Bowles creates a flexible and responsive rhythmic scheme of 6/8 combined with 9/8 measures, and adds a sense of spaciousness to the telling of the tale.

In "Heavenly Grass" we encounter one of the first-person monologues, in this case spoken by a simple, devout individual whose plain speech is transformed by Williams into intensely poetic imagery. One is reminded of Agee's view of "the mountain people" as drawing both poetry and spirituality from their closeness to the earth, as the protagonist likens the journey of the soul to a walk from "heavenly grass" to earthly terrain, and back again. Bowles first provides a lightly textured, poignant piano introduction in which twanging major ninths underlie the melodic motif of a minor third plus a second.

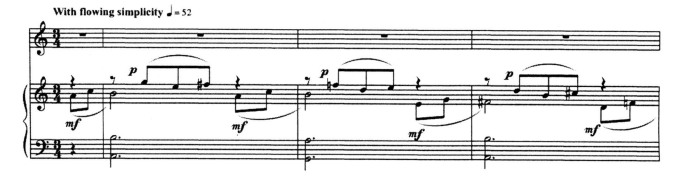

Example 6.56, mm. 1–3

This motif takes on a "question and answer" quality, as each statement is followed by its inversion (see Ex. 6.56), and the minor third (a favorite interval of Bowles's) is also prominent in the contour of the vocal line (see Ex. 6.57).

As the voice enters, the composer continues to employ musical device in a perfect correspondence to the artful simplicity of the poetry. The overall form is a recurring AB pattern in which the first line of each couplet is given a modal setting and a faster-moving 5/4 meter, while the second line takes on a slower, wandering 4/4 meter and the contrastingly ecstatic brightness of the G major key.

Example 6.57, mm. 4–7

The only exception to this scheme is the setting of the third couplet, which incorporates the birth experience. This is clothed in the faster tempo plus the urgency of a 3/4 meter, and the voice line descends with the weight of human pain, and the sorrow of heavenly loss.

Example 6.58, mm. 14–18

Glanville-Hicks had observed that "a peculiarity [Bowles's] music has in common with certain folksong material, and even with modal harmonization of folk tunes, is that a point of rest or complete finality can be arrived at on all manner of tonal degrees other than a tonic."[120] In the magical conclusion of "Heavenly Grass," Bowles repeats the final line ("But they still got an itch for heavenly grass") and changes the last note to end on the sixth degree of the scale, in a reverie of suspended longing.

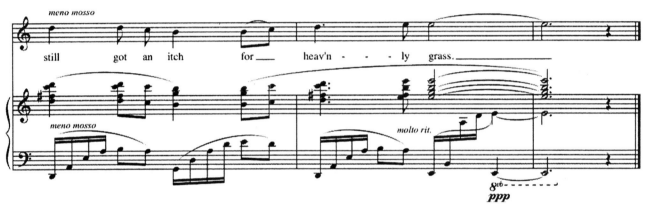

Example 6.59, mm. 25–27

"Sugar in the Cane" is a very different portrait. Here Tennessee Williams uses his considerable comic talents to bring before us a nubile young woman whose metaphorical allegations of innocence ("I'm potatoes not yet mashed," etc.) appear to be somewhat exaggerated. In the collection *In the Winter of Cities*, Williams had published two poems called "Kitchen Door Blues" and "Gold Tooth Blues" which clearly had the "feel" of song lyrics, particularly the second, whose structure included a refrain. "Sugar in the Cane" falls into the same category, and is a fine idiomatic imitation of the rhythm, language, and sexual innuendo of the typical "blues" lyric.
Bowles's style in the setting is a precisely perfect blend of elements taken from the appropriate areas of American popular music. He employs the tied-over syncopations and pianistic octaves of early ragtime (see Ex. 6.60) together with the ornamental "smears" and flatted thirds derived from the vocabulary of "blue notes" (see Ex. 6.61).

Example 6.60, mm. 1–5

Example 6.61, mm. 12–14

Stylistic quotation is, of course, in an art song framework, and therefore not slavishly derivative. Bowles uses a ten-measure vocal strain rather than the usual twelve measures of "the blues," and replaces the typical subdominant harmonic contrast with a secondary dominant to the V chord. The ending of both verses of the strophic form is also interesting in that it is idiosyncratic to the composer. Once again, as in "Heavenly Grass," Bowles selects the sixth degree of the scale as his final note, and also sets the concluding word with his "trademark" falling third.

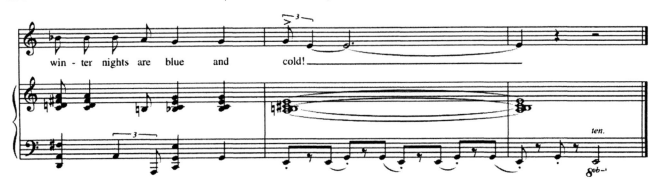

Example 6.62, mm. 24–26

Though the key (G major) and scalar relationship of the sixth is the same as the ending of "Heavenly Grass," the effect is a far cry from "heavenly," and indeed, in this context of low range, insistent rhythmic accent, and strident cluster harmonies, becomes insinuatingly provocative.

"Lonesome Man," the last of the *Blue Mountain Ballads*, is a swift, brilliant characterization of one of Williams's "outcasts" from society. The speaker in this case knows he is too old to win love for himself, refuses to pay for it, and at the same time mocks the suffering brought down by his pride on "an old fool's head." The poem itself has a rueful quality which Bowles turns to humor with his spirited use once again of ragtime syncopations in the accompaniment. This figure clearly derives from the opening line of text ("My chair rock-rocks by the door all day") and the recurring interpolations of 7/16 in the overall 4/8 meter suggest that an agitated state of mind is causing an occasional acceleration in the chair's regular rocking.

Example 6.63, mm. 5–10

In another instance of the composer's sensitivity to the dramatic action, two recitative-like passages over held piano chords set the poignant phrases "I don't want love from the mercantile store" and "While the moon grins down at an ole fool's head." The culturally but not musically incongruous comparison that springs to mind is Schubert's "Gretchen am

Spinnrade." Like the young girl's spinning wheel, the old man's rocking chair has momentarily stopped, as he muses over the joy and sorrow of love.

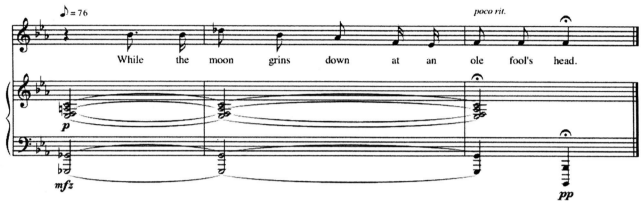

Example 6.64, mm. 35–37

"Three"[121] is a Bowles-Williams song published in 1947, slightly later than the *Blue Mountain Ballads*. It is a short, two-page setting of a simple but powerful poem about three loves. Again the text is in the first person, and the lover's sorrowful realization is that the one who died ("is sheltered under frost") is also the one who "stayed in [his] heart forever." Stylistically, the setting is somewhat reminiscent of "Heavenly Grass" with its modal constructions and unelaborated but convincing vocal contour. The piano interlude before the last stanza exhibits a meltingly effective use of pianissimo chords in parallel fifths and octaves. As the text returns, this figure is hauntingly continued in the accompaniment.

Example 6.65, mm. 14–19

A Tennessee Williams text called "Her Head on the Pillow"[122] was set by Paul Bowles in Tangier in 1961. Like "Cabin," this is a story centered on passion's destructive force, this time told by the man, who is filled with remorse as "her head on the pillow" reminds him of "Holy Mary's Crown." The poem is in three six-line stanzas, and in the fashion of many examples of folk-poetry and folk-song lyrics, lines five and six of each stanza are a subtle variant of three and four. This affords Bowles the opportunity for musical amplification and emotive intensification at the end of each verse setting, which occur in the form of more arching vocal lines, and fuller pianistic figurations. Dramatic contrast is skillfully achieved by the composer through a change of meter and tempo in the middle section of a three-part form. The outer sections, embodying the protagonist's repentant adoration, are in a slower reflective 4/4, while his painful memories ("when I took the lady by storm") are mirrored in an agitated, whirling 3/8.

Not surprisingly, Paul Bowles has also set his own texts on a number of occasions. One of the most successful of these, "Once a lady was here,[123] has been anthologized,[124] and appears frequently on recital programs.[125] Indeed, it was not only included in the recorded selections of the Rockefeller project's New World Records, but even provided the disc's title—*But Yesterday Is Not Today*—which is the last line of the poem.[126] This song and "In the Woods"[127] (also to a Bowles text) are both from the middle forties, the same period as most of the Williams settings, but Bowles setting Bowles produces a more emotionally complex, sophisticated product than the simple, direct expression of Blue Mountain's inhabitants. In these Bowles texts, he is the narrator/observer, who comments on the passing scene with a kind of detached compassion. It is as though the lady who once "sat in this garden and . . . thought of love" and the girl who "hears a bird . . . in the woods" are seen from a veiled distance, as microcosms in the universal scheme, rather than as possibilities for human involvement. The quality is the same as that which Glanville-Hicks describes in Paul Bowles's music as "an emotional-mystical quality . . . at once personal and remote."[128]

"Once a lady was here" has a musical-theater flavor, drawn from the composer's extensive experience in the style. The chordal constructions, dotted note patterns, and "off" notes are all out of ragtime and blues through Broadway and are elements that become increasingly common in American art song as the twentieth century progresses. Bowles's considerable skill at handling subtle, asymmetric rhythmic patterns is evident in his undulating metric scheme of 4/8 5/8, and his most uncommon melodic gift is once again revealed in the seemingly inevitable contours of the vocal line.

Example 6.66, mm. 1–8

"In the Woods" has a shifting, chromatic accompaniment of soft parallel tone clusters which seems to shed an Impressionistic haze over the scene.

Example 6.67, mm. 1–4

A striking contrast to the pianistic color is provided by the composer's request that the repeated descending fourth (see last two notes of Ex. 6.67) be whistled, in direct imitation of the bird's "music-making." Interestingly, in this context the whistle does not emerge as a cheerful sound. Rather, it becomes wistfully hypnotic in its repeated downward leaps, and emphasizes the aloneness of the girl with her "tears that careless thoughts can sometimes bring."

Notes

1. For Ross Lee Finney's comments on his studies with Berg and Boulanger, see Cole Gagne and Tracy Caras, *Soundpieces, Interviews with American Composers* (Metuchen, N.J.: Scarecrow Press, 1982), 182ff.

2. Ross Lee Finney, "Analysis and the Creative Process," *Scripps College Bulletin* 33, no. 2 (February 1959): 10.

3. Ross Lee Finney, "Composer in Residence," *Composer* 15 (April 1965): 5–6.

4. Ross Lee Finney, "The Composer in Academia," *College Music* 10 (1970): 76–77.

5. Ross Lee Finney, "Employ the Composer," *American Music Teacher* 11, no. 2 (1961): 9.

6. Finney, "Employ the Composer."

7. Ross Lee Finney, "Theory in a Period of Change," *American Music Teacher* 17, no. 1 (1967): 45.

8. Gilbert Chase, *America's Music* (New York: McGraw-Hill, 1966), 614.

9. Ross Lee Finney, *Three Seventeenth Century Lyrics* (Northampton, Mass.: Valley Music Press, 1948). Out of print. Available from the Smith College Department of Music Records, Box 9, Smith College Archives.

10. Paul Cooper, "The Music of Ross Lee Finney," *The Musical Quarterly* 53, no. 1 (January 1967): 4. This article by Paul Cooper contains a complete listing of Finney's works including publishers, recordings, and first performances, to 1966.

11. William Billings (1746–1800), an early New England composer.

12. For a discussion of the Ainsworth Psalter and its musical descendants, see H. Wiley Hitchcock, *Music in the United States* (Englewood Cliffs, N.J.: Prentice-Hall, 1969), 4.

13. The reader will notice that Benjamin Franklin, writing in the late eighteenth century, is the earliest American poet treated in this study.

14. Ross Lee Finney, "Poor Richard" (New York: G. Schirmer, 1950). Tenor. Range: d^1 to a^2.

15. Carl Van Doren, *Benjamin Franklin* (New York: Viking, 1938), 114–15.

16. Francis Hopkinson (1737–1791), the first native born American composer. For an extensive treatment of Hopkinson, see Hitchcock, *Music in the United States*, 33.

17. Personal letter to R. Friedberg, 23 September 1982.

18. Hitchcock, *Music in the United States,* 225.

19. Van Doren, *Benjamin Franklin*, 145.

20. W. Thomas Marrocco and Harold Gleason, *Music in America* (New York: W. W. Norton, 1964), 105.

21. Van Doren, *Benjamin Franklin*, 148.

22. Van Doren, *Benjamin Franklin*, 148.

23. (a) Letter to R. Friedberg, 17 August 1982. George Newton served as interim associate editor of music reviews for the *Bulletin of the National Association of Teachers of Singing* from 1980 to 1983. R. Friedberg was an assistant music review editor under both George Newton and Walter Martin. (b) Information on Naginski's family and the Koussevitsky correspondence is contained in an email from Howard Morris, the composer's second cousin, to R. Friedberg, 27 August 2011.

24. Charles Naginski, "Look down, fair moon" (New York: G. Schirmer, 1942). Medium voice. Range: d^1 to e^2. Charles Naginski, "The Ship Starting" (New York: G. Schirmer, 1942). Medium voice. Range: b flat to C^2. Both of these songs are out of print. They are available from G. Schirmer as archive copies and are also held by the Library of Congress Music Division. Recordings of "Look Down, Fair Moon" and Naginski's setting of "Richard Cory" are included in the Thomas Hampson CD *I Hear America Singing* (2006) available from ArkivMusic.com.

25. Walt Whitman, "The Last of the War Cases," *November Boughs* (Philadelphia: David McKay, 1888).

26. This essay, titled "Notes (such as they are) founded on Elias Hicks" is also in Whitman's *November Boughs*.

27. Charles Naginski, "Under the harvest moon" (New York: G. Schirmer, 1940). Medium voice. Range: d^1 to e^2. Out of print. Available from G. Schirmer as an archive copy and held by the Library of Congress.

28. Louis Untermeyer, ed., *Modern American Poetry* (New York: Harcourt, Brace and World, 1969), 197.

29. Charles Naginski, "Night Song at Amalfi" (New York: G. Schirmer, 1942). Medium voice. Range: d^1 to e^2. Out of print. Held by the Library of Congress.

30. See Billy Jon Woods, "The Songs of Sergius Kagen," *The NATS Bulletin* 27, no. 3 (1974): 24–25, for a complete listing of the songs. Also see Billy Jon Woods, "Sergius Kagen: His Life and Works" (Dissertation, George Peabody College for Teachers, 1969), for detailed biographical information and stylistic description of the songs.

31. No relation to R. Friedberg whose maiden name was Crane.

32. Sergius Kagen, "The Teaching of Carl Friedberg," *The Juilliard Review* 4 (Winter, 1956–1957): 28–32.

33. There were two daughters born of this marriage: Anna Lee (1944) and Ruth Greer (1950).

34. Sergius Kagen, "Training Accompanists at Juilliard," *The Juilliard Review* 7, no. 1 (1959–1960): 5.

35. Conversation of 9 October 1982, with R. Friedberg.

36. Sergius Kagen, *Music for the Voice* (Bloomington: Indiana University Press, 1968).

37. Sergius Kagen, *On Studying Singing* (New York: Dover, 1960).

38. Sergius Kagen, "Mack Harrell," *The Juilliard Review* 7, no. 2 (1960): 15.

39. Sergius Kagen, "The American Concert Song," *The Juilliard Review* 1 (Fall 1954): 11.

40. Kagen, "The American Concert Song."

41. Kagen, "The American Concert Song," 16.

42. Sergius Kagen, "I Think I Could Turn" (New York: Mercury Music, 1952). Bass. Range: A-sharp to d^1. This song, as well as "Mag," is dedicated to Howard Swanson, himself a writer of many fine songs in the forties and fifties. Both pieces are out of print.

43. See chapter 3 for a discussion of "Walt Whitman," an Ives setting of another portion of "Song of Myself."

44. Sergius Kagen, "Mag" (New York: Weintraub Music, 1950). Baritone. Range: B-flat to e^1. Out of print.

45. Sergius Kagen, "Maybe" (New York: Weintraub Music, 1950). Soprano. Range: d^1 to g^2. Out of print.

46. Sergius Kagen, "A June Day" (New York: Weintraub Music, 1950). Soprano. Range: f-sharp^1 to b-flat^2. Out of print.

47. Sergius Kagen, "Let It Be Forgotten" (New York: Weintraub Music, 1950). High voice. Range: f^1 to f^2. Out of print.

48. "Quartal" is a harmonic system based on the fourth, as distinguished from the common system of "tertian" harmony, based on the third.

49. Interview with R. Friedberg, Philadelphia, 5 February 1975.

50. Anthony, Silvia and Guy. In 1950, G. Schirmer published Nordoff's *Anthony's Song Book* that was a collection of ten play songs for children set to his own texts.

51. For a comprehensive listing of Nordoff's works, see R. Friedberg, "Nordoff, Paul," in Stanley Sadie, ed., *The New Grove Dictionary of Music and Musicians* 13 (London: Macmillan, 1980), 277.

52. For a clear presentation of Steiner's life and thought, see A. P. Shepherd, *A Scientist of the Invisible*. Reprinted in paperback, 1990, and available from Amazon.com.

53. Friedberg, "Nordoff, Paul" (see n51).

54. All of this musical material has been published by Theodore Presser.

55. Nordoff described to R. Friedberg (see n49) a letter in which e.e. cummings had written "I not only like Paul Nordoff's settings, I love them." The relationship between Nordoff and cummings is also discussed in Richard S. Kennedy, *Dreams in the Mirror* (New York: Liveright, 1980), 383–34.

56. Wife of Judge Bok and mother of Derek Bok, president of Harvard University from 1971 to 1991.

57. Telephone conversation with R. Friedberg, 4 July 1973.

58. A further quotation from the Nordoff interview appears in the Introduction.

59. Frederick J. Hoffman, *Conrad Aiken* (New York: Twayne, 1962), Preface.

60. Hoffman, *Conrad Aiken*.

61. Hoffman, *Conrad Aiken*, 70.

62. Stanley Kunitz and Howard Haycraft, eds., *Twentieth Century Authors* (New York: H. W. Wilson, 1942), 13.

63. Paul Nordoff, "White Nocturne" (Philadelphia: Oliver Ditson, 1942). Medium voice. Range: e^1 to e^2. Out of print. Held by the Library of Congress. This song is recorded in John Hanks and Ruth Friedberg, *Art Song in America*, 1997, Duke University Press.

64. Neil Corcoran, "Conrad Aiken," *Great Writers of the English Language—Poets* (New York: St. Martin's, 1979), 14.

65. Untermeyer, *Modern American Poetry*, 419.

66. Paul Nordoff, "Music I heard with you" (London: Schott, 1938). High voice. Range: d sharp^1 to f sharp^2. Out of print. Held by the Library of Congress (foreign copyright deposits).

67. Untermeyer, *Modern American Poetry*, 420.

68. Paul Nordoff, "This is the shape of the leaf" (London: Schott, 1938). Medium voice. Range: b to e^2. Out of print. Held by the Library of Congress (foreign copyright deposits).

69. Paul Nordoff, "Fair Annette's Song" (London: Schott, 1938). High voice. Range: e^1 to f^2. Out of print. Held by the Library of Congress (foreign copyright deposits). Notice that Nordoff changes the spelling of the title that reads "Fair Annet's Song" in Howe's setting and in the original poem. This could, of course, have been a printer's error.

70. Samuel Barber, "On Waiting for a Libretto" *Opera News* 22, no. 13 (January 27, 1958): 4.

71. Nathan Broder, *Samuel Barber* (New York: G. Schirmer, 1954), 9.

72. Harold Randolph also taught John Duke, as discussed in chapter 5.

73. Mary Curtis Bok was the mother-in-law of Nellie Lee Bok, a next generation patron of the arts, and friend of the composer Paul Nordoff.

74. Marcella Sembrich, later at Juilliard, was on the voice faculty of Curtis at its opening. (For her connections with the composer Sergius Kagen, see the discussion of this composer earlier in this chapter).

75. Barber, "On Waiting for a Libretto," 5.

76. Broder, *Samuel Barber*, 19.

77. "Dover Beach" (G. Schirmer) is scored for baritone and string quartet, and was recorded with Barber himself singing the voice part. The other three songs all appear in the *Collected Songs of Samuel Barber* (New York: G. Schirmer, 1971), which are available for high and medium voice.

78. See Irvin Kolodin, "Farewell to Capricorn," *Saturday Review/World* 1 (June 1, 1974): 44–45.

79. All songs by Samuel Barber written and published up to 1969 are in the Schirmer collection (see n77). *Three Songs* written in 1972 are published separately by Schirmer.

80. Nicolas Slonimsky, comp., *Baker's Biographical Dictionary of Musicians* (New York: G. Schirmer, 1978), 97.

81. The James Joyce settings include "Rain Has Fallen," "Sleep Now," and "I Hear an Army."

82. Mark A. Doty, *Tell Me Who I Am* (Baton Rouge: Louisiana State University Press, 1981), 3.

83. Genevieve Moreau, *The Restless Journey of James Agee* (New York: William Morrow, 1977), 29.

84. Samuel Barber, *Knoxville, Summer of 1915* (New York: G. Schirmer, 1949). Actually, Barber sets only excerpts from this work, begun by Agee in the middle thirties, and republished posthumously as a preface to his autobiographical novel, *Death in the Family*. *Knoxville* is dedicated to Roy Barber, the composer's father, who was suffering his terminal illness during its composition. For a discussion of Barber's meeting Agee and identifying with his paternal loss, see Barbara B. Heyman, *Samuel Barber; The Composer and His Music* (New York: Oxford University Press, 1992), 278–79.

85. See *Letters of James Agee to Father Flye* (Boston: Houghton Mifflin, 1971).

86. For a graphic description of James Agee's piano playing, see the introductory "Memoir" in Robert Fitzgerald, ed., *The Collected Short Prose of James Agee* (Boston: Houghton Mifflin, 1958), 42.

87. Moreau, *The Restless Journey*, 94.

88. *Letters to Father Flye*, New York City, 21 September 1941.

89. Peter H. Ohlin, *Agee* (New York: Ivan Obolensky, 1966), 3.

90. Moreau, *The Restless Journey*, 276.

91. Dwight MacDonald, "Death of a Poet," *New Yorker* 33, no. 38 (1957): 226.

92. James Agee, *Permit Me Voyage* (New Haven, Conn.: Yale University Press, 1934).

93. This song appears in the 1971 collection, and an orchestration is available from the publisher. Recorded performances are to be found in: (a) Hanks and Friedberg, *Art Song in America*; (b) Bethany Beardslee and Robert Helps, *But Yesterday Is Not Today* (New York: New World Records, 1977).

94. Compare the following quotation from *Knoxville, Summer of 1915* with the text of "Sure on this Shining Night": "Now is the night one blue dew . . . The stars are wide and alive, they seem like a smile of great sweetness, and they seem very near."

95. See Introduction.

96. This quotation from the *Collected Prose* (Fitzgerald, ed.) is given by Moreau, *The Restless Journey*, 93.

97. Radcliffe Squires, *Frederic Prokosch* (New York: Twayne, 1964).

98. This song is also published in the 1971 collection (see n77), and recorded by Hanks and Friedberg (see n63).

99. See Peter Garland, "Paul Bowles and the Baptism of Solitude" in *Americas: Essays on American Music and Culture 1973–80* (Santa Fe, N.M.: Soundings Press, 1982).

100. Paul Bowles, *Without Stopping* (New York: Putnam, 1972), 69. See also (a) Millicent Dillon, *A Little Original Sin—The Life and Work of Jane Bowles* (New York: Holt, Rinehart and Winston, 1981); (b) Millicent Dillon, ed., *Selected Letters of Jane Bowles* (Santa Barbara, Calif.: Black Sparrow Press, 1985).

101. Dillon, *Selected Letters*, 43.

102. Dillon, *Selected Letters*, 103.

103. Only 100 copies of each composition were printed by this company, and most are long gone. A few are held in the Harry Ransom Center, The University of Texas at Austin, which has a considerable Paul Bowles collection.

104. Paul Bowles, "Letter to Freddy" in *Selected Songs* (Santa Fe, N.M.: Soundings Press, 1984). Medium voice. The collection also contains a number of Bowles songs being published for the first time. Among these are settings of poetry by Paul Bowles, Jane Bowles, and other Tennessee Williams texts, as well as four poems in Spanish by Garcia Lorca. The collection is now out of print but republication efforts are in process.

105. Bowles composed three songs for Saroyan's play *Love's Old Sweet Song* (1940). One of these, "A Little Closer Please (The Pitchman's Song)" is included in Paul Bowles, *Selected Songs* (see n104).

106. Bowles, *Without Stopping*, 229.

107. Peggy Glanville-Hicks, "Paul Bowles—American Composer," *Music and Letters* 26, no. 2 (April 1945): 94.

108. Glanville-Hicks, "Paul Bowles," 88.

109. Quoted in Garland, "Paul Bowles and the Baptism of Solitude," 216.

110. Bowles, *Without Stopping*, 336.

111. Bowles, *Without Stopping*, 369.

112. These letters are held by the Harry Ransom Center (see n103).

113. T. E. Kalem, "The Laureate of the Outcast," *Time* (7 March 1983), 88.

114. Ironically, Dakin Williams had his brother buried in St. Louis (a city which Tennessee had always disliked) because he felt it was centrally located for the many people who would want to visit the grave.

115. Kalem, "The Laureate," 88.

116. Felicia Hardison Londré, *Tennessee Williams* (New York: Frederick Ungar, 1979), 23.

117. Glanville-Hicks, "Paul Bowles," 94.

118. Letter to R. Friedberg, 26 April 1983.

119. Paul Bowles, *Blue Mountain Ballads* (New York: G. Schirmer, 1979). Medium voice. "Lonesome Man" and "Sugar in the Cane" are also included in the Soundings Press Collection. All four songs were recorded by Donald Gramm in *Songs by American Composers* (Desto, 6411/6412). The Hanks/Friedberg recording (see n63) includes "Cabin" and "Heavenly Grass." Most recently, all four songs are included in *I Hear America Singing* (see n24).

120. Glanville-Hicks, "Paul Bowles," 93.

121. Paul Bowles, "Three," Soundings Press collection (see n104). Medium voice.

122. Paul Bowles, "Her Head on the Pillow," Soundings Press collection (see n104). Medium voice.

123. Paul Bowles, "Once a Lady Was Here," Soundings Press collection (see n104). Medium voice.

124. This song is included in Bernard Taylor, ed., *Songs by 22 Americans* (New York: G. Schirmer, 1960).

125. At the First International Art Song Festival in Petit Jean, Arkansas (May 1983), this song was performed in a Paul Bowles group presented as part of Paul Sperry's American art song recital.

126. *But Yesterday Is Not Today: The American Art Song 1927–1972*, Donald Gramm (baritone), Bethany Beardslee (soprano), Robert Helps (piano), Donald Hassard (piano), New World Records 80243.

127. Paul Bowles, "In the Woods," Soundings Press collection (see n104). High voice.

128. Glanville-Hicks, "Paul Bowles," 94.

Chapter 7

The Second Decade

Hugo Weisgall (1912–1997)

Hugo Weisgall was born in Ivancice, Czechoslovakia, and in 1920 his family emigrated to America from a Europe suffering the chaotic aftermath of World War I and the Russian Revolution. Like Sergius Kagen and other European-born artists of his generation, Weisgall became a rich contributor to the creative life of this country. He also became an ardent advocate of American music, and, in a 1965 article, roundly castigated *The Musical Quarterly* for devoting its fiftieth anniversary issue to a survey of European rather than American music.[1]

Weisgall's mother came from a highly cultured family, and his father was a professional opera singer and cantor. From an early age, the boy developed his vocal and instrumental skills as he sang in synagogue choirs and played piano accompaniments while his father performed lieder and operatic arias. In 1921 the family settled in Baltimore, and except for the period of World War II and the travel demands of a busy career, Weisgall remained a Baltimore resident until 1960. Peabody Conservatory, then, was a natural place to start his professional musical training. He won a scholarship there and studied from 1927 to 1930, at the same time beginning an overlapping course of study in Germanic literature at Johns Hopkins University that would eventually result in a doctorate (1940).

During these early years, Weisgall was performing professionally as a singer, an actor, and a conductor of choirs and amateur orchestras. In 1936 he accepted a conducting scholarship at Curtis with Fritz Reiner and for the next three years also worked in composition with Rosario Scalero. The latter's conservatism, however, had less influence on Weisgall's developing style than did his intermittent studies (1933–1941) with Roger Sessions. As he had done with Finney and Naginski (see chapter 6),[2] Sessions opened the young composer's mind to the musical innovations of Stravinsky and Schoenberg as well as of contemporary Americans such as himself.

In 1942, Weisgall enlisted as a private to serve in World War II. He soon found himself assigned on diplomatic missions to England and the continent, after U.S. military intelligence discovered his command of languages and European background. In 1946–1947, he remained as American cultural attaché in Prague, during which time he took advantage of frequent "guest conductorships" to perform many contemporary American scores throughout Europe. On his return to the United States, Weisgall developed an impressive teaching career which included appointments at Juilliard, Peabody, and Queens College, and at the same time emerged as one of America's leading composers of opera. His numerous contributions to the synagogue liturgy, and wide experience in the performance of Jewish music, had also brought him an appointment in 1952 to the chairmanship of the Faculty of the Cantors' Institute of the Jewish Theological Seminary. In 1992 he was commissioned by the seminary's Friends of the Library to compose the song cycle *Psalm of the Distant Dove* commemorating the five hundredth anniversary of the expulsion of the Jews from Spain. Weisgall continued to teach and compose in Great Neck, Long Island, until the end of his life in 1997.

As Bruce Saylor has pointed out, "the vocal impulse is primary" in Hugo Weisgall's music,[3] and the composer himself had said "If I can't sing it, I don't write it."[4] In 1931, he had won Columbia University's Bearns prize with a set of songs called *Four Impressions*, and in 1933 he composed *Five Night Songs*. Both of these works remain in manuscript, and the only American poet whose texts appear therein is Amy Lowell in the *Four Impressions*. However, in 1934 Weisgall set another American poet, this time so successfully that the *Four Songs* to Adelaide Crapsey's poetry became, as Opus 1, his first published work.

In a letter to R. Friedberg dated September 7, 1983, Hugo Weisgall commented on the poets that had attracted him in this and subsequent periods of his composition. "Specifically concerning Crapsey," he said, "I discovered her poetry way back in the late twenties or early thirties while I was still an undergraduate. I had always written songs from early childhood and among my early unpublished work there are settings of Amy Lowell. Somehow or other I seemed to have set a large number of women poets. I don't know why that is. I have known and do know," he concluded, "a great many American poets, some of them quite well, and at present I am working on a large cycle of texts by John Hollander."

Adelaide Crapsey (1878–1914)

Adelaide Crapsey's life has been treated at some length in chapter 5. It was a tragic life in which a brilliant, creative woman who had been elected to Phi Beta Kappa at Vassar, taught poetics at Smith College, and invented a compressed and elegant five-line verse structure called the "cinquain," was doomed to an early death from tubercular meningitis. Her health waned during the last decade of her life, and after a complete collapse in 1913 she was taken to Dr. Trudeau's widely recognized nursing home at Saranac Lake, New York. Here she spent the year before her death looking out the window at the graveyard she called "Trudeau's Garden" and using her poetic gift to record her muffled anguish over the approaching end.

Except for the Asian influences that had prompted the "cinquains" of 1911–1913, Crapsey's verse shows little evidence of the experimentalism in poetic form and language of her contemporaries. But study of the Japanese hokku models had contributed a Dickinson-like brevity and directness to the author's expression, and her "courageous refusal to soften . . . despair with vague appeals to the immortality of the soul,"[5] was a direct precursor of the growing twentieth-century tide of Existentialism.[6] Weisgall's *Four Songs*[7] use an apparent minimum of musical device so as not to lessen the stark poignancy of the textual message, and the result is a devastatingly powerful example of a musical "soft sell."

Each of the four takes its title directly from the poem. In number one, which is only one page long, the "Old Love" of the title seems fittingly interpreted as the dimly remembered face of Death, a "ghost" whose "eyes most strangely glow." Weisgall makes of the six verse lines a small three-part form in which the two A sections, and the piano introduction, employ a circular, chant-like figure hovering around three adjacent scale degrees. This figure suggests the terrible hypnotic power of the phantom's gaze, while the variously changing 3/4 2/4 meter and continuous small waves of dynamic rise and fall add the ambivalent victim's attraction and revulsion.

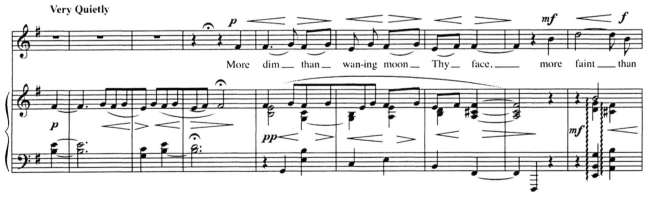

Example 7.1, mm. 1–8

Number two, called simply "Song," uses an all treble register, tinkling piano part, and regular, flowing vocal rhythms to create the semblance of a springtime ballad. But the opening E minor key and softly clashing dissonances provide the clue to the chilling deception soon revealed by the text ("I make my shroud, but no one knows").

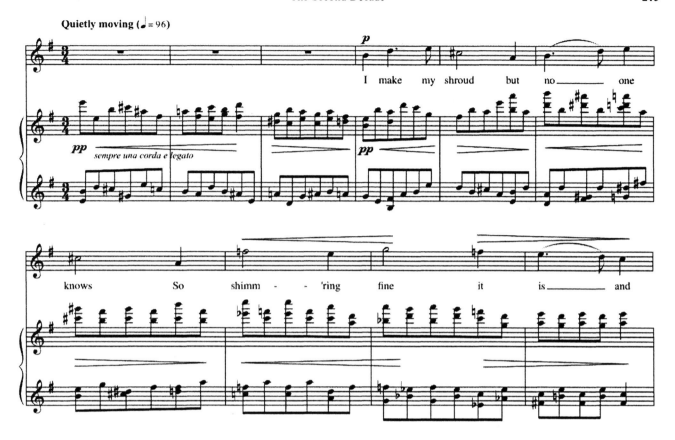

Example 7.2, mm. 1–10

In the most telling, eerie moment of the setting, Weisgall moves to G major for a seemingly innocent, light-hearted melisma on "a little wandering air" over a folkish, drone-like bass in the accompaniment.

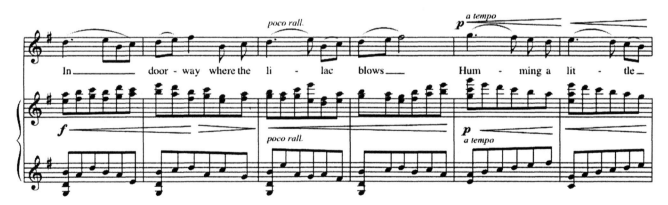

Example 7.3, mm. 22–33

The poetic contrast between the visual and aural images of life and the secret knowledge of Death is perfectly captured in this setting by its use of the myriad available contradictions of musical language.

In number two, Weisgall had repeated Crapsey's final line ("So shimmering fine it is and fair") to form a coda for his mock folk-ballad structure. For his third setting, "Oh, Lady, Let the Sad Tears Fall," the composer uses text repetition three times in a litany of sorrow whose lyric contours, long sustained tones, and pauses in the vocal line suggest a struggle with overwhelming emotion. The familiar Baroque "affection" of chromaticism in the context of anguish is expanded to a moving bi-tonal climax in the accompaniment following the word "pain."

Example 7.4, mm. 6–14

In two other skillful instances of "word painting," Weisgall writes a brief vocal rest before the word, "sigh," and applies a descending line in the lowest tessitura of the cycle to "where / Pale roses die."

Example 7.5, mm. 28–33

The fourth and final setting is of a poem called "Dirge" [8] which is a polite, understated description of Death as an approaching absence of sensation, particularly the sense of hearing. The music has the restraint of the text (this setting, too, is one page long) with only subtly altered chords attesting to the sharpness of the coming loss.

Example 7.6, mm. 7–14

In the foregoing example, the apparently simple rhythmic repetition in the vocal line which clothes "Tap at thy window-sill" becomes an inspired closing of the cycle, as it suggests both a lively, feathered visitor, and the bony finger of Death itself.

Hugo Weisgall's next song cycle was *Soldier Songs*,[9] written a decade later (1944–1946) as a direct result of his war-time service. Deeply moved by the futility and horror of war, the composer chose for setting nine poems by British and American authors that had been written as a result of the poets' personal experiences. To these he added his own experience, and recalls writing one of the set in an air-raid shelter of the Brussels Radio Station; another after returning from a "tour" of a German concentration camp. The work was premièred in New York in 1954 by Grant Garnell, baritone, and Stanton Carter, pianist. In 1966 the orchestral version received its first performance with Robert Trehy, baritone, and the Baltimore Symphony conducted by Peter Herman Adler.

e.e. cummings (1894–1962)

Two of the *Soldier Songs*, which are both settings of American texts, demonstrate the wide variety of poetic mood and musical treatment found in the cycle. Number four sets "my sweet old etcetera," written by e.e. cummings, whose initial treatment by these authors can be found in chapter 5. Basically, cummings was a pacifist, but had felt impelled toward some type of humanitarian service as World War I decimated a generation of European youth. In April 1917, having only recently moved to New York and begun to work for *Collier's*, he enlisted with the Norton Harjes ambulance group which was based in France. The entire enterprise was to prove ill-fated, after a bad beginning in which cummings failed to find his unit and located it only after a week's delay in Paris. Then a misinterpretation by French censors of apparently pro-German comments in cummings's letters resulted in his internment in a kind of concentration camp at La Ferté-Macé. He was eventually released through intervention by the American government, but it was a bitter experience which became the basis of *The Enormous Room*, his first long prose work, published in 1922.

Back in the United States, he was drafted and sent to Camp Devens, forty miles west of Cambridge. This proved physically beneficial, but psychologically difficult for cummings, and his wartime experiences left him with a value system that included a deep need for personal freedom from social structures, as well as the recognition of human vulnerability to chance and the forces of nature.[10] In 1926, the continuing bitterness surfaced again in his writing, with a group of anti-war poems that were included in *is 5*. This volume had been contracted by Horace Liveright following the promising appearance of *Tulips and Chimneys*, cummings's first collection of verse, three years earlier. This time the publisher requested an introduction that would help people understand the poet's style, but the one which cummings supplied did little to accomplish this purpose. The poems of *is 5* show much of the same visual experimentation and word-play of his first volume, but there is a marked increase in satire: in the war poems, in those commenting on contemporary American life, and in lyrics such as "my sweet old etcetera" which combine both elements.

The picture presented here is of a useless flurry of home front activity ("my sister isabel created hundreds of socks") and of the empty talk by elderly relatives about the meaning of the war and the "privilege" of participating. As a final ironic touch, cummings, whose sexual initiation had occurred during his week in Paris in 1917, ends the poem with himself, lying "quietly in the deep mud," dreaming, not of the glories of combat, but of "Your smile/eyes knees and of your Etcetera." The poem has the poet's typical visual distortions of word groupings, but parts of speech are all used conventionally except for "Etcetera" which after previous heavy employment in its usual function, becomes a noun in the final line quoted above.

In Weisgall's setting, the distorted word groupings disappear, and connected verbal ideas become musical phrases. Thus lines such as

> what everybody was fighting
> for
> my sister
> isabel created hundreds

are rejoined into the following:

Example 7.7, mm. 8–17

The composer demonstrates, in this song, his tendency to underline strong emotion by musical repetition not in the poetic original. Suggesting the poet's suppressed rage at his father's facile and fatuous statements, Weisgall incorporates one repetition each of "my father" and of "if only he could," while "a privilege" receives four repetitions, a series of sharp staccato leaps, and a hysterical crescendo of sound.

Example 7.8, mm. 30–34

As can be seen in these examples, Weisgall's style remains basically tonal in these pieces, but incorporates a more dissonant, disjunct vocal line, and considerably more chromaticism in the harmony than the *Four Songs* of 1934. The change was discernible throughout his works of the forties and is certainly appropriate to the grim and often tragic texts of the *Soldier Songs*. A unifying element in the cycle is the interval of a major sixth (which opens the cummings setting) and the minor third, its inversion (which closes it).

Example 7.9a, mm. 1–3

Examples 7.9b, mm. 47–49

Finally, one of the most striking features of the song is Weisgall's use of popular dance rhythms, such as the dotted-note patterns of ragtime in Example 7.8, measures 30–31, and the syncopated "beguine" accompaniment of Example 7.9a, which pervades much of the setting. This device characterizes with a dramatic stroke the poet's vision of wartime America's selfishness and merely superficial concern for her soldiers.

Herman Melville (1819–1891)

The last song of the set is "Shiloh," a musical treatment of a poem from the collection titled *Battle-Pieces* written by Herman Melville, whose life will be discussed at some length later in this chapter. Melville had dedicated *Battle-Pieces* "to the memory of the three hundred thousand who in the war for the maintenance of the union fell devotedly under the flag of their fathers."[11] Although largely ignored at its publication in 1866, the volume is now ranked with Walt Whitman's *Drum Taps* (see chapter 2) as among the best of the Civil War poetry.

"Shiloh's" subtitle is "A Requiem (April, 1862)" which date refers to the terrible "Sunday fight / Around the church of Shiloh" in southern Tennessee which resulted in the slaughter of nearly 25,000 Union and Confederate troops. The moving poem contrasts the peaceful present as swallows skim the field, with the remembered scene of desolation, filled with groans of the dying, who had been "Foemen at morn, but friends at eve."

Weisgall's setting is in the key of E minor, established at the outset by the lowest voice of the accompaniment which outlines the tonic triad in steady quarter note motion. On top of this, the rest of the accompaniment and the voice line participate in the creation of dissonant seconds and sevenths, whose pianissimo dynamic context suggests a shimmering veil of lingering horror over the peaceful surface. (Although the dramatic mood is quite different, the technique is reminiscent of "Song," discussed previously in the Crapsey settings.)

Example 7.10, mm. 1–7

The song has a basically three-part structure with a shortened return to A. The middle section, which describes the battle itself, has an agitated leaping vocal contour (see Ex. 7.11) while the two outer sections present a more lyric and stepwise line:

Example 7.11, mm. 31–33

Two startlingly dramatic portamentos, one of an octave and the other of a tenth, occur in a crescendo context (piano to a sudden forte) and are totally shocking, like the bloody events of the day (see Ex. 7.11). Two brief but powerful instances of musical pictorialization further heighten the drama. One is a measure in which the soft, staccato pulse of the pianist's left hand recalls the menacing march with its accompanying drumbeat (see Ex. 7.10, m. 6) and the other is the sharply accented, bi-tonal, fortissimo chords which suggest the deadly impact of a bullet (see Ex. 7.11).

The poem's refrain-like fourth line ("The forest-field of Shiloh") and final line ("And all is hushed at Shiloh") receive similar melodic and harmonic treatment which serves to unify the individual setting, while the minor third concluding the vocal line ties this song to the rest of the cycle (see Ex. 7.12). The sense of ancient ceremony that Weisgall achieves at the end of "Shiloh" is largely due to the last two accompanying chords. The first chord uses a lowered second step (found in the Phrygian ecclesiastical mode) and the second is an empty, open fifth sonority in the medieval and Renaissance tradition.

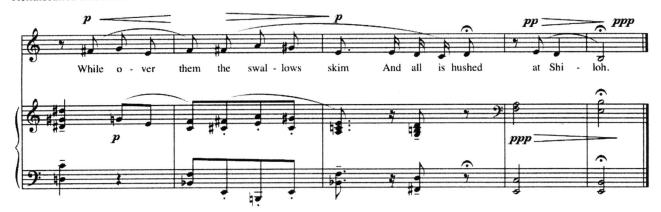

Example 7.12, mm. 38–42

Norman Dello Joio (1913–2008)

Music was always a natural element to Norman Dello Joio, and the lyricism that dominates his vocal and instrumental works was seeded by heredity and nourished through environment. His father, Casimir Dello Joio, was an Italian organist and composer who emigrated to the United States and settled in New York City. He married an American and assumed the post of organist at the Church of Our Lady of Mt. Carmel. Norman's earliest memories were of creeping out of bed to listen to his father's musician friends, all ardent fans of Italian opera, performing Verdi arias far into the night.

The boy soon demonstrated his native talent by beginning to pick out the major arias on the piano. Casimir then undertook his formal instruction in piano and organ and, at the age of fourteen, Norman Dello Joio was given the first of several subsequent positions as organist and choir director in a church of his own. During his teens, he composed music for recreation, and in his remaining leisure hours became so proficient at baseball that he is probably the only American composer ever to have been offered a place on a professional ball team.

Having chosen to sacrifice immediate glory for the longer lasting satisfaction of an artistic career, Dello Joio undertook his advanced musical training at City College and the Institute of Musical Art, after which he won a fellowship in composition under Bernard Wagenaar[12] at the Juilliard Graduate School. One of the teachers who influenced him the most was Paul Hindemith, with whom he studied in the opening session of the Berkshire Music School. This program had been established by Serge Koussevitzky as part of the summer festival at Tanglewood, and Dello Joio's classmates in that exciting 1940 season included Leonard Bernstein, Harold Shapero, and Lukas Foss. Dello Joio continued to study with Hindemith during the next winter at Yale University, and returned to Tanglewood with him the following summer. By the end of this time, the young composer had been encouraged by the older master to follow his own creative instincts, and the clarification and development of the Dello Joio style were well under way.[13]

During the middle decades of the twentieth century, Norman Dello Joio was not only one of America's most established and prolific composers, but also a major force in the philosophy and practice of music education in this country at many levels. He taught composition for a number of years, first at Sarah Lawrence College from 1945 to 1950, and subsequently at Mannes College of Music from 1956 to 1972. He then continued his university career at the administrative level, as dean of the School for the Arts at Boston University (1972–1978). After his retirement from academe, he continued to compose during the last three decades of his long life until his death in 2008 at his home in East Hampton.

Dello Joio had become involved, in the late fifties, with a Ford Foundation project, which placed young composers in the public schools to write for their performing groups. As an outgrowth of this, Dello Joio served as chairman of the Contemporary Music Project for Creativity in Music Education, under the joint sponsorship of the Music Educators' National Conference and the Ford Foundation. In his comments that were part of a long retrospective article published in 1968 on the work of the Project, the composer dated his personal concern with the teaching of musicianship from his Sarah Lawrence appointment. Here he had come to realize that students who wanted to be musically creative through their "intuition" were hampered by their lack of musical knowledge and discipline. Having then committed his energies to the introduction of this discipline at the public school level, and as a result of his work for the Ford Foundation, he began asking himself a series of such fundamental questions as: "Is an academic degree a guarantee of professional competence?" and "Are our teacher training programs and curricula adequate?"[14]

These questions were particularly relevant in the 1960s, that long-vanished decade of seemingly unlimited university funding which appeared to promise a haven of support for all types of artistic activity. In "The Composer and the American Scene," Dello Joio warned that the proliferating fine arts centers would be no better than the level of activity taking place inside them, and that teachers' colleges must beware of spending "more time on methods of teaching than on music itself."[15] At the same time, he emphasized the importance of the creative artist's mission in a world dominated by the destructive potential of nuclear warfare. "The fruit of his labor," said Dello Joio, "is an expression of humanity's will to survive," and added "The artist is also in a sense today's penitent, for he atones for much of modern man's abandonment of his own soul."[16]

In the course of his career, Norman Dello Joio composed several operas, and a number of choral works. Among these choral pieces are settings of texts by the American poets Stephen Vincent Benét and Walt Whitman. Concerning the latter, the composer stated "I have written extensively to the poetry of Walt Whitman because his thought was so all embracing and . . . lent itself to epic musical expression."[17] Another American setting of sweeping proportions is Dello Joio's *Songs of Remembrance*[18] for baritone and orchestra, written to the poetry of John Hall Wheelock, "a neighbor and close friend in my town of East Hampton, New York. Unfortunately," added the composer, "he did not live to hear the premiére of the work with the Philadelphia Symphony."[19]

It is clear then, that Norman Dello Joio was drawn to set the work of American poets on a number of occasions. What did not appear to attract him strongly was the intimate medium of the art song with piano, although the *Six Love Songs* of 1949,[20] his major effort in this genre, remain a valuable addition to the literature. Only one of the six, "The Dying Nightingale,"[21] is to an American text, and the composer had this to say of its origins: "Stark Young wrote the poem for me. It was to be an aria in a projected plan I had for a short opera based on Oscar Wilde's fairy tale, *The Nightingale and the Rose*. The opera was never completed."[22]

Stark Young (1881–1963)

Stark Young was an extremely versatile man of letters who never forgot his birthplace and his early influences in the town of Como, Mississippi. His father was a respected family doctor and his mother a beautiful, dark-haired, blue-eyed young woman who died when Stark was only eight, leaving him unable to speak of his profound loss for many years. The society that surrounded his childhood was still suffering the painful aftereffects of the Civil War and Reconstruction, but Young perceived this environment as gentle and loving, and recounted the colorful reminiscences of his youth in an autobiography called *The Pavilion* published in 1951.[23]

Young's father and other relatives supported Stark through his university education with great determination, despite limited family resources. He took his undergraduate degree at the University of Mississippi, and while in the city of Oxford, came to know William Faulkner, who was then a young man beginning to write verse. After earning an M.A. in English at Columbia University, Young began a teaching career that lasted from 1904 to 1921, and included positions on the faculties of English literature at the University of Mississippi, University of Texas, and Amherst College. In 1921, he abandoned teaching for journalism and joined the editorial staff of the *New Republic* and *Theatre Arts Monthly*. After a two-year stint (1924–1925) as drama critic of the *New York Times*, he returned to the *New Republic* and stayed on as drama editor until his retirement in 1947.

Stark Young's criticism was greatly prized by his literary contemporaries, and his pivotal position in the theatrical world during his working years is clear from that portion of his correspondence now held by the University of Texas.[24] In this collection are letters from and to such playwrights as Sherwood Anderson and Eugene O'Neill, and actors and actresses of the stature of Alfred Lunt, Katharine Cornell, and Eleonora Duse. Composers are also represented, with a Christmas card from Igor Stravinsky and thank you notes to Gian Carlo Menotti and Norman Dello Joio.

Besides his high-level criticism, Stark Young also wrote a number of his own plays, as well as several novels. He was identified as a writer with the so-called Southern Renaissance that emerged in the middle decades of the twentieth century, and he had indeed contributed an essay in 1930 to a collection called *I'll Take My Stand* that was a manifesto of American Southern agrarianism. Young's attachment to Southern soil had been strengthened by a number of months spent living in the North Carolina mountains, both before and after his graduate year at Columbia. In time, he also began to perceive meaning in the social patterns of the South, which growth in perception he described in these terms:

> The affability and grace of Southern manners . . . made the surface of things easier and pleasanter; but I felt that it was merely the surface. It was only much later that I came to understand the value of forms and ritual and symbols [and to] understand that to think within a tradition of forms and words may be to think within what is solid and human.[25]

Like many creative individuals, Stark Young was gifted in more than one art form. Although his father denied his request for painting lessons at the age of eleven, the writer eventually became a painter as well and exhibited in the New York galleries in the years following his retirement. His earliest creative medium, however, was poetry, and in 1906 he had published a collection of poems called *The Blind Man at the Window* and a verse play entitled *Guinevere*. It is easy to see why his years of experience with dramatic and poetic forms made him desirable to Norman Dello Joio as the librettist for his projected opera, *The Nightingale and the Rose*.

The Oscar Wilde tale, which was to have been the basis of the work, is taken from his *Complete Fairy Stories*, and like so many of this genre, is almost too painful for adult contemplation. In it, a young student is desperate for lack of a red rose to give to the lady of his choice, and a nightingale who loves him, sings all night pressing her breast against a thorn, so that her dying heart's blood may color the flower. Stark Young's text for "The Dying Nightingale" represents the dramatic climax of the story: the final moments during which the bird invokes Death to "Come with thy sweet darkness," as she willingly enters a night in which she will "sing forever." The lines are unrhymed, mostly containing four stresses in varying poetic meters, and the phrase "Come, sweet Death" occurs at the beginning of the outer sections of a three-part form. The middle section is an inspired transfer into the first person of Wilde's passage describing the effect of the nightingale's last faint notes on the listening natural world. "Does the white moon hear me?" she asks. "Do the river reeds carry my voice to the sea?"

Dello Joio has set this poignant text in a freely moving, arioso style in which the rhythmic pulse holds to the quarter note throughout, but variously contains three, four, five, or six beats per measure. The free flow of rhythm is counterbalanced by several tightly controlled formal elements, even as the bird's movement is constrained by the terms of her sacrifice. The first of these is the motivic germ of a perfect fourth, expressed in the rhythmic pattern of a dotted quarter and eighth note that is announced in the piano introduction and restated in inversion as the voice enters.

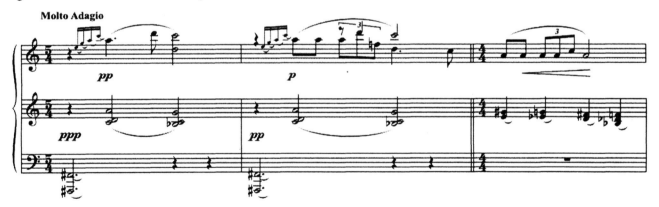

Example 7.13, mm. 1–7

The second is a pandiatonic harmonic scheme that opens in D major and proceeds to vary this tonality with passages in other aspects of D (i.e., D-flat major, C-sharp minor, and the Dorian mode). This aspect of the writing comes together with the third element, a three-part musical structure that coincides with the poetic one indicated in Example 7.13. Thus, section three entering with "Come, sweet Death" repeats its original Dorian context in D-flat major, with the motif transposed up to a passionate statement beginning on the chordal seventh.

Example 7.14, mm. 23–24

Finally, the harmony ends its restless wandering with a quiet return to the opening piano material in the original key, as the text portrays the end of the nightingale's pain in peaceful death.

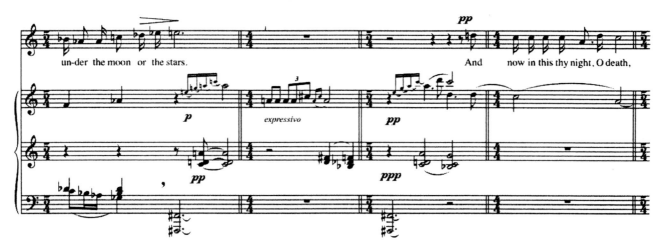

Example 7.15, mm. 32–37

The motivic fourth in a dotted note pattern which recurs in Example 7.15 suggests an actual component of birdsong, and the topmost line in the opening three measures state this basic interval followed by two variants thereof (see Ex. 7.13). Also reminiscent of the nightingale's cadence are the many instances of syllabic vocal setting on rapidly moving sixteenth notes, which are suggestive of gentle, bird-like twittering.

Example 7.16, mm. 19–21

David Diamond (1915–2005)

David Diamond was born in Rochester, New York, a city that remained a focal point in his life, and which he chose, in 1964, to again make his home after many years' absence. Diamond's parents were Austrian-Jewish immigrants, his father a carpenter by profession, and his mother a former dressmaker with a deep-rooted love of music and theater. Early on young David early began to exhibit his mother's musical propensities. By the age of seven he had taught himself to play the violin on a borrowed instrument, and had begun to write down original melodies in an ingenious notation of his own devising.

Unfortunately, there were no family funds to assure the growth of this precocious talent, and David Diamond's musical training was to be gained in years of struggle during which his studies were supported entirely by scholarship. In 1925, his family was forced to leave Rochester for financial reasons and go to live with relatives in Cleveland. Here he attracted the attention of a Swiss musician named André de Ribaupierre, and was enabled to attend the Cleveland Institute of Music from 1927 to 1929. When the family returned to Rochester in 1930, Diamond became a scholarship student at the Eastman School and remained there for four years, studying composition with Bernard Rogers, and playing second violin in the conservatory orchestra.

His next mentor in composition was Roger Sessions, with whom he studied at the New Music School and the Dalcroze Institute in New York. Once again there was scholarship aid, but living was now a problem as well, and Diamond held a series of menial jobs to earn expense money. In 1935, his work began to be recognized, and he won the $2500 Paul Whiteman award for his *Sinfonietta*, based on a Carl Sandburg poem. The same summer, he received a fellowship to the MacDowell Colony in Peterborough, New Hampshire, and in 1936 was elated when e.e. cummings accepted him as the composer of music for his ballet *Tom*.

The commission proved important not only for itself (the ballet was never actually produced) but because its financial backers sent Diamond to Paris to collaborate with Leonid Massine, the choreographer. Having been already attracted to contemporary French musical influences, the young composer was now excited to find himself in their midst, and returned to France a second and third summer to study at Fontainebleau with Nadia Boulanger. Germany's declaration of war against France brought an end to this fruitful and pleasant period. Back in the United States, the struggle for acceptance began again, and again the forces were mustered by which America supported her promising composers in mid-twentieth century. Diamond was given successively a residence at the Yaddo estate in Saratoga, a renewal of his 1938 Guggenheim fellowship, the cash prize of the Prix de Rome (war preventing residence in Italy), and finally the National Academy of Arts and Letters grant.

The citation that accompanied the National Academy's 1944 grant mentioned "the high quality of [Diamond's] achievement as demonstrated in orchestral works, chamber music, and songs."[26] Although this was relatively early in his career, solo song did indeed prove to be a major genre in Diamond's prolific catalog, and he published forty settings between 1940 and the early 1950s. This same period also saw him engaged in composing music for theatrical productions, which included three film scores and incidental music to Shakespeare's *Tempest* and *Romeo and Juliet* as well as Tennessee Williams's *The Rose Tattoo*.

At the age of thirty-five, David Diamond began a series of sporadic teaching appointments in Europe and the United States with a year spent at the Metropolitan School of Music in New York City. In 1951, he went to Europe as a Fulbright professor, eventually settling in Florence where he remained until 1965 except for brief appointments at the University of Buffalo in 1961 and 1963. He chaired the composition department at the Manhattan School of Music from 1965 to 1967, was visiting professor at the University of Colorado in Boulder in 1970, and in 1973 began a twenty-five year tenure as professor of composition at Juilliard. (Between the last two positions, he had returned to Italy as composer-in-residence at the American Academy that had awarded him the Prix de Rome thirty years earlier.)

Diamond's remarkable works of the 1930s and 1940s had fallen out of favor during the serial oriented mid-twentieth century decades, but were rescued from obscurity in the 1980s by Gerard Schwarz who performed and recorded over thirty of his orchestral works with the Seattle Symphony and the New York Chamber Symphony. This renewed interest in Diamond's music brought the composer a number of important awards, among them the gold medal of the American Academy of Arts and Letters in 1991, the American National Medal of the Arts in 1996, and an honorary Doctor of Music degree from Juilliard in 1998. David Diamond died in Rochester in 2005, shortly before his ninetieth birthday.

As Slee Professor of Music at the University of Buffalo in 1961, Diamond had delivered a series of three lectures entitled "Integrity and Integration in Contemporary Music," "The Babel of Twentieth Century Music," and "Beethoven and the Twentieth Century." In the first of these, discussing contemporary aspects of the American scene, he remarked that "nowhere else in the Western World have so many disparate cultural influences worked advantageously and productively,"[27] and described the merging of contributions from Europe, Africa, China, Japan, and Latin America with folk, jazz, and popular theater music in the melting pot of our national style. Three years later, the articulate composer aired his views in the *Music Journal* on the future of a contemporary music that seemed to many, in 1964, to be floundering for direction. "It is my strong feeling," he said, "that a romantically inspired contemporary music, tempered by reinvigorated classical technical formulas, is the way out of the present period of creative chaos in music. . . . A composer's greatness," he added, "is gauged by how he enlarges and extends spiritual communication between himself and humanity."[28]

One of the areas of David Diamond's most successful communication with humanity had certainly been that of the art song. Hans Nathan observed in *A History of Song* that Diamond "has cultivated the art song more consistently than any other American composer of his standing" and that "among the variety of forms that he commands, his songs represent his finest achievements."[29] His ability to set a wide variety of literary styles was most striking, as William Flanagan, a song composer himself, remarked in 1952: "Diamond's choice of textual material knows practically no limit in diversity."[30] About half the writers set by David Diamond were American, and he had this to say of the selection process:

> My friendship with the poet e.e. cummings . . . produced a full flowering of my taste in choosing texts for settings; also my friendship with Carson McCullers and Katherine Anne Porter, miraculous women, alas, gone forever. My love of Melville stems from my adolescent years reading his poetry—then *Moby Dick* and *Billy Budd* and eventually everything else between 1939–51. Melville to me is like reading Job or Isaiah. But he is also a kind of Great Father, Great Lover, Great Prophet, Great Martyr. He nourishes me when I am most depressed.[31]

Herman Melville (1819–1891)

It is easy to understand why David Diamond, who had known years of physical and psychological struggle toward recognition as an artist, would identify with and draw strength from Herman Melville, whose rightful place in American literature was denied him until twenty years after his death. Melville was born in New York City, to parents whose families had old roots in America. His mother's ancestors, the Gansevoorts, were linked to the greatest Dutch patroon families who had settled New York, and his father had traced his line even farther back to Scottish Renaissance courtiers and a Queen of Hungary. Melville's early childhood was spent in luxury, but his father's business reverses and subsequent death in 1832 made "poor relations" of his whole family, who moved to Albany and became dependent on the care of the Gansevoorts. Herman left school at twelve, holding various jobs (including a year of teaching) until 1839, when he began the five years at sea which would form the basis of much of his writing and life experience.

In 1846, with two successful novels, *Typee* and *Omoo*, behind him, he married Elizabeth Shaw, daughter of the Chief Justice of Massachusetts, and bought a house in New York City, to which he brought not only his bride, but his mother, four sisters, and his younger brother Allan and wife as well. Success, however, was to prove short-lived. Subsequent novels gained only intermittent approval of critics and the public, and in 1850 he moved his family to a farm at Pittsfield, Massachusetts, where he continued work on *Moby Dick* despite his publisher's refusal to advance him money. Melville's responsibilities were growing (by 1855 he had two sons and two daughters), and he now began a new career as short-story writer for *Harper's* and *Putnam's*, the *Putnam's* stories being published eventually as *The Piazza Tales*.

In 1856, Melville was forced to sell part of his farm and, close to a nervous collapse, was sent by his father-in-law on an extensive trip to Europe and the Levant. These travels, during which he kept a journal, also nourished his later work, although on his return, he did not write for several years.

The decade of the 1860s proved to be the most difficult of all for Herman Melville and his family. Devastated by the collapse of his literary career and the repeated failures of his attempts to find a government job in Washington, Melville's behavior suffered to the extent that his wife began to fear for his sanity. A turning point was reached in 1866 when the writer obtained a political job as deputy customs inspector in New York City, and after the suicide of their son, Malcolm, in 1867, Melville and his wife drew closer together. He remained in his position as customs inspector for the next twenty years, when a series of legacies finally enabled him to retire and spend all his time writing.

During the last thirty years of Melville's life, he produced a considerable body of poetry, most of which attracted very little attention at the time. *Battle-Pieces* (see the earlier discussion of Hugo Weisgall in this chapter) was published in 1866 by *Harper's* and by 1868 had sold only 486 copies. "Clarel," a long, philosophical poem which has been characterized as one of America's most thoughtful contributions to the conflict between religious faith and Darwinian skepticism,[32] was published with funds designated in a specific bequest from his dying uncle Peter Gansevoort. The majority of the poems written after "Clarel" were collected into two volumes and printed privately by Melville through the Caxton Press shortly before his death in 1891. At about this same time, something like a Herman Melville "revival" was beginning to get underway, particularly in England, but it ended with his death. The works remained in relative obscurity until the centennial of his birth in 1919, which occasioned a wave of new scholarship and a reevaluation of his many long-neglected masterpieces.

Although largely self-educated, Herman Melville possessed an unusually reflective and philosophical mind, and spent a lifetime trying to construct a moral and metaphysical system that would account for the inequities and ambiguities of human experience. His preoccupations with the ultimate problems of life, death, and the vagaries of Destiny pervade his poetry as well as his prose works, and find a perfect musical counterpart in David Diamond's settings. Reflecting the fact that Diamond's performing instrument was the violin, these settings have accompaniments that are for the most part contrapuntally conceived and show little exploitation of pianistic figuration. This affords prominence to the "great and tender texts"[33] (the phrase is the composer's) and to the vocal line which carries them in a highly sensitive prosodic rendering that clings to the original poetic accents.

"Epitaph,"[34] composed in 1945, sets another of Melville's *Battle-Pieces*, this one included in a group designated as "Verses Inscriptive and Memorial." Its original title, printed by Diamond as a subtitle, was "On the Grave of a Young Cavalry Officer Killed in the Valley of Virginia," and the mood of the poem forms a peaceful contrast to the bloody memories of "Shiloh" (see the earlier discussion of Hugo Weisgall in this chapter). In five skillfully concentrated lines, a swift portrait is painted of a young man gifted in his "beauty . . . manners . . . and friends," and who possessed "gold— yet a mind not unenriched." The final line that describes "his happier fortune in this mound" is surprising in the face of Melville's avowed and uncomfortable agnosticism, and of his many *Battle-Pieces* that deplored war's waste of youthful promise. The line, therefore, may represent a mellowing toward hope that is observable in some of the poetry of the later years or it may also be seen as an almost intolerably ironic view of "heroic" death in battle.

Diamond chooses to interpret the "inscription" positively and creates an atmosphere of serenity not unlike that of Hugo Wolf's "Anakreon's Grab" in which another noble life and well-deserved rest in death are commemorated. A corresponding quality of musical "tenderness" is achieved through the quiet simplicity of a transparent texture, steady rhythmic flow in quarter notes (predominantly 3/4), and an unassuming but poignant melodic motif stated in the opening piano phrase.

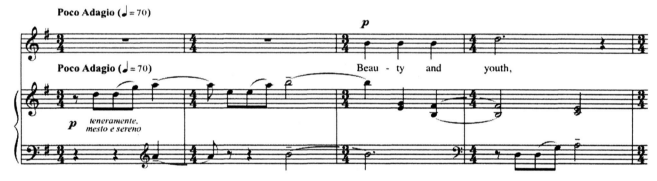

Example 7.17, mm. 1–4

This motif is carried into the vocal contour to set "with manners sweet," and also functions structurally in the accompaniment during the singer's rests.

Example 7.18, mm. 5–9

The effect of these carefully calculated vocal pauses in this and other Diamond settings is twofold: they at once afford added emphasis to the words thus highlighted in temporal space, and at the same time suggest an imaginatively inflected verbal reading of the text. Also notice in Example 7.18 the many chordal sonorities containing open fifths and fourths which tend to emphasize the lightness of texture and its analogy to the undeveloped life cut off before its flowering.

"Monody" comes from Melville's *Timoleon*, one of the poetry collections he had printed in 1891, in an edition limited to twenty-five copies. The book was dedicated to Elihu Vedder, an American artist whom Melville admired but had never met, and the poem "Monody" is widely believed to refer to another creative artist admired by Melville: the writer Nathaniel Hawthorne. Melville and Hawthorne had begun a friendship around 1850 when Melville had reviewed Hawthorne's *Mosses From an Old Manse* for *Literary World* in most favorable terms. "Monody" is a lament for a beloved friend from whom the protagonist has become "estranged in life," and literary historians point out that no estrangement occurred in this case except that of distance and intervening events in the writers' lives. It is also true, however, that by the time of the Melville "revival," many valuable biographical materials had been lost, including Hawthorne's letters, which had been burned by Melville himself. An undocumented estrangement therefore remains a possibility.

Though the genesis of the poem is in doubt, its artistry is not, and it falls into that category of "elegiac subjects" which, as Hans Nathan points out, are particularly suited to Diamond's idiom: those subjects, that is, that "speak of a valuable person or a moral quality that has disappeared but is remembered with sad affection."[35] "Monody"[36] was also composed in 1945 and together with "Epitaph" seemed to have captured the particular devotion of the American public. In speaking of his Melville songs, Diamond said "I am always being written to about them, especially 'Epitaph' and 'Monody.'"[37]

"Monody" shows the same contrapuntal interweaving of voices, pauses between poetic phrases, and meticulous attention to prosodic detail as "Epitaph," and adds an arching lyrical voice line whose convincing contours follow the rise and fall of passionate grief and wintry resignation. The harmonic language is tonal but highly colored with Diamond's frequent chords of the seventh and ninth, and a brief excursion into chromatic alterations occurs for the setting of the crucially painful line "And now for death to set his seal." Neither "Monody" nor "Epitaph" exhibits much use of "word-painting" or descriptive musical device. The composer concentrates rather on the overall mood of the text and with a broad palette enlists all stylistic elements in its service.

"A Portrait,"[38] set by Diamond in 1946, is rather different. This setting is of another poem from *Timoleon*, originally titled "The Marchioness of Brinvilliers," and describes a painting viewed during Melville's travels in the late 1850s. The lady in question, though obviously beautiful, was also ruthless and amoral, and the painter's task, according to the custom of the time, seems to have been to record the surface while merely suggesting what lay beneath. The poet, describing the painter's art, reflects this in such ambiguous verbal constructions as "Light and shade did weave," "mystery starred in open skies," and "her fathomless mild eyes"—all of which recalls the lethal sweetness of the Gioconda smile.

Irony is a state of mind difficult to depict in musical terms, and if he recognized it, David Diamond chose to ignore it in favor of a more straightforward interpretation of the text. The result is a lively piano figuration inspired by the opening line ("He toned the sprightly beam of morning"), which pervades the entire song, while a lyric vocal line in longer note values represents the gentler aspects of the lady's nature.

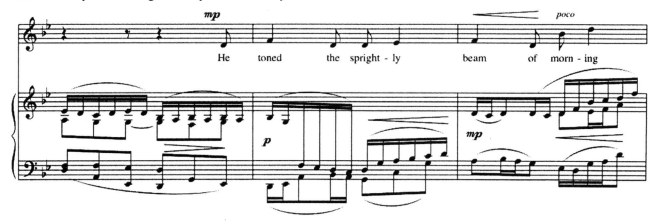

Example 7.19, mm. 4–6

The many metric alterations between 5/8 and 6/8 also give a sense of "light and shade," i.e., the fluctuations of her personality, and the move from B-flat major up to D major for the melodic outline of "Brightness" seems a direct response to the verbal call for an increase in musical brilliance, through the addition of upper overtones.

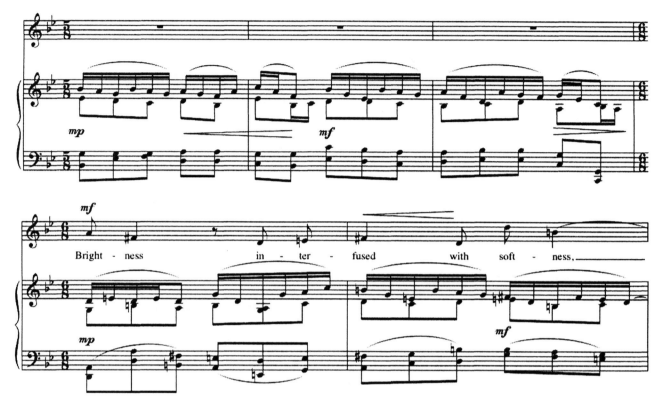

Example 7.20, mm. 10–14

Diamond's versatility as a musical dramatist is evident in the juxtaposition of the graceful, ornamental, and somewhat artificial style of "A Portrait" with the rugged, folk-ballad milieu of his "Billy in the Darbies."[39] This song, written in 1944, was the earliest of his Melville settings, and like all the others is faithful in every syllable to the original poetic text. The poem is from the middle 1880s, and is based on the hanging of an American seaman in 1842 that Melville transposed to a British warship in 1797. An expanded and re-expanded head-note to the poem eventually became *Billy Budd, Sailor*, a story left almost finished at his death, in which Melville examined for the last time the conflicting claims of authority and individuality.

"Billy in the Darbies" shows the young sailor, condemned to die for an act of violence against his nature, awaiting his imminent death, and imagining the events and aftermath of the hanging. The pervading folk atmosphere of the setting is established immediately by the drone-bass of the accompaniment figure's tonic-dominant emphasis, by the modal (Dorian from G) scale, and by the meter and accent pattern drawn from the British sailor's "hornpipe."

Example 7.21, mm. 1–3

As the ballad progresses, the vocal line becomes increasingly agitated with accented syncopations and a rising tessitura. A pianistic drum roll depicts the call to grog that a dead Billy will not hear, and a pair of octave leaps is his last outcry before resigning himself to sleep and dreaming of "oozy weeds."

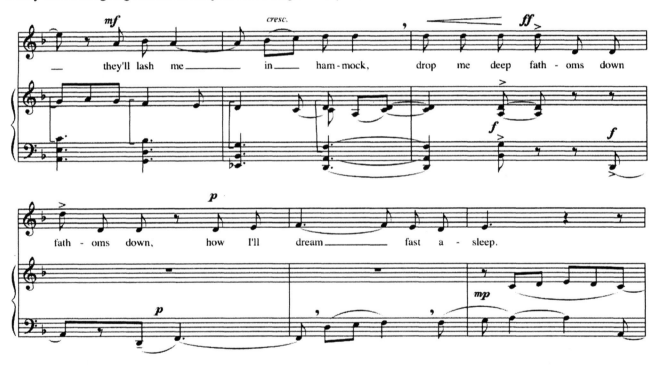

Example 7.22, mm. 86–91

Example 7.22 climaxes one of the song's most vivid passages (in the contrasting Mixolydian mode transposed to F) and the reader is referred to Hans Nathan's article for an extended quotation and treatment of this section.[40]

Vincent Persichetti (1915–1987)

Vincent Persichetti's contributions to the musical life of twentieth century America were of staggering proportions. As well as the composer of a large catalog of works in almost all media, Persichetti was also a virtuoso performer, a teacher, administrator, governmental advisor, editor, reviewer, and writer of important musical texts. Philadelphia was his birthplace as well as the center of much of his musical activity, and he died in that city at the age of seventy-two.

Like many of the most creative musical talents, Persichetti was a child prodigy. At five, he began to study piano and organ, and soon added double bass, tuba, theory, and composition. His early musical education was materially aided by a fantastic sight-reading ability at the keyboard which enabled him to play at the piano all the scores heard at weekly concerts of the Philadelphia Orchestra. In later years, this ability, coupled with an insatiable musical curiosity, would lead him to play through the vast majority of the twentieth century vocal and chamber music repertoire.

In 1935, he earned a bachelor of music degree at Combs College, and immediately thereafter was appointed to head its theory department, while simultaneously studying conducting under Fritz Reiner at the Curtis Institute, piano with Olga Samaroff at the Philadelphia Conservatory, and composition with a number of mentors including Paul Nordoff (see chapter 6). Six years later, he became head of the Philadelphia Conservatory's theory and composition department, and also married a pianist and teacher named Dorothea Flanagan. The composer recalled that "when Dorothea and I were married in 1941, we absolutely had no money, but . . . for my birthday, she came in with this big package for me [of] the Sandburg Lincoln books—all of the volumes. That cost . . . a fortune for us in those days and I still don't know how she did it," he added in appreciative admiration.[41]

A daughter and son were born to the Persichettis in 1944 and 1946, respectively. In 1947, the composer joined the faculty of the Juilliard School of Music, becoming chairman of the Composition Department in 1963. He held this position until the end of his life, as well as that of Director of Publications for Elkan-Vogel, Inc. (a division of Theodore Presser Co.), which he had assumed in 1952. R. Friedberg had the privilege of observing Vincent Perischetti both in the role of an exciting teacher/performer during his visit to the Duke University campus in the mid-1960s, and as a discerning, articulate music editor during an interview in his high-ceilinged, manuscript-laden office in Bryn Mawr, Pennsylvania, in 1975. In all situations, his was an impressive musical presence which drew the accolades of such colleagues as William Schumann ("Persichetti is a teacher with remarkable insights")[42] and Virgil Thomson ("Persichetti is a marvelous pianist and his piano writing is suited to the instrument better than almost anything written in America today").[43]

The composer's writings on musical subjects indeed constituted almost a mini-career of their own and kept him at the vital center of the American musical scene of his era. In the 1940s, he reported and commented on performances of twentieth-century works in his city of Philadelphia for the League of Composers' journal *Modern Music* and for the "Current Chronicle" section of the *Musical Quarterly*. Through the fifties, he wrote book and record reviews for *Musical Quarterly*, and during the same period, contributed occasional reviews of new music publications to *Notes*, the journal of the Music Library Association. All of these articles, which are of varying lengths, are written in a uniquely attractive style and are full of cogent observations clearly stemming from a highly trained, objective, compassionate, and creative musical mind. These same characteristics were brought to bear on essays concerning twentieth-century choral and orchestral music in two books edited by Robert Hines,[44] and in a biography of William Schumann of which Persichetti was co-author.[45] But the crowning literary achievement of all was certainly his *Twentieth Century Harmony, Creative Aspects and Practice*, which was published in 1961. Herein the composer brilliantly accomplished his announced objective of "defining the harmonic practice of the first half of the twentieth century and making it available to the student and young composer."[46] He did so in a work that is far from standard textbook fare and which William Schumann characterized as containing "penetrating insights into the materials of music" in writing which has "an élan—a dash that even includes—shades of e.e. cummings—the invention of words."[47]

Persichetti was uniquely qualified to define the parameters of twentieth-century harmonic practice, given his lifelong approach to his own composition. He saw himself as an "amalgamator"[48]—one who had drawn from many diverse elements of contemporary musical practice, yet without abandoning what was useful and meaningful in traditional techniques. Persichetti's opus 1 (a serenade for wind instruments) was written in 1929, but it was not until sixteen years later that he made his first essay into vocal music, with his e.e. cummings songs. The composer explained that although he had always read poetry and had great love and respect for the medium, he hesitated to set it to music, feeling that a good poem was already complete in itself. Finally, he realized that "poetry is, in reality a distilled concept full of implications that you can interpret many ways [and] my composition is a statement of one of the implications of the poem."[49]

Of Persichetti's eleven opus numbers devoted to solo songs, six are settings of American poets, and of these only the Wallace Stevens and Emily Dickinson settings have been published. The e.e. cummings, Sara Teasdale, Carl Sandburg, and Robert Frost songs remain in manuscript, and Persichetti did not pursue their publication because of the commonly encountered problem of clearing copyrights on the poetry. There was some feeling on the part of the composer that his songs had not been afforded the same public acceptance as his instrumental music ("People think they've heard my songs when they haven't").[50] He also was of the opinion that "voice teachers pay lip service to American songs but teach few, maybe because they're afraid of the medium."[51]

Wallace Stevens (1872–1955)

Persichetti's major solo vocal work in size and scope is the song cycle *Harmonium* (1951) based on poetry by Wallace Stevens, whose writing embodied the composer's own qualities of sensuous elegance, and deep feeling held under classical restraint. Stevens, too, was from Pennsylvania, having been born in Reading, which was both an industrial and a provincial city, being surrounded by woods and farmland. It was, however, a city not without culture, and its traditions, extending back to William Penn, included a love of music and pageantry. Stevens's father was a lawyer by profession who contributed poetry to the *Reading Times* and who was interested in both the intellectual and aesthetic development of his son. Wallace Stevens's own literary talents began to surface in high school where he won prizes for oration and essay writing. Entering Harvard in 1897, he began to publish both prose and poetry in the *Harvard Advocate* during his sophomore year, and had become its president before leaving in 1900. Witter Bynner and Arthur Davison Ficke (see chapter 5), who would also become notable poets, were friends of Stevens' undergraduate years. It was a period of general sterility in English and American poetry, which would soon be revitalized by the growing influence of the French Symbolists, and the rediscovery of Whitman and Dickinson.

Stevens spent the year after graduation as a reporter for the *New York Herald Tribune*. Having by then decided against the life of a professional writer, he attended New York University Law School and adopted the parental pattern of legal vocation/poetic avocation. He married in 1909, and in 1916 moved with his wife to Hartford, Connecticut, where he entered the legal department of the Hartford Accident and Indemnity Company. The Stevens's only child, Holly, was born in 1924, and ten years later the poet followed in Charles Ives's footsteps by becoming the vice-president of the insurance company, a position he held until the end of his life. It was not an unconflicted combination of professions, and there were a number of "dry" years during which Stevens wrote little or not at all. In retrospect, these emerged as periods of gestation which preceded changes in the direction of his poetic thought, and his life as a whole yielded a substantial body of work.

The first public recognition of Wallace Stevens's writing came from Harriet Monroe's publication of *Phases* (four poems) in the November 1914 edition of *Poetry* magazine.[52] This was a "war" issue which had been about to go to press, but which was torn apart to make room for the talented unknown. In late 1915, *Poetry* also awarded Stevens a prize of one hundred dollars for his one-act play in free verse, *Three Travelers Watch a Sunrise*. This play was produced five years later at the Provincetown Theater in New York City, and another one-act play, *Carlos among the Candles*, received productions in both Milwaukee and New York. The writer had, however, been in no hurry to publish a book of poetry which, in his frequently quoted phrase, he held to be "a damned serious affair." The first such volume, therefore, which was *Harmonium*, did not appear until 1923, in the writer's forty-fourth year (a second edition following eight years later).

In fact, Stevens had waited none too long, for neither the public nor the critics were as yet totally prepared for the form or the content of *Harmonium*. Early criticism characterized him as an "intellectual poet," as a "poet's poet," and the final pejorative, as a "critic's poet," who had never sought, and was unlikely to gain, a popular audience. The passage of time, however, has brought a wider acceptance and a clearer perspective on Stevens's work. Robert Buttel, among others, has come to see him as "a direct descendant of the Romantic poets in his unceasing exploration of the relationships between the inner, subjective, human point of view and outer, objective nature—or as he so often stated it himself, between 'imagination and reality.'"[53] Yet, despite this philosophical preoccupation, Stevens's poetic world is full of light, color, and sound, and Babette Deutsch holds that "none of Stevens' juniors has celebrated being with a like sensual precision, sparkle, and energy."[54]

The contemporary reader, struck by Stevens's "bold, bizarre, and immaculate phrasing, imagistic concreteness, (and) incisive prosody,"[55] can also identify with the poet's emphasis on the "process of seeing the world, (and his) exercises in creative perception,"[56] particularly in the light of suggestions by quantum physicists concerning the possible influence of the observer on observed systems. The strong appeal of Wallace Stevens's thought and poetic language to Vincent Persichetti is evidenced by the composer's statement in 1973. "I guess I really got into working for the voice through Wallace Stevens. My song cycle *Harmonium* is based on a book of poetry of his by the same title. I wrote him for permission to use his poetry, and he replied that his permission was not needed—for me to go ahead."[57]

Although the affinity of a composer for a poet cannot be successfully predicted before the event, ex post facto examination reveals several interesting parallels between Stevens and Persichetti. One thinks, for example, of the poet's debt to the philosophy and techniques of the French Symbolists and compares it to Persichetti's finding influences in his own work from Honegger and Stravinsky,[58] both purveyors of the French musical traditions. Equally striking are the similarities between two quotations which describe the eclectic orientations of these two creative artists. Stevens, says Joseph Riddel, is "a traditional poet, yet experimental; an imagist, but also a symbolist; a romantic, but disconcertingly impersonal."[59] Robert Evett counters with "Persichetti enjoys the almost unique distinction of never having belonged to the Right or the Left, or for that matter, the Middle of the Road."[60] Not surprisingly, Stevens, whose musical preoccupations speak clearly in the very title of *Harmonium*, liked Persichetti's settings very much. The two men had, indeed, planned to collaborate on an opera based on *Three Travelers Watch a Sunrise*, but to Persichetti's great sorrow, Stevens's death put an end to the project. "I was very angry at him," the composer admitted, and added ruefully, "I had lunch with his daughter, but it wasn't the same thing."[61]

Persichetti's monumental cycle[62] sets twenty poems selected from Stevens's *Harmonium*. There are no narrative connections between them, but a number of recurring themes lend cohesiveness to the set, in the manner of Copland's *Twelve Poems of Emily Dickinson*. Number one, "Valley Candle," can be seen as a succinct statement of Stevens's continual speculation on the relationship between the individual consciousness (the candle and remembered image thereof) and its environment (the valley, the night, and the wind). Persichetti's angular, leaping vocal line serves a word-painting function for the phrases "immense valley" and "beams of the huge night."

Example 7.23, mm. 21–31

Besides the alternation of scale passages and large interval leaps in the voice line, another musical style characteristic that will pervade the cycle appears in "Valley Candle." This, as seen in the introductory measures for piano, is the polytonal implication of much of the harmony, an appropriate musical symbol for the conflict between "imagination and reality" which much of the poetry delineates.

Example 7.24, mm. 1–5

The second song sets "The Place of the Solitaires," which the poet indicates should be "a place of perpetual undulation." There are several different definitions of the word "solitaires," both in English and in French, a language with which Stevens felt very much at home and to which he often alludes in his poetry. All of them point toward a poetic meaning based on the primacy of movement ("motion," "noise," "thought") in the constitution of our universe, a movement which is incomplete without the lone consciousness that perceives, and that is perhaps, in some mysterious way, the source of the "manifold continuation." Since the second poem is clearly tied to the theme of "Valley Candle," Persichetti chooses to relate the musical material also, and brings back both the angular intervallic leaps and the unisons that often precede them, now expanded in chant-like repetition. A new device, that of a "perpetual motion" figure in the accompaniment, is also introduced, which at once grows out of the textual emphasis on movement, and also prefigures the texture of "The Snow Man," a focal point of the cycle.

Example 7.25, mm. 1–3

In number three, "Theory," the poet presents the notion that human personality is tied to its physical surroundings ("One is not Duchess / A hundred yards from a carriage.") Persichetti's vocal contour now becomes more rounded, with an opening vocal phrase in consecutive fourths that will expand into the full-blown lyricism of number nineteen ("Of the Surface of Things"). The quiet, slowly moving syncopations and "white-key" chordal dissonances of the piano opening introduce an "American" sound that is frequently associated with Copland.

Example 7.26, mm. 1–11

The song ends in quite a different mood, however, as the dynamic profile of the last line adds an intensity in the musical setting which is lacking in the poem.

Example 7.27, mm. 37–47

Number four sets "Lunar Paraphrase," one of three poems in *Harmonium* that were based on the *Lettres d'un Soldat* of Eugène Emmanuel Lemercier. He was a young painter who had been lost in action on the Western Front in 1915, and these records of war, as seen through an artist's eye, took on considerable importance to Stevens. Nine poems of this series had originally appeared in *Poetry* magazine in 1918, on which occasion fragments of the original letters were published as epigraphs. The fragment that preceded "Lunar Paraphrase" described a night march in late November when the moonlight fell tenderly on bare branches, ruined houses, and suffering soldiers ("le pathétique de calvaires"). Stevens takes over most of this scene into the poem, but uses Jesus as a universal symbol for suffering, thus making this a "war" poem only by association with its origins.

The restrained compassion of these powerful lines is well matched by Persichetti's setting, a twentieth-century recitative with a strong emotive contour. The composer chooses to repeat the poem's first line, in a narrow-range hypnotic chant that is organized by softly insistent rhythmic impulses from the piano.

Example 7.28, mm. 1–5

With the establishment of an ominous C sharp minor, the scale passages which describe the figures of Jesus and Mary begin an episode of growing intensity, culminating in the desperate reiteration of the major sixth interval.

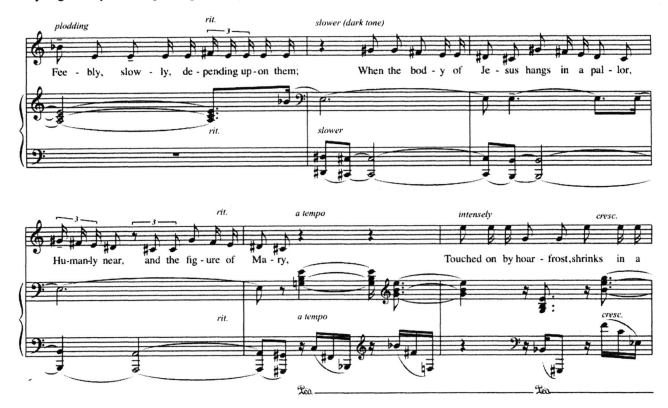

Example 7.29, mm. 11–16

The song ends as it begins, with a chant-like repetition of the dominant phrase ("The moon is the mother of pathos and pity"). This time it deserts the unison to conclude with a descending diminished fifth, whose coldness gives the lie to the moonlight's illusory comfort.

The fifth setting, "Death of a Soldier," is also based on the Lemercier *Lettres*, and the poem is generally conceded to be one of the strongest in the *Harmonium*. The epigraph (translated) had read "The death of a soldier is close to natural things." Stevens equates this occurrence with the expected passing of life forms in autumn, the season of death, and contrasts the unmarked fall of the soldier with the ceremonial passage of a "three days personage" who "imposes his separation." The poem's structure is carefully chiseled into four diminishing tercets in which, as one critic has graphically suggested, "each end-stopped stanza is like a tombstone."[63]

Persichetti's setting is as strong and economical as Stevens's verses. For the most part, it alternates lines of text sung over sustained chords, with incisive comments from the piano, whose dotted figures and accents carry an ironic reference to martial rhythms.

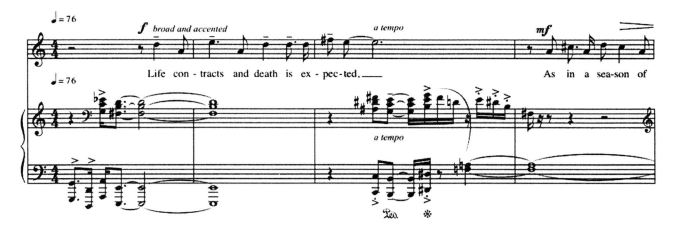

Example 7.30, mm. 1–4

Two instances of word-painting are absorbed into the starkness, as "the soldier falls" takes a descending arpeggio to the lowest note of the song, and "calling for pomp" is given a pseudo trumpet-call figure in a brilliant upper register.

Example 7.31, mm. 11–12

Unifying devices in the song are the melodic interval of the perfect fourth, which is seminal to the whole cycle, and a chordal figure of two minor triads in the second inversion, usually presented as a sixteenth followed by a dotted eighth note, with an accent over the first (see Ex. 7.30 and Ex. 7.31). At the end of the song, after the text has philosophically concluded that life goes on ("The clouds go, nevertheless, / In their direction"), the sudden, brutal reiteration of this chordal figure carries a reminder of individual loss.

Example 7.32, mm. 23–24

In number six, "The Wind Shifts," Stevens has once again used a favorite symbol, the wind, to stand for the consciousness of human beings who, in this instance, are the old, the disillusioned, and the defeated. Persichetti employs stepwise, largely chromatic triplets to portray the subtle movements and gradations of thought.

Example 7.33, mm. 4–7

He also brings in some of his most expansive piano writing in instrumental interludes that suggest the successive emotions of tenderness, passion, and desperation implied by the text. All of this contracts at the end to a single, repeated vocal note over sparse piano figures, signifying the depressed silence of a "human . . . who does not care."

Example 7.34, mm. 74–82

Stevens's small gem of a poem called "Tea" appears as number ten of the cycle, and reminds us of the poet's ability to celebrate the visual. As he contrasts the colorlessness of the outside world ("Shrivelled in frost") with the indoor warmth and exoticism of "shining pillows" in "sea-shades and sky-shades," the poet conjures the Asian-French atmosphere of a Matisse painting. He also reminds us, as Deutsch has pointed out, that blue is a color which predominates in his scenery, and is often "associated . . . with the adventures of the mind."[64]

Persichetti's appealing setting of "Tea" creates a musically analogous atmosphere of cozy intimacy with its transparent texture and low dynamic level. The opening vocal line and accompaniment figures carry an echo of the amusement "park," remembered from crowded summer days, while the "jazzy" added sixths and seconds of the piano's right-hand chords lend a sophisticated, urban flavor.

Example 7.35, mm. 1–12

For the setting of the last line, "Like umbrellas in Java," Persichetti moves to a melisma in the exotic (in this context) key of C-sharp major. In the piano postlude, reality, in the form of C major, gradually regains the upper hand, although the penultimate measure includes a single C-sharp as a remaining trace of the fantasy.

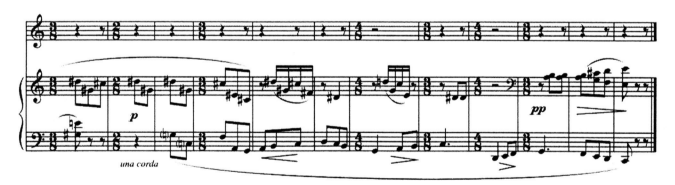

Example 7.36, mm. 62–73

"The Snow Man" of number eleven is a prime example of Stevens's many "mind of winter" poems in which his other preoccupation (with summer and the South) gives way to the frozen bleakness of the North. These verses are also cast in the typically simple diction and flexible, unrhymed tercets characteristic of much of the poet's work, and all five stanzas constitute a single, complex sentence. Although on the surface the wintry scene seems equivalent to a climate of negation, many critics see the figure of the "Snow Man" as an affirmation of the role of the poet, who must summon the courage to confront primary, unadorned reality and to see "nothing that is not there and the nothing that is."

The composer's setting uses a filigree of crystalline, unpedalled pianistic scales to create most successfully an aural context of icy cold.

Example 7.37, mm. 1–5

The vocal line frequently imitates these scale passages at a slower rhythm (see Ex. 7.37, mm. 4–5), but also incorporates some jagged, accented leaps in a high tessitura to suggest the rough outlines of the ice-laden trees.

Example 7.38, mm. 12–17

The scales stop for a few phrases as the "listener . . . listens in the snow" to the wind "That is blowing in the same bare place." They resume in the piano postlude, which takes on a circular, never-ending aspect from the direction of the figures, and from the unresolved, polytonal overlap of the final measure.

Example 7.39, mm. 48–50

One of the most haunting moments of the cycle is the setting of "Infanta Marina," number fourteen, which Persichetti transcribed for viola and piano in 1960 as his opus 83.[65] This poem is a prime example of a Stevens tropical land-and-seascape, complete with sand, sails, and palm trees, as well as a mysterious, fascinating creature (the "Infanta") who has dominion over the magical kingdom. The rich visual images of the text are well matched by Persichetti's rapidly shifting harmonic color, and the reader is recommended to Robert Evett's analysis of the piano introduction and its implications of an E tonality.[66] The last phrase of the song, in fact, fulfills all the originally suggested pandiatonic elements of E, with the repeated F and final vocal interval on "sound" deriving from the Phrygian mode, while the accompaniment G sharps establish the overlapping claims of E major. Notice also the added sixth (C sharp) of the last chord, which contributes still another shade of warmth to an already lush harmonic palette.

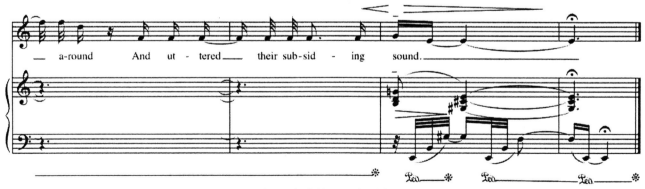

Example 7.40, mm. 31–34

"Of the Surface of Things," number nineteen, sets a poem in which seemingly Romantic images clothe the contemporary concept that the poet's true reality can be drawn only from the evidence of his own perceptions. Therefore, "the gold tree is blue" (with blue once again standing for the processes of the mind) and the moon's true existence is in "the folds of the [singer's] cloak," that is, in his own individual picture of his environment. Persichetti skillfully captures the duality of mood between the thought and language of this poem. In a flowing, sustained 6/4 meter, he lets the previously mentioned germ phrase of number three flower into a lyrical line of melting contours, then structures this line as a tightly controlled canon at the unison between the right-hand of the accompaniment, and the voice, which follows it one and a half measures later.

Example 7.41, mm. 1–6

"Thirteen Ways of Looking at a Blackbird" completes the cycle and is like an apotheosis of the settings that have preceded it. "In this poem," said Persichetti, "I found that all of the previous nineteen poems were related in one way or another and so I did this with all the music. I wrote Stevens about this," added the composer, "and he replied that he had not realized this connection.[67] "Thirteen Ways" therefore includes a number of musical quotations from the rest of the cycle, particularly in the piano writing. These appear where the textual content is reminiscent of an earlier song or where it serves the musical structure. The last "way of looking" is introduced by the masterful stroke of a quotation from "Infanta Marina," which recalls a far different "evening" and a colorfully dramatic contrast to the stark black and white of the bird as it is seen for the last time on the snowy cedar limbs.

Example 7.42, mm. 275–82

Persichetti extends the text for this lyrical conclusion with two repetitions of "the blackbird" which arch up to an expressive climax, and then fall back to a thoughtful, mid-range retreat. This final phrase might well be seen as a representation of the dichotomy between the artist's passionate perceptions, and his need to subject them to the linear processes of technical structuring.

Example 7.43, mm. 285–90

Emily Dickinson (1830–1886)

The poetry of Emily Dickinson has been treated earlier in this series in connection with the settings of Bacon and Copland (chapter 3) and John Duke (chapter 5). Vincent Persichetti's opus 77,[68] written six years after *Harmonium* (i.e., in 1957), also sets four poems by Dickinson, one of the writers to whom he felt strongly connected, by virtue of her poetic "message."[69] The rediscovery of Walt Whitman and Emily Dickinson during the teens and twenties of the last century had of course led to new publications of their poetry, and Persichetti's settings follow the Dickinson poems as they appear in the 1937 edition put out by Martha Dickinson Bianchi and Alfred Leete Hampson. As mentioned in connection with the Copland settings, the definitive Thomas H. Johnson edition, published by Harvard University Press, did not appear until 1958. This was the same year in which the Persichetti songs came into print, but there are only a few discrepancies in these texts from the poetic originals, and for the most part, they do not involve major changes of meaning where they occur.

The style of Persichetti's Dickinson settings is markedly different from his *Harmonium*. In general, these songs have a thinner texture, less complex rhythmic treatment, and a more diatonic harmonic orientation. The piano writing is more transparent, and the vocal lines more stepwise and lyrical in contrast to the frequently angular and declamatory lines of the other work. It is as though the composer were attempting to capture both the childlike innocent wonder of Dickinson's original perceptions of the world, and the barebones simplicity that is another hallmark of her greatness. The attempt was successful, and these songs have attracted considerable attention from performers and teachers.

The four poems of this set were all written between 1859 and 1863, an exciting yet disturbing period in Emily Dickinson's life (see chapters 3 and 5 for a more detailed discussion). These selections, however, are mostly sunny, affirmative poems, celebrating nature and human affection, with only occasional undertones of her growing sense of alienation from the "normal" patterns of society. Number one, "Out of the Morning," asks "where the place called morning lies" and "could I see it from the mountains": refusing to take for granted the daily miracle by which darkness is ended. Persichetti sets his vocal lines, which mostly descend in a questioningly doubtful inflection, against an arpeggio figure spread widely over the keyboard, like the verbal suggestion of a stretch to see the sunrise.

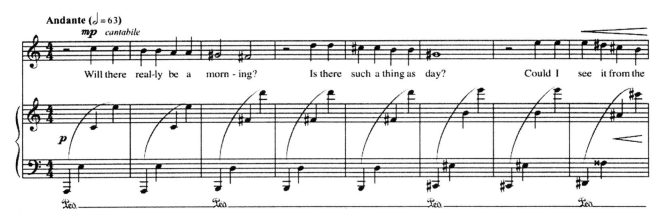

Example 7.44, mm. 1–8

The poetic rhythm has here been quietly assimilated by the increased note values of the phrase endings ("morning," "day," etc.) and this device also serves to lend a note of wide-eyed pathos to the conclusion of each question (see Ex. 7.44).

In the second poem of the group, "I'm nobody! Who are you?," Dickinson's disdain of notoriety is couched in the images of her playful wit ("How dreary to be somebody! / How public, like a frog"). The fact is, of course, that Emily Dickinson was already "somebody" by birth and association. Her father had been one of the founders of Amherst College; her brother became a respected lawyer; and she herself "was not . . . a rural poetess or spinster, but a princess."[70] Nevertheless, by 1861, when the poem was written, it was already clear to Emily, now entering her thirties, that she was doomed to find little understanding among friends or members of the literary Establishment, and her gradual withdrawal from society dates from about this time.

The Johnson version of this poem differs only in the last word of the penultimate line which is "June," instead of the more euphonious but less original "day" of the 1937 edition. Rhythm is one of the most important elements that Persichetti uses to establish the mockingly humorous mood of the setting. The piano introduction seems like a cross between American folk derived and syncopated jazz figures, and this instrumental material returns between vocal phrases like a teasing refrain.

Example 7.45, mm. 1–10

The vocal line throughout most of the song shares in the syncopated patterns which suggest the darting, secretive movements of a pair of conspiratorial children (see Ex. 7.46), but achieves telling contrast at the end with a string of accented quarter notes that describe the horrifying picture of fame (see Ex. 7.47).

Example 7.46, mm. 20–24

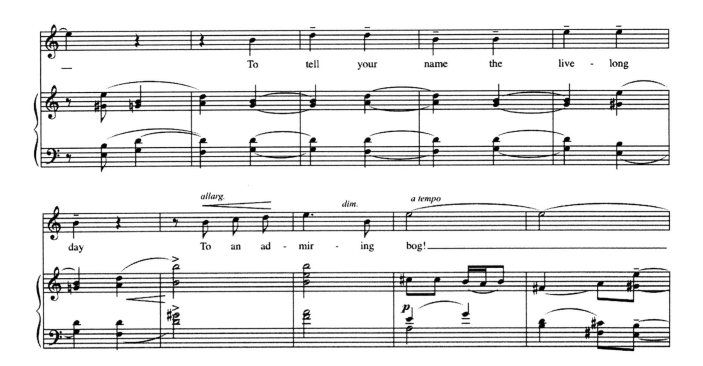

Example 7.47, mm. 39–48

"When the Hills Do" is a statement of devotion to an unknown person whom the 1937 version identifies as "O friend" (end of line seven), whereas the Johnson edition reinstates the more revealing "Sir." The latter echoes the tone of the "Master" letters, which were written by Dickinson between 1858 and 1862, in deep affection and respect, but whose source of inspiration is still shrouded in mystery and conjecture.[71] Whoever the object might have been, the poem, written in 1863, is a compressed and elegant statement of unending love, for which Persichetti finds a remarkably appropriate musical framework. He writes a series of legato and expressive harmonic sequences for the piano, then has the voice join with the upper chord tone at the end of each, like a coming together in gentle embrace.

Example 7.48, mm. 1–6

This method of embedding the text within the musical phrase has the effect of preserving some of the original poetic meter, whose square simplicity carries much of the strength of these verses.

"The Grass" is the fourth and longest poem, and also incorporates an interesting deviation from the original. The lines which Persichetti sets as "As lowly spices gone to sleep / Or amulets of pine" appear in the Johnson edition as "Like lowly spices, lain to sleep / Or spikenards perishing." This is yet another instance of Dickinson's courageous and exciting use of language being smoothed over by her "helpful" editors, and it is challenging to speculate on how differently Persichetti would have set the original lines had he had them available. The composer himself appears to have changed "a" hay to "the" hay in the last line of the song, but this seems likely to be a printing error in view of his usually unremitting faithfulness to the poetic text.

The poem personifies the grass, and envies the sights and sounds with which it is surrounded: butterflies, bees, sunshine, breezes, and all the accoutrements of the outdoors in a New England summer, of which the writer was so fond. Once again, in this setting, rhythmic factors are of prime importance. Persichetti uses a recurring accompanying figure of an eighth note and dotted quarter which dovetails with the opposite vocal figure to set up a peacefully rocking pattern, suggestive of a child moving aimlessly and happily through a meadow.

Example 7.49, mm. 1–3

Persichetti sets the first two stanzas without a break in the vocal line, changing his 4/4 meter to 3/4 just before the piano interlude takes over the melodic material. Again the dramatic reference is to the world of childhood, and to an enthusiastic storyteller who runs on and on in excitement, and as suddenly stops.

Example 7.50, mm. 10–15

In the last verse, the composer repeats the phrase "and dream the days away," setting the repetition with a contrapuntal interweaving of voice and piano, like the texture of a mind woven through with fantasy.

Example 7.51, mm. 33–38

Persichetti also adds a repetition to the last poetic line ("I wish, I *wish* I were the hay") and has his concluding statement of the melodic theme turn wistfully downward in the piano postlude, as though the wish were destined to denial.

Example 7.52, mm. 39–44

Finally, it should be noted that Vincent Persichetti used his setting of "The Grass" as the basis for a one-act opera called *The Sibyl*. The libretto, based on the "Chicken Little" fable was his own, and it was premiéred in 1985 at the Pennsylvania Opera Theater.

Notes

1. Hugo Weisgall, "The 201st Quarterly," *Perspectives of New Music* 3, no. 2 (1965): 133–36.
2. Another notable Sessions student was David Diamond, whose life and training are discussed later in this chapter.
3. Bruce Saylor, "The Music of Hugo Weisgall," *Musical Quarterly* 49, no. 2 (1973): 241.
4. Saylor, "The Music of Hugo Weisgall."
5. Edward Butscher, *Adelaide Crapsey* (Boston: Twayne, 1979), 16.
6. "Existentialism" is a philosophical system which postulates Man as alone in an unfriendly universe, doomed to an existence which can be given meaning only by his own courage.
7. Hugo Weisgall, *Four Songs* (Bryn Mawr, Pa.: Theodore Presser, 1940). High or medium voice.
8. John Duke has also set this poem in a song that is included in: *Songs by John Duke*, Vol. 2 (San Antonio, Tex.: Southern Music Co., 1985). See chapter 5 for a discussion of Duke's song "Rapunzel," which is another Crapsey setting.
9. Hugo Weisgall, *Soldier Songs* (New York: Merrymount Music Press, 1953). Baritone. A recording of "Shiloh" is included in the Thomas Hampson CD *I Hear America Singing* (2006), available at ArkivMusic.com.
10. The foregoing sentence is based on material in Richard S. Kennedy, *Dreams in the Mirror* (New York: Liveright, 1980), 172–88.
11. Herman Melville, *Works: vol. 16, Poems* (New York: Russell and Russell, 1963).
12. Bernard Wagenaar was also an important teacher of John Duke (see chapter 5).
13. For further discussion of the connections between Norman Dello Joio and Paul Hindemith, see (a) Madeleine Goss, *Modern Music-Makers* (New York: Dutton, 1952), 437; (b) Edward Downes, "The Music of Norman Dello Joio," *The Musical Quarterly* 48, no. 2 (April 1962): 151.

14. The foregoing paragraph is based on the following article: Norman Dello Joio, "The Contemporary Music Project for Creativity in Music Education," *Music Educators' Journal* 54 (March 1968): 4–72.

15. Norman Dello Joio, "The Composer and the American Scene," *Music Journal* 22 (March 1964): 100.

16. Dello Joio, "The Composer and the American Scene," 31.

17. Letter to R. Friedberg, 9 February 1983.

18. Norman Dello Joio, *Songs of Remembrance* (New York: Associated Music Publishers, 1979). Baritone. The keyboard reduction of this orchestral work was reviewed by R. Friedberg in the March/April 1980 issue of the *Bulletin* of the National Association of Teachers of Singing and is available from G. Schirmer (distr. Hal Leonard).

19. Letter to R. Friedberg, 9 February 1983.

20. The other five are "Eyebright," "Why so Pale and Wan, Fond Lover?," "Meeting at Night," "All Things Leave Me," and "How Do I Love Thee?" Two of these, "Meeting at Night" and "Eyebright" are recorded in the Hanks-Friedberg anthology (see chapter 1, n7). For further information on all of Dello Joio's solo vocal music to date of publication, see Thomas A. Bumgardner, *Norman Dello Joio* (Boston: Twayne Publishers, 1986), 42–47.

21. Norman Dello Joio, "The Dying Nightingale" (New York: Carl Fischer, 1954). High voice.

22. Letter to R. Friedberg, 9 February 1983.

23. Stark Young, *The Pavilion* (New York: Scribner, 1951).

24. Harry Ransom Center, The University of Texas at Austin.

25. Young, *The Pavilion*, 164.

26. Madeleine Goss, *Modern Music Makers* (New York: Dutton, 1953), 453.

27. David Diamond, "Integrity and Integration in Contemporary Music," *The Alice and Frederick Slee Lectures* (University of Buffalo, Spring 1961).

28. David Diamond, "From the Notebook of David Diamond," *Music Journal* 12 (April 1964): 25.

29. Hans Nathan, "The Modern Period—United States of America," *A History of Song*, edited by Denis Stevens (New York: Norton, 1960), 444.

30. William Flanagan, "American Songs: A Thin Crop," *Musical America* 72 (February 1952): 23.

31. Letter to R. Friedberg, 7 February 1983.

32. Frances Murphy and Hershel Parker, eds. *The Norton Anthology of American Literature*, Vol. 1 (New York: Norton, 1979), 2043.

33. Goss, *Modern Music Makers,* 454.

34. David Diamond, "Epitaph" (New York: Associated Music Publishers, 1946). Medium high voice. This song is now available from G. Schirmer (distr. Hal Leonard).

35. Nathan, "The Modern Period," 444.

36. David Diamond, "Monody" (Philadelphia: Elkan-Vogel, 1947). Medium voice.

37. Letter to R. Friedberg, 7 February 1983.

38. David Diamond, "A Portrait" (Philadelphia: Elkan-Vogel, 1947). Medium high voice.

39. David Diamond, "Billy in the Darbies" (Philadelphia: Elkan-Vogel, 1946). Medium high voice.

40. Nathan, "The Modern Period," 446–47.

41. Robert Page, "In Quest of Answers—An Interview with Vincent Persichetti," *Choral Journal* 14, no. 3 (November 1973): 6.

42. William Schuman, "The Compleat Musician: Vincent Persichetti and Twentieth Century Harmony," *The Musical Quarterly* 47, no. 3 (July 1961): 380.

43. Virgil Thomson in the *Colorado Springs Gazette Telegraph.*

44. University of Oklahoma Press, 1963 and 1970.

45. G. Schirmer, 1954.

46. Vincent Persichetti, *Twentieth Century Harmony, Creative Aspects and Practice* (New York: Norton, 1961), 9–10.

47. Schuman, "The Compleat Musician," 381.

48. Page, "In Quest of Answers," 6.

49. Page, "In Quest of Answers," 5.

50. Interview with R. Friedberg at Theodore Presser Co., Bryn Mawr, Pennsylvania, 3 February 1975.

51. Interview with R. Friedberg, 3 February 1975.

52. See index for further references to Harriet Monroe and *Poetry* magazine.

53. Robert Buttel, *Wallace Stevens: The Making of Harmonium* (Princeton, N.J.: Princeton University Press, 1967): x.

54. Babette Deutsch, *Poetry in Our Time* (Garden City, N.Y.: Doubleday, 1963), 285.

55. Buttel, *Wallace Stevens,* x.

56. Joseph N. Riddel, *The Clairvoyant Eye* (Baton Rouge: Louisiana State University Press, 1965), 65.

57. Page, "In Quest of Answers," 5.

58. Interview with R. Friedberg, 3 February 1975.

59. Riddel, *The Clairvoyant Eye*, 11.

60. Robert Evett, "The Music of Vincent Persichetti," *The Juilliard Review* 11, no. 2 (Spring 1955): 16.

61. Interview, 3 February 1975.

62. Vincent Persichetti, *Harmonium* (Philadelphia: Elkan-Vogel, 1959). Soprano. Recorded performances: (a) Hanks and Friedberg, *Art Song in America*, contains "The Death of a Soldier," "The Snow Man," and "Of the Surface of Things," (see chapter 1, n7); b) *Songs of American Composers*, "Sonatina to Hans Christian," sung by Mildred Miller.

63. A. Walton Litz, *Introspective Voyager* (New York: Oxford University Press, 1972), 76.

64. Deutsch, *Poetry in Our Time*, 271.

65. R. Friedberg had the pleasure of performing this work with Julia Mueller, violist, during Vincent Persichetti's previously mentioned visit to the Duke University campus in the mid-1960s.

66. Evett, "The Music of Vincent Persichetti," 22–23.

67. Page, "In Quest of Answers," 5.

68. These four songs are published separately: (a) Vincent Persichetti, "Out of the Morning" (Philadelphia: Elkan-Vogel, 1958). Medium voice; also available in *Contemporary American Art Songs,* B. Taylor, ed. (publ. Theodor Presser); (b) Vincent Persichetti, "I'm Nobody" (Bryn Mawr, Pa.: Elkan-Vogel, 1958). Medium voice; (c) Vincent Persichetti, "When the Hills Do" (Philadelphia: Elkan-Vogel, 1958). Medium voice; (d) Vincent Persichetti, "The Grass" (Bryn Mawr, Pa.: Elkan-Vogel, 1958). Medium voice. This song is recorded in the Hanks-Friedberg anthology (see chapter 1, n7).

69. Interview, 3 February 1975. In a letter to R. Friedberg dated "Early August, 1983," the composer added "Stevens and Dickinson . . . both say more about less, rather than less about more, and that is for me."

70. Austin Warren, "Emily Dickinson," *A Collection of Critical Essays*, edited by Richard B. Sewall (Englewood Cliffs, N.J.: Prentice-Hall, 1963), 111.

71. Richard B. Sewall, *Life of Emily Dickinson,* Vol. 2 (New York: Farrar, Straus and Giroux, 1974), 512–31.

Chapter 8

The Third Decade I

Jack Beeson (b. 1921)

The life and career of Jack Beeson represent a triumph of the human spirit operating through one of its principal manifestations—the impulse toward artistic creativity. Beeson was born with a serious metabolic disorder and was given just a few months to live when he was six years old. The following year, instead of dying, he began to study the piano at his own request, and to nurture an inner compulsion toward music making which could have received but little stimulation within the family circle or in his hometown of Muncie, Indiana.[1]

The medium of radio, and the Saturday afternoon broadcasts from the Metropolitan, enabled the boy to identify and begin to cultivate a life-long passion for opera. Buying piano scores of operatic works with his savings, he would play along with the performances, and in his teens made three abortive attempts to write music and libretti for operas of his own. In 1936, his first piano teacher, Luella Weimer, turned him over to Percival Owen, who had come from Canada to join the music faculty of Ball State College, and who, like many of the first-rank piano instructors of that era, had trained under Leschetizsky. With Owen's assistance, Beeson began to study theory and music history, and at the same time was learning to play the clarinet and xylophone.

In similar fashion to Westchester's creating special dispensations for Samuel Barber, the Central Senior High School of Muncie rewarded sophomore Jack Beeson's A student status with permission to attend classes only in the morning, in order to have afternoons free for practicing and composing. When he was seventeen he followed Percival Owen's advice and began studies at the Royal Conservatory in Toronto, where he earned certificates in piano and theory. Following his high school graduation, Beeson was awarded a fellowship to the Eastman School in Rochester, where he studied composition with Bernard Rogers, Burrill Phillips, and Howard Hanson, and enrolled in the many liberal arts courses prompted by the broadening scope of his interests.

By 1944, he had received bachelor's and master's degrees from Eastman and was working toward a doctorate in music, when his father's death and a resulting legacy conferred temporary financial independence. Beeson interrupted his doctoral studies to spend a privileged year studying composition with Béla Bartók, who had recently fled the Nazi takeover of Hungary, and was suffering the lean years of neglect that became the retrospective shame of the American musical community. Having already begun to compose songs at Eastman (in the absence of opportunities for opera, his first love), Beeson showed Bartók his settings of W. B. Yeats, and was told by the master composer that he couldn't attempt to judge poetic settings in a language not his own. He added that he himself had written few songs because there was so little lyric poetry in Hungarian, and, as he put it, "I have too much respect for one's native language to set another language's poetry."[2]

During the period of his graduate studies at Eastman (1942–1944), Beeson had commuted to New York City and a teaching fellowship in theory at Columbia University. After his year with Bartók, he returned to the University to study conducting and musicology, and to begin a long series of faculty appointments culminating in his selection as MacDowell Professor of Music in 1967, and the conferral of Columbia's Great Teachers' Award in 1979. In addition to the fostering of his teaching career, the University also provided the long-sought opportunity for Beeson's development in the art and craft of opera. He served as coach and conductor of both the Columbia Opera Workshop (1945–1950) and Columbia Opera Theater Associates (1945–1952), and in a natural flowering of events, had his own first operatic production (*Hello Out There*—a one-act work with libretto adapted from a William Saroyan play) presented at the university in 1954.

For many years, Jack Beeson occupied a large office, filled with books and scores, on the fourth floor of Columbia's venerable Dodge Hall at 116th Street and Broadway. Columbia University was indeed a kind of anchor point to Beeson's career, during which he served it in a number of administrative capacities: as chairman of the Music Department, member of the Senate, head of new music publications for Columbia University Press, and officer in charge of the Alice M. Ditson Fund. He elected early retirement in 1988 but afterward returned as a member of the Society of Senior Scholars.

In 1947, Beeson had married Nora Sigerist, and they had a daughter and a son, the latter being fated to die in a tragic auto accident at the age of twenty-five. The years 1948–50 saw the Beesons in Rome, supported by the Prix de Rome and a Fulbright Fellowship, and it was here that the composer completed his first opera. Called *Jonah*, it used Beeson's own libretto, adapted from a play by Paul Goodman (see chapter 9) and although it won special mention in a La Scala competition, remains unproduced to this day. Another American artist in Rome on a Guggenheim Fellowship during this time was Peter Viereck and the Beesons got on very well with him. "He was tone-deaf," says the composer, "but he kept showing me his poetry, and at the time I didn't feel it was appropriate for musical setting."[3]

Back in the United States, Beeson proceeded to make a name for himself as an opera composer, following *Hello Out There* (mentioned above) with a production of *The Sweet Bye and Bye* (libretto by Kenward Elmslie) at the Juilliard Opera Theater in 1957. In an article in the *Opera News* of January 5, 1963, entitled "Grand and Not So Grand," he predicted that the future of American opera did not lie with Broadway, nor in the old established houses, nor in the University opera workshops. Rather, he felt, it would emerge from the newly developing metropolitan and regional opera companies around the country and from new developments in the artistic use of the media. His prophecies were proven accurate by his own subsequent productions. It was the innovative New York City Opera who commissioned his *Lizzie Borden* in 1965; the growing medium of National Educational Television which produced *My Heart's in the Highlands* in 1970 (again, a Saroyan adaptation, with Beeson as a walk-on bit player); and an excellent regional company, the Kansas City Lyric Theater, which in 1975 presented *Captain Jinks of the Horse Marines*, under a bicentennial commission from the National Endowment for the Arts. His most recent musico-dramatic ventures have been *Cyrano* in 1992 with libretto by Sheldon Harnick (which he called a heroic comedy in music) and *Sorry Wrong Number* in 1996.

Other journal articles by Beeson have recorded his appreciation of and sense of indebtedness to his elder colleagues in the composing world. His memorial to Douglas Moore[4] (see chapter 3) who had been an esteemed fellow faculty member at Columbia for over twenty years, traces the geographical and historical roots of Moore's musical "Americanism," and lauds his expressive and dramatic gifts as an opera composer. In a 1977 article on Virgil Thomson,[5] published in the literary magazine *Parnassus*, Beeson discussed the older composer's important contributions to our contemporary understanding of English language word setting. Beeson, on interview, had indicated his own constant awareness in his vocal writing of the faster pace of English vowels ("People set it as though it were German"),[6] the necessity for fixed accents, and for the verbal syncopations which have inevitable musical consequences. In the *Parnassus* article, he acknowledges Thomson's scattered writings on declamation and his widely given lecture "Words and Music" as the partial stimulus for his own thinking, while taking mild exception to Thomson's overstated claim in 1976 that "Nobody else was doing anything about (setting English properly)."[7]

After his initial encounter with songwriting in Eastman days, Beeson returned frequently to this form throughout his composing career, and feels that his songs "are different from the songs that others write. The texts chosen," he says "are different from others' choices, and are often not conventional lyrics. Often they are inherently dramatic, which, of course, makes the songs tend to be more dramatic."[8] It might be noted here that Jack Beeson has himself written a fair amount of poetry, including 100 lines of the challenging "terza rima" form. He also reads much poetry, and within two lines knows whether or not a poem appeals to him as a possible song text.

Edgar Allan Poe (1809–1849)

Beeson's first setting of an American text was Edgar Allan Poe's "Eldorado." Written in 1951 and revised in 1967 and 1977, this song was published for the first time in a 1982 Galaxy collection[9] of twenty previously unprinted American songs. Poe, who is treated initially in chapter 1, had published his fourth volume of poetry, *The Raven and Other Poems*, in 1845. During the four agonizing years that remained to him, years that encompassed the death of his wife and his own physical and emotional deterioration, a dozen of his poems appeared in various periodicals and "Eldorado" is one of them. Although a seemingly straightforward tale of a "gallant knight" who spends his life in a vain search for the mythical city of gold, it has proved enigmatic to its interpreters, some of whom see it as embodying "the pursuit of the ideal"[10] while others find it an "ironic" and "worldly wise"[11] mockery of such a quest. Historical perspective is helpful here, for it must be remembered that 1849 was the year of a major American epidemic of "gold-fever." Poe had responded to this phenomenon with satirical essays decrying his countrymen's materialism, and with the last of his fictional hoaxes—"Von Kempelen and His Discovery"—which purported to be a scientific method for turning lead into gold.

Given this background, it seems most likely that the knight's journey is an ironical representation of the national madness: a frenzied search for wealth that could carry a man "Down the Valley of the Shadow" to the very gates of Death. This poem of four six-line stanzas has Poe's typically tight control of rhyme and rhythmic elements, and a resultant musical flow that tends to obscure the deeper level of metaphysical speculation that has a parallel if not primary function. Besides the creation of nightmare visions and detective stories which the twentieth century chose to consider his most important legacy to us, Poe's gifts included a curiously contemporary mystical sensibility which saw the material world as an emanation of divine consciousness ("The Universe is a plot of God") in which each man must recognize his own existence "as that of Jehovah."[12] It would seem that Poe's worldview, although never his poetic style, has strong ties to that of Stephen Crane, another unique literary figure who defies categorization, and who raised a despairing cry against the compassionless God of common acceptance. The reader is invited to compare Poe's gold-crazed knight whose courage sustained his misguided quest, with Crane's "man pursuing the horizon" (to be treated in the following section) and his endless, Existential journey.

Although Poe was preeminently a lyric poet, "Eldorado" does possess the dramatic elements that Beeson indicates are a prime consideration in his settings. The figure of the knight and his changing patterns of movement are clearly delineated by manipulation of tempo, rhythm, and phrasing. The opening indication for the "gaily bedight" figure is "Swinging," but already the asymmetrical effect of cross-accents between vocal and instrumental phrases introduce a suggestion of the jerky, uncontrolled trotting of a stumbling, Don Quixote-like nag.

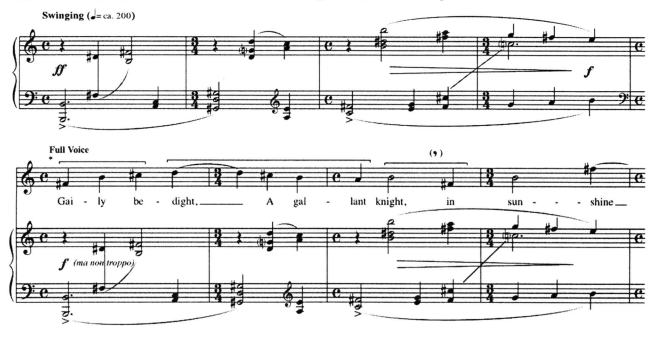

Example 8.1, mm. 1–8

The beginning tempo is almost hysterically fast but slows to nearly half "as his strength (fails) him" in verse three. Harmonic factors parallel this change, and the opening sharps of the pandiatonic B major/minor context (see Ex. 8.1) give way to the more somber B-flat elements.

Example 8.2, mm. 33–39

As the misleading "shade" spurs the rider on in his fruitless travels, the deceptively hopeful original tempo and sharp dominated harmony return. This time the contour of the vocal line rises to its highest point as the phantom mocks the other's desperate obsession.[13]

Example 8.3, mm. 57–63

Abraham Lincoln (1809–1865)

In contrast to "Eldorado's" agitated vignette of the wanderings of an anti-hero, "Indiana Homecoming,"[14] written in 1957, is a gentle landscape in which a sensitive observer's view of the present is overlaid by the hazy scrim of memory. The text is adapted from a rare poem of Abraham Lincoln's which was included in his letter of April 18, 1846, to John D. Johnston, his stepbrother.[15] Lincoln's family, it will be remembered, had moved in 1816, when he was eight, from Kentucky to Indiana, partly over the slavery issue, and partly because of the difficulty of land titles in Kentucky. The family endured hard times until the land was cleared and a cabin built, and the boy's mother died in 1818. The following year his father married Mrs. Sally Johnston, a widow with three children, who proved to be a kind stepmother to young Abe. In 1830, all the Lincolns, including Mrs. Johnston's two daughters and sons-in-law came in ox-drawn wagons to settle in Illinois on the Sangamon River, and Abe began a series of jobs that eventually led to law, politics, and the historical role for which Destiny had prepared him.

The year 1844 had found Lincoln practicing law in Springfield as part of the Lincoln and Herndon partnership, recently rejected as a delegate to the Whig convention, and two years away from the Congressional nomination he would receive in 1846 after General Hardin's withdrawal from the race. In the aforementioned letter, he describes the circumstances of his Indiana visit, and its attendant poetic genesis in these terms:

> In the fall of 1844, thinking I might aid some to carry the State of Indiana for Mr. Clay, I went into the neighborhood in that state in which I was raised, where my mother and only sister were buried, and from which I had been absent about fifteen years. That part of the country is, within itself, as unpoetical as any spot of the earth; but still, seeing it and its objects and inhabitants, aroused feelings in me which were certainly poetry; though whether my expression of those feelings is poetry is quite another question.

Lincoln indicates that the ten stanzas he now quotes constitute one of a projected four cantos,[16] not an easily manageable length for an amateur poet. Although the lines are couched in the typically flowery mid-nineteenth century "literary" language, their author's skill at versification amazes us as much as the strength of his prose writings, coming from a man whose formal schooling totaled approximately one year. Jack Beeson, whose "Bear Hunt" for male chorus (1961) sets another of the cantos, has a very personal identification with "Indiana Homecoming." The song title is his own (the poem being untitled) and he now views it as a "nostalgia piece" reflecting his own Indiana origins, and the fact that he had not been back there for many years.[17]

The song indicates that the text has been "adapted" and Beeson's changes are of two types: word alteration and stanza omission. He substitutes the word "between" for "twixt" in line six, "seen" for "seem" in line eight (possibly a printer's error) and makes the last two lines of the song read

> Where memory will hallow all
> We've known, and know no more.

instead of Lincoln's original

> But seeing them, to mind again
> The lost and absent brings.

The latter change destroys the rhyme scheme, but Beeson's purpose is clear. In the desire to have a text of more workable length, he has cut stanzas four and five and the last three. The omission of these final ones, in which Lincoln dwells at melancholy length on the death of many former friends and loved ones, also changes the mood of the song text, removing the air of heavy sorrow, and conferring the peace of "hallowed memory" on what is "known no more."

Despite its lyrical flow, "Indiana Homecoming" has dramatic possibilities as well, and could easily be seen as a major aria in an opera on the life of Lincoln, with the protagonist alone on stage, surrounded in remembrance. The melodic lines, mostly in chordal skips and stepwise motion, are broadly arching, and a particularly felicitous contour outlined by an octave leap is repeated twice at other pitch levels, always at the low dynamic level of suppressed emotion.

Example 8.4, mm. 5–6

The song exhibits mostly diatonic language with flexible movement between tonal structures. Occasional polytonal elements are imaginatively tied to the text as in the following measures where memory rises, "pure and bright" toward a vocal cadence in F major (supported by the piano's right hand) having been "freed from all that's earthly vile," as symbolized by clashing chords and scale passages.

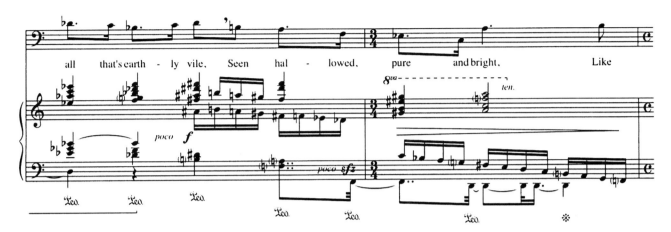

Example 8.5, mm. 9–10

Peter Viereck (1916–2006)

In 1951, the year of "Eldorado," Jack Beeson recanted on his earlier rejection of Peter Viereck's poetry, and composed the first of three settings based on his texts. Viereck had been born in New York City, and was the son of George Sylvester Viereck, a freelance writer who attracted considerable notoriety during both World Wars for his pro-German views. These were emphatically not shared by his son, who, after his academically illustrious years of preparation at Harvard and Oxford began a long career as teacher and writer on historical subjects, which enabled him to express his opposing points of view. Ironically, his brother, George Sylvester Viereck Jr., had been killed fighting with the Allied forces at Anzio, and Peter Viereck had served in Africa and Italy with the Psychological Warfare Branch in 1943–1944. The following year brought two life-changing events: Viereck met and married Anya de Markov, the daughter of Russian émigrés, and served as history instructor at the U.S. Army University in Florence. It was the latter experience that turned him away from freelance writing and toward teaching, and on his return to America, he taught briefly at Harvard and at Smith College. After 1948, except for periodic appointments to visiting professorships in the United States and Europe, he was firmly ensconced on the history faculty of Mount Holyoke until his retirement in 1987. Thereafter, as Professor Emeritus, he continued to teach his Russian history course for another decade. He died in South Hadley in 2006, close to the age of 90.

Besides his numerous published works on history and social philosophy, Viereck also wrote four volumes of poetry during the 1940s and 1950s, and a collection of *New and Selected Poems* in 1967. He felt that he had an advantage as a professor of history, claiming that a poet who teaches English "becomes self-conscious," and further that "academic poets tend to be critics and analysts rather than [to] feel the joy of spontaneity."[18] Conservative in both politics and literature, he found much modern poetry to be "too critical, too intellectual, too dry, and too lacking in music,"[19] and sought a "return to romantic wildness . . . and lyrical passion."[20]

Other strong strains in Viereck's poetry, particularly the early verse, are a kind of "classicism of the industrial age,"[21] and an acceptance and reconciliation of the uncouth aspects of life in New York and in the rest of the country. All three of Beeson's poetic choices fall into this category. "Big Crash Out West" (1951), originally printed in *Strike through the Mask* and included in the "Wars" section of *New and Selected Poems*, chronicled a senseless auto accident encouraged by the invitingly open spaces and smoldering boredom of western America. The setting, now reprinted by Boosey and Hawkes,[22] is in the lyrical/dramatic, largely diatonic, melodically expansive style of "Indiana Homecoming." The other two, composed twenty years later, use poems that Viereck grouped under "Grotesques" in 1967. They present contrasting Midwest farmland, and eastern big-city themes, and each affords Beeson the opportunity to employ his impressive command of musical characterization in a lighter, quasi-humorous vein.

"To a Sinister Potato" had initially appeared in *Terror and Decorum*, Viereck's first poetry collection, published in 1948. Its strong element of satire is typical of many of these early poems, as is its personification of an inanimate object in order to make "a witty comment on human existence."[23] In a rapid verbal rhythm accelerated by the refrain "In Indiana or in Idaho," the potatoes "bide their hour" underground, "puffed up by secret paranoia" and envious of the stars moving unconfined through the vastness of space. Jack Beeson's setting, written in 1970,[24] shortens the text by omitting the poem's fourth stanza, which describes the bland potatoes on Kiwanis Club plates deceiving Indiana as to their actual sinister intent. Otherwise, Beeson follows the process that he describes as being "quite literal in his settings, with word repetition as the only change."[25] In fact, only the word "silent" is repeated in this song, and that because it is followed by a melisma, a not infrequent device of the composer's to ensure comprehension of a word before its decoration.

Example 8.6, mm. 14–15

The dramatic effect of this upward curving melisma is to suggest the softly gathering menace of the "watchers" (see Ex. 8.6), and it forms an interesting contrast to the predominantly fast-moving, syllabic setting with which Beeson matches Viereck's verbal rhythm.

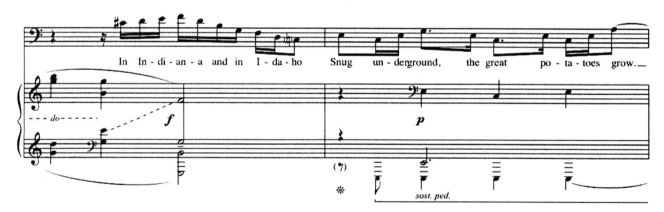

Example 8.7, mm. 7–8

Other dramatic moments are the opening, reiterated, forte low D in the piano part which establishes the "vastness" of this "earth-apple" together with the dimensions of its threat,

Example 8.8, mm. 1–2

and the crescendo of doom created in the final measures by cluster chords, undamped strings, and a leaping vocal contour which forms an unsettling augmented fourth with the last piano note.

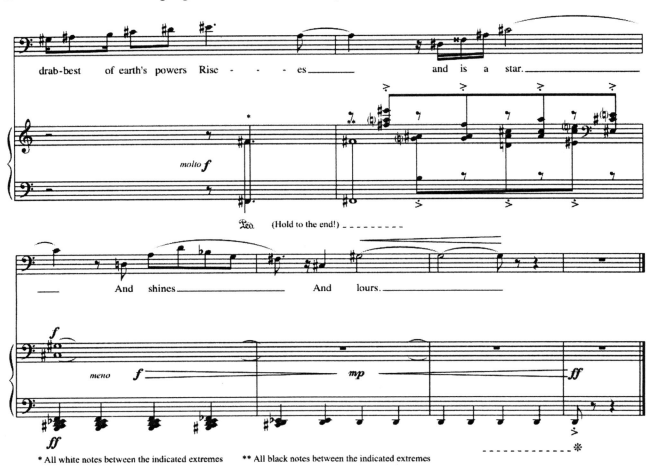

* All white notes between the indicated extremes   ** All black notes between the indicated extremes

Example 8.9, mm. 29–34

As befits the agitated mental state of the power-mad potato, the vocal line of this song is considerably more jagged than the Lincoln setting, and its harmonic structure shows the typical Beeson procedures of a suggested tonal center at the beginning and/or end of the song (D in this case) with freely ranging cadences in other tonal areas (C, F-sharp, A-flat, etc.). An infrequent but effective instance of word-painting is the treatment of "coiled-up springs," set with a long piano trill and tremolo that finally "uncoil" in an arpeggiated release.

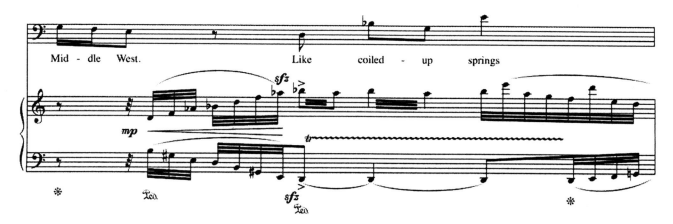

Example 8.10, m. 11

Beeson's third Viereck setting, called "The You Should of Done It Blues"[26] uses a 1965 poem whose original title was "The Lyricism of the Weak." Another poem in the "Grotesques" section of Viereck's 1967 collection, called "The New Cultural Blues," had been performed to music at Harvard's Loeb Theater in 1961, and one wonders if these factors might have influenced Beeson's view of the poem he chose to set as a musical blues lament. Interestingly, the song emerges on a note of ironic, "gallows-humor" self-deprecation, with an objectivity contributed by the formal "blues" setting, whereas the poem, lacking that formalized structure, seems to emphasize the victimization and deep, though ungrammatical, grief of the protagonist.

Beeson, despite his commitment to "literal" settings, makes two small changes in this text. One is the omission of the second "it" in the tenth line: "You should of done it (which it is no crime)"; and the second is the addition of the word "be" to line eight: "She is they say, 'no better than she ought to.'" Both of these alterations appear to serve the purpose of convincing rhythmic patterning in the vocal line, which displays throughout the syncopated accents, tempo, melodic shapes, and "off" notes of the "blues" idiom.

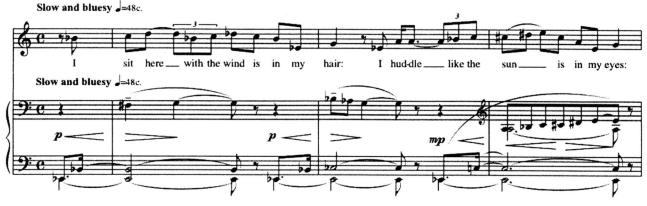

Example 8.11, mm. 1–3

The original poem, in an unrhymed iambic pentameter with the opening line repeated at the end, has an interesting structure of four three line stanzas. As Beeson sets this affecting monologue according to its expressive content, the corresponding musical "verses" occupy six, four, six, and eight measures respectively. The prosodic reasons for this discrepancy can be seen as he builds to the emotive climax, with a rapid, syllabic sequence ("It figures who I heard there," etc.) followed by drawn out melismas in the "blues" manner.

Example 8.12, mm. 8–13

The clearly defined E-flat tonal center of the opening and closing verses seems appropriate to the derivation of the musical style, but the rich coloration of the chromatic overlay carries it far from its "popular" origins. In another device for unification, Beeson applies the original melodic shape to Viereck's repetition of line one as the final line of the song except for a rhythmic augmentation, inversion, and substitute of seventh for tonic, in the last two notes (compare with Ex. 8.11).

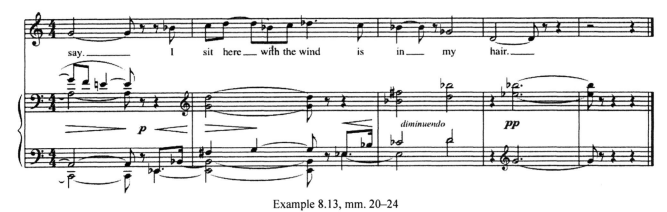

Example 8.13, mm. 20–24

Richard Owen (b. 1922)

"I believe in my double life," says Richard Owen, and adds "The scales of music and the scales of justice lend a balance to each other."[27] This composer, like the poet Wallace Stevens (see chapter 7), has spent a lifetime juggling a notable career as a lawyer with the demands of the creative avocation to which he is devoted. Owen's father, also a New York City lawyer, was a great lover of opera, and Richard attended many Metropolitan performances with his parents during his boyhood. Having dropped the piano after a few months of study at the age of six, Owen eagerly resumed his lessons at twenty-nine. Over the ensuing years, he studied composition privately with Vittorio Giannini and Robert Starer and took classes from time to time at the New York College of Music, the Mannes School, and the Berkshire Music Center at Tanglewood. From 1960 to 1963 he studied at the Manhattan School of Music and eventually was awarded an honorary Doctor of Music by that institution.

In his other life, Owen had completed his undergraduate degree at Dartmouth in 1947 after serving as a navigator in the Army Air Corps during World War II. Three years later, in 1950, he finished Harvard Law School, passed the New York State bar, and began many years of practice (in government service, in various partnerships, and by himself) in the city of New York. In 1956, while working as a Senior Trial Attorney with the Anti-Trust Division of the Justice Department, Owen had his initial public recognition as a composer, with the performance of his first opera at the local Bar Association. It was a one-act opera about a lawyer and his client, and the singers included a young Juilliard soprano named Lynn Rasmussen whom Owen married in 1960. Now there was a new partner in the family juggling act, as Mrs. Owen divided her time between an operatic career which included performances at the Hamburg and Zurich operas, and a home life which grew to encompass city and country residences and the birth of three sons.[28]

During his busy years of law practice, Richard Owen composed two more operas. The first, on commission from the After Dinner Opera Company, was a one-act called *A Moment of War*, given in concert form in 1958, and subsequently in a number of staged Spanish translation performances in Buenos Aires. The second, a religious work titled *A Fisherman Called Peter*, was premièred in 1965 in a New York production under the supervision of Dorothy Maynor. In 1974, Owen was appointed United States District Judge of the Southern District of New York and since that appointment he has written *Mary Dyer* (1976), based on the life of the Quaker martyr, *The Death of the Virgin* (1983), *Abigail Adams* (1987), and the children's opera, *Tom Sawyer* (1989).

Stephen Crane (1871–1900)

In the sixties and early seventies, Richard Owen wrote a number of songs, in which settings of American poetry predominated. Among these were two poems by Stephen Crane, an enormously interesting writer whose works had, until then, attracted very little attention from composers. Crane was born in Newark, New Jersey, a city which one of his ancestors helped to establish. Descended from a line of Methodist ministers, he had a grandfather who was a bishop and founder of Syracuse University. Stephen's father, the mild, unworldly Reverend Jonathan Townley Crane, died when the boy was eight, while holding a Methodist pastorate at Port Jervis, New York. His mother, a forceful religious journalist who doted on this last of her fourteen children, then took him to live in Asbury Park, where at seventeen he began to work summers on his brother Townley's Press Bureau.

Crane's university education was spotty and brief. He failed in his first semester as an engineering student at Lafayette College, then spent a single semester (spring, 1891) at Syracuse where he attended but few classes, played on the varsity baseball team, and probably started *Maggie: A Girl of the Streets*, the landmark naturalistic novel which was to profoundly shock his contemporaries. The next few years brought a series of intermittent jobs as a newspaper reporter, alternating with periods of extreme poverty, romantic attachments to unattainable objects, and a constant, passionate concern over the moral and social ills of society. A chance meeting with the writer Hamlin Garland led to an introduction to William Dean Howells, and both men became interested in the developing talent of the younger man. Howells, in fact, invited Crane to tea and read Emily Dickinson's poetry to him, and it is a commonly accepted belief that the brevity and power of her verses inspired Crane's major collection of poems, *The Black Riders and Other Lines*, to be written soon after.

The Black Riders was published in 1895, the same year in which the publication of *The Red Badge of Courage*, Crane's famous Civil War novel, brought international renown. During the last four years of his life he traveled as a war correspondent to the most dangerous sectors of the Greco-Turkish, Cuban, and Spanish-American conflicts, returning to interludes of relatively peaceful living in England with Cora Taylor. In her, he had finally found a woman who could match his unconventional, free-spirited approach to life, and appreciate his artistic goals and sensibilities. She was, however, dedicated to surrounding her celebrated author with an overly lavish lifestyle, which necessitated his writing furiously against a growing mountain of debt. In 1900, after a considerable period of failing health, he succumbed to tuberculosis at the age of twenty-nine, ending a short lifetime that had been crowded with adventure, intensity, and literary accomplishment.

It is widely believed that Stephen Crane's title of *The Black Riders* for his poetry collection, refers to a childhood dream of his at Ocean Grove, New Jersey, in which black riders on black horses were charging at him from the surf.[29] The poems themselves proved more confusing to contemporary critics who were put off by the angular, short-line, free-verse structures and the troublesome themes of man's alienation in an uncaring universe dominated by a vengeful God. British criticism managed a truer perspective from a greater geographical distance, and H. G. Wells wrote, shortly after Crane's death, that "he is the first expression of the opening mind of a new period . . . beginning . . . with the record of impressions . . . of a vigor and intensity beyond all precedent."[30] Two decades later, Carl Van Doren pointed out that during the American "poetic twilight" of the 1890s, only Crane had challenged the conventions of poetic form and diction of late Victorian verse: a challenge curiously similar to that of French Symbolism, despite Crane's ignorance of Symbolist verse and philosophy.[31] Following the appearance of Crane's *Collected Works* in 1926, his poetry became more widely available, and it was now clear that he had indeed been a forerunner of many of the movements of the "poetic renaissance." By 1950, John Berryman was able to proclaim him as "the important American poet between Walt Whitman and Emily Dickinson on one side, and his tardy-developing contemporaries Edwin Arlington Robinson and Robert Frost and Ezra Pound on the other."[32]

Two characteristics of Crane's style in *The Black Riders* set him apart as unique despite twentieth-century literature's belated attempts to draw him in: one is his extreme brevity and concentration which relates only to the isolated attempts by Crapsey, Lowell, and Pound to adapt Japanese haiku forms; the other is his narrative emphasis, which spawned few followers in an era dominated by lyric and dramatic expression.[33] These two characteristics prove to be energizing points of correspondence in Richard Owen's settings, for his declamatory vocal style is appropriate to the "story-telling" verbal mode of the narratives, while the brevity of the verses permits musical amplification through both temporal and expressive elements.

"There were many who went in huddled procession" contrasts "mass-man" with a single, courageous soul "who sought a new road . . . and ultimately died alone . . . (in) direful thickets." It perfectly represents Crane's sense of the individual's isolation in a menacing world, and could, indeed, be his own epitaph. Owen begins his setting[34] with a repeated piano figure in the hypnotic march rhythm of the blindly moving "procession." The empty, parallel fifths drawn from the Phrygian mode lend an ancient quality to the universal tale, and the ingenuous little stepwise eighth note motif introduced here will later expand to a dramatic vocal series of leaping fourths ("There was one").

Example 8.14a, mm. 1–5

Example 8.14b, mm. 19–21

Halfway through the song, the parallel fifth figure intensifies and broadens with the addition of the upper octave, and in the final phrase, it is transposed down a half step to match the somber verbal irony. The latter finds vocal representation through a slower, triplet rendering of the leaping fourth figure, suggesting the weariness of bitter reflection.

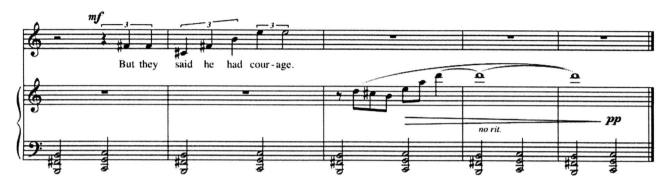

Example 8.15, mm. 28–32

In Stephen Crane's parable "I saw a man pursuing the horizon," he draws close to the allegorical mode of his literary forefathers, Hawthorne and Melville. This poem has been mentioned previously as an updated parallel to the search for the Ideal in "Eldorado," although in this case, unlike the knight's encouraging "shade," the observer states "It is futile" with merciless clarity. Owen's setting[35] provides in musical terms a sense of the protagonist's ceaseless running, a physical activity which at once embodies his cosmic helplessness, and Existential dedication to courageous movement through life. The 6/8 "perpetual motion" figure, and circular shapes of the vocal and piano lines both contribute to this effect.

Example 8.16, mm. 1–6

At the climactic moment of confrontation, the composer stops the motion somewhat in "freer" recitative. The anguished rebuttal ("You lie") rises to the song's largest vocal leap, and touches off a frantic renewal of motion that fades dynamically in representation of a visually receding form.

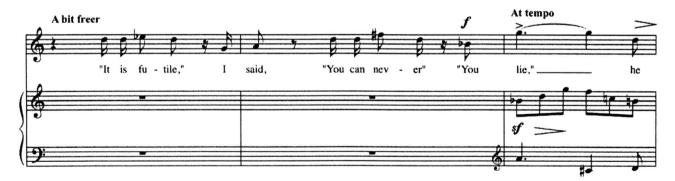

Example 8.17, mm. 16–22

Robert Frost (1874–1963)

In 1966, the year in which the Crane settings had appeared, Richard Owen also published "The Impulse ,"[36] to a poem by Robert Frost. (The reader is referred to chapter 5 for a major treatment of Frost in connection with John Duke's settings.) "The Impulse" was originally included in the collection *Mountain Interval*, which Frost published in 1916, soon after he returned from England to receive America's belated recognition and to take up his life on the farm at Franconia, New Hampshire. The pressure was gone from his farming now, for he was in great demand as a teacher and lecturer and no longer depended on the land for a living. But his eye for nature and its interactions with man remained as keen as the ear that had raised the New England idiom "to the dignity of a literary language."[37] In poem after poem, he records the many faces of mountain life: its beauties, and its terrors.

"The Impulse" is the last of five sections in a longer poem called "The Hill Wife." The titles of the first four sections, "Loneliness," "House Fear," "The Smile," and "The Oft-Repeated Dream," partially suggest the state of mind of the protagonist whose spirit is crushed by years of isolation with only her husband for company. In "House Fear" and "The Oft-Repeated Dream," surrounding trees and eventually the house itself come to be seen as increasingly malevolent, until in "The Impulse" she is driven to a sudden, unexpected flight through the woods from which she never returns.

The poem is in seven stanzas, exhibiting Frost's favorite four line verse form in an unusual pattern of alternating four and two stress lines. For the most part, Owen's setting treats the stanzas as consisting of two lines with six stresses each, and creates a rhythmic scheme based on the quarter note in groupings of 4, 6, 2, and 3 per measure. An exception to this is the pictorial effect of a single 4/8 measure that uses the smaller note values and an even faster moving triplet to suggest the woman's flight.

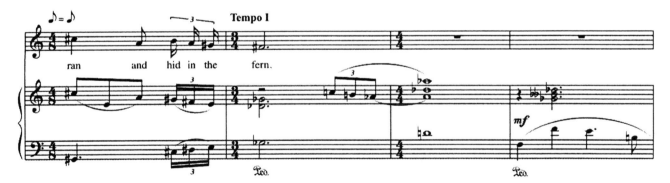

Example 8.18, mm. 40–43

The overall style of "The Impulse" is similar to Owen's Crane settings, in which a declamatory vocal line, with many repeated notes, is supported by a lightly textured accompaniment. This piano writing also contains a recurrent melodic motif (F, E, B) that is first stated just before the voice enters.

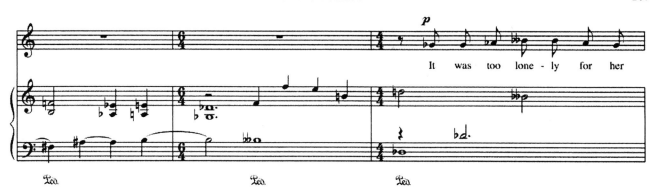

Example 8.19, mm. 5–7

This motif reappears many times in transposition, inversion, and its original form, and finally transfers to the vocal line at a moment of profound emotion ("he looked ev'rywhere").

Example 8.20, mm. 44–46

Free use of tonal elements characterizes the harmony, with considerable polytonal juxtaposition of simultaneous D and D-flat structures. The resulting dissonance is occasionally parted by a clear diatonic function, such as in Example 8.21 where the widely spaced cadential chords on "felled tree," give a Copland-esque, "American" sense of the spacious natural environment.

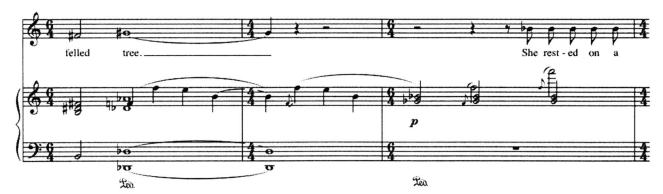

Example 8.21, mm. 20–22

Amy Lowell (1874–1925)

Six years after the Crane and Frost songs, Richard Owen published a setting of "Patterns,"[38] a widely known poem by Amy Lowell who is originally discussed in chapter 4. "Patterns" was written in the spring of 1915, at a time when Amy

Lowell and her championship of free verse were a subject of attack and ridicule in many circles.[39] One weekend, when Lowell's devoted companion, the former actress Ada Dwyer Russell, was out of town, the poet composed "Patterns" with an easy flow and mounting excitement. On Ada's return, she insisted on reading it to her at once, after which they agreed that Lowell had made a masterful statement against literary conservatism, armed conflict between nations, and the restricted lives of women, beneath the cloak of an eighteenth century historical romance. Sensing that "the piece was a trifle risqué for the general public,"[40] the poet sent it off to the *Little Review*, one of the foremost "little magazines"[41] of the period, whose editor, Margaret Anderson, readily accepted it for the August issue. The poem was an instant success, and a year later was printed as the opener to Lowell's poetry collection called *Men, Women and Ghosts*, published in the fall of 1916. It is still widely quoted and anthologized more than any other Amy Lowell poem, including an appearance in a 1972 anthology of anti-war poetry.

Written with an irregular but carefully controlled rhyme scheme, "Patterns" is a dramatic monologue in which a woman, who has just learned of her betrothed's death in battle, cries out against the stiff materials that confine her body and the rigid mores of society that have destroyed her life. Richard Owen had already written three operas when he undertook to set this poem, and treated the text as he would have one of his own libretti, cutting where compression seemed necessary for heightened musical effect. Out of an original 107 lines, approximately 66 remain in an extended "scena" of operatic dimensions that Owen, not surprisingly, dedicated to his wife.

The vocal style of the work is a flexible arioso that ranges from recitative-like passages to widely spaced lyrical contours that seem to break loose from their restricted "patterns" at climactic moments. The piano writing is more expansive and more orchestrally conceived than in the settings treated previously, and from the outset, establishes a motivic life of its own.

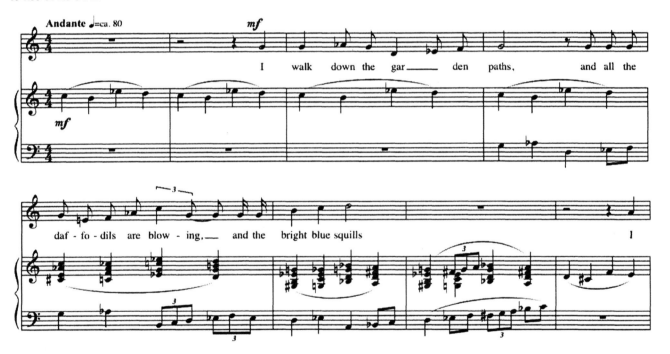

Example 8.22, mm. 1–8

The device of "word-painting" is also employed by the composer in this dramatic context as he uses rapidly repeated vocal notes to suggest drops of water (see Ex. 8.23) and ornamented piano tremolos to portray the visual distortion wrought by the terrible import of the Duke's letter (see Ex. 8.24).

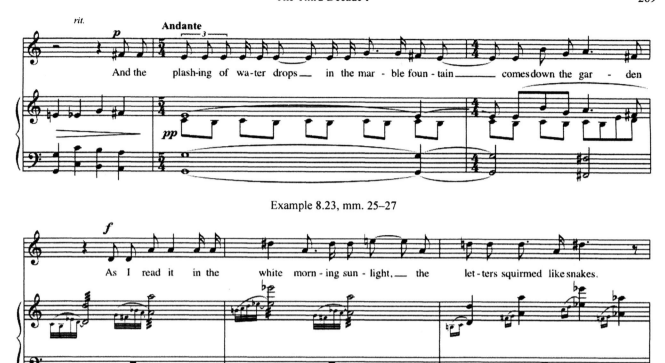

Example 8.23, mm. 25–27

Example 8.24, mm. 82–84

C is the tonal center that Owen holds as a reference point, and the song begins (see Ex. 8.22) and closes in its minor mode. The final phrase, set in the rhythmic freedom of an a capella cry of anguish, ends tellingly with the unresolved despair of the second scalar degree.

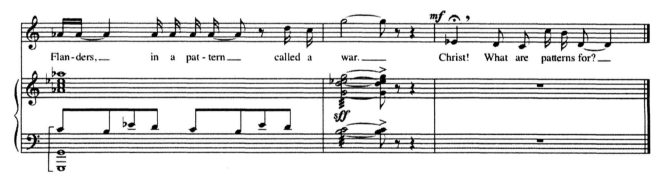

Example 8.25, mm. 123–25

Jean Eichelberger Ivey (1923–2010)

It is interesting to observe the several parallels that exist between the life of Jean Eichelberger Ivey and that of Mary Howe, another outstanding woman composer who is treated in chapter 4. Both of these women centered the major part of their lives in the Washington-Baltimore area; both were professional pianists before they became established composers; and both had important connections to the Peabody Conservatory, where Howe received a diploma in composition, and Eichelberger Ivey a Masters of Music in piano as well as subsequent major faculty appointments.

The Eichelberger family's Baltimore roots extend back to colonial times, and the composer had celebrated this paternal heritage in a vocal chamber work called *Notes Toward Time*, which premièred in March 1984, having been commissioned by the Baltimore Chamber Music Society for the 350th anniversary of the founding of Maryland. "Although I have written for virtually every medium" said Ivey, "my favorite medium is the voice,"[42] and she attributed this fact to early influences from her mother, a semi-professional singer, and from two of her father's sisters, who were voice teachers.

Like many musically gifted children, the young Jean quickly became fluent at the keyboard, and by the age of eleven held a position as organist at St. James Church in Mount Rainier. In this capacity, she was able to experiment with the building of timbres on the parish's Hammond organ, an interest that would expand in later life to the composition of electronic music and to her establishment of Peabody's Electronic Music Studio. The development of her precocious talent, however, was seriously threatened by the Depression, which brought about the demise of *The Woman Patriot*, an anti-feminist newspaper that her father had edited for a number of years. Fortunately, she was able to win a full tuition scholarship at Trinity College in Washington, and her 1944 bachelor's degree was soon followed by the master's in piano at Peabody, and a second master's degree in composition earned during the summers at the Eastman School in Rochester.

Over twenty-five years were to intervene before Eichelberger Ivey was awarded a doctorate of music in composition by the University of Toronto, whose music school at that time (1972) was a leading center of electronic music in North America. The years between had been crowded: with a marriage that lasted "long enough to establish her professional reputation as Jean Eichelberger Ivey;"[43] with teaching appointments in piano, organ, and theory at middle-Atlantic colleges such as Peabody, Trinity, and Catholic University; and with recital tours as a concert pianist to Mexico, Germany, and Austria as well as the United States.

A review by Paul Hume, writing for the *Washington Post* in June 1956, attested to the young performer's technical and interpretive talents as well as to her musical taste and versatility in a program which included the Haydn F-minor variations, Beethoven sonata opus 109, and her own promising composition titled *Prelude and Passacaglia*.[44] Increasingly, with the passage of years, the pianist gave way to the composer. Ivey gained renown for performances by soloists and orchestras of her works in many media.[45] In 1969 she returned to Peabody as a major teacher of composition, and in 1982 acceded to the position of coordinator of the composition department. She held this position until her retirement in 1997, and died on May 2, 2010, in Reisterstown, Maryland, after a long illness.

The 1983–1984 season was a memorable one for the composer, as her sixtieth birthday occasioned all-Ivey concerts at Trinity College, Peabody Conservatory, and at the convention of the Music Teachers' National Association in Louisville. Surrounding these were major performances of Ivey works by the Oakland Symphony, Fort Wayne Philharmonic, and Peabody Chamber Orchestra. The Baltimore Symphony had premièred two of her earlier works: *Testament of Eve* for mezzo, tape, and orchestra in 1776 and *Sea-Change* for tape and orchestra in 1982.

Musical sounds, both traditionally and electronically generated, had long created a comfortable ambiance for Jean Eichelberger Ivey. She was equally at home in the world of words, and had published a number of journal articles. These included "The Contemporary Performing Ensemble"[46] which described American college groups dedicated to new music; "Electronic Music Workshop for Teachers,"[47] a review of the goals and achievements of this pioneering effort held at Peabody in 1967; and "The Composer as Teacher,"[48] in which Ivey's own keen pedagogical insights were revealed. She herself had also been the subject of many articles by others, as well as of radio interviews and a half-hour television documentary filmed by WRC-TV (NBC) in Washington for their series *A Woman Is*.

Poetry was another preferred literary medium of the composer's. "I have always loved poetry," she said, "and have written a fair amount of it, including texts for some of my vocal works, notably *Solstice* (1977) and *Testament of Eve*. I have also set to music poems I have come upon and liked,"[49] and one of the earliest of these, written for medium voice in 1956, was an attractive, lyric-dramatic setting of "Morning Song" from *Senlin* by the poet Conrad Aiken (see chapter 6). This song received its Baltimore première on April 10, 1984, in a performance by Wayne Connor, tenor, and Ernest Ligon, pianist. Surprisingly, it has never been published but is available from the American Music Center which holds a complete collection of Ivey works.[50]

As the composer pointed out, her attention had often been captured by the work of women poets, such as Carolyn Kizer's text for *Hera, Hung from the Sky* which setting was recorded by CRI, and which treated the ancient myth from the woman's point of view. Ivey interpreted this poem as describing the goddess' punishment "for daring to question the established male-dominated order of things,"[51] and her own text for *Testament of Eve* saw Eve non-traditionally as a heroic figure "choosing knowledge and growth for herself and her children."[52]

Sara Teasdale (1884–1933)

Perhaps the earliest feminine voice to capture Ivey's attention was that of Sara Teasdale, who has been treated at length in chapter 5. The composer explained: "I became interested in Sara Teasdale's poetry in college and later read a biography of her. . . . In the case of *Woman's Love* I was interested in the fact that she brought a special, feminine point of view to love poetry—not the only woman poet to do so, of course."[53]

Woman's Love is Ivey's title for a cycle of five songs composed in 1962, from which two have been published in Galaxy Music's American Artsong Anthology, Volume I.[54] The first of these, "I Would Live in Your Love," has a text taken from *Helen of Troy* (1910), Teasdale's second volume of poetry, and the one which established her reputation. The second song, "To One Away," plus the three which remain unpublished ("The Kiss," "The Old Maid," and "Peace") all set poems from *Rivers to the Sea*, which appeared in 1915, the first year of the poet's marriage to Ernst Filsinger in a seemingly fulfilling resolution to "her search for the love that would justify the giving up of the separate self."[55] That the separate self eventually reasserted its claims appears unmistakably clear both from the poet's divorce of Filsinger in 1929 and from the internal evidence of the later poetry. "It was myself that sang in me"[56] writes Teasdale in *Dark of the Moon* (1926) that contains some of her finest work, and again, "Let them think I care, though I go alone. . . . Who am self-contained as a flower or stone."[57] But in the 1910 and 1915 poems, the point of view that Ivey found so typically feminine was that of a young woman in love, longing for a sense of completion by and absorption into the object of that love, and focusing her energies toward response to the other's needs and emotions.

The musical language and devices of *Woman's Love* show a sensitive adaptation by the composer to serve the expressed meaning and implications of the texts. In "I Would Live in Your Love," both the voice part and linear accompaniment are dominated by lines of scalar eighth notes, moving variously in unison, imitation, inversion, and/or contrary motion. These lines carry both an aural and visual suggestion of the waves that draw the sea-grasses in their wake:

Example 8.26, mm. 4–8

They also create, through their harmonic ambiguity (C major combined with Aeolian modal elements) and through their never-ending undulations of pitch, a sense of almost a hypnotic process at work, in which the protagonist is drawn up and down as though by an outside will.

This process is intensified at the emotive climax of the song by a shortening of the "wave" length to half a measure each at the end of the line "I would empty my soul of the dreams that have gathered in me." Suddenly, then, it is shattered by a subito forte, and a series of "heart beat" accents on the strong beats of the piano accompaniment. It is as though the submerged will had suddenly broken free to commit an impassioned act of total self-dedication.

Example 8.27, mm. 12–16

"To One Away" presents a sharp musical contrast to the flowing, tranquillo atmosphere of its companion piece. Here the tempo is agitated, and the unease of lovers separated takes the form of an unrelenting chromatic ostinato in the left hand of the accompaniment. The urgency of this figure is further underlined by the syncopated accent patterns of both the vocal line, and the piano's right hand chords.

Example 8.28, mm. 4–6

The "cry in the night" is not actually heard in musical terms until m. 10, when "my name" is set with a sudden dynamic increase imitated and confirmed by the piano an octave higher, and then repeated quite softly, in the awed whisper of overwhelming emotion.

Example 8.29, mm. 10–12

The second verse of this modified strophic form sets "I know," which is the woman's answer to her lover's call, with a similar three part repetition, followed by yet another high, soft chordal echo of never-ending response.

Example 8.30, mm. 22–25

Of the three remaining unpublished songs,[58] "Peace" is a particularly attractive setting which demonstrates a changing metric organization well adapted to textual needs and the composer's always sensitive and fresh harmonic structures. *Woman's Love* was performed in a New York recital on April 8, 1984, by Dilly Patrick, soprano, and Daniel Ragone, pianist, and was called "an exquisitely crafted song cycle" by the *New York Times* reviewer.[59]

William Flanagan (1923–1969)

Throughout his crowded, intense, and tragically shortened life, William Flanagan was slightly out of step. Not only was he marching to a different drummer, but indeed it must often have seemed to him as though he was part of a whole different parade than the one which engaged the rest of his world. To begin with, he was born in Detroit to a non-musical family, and received little early training besides exposure to Max Steiner's scores in the movie-houses of the thirties which he then reproduced "by ear" as chapel organist for the University of Detroit High School.[60] Having begun his college work in Detroit and Ann Arbor aiming at a more "acceptable" career as a journalist, Flanagan capitulated, after two years, to the strength of his inner pull toward music. It was only at this point, at the age of twenty, that he started, in his own words, "to learn musical notation, and to grapple with the bare concept of imposing control over my random improvisations."[61]

The youthful talent ripened in three years of study at the Eastman School under Burrill Phillips and Bernard Rogers. By the late forties, Flanagan had shown sufficient promise to be taken on as a scholarship student at the Berkshire Music Center where he studied under Arthur Honegger, Samuel Barber, and Aaron Copland. Settling in New York City, he sharpened his compositional technique in two years of work with David Diamond, and also began to share a Greenwich Village apartment with a young man named Edward Albee who was trying to find his place in the world of literature.

Except for a brief stint as instructor at the now defunct School of American Music, William Flanagan was to earn his living for the next twenty years primarily as a journalist, his supposedly abandoned profession, while trying to come to terms with his own conclusion that "only three classical composers in the United States today . . . can make a living from their music: Barber, Copland, and Thomson."[62] As a further irony, it was Flanagan's sending *The Zoo Story* (Edward Albee's first major play) to David Diamond in Italy that eventually led to its German and American productions, and to the meteoric rise of Albee's theatrical career. Yet Flanagan's composing career could, it seemed, gain little luster by creative association with his friend. Their collaboration on the opera *Bartleby*, based on a Melville story, opened in 1961 to a cool reception by the New York critics; Albee's dramatic adaptation of James Purdy's novel *Malcolm*, with Flanagan's music, fared no better in 1966; and a final collaboration, commissioned by the New York City Center, on an opera called *The Ice Age*, remained uncompleted at the composer's death. The single exception to this discouraging list received comment in Flanagan's rueful article written in 1963 and titled "How to Succeed in Composing without Really Succeeding." Here he describes how seven minutes of incidental music for Albee's one-act play, *The Sandbox*, had, since its 1961 opening, earned him two thousand dollars in royalties, "at least as much," he says, "as the many performances and recordings of my music have over the thirteen years of my career as a professional composer."[63]

Albee and Flanagan had, in fact, moved to separate living quarters after the late fifties, but had remained friends and continued to work together. Despite their diverging fortunes, the composer commented in an interview with John Gruen that although "people have often thought it odd . . . to this day I have never known a moment of jealousy about Edward's fame (and) have always taken great pride in his success."[64] One of Gruen's own memories which confirmed Flanagan's generosity of spirit concerned a night when both were writing concert reviews for the *New York Herald Tribune*, and Flanagan "had left his own review waiting in the typewriter"[65] to ease Gruen's anxiety on this, his first encounter with a deadline. Other of Gruen's recollections portray William Flanagan as "one of the most intellectually stimulating people I have ever known," as well as a "deeply unhappy, somewhat sullen and bitter person," who was prone to periods of heavy drinking during which, "as he lived alone, it was often difficult for him to call for help."[66]

Although peripheral by his own perceptions, Flanagan's position in the New York musical scene of the fifties and sixties was actually quite central. He was music essayist for many magazines and newspapers and served as an important critic and reviewer for successively, *Musical America*, the *New York Herald Tribune*, and *Stereo Review*; he wrote well over a hundred "sleeve" commentaries for almost a dozen record companies; and between 1959 and 1962 he was heavily involved in a concert series called Music for the Voice by Americans which presented and often premièred major songs by Ned Rorem, Virgil Thomson, David Diamond, Daniel Pinkham, John Gruen, and Lou Harrison as well as Flanagan himself.

This series was, according to Edward Albee, William Flanagan's "brainchild,"[67] but the actual work of organization and implementation was, from the outset, shared by Ned Rorem, who was his "close, if competitive ally for twenty-three years."[68] Rorem's diaries contain numerous references to dinner parties and correspondence shared, and an article about his friend published in *Critical Affairs* suggests how alike they were in their fundamental musical convictions. "We were the same age," says Rorem, "and of similar convictions, namely that there was still blood in tonality, breath in the simple line, and that the flesh of music could be grafted onto the skeleton of poetry and given life by the singing voice, with a feeling of heightened naturalness for the listener."[69]

Lester Trimble, still another American composer of about the same age, had known William Flanagan at Tanglewood, in Paris, and as a fellow critic for the *Herald Tribune*. In his memorial tribute, written two months after Flanagan was found dead in his New York apartment from an overdose of barbiturates, Trimble recounted the twofold "nature of the battle Flanagan was fighting in his creative and professional life."[70] The first major strain he delineates was the composer's refusal to adopt the seemingly mandatory serial techniques of the successful avant-garde. The second was the advantage held by composers only five or six years older than Flanagan, whose careers had been solidly established before the traumatic interruptions of World War II. "I have no doubt," added Trimble "that the special obstacles posed against his generation have produced special inner tensions which . . . were the underlying cause of his death." As a final irony, the last decade of William Flanagan's life had brought him the National Institute of Arts and Letters Award, a Pulitzer nomination, several major recordings, and commissions and performances of his works by leading orchestras. Out of step to the end, Flanagan, on the threshold of the recognition he had long desired, brought it all to a crashing halt.

Song had remained a favorite medium of William Flanagan's ever since his early settings, in 1946, of poetry by W. B. Yeats ("After Long Silence") and Siegfried Sassoon ("The Dugout").[71] He explained its early appeal as stemming from his lack of technique adequate to longer forms,[72] but as time went on, his innate vocal orientation became apparent even in the symphonic and chamber works,[73] as did his dedication to the art of word-setting in a growing body of songs. "The vocal line" wrote Flanagan "is a song's most elusive property. Its curves, its metrical pulse should be one with the rhythmic flow of the language."[74] The comments were scarcely surprising coming from an artist who, in a 1967 article, had listed Mozart, Mahler, Debussy, Poulenc, and Britten as among his ten favorite composers.[75]

On examining a complete listing of Flanagan's vocal works, one finds settings of a number of American poets, including Gertrude Stein,[76] e.e. cummings,[77] Herman Melville,[78] and Walt Whitman.[79] The composer also collaborated twice in this medium with Edward Albee, once in 1959, in a long cantata-like work for two singers and seven instruments called "The Lady of Tearful Regret," and on another occasion, nine years earlier, in a small masterpiece for solo voice and piano called "Song for a Winter Child."[80]

Edward Albee (b. 1928)

Edward Albee had been born in Washington, D.C., to natural parents whom he never knew, for at the age of two weeks he was adopted by millionaire Reed Albee and taken to Westchester County, New York. Here he grew up in the midst of physical luxury but almost unrelieved emotional poverty. His adoptive father was a silent man, twenty-three years older than his wife, Frances—a strong-willed former fashion model who dominated the marriage. As a child, Edward was not very close to the Albees, and also harbored deep-seated resentment toward his natural parents. The only warmth in his early years stemmed from his relationship with "Grandma Cotta," Mrs. Albee's mother, who would leave him the inheritance that supported his decade of artistic struggle.[81]

School represented a series of traumas for the "spoiled . . . plump, precocious and unhappy" youth.[82] Expelled from boarding school in Lawrenceville, New Jersey, and from Valley Forge military academy, Edward finally found a congenial atmosphere at the Choate School in Connecticut, where he began to write seriously and to turn out large quantities of prose and poetry. After a short interlude at Hartford's Trinity College, Albee ended his formal education and got a job writing continuity for musical programs on radio station WNYC. This position reflected a strong interest in music which had first surfaced at Lawrenceville and which would eventually carry over into his concepts of playwriting. "I always find," said Albee from a later vantage point, "a great association between plays and musical composition, [and] composer friends of mine have told me that my work is related very strongly to musical form as they understand it."[83]

At the age of twenty, Albee left home after a family argument, settled in New York, and held a series of odd jobs until the production of *The Zoo Story* in 1959 brought him recognition as a major young dramatic talent. For nine years of this unsettled period, Albee and Flanagan shared an "airy and comfortable . . . floor-through flat"[84] in the Village. On one occasion in 1950, Albee recalls, "Flanagan asked me to write a brief poem, which I did, which he set."[85] This, then, was the genesis of "Song for a Winter Child."

The poem, which is metrically free with a subtle rhyme scheme, and full of compelling imagery, has not, to the authors' knowledge, ever been published. Its message is that of welcome to a new infant whose coming has set "winter to flight as new grasses crack the hoping winter earth." One cannot help wondering whether Albee, who was himself born on March 12, 1928, was not perhaps imagining on some level a poetic welcome for his own birth from all of spring-intoxicated Nature, having been denied by harsh circumstance the celebrations of mother and father as traditional welcomers.

Flanagan's setting, written only four years after he had begun composing, certainly demonstrates "a melodic style that is part and parcel of the language"[86]—his own description of a goal he felt had already been achieved by "popular" composers and should be imitated in serious music. Flexible quarter note groupings of 2, 3, 4, or 5 to the bar follow the poetry's changing accents; the prosody shows a keen ear for the rhythms of American speech; and the vocal contours rise and fall convincingly to the emotive context of the words.

Example 8.31, mm. 1–8

The diatonic dissonances of the harmony, and largely chordal accompaniment with broadly arching counter melodies attest to Flanagan's years of study with David Diamond (see chapter 7). But the key movements (E to F to F-sharp major with a brief interlude in C) are the ascending half-step relationships of Broadway, and the synthesis of all these elements with Flanagan's unerring instincts in text setting produces a new and exciting flavor that is unique in mid-twentieth century American song. Although the overall orientation of "Winter Child" is dramatic, with little lied-like verbal correspondence, there is one very effective instance of musical pictorialism in the last phrase. While the piano moves in legato augmentation, the voice sings a dropping line of tender eighth notes to set "And gentle rain will fall tonight."

And gen - tle rain will fall to - night._____

Example 8.32, mm. 19–23

Howard Moss (1922–1987)

On March 11, 1962, the fourth yearly concert in the Music for Voice by Americans series was given in Carnegie Recital Hall. There were nine composers represented and the conclusion of Musical America's reviewer was that "Flanagan's new cycle, *Moss*, was the strongest collection of songs at the concert."[87] Indeed, in Howard Moss, William Flanagan appeared to have found an ideal poetic counterpart and the five products of this combination, still barely known to the American public, are a major contribution to the genre.

There were two important contrasts in Howard Moss's early life that broadened his worldview beyond that of the average American schoolboy. The first was cultural, and stemmed from the "old country" influence in the house of his paternal grandparents, whom his father had brought over from Lithuania after himself "making it," as an immigrant, into middle-class American society. The second was geographical, for the family had settled in Rockaway Beach (a brief train ride from Manhattan) as a healthly place to raise a child, thus providing Howard's growing years with an ambiance that was "half sea-soaked, half citified."[88]

Well-nourished by all the gifts of nature, family tradition, and the metropolis, Moss began to write in grammar school, and in high school was already producing short stories and poetry. Reversing William Flanagan's progression, he left the New York area to spend his college years in the Middle West that beckoned with a "romantic aura."[89] He attended the University of Michigan for one year, and finished his B.A. at the University of Wisconsin, where, as a sophomore, his first poem was accepted for publication by *Accent*.

Finding his proper niche in the literary world, however, involved a number of "tries." Even before graduation from college, he had had a dazzling rise from copyboy to book reviewer during a period of employment by *Time* magazine. After graduation, there was a short stint with the Office of War Information as World War II came to a close; some graduate work at Columbia never completed; two years teaching English at Vassar College; and a year as fiction editor of *Junior Bazaar*. In 1948 he joined the editorial staff of the *New Yorker*, where he remained as poetry editor from 1950 until his death in 1987.

His own poems had brought him *Poetry* magazine's Janet Sewall David award in 1944, as the first of many subsequent prizes. Two years later he published his first book, *The Wound and the Weather*, a volume of poems that would be followed by ten more in the ensuing quarter of a century. In *Selected Poems* of 1971, he made choices from the seven preceding volumes, and for this collection he was co-winner of the 1972 National Book Award in poetry. Moss said he had given up fiction, since "none of it was any good"[90] but he wrote a number of plays which had small productions. Interestingly, his *The Palace at 4 A.M.* was produced in the summer of 1972 at the John Drew Theater in East Hampton with Edward Albee as its director.

In 1975 Moss described having lived in the same garden-terraced Greenwich Village apartment for the past twenty years. Moving no doubt, in the same Village circles as Flanagan and Albee in the fifties, the poet and his work evidently had come to the attention of the composer, and the flood of Flanagan-Moss settings began in 1959. William Flanagan's attraction to Howard Moss's poetry might well have been predicted, for Flanagan's resistance to the stylish musical fads of his time was paralleled by Moss's stated position that "Schools of poetry (and) insistences on the way to write or not to write are deadening."[91] Stylistically, too, they were well matched, for Moss's ability to "convey complex states of feeling"[92] in his poetry was equaled by Flanagan's plastic and subtle command of rhythmic, melodic, and harmonic nuance.

William Flanagan, in a 1968 article, had credited Leonard Bernstein with "more influence on popular music than any other composer of his time. What he did" added Flanagan, "was to take the vocabulary of Copland and Stravinsky and sneak it onto Broadway [which] filtering through of these sources has created a whole new musical vocabulary."[93] In the Moss cycle, Flanagan takes this new vocabulary and brings it back into the art song, with its Broadway experience still clinging to it—a direction that Paul Bowles had begun to explore some fifteen years earlier (see chapter 6). The influences are clearly seen in the theatrical waltz background and sudden dynamic spurts, plus the added sixth and seventh chords of "Plants Cannot Travel"[94] (written in 1959).

Example 8.33, mm. 1–6

The text of this song is a single ten-line verse of a longer, seven-sectioned poem called "Cliché's for Piano and Orchestra," and the pervasive accompaniment figure (see Ex. 8.33) could be easily related to the pianist's contribution in a theater orchestra. This verse, which echoes e.e. cummings's preoccupation with love as the universe's enabling mystery, suggests that love's "miracle" can invest the natural world with at least the appearance of consciousness. The rest of the "Cliché's," however, turn toward doubt and depression, thus making Flanagan's abruptly joyful vocal leaps followed by a swift descent of pitch and dynamics appropriate to the overall poetic context.

Example 8.34, mm. 14–23

The other four Moss settings were all composed in 1961 and 1962 and published two to three years thereafter. For the text of "If You Can,"[95] Flanagan used a complete poem, without change or deletion, taken from *A Winter Come, A Summer Gone*, which was Moss's third volume of poetry, published in 1960. The form of this poem is interesting, having a complicated rhyme scheme that interrelates the four four-line stanzas, plus a refrain that adds one line after each stanza to achieve its final form:

> For I have loved
> But not loved well
> If I have loved
> At all.

The theme of the poem is closely tied to that of "Plants Cannot Travel" and the two songs were originally published together. This time the poet sees the physical world as a mystery that can be given meaning and reality only through love—an emotion that he is not certain he has ever truly experienced. Here, in one of his strongest settings, Flanagan demonstrates his dramatic flair and lyrical gifts, as musical-theater derived modulations and chordal constructions are subsumed in a fabric of inspired prosodic choices and motivic manipulation.

Having begun in F-sharp major, a favorite Flanagan key, the thematic construction eventually lowers into a quasi-operatic contour in C major.

Example 8.35, mm. 35–36

It then combines the germinal motivic intervals of a minor second and major sixth into a final vocal phrase ("I have loved at all") which blossoms as a piano postlude.

Example 8.36, mm. 44–52

As a final elegant detail, the last two measures (see Ex. 8.36) are a transposed repetition of the voice line's opening melody on "Country-man, tell me if you can." The resulting sense of formal and conceptual unity has been masterfully achieved.

The March 1962 concert which premièred the *Moss* songs had included two settings of his poem "See How They Love Me," one by Flanagan,[96] and another by Ned Rorem. As indicated in a letter from Howard Moss to R. Friedberg, "See How They Love Me" was originally a poem on its own [and] was then incorporated as section 7 of a much longer poem, 'King Midas.'"[97] Setting aside its later inclusion into the myth of the "golden king," the poem standing alone is a succinct, moving lyric which juxtaposes human rejection to the poet's loving acceptance by natural elements ("green leaf, gold grass, blue sea," etc.).

The 1962 reviewer had found it "interesting to compare the strophic-like setting by Rorem with the freer improvisatory one by Flanagan."[98] Evidently he missed the equally strophic flavor lent by Flanagan's basic motif which, with only slight pitch or rhythmic changes, begins each of the song's four verses (mm. 1 and 2).

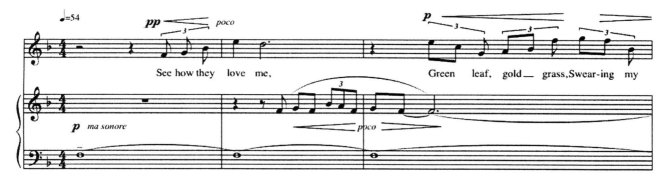

Example 8.37, mm. 1–3

It is true, however, that the piano accompaniment markedly changes in figuration as the verses gain in intensity, and that the third verse culminates in a dramatic a cappella line beginning with a high subito piano on F-sharp, Flanagan's frequently encountered "note of ecstasy."

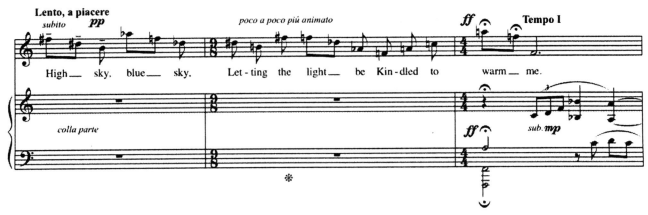

Example 8.38, mm. 16–18

The fourth and final verse introduces a nervous sixteenth note triplet into the piano part which seems to contrast the niggardly human emotion of "rebuke" with the more expansive eighth note triplet of nature's warmth (see Ex. 8.37).

Example 8.39, mm. 22–24

"Horror Movie"[99] is a setting of a poem from *A Swimmer in the Air*, Moss's third collection, published in 1957. In this setting, both artists prove themselves thoroughly at home in contemporary farce: the poem's rhymed couplets frequently recall Ogden Nash ("You took the gold to Transylvania / Where no one guessed how insane you were") and the piano figurations are a send-up of melodramatic movie music from the silent films on out.

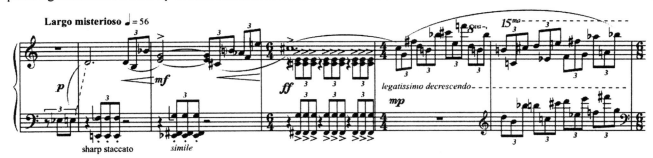

Example 8.40, mm. 1–5

Most of the vocal writing is declamatory in the interests of the text's narrative emphasis, while the form is through-composed and sectional with motivic interweaving suspended as inappropriate. An especially notable moment is the pianistic tango figure that emerges rather suddenly to set the stage for the appearance of two exotic figures: the Spider Woman and Dracula.

Example 8.41, mm. 22–24

"The Upside Down Man"[100] was completed in January 1962, just two months before its concert première. Although written earlier, the poem was first published in a Moss collection when it appeared in *Finding Them Lost* (1965). The interesting thesis of this poem is that man, formed as he is, suffers from having his feet "chained to earth," and the poet here imagines the soliloquy of a more fortunately formed being who experiences the world in positional reverse. The needs of the text give rise to a very angular, leaping vocal line, as well as a mostly linear accompaniment in which the hands frequently imitate each other at the interval of an octave or a tenth.

Example 8.42, mm. 5–7

Most of the song is in C major with much overlay of chromatic dissonance, but a single passage of diatonic lyricism pulls to one of Flanagan's favorite heavily laden sharp keys, in this case B major (See Ex. 8.43).

Example 8.43, mm. 24–26

In 1970, a memorial concert of Flanagan's music took place at the Whitney Museum. Ned Rorem accompanied some of his songs, Albee's *Sandbox* with music by Flanagan was presented, and the late composer's talents were praised by no lesser figures than Aaron Copland and Virgil Thomson. Shortly before, Thomson had written in *American Music Since 1910* that although "the English art song is not yet a major form" and "has never achieved psychology or drama as we know these qualities through the German or French," the songs of William Flanagan nevertheless "have a soaring intensity all unusual to the English language."[101] Bill Flanagan's songs, it seemed, had conquered even the redoubtable Virgil Thomson. It is past time for their rediscovery by the rest of us.

Notes

1. Most of the biographical information on Beeson's early life is drawn from David Ewen, *American Composers* (New York: Putnam, 1982), 48–50.
2. Interview with R. Friedberg, 1 December 1982.
3. Interview with R. Friedberg.
4. Jack Beeson, "In Memoriam: Douglas Moore," *Perspectives of New Music* 8 (Fall/Winter 1960): 158–60.
5. Jack Beeson, "Virgil Thomson's *Aneid* (The Operas)," *Parnassus* 5, no. 2 (Spring/Summer 1977): 457–78.
6. Interview with R. Friedberg.
7. Beeson, "Virgil Thomson's *Aeneid*," 471.
8. Interview with R. Friedberg.
9. Jack Beeson, "Eldorado" in John Belisle, ed., *American Artsong Anthology,* Vol. 1: *Contemporary American Songs for High Voice and Piano* (New York: Galaxy, 1982).
10. Robert E. Spiller, Willard Thorpe, Thomas J. Johnson, Henry Seidel Canby, and Richard M. Ludwig, eds., *Literary History of the United States* (New York: Macmillan, 1963), 338.
11. Floyd Stovall, ed., *The Poems of Edgar Allan Poe* (Charlottesville: University Press of Virginia, 1965), xxvi.
12. From "Emelia (an Essay on the Material and Spiritual Universe)," quoted in Spiller, et al., *Literary History,* 337.
13. Another interesting comparison in connection with "Eldorado" is John Duke's setting, "The Mad Knight's Song," of a poem by John Heath-Stubs (*Three Gothic Ballads*, Southern Music, 1959). Both describe an endless journey, but whereas "El Dorado's" knight seeks for gold, "the Mad Knight's" quest is to escape the searing pain of unrequited love.
14. Jack Beeson, "Indiana Homecoming" in *Nine Songs and Arias* for Baritone and Piano (New York: Boosey & Hawkes, distr. Hal Leonard).
15. The letter and poem are in: Nathaniel Wright Stephenson, comp., *An Autobiography of Abraham Lincoln* (Indianapolis: Bobbs-Merrill, 1926), 57–59.
16. Only three were actually written.
17. Interview with R. Friedberg.
18. Marie Hénault, *Peter Viereck* (New York: Twayne, 1969), 18.
19. Hénault, *Peter Viereck*, 18.
20. Hénault, *Peter Viereck*, 34.
21. Hénault, *Peter Viereck*, 36.
22. Jack Beeson, "Big Crash Out West" in *Nine Songs and Arias* for Baritone and Piano.
23. Hénault, *Peter Viereck*, 38.
24. Jack Beeson, "To a Sinister Potato" in *Nine Songs and Arias* for Baritone and Piano.
25. Interview with R. Friedberg.
26. Jack Beeson, "The You Should of Done It Blues" in *Nine Songs and Arias* for Soprano and Piano (New York: Boosey and Hawkes).
27. Richard Owen, "Husband, Father, Attorney, Composer," *Music Journal* 25 (April 1967): 37ff.
28. Lynn Owen, "Wife, Mother, Opera Singer," *Music Journal* 25 (April 1967): 36ff.
29. Cf. "I Hear an Army," a strikingly similar James Joyce poem set by Samuel Barber. This setting is found in the Schirmer collection of Barber's songs (see chapter 6, n77).
30. Quoted in John Berryman, *Stephen Crane* (New York: Octagon Books, 1975), 266.
31. Daniel Hoffman, *The Poetry of Stephen Crane* (New York: Columbia University Press, 1956), 4.
32. Berryman, *Stephen Crane,* 269.
33. Hoffman, *The Poetry of Stephen Crane,* 262–64.

34. Richard Owen, "There were many who went in huddled procession" (New York: General Music Publishing, 1966). Medium voice. Out of print. This song, together with "I saw a man pursuing the horizon," has been recorded by John Reardon, baritone, and Bliss Hebert, pianist, on the Serenus label (SRE-1019/SRS-12019).

35. Richard Owen, "I saw a man pursuing the horizon" (New York: General Music Publishing, 1966). Medium high voice. Out of print.

36. Richard Owen, "The Impulse" (New York: General Music Publishing, 1966). Medium voice. Out of print.

37. Malcolm Cowley, "The Case Against Mr. Frost," in *Robert Frost*, James M. Cox, ed. (Englewood Cliffs, N.J.: Prentice-Hall, 1962), 39.

38. Richard Owen, "Patterns" (New York: General Music Publishing, 1973). Medium high voice. Out of print.

39. e.e. cummings had quoted from Lowell's "Grotesque" in his Harvard commencement address on the "New Art." The effect on the audience was mostly shock and embarrassment on behalf of Harvard's president, Abbott Laurence Lowell, who was Amy's brother.

40. Jean Gould, *Amy* (New York: Dodd, Mead, 1975), 181.

41. See the Introduction for a discussion of the "little magazines" and their contribution to the "poetic renaissance."

42. Letter to R. Friedberg, 26 August 1983.

43. "Jean Eichelberger Ivey—a Retrospective," *Peabody News*, July 1983.

44. This review is reprinted in the chapter on Jean Eichelberger Ivey that appears in Jane Weiner LePage, *Woman Composers, Conductors and Musicians of the Twentieth Century* (Metuchen, N.J.: Scarecrow Press, 1980).

45. The principal publishers of Jean Eichelberger Ivey's works are Carl Fischer, Inc., Boosey & Hawkes, and E. C. Schirmer.

46. Jean Eichelberger Ivey, "The Contemporary Performing Ensemble," *College Music Symposium* 8 (Fall 1968): 120–28.

47. Jean Eichelberger Ivey, "Electronic Music Workshop for Teachers," *Music Educators Journal* 55 (November 1968): 91–93.

48. Jean Eichelberger Ivey, "The Composer as Teacher," *Peabody Conservatory Alumni Bulletin* 14, no. 1 (Fall/Winter 1974).

49. Letter to R. Friedberg.

50. The American Music Center's address is 322 8th Avenue, Suite 1401, New York, NY 10001, or the url: www. http://www.amc.net.

51. "Jean Eichelberger Ivey," *Peabody News*.

52. "Jean Eichelberger Ivey," *Peabody News*.

53. Letter to R. Friedberg.

54. See n9.

55. See the discussion of Teasdale's emotional turmoil in chapter 5.

56. From "On the Sussex Downs" to be found in Sara Teasdale, *Collected Poems* (New York: Macmillan, 1966).

57. From "The Solitary," also in Teasdale's *Collected Poems*.

58. Available from the American Music Center, see n50.

59. Tim Page, "Music-Debuts in Review," *The New York Times*, Sunday, April 8, 1984.

60. Edward Albee, "William Flanagan," *Bulletin of the American Composers' Alliance* 9, no. 4 (1961): 12.

61. Lester Trimble, "William Flanagan (1923–1969)," *Stereo Review* 23 (November 1969): 118.

62. Peter Reilly, "William Flanagan," *Stereo Review* 21, no. 5 (November 1968): 134.

63. William Flanagan, "How to Succeed in Composing without Really Succeeding," *Bulletin of the American Composers' Alliance* 11, no. 1 (1963): 8.

64. John Gruen, *The Party's Over* (New York: Viking, 1972), 114. This is an excellent series of memoirs of New York artistic life in the fifties by John Gruen who is himself a writer, composer, and art historian.

65. Gruen, *The Party's Over,* 110.

66. Gruen, *The Party's Over,* 110, 118.

67. Albee, "William Flanagan," 12.

68. Ned Rorem, *Critical Affairs* (New York: George Braziller, 1970), 119.

69. Rorem, *Critical Affairs*, 73.

70. Trimble, "William Flanagan," 118.

71. A complete listing of Flanagan's works up to that date can be found in the following article, Ned Rorem, "(William Flanagan) and his music," *Bulletin of the American Composers' Alliance* 9, no. 4 (1961): 13–19.

72. Trimble, "William Flanagan," 118.

73. Rorem, "(William Flanagan) and his music," 14.

74. Rorem, "(William Flanagan) and his music," 15.

75. William Flanagan, "My Ten Favorite Composers," *Hi-Fi/Stereo Review* 19 (September 1967): 68–69.

76. (a) William Flanagan/Gertrude Stein, "Valentine to Sherwood Anderson" (New York: Peer International Corp., 1948). Mezzo-soprano; (b) William Flanagan/Gertrude Stein, "A Very Little Snail" (New York: American Composers' Alliance, 1949). Soprano. Out of print.

77. William Flanagan/e.e. cummings, "Buffalo Bill" (New York: American Composers' Alliance, 1947). Out of print.

78. William Flanagan/Herman Melville, *Times Long Ago* (New York: Peer International Corp., 1951). Cycle of six songs for soprano. Out of print.

79. William Flanagan/Walt Whitman, "Goodbye, My Fancy" (New York: Peer International Corp., 1959). Soprano, flute, and guitar.

80. William Flanagan, "Song for a Winter Child" (New York: Peer International Corp., 1964). Medium voice.

81. Information in preceding paragraph from John Wakeman, *World Authors*, 1950–1970 (New York: H. W. Wilson, 1975), 22.

82. Wakeman, *World Authors*.

83. Richard E., *Edward Albee* (New York: Twayne, 1969), 37.

84. Amacher, *Edward Albee,* 18.

85. Letter to R. Friedberg, 30 November 1983.

86. Back cover notes to: William Flanagan, "See How They Love Me" (New York: C.F. Peters, 1965). High voice.

87. John Ardoin, "Rorem-Flanagan Concert," *Musical America* 82 (May 1962): 37.

88. Wakeman, *World Authors*, 1038.

89. Wakeman, *World Authors*, 1037.

90. Wakeman, *World Authors*, 1038.

91. Howard Moss, *Writing against Time, Critical Essays and Reviews* (New York: Morrow, 1969), 194.

92. Wakeman, *World Authors*, 1038.

93. Reilly, "William Flanagan,"134.

94. William Flanagan, "Plants Cannot Travel" in *Songs (2)* (New York: C.F. Peters, 1963). High voice. This song, together with "Horror Movie," "If You Can," and "See How They Love Me," was recorded by Carol Bogard, soprano, and David Del Tredici, pianist, on the Desto label (DC-6468).

95. William Flanagan, "If You Can" in *Songs (2)* (New York: C.F. Peters, 1963). High voice.

96. See n86.

97. Letter to R. Friedberg, 18 August 1983.

98. Ardoin, "Rorem-Flanagan Concert."

99. William Flanagan, "Horror Movie" (New York: C.F. Peters, 1965). Medium high voice.

100. William Flanagan, "Upside Down Man" (New York: Peer International Corp., 1964). Medium high voice.

Chapter 9

Ned Rorem (b. 1923)

Ned Rorem would probably be the first to agree that his life has been founded in a series of contradictions, some of which have proved forceful, if occasionally painful, spurs to artistic creativity. To begin with, although raised in geographically insular Chicago, Rorem's earliest musical allegiance was to the sophisticated nuances of French Impressionism. Secondly, this son of Quaker converts whose strongest values were intellect and discipline, spent his youth as the dissolute, often guilt-ridden (but always industrious) "golden boy" of Paris and New York artistic society. And finally, after becoming, in his maturity, one of the best-known names in American art song, Ned Rorem turned much of his energy toward writing in the instrumental forms, and building a notable reputation as a musical journalist.

In his diaries and journal articles, Rorem describes with warm affection his parents' supportive role in his developing talent. "Although not specifically musical, [they] exposed my sister Rosemary and me to concerts, mainly high-class piano recitals"[1] says the composer who, at the age of seven, began a decade of keyboard study under a series of seven teachers. Notable among these were Nuta Rothschild, who introduced him to the magic of Debussy; Margaret Bonds, who "played with the authority of a professional and showed [him] how to notate [his] ramblings"[2]; and Belle Tannenbaum whose instruction was supplemented by harmony classes in the Chicago Loop area with Leo Sowerby. Writing in 1969 at the time of Sowerby's death, Rorem recalled that, "his encouragement during my adolescence was the springboard of my career."[3] Having emerged from high school at the age of sixteen, Rorem turned toward the area of music that was increasingly absorbing him and entered Northwestern University's School of Music as a composition major. This plan had the full cooperation of his father who was America's leading medical economist, the founding father of Blue Cross, and a "not so sublimated baritone"[4] as well.

Dr. Alfred Nolte, a former protégé of Richard Strauss, now became Rorem's professor of composition, but he remembers less about those lessons than about his piano instruction with Harold Van Horne. Setting out to enlarge his keyboard repertoire beyond its heavy emphasis on Debussy and Stravinsky, Rorem learned "all thirty-two Beethoven sonatas and the entire keyboard catalogue of Bach and Chopin"[5] in his two years at Northwestern. A Curtis scholarship brought him to Philadelphia in 1943, but Rosario Scalero's counterpoint exercises proved too limiting to the young composer. Against the advice of his parents, who cut off his allowance, Rorem moved to New York the following year to become Virgil Thomson's copyist in exchange for twenty dollars a week and orchestration lessons.

The New York experiences in "the real world of music"[6] came thick and fast, punctuated by pilgrimages to Aaron Copland's tutelage at Tanglewood in the summers of 1946 and 1947. Rorem became the accompanist for Martha Graham's dance classes, studied composition with Bernard Wagenaar at the Juilliard School where he earned a master's degree in 1948, and began to establish some long-lasting friendships. In the *New York Diary*, Rorem remembers 1947 in Mary's Bar on Eighth Street, noting that "it is already eleven summers ago that John Myers and Frank Etherton worked there, whining the tunes Paul Goodman and I composed for them: Bawling Blues, Jail Bait Blues, Near Closing Time."[7] Paul Goodman, then, was already an artistic collaborator and important force in Ned Rorem's life. Looking back from the 1960s, the composer would refer to him as "my Manhattan Goethe,"[8] and indeed, it was Rorem's setting of a Goodman poem ("The Lordly Hudson") that won recognition as the best published song of 1948. In the same year, Rorem received the Gershwin Award for the Orchestral Overture that was his master's thesis at Juilliard, and by 1949 he was off to Paris, having been awarded a Fulbright scholarship to study there with Arthur Honegger.

After only a few months in France, Ned Rorem followed the path to Morocco pioneered by Paul Bowles. Although this move had nothing to do with Bowles, it is also true that the older composer had fascinated him from their first meeting in Taxco when Rorem was sixteen. He stayed in Morocco for two years, and even after his return to Paris, would be drawn back at intervals to the colorful, mysterious ambiance of Fez, Marrakech, and Tangier. France, however, remained his principal residence until 1958, and he spent most of his time in the luxurious homes maintained in Paris and Hyères (on the Mediterranean coast) by the Viscountess Marie Laure de Noailles, his patroness. During these years in France, Rorem won acceptance in the artistic circles headed by Poulenc, Auric, and Cocteau, but did not allow the active and brilliant social life of Marie Laure's "salon" to deter him from serious application to musical composition in many forms, including a large number of song settings.

In the John Gruen collection of "fifties" reminiscences, Ned Rorem made some interesting observations on his decade as an expatriate. "I was always attracted by things French," said the composer, "so I didn't become French by living in France. I was already French at home in Chicago, and later in New York. . . . I went to France for the same reason everybody else in America went to France—we went looking for what were then stylishly called 'our roots.' I found out," he added, "that my roots were not in France but America."[9] In the same memoir, Rorem commented on *The Paris Diary*, the book that began his flourishing literary sub-career as journalist and critic. He recalls that Marie Laure had encouraged him to keep a diary, and states his feeling that what this early writing reveals is "terribly fifties . . . full of self-pity and self-advertisement."[10] He is quick to note, however, that his diary also "reflects the fact that ninety percent of my time was spent at home working hard, writing music, and not out getting drunk or crying or lacerating myself for love."[11]

During the mid-fifties, Rorem made several trips to America for premières of major symphonic works. He was beginning to realize that, unlike Frederic Prokosch (see chapter 6), who had confided that he needed to live far from America's "vulgarity," Rorem himself wanted "more and more to leave the France [he knew]."[12] In 1958, he resettled in New York City, having come to believe that "an American composer must live here whether he likes it or not . . . [for] it is here that his most interesting problems will at least be presented if not solved."[13] One of the problems which did present, and which is movingly delineated in the *The New York Diary* is a form of early mid-life spiritual crisis that began to envelop the thirty-five-year-old composer. Entry after entry speaks of boredom, uncaring, joylessness, the failures of religion, and the consideration of suicide. Alcohol, perhaps as an antidote to meaninglessness, had become a friend and enemy (says Rorem, "the fifties to the sixties was my drinking decade"[14]) bringing both surcease of pain, and guilt-laden aftermath.

Work, however, remained a driving and salutary force. In the decade following his return to America, Rorem added to his catalog of works several song cycles, two operas, and many choral, orchestral, and chamber works. Other directions opened up as well, with teaching appointments at the University of Buffalo (1959–1961) and Utah (1966), and the publication of *The Paris Diary* (1966), *The New York Diary* (1967), and the essay collection *Music from Inside Out* (1967). Yet another venture, this time in behalf of the song literature which was always close to the composer's heart, was recorded proudly in 1959: "Last February, Bill Flanagan and I . . . inaugurated to Standing Room Only the first in what we hope will be a series called Music for the Voice by Americans"[15] (see chapter 8).

The Later Diaries chronicles the years from 1961 to 1972 and is crowded with the names and events of the artistic life of the period. In New York we follow Rorem's interactions with such literary figures as John Ashbery, Frank O'Hara, Paul Goodman, Edward Albee, and James Purdy, as well as an endless stream of conductors, singers, instrumentalists, and fellow composers. On visits to France we see him with Nadia Boulanger and the Milhauds, and in Morocco with Paul and Jane Bowles. One name that recurs constantly is that of Bill Flanagan, whom he reports in a 1964 entry seeing daily, and whose many hospitalizations and final solitary death in a losing battle against drugs and alcohol is a historically valuable while personally tragic aspect of this journal. The overall tone of this diary, despite the mourned losses to mortality of important friends such as Flanagan, Goodman, and Marie Laure, is far more positive than the earlier two. By the end of the volume, Rorem has stopped drinking, and reports his mental condition on a number of occasions to be that of "happiness, [a state in which] nobody is much interested."[16]

During the late sixties and early seventies, Rorem published three more volumes of essays, which were mostly drawn from lectures delivered in university settings, or articles previously printed in various periodicals. *Music from Inside Out* had devoted a fourth of its content to the composer's valuable insights on vocal music in the section titled "Variation Two: Music for the Mouth." The newer collections revealed his continuing literary preoccupation with the philosophy of and contributors to art song in articles such as "Poetry of Music" and "Bill Flanagan" in *Critical Affairs* (1970); and "Paul Bowles" and "Remembering a Poet" in *Pure Contraption* (1973).

Rorem's next published books were *An Absolute Gift* (1978) and *Setting the Tone* (1983), which combine some personal memoirs with criticism, reviews, and the author's unique observations on the contemporary artistic scene. Both of these volumes are dedicated to James Holmes, a fellow musician whose friendship had become one of the stabilizing factors in a life which the composer described in 1974 as no longer incorporating "a strong need for novelty [or] for possibilities around the corner."[17] R. Friedberg's interview with Ned Rorem, previously quoted in chapter 1, took place at just about this time (April, 1975) in the composer's pleasant apartment in Manhattan's West Seventies. The interview had been graciously granted, with little advance notice. Rorem not only patiently answered questions, but also contributed generously to the interviewer's grasp of her subject, by putting her in touch with Alice Esty, who commissioned so many American art songs of the sixties,[18] and with a whole group of song composers who will be represented later in this series.

By the end of the twentieth century, Rorem had published five more books. They were *The Nantucket Diaries* (1989) and *Knowing When to Stop* (1994) in his memoir series; two volumes of essays called *Settling the Score* (1988) and *Other Entertainment* (1996); plus his correspondence with Paul Bowles titled *Dear Paul, Dear Ned* (1997). The year 1994 saw a revival at the Manhattan School of *Miss Julie*—besides *Our Town* (2005), Rorem's only full-length opera— and in 1998 the New York Festival of Song gave the première of his *Evidence of Things Not Seen*, a set of thirty-six poems by twenty-four authors. The twenty-first century found the composer still at work on his literary legacy. Two more additions to his memoir series were published: *Lies: A Diary* (1986–1999) and *Facing the Night* (1999–2005) as well as *Wings of Friendship*, a selection drawn from his nearly six decades of correspondence from the years 1944 to 2003.

Back in 1982, an interesting and useful summary of the composer's lifelong thinking about the art song had appeared as a conversation with Ned Rorem reported in the November/December issue of the *NATS Bulletin*. Herein Rorem reiterated that for song texts he chooses "whatever, as the Quakers say, speaks to my condition," and that in his settings he adheres "to two moral principles: follow a natural prosodic flow [and] never repeat words not repeated by the poet."[19] Asked about French influences on his songs, he replied "I'd like to suppose that after years and years . . . of emerging into myself I finally speak my very own dialect,"[20] and he underlined his continuing advocacy of American songs sung by American singers. "We Americans," said Rorem, "now lead the world in weaponry, but still follow sheepishly in artistic standards. Yet the future will judge us not by our destruction but by our creation."[21]

Toward the end of this conversation, Rorem states that his earliest songs "were made not from love of the human voice but from the love of poetry, and from a need to meld two passions—music and literature—into one entity."[22] Discounting those composed at the age of eleven while studying with Margaret Bonds, he feels that "the first songs of any quality at all were written . . . when [he] was a student at Northwestern . . . mostly on poetry of e.e. cummings."[23] His literary "passion" then, had, by 1939, already become attached to American poetry as an important focus. In the years to come, the focus would grow even stronger as Rorem's single songs and cycles came to include settings of a long list of American poets. Paul Goodman, Theodore Roethke, Howard Moss, Walt Whitman, Kenneth Koch, John Ashbery, Elizabeth Bishop, Wallace Stevens, Sylvia Plath, and Witter Bynner were all grist to his mill, as Rorem continued to prove his own claim, that "in general a composer prefers to set poetry of his national contemporaries."[24]

Paul Goodman (1911–1972)

Paul Goodman, one of Rorem's major poetic sources, was a complex and dramatic figure whose poetry formed a little-known but critical part of a wide-ranging literary output. He was born in New York City's Greenwich Village, the fourth child in a remarkably atypical middle-class German Jewish family. Goodman's father, having failed in business, abandoned the family before Paul was born; his mother, a "bourgeois gypsy,"[25] was a traveling saleswoman, seldom at home; and he was mostly cared for, even through his college years, by his sister Alice, who was ten years his senior.

Though unconventional, the atmosphere of his childhood was clearly a nurturing one. Goodman later described himself as "an orphan who had had a home" and as a "fatherless [child] free on the streets of the Empire City and the wild rocks along the Hudson River."[26] The rich resources of New York's free educational opportunities fed his developing mind, and he proved an exceptional student of literature and languages at Townsend Harris Hall High School, and of philosophy at the City College of New York (A.B., 1931). During his college years, he not infrequently hitchhiked to Cambridge to sit in on courses at Harvard, and observed the same process of "informal audit" at Columbia University during the five years after graduation when he was an unemployed writer living with his sister.

From 1936 to 1940 he was a graduate student, research assistant, and part-time instructor in literature and philosophy at the University of Chicago, but did not complete his doctoral dissertation (published as *The Structure of Literature*) until 1954. In 1940 he returned to New York City and for the next two decades attracted a small but dedicated group of young intellectuals who followed his career as editor and contributor to *Partisan Review, Kenyon Review, Commentary* and other journals; as teacher at Manumit, a progressive boarding school, and at Black Mountain College; and as author of novels, plays, short stories, and many essays. These essays, considered by some critics to be among his finest work, included forays into social criticism, such as *Communitas*, a description of the ideal city written with his architect brother, Percival, and a volume on psychoanalytic process called *Gestalt Therapy*, drawn from his own experiences in analysis and later as a practicing therapist. Even music did not escape this Renaissance mind for Goodman not only wrote critically and philosophically on musical subjects, but also, from time to time, tried his hand at composing.

An earlier common-law marriage of five years to Virginia Miller had produced a daughter, Susan, in 1939. From 1945 to the end of his life, Goodman was married to Sally Duchsten who often functioned as his secretary and informal bibliographer. They had two children (a son Matthew Ready born in 1946, and a daughter, Daisy, born seventeen years later) and family life followed the "bohemian" model of artistic struggle and material poverty. In 1961, however, the successful publication of *Growing up Absurd* (subtitled "Problems of Youth in the Organized Society") brought not only many requests for lecturing and teaching engagements and a substantially increased income, but the adulation, as well, of a whole generation who saw Goodman as their hero and spokesman.

During the last decade of Goodman's life, a number of volumes of poetry were added to the novels, short stories, and social criticism that he continued to publish. In 1962 his first volume of verse, titled *The Lordly Hudson*, appeared, and was soon followed by *Hawkweed* (1967), *North Percy* (1968), and *Homespun of Oatmeal Gray* (1970). The seemingly new literary mantle was no surprise to his friends, in whose company there would always "come a moment when he handed around five or six sheets of new poems"[27]; in fact, he had been a frequent contributor to *Poetry* magazine during the forties and fifties, and had published poems in small editions throughout his life. His final decade also encompassed tragedy, for Goodman's son Matthew was killed in a 1967 mountaineering accident, and the writer's lifelong charismatic vitality gave way to depression and ill health. He died of a cardiac ailment at his New Hampshire farm in August 1972, having spent the summer working on a new collection of poetry, *Little Prayers and Finite Experience*, as well as the editing of his *Collected Poems*, both of which were published posthumously.

Goodman historians are for the most part in agreement as to the major influences on his thinking. Alicia Ostriker lists "Aristotle, who taught him to observe human institutions and Kant, who taught him the moral imperative"[28] as well as Freud, Reich, John Dewey, William James, Maimonides, Buber, and Marx (Goodman was not a Communist, but an anarchist). There is less critical consensus, however, on the position of the poetry in his work, or, indeed, in American letters. Kingsley Widmer finds him to have "had little sense of poetry and an absurdly wooden sense of language"[29] while Robert Merideth calls Goodman "a major American poet, though almost completely ignored," partly because "his technical skill and knowledge are so considerable as to be nearly invisible."[30] Ostriker, another advocate, opines that "there has not been a thoughtful and passionate personal voice like this in our poetry since Robinson Jeffers" and sees him being criticized as too pragmatic to be a good poet because he writes "without decorum and the manners which protect the private self."[31]

Emile Capouya adds that the power of Goodman's rhetoric which is "direct and hopelessly unsophisticated" draws upon strong, fundamental emotions like patriotism, and he offers as proof a quotation in entirety of "The Lordly Hudson," calling it the greatest poem about New York since Walt Whitman.[32] This poem had been published with the Goodman selections in the second series of *Five Young American Poets* in 1941. Three years before, Ned Rorem, who was then fourteen years old, had met Paul Goodman, a graduate student at the University of Chicago, and the two had formed part of a group that attended Thursday evening poetry sessions at Monroe Library.[33] In the essay "Remembering a Poet,"[34] written in the month of Goodman's death, Rorem recalls that, in the years after their meeting, the writer became his "most pertinent influence, social and poetic," and that he (Rorem) "never in the following decades wearied of putting his words to music."

In the 1975 interview, Ned Rorem told R. Friedberg that when he wrote "The Lordly Hudson"[35] he knew no other American songs, and only later became familiar with settings by Chanler, Diamond, and Bacon. It is interesting, however, to learn that the French song literature played a crucial part in the inspirational genesis of this seemingly prototypical piece of Americana. In *The Paris Diary*, Rorem describes a New York Christmas party of 1946 during which he was much taken by his first hearing of Poulenc's "C," particularly the vocal interval which sets "de la prairie."

The next day, moved to compose a song himself, he fastened on "The Lordly Hudson" (then called "Poem") which he had already tried unsuccessfully to set.

In one sitting, I wrote the song . . . deciding on 6/8 because that means "water," I suppose. I first wrote the vocal phrase "home, home" and "no, no"—skipping a seventh and rising in the sequence, because Poulenc had skipped a fifth and dropped. Then I decided on the accompaniment pattern, and for the rest of the words I simply used taste and a melodic stream of consciousness.[36]

Rorem then gave the song, without changes, to Janet Fairbank, a young soprano who during the forties presented concerts of new American songs, and it was she who premièred the setting of "Paul's soaring words that still so grandly extol his beloved Manhattan."[37] It was sung first under the title of "Poem," later "Driver, What Stream Is It?" (the opening line); and finally, when Richard Dana offered to print it, was given its present title by the author. The song was dedicated to Janet Fairbank who died in 1947 on the day it was published, and who was mourned by the whole community of poets and musicians whose work she had fostered.

Although an early song, "The Lordly Hudson" already demonstrated the composer's highly developed instinct for poetic setting. Using melodic variations on the original seminal interval, Rorem allows the welcoming rush of feeling to expand vocally in arpeggiated ninths, and pianistically in a similar, chordally amplified line.

Example 9.1a, mm. 40–42

As is true in many Rorem settings, the more intricate and developed melodic structure is carried by the piano. In this case, the slower rhythms and frequent pauses in the vocal line seem to suggest the protagonist's attempt at control ("Be quiet, heart!") while the accompaniment releases the overwhelming flood of emotion (see Ex. 9.1b).

Harmonic usage, too, feeds textual needs. The basic tonality of F minor appears in its modal form (Aeolian) for the cloudy, dreamlike opening and contrasts with the raised pitch and greater brilliance of A minor for each impassioned setting of "Home! Home!" In the last three measures, Rorem sets an F pedal point in two voices against a wandering, downward scale in the Phrygian mode that finally and joyfully comes "home" to the brightness and resolution of an F major chord.

Example 9.1b, mm. 50–56

Paul Goodman's poetry was in a continual state of revision throughout his life and "The Lordly Hudson" as it appears in the *Collected Poems* shows changes that, in the authors' opinion, are weaker than the original version (fortunately that of Rorem's setting). The same is true of "Absalom," another poem published in the *Five Young American Poets* of 1941, and a prime example of the prodigious albeit invisible technical skill that Robert Meredith claims for Goodman. "Absalom" presents three verses of five lines each in which the second and third lines rhyme, as do the first, fourth, and fifth. The use of language is strong and original, and paints a dramatic picture of the dead, bloodstained prince hanging from his hair amid frightened birds in the agitated oak tree.

As is often the case, Rorem's 1946 setting of "Absalom"[38] swallows the original metric structure, and replaces it with a plastic, freely flowing alternation of 3/4 and 4/4. Once again, as is his custom based on conviction, Rorem sets the text precisely as given (the word repetition in the final line is Goodman's) but creates dramatic space by devices like the two-measure vocal hold on the climactic word "blood." Perhaps the most interesting aspect of this remarkable song is that it is entirely built around the motif of two conjunct descending scalar steps, first announced in the introduction:

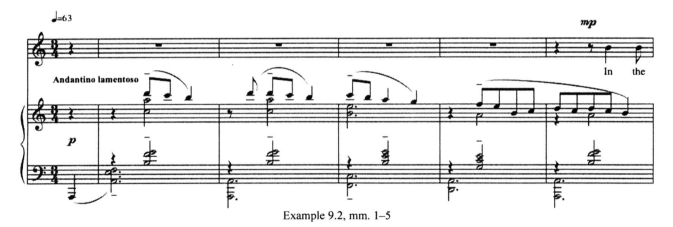

Example 9.2, mm. 1–5

This motif continues to appear in the piano, often in sequence, throughout the song, but is never taken into the voice part until it becomes the father's despairing cry:

Example 9.3, mm. 39–45

In 1949, newly arrived in Paris, Rorem set a short, charming lyric of Goodman's called "Rain in Spring,"[39] which he appropriately completed and dated on the seventh of June. This poem recalls a season when a "clear and refreshing rain, falling without haste or strain" marked the very moment when spring began. Taking his cue from the text, Rorem creates a "very languid" (his indication) setting whose double-dotted accompaniment figures seem to hold back any urge toward "haste," while the simple diatonic voice line and thinly textured piano chords suggest the clarity of the water:

Example 9.4, mm. 5–7

Influences of the French cabaret and jazz scene filtered through Poulenc seem to hover in this song around the pianistic figurations as well as the heavy sprinkling of seventh, ninth, and thirteenth chords. One is reminded of the mood, if not the meter, of "Hôtel" from *Banalités*.

An entry dated October 28, 1972, in *The Later Diaries* recalls that twenty autumns earlier, Rorem had returned from France for the first time to spend three months in New York's Chelsea Hotel. "My 1952 agenda shows," he writes, ." . . that Paul Goodman handed over thirteen new poems (which I made into songs the next summer)." The next seven Goodman settings that Rorem published (all completed during the fifties) are drawn from this group, and the first five to be treated here bear the legend "Hyères, September 1953."

The poem that Rorem sets in "The Midnight Sun"[40] had originally appeared in *Poetry* magazine[41] under the title of "Stanzas." It is a strange, haunting poem wherein a dream of floating people, droning bagpipes, and a midnight sun takes on a mystical air uncommon to Goodman through the line "I hastened to behold him there." Rorem's setting enhances this mystical quality with its chant-like melody full of repeated notes and melismas set off against the bareness of single or superimposed empty fifths in the accompaniment:

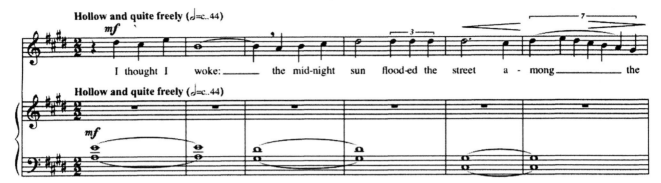

Example 9.5, mm. 1–6

Harmonic treatment intensifies the strangeness of the atmosphere in the final phrase ("and where the shadows fell they lay") by means of soft, polytonal chords that create a powerful, though whispered dissonance with the vocal line in the last two measures:

Example 9.6, mm. 28–31

"The Midnight Sun" forms an interesting pair with "The Tulip Tree."[42] In the text of the latter, an apparently straightforward story is told of a boy in a tree tossing blossoms to the girls below and then engaging in a game of catch-ball with the poet as a thunderstorm gathers. Literalness fades, however, as the composer, again using a single, constantly recurring, accompaniment motif as announced in the introduction

Example 9.7, mm. 1–2

changes and amplifies it, sometimes to exuberant heights, to match the mood of the text.

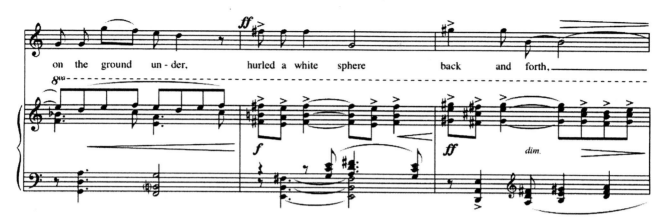

Example 9.8, mm. 29–31

This device serves to unify the song, and also seems to hold the suggestion of an ongoing event in which the boy and the poet become symbolic figures, woven into the fabric of eternity.

"Sally's Smile" appeared in Goodman's first published collection of poetry (*The Lordly Hudson*, 1963). Included in the section called "Love Poems," it is the poet's tribute to the compelling smile and presence of his wife. Allusions to "caution and resentment, both my wardens," and their connection with the Miami grave of the mother he rarely saw, hint that a strong maternal influence has been overcome by the nuptial alliance. In any case, Rorem opts for a light-handed treatment[43] suggested by the endearment "Sally-o" and by the fact that the two-stanza poem is one unbroken sentence. He makes it a fast-moving patter song with a mostly diatonic scalar melody in the voice part and in the elaborated sixteenth note piano figurations. There is only one major break in the two page vocal line, and the whole effect is of breathless, unabashed joy.

The last two of the "Hyères, 1953" Goodman settings are "For Susan" and "Clouds," both published in 1968 together with "What Sparks and Wiry Cries" under the heading of *Three Poems of Paul Goodman*.[44] "For Susan" compares Goodman's older daughter as a child to a "wildflower untended among garden flowers no fairer" and praises the "wild strain of blood and wit" that is somehow nourished by nature, even in our "disastrous homes." Rorem looses his lyrical vein on this fatherly fancy, in a vocal line whose frequent chordal leaps seem a musical representation of the young lady's labile nature as poetically portrayed:

Example 9.9, mm. 13–15

"Clouds" is a technically interesting eight-line poem in which lines three and four rhyme, as do five and six, while the other four do not. It is a skillful portrayal of the movement of clouds as they gather, pile into great heights, and disperse, without effort or desire. The composer captures the emotionless, "now-centered" atmosphere of the poem in one of his most impressionistic settings. With perhaps a subconscious nod to Debussy, his earliest musical mentor, and *his* "Clouds" (i.e., the orchestral "Nuages"), Rorem writes a "highly pedaled" piano part full of non-resolving chords built in fourths and fifths. To the singer, whom he instructs to begin "in a 'half-voice,'" he gives two musical stanzas whose me-lodic contours emphasize and end on the suspended second degree of the E major scale. Thus all musical elements serve the textual aspects of haziness, lack of effort, and an endless cycle of becoming.

The notation that concludes "What Sparks and Wiry Cries" is "France, 1952–1956," and from this we learn that Ro-rem took somewhat longer to complete what emerged as possibly the strongest setting of the *Three Poems* group. Goodman had titled this poem "1943" when it appeared in *The Lordly Hudson* collection, and one assumes that it was inspired by a failed love affair of that year. The rather unique idea therein expressed is that the sorrow of parting is tem-pered by the "furious joy" of a "heart [now] undivided by hope or fear." This is presented in harshly powerful verbal images of a "skirl of glee" being played with a "pick of flint" on "twangled . . . iron strings." In Rorem's setting, the twangling of these strings is clearly heard in the accompaniment, and the folk-like contours and modal context of the vocal melody deepen the atmosphere of an ancient, keening troubadour.

Example 9.10, mm. 1–5

In the middle, recitative-like section of this ABA form, the remembered pain of separation becomes a growing la-ment. It rises to a despairing cry on a sudden, triple forte high B-flat, by which the composer may be letting us know that the poet's "furious joy" is self-delusion.

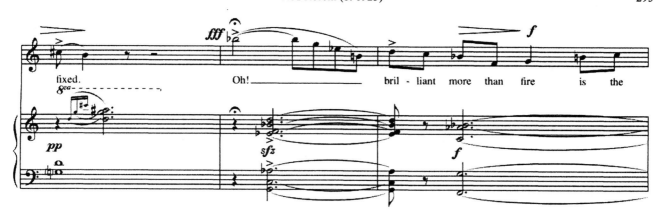

Example 9.11, mm. 15–20

The last of the Goodman settings, "Such beauty as hurts to behold "[45] was completed at Hyères, in July 1957, when Rorem was soon to leave France for his return to New York. The poem, which also appeared in the "Love Poems" section of the 1963 collection, describes a passion so deep as to be beyond desire, giving rise to a muttered prayer of thanks for the existence of the beloved. The tone here is far more serious than "Sally's Smile" and Rorem accordingly sets it with an arioso-like vocal line ("very slow, very free") over a mostly chordal background. Metric insertions of 5/4 and 3/4 into the basic 4/4 combine with melodic contours that sensitively follow the inflexional rise and fall of the language. The result is to throw the emphasis on the poetic text in a kind of musically heightened speech that relates to what Debussy achieved for the French language in *Pelléas* and the late songs.

Theodore Roethke (1908–1963)[46]

Roethke, like Ned Rorem, spent his formative years in the Midwest. He was born in Saginaw, Michigan, where his grandparents had settled in 1872 as immigrants from East Prussia. Theodore was a small and sickly child who would in maturity attain a height of six feet and the physical stamina to become a skilled tennis player and coach. Artistic leanings surfaced early, and Roethke recalled "an intense period of pleasure in nursery rhymes in English and German and songs my mother and nurse sang me."[47] He became an avid reader when quite young and began subscribing to *The Dial* in the seventh grade.

Roethke's father, who inherited the family greenhouse and gardening business, died when the boy was fifteen, but remained a strong influence throughout the poet's life. Although drawn to Harvard, Roethke enrolled at the University of Michigan to placate his mother's fears of "the mysterious East"[48] and received his B.A. in 1929. He had begun to write short stories and poetry while still at Ann Arbor. During an abortive post-graduate year at Harvard Law School, he was encouraged by Robert Hillyer to begin marketing his poetry, and thereafter turned gratefully to a career as teacher and writer.

By the time Roethke received his M.A. from the University of Michigan in 1936, he had taught English for four years at Lafayette College, for less than a semester at Michigan State University, and had been hospitalized with the first of the periodic mental breakdowns that were to afflict him all his life. At the 1967 inauguration of the Theodore Roethke Memorial Foundation in Saginaw, Stanley Kunitz recalled "the outbreaks and absences and silences that he had to cover up, partly because he realized what a threat they offered to his survival in the academic world."[49]

Despite this ever-present threat, Roethke proceeded to forge a name for himself in academic circles. He held faculty positions at Pennsylvania State University (1936–1943) and Bennington College (1943–1946), and by the time he came to the University of Washington (1947), where he would remain for the rest of his life, he had become "the greatest teacher of poetry in the country."[50] His friends also remember that Roethke had "a girl" every place he taught, but no serious alliances occurred until 1953, when on a trip to New York, he ran into Beatrice O'Connell, a former Bennington student. They were married a month later.

With the publication in 1941 of *Open House*, his first poetry collection, Roethke's position as a major American poet began to be recognized. He was awarded a Guggenheim fellowship in 1945, and a second one followed after the publication of *The Lost Son* in 1948. *The Waking* brought him the Pulitzer Prize in 1954, and the remaining decade of his life was crowded with European travel and lecturing made possible by Fulbright and Ford Foundation grants. Continuing to write and publish (including several books for children) during these years, Roethke had barely returned to the United States as Poet-in-Residence at the University of Washington when his life abruptly ended. On the fourth of August, 1963, Ned Rorem wrote "Theodore Roethke has dropped dead in a Seattle swimming pool. Is no one immune? Who will write my songs now? and those others he'll never hear?"[51]

Paul Goodman had been characterized by Ostriker as a poet with "a bias toward the literal [who] sees the world as ethics, not metaphysics."[52] When Rorem began to set Theodore Roethke in the late fifties, it was almost like a turning to the opposite principle, for all of Roethke's life and work seem in retrospect to take on the aspect of a metaphysical journey. William Heyen described him as "an artist who experienced moments of deep religious feeling and almost inexpressible illumination" whose "choice was not traditional Christianity or Atheism, but a reliance upon the mystic perceptions of his own imagination."[53] Neil Bowers[54] sets forth the further premise that it was Roethke's manic-depressive illness that produced a propensity for mystical insight, and the poet himself, according to Kunitz, "eventually more than half believed that the springs of his disorder were inseparable form the sources of his art."[55] From the reader's viewpoint, however, the precise relationship between Roethke's illness and his poetic gift is immaterial. Of far greater moment is the incredible power and concision of his verbal imagery as he chronicles his descent into his own unconscious, followed by emergence and growth toward loving union with the finite and the absolute.

Alice Esty, "a soprano of style and means,"[56] together with her knowledgeable pianist, David Stimer, had performed and recorded French and American songs during the years 1954 to 1959. In the latter year she began commissioning major cycles which she premièred in Carnegie Hall to an eventual total of nine by American and seven by European composers. (For a listing of the former, see the source cited in n56.) Ned Rorem's *Eight Poems of Theodore Roethke* was the first of the American cycles. It was presented on April 3, 1960, and Rorem marks its completion with an entry in *The New York Diary* written from the University of Buffalo where he was, at that time, Slee Professor of Composition: "After a labyrinthine correspondence with Theodore Roethke, letters of practical suspicion and mutual praise, the settings of his eight poems are finally completed for Alice Esty. Because—and not despite the fact that—my heart wasn't in them, they've turned out to be great songs. (For musicians, the heart is a dangerous vulgarian.)"[57]

Five of the eight poems that Rorem had chosen for setting came from Roethke's collection *The Lost Son*. In this volume, the poet turned from the more formal structures of *Open House* to the liberating cadences of free verse as he sought the origins of his life and thought. "Root Cellar" and "Orchids" borrow their imagery from memories of his father's greenhouse, and in them the poet is struck by the stubborn and strong attachment to life of plant forms. It is interesting to observe how Rorem in his settings dramatizes this attachment and suggests its menacing aspect. He does this in "Root Cellar"[58] through a series of highly dissonant chords harshly struck on the piano, while the voice intones repetitively, as though hypnotized by fear.

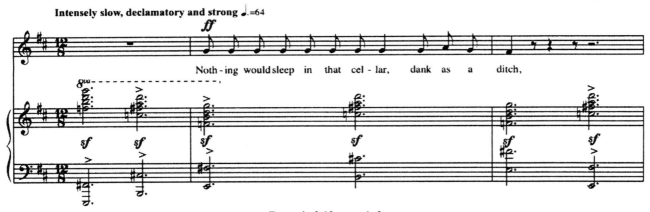

Example 9.12, mm. 1–3

The terror rises as the contours of the vocal line take on the shape of the shoots that "dangled and drooped,"

Example 9.13, mm. 7–8

and ends in a muffled whisper at the recognition that even the dirt seems alive.

Example 9.14, mm. 19–21

In comparison to "Root Cellar," "Orchids"[59] is a more gently insinuating horror story. The orchids are very beautiful, but therefore more dangerous, and the vocal lines take on a more arching contour, like the graceful flowers as they "lean, addermouthed, over the path." The chordal background, too, is different here. Softly struck, less dissonant harmonies built often of superimposed fourths and fifths exploit the extreme ranges of the piano, to create an Impressionistic, seductively enveloping haze of sound.

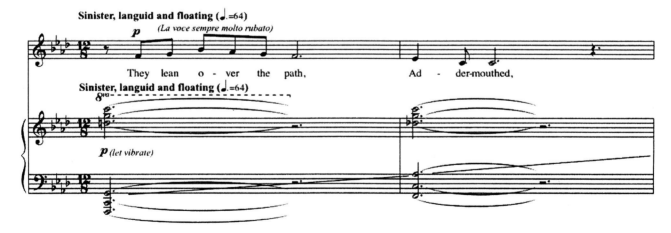

Example 9.15, mm. 1–2

"Night Crow" is a short, evocative eight-line poem that explores levels of awareness. Seeing the "clumsy crow" in flight causes the image of a "tremendous bird" to rise from the unconscious, but the poet barely grasps its meaning before it retreats again into the "moonless black." In Rorem's "Night Crow,"[60] musical device expands the verbal suggestion. The piano prelude, postlude, and interludes with their restlessly moving triplets and sixteenth note figures become the seething, fertile contents of the unconscious mind (see Ex. 9.17). Over this, a lyrical vocal line employs a recurrent melodic formulation, moving in the slower, more controlled cadences of the conscious mind, while the piano sinks back to sustaining chords:

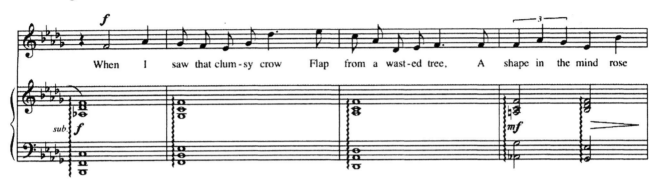

Example 9.16, mm. 4–7

The two levels are masterfully joined at the song's climax. As the image of the bird recedes, Rorem moves up a major third from D-flat to F major. In the more brilliant key, the voice line repeats the melodic pattern but in agitated rhythms over an accompaniment now in moving eighth notes. Conscious and unconscious have come together for a brief moment, only to give way again to the separation announced by the piano postlude.

Example 9.17, mm. 13–20

Since the *Eight Poems* were intended to be performed as a cycle, contrast was essential. "My Papa's Waltz" differs from the other seven in that it is not metaphysically oriented but a clearly held memory of being waltzed off to bed by an intoxicated but beloved father. The poem is four verses of iambic trimeter with rhymes or half-rhymes linking lines one/three and two/four. Rorem's setting[61] maintains the verse divisions with pianistic interludes of swooping arpeggios that propel the wild gyrations of the dance.

Example 9.18, mm. 18–28

The three-stress line that Roethke used to suggest a waltz easily becomes a 3/4 meter as Rorem expands the accented syllables to half notes (see Ex. 9.18). Although the tempo is the fastest of the cycle, the composer makes it clear by his marking that this is not a totally happy situation ("very fast but joyless, breathless, crude and free"). The boy's ambivalence, torn as he is between fear and excitement, is musically clear in the strong dissonances on pianistic downbeats, and the octave vocal leaps which suggest "papa's" drunken lurches (see Ex. 9.18, m. 20).

"I Strolled Across an Open Field,"[61] the last of the *Lost Son* texts, carried the original poetic title of "The Waking." It was no doubt changed because another song in the cycle sets another poem called "The Waking"—that one the title poem from the Roethke collection published in 1953. From this it becomes clear that the idea of "waking" (i.e., the coming of understanding or sudden illumination) was important to Roethke's thought. In "I Strolled across an Open Field" the mechanism of illumination is an early morning walk through spring fields full of flowers and singing birds, and its effect is the sense of merging the poet's own identity with the rich life around him ("and all the waters of all the streams / sang in my veins that summer day"). Notable also is the presence of the river in verse six of this poem, which can be compared with the even greater prominence of the symbol in "Song"—a Douglas Moore setting of Theodore Roethke discussed in chapter 3.

Rorem's setting of this poem deals more with the physical than the metaphysical aspects of the stroll. His tempo marking is "fast and exuberant" and a steady eighth note motion in pianistic cluster chords establishes the rapid pace of the walker, while a filigree of sixteenth notes in the right hand breaks loose in joyful roulades.

Example 9.19, mm. 4–6

In the middle section of the ABA form, Rorem moves from the brighter key of A major to the greater warmth of D-flat and lets his voice line take on jazz-like syncopations as the flowers jump "like small goats." The returning A material brings a resumption of purposeful walking, which continues without abatement until with the closing pianissimo scale the "stroller" vanishes from sight.

Example 9.20, mm. 36–38

The Roethke volume called *The Waking* (see Ex. 9.20) included poems written between 1933 and 1953. Its title poem demonstrates a technically impressive command of form: six stanzas of three lines each in strict iambic pentameter, wherein all second lines, and all first and third lines throughout share a single rhyme (or near rhyme). Further there is a poetic "motif" built of two separate lines that come together at the end in refrain and recapitulation. "I wake to sleep and take my waking slow. / I learn by going where I have to go." As always with Roethke, the language is simple, but the thought complex. The poet appears to be saying that in sleep comes the real waking, when the unconscious mind delivers its uncensored messages. He goes on to celebrate intuition over cerebration ("we think by feeling") and experience over analysis (see second line of refrain). When Ned Rorem chose to set "The Waking,"[64] he wisely selected a musical style that would highlight rather than compete with this intriguing text. The rhythmic structure is a square, steadily moving 4/4 with the voice in constant quarter notes and the pianist's left hand in chordal or arpeggiated eighths. The right hand of the accompaniment either doubles the voice or engages in a complementary counterpoint that opens up as the voice holds the last note of the refrain lines.

dance from ear to ear. I wake to sleep, and take my wak - ing

slow. Of those so close be - side me, which are

Example 9.21, mm. 16–23

The song opens and closes with simple C major chords, but in between employs free chromatic movement, with many polyharmonies and other forms of dissonance. The intuitive state, it seems to say, is clear and organically whole, but the mind (witness this poem) weaves tangled webs trying to attain it.

Words for the Wind was published in 1958, and its section designated "Love Poems" reflects a new area of Roethke's growth stemming from his marriage five years earlier. "Memory" is from this group, and seems to bear out Bower's contention that Roethke's love poetry "functions simultaneously on sensual and spiritual levels" with his lady often becoming the embodiment of his striving toward the Absolute (see n54). The poem, which is three four-line stanzas of free verse, begins (again) in the dream world with the lovers merged into one ("we breathe in unison"). The woman turns, then, and moves away toward a doe and her fawn, as everything becomes frozen in the eternal moment ("the grass changes to stone"). Rorem's "Memory"[6] captures the alluring strangeness of the poetic atmosphere quite remarkably, with restricted but highly appropriate musical means. The repetitive melodic motifs that center around an open fifth and derive from the pentatonic scale create an exotic, Asian feeling, as does the overall sparseness of the setting. (See Ex. 9.22). Notice, also, that the earlier, "together" part of the dream unfolds in smooth, diatonic harmonies. As separation and uncertainty take over, the vocal melody repeats strophically but the accompaniment incorporates increasing dissonance and polytonal ambiguity.

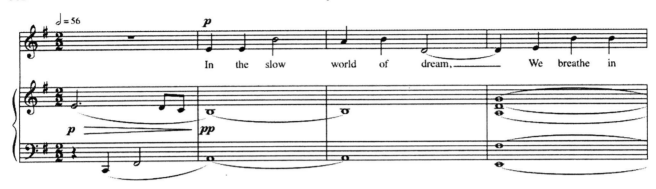

Example 9.22, mm. 1–4

"Snake,"[65] the last of the *Eight Poems*, comes from the section in *Words for the Wind* called "Voices and Creatures." It is a masterful verbal portrait of the appearance and movement of a young snake whose "pure, sensuous form" raises the poet's longing "to be that thing" and the hope that he might be, in some way, at some time. As B. Middaugh has pointed out,[66] Ned Rorem's setting employs three ostinato figures, and it is interesting that despite the composer's expressed disdain of musical "word-painting," two of these take on the coiled, circular contours of the reptile in question.

Example 9.23, mm. 3–5

The "Presto" tempo marking and recurrent opposition of F minor voice patterns to A-flat chordal outlines in the bass lend a possibly humorous note which can be overemphasized in performance. This was clearly not Roethke's intent, and it is doubtful that it was Rorem's, since he assigns two and a half lines at the song's end to a pianistic spinning out of the philosophical speculation on the possibilities of reincarnation.

In 1965, Ned Rorem published a song cycle called *Poems of Love and the Rain*[67] that was without precedent in the literature. The composer begins this cycle with settings of eight poems, and after an "Interlude" (number 9) proceeds to contrasting settings of the original eight, in reverse order. The pair that appears as numbers five and thirteen sets a Roethke poem "Apparition" from *The Far Field*, a collection published posthumously in 1964. Although the poet's mysterious references to "the softfooted one" make it uncertain as to whether the apparition is a spirit, fantasy, or dream figure, the three verses of conventionally rhymed four lines each, have the unmistakable flavor of a folk ballad. Rorem's second setting (number 13) picks up this atmosphere with a flowing 9/8 meter, a lyrically contoured voice line doubled in the accompaniment and a largely homophonic texture.

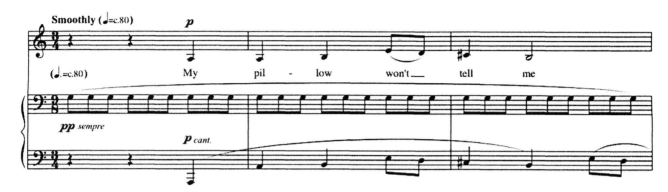

Example 9.24, mm. 1–3

In the first setting, however (number 5), he adopts the always-arresting theatrical device of "playing against the mood." Now the voice line becomes highly angular, with much chromatic movement and many jagged leaps. The singer is sometimes alone, recitative style, and at other times shares a polyphonic, even imitative texture. The tempo is allegro agitato, the dynamic level mostly fortissimo, and the effect, one of dramatically portrayed desperation.

Example 9.25, mm. 1–6

Number 9, which Rorem calls "Interlude," sets a Roethke poem by that same title, and is the only poem that Rorem ever used from Roethke's first published collection, *Open House*. In rich verbal images, and the tight formal structuring of the poet's early period, it describes the time of anxious waiting for a threatening thunderstorm which does not "come to pass." The Rorem "Interlude" has two distinct sections. The first is an unaccompanied vocal recitative in the chromatic, angular style of the first "Apparition." The second is a solo piano passage in rapidly moving chromatic figurations that reach a towering dynamic climax at the upper range of the keyboard and then recede. Each section alone and the combined effect are skillful musical portrayals of gathering excitement with a disappointing end.

Ned Rorem's next to last Roethke setting was written in 1971 and dedicated to Phyllis Curtin, one of the singers whom he has most admired and who has given many performances of his songs. This was "The Serpent,"[68] a poem published in *Words for the Wind* in the section titled "Lighter Pieces and Poems for Children." In these amusing verses, we see an entirely different side of the obscure and mystical Roethke, and indeed this story of the "serpent that had to sing" is attracting settings by a number of composers who appreciate its possibilities for musical humor. As a matter of fact, the humorous is an unaccustomed area for Rorem, too, but he rises magnificently to the occasion. A lively, "perpetual motion" figure in the piano mocks the reptile's urge toward a "Singing Career," while the vocal line modifies its strophes with occasional melismas of an appropriately operatic contour.

Example 9.26, mm. 47–52

Although Rorem's vocal lines become increasingly chromatic into the seventies, this one remains largely diatonic, in keeping with the ingenuous nature of the text. Notice also the jazzy, syncopated vocal rhythms that contribute to the lightheartedly contemporary atmosphere.

The final Rorem/Roethke setting to be treated here opens the cycle called *The Nantucket Songs*,[69] that was commissioned by the Elizabeth Sprague Coolidge Foundation and premièred in 1979 by Phyllis Bryn-Julson and the composer at the Library of Congress. Rorem titles this opening piece "From Whence Cometh Song," a phrase that serves as the first line of a poem called simply "Song" in Roethke's collection *The Far Field*.

In his jacket notes for the CRI recording of the cycle, the composer tells us that it was written at his house on Nantucket Island, and that the songs "are emotional rather than intellectual," being aimed "away from the head and toward the diaphragm." Roethke's compressed, dramatic exploration of the sources of song, love, and death was an inspired poetic choice to establish the desired "emotional" ambiance of the work. The setting has an equally visceral impact, as the wide-ranging vocal line, highlighted against a spare accompaniment, poses and answers Roethke's uneasy questions in stark, unrelenting contrasts of pitch, dynamics, and contour.

Notes

1. Ned Rorem, "The Piano in My Life," *Setting the Tone* (New York: Coward-McCann, 1983), 18.

2. Rorem, "The Piano in My Life," 20.

3. Ned Rorem, *The Final Diary* (New York: Holt, Rinehart and Winston, 1974), 310. Reprinted by North Point Press under the title, *The Later Diaries*.

4. Rorem, *Setting the Tone*, 20.

5. Rorem, *Setting the Tone*, 22.

6. Rorem, *Setting the Tone*, 23.

7. Ned Rorem, *The New York Diary* (New York: George Braziller, 1967), 174. The three songs are now printed in a private edition as *Paul's Blues* (Red Ozier Press).

8. Ned Rorem, *Critical Affairs* (New York: George Braziller, 1970), 32.

9. John Gruen, *The Party's Over* (New York: Viking Press, 1972), 74.

10. Gruen, *The Party's Over*, 80.

11. Gruen, *The Party's Over*, 81.

12. Rorem, *The New York Diary*, 105.

13. Rorem, *The New York Diary*, 155.

14. Gruen, *The Party's Over*, 81.

15. Rorem, *The New York Diary*, 184.

16. Rorem, *The Later Diaries*, 144.

17. Rorem, *Setting the Tone*, 85.

18. See *Setting the Tone*, 230–31, for a listing of these commissions.

19. Ned Rorem, "Interview," *The NATS Bulletin* 39, no. 2 (1982): 5. This interview ends with a complete catalog of Rorem songs to this date plus a discography. An addition to the latter is Rosalind Rees and the composer performing Ned Rorem's songs (GSS 104) that includes ten of the twenty-one Goodman and Roethke settings discussed in this chapter.

20. Rorem, "Interview," 46.

21. Rorem, "Interview," 46.

22. Rorem, "Interview," 47.

23. Marvin Robert Bloomquist, *The Songs of Ned Rorem* (Kansas City: University of Missouri Dissertation, 1970), 2.

24. Quoted in Philip L. Miller, "The Songs of Ned Rorem," *Tempo* 127 (December 1978): 25.

25. George Dennison's "Memoir" in Paul Goodman, *Collected Poems* (New York: Random House, 1973), xiii.

26. Kunitz and Haycraft, eds. *Twentieth Century Authors. First Supplement* (New York: H.W. Wilson, 1961), 372.

27. Dennison, "Memoir," xv.

28. Alicia Ostriker, "Paul Goodman," *Partisan Review* 43, no. 2 (1976): 286.

29. Kingsley Widmer, *Paul Goodman* (Boston: Twayne, 1980), 23.

30. Robert Meredith, "Everywhere a Single Voice," *Poetry* 128, no. 2 (1976): 105.

31. Ostriker, "Paul Goodman," 294.

32. Emile Capouya, "The Poet as Prophet," *Parnassus* 3, no. 1 (1974): 30.

33. Rorem, *The Later Diaries*, 432.

34. Ned Rorem, *Pure Contraption* (New York: Holt, Rinehart and Winston, 1974), 97–101.

35. Ned Rorem, "The Lordly Hudson" (New York: Mercury Music Corp., 1947), Medium high. Now available in *50 Collected Songs* (Boosey & Hawkes, distr. Hal Leonard Corp.), High voice, Medium/Low voice; also available through Theodore Presser.

36. Ned Rorem, *The Paris Diary* (New York: George Braziller, 1966), 10.

37. Rorem, *Pure Contraption*, 101.

38. Ned Rorem, "Absalom" (Boosey & Hawkes, 1972). Medium voice. Now available in *50 Collected Songs* (Boosey & Hawkes, distr. Hal Leonard Corp.), High voice, Medium/Low voice.

39. Ned Rorem, "Rain in Spring" (Boosey & Hawkes, 1956). Medium voice. Now available in *50 Collected Songs*. See n38.

40. Ned Rorem, "The Midnight Sun" from *Four Songs* (Boston: E.C. Schirmer, 1968). Medium high.

41. See Daryl Hine and Joseph Parisi, eds., *The "Poetry" Anthology* (Boston: Houghton Mifflin, 1978), 275.

42. Ned Rorem, "The Tulip Tree" from *Four Songs* (Boston: E.C. Schirmer, 1968). Medium high.

43. Ned Rorem, "Sally's Smile" (New York: Henmar Press, 1957). Medium high. Now available from Edition Peters. Also available in Ned Rorem, *Fourteen Songs on American Poetry* (New York: Edition Peters).

44. Ned Rorem, *Three Poems of Paul Goodman* (New York: Boosey & Hawkes, 1968). Medium high. "Clouds" is now available in *50 Collected Songs*. See n38.

45. Ned Rorem, "Such beauty as hurts to behold" (New York: Henmar Press, 1961). Medium high. Now available in *50 Collected Songs*. See n38.

46. The reader is referred to chapter 3 for a brief discussion of Roethke in connection with a song by Douglas Moore.

47. Stanley J. Kunitz and Howard Haycraft, *Twentieth Century Authors* (New York: H. W. Wilson Company, 1967), 837.

48. William Heyen, comp., *Profile of Theodore Roethke* (Columbus, Ohio: Charles E. Merrill, 1971), 5.

49. Heyen, *Profile*, 13.

50. Heyen, *Profile*, 8.

51. Rorem, *The Later Diaries*, 65.

52. Ostriker, "Paul Goodman," 292.

53. Heyen, *Profile*, 101.

54. Neil Bowers, *Theodore Roethke* (Columbia, Mo.: University of Missouri Press, 1982).

55. Heyen, *Profile*, 13.

56. Rorem, "The American Art Song" in *Setting the Tone*, 230. Although listed here as a cycle, Ned Rorem pointed out in a 20 November 1985 letter to R. Friedberg that the *Eight Poems of Theodore Roethke* were not necessarily intended to be performed as a group and have never been done that way since their première.

57. Rorem, *The New York Diary*, 121.

58. Ned Rorem, "Root Cellar" (New York: Henmar Press, 1963). Medium high. Now available from Edition Peters. See n43.

59. Ned Rorem, "Orchids" (Boosey and Hawkes, 1969). Medium voice. Now available in *50 Collected Songs*. See n38.

60. Ned Rorem, "Night Crow" (New York: Henmar Press, 1963). Medium high. Now available from Edition Peters. See n43.

61. Ned Rorem, "My Papa's Waltz" (New York: Henmar Press, 1963). Medium high. Now available from Edition Peters. See n43.

62. Ned Rorem, "I Strolled across an Open Field" (Boosey and Hawkes, 1969). Medium high. Now available in *50 Collected Songs*. See n38.

63. Ned Rorem, "The Waking" (New York: Henmar Press, 1961). Medium high. Now available in *50 Collected Songs*. See n38.

64. Ned Rorem, "Memory" (New York: Henmar Press, 1961). Medium. Now available from Edition Peters. See n43. Also available in Ned Rorem, *Another Sleep: Nineteen Songs for Medium Voice and Piano* (New York: Boosey and Hawkes).

65. Ned Rorem, "Snake" (New York: Henmar Press, 1963). Medium high. Now available from Edition Peters. See n43.

66. Bennie Middaugh, "The Songs of Ned Rorem," *The NATS Bulletin* 24 (May 1968): 36.

67. Ned Rorem, *Poems of Love and the Rain* (Boosey and Hawkes, 1965). Mezzo-soprano.

68. Ned Rorem, "The Serpent" (Boosey and Hawkes, 1974). Medium high. Now available in *50 Collected Songs*. See n38.

69. Ned Rorem, *The Nantucket Songs* (Boosey and Hawkes, 1979). Soprano. "Ferry me across the river" and "Nantucket" are also available in two collections of Rorem songs published by Boosey and Hawkes, *50 Collected Songs* and *10 Selected Songs*, a selection of songs suitable for student singers.

Chapter 10

The Third Decade II

Ruth Schonthal (1924–2006)

Ruth Schonthal belongs in the category of American composers who were not born in this country, but who, like Charles Loeffler and Sergius Kagen, emigrated here as young adults, and soon became firmly woven into the fabric of the American musical scene. Schonthal's birthplace was Hamburg, Germany. Her parents were Viennese, and they actively encouraged their precociously talented daughter, who began to compose at the age of five and in the same year became the youngest student ever accepted at the Stern Conservatory in Berlin.

In 1937, the Schonthals fled Hitler's Germany, leaving everything behind. The composer's father, who had a weak heart, would never thereafter discuss this extremely painful loss of home, friends, and possessions. Stockholm provided a temporary and uneasy refuge as Schonthal continued her studies there at the Royal Academy of Music, but the family moved again just three months before the completion of her degree. This time they located in Mexico City (where Schonthal's mother owned a shop for many years), and the young woman was taken on as a composition student by Manuel Ponce.

While traveling in Mexico on a concert tour, Paul Hindemith heard about Ruth Schonthal's talent, and shortly thereafter arranged for her to study composition with him on scholarship at Yale University. She came to the United States in 1946, earned a bachelor of music degree at Yale, and remained to become a U.S. citizen, marry, and raise a family of three boys. Her husband was a painter and lithographer and one son followed in his artistic parents' footsteps by attending Juilliard and becoming a violist and composer.

Ruth Schonthal was a concert pianist as well as composer and she had an active teaching career in the areas of piano, composition, and music literature. In 1973, after a number of years of private teaching, she joined the faculty of Adelphi University. Three years later she began to teach at Westchester Conservatory and eventually bought a home in New Rochelle after constantly missing trains back to her Manhattan apartment because of her unwillingness to cut a lesson short. At the time of R. Friedberg's interview with Ruth Schonthal on December 3, 1982, she had also held a part-time position teaching "period" and "genre" courses at New York University for four or five years. She described this as a difficult situation, due to lack of tenure and fringe benefits plus the financial uncertainty of a teaching load tied to unpredictable course enrollments.

Schonthal was at that time a small, vital, personable woman with black, slightly graying hair and dark, intense eyes. The composer and writer met on the steps of Carnegie Hall, talked in a nearby coffeehouse, then drove to Town Hall to pick up programs for an upcoming concert in the International Chamber Artists series that would include a world première of her chamber work "Aranjuez." Schonthal maintained humor and perspective despite the many struggles of her life that included the raising of her mentally retarded oldest son, who was living in a group home. Nor did recognition of her creative work come easily, for as Schonthal explained, she "did everything herself for her career and it was hard to get the music out to publishers."

During the decade of the 1980s, however, Ruth Schonthal's reputation as an important contemporary composer became firmly established. For her one-act opera, *The Courtship of Camilla*, she became a finalist in the 1980 New York City Opera Competition, and the previous year she had been nominated for the Kennedy Center–Friedheim Award for *In Homage of . . .* (a set of twenty-four piano preludes). She won a number of ASCAP music awards and "Meet the Composer" grants; her music was being played in major American and European music centers, and she herself was in demand for lectures, workshops, and guest appearances on radio and television. Her song cycle *Totengesänge*, that sets her own poetic texts, was recorded by Leonarda Records, and Capriccio Records released her piano works performed by pianist Gary Steigerwalt.

Schonthal then went on to compose two more operas: *Princess Maleen* in 1988 and *Jocasta* in 1998, the latter a feminist retelling of the Oedipus story in which both main characters are represented by an actor, a singer, and a dancer. In 2003, Schonthal was invited to be one of the principal U.S. composers present at the Songs Across the Americas conference in Bolivia. Here, author R. Friedberg who was on the program as a scholar and performer, had the pleasure of meeting Ruth Schonthal again after the passage of twenty years. Having lost none of her energetic charisma, Schonthal was an exciting and instructive presence to the many young singers and pianists gathered at the conference. But failing health caused the composer's brief collapse on arrival at the La Paz airport (whose altitude is a daunting 13,000 feet) and within a few more years, she died in the environs of New York City, her home of many years.

A number of publishing houses currently carry Schonthal's works, and facsimiles of unpublished scores are available from the American Music Center. Her catalog includes instrumental works for orchestra, solo instruments, and chamber groups; works for solo voice and vocal chamber music; three operas; and the film score for *Lantern Love*. Southern Music Co. of San Antonio issued two collections of her art songs in the nin1990s that have proven to be much in demand. They are *Early Songs* that are settings in German of Rilke's poetry and *Four Songs* that include two Emily Dickinson texts and two poignant settings of Spanish poetry by Garcia Lorca.[1]

As these song settings indicate, Ruth Schonthal was fluent in five languages: the German, French, Spanish, and English gleaned from her world travels, and the Italian that she taught herself. It is interesting, therefore, that the texts of her vocal works are primarily in German (she set Rilke at the age of fourteen) or in English (the majority of these are British, such as the poetry of Yeats and Wordsworth). Commenting on the different problems in setting German and English texts, Schonthal said:

> Of course the language changes the style of the music because of its sound qualities and accents. But besides this, I change my personality and the tempo of my speech when I change languages. Even English and American speech are different: English is more elaborate, mannered, civilized with a sheen, while American is open, direct, and deliberate. After all, American immigration was self-selected—those who wanted to get away from traditions to a more open society.

Walt Whitman (1819–1892)

Given this view of America, it is not surprising that Walt Whitman was one of the few American poets that Schonthal chose for setting. She explained that she loved Whitman, "and when [she] wanted to write an American work, felt that he was typically American." Schonthal was also drawn to "the conciseness of the short poems" since she loved "conciseness in general" and found a strong appeal in the "emotional climate"[2] of this writing. The poems to which she refers come from the section of *Leaves of Grass* that is subtitled "By the Roadside" and this is the same title that Schonthal assigned to a remarkable ten page song cycle which sets six of them.[3]

The authors have already discussed Walt Whitman's life,[4] and have provided an exploration of Whitman texts drawn from the exultant, life-celebrating *Song of Myself* (1855)[5] and from the more reflective, sometimes somber poetry of *Inscriptions*[6] and *Drum Taps*,[7] written ten years later. Thomas Crawley, in his structural analysis of *Leaves of Grass* postulates that a bridge "was needed between the exuberant story of material and social development and success of 'Song of Myself' . . . and the dark, critical [Civil War] experiences of 'Drum-Taps.' To perform this function," he continues, "scattered poems of doubt and turmoil were collected under 'By the Roadside.'"[8] It is also true, that in this transitional phase of Whitman's verse, the expansiveness and the catalogs of the earlier writing give way to sharply focused portraits, delineated with the conciseness that Schonthal found so appealing. And perhaps, too, this composer, whose youth had been traumatized by man's inhumanity to man, felt herself to be on familiar ground with Whitman's increasingly pessimistic view of America's capacity for self-delusion and destruction as the country moved uneasily toward and over the brink of war.

The six poems that Schonthal selected are all very short (between one and four lines in length), all unrhymed, and with varying poetic meters, although there is a preponderance of three and six stress lines. They are not all alike in mood, however, and seem to fall into two distinct groups: those written in 1860 ("Thought," "Visor'd," "To Old Age") which are philosophical reflections on man's condition and behavior; and those from 1865 ("Mother and Babe," "A Farm Picture," "A Child's Amaze") which present vignettes of American life drawn from observation or memory. Schonthal has not opted for a chronological arrangement in the cycle, but for an artistic one, which resembles a circular structure. She opens with the pictorial "Mother and Babe," continues with the three reflective verses of 1860, and concludes with the Americana pieces "A Farm Picture" and "A Child's Amaze."

In "Mother and Babe," the poet sees a mother nursing her infant, and gazes at them "long and long" in a state of "hush'd" contemplation that suggests his awed tribute to the miracle of life and its processes. Schonthal sets this text and begins her cycle with an appropriately soft dynamic level and gently rocking 6/8 (or 9/8) meter.

Example 10.1, mm. 1–3

In a middle section marked "Quasi doppio movimento" the eighth notes move twice as fast in contrary motion, hinting at a rush of emotion arising in the poet as he "studies them."

Example 10.2, mm. 16–18

As can be seen in Example 10.1, the opening harmonic scheme uses the superimposed tonalities of C major and E major in the piano part, with the voice joining in the right hand's E major but at mostly dissonant intervals to the accompaniment. The vocal line by itself is an arching diatonic contour, as are the individual lines of the "doppio movimento" which nevertheless clash in consort. Similarly, the song ends with warm, softening B major chords, and their ambiguous echoes of dissonant minor seconds. The combined effect of all these harmonic juxtapositions is that of a timeless lullaby filtering through a contemporaneous and possibly threatening haze.

"Thought" is the most pessimistic poem of the whole "By the Roadside" series and contains Whitman's discouraged observation, no doubt occasioned by pre–Civil War politics, of how easily men could be led by demagogues "who do not believe in men." Schonthal begins this setting in dramatic contrast to number one with a forte, accented, sixteenth to quarter note accompaniment pattern of consecutive fourths, with the two hands almost on top of each other as they clash angrily in the bass register.

Example 10.3, mm. 1–4

As the soprano enters softly in the bottom of her range, the piano remains in its depressed lower octaves, and the tempo changes to a musing andante. Gradually then, the vocal and right hand pitches rise (over a grimly repetitive D pedal point) while the tempo accelerates to a climactic point of despair.

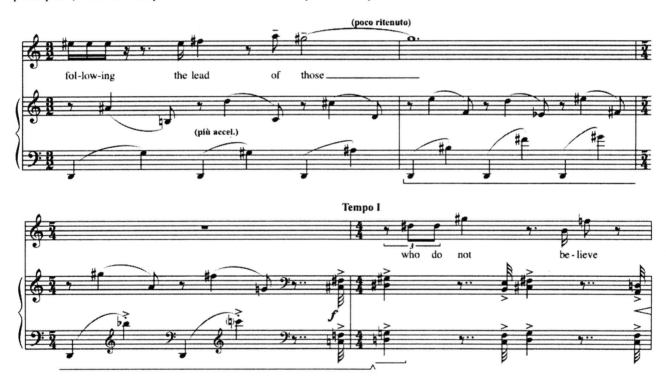

Example 10.4, mm. 12–15

Now the battering fourths of the introduction return (see Ex. 10.3), again serving to escalate the original poetic negativity from sorrow to disgust.

Number three of the cycle sets "Visor'd," Whitman's evocation of a woman whose face was always a changing mask of concealment, even in sleep. Schonthal takes off brilliantly from the text line "Changes and transformations every hour, every moment" to create a musical climate of constantly altering meters, tempos, vocal rhythms, and broken chordal structures. "Even when she sleeps" the changes continue, now in a whispered pianissimo dynamic with tiptoeing staccato accompaniment.

Example 10.5, mm. 13–20

Interestingly, this song contains the only instance of the composer's changing Whitman's original texts. In the line "a perpetual natural disguiser of herself," she chooses to omit the word "natural," probably in pursuit of a more forceful vocal contour which is rising at that point to a climax in solo recitative.

Example 10.6, mm. 1–6

In the fourth poem, "To Old Age," the poet compares the late years of human life to an "estuary that enlarges . . . as it pours into the great sea." This powerful metaphor for Whitman's concept of the individual soul preparing to return to universal consciousness gains further strength in its musical mating. Large-interval arpeggios, with the right hand climbing into the upper register, create an appropriate pianistic context of expansion as the voice also rises to the climactic moment of fulfillment:

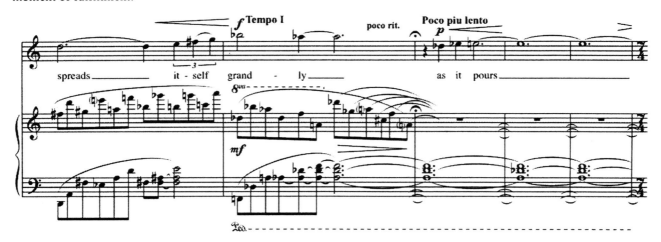

Example 10.7, mm. 4–8

There is greater consonance between voice and accompaniment in this setting, and a clear D major is carried upward in scalar fashion by the vocal line to the very moment of transformation ("grandly"), signified by the sudden appearance of D-flat major. Thereafter the original key quietly reasserts itself, as the soul loses itself in God (see Ex. 10.7).

"A Farm Picture," painted by Walt Whitman in number five, was a scene of daily life to the poet, but "the peaceful country barn" and "sunlit pasture field" take on the aspect of a nostalgia piece in the face of contemporary encroachments on a farmer's tranquility. The setting enhances this flavor, with its forthright C major opening in a swinging 6/8 folk-like pattern. Toward the end, a sudden slowing of tempo and rhythmic movement, and a drift to "hazy" A major/minor key references set up the musical "fading" of the picture into the "far horizon" of the past.

Example 10.8, mm. 7–11

In the final song, "A Child's Amaze," Schonthal adds her lively sense of humor to Whitman's irony and creates a bravura ending to the cycle. The verse is a recollection of the poet's boyhood amazement while listening to the preacher speak of God as though "contending against some being or influence." Schonthal surrounds this text with a pseudo chorale-prelude accompaniment as it would be played by a bad church piano player on a worse instrument ("non legato, clangy, with much pedal"):

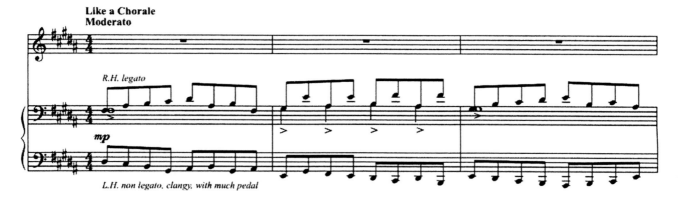

Example 10.9, mm. 1–3

The voice then enters timidly ("hymnlike, as sung by a child") but as the memory unfolds, begins to imitate the pomposity of the preacher, while the piano pounds away with increasing vigor.

Example 10.10, mm. 19–25

As the Ivesian scene draws to a close, the piano player strikes the triumphant final chord and hits a few wrong notes out of sheer exuberance (see Ex. 10.10).

Lee Hoiby (b. 1926)

There are interesting parallels between the musical careers of Lee Hoiby and that of John Duke (see chapter 5) who had been born almost thirty years earlier in 1899. Both had originally intended to be concert pianists, an intention which would inform the virtuosic demands of their song accompaniments and chamber music with piano. Both were historically out of step for many decades with the prevailing serial and experimental style of mid-twentieth century musical composition. And both chose to live in relative geographic isolation from the distracting competition of the centers of the musical marketplace: John Duke in the calm heart of academia at Smith College and Lee Hoiby in the peaceful countryside of Long Eddy, New York.

Lee Hoiby, born in Wisconsin, had a maternal grandfather who had emigrated from Denmark and was a professional violinist and teacher. His aunts performed as an all-girl saxophone band, and the family musical gifts were early evidenced in Lee who began serious piano study at the age of five. As his talent matured, in a replay of the Johannes Brahms experience, he was forced by his father to play in unsavory bars, where he developed an antipathy to popular music while imbibing some aspects of the idiom.

Enrolled in the wartime music department of the University of Wisconsin at Madison, Hoiby was exposed to many fine musicians who had fled Hitler's Germany. Among these was Arnold Schoenberg's son-in-law, Rudolph Kolisch, who led the Pro Arte Quartet. From these performers he learned thoroughly the European stylistic tradition of the common practice period, but rejected the newer serial language of Schoenberg and Webern. Hoiby likewise rejected the experiments of Harry Partch, who was also on the Madison campus, although he enjoyed playing the kithara in Partch's ensemble of garage-made instruments.

The most important aspect of Hoiby's Madison years was the continuation of his studies with Gunnar Johansen, the Danish virtuoso who had been persuaded by the youth's talent to accept him as a student while he was still in high school. After completing his bachelor of arts degree at the University in 1947, Hoiby was sent on to Johansen's mentor, Egon Petri, whose master classes he attended at Cornell University and afterward at Mills College in Oakland, California. At Mills, he was granted a master of arts degree in 1952, and it was here, while studying composition with Darius Milhaud, that the seemingly straight path to a concert pianist's career hit a major detour.

On the basis of a few compositions submitted by a friend without his knowledge, Hoiby was invited by Gian Carlo Menotti to come and study with him at the Curtis Institute in Philadelphia. They worked together for three years (1949–1952) after which the young composer's promise was recognized by a Fulbright grant (1953), an award from the National Institute of Arts and Letters (1957), and a Guggenheim fellowship (1958). The years under Menotti's tutelage (two of them spent writing strict Palestrina counterpoint) developed Hoiby's gifts as an opera composer, and the presentation of his one-act work, *The Scarf* (with a libretto after Chekhov) at the first Spoleto festival of 1957, was followed by many more successful works in this genre. These have ranged from *Summer and Smoke* in 1970 with a libretto by Lanford Wilson adapted from the Tennessee Williams play, all the way to Shakespeare's *Tempest* (1986) and *Romeo and Juliet* (2008) with libretti by Mark Shulgasser.

Throughout his composing career, numerous choral works and solo songs also evidenced Hoiby's strong affinity for vocal composition. But at the same time, his many piano solos, two piano concerti, and a number of chamber pieces with piano attested to the concert performer's ongoing attraction to his instrument. In 1978, at the age of 52, Lee Hoiby made his New York recital debut and thereafter gave a number of recitals throughout the United States. In the years that followed, he maintained that the unique discipline involved in concert performance informed all of his subsequent musical undertakings.

Hoiby's return to the piano in the seventies and the scarcity of new compositions in that decade partly represent the composer's growing sense of isolation from a musical world still dominated by avant-garde and serial techniques. However, another important, and very positive aspect of this period was Hoiby's spiritual awakening, initiated by his experiences with a New Age group called "The Pathwork" whose beliefs emphasized learning and growth as the principal goals of human existence.

Following these life-changing events, Lee Hoiby returned to writing music in a world increasingly reverting to the pre-serial musical idioms of "late Romanticism"—Hoiby's own preferred characterization of his compositional style. After 1979, Hoiby was usually assisted by Mark Shulgasser, his librettist, in what he saw as the challenging task of choosing texts for vocal works. Interestingly, Hoiby had always been drawn to strong American poets, and by the early sixties had set Adelaide Crapsey, Ezra Pound, Robert Frost, and Thomas Wolffe. In the eighties and nineties, the works of Walt Whitman, Wallace Stevens, Emily Dickinson, and Elizabeth Bishop were selected for major song cycles. And a humorous poem by Theodore Roethke, "The Serpent" (also set by Ned Rorem, see chapter 9) became a tour de force for Leontyne Price as one of the set that Hoiby titled *Songs for Leontyne*.[9]

Ezra Pound (1885–1972)

Ezra Pound has been a controversial figure in twentieth century literary history and an infrequent choice for setting by American composers. Pound was born in Hailey, Idaho territory, in 1885, and his maternal grandfather had been the Lieutenant Governor of Wisconsin, but the family moved east to the Philadelphia suburbs when he was only eighteen months old. By the age of fifteen, he was ready for college, and entered the University of Pennsylvania only to transfer two years later and complete his undergraduate studies at Hamilton College. Returning to Penn, he not only acquired an M.A. in Romance philology, but fortuitously crossed paths with William Carlos Williams and with Hilda Doolittle (H.D.), who became his fiancée for a time.

Pound had visited Europe twice in his younger years and in 1908 moved there permanently, settling first in London where he became secretary to William Butler Yeats whom he considered to be the world's greatest living poet. Pound's own early poetry had been modeled after nineteenth century and medieval Romance literature, but in England he began to search for new directions, and spear-headed the Imagist movement on both sides of the Atlantic. Moving to Paris in 1920, he quickly became part of the circle of Parisian and expatriate artists who dominated the decade, and as a largely self-taught composer, wrote two complete operas (with the assistance of George Antheil) plus several works for solo violin. In 1924 he moved to Italy and collided with history. His support of the Mussolini regime would, by the end of World War II, lead to a charge of treason against the United States and, subsequently, to an insanity plea which resulted in his incarceration at St. Elizabeth's Hospital in Washington, D.C., from 1946 to 1958.

During those years he continued to write, receive visitors, and collaborate with other authors. Opinion was strongly divided between those who were affronted by his anti-semitic statements and those who indignantly campaigned for his release from an inappropriate situation. The latter group, headed by Robert Frost and Archibald Macleish eventually won out, and on his release, Pound returned to Italy for fourteen years and died in Venice just before his eighty-seventh birthday.

In 1912, Ezra Pound had written a group of verses called *Ripostes*, which were included in the posthumous *Collected Early Poems*, published in 1976.[10] The volume contains ninety-nine works that Pound had published early on, but rejected in later collections. The poet's opinion notwithstanding, "An Immorality" (from *Ripostes*), which was set by Hoiby in 1952 when he had barely completed his years at Curtis, is a perfect confluence of the composer's and the author's early fresh, lyrical writing. Louis L. Martz in the Introduction to *Early Poems* admires the "supple language and clear imagery" of *Ripostes*, while also quoting Pound's developing conviction that "a renaissance for American poetry might lie in foreign literature,"[11] which for him came to mean the concision and structures of Asian verse.

In "An Immorality," Pound seems already to be pulling away from flowery nineteenth-century literary Romanticism and toward the concise forms that were beginning to attract him. The poem consists of eight brief lines of alternating four and three stresses, and the underlying message might well have seemed "immoral" in the post-Victorian era of his surroundings. "Sing we for love and idleness" is his manifesto, for "Naught else is worth the having."

Lee Hoiby begins his equally brief, three page setting,[12] with the disarming simplicity that is his trademark. He opens in the warm, diatonically stated key of A-flat major with a little eighth note piano motif in the right hand that will then blossom upward as the vocal line joins it in a downward direction.

Example 10.11, mm. 1–4

The first page remains solidly in the opening key and in a 2/2 meter that closely follows the prosody. Then, everything begins to change with the poet's intensified declaration: "I would rather have my sweet . . . than do high deeds in Hungary." Now, Hoiby changes meters constantly, lengthening words for emotive content and removes the key signature

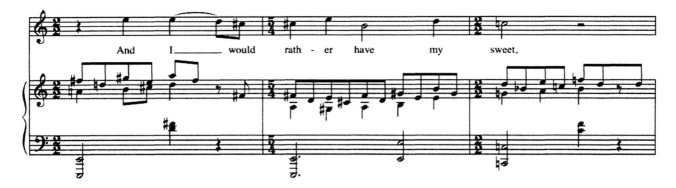

Example 10.12, mm. 12–14

in order to create a crescendo of rapidly changing harmonic movement up to the climactic moment ("high deeds").

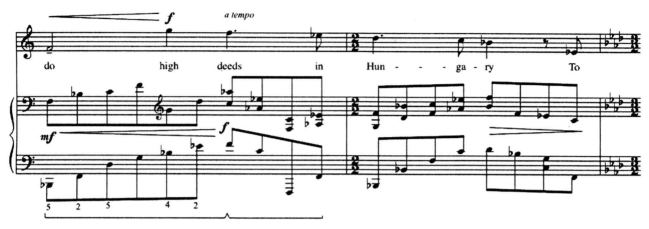

Example 10.13, mm. 18–19

The rush of feeling then comes to a peaceful conclusion as the original key and piano motif make a quiet return.

Emma Lazarus (1849–1887)

Emma Lazarus was a well-known figure in New York literary circles of the latter half of the nineteenth century. Nevertheless, the only work in her own catalog of writings to have stood the test of implacable time is a sonnet called "The New Colossus" [13] which, about a hundred years ago, was inscribed on the pedestal of the Statue of Liberty.

Lazarus was born into a wealthy, cultured family of New York Sephardic Jews. Their Portuguese ancestors had been settled in the United States for a number of generations and the writer grew to womanhood feeling much more attached to American life than to Judaic traditions. Her precocious literary talent was warmly supported by her father, who had her first poems privately printed when she was seventeen. This volume (*Poems and Translations*) achieved a publication in 1867 and was soon followed by *Admetus and Other Poems* in 1871. These poems and the youthful promise of their author were much admired by Ralph Waldo Emerson who invited Lazarus to visit him. The visit initiated a long correspondence with Emerson and with his daughter, but the friendship cooled when he failed to select her poetry for inclusion in an edited collection, and thereafter when Alzheimer's disease erased all his relationships.

During the 1870s, Lazarus's work appeared regularly in *Lippincott's Magazine* and *Scribner's Monthly*. Her first prose publications were *Alide: An Episode of Goethe's Life* (1874) and a five-act play called *Spagnoletto* (1876), but critics agreed that poetry, not drama, was her forte, and her 1881 translation of Heinrich Heine's *Poems and Ballads* was universally admired as the best version of Heine in English at that time.

In the next decade, Emma Lazarus's life, like that of Ezra Pound, was materially affected by historical events. The violent anti-Semitism that broke out in Russia and Germany during the early 1880s produced in her a strong sense of identification with her Jewish heritage, as well as with all oppressed and helpless victims worldwide. Her writings began to reflect these feelings in the poetry collection *Songs of a Semite* (1882); a play based on twelfth century Jewish life called *The Dance of Death*; and a series of articles for the magazine *American Hebrew*. At this time, Lazarus was also swept by a rising conviction that Zionism was the obvious answer to persecution of the Jews, and she made trips to Europe in 1883 and 1885 seeking to advance the cause, until her life was cruelly cut short by Hodgkin's disease in 1887, at the age of thirty-eight.

For about a century, Lazarus's historical reputation was that of a demure recluse, but this view was destroyed by the scholar Betty Roth Young in 1995 with her publication of *Emma Lazarus in Her World: Life and Letters*.[14] Herein, the writer's correspondence, mostly with Helena de Kay Gilder, wife of Emma's publisher, Richard Gilder, shows her to be a clever, assertive, and courageous woman, interacting with artists and politicians, and dedicated to many contemporary causes. Other correspondents in the collection are Rose Hawthorne Lathrop, Henry James, and the Emersons (mentioned earlier), and with this rich material now available to her, Esther Schor was able to create the first in-depth biography of the writer that was published in 2006 and called simply *Emma Lazarus*.[15]

A literary auction had been held in New York City in 1883 to raise funds to build a pedestal for the Statue of Liberty, a recent gift from the people of France. Emma Lazarus's sonnet, "The New Colossus," was submitted, sold, and forgotten until 1903 when a memorial plaque engraved with the poem was placed inside the pedestal, through the efforts of Lazarus's friend, Georgina Schuyler. Even then, it went largely unnoticed until Louis Adamic used it in a collection intended to celebrate the contributions of the more recent groups of immigrants in America.[16]

Lee Hoiby, for his moving setting which he calls "The Lady of the Harbor,"[17] chooses only the final and most cherished lines of the sonnet which begin "Give me your tired, your poor" The sonnet as a whole has a complex rhyme scheme and much flowery, over-blown language, but in the lines used in this setting the poet seemed to have suddenly tapped into a source of powerful inspiration which for years has encapsulated for us the immigrant's dream of salvation in America and America's vision of her life-saving mission to the world.

The musical imagery is unmistakably clear. Hoiby says "Moderato, rocking," so that we are immediately aware that the piano introduction, with the 9/8 time signature and alternating eighth and quarter note figures, is portraying the motion of the ship entering the harbor, with occasional groups of two sixteenth notes signifying dips in the otherwise smooth motion.

Example 10.14, mm. 1–2

The voice of "the Lady" enters in its own rhythm that has destroyed the prosody of the sonnet by means of long held notes on words of emphasis

Example 10.15, mm. 5–11

but it also incorporates occasional echoes of the piano's lurching sixteenth note figure (see Ex. 10.15, mm. 8 and 11) as if she would share in the experience of the anxious passengers.

The opening key looks like C major but Hoiby ingeniously clouds it with a recurring B-flat that draws it into the modal scale built on G (Mixolydian) and increases the atmosphere of aural ambiguity. Now, as the Lady's invitation begins to gain force, the rocking motion continues but Hoiby commences a free, diatonic sequence of ever-changing harmonic movement in an upward direction following the ascent and temporal extension of the vocal line.

Example 10.16, mm. 15–18

Hoiby chooses to repeat the beautiful metaphor of the final line ("I lift my lamp beside the golden door") and he makes the second setting of "lamp" his musical and emotive climax. The approach begins on A major vocal and instrumental arpeggios, but the A at the top of the vocal contour turns into the mediant of an F major chord signaling an eventual return to the opening key.

Example 10.17, mm. 26–27

The mood now, unlike the opening of the song, is anything but tentative. Rather, as made clear by the piano's fortissimo and allargando conclusion, it is triumphant, and we sense that the ship has arrived to an embracing welcome.

Example 10.18, mm. 30–33

In 1973 (with revisions in 1986), Lee Hoiby composed, to his own poetry, what would become one of his most popular songs. He called it "Where the Music Comes From"[18] and dedicated it to "The Guide," thus suggesting that this may well be a musical summation of the projected spiritual journey that he had chosen to travel with the "Pathwork" group. The message of the text is close to the stated goals of "Pathwork," particularly as the poet speaks of wanting "to grow," "to feel," and "to love" in his search for "the living spirit" and for oneness with all of nature. There is more than a hint of Broadway in the repeated rising transposition of the material for three verses of text and in the nature of the poetry that resembles stage lyrics rather than complex literary thought. But the increasingly virtuosic demands of the piano writing in verses two and three as well as the rising tessitura of the vocal line to an arching largamente finish are clearly intended for seasoned concert performers. This is Lee Hoiby at his lyrical best with a sophisticated command of vocal and pianistic detail that belies the apparent simplicity of this seemingly inevitable setting.

As a final note and caveat, Richard Jackson's words of stylistic summary should be noted:[19] "Though much of [Hoiby's] music is characterized by a disarming diatonic simplicity, his ambitious works tend toward greater harmonic and textural complexity." An example of this alternate style is *I Was There*, five settings of texts by Walt Whitman that began as *Four Whitman Songs* in 1988. They were published under the new title in 1993 with the addition of "O Captain! My Captain!" and a subsequent orchestral version created a broader dimension for performance.[20]

Emma Lou Diemer (b. 1927)

Emma Lou Diemer began to write music at the age of six and never doubted that she was destined to be a composer. While a number of other women musicians born in the same decade turned their principal energies toward musicology or publishing,[21] Diemer steered the course of her career steadfastly ahead despite the discouraging climate for women composers in mid-twentieth century.

She had been born in Kansas City into a highly musical family. Both sets of grandparents were church musicians and George Diemer, her father, initiated a new bachelor of music program at Central Missouri State Teachers' College that he also served as president. Emma Lou's sister, Dorothy, and twin brothers, John and George Jr., all played the piano plus other instruments. Diemer herself reproduced Paderewski's Minuet perfectly by ear at the age of five and her talent as a keyboard performer on both piano and organ then began to develop alongside her gift as a composer. During her teenage years, she started to play professionally as church organist; regularly wrote music in the morning before going to school; and also began to receive public recognition in the form of awards for both performing and composition.

Diemer's undergraduate studies began at Eastman continued back home at Central Missouri State Teacher's College, and ended at Yale University which had the strong offerings in composition that Diemer's burgeoning skill required. At Yale she also earned a master's degree although interestingly, she studied counterpoint, but not composition, with Paul Hindemith, following her stated instinct of not wanting to be overly influenced by a mentor's style. A Fulbright fellowship awarded for 1952–1953 brought her to Brussels to study both piano and composition at the Royal Conservatory. Back in America, she taught in regional schools, and in the summers of 1954 and 1955 studied composition at Tanglewood with Ernst Toch and Roger Sessions. At this time, her growing reputation brought her a scholarship award in the Ph.D. program at Eastman, where she would work with Bernard Rogers and Howard Hanson . The latter conducted her dissertation work, the *Symphony on American Themes* with the Eastman-Rochester Orchestra and pronounced her to be one of America's most gifted women composers.

In truth, Emma Lou Diemer's composing career has not been relegated to the narrow annals of "women composers." She has been as prolific, and as widely performed and published as her male confrères. She herself points to only two occasions when gender became a prominent issue: the first when she was only the second woman to receive the Louisville Symphony Orchestra Student Award (1955) and the other, when she was the lone woman among the dozen composers selected for the Young Composers Project in 1959, which linked twelve composers with twelve school systems nationwide.

Her first destination as one of the Young Composers was Arlington, Virginia, and here she was able to put into practice a philosophy of hers, partially modeled on Hindemith's "Gebrauchsmusik" principle, that music should be accessible to both audience and performers. In 1965, Diemer was invited to teach theory and composition at the University of Maryland College Park, and in 1971 she accepted a similar faculty position at the University of California Santa Barbara, which she would hold until her retirement in 1991. Just before moving to California, Diemer had attended an electronic music workshop in Washington, D.C., and she carried her excitement over this new world of musical sound into the creation of an electronic and computer music lab at UCSB, which she directed for the next fifteen years.[22]

During all of her teaching appointments and in the ensuing years as Professor Emerita, Emma Lou Diemer continued to hold church organist positions and to compose prolifically in all genres. From 1990 to 1992, she was composer-in-residence for the Santa Barbara Symphony, which resulted in premières of four orchestral works. And throughout the decades of teaching and composing, Diemer somehow found time to write a number of articles on her experiences as a composer in the schools, as a professor of composition, and as organist and composer in the area of church music.[23]

At this writing, Emma Lou Diemer has been invited to be guest composer at the 2010 Women in Music Festival at the Eastman School of Music, marking approximately sixty years of remarkable creativity since the awarding of her doctoral degree from that venerable institution. Looking over her impressive catalog, one finds that the majority of vocal works have been for chorus, but in fact, she has also set a substantial number of texts for solo voice. These have included sacred texts drawn from the Psalms, Koran, and Hindu Upanishads, and the secular poetry of a number of English and American authors.

Dorothy Diemer Hendry (1918–2006)

One of Diemer's favorite American poets was her sister, Dorothy Diemer Hendry, who was ten years older and a strong influence in her life. The composer began to set her poetry in 1945 and continued for many decades to a total of twenty-two secular settings and six hymn texts for solo voice and piano. Hendry had a long career as an English teacher, as department chair in the high school of Huntsville, Alabama, and as an active participant in the education field in Alabama and the surrounding states. She also had a stable marriage of sixty-two years to an army colonel engineer named Wickliffe B. Hendry, which produced four children plus a baby son who died in infancy. Diemer describes her sister's personality as loving but forceful—a "steel magnolia type"[24]—whose wisdom and sense of humor informed even her terminal illness of three years duration. Hendry had published a number of her works in poetry journals such as *Columbia Poetry* and the *Alabama Anthology of Poetry*, and iUniverse is now offering a collection of her poetry called *Burnished Pebbles* and a biography of the author's maternal grandmother titled *Looking for Jencey*.

The two Hendry settings, published five years apart (1995 and 2000), present very different poems and an equal contrast in musical style. Both, however, demonstrate the sharp mind and incisive wit that characterized the author's approach to her life and writing. "October Wind (in New York)"[25] was one of four Hendry settings composed by Diemer in 1948 as her earliest group of solo vocal works. The poem is a wry comment on city life, as the writer points out that although "There is an autumn somewhere/I know it by the breeze," she is only able to see "through my small window/A little grimy court." The wind, however, brings her hints of "smoky trees and gorgeous oaks" while bestowing a final gift of a "frosted kiss."

Emma Lou Diemer has said that she sees herself as "a composer most comfortable with free tonality . . . who enjoys creating an indeterminate tonal center." She also views herself as "basically conservative, with periodic forays into the experimental and avant-garde."[26] The musical style of "October Wind" epitomizes this self-profile, as a piano interlude in mm. 10–13 briefly suggests a B-flat tonal center (with chromatic overlay),

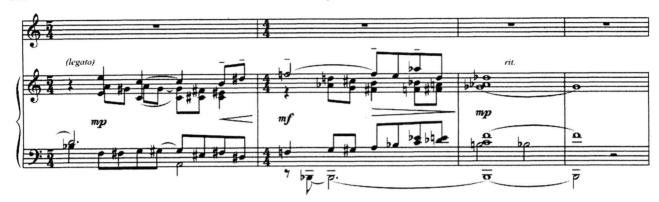

Example 10.19, mm. 10–13

but soon wanders toward B natural and other goals of harmonic motion. The "avant-garde" elements of the setting include polytonality,

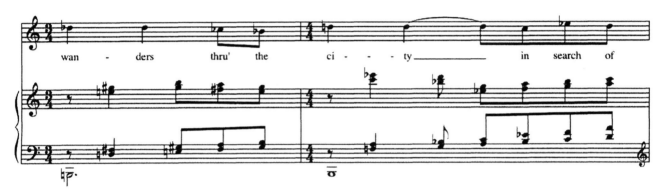

Example 10.20, mm. 18-19

cluster chords, modal melodic fragments,

Example 10.21, mm. 39–43

and quartal harmony.

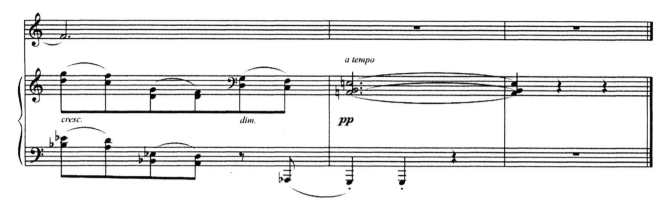

Example 10.22, mm. 59–61

But the "basically conservative" Diemer is evidenced in the overall structure of the song which incorporates considerable repetition of rhythmic, melodic, and harmonic motifs, and ends with a classic example of textual word-painting when the piano provides the "frosted kiss" in the left hand's final notes. (see Ex. 10.22, mm. 59–60). The overall sound-world which the composer has created is perfectly calculated to portray the emotional tone of the poem: sardonic, frustrated, and minimally hopeful.

"The Caller"[27] is so different in every way from "October Wind" that it almost seems a product of a different poet and composer, thereby attesting to the artistic range and versatility of the duo. Diemer finds it "ironic that 'The Caller,' written three years before [Dorothy] was diagnosed with multiple myeloma is a quasi-amusing encounter with Death. I chose to give it a jazzy setting—," she continues, "a thumbing your nose attitude addressing that specter."[28] The poem is actually in the form of a monologue in back-country dialect, which begins with the speaker's welcome to Death's knocking on the door, reminisces about their former encounters, and ends with the two going off together. Now, fifty years after "October Wind," Diemer's language still incorporates shifting tonal centers but there is much less dissonance here and the encounter is propelled to the chilling conclusion of this powerful setting by the insistent jazz rhythm. The piano figurations create much of the atmosphere but the syncopations of the vocal line share it equally.

Example 10.23, mm. 5–8

As the scene draws to its dramatic conclusion, the piano writing becomes more elaborate and the key center, which has gone from D to E-flat and back to D, now moves up to G for a shattering finale.

You ain't much of a prize, but Neith-er am I, Mis-tah
Death! Mis-tah Death!

Example 10.24, mm. 54–59

Dorothy Parker (1893–1967)

Directly following "The Caller" in the 2000 publication of Diemer's *Four Songs* are two settings of Dorothy Parker poems that appeared in *Enough Rope*, her first "blockbuster" collection. These settings, "One Perfect Rose" and "Comment," were originally part of the composer's *Seven Somewhat Silly Songs* that she "intended to fill a need in the repertoire of the singer who [was] looking for light, amusing, entertaining songs."[29] And indeed, after the macabre nature of "The Caller," they tend to take on an air of "comic relief" in theatrical terms. Ironically, Dorothy Parker's life was anything but comic.[30] Her mother died when she was five, and a stepmother several years later, so the young Dorothy felt both abandoned and possibly guilty in the mysterious logic of childhood. Both mothers had been Protestant, but her father, Jacob Henry Rothschild,[31] was of German Jewish descent, leading to Parker's later self-characterization as a "mongrel." Rothschild made a comfortable, upper-middle class living as a factory owner in the garment industry, and seems to have been a loving father. But the writer's later adoption of civil rights issues and increasingly radical left-wing causes may well have stemmed from an uncomfortable early recognition of the "sweatshops" that provided her family's privilege.

Parker attended, but did not graduate from the Blessed Sacrament Academy and Miss Dana's boarding school, and her formal education ended at the age of fourteen, after which her obvious literary talent was cultivated by her own reading. Two brothers and a sister were considerably older so Parker was "at home" with her father until her twentieth year, when Henry Rothschild died of a heart attack. At this point, she set out to reinvent herself in the world of high-end New York periodicals. She eventually wrote for *Vogue* and *Vanity Fair*, was a founding editor of the *New Yorker*, and became a central figure of the Algonquin Round Table, a lunchtime gathering of New York literati in the early 1920s which included Robert Benchley, Alexander Woolcott, and Franklin P. Adams.

In 1917 she had married a Wall Street stockbroker, Edward Pond Parker II, whom she often jokingly claimed to have wed for his name, in light of the anti-Semitism of the era and her minimal connection to her Judaic heritage. (Interestingly, she would be a leading organizer of an anti-Nazi organization in the Hollywood of the thirties.) But the newlyweds were quickly separated by World War I, and the marriage foundered as her career blossomed. Between 1920 and 1935, Dorothy Parker became a well-known writer of book reviews, drama criticism, short stories, and particularly light, satirical verse. The poems collected in volumes called *Enough Rope* (1926), *Sunset Gun* (1928), and *Death and Taxes* (1931) sold widely, as her frequent love affairs and free-wheeling, "speakeasy" dominated lifestyle[32] provided rich material for her sardonic, self-deprecating but always humorous comments.

Dorothy Parker finally divorced Edwin in 1928 and in 1934 married Alan Campbell, an actor who aspired to be a screenwriter. With him, she moved to Hollywood, as together they worked on fifteen films over a period of nearly three decades which included several returns to the East, marital separations and reconciliations, and his sudden death in 1963. Campbell had taken over the handling of all the formerly slipshod details of Parker's life and household, and she flourished during these periods of more ordered living and less alcohol. But the writer's need for affection and attention coupled with a life-long self-hatred caused her to destroy the majority of her most important relationships. In 1967, she died alone in the Volney hotel in New York City and was discovered the next day by a chambermaid.

Money, or sometimes, the lack of it, was always an issue in Dorothy Parker's life. In "One Perfect Rose," she shares with us her disdain for the romantic offerings of her current lover (such as "one perfect rose") with the wry comment that "one perfect Cadillac" would be a lot more welcome. As Emma Lou Diemer points out, this is one of the many Parker poems that have to do with disappointed love affairs. "I chose to set it," says Diemer, "in a restless, rapid repeated chords, changing harmonies, rather lyrical way, because I think behind every witty handling of disappointment is a bit of wistfulness and agitation."[33]

Example 10.25, mm. 3–7

The syncopated accents that pervade the setting (see Ex. 10.25) create the aural atmosphere of the "jazz-age" of the twenties that produced the Dorothy Parker ethos. Diemer captures the "wistfulness" underlying the comedy in the melodic contours of the vocal line, and the "agitation" builds as she alters the repetition of "It's always just my luck to get/One perfect rose" with an exasperated, elongated climax on F natural.

Example 10.26, mm. 77–80

Diemer adds a further masterful touch to the drama by ending with two repeated settings of the phrase "one perfect Limousine" at a diminishing dynamic level. It is as though the storms of disappointment have given way to a meditative conjuring of the heart's desire.

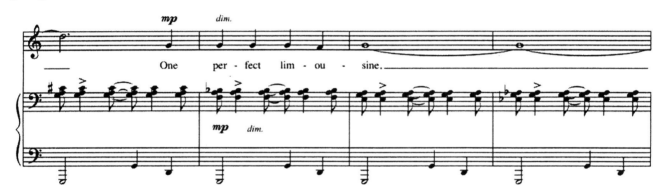

Example 10.27, mm. 83–86

The second Diemer/Parker setting begins with the title's "Comment" to the effect that "Life is a glorious cycle of song." Since we know that Parker's life encompassed two divorces, one abortion, several miscarriages, and a scattering of suicide attempts, we are prepared for the end of the "Comment" to be an ironic reversal of the original position—(i.e., "And I am the Queen of Romania"). Diemer tells us that this poem suggested to her "a diva, pompous and self-important, who 'pokes fun at herself' . . . in a grandiose manner. I used big chords," she explains, "big gestures, and asked for the singer to ham it up at will, even with a bit of swooping up to notes in places."[34]

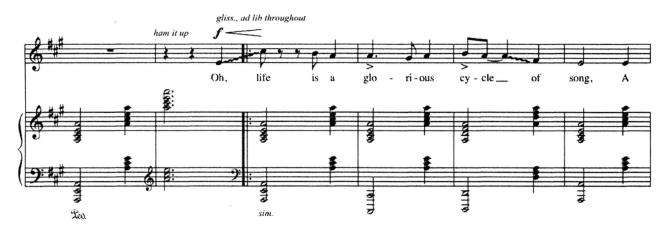

Example 10.28, mm. 3–8

The short, four-line text is repeated three times, with increasing dramatic exaggeration, and the setting of the final punch line provides a choice of a bravura melodic climb to high A or an Anna Russell-like gleeful octave glissando up to the same note.

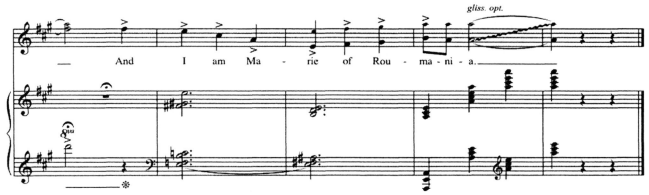

Example 10.29, mm. 35–39

Richard Cumming (b. 1928)

Richard Cumming's early life was centered in the West Coast and the Orient that it faces. Born in Shanghai to American parents, he was brought back to the States to settle in California and graduated in 1945 from George Washington High School in San Francisco. For the next six years he attended the San Francisco Conservatory of Music, spending the summers of 1947 and 1948 at the Music Academy of the West in Santa Barbara and those of 1949 and 1950 at the Griller Quartet Summer School in San Francisco. During these same years he studied the piano with Herbert Jaffe and Lili Kraus, and, as a talent for composition began to emerge, was able to develop it through lessons with three towering figures who were teaching nearby: Roger Sessions, then professor of music at Berkeley; Ernest Bloch who left his Oregon retreat each summer to teach, also at Berkeley; and Arnold Schoenberg who was at that time seeing just a few private students in his Los Angeles home.

From 1951 to 1956, Cumming did a great deal of performing as a concert pianist. There were solo recitals, appearances as soloist with a number of West Coast orchestras, and as chamber player with the Griller and San Francisco Quartets and the Corinthian Piano Quintet. During the early fifties, he spent several summers at Aspen where he continued piano study with Rudolph Firkusny, and in the summer of 1954 served as assistant to the directors of the Aspen Institute (Victor Babin and Richard P. Leach). Through all these formative years, a strong empathy for the vocal repertoire was developing and in 1950 Cumming began a twenty-five year stint as concert accompanist during which he would play for Phyllis Curtin, Donald Gramm,[35] Frank Guerrera, Florence Kopleff, Martial Singher, Jennie Tourel, and many others.

Around 1955, Richard Cumming met Philip Minor, who at that time was spending his summers acting and directing with the Princeton University Players. As Minor puts it, he "got Richard Cumming into the theater,"[36] and from that point on, Cumming turned his talents increasingly to use in musical/dramatic contexts. He, too, joined the Princeton University Players (as composer-in-residence) through the summers of 1957 to 1960, and for the three following years served as an assistant conductor at the Santa Fe Opera in New Mexico. From 1963 to 1967 he alternated winters and summers as composer-in-residence for the Milwaukee Repertory Theatre, and the Marin Shakespeare Festival at San Rafael, California. In 1966 he moved his home and the center of his artistic activities, to Providence, Rhode Island. There he remained composer-in-residence at the Trinity Square Repertory Company for several decades, besides serving as their director of educational services until 1980, when he became the company's literary manager. After taking up residence in Rhode Island, Cumming also taught in the Providence Arts Magnet Program and the Rhode Island Governor's School for Youth in the Arts, and spent several years as both a music and theater consultant to the Rhode Island State Council on the Arts. Currently, he has left Rhode Island and makes his home in Attleboro, Massachusetts.

Richard Cumming's impressive catalog of works includes scores for nearly seventy-five plays, ranging from Euripides and Shakespeare to Brecht and Saroyan. By the 1970s, having had wide experience with the literary demands of the dramatic situation, he became the co-author and adaptor, with Adrian Hall, of a number of dramatic pieces for stage, radio, and film such as *Ethan Frome*, an adaptation of the Edith Wharton novel, and Dicken's *A Christmas Carol*. In 1999, the Trinity Square Repertory Company staged the première of Cumming's first opera, *The Picnic*, with libretto by Henry Butler.

As regards the non-dramatic areas of his composition, it is interesting to note that, outside of a sizable group of piano works,[37] almost all the rest are text-oriented. The large majority of his chamber and orchestral works are for voice plus instruments, and the catalog also shows seventeen choral settings and over seventy songs.[38] Of the seventy, fully half are based on the work of American poets. There are two settings of Robert Frost, two of Muriel Rukeyser, five of Walt Whitman, and a number by less familiar writers some of whom, like Philip Minor, are primarily known for their work in other fields.

Philip Minor (1927–1991)

Philip Minor was born, one year earlier than Richard Cumming, in the town of Butler, Pennsylvania. His parents lived, for the first twenty years of their married life, in various countries of South America, and in Mexico. The longest period in one place was 1935 to 1944 in Buenos Aires, where Minor attended an American school, fulfilling the Argentine government's curriculum while preparing to enter an American college. In 1944, he graduated from high school, came to the States, and attended Princeton University for one year. Minor was then drafted into the United States Army Air Force where he claimed to have spent "thirteen totally unproductive months, but as the first lengthy exposure to life in these United States," he added, "it was quite an eye opener."[39] He then returned to Princeton, and graduated in 1950 with a degree from the Woodrow Wilson School of Public and International Affairs.

At this point occurred one of those complete changes of direction often made by people who are beginning to feel impelled toward an artistic career. This is how Minor describes what happened:

> The next few years were spent in an attempt to carve out some sort of a career as an actor, and eventually, as an actor-director. I lived in Greenwich Village—where else?—and did the usual things: odd jobs to keep body and soul together; small productions hither and yon. I attended the Royal Academy of Dramatic Art in London, 1952–53. On returning, I began to work with the University Players in Princeton, New Jersey, for approximately seven summers, which is where I received whatever real theatrical training I have.[40]

Minor lived in New York after 1951, except for the time spent in London while at the Royal Academy. He worked extensively with the APA-Phoenix Lyceum Theatre and the Sheridan Square Playhouse in New York City, and also traveled around the country to such regional theaters as the Guthrie Theater in Minneapolis, Alley Theater in Houston, and the Trinity Square Repertory Theater in Providence. He continued for many years to both act and direct, but admitted to spending most of his time and energy on the latter. Teaching had been another phase of his career. Besides shorter appointments at New York University, Circle in the Square, and the American Academy of Dramatic Art, his most important academic connection was to Bennington College, which continued, off and on, from 1970 to 1980. Minor died in 1991 at his brother's home in Pennington, New Jersey, at the age of sixty-three.

On the occasion of his meeting with Richard Cumming in 1955, Minor, who said he was "not a musician, but plays the piano,"[41] recalled that the two of them "played four-hand Mozart, Haydn, and von Weber, and listened to a recording of Strauss' *Four Last Songs* with Elizabeth Schwarzkopf."[42] He also disclaimed the title of poet and said he did not write verse very often, but admitted that he never knew when the muse might strike.

Richard Cumming has a different view of Minor's poetic talents, and described the genesis of the song cycle on which they collaborated in these terms:

> Philip Minor has been an old, dear, and valued friend of mine for almost thirty years. In 1959, he made his own translation of Jacinto Benavente's *The Bonds of Interest* that was produced in New York City. Act III of that play closed with a ravishing serenade, the words of which I liked so much I asked him to think of writing me some more poems for concert songs. *Other Loves*[43] resulted. They were written for Helen Vanni and first sung by her in 1974 at the Cleveland Institute of Music.[44]

The première of Cumming's other song cycle, *We Happy Few*,[45] had been presented in 1964 by Donald Gramm who had commissioned the work through the Ford Foundation Program for Concert Soloists. Reviewing it, *Musical America* called Richard Cumming a "notable vocal composer" who, in all the songs, found "interesting things for the voice to do, and things that set the voice off well."[46] Nineteen years later, in his liner notes for the 1983 issuance of Cambridge Records' retrospective Cumming disc (see note 35c), Ned Rorem describes his songs similarly, but more colorfully, as "delectably singable goodies." Rorem further characterizes Cumming as "a survivor, being of that handful of Americans who were writing first-rate tonal songs thirty-five years ago, and who, in their madness, persisted in writing such songs to this day." Finally he recalls his first meeting with Richard Cumming, now a long-time friend, in New York in 1956, and discovering that "we and only a few others (Flanagan, Daniel Pinkham, who else?) were playing the game."

The impressive degree of skill with which Richard Cumming continues to "play the game" is clearly evident in *Other Loves*. "First rate tonal songs" they are, but with a tonality constantly adapting to the needs of the text and the times, and with a buoyant, effortless clarity of texture that is a Cumming trademark. The three free-verse poems that provide the text of this mini-cycle immediately invite musical setting with their titles: "Summer Song," "Night Song," and "Love Song." As it happens, the unity of this set is found mostly in the titles. All, it is true, are "Songs," but of a riveting diversity, with the first a languid portrait of fulfillment, the second a lament for lost love, and the third a rollicking celebration by a "torch carrier"[47] who is about to drop his torch.

Minor's "Summer Song" is haiku-like in feeling, if not in form, with its images of satiated bees, lolling catfish, and branches barely moving in a light breeze. Striving is erased and meaning is implicit in the moment as the poet intones "Now. Now!" Cumming rises to this challenge with a series of choices that effectively annihilate musical drive. His triplet piano figures circle back on themselves, and the "lento e languido" 5/4 meter incorporates long, lazy pauses on beats two, four, and five.

Example 10.30, mm. 3–4

"G" is clearly the tonal center, but it is softened with desultory lowerings of the third and sixth degrees (see Ex. 10.29). More importantly, the seventh scalar degree appears most prominently as F rather than F sharp, thus sacrificing its pull to the tonic.

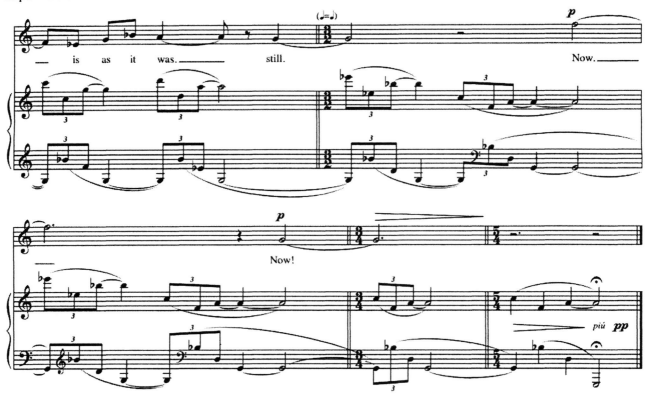

Example 10.31, mm. 19–23

Notice that as the song ends (Ex. 10.31), the measures lengthen from five quarter-note beats to six, and then the triplet figures disappear. It is as though time itself has stopped.

"Night Song" is a poignant farewell to a lover who was so "eager to be gone" that the poet has been left with "unclaimed treasures in [his] weeping hands." It is unclear from the poetry whether it is a rival or death whose hand now "lies softly" on the absent one's throat, but Cumming's "blues" setting seems to opt for the lesser tragedy of the former. Over a recurrent chordal background full of the sixths, sevenths, ninths, and thirteenths of "popular" harmony, the composer sculpts an artfully contoured vocal lament that rises and falls in the familiar framework of two choruses, verse, and chorus.

Example 10.32, mm. 1–5

One may find, in this song, some parallels to Paul Bowles's settings such as "Sugar in the Cane" and "Once a Lady was Here" (see chapter 6). It is worth remembering that Bowles, like Cumming, composed heavily in the areas of musicals and theater scores, both of which have become increasingly strong and vitalizing influences on the American art songs of recent decades (see chapter 8 for a discussion of William Flanagan's participation in this trend).

Cumming and Minor end their trilogy with a nicely contrasting touch of sophisticated humor. "Love Song" proves to be an ironic title, for the poet's heart is longing to be released, "like a rampant kite" that is constantly pulled back by the "candied chains" of his passion. The bright, brassy tone of Broadway is never far from the surface as Cumming writes a jazzy, syncopated introduction, simple but propulsive chordal piano part, and a voice line that borrows the rhythmic emphasis and dramatic leaps of the musical comedy idiom.

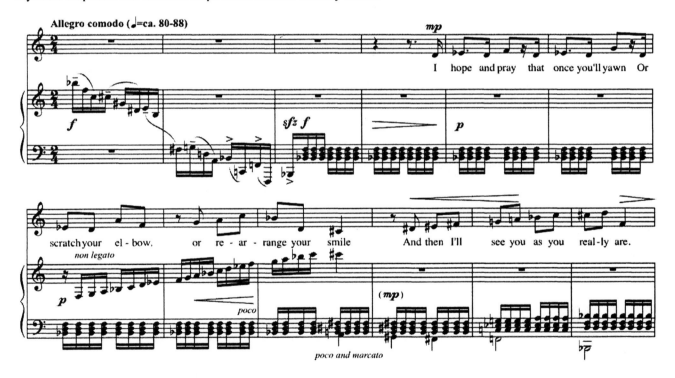

Example 10.33, mm. 1–12

The agitated speed of the "allegro commodo" keeps a steady pace with the lover's desperation. As he begins his vision of freedom, the intensity is increased by a tango-like syncopation in the melodic line that releases into an unmeasured "liberamente" declaration and a final, child-like shout of glee.

Example 10.34, mm. 38–44

Notes

1. Ruth Schonthal, *Four Songs* (San Antonio, Tex.: Southern Music Co., 1995). Medium voice. Ruth Schonthal, *Early Songs* (San Antonio, Tex.: Southern Music Co., 1996). Medium voice.

2. All the foregoing quotations are from an interview in New York City with R. Friedberg, December 1982.

3. Ruth Schonthal, *By the Roadside* (New York: Oxford University Press, 1979). Soprano.

4. See chapter 2, "Charles Ives: Walt Whitman."

5. See chapter 2, Ex. 2.17 of the song "Walt Whitman" by Charles Ives; see also chapter 6, Ex. 6.25 and 6.26 of "I think I could turn . . ." by Sergius Kagen.

6. See chapter 6, Exs 6.19, 6.20, and 6.21 from "The Ship Starting" by Charles Naginski.

7. See chapter 6, Exs. 6.16, 6.17 and 6.18 from "Look down, fair moon" by Charles Naginski.

8. Thomas Crawley, *The Structure of "Leaves of Grass"* (Austin: University of Texas Press, 1970), 219.

9. The majority of the information in the foregoing paragraphs is based on material contained in Colleen Gray Neubert, "Lee Hoiby: His Life, His Vocal Writing Style, and an Annotation of Selected Songs for High Voice with Performance Considerations" (DMA Dissertation, University of West Virginia, 2003).

10. Michael John King, ed., *Collected Early Poems of Ezra Pound,* with Introduction by Louis L. Martz (New York: New Directions Books, 1976).

11. See King, *Collected Early Poems.*

12. Lee Hoiby, *Thirteen Songs for High Voice and Piano* (New York: G. Schirmer, 1990). Contains "An Immorality," "The Lady of the Harbor," and "Where the Music Comes From."

13. Emma Lazarus, *Emma Lazarus: Selected Poems* (New York: Library of America, 2005).

14. Betty Roth Young, *Emma Lazarus in Her World: Life and Letters* (Philadelphia: Jewish Publication Society, 1995).

15. Esther Schor, *Emma Lazarus* (New York: Schocken Books, 2006).

16. Adamic's work is described in John Higham, *Send These to Me: Immigrants in Urban America,* Rev. Ed. (Baltimore: Johns Hopkins University Press, 1984), 77–78.

17. See Hoiby, *Thirteen Songs.*

18. See Hoiby, *Thirteen Songs.*

19. Richard Jackson in *The New Grove Dictionary of Music and Musicians,* edited by Stanley Sadie, (London: Macmillan, 2001).

20. Lee Hoiby, *I Was There* (New York: G. Schirmer, 1993).

21. Edith Boroff and Claire Brook, both talented musicians born in 1925, originally intended to be composers. In the unfavorable climate of the era for women composers, Boroff became a noted musicologist at the University of Michigan and Brook had a distinguished career in music publishing, primarily at W. W. Norton and Co.

22. For a detailed treatment of Emma Lou Diemer's early and middle years and university career see Jane Weiner LePage, *Women Composers, Conductors, and Musicians of the Twentieth Century: Selected Biographies* (Metuchen, N.J.: Scarecrow Press, 1980).

23. For further information on the life and works of Emma Lou Diemer, see Ellen Grolman Schlegel, *Emma Lou Diemer: A Bio-Bibliography* (Santa Barbara, Calif.: Greenwood Press, 2001).

24. Email to R. Friedberg, 26 May 2009.

25. Emma Lou Diemer, *Two Songs* (San Antonio, Tex: Southern Music Co., 1995). Contains "Shall I Compare Thee to a Summer's Day?" and "October Wind (in New York)."

26. Ellen Grolman Schlegel, "Emma Lou Diemer: A Consummate Musician," *International Alliance for Women in Music,* http: //www.iawm.org/articles_html/ schlegel_diemer.html (24 July 2011).

27. Emma Lou Diemer, *Four Songs* (San Antonio, Tex: Southern Music Co., 2000). Contains "Strings in the Earth and Air," "The Caller," "One Perfect Rose," and "Comment."

28. Email to R. Friedberg, 26 May 2009.

29. Introduction by the composer to *Four Songs* (see n27).

30. For details beyond the following synopsis of Dorothy Parker's life, see Marion Meade, *What Fresh Hell Is This?* (New York: Villard Books, 1988).

31. Not a member of the famous, wealthy Rothschild family.

32. "Speakeasies" were clandestine bars selling contraband liquor, proliferated during Prohibition (1920–1933).

33. Email to R. Friedberg, May 2009.

34. Email to R. Friedberg, May 2009.

35. Richard Cumming appears as pianist accompanying Donald Gramm on the following recordings: (a) *Recital by Donald Gramm,* Music Library Recordings, MLR 7033; (b) *And If the Song Be Worth a Smile—Songs by American Composers*, 2009, Desto DS 6411B; (c) *Cycles and Songs by Richard Cumming,* Cambridge Records CRS 2778.

36. Telephone interview with R. Friedberg, 15 June 1985.

37. Cumming's *Piano Sonata* was published by J. & W. Chester in 1953 and recorded by the composer on Music Library Recordings, MLR 7053. His *Twenty-Four Preludes* were published in 1971 by Boosey & Hawkes and recorded by John Browning on Desto, DC 7120.

38. The major recordings of his songs are the discs listed in n35c, and John Hanks and Ruth Friedberg, *Art Song in America,* 1997, Duke University Press that contains "Go, Lovely Rose," "Memory, Hither Come," and "The Little Black Boy."

39. Letter to R. Friedberg, 25 June 1985.

40. Letter to R. Friedberg, 25 June 1985.

41. Telephone interview with R. Friedberg, 15 June 1985.

42. Letter to R. Friedberg, 25 June 1985.

43. Richard Cumming, *Other Loves* (New York: Galaxy Music Corp., 1982). High voice. The work is included in John Belisle, ed., *Contemporary American Songs for High Voice and Piano.* Vol. 1, *American Artsong Anthology* (New York: Galaxy, 1982) .

44. Letter to R. Friedberg, 9 September 1984.

45. *We Happy Few,* that appears on the recording *Cycles and Songs* (see n35c), is a cycle of ten songs based on mostly British poetry, the majority of which relates to war. American poets are represented by two of the settings: Walt Whitman's "A Sight in Camp" and Archibald MacLeish's "The End of the World."

46. "Reviews," *Musical America* 54 (February 1964): 34–35.

47. The authors are using the term "carry a torch" in the colloquial sense of trying to hang on to a failed or failing love affair.

Chapter 11

The Fourth and Fifth Decades

Richard Hundley (b. 1933)

Richard Hundley's early life straddled the states of Ohio and Kentucky. He was born in Cincinnati, into what the composer describes as a "very emotional, Protestant-revival-type"[1] family. Two weeks after his birth, the Hundleys moved to Kentucky, and it was here that young Richard learned the fundamentals of music from a Hungarian teacher, and began piano study with a Mrs. Wyman whose fee was a dollar an hour. The composer recalls performing at a ladies' tea party, and being unable to finish the piece through lack of self-discipline in his preparation. "I started writing my own pieces," says Hundley, "so I'd be able to finish!"[2]

When he was eleven years old, Hundley began commuting from his home in Kentucky to the Cincinnati College Conservatory. Here he came under the imposed discipline of a teacher who dismissed him from lessons when assignments were not completed. By the age of fourteen he was able to perform a Mozart piano concerto with the Northern Kentucky Symphony Orchestra, and at sixteen, he soloed with the Cincinnati Symphony under Thor Johnson's conducting.

In 1952 came his first visit to New York, a city which he quickly came to love because there he "could be free and not have to conform." For most of the fifties, he traveled back and forth between New York and the Cincinnati Conservatory. Finally, at the death of his grandmother, Hundley severed his last emotional tie to the Midwest and, with fifty dollars in his pocket, took up residence in Manhattan.

While growing up in Kentucky, Hundley's musical gods had been Stravinsky, Beethoven, and Wagner, but a chance hearing of Samuel Barber's "Knoxville, Summer of 1915" had effected a radical change that steered him toward the voice as a medium of expression. By the time he settled in New York, he had already begun to compose songs, and to center the rest of his musical activities on singers as a vocal coach and accompanist. Hundley, himself, possesses a very pleasant singing voice, and after performing with various choral groups, he took and passed an audition in 1960 for the Metropolitan Opera Chorus. To prepare for the position he "went to school to learn ten operas in four languages," and in retrospect, Hundley feels that his concept of writing vocal music is strongly related to the bel canto influence from his four years with the Met chorus.

During this period, Hundley wrote music in the summertime and studied counterpoint with Israel Citkowitz and harmony with William Flanagan, both of whom were strongly oriented toward vocal composition. He also began to show his music to some of the leading Metropolitan singers, and soon Annaliese Rothenberger was singing his "Softly the Summer" (see below) all over the country. Anna Moffo, too, was taken with the songs that Hundley played for her while she was changing in her dressing room. When she started to program them on recitals, the composer felt that "[he] was made."

For the next twenty years, however, Hundley's reputation was to achieve a steady, but frustratingly slow growth. One notable event in this growth was an Overseas Press Club concert in 1966 at which the tenor Paul Sperry, who is a well-known specialist in American song repertoire, was so favorably impressed by two of the composer's works that he has been singing and promoting Hundley's songs ever since. By the early seventies, the songs were also appearing in concerts by members of the Metropolitan Opera Studio[3] and by many stars of the opera such as Judith Blegen, Rosalind Elias, and Giorgio Tozzi.

It was not until the decade of the eighties, however, that the recognition that had taken him thirty years to achieve seemed finally to be descending on Richard Hundley. Frederica von Stade performed his "The Astronomers" on a 1982 CBS recording (Digital 37231); his *Eight Songs* were selected for inclusion in the repertoire for the 1982 International American Music Competition for vocalists; and his work was featured at the Newport Music Festivals of 1983 and 1984 (at the latter, he was the festival's first composer-in-residence). In August 1983, the *Eight Songs*, originally published two years earlier, had gone into their third printing, and were finding their way, along with other Hundley songs, onto recital programs throughout the United States. Not content, however, to rest on his laurels, Hundley published two more stunning song collections around 1990: *Ten Songs for High Voice*, commissioned by Joy in Singing, and a cycle called *Octaves and Sweet Sounds* which had also been a commissioned work, this one by Art Song Minnesota.

A small amount of support for his creative activity had come to Hundley through the years in the form of scattered ASCAP and "Meet-the-Composer" awards as well as three summer fellowships at the MacDowell colony in New Hampshire (see chapter 4). Nevertheless, Hundley has paid a price for being what he terms a "maverick" and for forging an "independent career outside of academia and [the] grants" that are available to those pursuing conventional teaching careers and writing in the large forms acceptable to the musical establishment. Hundley continues to live very modestly in the apartment at West Street and Bethune where R. Friedberg interviewed him. It is an artists' low rent housing project, located one block from the East River. Here, a huge yellow-brick building whose entrance is guarded by security policemen, has been cut up into large, loft-like spaces, which the residents divide into sleeping, working, and eating areas.

The piano was not a grand, but Hundley made it sound like one as he played his songs and sang them in a pure, lyric tenor voice. He was anxious to communicate his feelings about the texts he sets and how he sets them, and the warmth of his personality was striking. "What I am interested in," said Hundley, "is the crystallization of emotion. I memorize a text and live with it, then set it according to how I feel about the poem. I have to tell the listener what it's about when the pianist starts—like a short story."

Hundley went on to say that what he looks for in a poem is "something [he] can identify with" and that he "finds much contemporary poetry unsuitable for setting because it is alien to nature." He reads a great deal of poetry, recites it at the drop of a hat, and knows "by heart" every text he has ever set. He mentioned James Purdy, who is a close friend, as one of his favorite poets, and pointed out that Dorothy Parker had thought him the wittiest writer in America.

Questioned about influences on his compositions, he listed Barber as the first, and continued "Harris, Copland, and the young David Diamond were the reasons I went into serious music. Virgil Thomson's wit was also an influence, and his use of simple chords for interesting effects. William Flanagan, of course—his music had a kind of pre-Sondheim 'gorgeousness' about it," and sadly added, "no one knows exactly how he died."

Richard Hundley's list of compositions includes, besides the many songs, some choral works, a piano sonata, some chamber music for winds, and a few songs with orchestra. Hundley believes that the uniquely American musical theater has had a strong influence on the country's art song, and he also feels that "the academic serial school that dominated American music in the 1960s simply lost its audience."[4] This means, therefore, that with "the subsequent resurgence of romantic feeling, tonal harmony, and melody, conservative composers like himself are the new 'avant garde.'"[5]

There is, however, a caveat about Hundley's conservatism, for, as he explains, he "uses conventional harmonic and melodic material but rethinks it so that it comes across freshly in the contemporary spirit." A more apt description could hardly be made of "Softly the Summer,"[6] one of the earliest, and still one of the composer's most successful songs, which Hundley wrote to his own text. It had been begun in the unsettled year of 1954, was completed on moving to New York City in 1957, and finally published in 1963. Around 1956, Hundley had showed it to "an academic" who called it a popular song. Conversely, "the popular folks said it was too serious" for their categories. Once discovered by Rothenberger, discussed earlier, however it has been sung with enjoyment by many sopranos who simply and correctly saw it as an art song with an unusual flavor.

The poem describes the moment when the "lovely green" of summer begins to fade into darkness, and the key to the composer's "crystallized emotion" in this setting is in the first line: "Softly the summer lies down in sleep." Hundley wanted a gentle, hushed atmosphere to prevail from the first word, and so he "wrote 'softly' on the high A flat so that singers couldn't sock it."

Example 11.1, mm. 4–9

In the fourth stanza of the modified strophic form, the soft, sustained A-flats extend to B flats in an exquisitely shaped contour that sets "High in the heav'ns" with a shimmering quality appropriate to the verbal description of silver light. It need hardly be pointed out that the tessitura and expressive demands of the vocal line are not only totally foreign to the realm of "popular" music, but require the artistry of a highly trained singer.

The song, indeed, is a brilliantly conceived wedding of sophisticated art song procedure to musical theater elements such as the simple, recurring waltz bass patterns of the left hand, and the encouraged freedom in performance of all the colla voce sections (see Ex. 11.1). As in all Hundley settings, the vocal writing is extremely grateful, the texture is classically transparent, and the piano writing extremely idiomatic as the right hand weaves its graceful filaments of sound around the sleeping figure of personified Summer.

Kenneth Patchen (1911–1972)

Life as a dedicated artist would have seemed a most unlikely result from Kenneth Patchen's origins. He, too, was born in Ohio but not into the metropolitan environment of Hundley's Cincinnati. Patchen's birthplace was Niles, a town that typified the mining and industrial atmosphere of the Mahoning Valley. Descended from English, Scotch, Irish, and French forbears, Patchen had one grandfather who had worked in the coal mines and another as a farmer-blacksmith. His father was a "roller" in the steel mills of the area for over twenty-five years, and Patchen never lost his youthful memories of grimy houses and the daily struggles of the workers against weariness, fear, and boredom.

In his early childhood, Patchen moved with his family to nearby Warren where he, a brother, and two sisters attended school. His mother, a devout Catholic, raised the children in her faith and cherished the hope that Kenneth would become a priest. Instead, he became a poet, whose lifework was infused with the priestly qualities of compassion and visionary hopes for mankind. He began to write in his twelfth year, at fourteen had two sonnets published in the *New York Times*, and became a frequent contributor to school publications until his graduation from Harding High School.

In order to pay for a college education, Patchen had worked alongside his father and brother in the steel mills for two summers. Entering the University of Wisconsin in 1929, he was accepted, after a battery of tests, into Alexander Meiklejohn's experimental college, the aim of which was to educate by focusing on a single great period of cultural history. The subject for Patchen's class was Athens in the fifth century B.C., "an exposure to a civilization that Patchen never forgot and which influenced his work decisively in terms of social viewpoints."[7]

During his year at Wisconsin, Patchen continued to play football, an activity begun in high school partially to promote his acceptance in a milieu that took a dim view of writers. Nevertheless, the break with home and family was complete after 1929. He transferred for one semester to Commonwealth College in Mena, Arkansas, into another experimental program, run by Meiklejohn's son; then turned to the self-education often preferred by artists, for a four-year period of writing, working at odd jobs, and wandering across the United States and Canada.

Patchen, like his father before him, was a powerfully built man with a passionate ideological commitment to pacifism. The strain was no doubt inherited from a family ancestor, Sir Aaron Drake—a British general who had deserted during the Revolutionary War to marry a Pennsylvania farm girl. When Patchen's wanderings found him in Boston on Christmas Eve of 1933, Destiny arranged his meeting with Miriam Oikemus, an attractive University of Massachusetts coed who had been involved that year as an anti-war organizer at Smith College. "We met at a party," she later remembered. "He was very rude and unsociable. He looked . . . sad and thin . . . and I was very impressed with him. Five months later we were married."[8]

Thus began a marriage that was to prove the poet's chief sustenance through a lifetime of prolific writing and almost constant pain. The pain resulted from a series of back injuries and operations that began in 1936, and left him crippled and bedridden from 1959 until his death thirteen years later. The Patchens began their married life in Greenwich Village, and lived in and around it from 1934 to 1950 except for two periods of travel. The first of these was to Santa Fe in 1936, a trip made possible by the Guggenheim fellowship awarded after the publication of *Before the Brave*, Patchen's first book of poetry. The second was a short time spent in Hollywood in 1937, where the lure of quick money to be earned in film writing could not allay the couple's unease in the "sordid small town with the psychology of a big city."[9]

Returned to the East, Patchen was an important presence in the avant-garde Village environment, which included e.e. cummings, Henry Miller, William Carlos Williams, and Stephen Vincent Benét. In 1950 Patchen left for the West Coast, moved into the north bay area of San Francisco, and soon formed ties to Kenneth Rexroth, Lawrence Ferlinghetti, and the West Coast literary movements. His defiance of academia and his anti-war, anti-materialist philosophy made him an immediate and important influence in "Beat" circles, but he fought to maintain his unique artistic identity since the nihilism of the "Beat" credo was totally foreign to him.

In 1956, the Patchens moved to the house in Palo Alto that would be the last home they shared. The next year, Patchen began his pioneer work in the Poetry-and-Jazz movement. For three years, before the final disabling injury, he toured the United States and Canada reading his poetry to the music of such jazz players as Charlie Mingus, the Alan Neil quartet, and the Chamber Jazz Sextet. Incredibly, the stream of writing never stopped. Between 1936 and the heart attack which killed him in 1972, Patchen produced an average of a book a year, in the genres of poetry, poetry-prose, concrete-poetry, "anti-novels," and "picture-poems," most of which he created as radically new forms.

Two of these genres came into being because Patchen, like his friend e.e. cummings, was strongly gifted in visual as well as verbal art forms. Concrete poetry was based on reduced elements of language, with an emphasis on arrangement and appearance on the page of the selected elements. The "picture-poems" and "painted-books" which he increasingly fashioned in his isolating disability, took on sufficient stature to merit a one-man show of Patchen graphics, held at the Corcoran Art Gallery (Washington, D.C.) in 1969.

With the passage of time, Kenneth Patchen, who had started out as a proletarian poet in protest against society and its ills, enlarged his focus to perceive a vision of individual growth and universal love. Love had indeed been one of the most powerfully sustaining forces in his life of physical torment. He had dedicated all his books "For Miriam" and had written a group of poems to her, through the years, that are perhaps his best-known work, and which have appealed to a number of composers as texts for setting.[10]

One poem of Richard Hundley's choice, "O Sleeping Falls the Maiden Snow," had first appeared in *Pictures of Life and Death* (1946), and was reprinted in the little volume called *The Love Poems* which City Lights Books of San Francisco published twenty years later. It is a short, free verse poem of three three-line stanzas whose deep feeling is heightened by the tightness of structure deriving from the preponderance of four-stress lines and the repetition of the opening one. Within this confining but enabling form, Patchen's characteristic perceptions unfold: the sharp visual image of the cold, clean snow on the "bitter roofs of the world"; the hostile world's menace in the "rush of dark wings"; and the impassioned commitment to protect the love who lay "safe in [his] arms."

The setting of this poem,[11] that Hundley dedicated to Anna Moffo, is dated December 27, 1960, and shows the composer's early mastery of serious, dramatic writing. Now titled "Maiden Snow," it is far removed from his light, sophisticated vein, and combines the expressive intensity of a short Puccini aria with the subtle interweaving of voice and piano that is characteristic of art song. The vocal line has many arioso-like repeated notes but the tension thus created always breaks out into a lyrically curving contour:

Example 11.2, mm. 1–7

The piano, which begins with the unobtrusive chordal support of a recitative, grows to full partnership in m. 6 (see Ex. 11.2) with an inspired rhythmic suspension in the right hand serving to delay the instrumental motivic thrust.

Strong dissonance is used sparingly but effectively as major and minor seconds fall with anguished force at the beginning of mm. 14 and 15.

Example 11.3, mm. 14–17

The setting of the final phrase uses musical device most skillfully to create two levels of meaning. The vocal line resolves to "safety" in a C minor/major context, reiterated by the uppermost chords of the piano postlude, while the rest of the accompaniment holds to the stolid G minor of the outside world's continuing threat.

Example 11.4, mm. 24–29

A more recent Hundley/Patchen setting, "O, My Darling Troubles Heaven with Her Loveliness," is one of the *Ten Songs for High Voice* published in 1988.[12] It uses a poem included by the writer in his 1943 collection, *Cloth of the Tempest*, one of Patchen's "painted-books" discussed earlier, and was also selected as one of the *Love Poems* of 1966. Unlike the underlying menace of "Maiden Snow," this poem is a rapturous tribute to the beauty of the poet's beloved and of their relationship. Hundley, in his Notes to the *Ten Songs*, calls it a "passionate love song" and tells the performers that, "its expressive content requires some rubato and a wide range of dynamics and colors."

In truth, the composer has largely written in his desired range of dynamic and colors and he creates an effective ebb and flow of emotion with frequently changing time signatures and tempo markings.

Example 11.5, mm. 5–9

The musical movement increases to "agitato" as the poet writes, "at night we step into other worlds" but soon pulls back to a forte broadening for the poem's climactic phrase ("O she touches me with the tips of wonder").

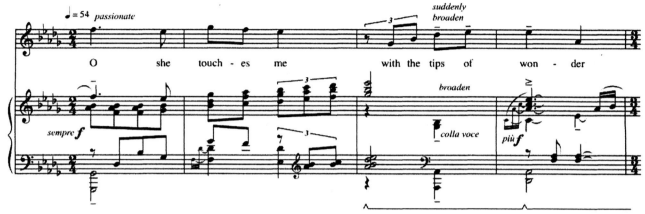

Example 11.6, mm. 24–27

The entire setting is one of Hundley's most gorgeous lyrical outpourings, and he follows Patchen's lead in ending it "calmly" and "languidly" as the lovers rest from their passion and the "angels cuddle like sleepy kittens."

Example 11.7, mm. 29–32

James Purdy (b. 1923)

James Purdy is also a fellow Ohioan of Richard Hundley's, having been born ten years before the composer near the town of Fremont. He was educated at the University of Chicago in 1941 and 1946, and also spent some time studying at the University of Puebla in Mexico. Purdy worked as an interpreter in Latin America, France, and Spain, and taught at Lawrence College in Appleton, Wisconsin, from 1949 to 1953. Since that time he has devoted himself to full-time writing, except for a Visiting Professorship held in 1977 at the University of Tulsa, Oklahoma.

Purdy has been the recipient of a number of major awards: a National Institute of Arts and Letters grant in 1958; Guggenheim fellowships in 1958 and 1962; and a Ford Fellowship for drama in 1961. His novel, *On Glory's Course*, was nominated for the William Faulkner Pen Award, and in 1993 he received the Morton Dauwen Zabel Fiction Award from the American Academy of Arts and Letters. Now, as a result of several reissues of previously out-of-print novels and a critical appreciation by Gore Vidal in the *New York Times Book Review*, Purdy's work is enjoying a twenty-first century renaissance.

His works have included short stories, novels, plays, and poetry, and he is widely considered to be a master of the short story genre. The writer lived at the same Henry Street address in Brooklyn for many years and was an integral part of the literary and musical scene that Ned Rorem chronicled in his *Diaries* (see chapter 9). A sense of this can be gleaned from two items of the Rorem-Purdy correspondence dating from the middle sixties. In 1965 Rorem writes, "Edward A. tells me he's deep in work on *Malcolm*. No doubt, if the production ultimately requires music, this will be allotted to Bill Flanagan, since he's Albee's official composer. But it goes without saying that I'd also love to do it if *you* want me!"[13]

The reader will recall (see chapter 8) that Bill Flanagan did write the music for this ultimately ill-fated production. Two years later, Rorem wrote again to congratulate Purdy on the publication of a new novel:

> Yesterday, in 2 fell swoops, I finished *Eustace Chisolm and the Works* and was overwhelmed. And though I'm a fan of almost everything you've written, this novel I like even better (if possible) than *Cabot Wright Begins*. . . . Everything pleased me: the horror and pity of love, the revival of my own adolescent Chicago years . . . the "importance of your theme"—as reviewers say—and above all: your musical ear. It's the best so-called fiction I've read in an age. . . . Thanks for reviving what in me is ever rarer: excitement.[14]

The keen aural awareness that Rorem characterizes as Purdy's "musical ear" comes through in the writer's own comments on his artistic goals. "As I see it," he says, "my work is an exploration of the American soul conveyed in a style based on the rhythms and accents of American speech."[15] The result of his exploration has been, in the prose works, primarily a dark vision, of a commercial culture in which "anything is sacred which brings in money"[16] and where "love . . . seems to be a sickness rather than a satisfaction."[17] Early in his career, Purdy had difficulty getting his writing published, and interpreted this, perhaps correctly, as a rejection by the literary establishment of his unconventional point of view. After Dame Edith Sitwell arranged British publication, however, his work rapidly gained recognition. Today he is regarded as a writer of extraordinary imagination who was able to mix realism, fairy-tale, and allegory in a unique combination of surrealism and a "meticulously rhetoric-free prose."[18]

Purdy's poetry, which shows many of these same qualities, was initially published together with short stories in collections titled *An Oyster Is a Wealthy Beast* (1967), *Mr. Evening* (1968), and *On the Rebound* (1970). In 1971 and 1973, two volumes of only poetry appeared, respectively called *The Running Sun* and *Sunshine Is an Only Child*. Reading the poetry, one senses that Purdy has lightened the weight of his satire to suit the compressed poetic form, and indeed, the titles themselves of the two verse collections are steeped in sunshine and the suggestion of increasing cheer.

In a December 1967, letter, Hundley begins to speak to Purdy of the settings he is making of his friend's poetry. Marcia Balwin, a singer from the Metropolitan, has come to his apartment and he has played "Sea Foams" (to a Purdy text) for her, plus sketches for other songs. She is anxious to have a cycle, and Hundley projects "the work will be a much welcomed addition to the nearly non-existent repertoire of humor in 'serious' music."[19] Curiously, the cycle was not to be performed for another fifteen years, but was finally premièred in 1982 in Alice Tully Hall, New York, under commission from Clarion Concerts for its twenty-fifth birthday celebration. It had by then become *The Sea Is Swimming Tonight*, a work scored for chorus, soloists, and four-hand piano.

In the summer of 1969, we can see from Hundley's correspondence that he is beginning the process that would lead to the Purdy settings for solo voice to be eventually published in the 1981 *Eight Songs*[20] collection. On August 3rd he writes to Purdy: "I read the poems in the *Mr. Evening* book by Black Sparrow Press and liked them again. . . . 'Come Ready and See Me, no matter how late' is real Purdy."[21] On the sixth of August he begins a directed study of their possibilities: "I'm working on the Purdy poems—grouping them according to subject and character. . . . If there is poetry of such extraordinary imagination being written today, I have never heard or seen it."[22] And on August 12, he prepares to share his enthusiasm with friends: "The poems are always a delight. Anne Cooper Dobbins and a pupil of mine, Cynthia Fleming, an educational editor, are coming here this evening and we will read you—and 'feel out' the poetry."[23]

The first composed of the four Purdy settings that constitute half of the *Eight Songs* was "Come Ready and See Me." Hundley finished it in January 1971, a year and a half after he had praised the poem extravagantly in the letters quoted earlier. In a flyer put out by the publisher, Boosey & Hawkes, in 1982, Hundley declared "My chief source of inspiration in these songs are the words themselves and I have tried to recreate in the music the emotion I experienced on first reading the poems. . . . 'Come Ready and See Me' concerns the poignancy of lost love."

A poignant poem it is, with its urgent plea to "come before the years run out," and its longing is in no way lessened by allusions to the contemporary scene such as "you must haste on foot or by sky." The ten-line poem is an unusual form, with lines three, five, and ten ending in the word "out," six and eight in "sky" and seven and nine in "forever." The lines are all short, and varyingly include two, three, or four stresses each. The particular combination of repetition and randomness gives the poem itself the feel of a song lyric, as does its verbal parodying of Tin Pan Alley.

Hundley's musical choices for this have the "inevitable" feel of skillful text setting. To underline the universality of the poetic message, he writes a spare, guitar-like accompaniment, and a simple 4/4 meter, which the textual rhythm is stretched to accommodate by means of tied-over half notes.

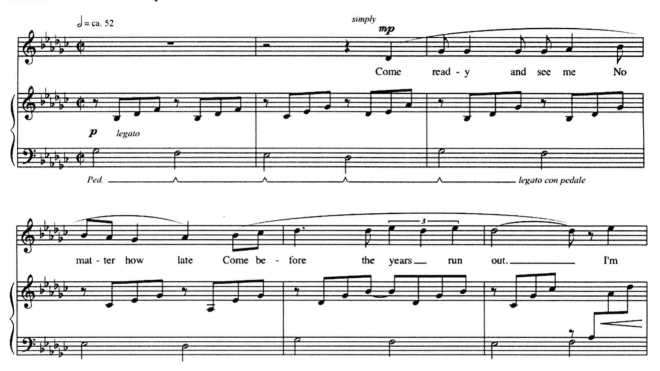

Example 11.8, mm. 1–6

Over this seeming simplicity are layered a broadly contoured vocal line of an octave and a half in compass, subtle use of lowered fourth and seventh steps in a basically diatonic context to emphasize "forever," and a masterful employment of formal repetition for dramatic purposes. The latter occurs when, after a piano "break" that restates the opening vocal material, Hundley brings the voice back, in popular ballad style, to repeat the entire chorus at a higher dynamic level, with quasi-hypnotic fervor. The modern-day incantation falls over into a coda that winds up from an elongated 3/2 measure, then continues to unfold after the voice ceases with a softly syncopated piano part. The final instrumental sound is a wistful, jazz-formula suspension signifying that the song, like the poet's years, has "run out."

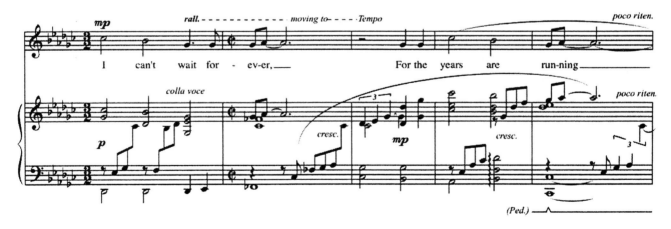

Example 11.9, mm. 43–53

"Birds, U.S.A.," like "Come Ready and See Me," was published in Purdy's *Mr. Evening* collection of 1968. Birds seem to be a frequently reappearing theme in Purdy's prose. They are mentioned in the short story "Home by Dark," while the novel *I am Elijah Thrush* (1972) is, as Tony Tanner puts it, "full of birds"[24] and their symbolic reference to the pure innocence lost by verbalizing humans. This five-line poem is given a humorous cast by its longish listing of the "principal birds of the U.S.A." which takes place in a jazzy, heavily accented anapestic tetrameter. Even the disillusion of the penultimate line ("Aren't the songsters that delighted you at seven") doesn't seem to stop its rush of headlong gaiety.

Hundley creates a musical satire from this text by means of two principal devices. One is the heavy use of syncopation in the vocal line over a "four square" chordal accompaniment that recalls popular America's ragtime roots.

Example 11.10, mm. 5–7

In the other, as Hundley himself tells us, he "paraphrases certain patriotic songs." Although the references are subtle, a perceptive listener can detect the outlines of "O, Say Can You See" in measures one and two,

Example 11.11, mm. 1–4

and "the home of the brave" in mm. 28–29 (just before the song's end).

Example 11.12, mm. 26–30

The "paraphrasing" piano carries out its task through the body of the song as well, and in mm. 11–12 takes off on "My country, 'tis of thee" while the voice sustains a joyful crescendo on F.

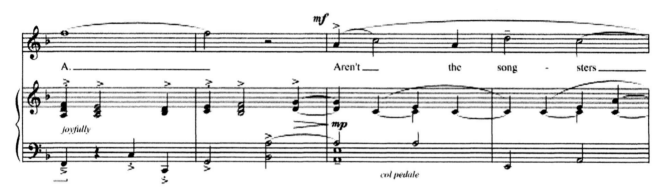

Example 11.13, mm. 11–14

"Birds, U.S.A." had been set by Hundley in 1972. "I do," which was completed in August 1974, is based on a poem from *The Running Sun*. Its four verses of a short four lines each present an interesting mixture of a conventional metric and rhyme scheme with an e.e. cummings style rejection of capitalization. Hundley calls it "a vocal valentine," reading the poet's proposal as a straightforward offer of delightful gifts in return for a promise to wed. This requires ignoring the tongue-in-cheek flavor of "This offer comes once in a lifetime or two" and of "pin on your wings (i.e., join the married establishment) and say 'I do.'" Be that as it may, the song "works" as a vocal valentine and Hundley seems to be tying it stylistically to both its predecessors by means of the running eighth note introduction and "tag" which recall "Come Ready and See Me" and the syncopated vocal line and chordal accompaniment which are a slowed-down, less accented, gentler version of those elements in "Birds, U.S.A."

Example 11.14, mm. 1–7

For the last of this group of Purdy settings, which he completed in November 1978, Hundley used a text from Purdy's 1967 volume, *An Oyster Is a Wealthy Beast*. In his conversation with R. Friedberg in 1982, Hundley had called this setting a "Hallowe'en or All Souls' Day piece," and in the Boosey & Hawkes brochure he mentions that he had "tried to capture the zany quality of [the] poem." The poem's title is "Bartholomew Green" and it consists of four rhymed couplets which center on four different, evocatively named personages: Bartholomew Green, Corliss Hart, Amelia Swan, and Isadore Gray. Following the composer's suggestion of a Hallowe'en piece, one is able to put together their minimal treatments into a ball scene in which the ladies flourish while the men, like the lusterless Green, are "seldom seen."

The "zany quality" Hundley sought has indeed been captured in this inspired setting which begins in the rapid, scurrying 5/4 rhythm of Bartholomew's diffidence.

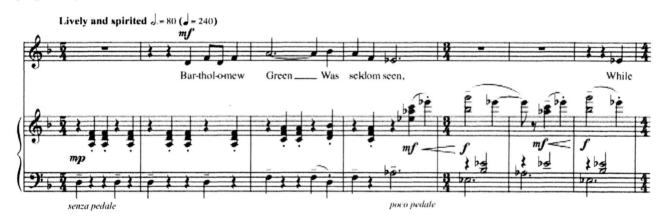

Example 11.15, mm. 1–7

An emphatic waltz rhythm takes over (see Ex. 11.15) as Corliss and Amelia enter, and continues until Isadore Gray's "fading away" which uses a transitional 3/2 meter on the way back to Green's awkwardly characteristic 5/4.

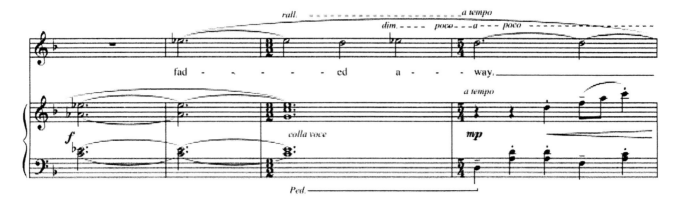

Example 11.16, mm. 28–31

Hundley chooses to repeat "faded away" for pictorial purposes and those of musical transition. He now creates a coda on three reiterations of "Bartholomew Green," with a soft, misterioso indication on the final one that supports the intriguing enigma of Purdy's rarely visible protagonist.

Example 11.17, mm. 38–41

In the *Ten Songs* of 1988, Richard Hundley included two more James Purdy[25] settings. The first one, "Waterbird," is from *An Oyster Is a Wealthy Beast* and reminds us of Purdy's ongoing preoccupation with the avian world. "Waterbird" was originally a choral movement in Hundley's cantata *The Sea Is Swimming Tonight* to texts by James Purdy, (discussed earlier) and tenor Paul Sperry had requested a setting of it for solo voice. Hundley turned the charming eight-line poem into an effective solo setting by varying text repetitions dynamically and by writing increasingly complex pianistic figurations that suggest the bird's watery "kingdom" under the sea.

Example 11.18a, mm. 13–17

Example 11.18b, mm. 46–49

The piano arabesques also hint of the "places remote" of the poet's longing, while the repeated melodic lines create the hypnotic effect called for by "sleepers like me." Hundley ends with a postlude on a partial poetic line that has the keyboard "gently float[ing]" to conclusion.

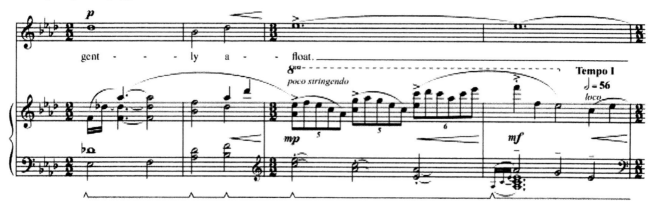

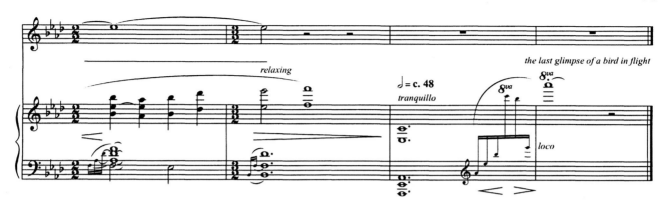

Example 11.19, mm. 71–78

"Lions," the other Purdy setting in *Ten Songs*, is a perfect example of the writer's tendency to employ fantasy and satire in his poetry. Hundley tells us[26] that "Henri Rousseau's painting 'Jungle with a Lion' in the Museum of Modern Art was his creative nourishment" while writing this song. The two verses of the poem state that trees and leaves "are choicer and much more fair" than lions and pale hares and that the animals should therefore be abandoned in favor of the vegetation. Hundley turns his setting into a humorous torrent of protest from the lions, which begins with a "roaring" tremolo and jungle drums in the piano introduction.

Example 11.20, mm. 1–4

By adding a repetition of the "lions and hares" lines at the end of the song, Hundley creates an ABA form in which the outer sections, in E-flat minor, carry the thumping menace of the king of beasts, while the word "lion" always presents the insistent rhythm of an accented eighth note tied to two and a half beats.

Example 11.21, mm. 15–17

The middle section portrays the "trees and the leaves" with a peacefully flowing treatment using F natural as its key center. Then the "lions" return in a furious cacophony of quasi-operatic ornaments in a rising tessitura.

Example 11.22, mm. 68–73

With seven accented reiterations of "lions" and a final tremolo roar, the setting leaves no musical doubt that the king of beasts has triumphed over the poet's deprecation.

Hundley's collection called *Octaves and Sweet Sounds*[27] was commissioned in 1989 and it was premièred a year later by Glenda Maurice and pianist Ruth Palmer. The fourth song of the cycle sets James Purdy's "Straightway Beauty on Me Waits" from *The Running Sun*, which was also the literary source of "Lions" and "I do." This poem begins with an evocative portrayal of the poet's response to the beauties of the natural world ("rain . . . sunshine. . . wind . . . snow," etc.) and ends with the reluctant acknowledgment that the beauty of love is as undependable as nature, since it either "waxes great or dies like the flower." Richard Hundley chooses to concentrate on the "waxing" phase as he composes a "love song whose music is as rapturous as its subject."[28]

In this setting, Hundley has indeed "pulled out all the stops," as it were, and combined hints of harmonic Broadway, the melodic flow of Italian opera, and exquisite structural details in one of the most affecting love songs in the late twentieth century literature. The lush lyricism of the vocal line is presented in the opening bars (see Ex. 11.23) and will recur at the end up a half-step and with a blossoming fioratura on "morning." Piano interludes contribute new melodic motifs that are then taken up by the entering voice (see Ex. 11.24). This imitation soon continues with the voice beginning the motif and the piano following in loving confirmation.

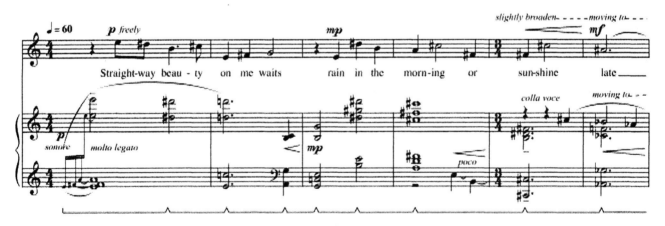

Example 11.23, mm. 1–6

Example 11.24, mm. 7–11

The word "love" is set with an expected extended lyrical line, but "dies like a flow'r" receives a surprising, rapid fluttering staccato treatment suggesting a sudden, wind-blown disappearance.

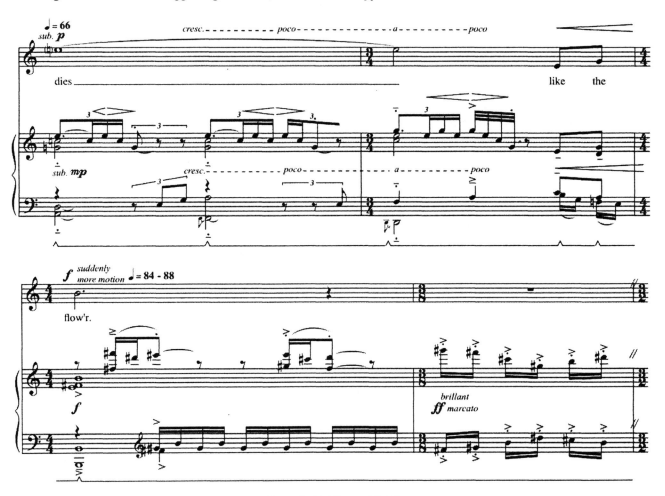

Example 11.25, mm. 27–30

The final postlude that alludes to an earlier piano interlude in mm. 16–17 is very reminiscent of the late, great, unsung song composer William Flanagan, and, like all good postludes, sums up the last lingering remnants of poignant emotion.

Example 11.26, mm. 40–43

Currently, Richard Hundley has completed a new cycle that he calls *Three Songs of Wonderment and Love*. The poets are Amy Lowell and Edna St. Vincent Millay, and the publisher was not yet determined at this writing.

John Corigliano (b. 1938)

"My father did everything he could to discourage me from being a composer,"[29] recalls John Corigliano—a not surprising paternal stance in mid-twentieth century America. It becomes more surprising, however, given the added information that his father, John Corigliano Sr., was concertmaster of the New York Philharmonic from 1943 to 1966, and his mother, Rose Buzen Corigliano, was a pianist and teacher. As a further curiosity of this unique path toward the making of a composer, Corigliano never gained proficiency on a musical instrument. A single piano lesson with his mother "ended in a fight,"[30] and lessons begun on the clarinet with Stanley Drucker of the New York Philharmonic finished when the instrument was stolen from his locker at Midwood High School in Brooklyn.

Although virtuosity did not interest him, music was becoming a growing force in young Corigliano's life, as he attended rehearsals and concerts of the Philharmonic, and began to buy recordings and scores for his own study. Despite his father's disapproval, which was based on personal observation of American composers' struggles for recognition, he began to study composition with Otto Luening at Columbia University and graduated in 1959 cum laude, with a B.A. in music.

At that point, Corigliano was faced with the problem of every young composer of serious music—how to "pay the rent" as he put it, with work that would leave him time to write. "When I left college," said Corigliano, "I bought my time to compose by working at other jobs. I was music director of WBAI, I worked on all the CBS TV music specials and *Young People's Concerts* for 12 years, I produced records for Columbia, I ran the Corfu Music Festival, . . . [and] I [taught] at Lehman College and the Manhattan School of Music."[31] Corigliano went on to reiterate the discouraging fact, noted fourteen years earlier by William Flanagan (see chapter 8) that only three or four American composers are able to live solely on the income from their serious music. (Currently, Corigliano teaches at Juilliard, where he joined the faculty in 1991.)

While working in all the above capacities, Corigliano had started to make a name for himself as a composer to watch. In 1962 he began a period of composition study with Vittorio Giannini and a year later finished the *Violin Sonata* that won first place in the Spoleto competition and effectively launched his career. Three other concert violinists had already performed it when Corigliano's father finally programmed the work on a New York recital in 1966. Convinced at last that his son was going to succeed as a composer, Corigliano Sr. became concertmaster of the San Antonio Symphony after retiring from the New York Philharmonic. In the new position, he led the violins in his son's *Concerto for*

Piano and Orchestra which had been written in 1968 on a Guggenheim fellowship, and which was performed the same year by Hilde Somer for the inaugural concert of the San Antonio Hemisfair.

Other major orchestral works by Corigliano followed. *The Concerto for Oboe and Orchestra* was commissioned by the New York State Council on the Arts for the bicentennial, and performed on November 9, 1975, by the American Symphony in New York, with Bert Lucarelli as soloist. A clarinet concerto was then commissioned by the New York Philharmonic, and in December 1977, Corigliano's longtime friend and erstwhile "teacher," Stanley Drucker, premièred it with Leonard Bernstein conducting.

In 1991, during his term as the first composer-in-residence of the Chicago Symphony Orchestra, Corigliano's Symphony No. 1, a moving work dedicated to the victims of the AIDS epidemic, was premièred with Daniel Barenboim conducting. This first symphony brought him the Gravemeyer award from the University of Louisville, and he received the Pulitzer Prize in 2001 for his Symphony No. 2.

Corigliano has also written several piano works, award-winning film scores for *Altered States* (1981), *Revelation* (1986), and *The Red Violin* (1999), and a multimedia updating of Bizet's classic called *The Naked Carmen*. Probably his best-known musico-dramatic composition is the opera *Ghosts of Versailles* based on Beaumarchais's third Figaro play with libretto by William Hoffman, which was commissioned by the Metropolitan Opera, premièred under James Levine's direction in 1992, and televised in 1993 with an all-star cast including Teresa Stratas and Renée Fleming.

His catalog further includes a number of choral compositions, one of the most important being a trilogy of Dylan Thomas settings, premièred in its entirety in Washington Cathedral in April 1976. R. Friedberg had the pleasure of helping to prepare two other Corigliano choral works—"L'invitation au Voyage" and "Psalm No. 8"—while employed as the San Antonio Symphony Chorus pianist in 1976–1977. This chorus, also known as the Mastersingers, made a recording in May, 1977, under the direction of Roger Melone, which included Corigliano's Psalm No. 8. Since it is scored for organ accompaniment, the recording took place in San Antonio's Temple Beth El, which had a suitable organ and acoustical environment.

Friedberg's interview with John Corigliano was held in the anteroom behind the temple sanctuary during intermissions in the recording process that the composer had come to San Antonio to supervise. Despite the unavoidable tensions of this project, Corigliano was able to relax and divert the intense focus of his energy to questions about his song writing. Asked why he has written relatively few solo songs, the composer replied that he has found "very few texts which he feels comfortable in setting."[32] Part of the reason for this is that he stays "very busy promoting [himself] as a composer," and therefore "has little time to read." The texts that he has chosen for solo or choral setting are either psalms or twentieth century poetry, both of which present the loosely structured meters with which he feels stylistically compatible.

In commenting on the position of the song medium in American music, Corigliano developed an interesting line of thought. "Twentieth-century American music," he said, "has a bare, uncluttered quality of simplicity in contrast to European music which equates complexity with progress. It follows that American composers would be drawn to songs, because you can't throw the voice around. A song is a direct, relatively simple statement of the vocal line and piano—not a big, complex, political decision like programming a symphony."

Corigliano's overall description of his personal approach to text setting is that "the structure of the piece comes out of the structure of the poem." He likes not to repeat words if possible, and before setting a text, types out the poem in double or triple spacing leaving room to plan the "emotional shape" of the piece. This includes "dynamics, interludes, words that reappear—always trying to follow the poet's intentions." In two of his vocal works, Corigliano was able to maximize the interrelationship of text and music by actual collaboration with the poet. One was the choral work "What I Expected Was" to a text by the British poet, Stephen Spender. The other was Corigliano's only major setting of American poetry, the cycle called *The Cloisters*,[33] in which three of the four component songs (all except "The Unicorn") were a collaborative effort with William M. Hoffman.

William M. Hoffman (b. 1939)

Hoffman was also born in New York City, a little more than a year after John Corigliano. He distinguished himself as an undergraduate at the City University of New York, and in 1960 earned a B.A. cum laude in Latin, as well as election to Phi Beta Kappa. Hoffman then began a seven-year stint as assistant editor and later drama editor at Hill and Wang publishers in New York. In this capacity, he edited three volumes of *New American Plays* (published between 1968 and 1971) and also began his own creative work as playwright and poet.

Hoffman's creative life has been largely oriented toward the theater in the capacities of playwright, director, and, occasionally, actor as well. Sixteen of his plays have been published and the earlier works were mostly produced in small, experimental, off-Broadway theaters. However, in 1985, he received critical acclaim when *As Is* opened in New York at the Lyceum Theater. This was one of the first plays to focus on the AIDS epidemic and it ran for 285 performances, garnering nominations, awards, and grants by way of public recognition.

Poetry is a congenial but less prolific medium for Hoffman and he writes that his poetry has been "published in magazines, set to music, and read in public."[34] A representative sampling, including three of the four *Cloisters* texts appears in the 1969 collection called *31 New American Poets.*

In the seventies, Hoffman held positions as literary adviser to *Scripts* magazine, and as playwright-in-residence for the Lincoln Center Student Programs, the Changing Scene Theater in Denver, and La Mama in New York. He has also served as visiting lecturer at the University of Massachusetts (1973) and as Star Professor at Hofstra University during the early eighties. His many awards have included MacDowell Colony and Guggenheim fellowships and grants from the Colorado Council on the Arts and Humanities, P.E.N., and National Endowment for the Arts. Currently, he is associate professor of journalism, communications, and theater at the City University of New York.

Besides the afore-mentioned operatic collaboration with John Corigliano, Hoffman has a number of other ties to the world of music. With songwriter John Braden he has written two musicals, *Gulliver's Travels* and *A Book of Etiquette* (both produced in 1978) and two of his three television plays have dramatized the lives of composers. These were *Notes from the New World: Louis Moreau Gottschalk* (1976) and *The Last Days of Stephen Foster* (1977). A poem of Hoffman's called "Screw Spring," which was also published in *31 New American Poets* has been set by Richard Hundley, and a 1969 letter from Hundley to James Purdy indicates that Hoffman, even at that time, was an accepted member of the New York musico/literary scene. "Bill Hoffman," says Hundley, "has just called to tell me his new play is on for four days at the same theater where we saw *Up Tight.* Maybe Virgil will like it, too."[35]

The Cloisters is a relatively early, but artistically mature work of remarkable intensity and power, written when both composer and poet were several years under thirty. Their overall plan for the cycle was that each song would treat a different season and a different aspect of love, all to be unified by the geographical setting of the medieval Cloisters that the Metropolitan Museum maintains and opens to the public in an upper Manhattan park area bordering the Hudson River.

The first text of the cycle, "Fort Tryon Park: September," brings us to the Cloisters as autumn begins. Falling leaves and berries, a waning sun, and a scarcity of visitors menace the lovers who "flee into dreams of permanence." Hoffman has written two stanzas of varyingly accented seven lines each, and Corigliano employs a metre-less rhythmic structure, with three to five eighth notes to a measure, that enhances the free flow of the poetry. In combination with this, the composer gives us a tightly worked, modified strophic form with two recurrent melodic phrases announced by the upper piano line and voice part as the song opens:

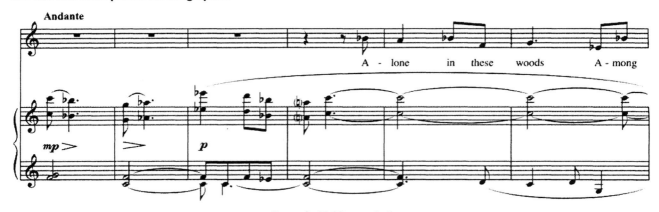

Example 11.27, mm. 1–6

The mingling of old and new stylistic elements continues as the "early-music" sounds of the spare counterpoint and modal melodic constructions are blended with later techniques of motivic development, and the idiomatic "Romantic" piano writing of the interlude between the verses.

Example 11.28, mm. 19–24

The result of this skillful mixing provides a sense of contemporary alienation cast in a medieval setting.

As Corigliano had pointed out in the 1977 interview, the creators of this song collaborated in a major poetic change that the composer felt necessary to the musical form and "emotional shape" of the piece. They decided together that the song should end on the wistfully haunting line "Homeless, we seek the cobbled court," and that the poem's ironic addition, "where our laughter rises like pigeons" should be omitted.

The seasons of this cycle do not all seem to follow in their natural order, and it appears likely that the songs have been arranged from the point of view of expressive contrast. The text of number two, "Song to the Witch of the Cloisters," suggests high summer, when the park is full of lovers who "wake . . . [and] sigh and fold." The poet, now alone, conjures an imaginary witch who has overpowered "Christ, [lying] unresurrected" and encouraged these lusty rites, and he begs her to "make the lovers be still." In a dramatic setting, Corigliano expands his use of melismatic vocal writing barely hinted at in the previous song. Writing many notes to one syllable, in the ancient fashion of Gregorian chant, he not only makes the medieval reference but uses the extended phrase to build powerful emotional crescendos.

Example 11.29, mm. 42–47

Chant-like repetition is another feature of this vocal line, and when this is used in the opening in conjunction with snickering grace notes and scampering staccato octaves in the accompaniment, the musical materials serve to give us a portrait of the very speech and movement of the wily witch.

Example 11.30, mm. 1–6

Number three is "Christmas at the Cloisters," a text which uses many short phrases to celebrate the Christ child's birthday and invoke His praise. The flexibility of this verbal structure allows Corigliano to weave a brilliant, rhythmically accented, jazzy accompaniment around a vocal line which alternately maintains repetitions of the G major dominant (D) or joins the churning syncopations.

Example 11.31, mm. 12–18

An exciting climax to this "joyful noise unto the Lord" is set up by a wild melisma structured in melodic thirds on the word "God." The tension of the two fermatas is then released in a crescendo of "Hallelujahs" which begins softly, rises to frenzied heights, and ends in a whispered "Amen."

Example 11.32, mm. 75–84

The last poem of the set, "The Unicorn," was actually the first to be written, and the one that had inspired planning for the cycle. It is spring now, and the poet sees himself in the guise of the unicorn, the mythical medieval beast whose savage behavior was purported to be soothed to gentleness by the sight of a virgin at mating time. The poetry is a seductive invitation to his virginal object not to let spring's return to the Cloisters catch either of them unfulfilled and "three nights sad." Corigliano bases his setting on a poignant melodic phrase announced in the first four vocal measures, whose chromatic intervals (three minor seconds and an augmented fourth) are filled with the unease of longing.

Example 11.33, mm. 1–4

This phrase returns many times in the voice part and accompaniment and is transposed to a number of different pitch levels. In an extensive piano interlude, it flowers to an imitative climax following the textual imagining of sensual fulfillment.

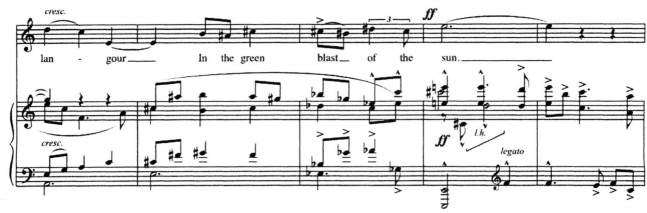

Example 11.34, mm. 18–22

The unicorn now intensifies his seductive plea, which emerges as the climax of the song. It is a ravishingly lyrical, dolcissimo passage in D major, replete with a bel canto vocal curve and a warmly supportive sequence of thirds in the pianistic harmony.

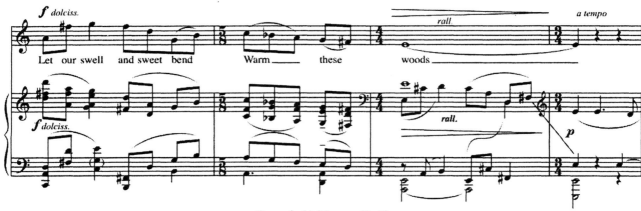

Example 11.35, mm. 40–43

In the penultimate phrase, a long, widely ranging vocal melisma on the first syllable of "unicorn" has a dual purpose. Stylistically, it relates "The Unicorn" to numbers two and three of the cycle where the device is heavily employed, and dramatically it suggests the barely controllable transports of desire.

Helen Medwedeff Greenberg (1939–2011)

The women composers treated in our survey up to this point have all used the keyboard as their primary connection to music. Now we take a fresh turn with the consideration of two women whose path to song composition, although fraught with many a detour, was primarily through the singing voice.

Helen Greenberg spent her childhood and youth in Baltimore, and as her mother was an excellent pianist, did begin to study that instrument at seven, but switched to voice lessons at the age of thirteen. Academically talented in a number of areas, she started premed studies at Oberlin, but after two years transferred to Goucher College in Baltimore and settled on a double major of English and secondary education. Greenberg married at twenty-two, moved to Canada (Montreal and later Toronto), and had begun to raise two children when she realized, at the age of thirty, that she wanted and needed to become a composer. At this point, she "had to start from scratch with the prerequisite theory, harmony, counterpoint, analysis, etc.,"[36] as well as continuing studies in voice and piano. The reader will be reminded of a similar blending of family and professional goals by Mary Howe (chapter 4) who received her degree in composition from Peabody Institute at the age of forty.

The Canadian composers Edward Laufer, Oscar Morawetz, and Srul Irving Glick were her chief mentors, and "because the human voice [was her] favorite instrument," Greenberg began to produce an impressive catalog of solo and choral vocal works. Her "training as an English major in college helped [her] to separate the wheat from the chaff" when choosing poetry for the art song medium which strongly attracted her, and her participation as member and director in a number of Jewish liturgical choirs proved a strong incentive to compose for these groups.

Another interesting parallel in Helen Greenberg's creative career to that of Mary Howe is that both composed in three languages, although they were native-born Americans. For Mary Howe, a French governess, travel abroad, and her own forays into European poetry led to her French and German settings. With Helen Greenberg, years of performing in and directing Temple choirs and her familiarity with the language occasioned many solo and choral settings in Hebrew. At the same time, her Jewish background also fostered an interest in art song settings of Yiddish poetry by women writers, and she formed a strong desire to musically enhance and "facilitate their additional exposure to audiences and performers." In the English language settings, she selected poetry by both British and American authors with equal enthusiasm. Her very active life as composer and performer in Toronto's rich musical scene came to an end on May 17, 2011 when she died, after battling a long illness, at Toronto's Baycrest Hospital.

Although somewhat of a late starter, Helen Greenberg had quickly compiled a large catalog of works that were performed throughout Canada, the United States, Europe, and Israel. Well-known artists such as Maureen Forrester, Paulina Stark, and the Elmer Iseler Chamber Singers of Canada programmed her music in prominent settings, among them the Aspen Music Festival, Washington, D.C. Holocaust Museum, and the 92nd Street YMHA in New York City. Her major instrumental compositions were works for oboe and clarinet with piano but, like John Duke (see chapter 5), she readily confessed that she had always been more strongly drawn to vocal composition since she derived major guidance and inspiration from the poetic text.

Kenneth Patchen (1911–1972)

One American poet who proved particularly compatible to Greenberg was Kenneth Patchen, whose life is discussed in the Richard Hundley section of this chapter. The two Patchen settings that she published in 2000[37] are highly contrasted, both poetically and musically, but both are elegant and affecting examples of their genres. The first poem, titled "Who'll that be?" was originally published in the 1957 collection *When We Were Here Together*. Just the year before, the Patchens had moved to Palo Alto and in 1957, Patchen became part of the poetry and jazz movement, which presented him reading his poetry to the background of music by the Chamber Jazz Sextet. One can only speculate as to the possible influence of the connection on this gently playful, very rhythmic address in folk dialect to a small child who is being questioned about her toys. It is interesting to observe Patchen's changes in the version that appears in the Collected Poems of 1968. In the first stanza, "Your little preachin' dog" has changed to "Your little pouty kitten"; the "bird" of verse three has become a "wren"; and the recurring refrain of "Honey, you wonder me" has now been amplified to "My little honey, you wonder me."

The amplification of the refrain helps to create a very regular poetic structure of three verses each containing four lines with four regular accents. One can almost hear the drummer of the Sextet lining out this rhythm. Indeed, Greenberg must have heard it too, for she writes a jazzy setting, with much syncopation, a relatively sparse, quasi-improvisational accompaniment, and many "blue" notes of the genre.

Example 11.36, mm. 1–5

The song opens in D major but verse two moves to B minor and begins to incorporate vocal and pianistic "riffs" reminiscent of jazz improvisation.

Example 11.37a, mm. 23–25

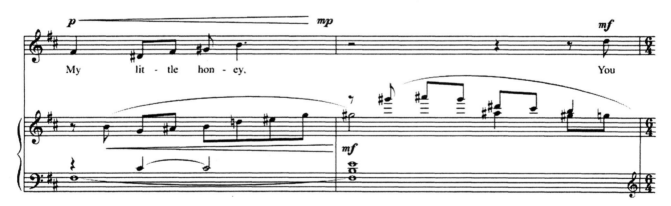

Example 11.37b, mm. 35–36

The last verse returns to D major and for a very effective conclusion, repeats both phrases of the final refrain in a challenging vocal elaboration that the piano joins in imitation and inversion.

Example 11.38, mm. 54–59

The second setting is of "Beautiful You Are," possibly the most perfectly fashioned of all the poems that Kenneth Patchen wrote for his wife, Miriam, who was clearly the lodestar of his difficult, pain-ridden life. It also appeared in the collection *When We Were Here Together*; was included in the *Love Poems of Kenneth Patchen* published in 1966 by San Francisco's City Lights Books; and made its way into the final definitive *Collected Poems* of 1968 virtually unchanged except for two very minor additions: the word "your" before "eyes, lips, and hair" in line four and the phrase "your lips" in the last line.

In the first stanza, Patchen captures, in two simple lines, the sight, smell, and kinesthetic feeling of a brilliant winter evening in the city. Greenberg presents this picture with an equally haunting simplicity as she begins to develop a diatonic, lyrical line.

Example 11.39, mm. 3–9

In the next two lines, and again with the sparest of verbal means, Patchen draws another picture, that of the woman who is beside him. Now Greenberg vocally introduces the four sixteenth and a quarter note motif that will pervade the two A sections of the song's three part form, imitates it in the accompaniment, and lets it develop into a piano line that intertwines with the voice before it blossoms into a rapturous interlude.

Example 11.40, mm. 10–12

In the B section, Patchen shows us, as in "Maiden Snow" (see the Richard Hundley section of this chapter) his shadow side: the darkness that is his fear of loss. In a wonderful metaphor, he compares these peaceful evenings to chalices "where little roofs and trees drink" until it is all shattered by a "rude hand." For this dramatic scene, Greenberg moves from the calmly flowing B-flat minor of the opening to a more dissonant B-flat major key signature with many altered chords. The melodic and harmonic tension mount with an upward melisma on "drink" and then a climactic "shattering" descent.

Example 11.41, mm. 22–23

Patchen now returns to his adoration of the one who brings "springtime" to "this winter place" and is seen in the candlelight to be more beautiful "than any legend's face." Greenberg is a match for this, as she moves to a warm E-flat major, expands her lyrical line, and ends with an exquisite pianissimo melodic suspension that is a glorious challenge to the soprano voice.

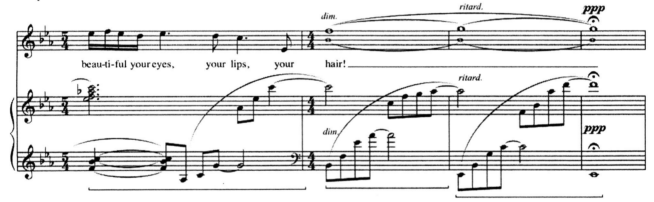

Example 11.42, mm. 43–46

Flicka Rahn (b. 1944)

Flicka Rahn's intimate understanding of composition for the human voice is based on an extensive career as a concert and opera singer as well as on many years in the studio as a professor of voice in academia.

Rahn was born in Corpus Christi, Texas, into a highly musical family. Her mother and aunt, Evelyn and Thelma Jackson, performed professionally as a string duo known as the Jackson Sisters. Her father, Henry Rahn, was a chemical engineer who sang in choirs (as did his two brothers) and also played the violin in a string quartet where he met (and later married) Evelyn Jackson. The family moved to Pittsburgh when Flicka was ten. As a young child, she had begun to compose pieces, which her mother wrote down for her, and she would often approach strangers asking "Can I sing for you?" The talented young musician studied piano through high school and began voice lessons at the age of fifteen. Attending Washington University in Saint Louis as an undergraduate in musical education, Rahn continued her vocal training and toured, with the University Madrigal Singers, all over the United States.

In 1965, Rahn married, moved to Philadelphia, and taught public school music until the birth of her daughter. A return to Texas for her husband's medical training in San Antonio proved fortuitous as Rahn now enrolled in the master of music education program at Texas State University where she studied voice with Lenore Sergi. Here, like Helen Greenberg, she discovered her strong pull toward composition just past the age of thirty, and was inspired to write and perform her own songs for her graduate recitals.

A continuing flood of works in different genres followed the completion of her master's degree. Under the mentorship of Rahn's most important composition teacher, Gerard Jaffe, she began to produce works for piano, choral settings for San Antonio's Temple Beth-El and St. Andrew's Methodist Church, and musical plays for children. At the same time, her singing career was gathering momentum, as she was regularly engaged by the San Antonio Symphony and the San Antonio Opera Company.

The academic teaching aspect of her career had its beginning at the University of the Incarnate Word in San Antonio, and it blossomed after a move to Boston where she taught for six years at Brandeis University. Drawn back once again to her native Texas, Rahn joined the music faculty of Texas A & M at Corpus Christi where she was professor of voice from 1988 until her retirement in 2011. During these teaching years, she remained an active concert performer with opera companies and symphony orchestras in Boston, New York, and Texas, and traveled the world in solo recitals of American art songs. The latter performances, which were often coupled with master-classes for local voice students, took place in Mexico, Bolivia, France, Spain, Hong Kong, and throughout the United States.

Publication of Rahn's songs brought her composing to national attention, and her Amy Lowell settings, to be discussed next, were chosen for inclusion on CDs recorded by Patricia Stiles of the Indiana University voice faculty and Linda MacNeil of Trinity University. Rahn was also an invited panelist at conferences on women composers held at Indiana University and Texas State University, and in 2011 was awarded a Fulbright fellowship to serve as scholar-in-residence at the Universidad Autonoma de Queretaro in Mexico. At this writing, Rahn is building a home in the Hill Country near San Antonio where she will maintain a private studio and do adjunct teaching at area schools.

It is not surprising to learn that Rahn is an amateur painter, after she lists some of her favorite composers as "Menotti, Bernstein, John Duke—composers who use keys as a way of painting aural landscapes with color."[38] She prefers "the loose harmonic colors of the twentieth century" and adds that, "as a performer, if I can see a picture or a color when I sing, I'm in love with the music." Although Rahn is fluent in Spanish and has set the poetry of Federico Garcia Lorca, the majority of her literary partners have been British and American writers. In comparing her "Four Sonnets of Elizabeth Barrett Browning" with her Amy Lowell settings,[39] she finds that "the Browning work carries a more complex energy, resulting in a larger concept and more dense piano writing.[40] The Lowell poems," she continues, "create a vivid drama in a few lines, so that a whole song was conceived before it was written."

Amy Lowell (1874–1925)

Amy Lowell's life has been previously discussed in chapter 4 in connection with the Mary Howe settings of "Three Hokku" from Lowell's posthumously published *What's O'Clock* (1925). The Rahn songs, "Vicarious" and "Shore Grass," set two poems from an earlier collection, *Pictures of a Floating World*, which appeared in 1919. At this point in her life, Lowell's interest in Asian poetry and her translations with Florence Ayscough had already begun, and in the foreword to the collection, she describes the writing of "Lacquer Prints," the section that includes "Vicarious." Says Lowell, "The first part of the book represents some of the charm I have found in delving into [Oriental] poetry. In the Japanese 'Lacquer Prints' . . . I have made no attempt to observe the syllabic rules [but] endeavored only to keep the brevity and suggestion of the *hokku*."

Interestingly, the *24 Hokku* which were the source of the Mary Howe settings do "observe the syllabic rules" of *hokku* but Flicka Rahn preferred the more pictorially developed and colorful "Lacquer Prints" as a richer background for musical setting. "Vicarious" portrays a woman "standing under the willow tree above the river" in a "straw-colored, silken garment" as she gazes at a beloved face painted on her fan. Rahn saw this scene in the "fresh greens of nature"[41] and made changes in the poem to heighten the dramatic immediacy of the monologue. She omits an opening "When," deletes a line describing the gown's embroidery, changes "I am gazing" to the stronger "I gaze," and leaves out a discursive "caused to be" before "painted on my fan."

The setting itself is beautifully crafted with a seemingly effortless flow that appears to attest to Rahn's description of hearing it in her inner ear in its entirety. Close examination reveals the finely wrought details. The harmonic world is tonal, although without key signature, and the keys underline the tight-knit but unobtrusive structure of an ABCA form.

Both A sections are for the keyboard and are based on a two-measure motif that surrounds the vocal statement like an Oriental triptych.

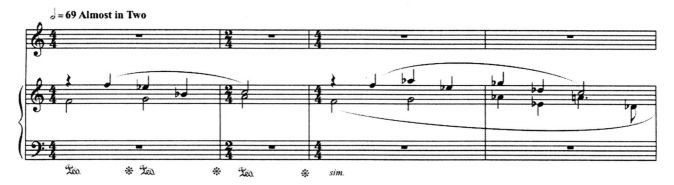

Example 11.43, mm. 1–4

The key is basically E-flat with softly colored chromatic alterations, and in section B the voice enters with a lyrical but leaping line encompassing one and a half octaves that suggests barely concealed depths of feeling.

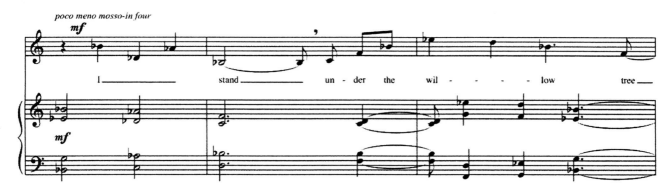

Example 11.44, mm. 9–11

Section C pulls into G major and the piano begins a surprising but effective waltz motif, soon imitated by the voice, which lightens the emotional climate and seems to reveal another aspect of the protagonist's persona. A finely calculated detail is the syncopated voice line of measure 21 that suggests the breathless excitement of a youthful passion.

Example 11.45, mm. 19–23

The song ends with a return to the opening A material now in a D centered tonality, and a final dominant chord with added second step lends an inconclusiveness that allows the scene to linger in our consciousness.

"Shore Grass" comes from a later subsection of *Pictures of the Floating World* which was titled "Two Speak Together." The other half of this imagined poetic conversation is generally believed to have been Ada Russell Dwyer, an actress eleven years older than Amy Lowell who was her friend and companion for many years and who helped to organize the poet's chaotic and often pain-invaded life. This poem, which Rahn has set without alteration, is almost an antithetical picture to "Vicarious." Instead of a warm, bright, wooded scene by a river, we are presented with a cold moon over sand dunes and sea-grasses and a "thin chime" of a watch that at "a quarter after midnight" brings no awaited step, only the "windy beating of the sea."

The coloristic world of "Shore Grass" is also much different from that of "Vicarious," and the composer tells us that the setting here calls for "muted greens, taupes, silver, and gray blue," and that she "has chosen piano sounds that elicit these colors."[42] Rahn has accordingly written a short instrumental prelude toward this end. It is in the form of a monophonic line for the piano of open fourths and fifths in the treble clef that is perfectly calculated to introduce the chill and loneliness of this scene.

Example 11.46, mm. 1–5

The voice line, throughout the song, will move in a narrow range (no joyful leaps here!), sometimes incorporating the well-recognized chromatic half-steps of musical suffering.

Example 11.47, mm. 14–17

In the dramatic climax of the song, the voice, on a long, reiterated E-flat, imitates the chiming of the watch. It also mirrors the poet's growing despair, which is underlined by the piano's dissonant chord that grows constantly faster and louder.

thin chime of my watch   tells the quarter after midnight   and still   and still   I   hear_____   No - thing

Example 11.48, mm. 20–24

The concluding return of the opening piano intervals at a lower pitch suggest that the rhythmic pattern of this motif was always intended to be heard as "the windy beating of the sea" which is as eternal as human sorrows are ephemeral.

Notes

1. Interview with R. Friedberg in New York City, 2 December 1982.

2. Unless otherwise indicated, all the ensuing Richard Hundley quotations are from the interview, 2 December 1982.

3. For further information on these Metropolitan Opera Studio concerts, see: (a) "Names, Dates, and Places," *Opera News* 386 (January 6, 1973): 6–7; (b) "Debuts and Reappearances," *High Fidelity/Musical America* 22 (June 1972): 18.

4. Robert Finn, "Richard Hundley, non-conformist," *The (Cleveland) Plain Dealer*, 3 June 1983.

5. Finn, "Richard Hundley, non-conformist."

6. Richard Hundley, "Softly the Summer" (New York: General Music Publishing, 1963). High voice. Out of print.

7. James Schevill, "The Search for Wonder and Joy," in *Kenneth Patchen: A Collection of Essays*, edited by Richard G. Morgan, (New York: AMS Press, 1977), 110.

8. Holly Beye and William McCleery, "The Most Mysterious People in the Village," in in *Kenneth Patchen: A Collection of Essays*, edited by Richard G. Morgan, (New York: AMS Press, 1977), 49.

9. Beye and McCleery, "The Most Mysterious People," 50.

10. For example, see David Diamond, "Be Music, Night" (New York: Carl Fischer, 1948). High voice. Out of print, available by contacting Carl Fischer Archive/Out-of-Print Service.

11. Richard Hundley, "Maiden Snow" (New York: General Music Publishing, 1961). Out of print.

12. Richard Hundley, *Ten Songs for High Voice and Piano* (Milwaukee, Wisc.: Hal Leonard, 1988).

13. Ned Rorem, letter to James Purdy, 16 January 1965, Harry Ransom Center (HRC), University of Texas at Austin.

14. Rorem, letter to James Purdy, 25 June 1967, HRC, UT Austin.

15. Quoted in James Vinson, ed., *Contemporary Novelists*, 2nd edition (New York: St. Martin's Press, 1976), 1130.

16. Vinson, *Contemporary Novelists*, 1130.

17. Tony Tanner, "Birdsong," *Partisan Review* 39 (Fall 1972): 610.

18. James Vinson, ed., *Great Writers of the English Language: Novelists* (New York: St. Martin's, 1979), 995.

19. Letter to James Purdy, 7 December 1967, Henry Ransom Center (HRC), UT Austin.

20. Richard Hundley, *Eight Songs* (New York: Boosey & Hawkes, 1981). Medium high.

21. Letter to Purdy, 3 August 1969.

22. Letter to Purdy, 6 August 1969.

23. Letter to Purdy, 12 August 1969.

24. Tanner, "Birdsong," 618.

25. For a complete edition of James Purdy's poetry see James Purdy, *Collected Poems* (Amsterdam: Athenaeum-Polak & Van Gennep, 1990).

26. Composer's "Notes" to *Ten Songs for High Voice.*

27. Richard Hundley, *Octaves and Sweet Sounds* (Milwaukee, Wisc.: Hal Leonard, 1990).

28. Composer's notes to *Octaves and Sweet Sounds*.

29. William Hoffman, "John Corigliano on Cracking the Establishment," *The Village Voice*, 21 February 1977.

30. David Ewen, *Composers since 1900, First Supplement* (New York: H. W. Wilson, 1981), 77.

31. Hoffman, "John Corigliano on Cracking the Establishment."

32. Unless otherwise indicated, all ensuing John Corigliano quotations are from the May 1977 interview held in San Antonio.

33. John Corigliano, *The Cloisters* (New York: G. Schirmer, 1967). Mezzo-soprano. The four songs of this cycle are published separately.

34. Ron Schrieber, ed., "Autobiographical Notes," *31 New American Poets* (New York: Hill and Wang, 1969), 255.

35. Letter to Purdy, 7 August 1969, HRC, UT Austin.

36. All Greenberg quotations in this and following paragraphs are from emails to R. Friedberg, 29 July 2009.

37. Helen Greenberg, *Two Songs with Texts by Kenneth Patchen* (San Antonio, Tex.: Southern Music Co., 2000).

38. All Rahn quotations in this and the following paragraph are from an interview in San Antonio with R. Friedberg, 15 July 2009.

39. Flicka Rahn, *Two Songs* (San Antonio, Tex.: Southern Music Co., 1995).

40. Flicka Rahn is currently in discussions with Walter Foster of Recital Publications who is interested in publishing *The Four Sonnets of Elizabeth Barrett Browning*.

41. Interview with R. Friedberg, July 2009.

42. Interview with R. Friedberg, July 2009.

Chapter 12

Half Century and Beyond

Libby Larsen (b. 1950)

Like Willa Cather, the writer she would later set so eloquently, Libby Larsen had a childhood that encompassed substantial geographic and psychological dislocation.[1] The first move occurred when Larsen was only six months old. At this time her father, who was a food chemist working for DuPont, had to move his family from Delaware to Chicago for a quartermaster corps assignment tied to the Korean War. Four years later, a post-war position with the Pillsbury Company brought the Larsens to Minneapolis where Libby was now old enough to experience the loss of Chicago and its attendant lifestyle.

Interestingly, loss of the major mid-western metropolis would not be the only one perpetuated in the family mythology. Larsen's mother, a great story-teller, would often describe at length their former genteel Eastern life in a small Pennsylvania town near Wilmington, Delaware, a life which had been complete with tennis tournaments, fox hunts coming through the back yard, and other patrician accoutrements. The direct parallel to this narrative with Willa Cather's family's forced abandonment of their ancestral farm in Virginia to relocate in the prairies of Nebraska would eventually find a strong response in the composer and it would color an important part of her creative life.

Libby Larsen is the only professional musician in her family, but her father is an amateur clarinetist, and all four of her sisters (two older and two younger) studied the piano. Seven was the designated age for beginning piano lessons, but years before her turn had formally arrived, Libby would watch her sisters' hands on the keyboard, and then climb up on the bench herself and play. The Catholic school that the children attended taught the medieval model of the quadrivium, with music considered essential for the logical development of the brain. Writing and reading music began in the first grade and continued for eight years, along with extensive singing of the chants and mass settings. By the third grade, Larsen was writing piano music, choral music, and elaborate playground operas with characters and choruses that would last an entire year.

The composer recalls that this early musical life seemed in no way remarkable to her ("doesn't everyone?") but that her junior year in high school was pivotal. Gaining entrance to a summer program for talented youth, Larsen's first choice was to study economics—also a strong interest. Since mores of the period decreed that females were not accepted into that area, her second choice was music, and she feels fortunate to have experienced the fine teaching of William Lidell who is currently an octogenarian and still a close friend. Lidell taught harmony on the Hindemith model and it was here that she first began to experience her deep love of the construction and architecture of music.

"But it was 1968," says Larsen, and women composers, far from being encouraged, were at best "merely tolerated" and at worst, subject to "benign neglect." With no formal vocal training, but years of chant singing behind her that had developed breath support and reading skills, she was accepted as a voice student in the University of Minnesota music department. Just after her sophomore year, Larsen decided to become an opera singer, and auditioned at Juilliard, the Mannes School, and Oberlin. Juilliard said "no," Mannes said "yes," and Oberlin, in their acceptance, was so impressed by her audition analysis of a Beethoven sonata that they convinced her to consider a career in composition.

The rest, as they say, is history. Libby Larsen went back to the University of Minnesota, earned a doctorate in composition with Domenick Argento as a major teacher, and co-founded the Minnesota Composers' Forum in 1973. During the ensuing decades, Larsen has become one of the most prolific and successful composers of either sex in America. She also holds the distinction of being one of a small handful that can live on the proceeds of their creative work without having to cope with the distractions of a university teaching position.

Through the years, Larsen has held many appointments as composer-in-residence with groups as diverse as the Minnesota and Colorado Symphonies, the Cincinnati Conservatory, and the Arnold Schoenberg Institute. At the same time, her deep interest in the broader issues of music in society has led to committed involvement with organizations such as the American Symphony League, American Music Center, National Endowment for the Arts, and the College Music Society. Not surprisingly, she is also in constant demand as a speaker, and one of Larsen's favorite topics is music education, an interest that has resulted in her appointment as the first holder of the Harrissios Papamarkon Chair in Education and Technology in the John W. Kluge Center of the Library of Congress.

Libby Larsen's compositional style has been characterized as "adventurous without being self-consciously avant-garde." Critical assessment has also noted its "energy, optimism, rhythmic diversity, . . . liberated tonality, . . . and pervading lyricism."[2] Larsen has a wide and varied catalog, having composed approximately 200 works in all genres, of which more than half are solo or choral compositions for the voice. This is not surprising in a composer who early on intended to be a professional opera singer and whose principal mentor in graduate school was Domenick Argento. Larsen also has a well-deserved reputation as a purveyor of the sounds and rhythms of American speech and has set texts by many American writers from both literary and vernacular derivations. Both sources were combined in one of her most admired and widely performed cycles, the *Cowboy Songs* of 1979, which sets texts by an American outlaw (Belle Star), an American poet (Robert Creely), and an anonymous American folk-singer.

But she has also set Spanish, German, and British English texts, and is keenly aware of how differently each must be approached. As a part of this process, Larsen has developed "a fairly complicated system" that enables her to take rhythmic dictation when people are speaking and thereby to find "the musicality of the speaking rhythms" of the language she is setting. A possible pitfall of which the composer is always aware is falling into musical clichés that the language invites. "The clichés," she says, "must be met head on and wrestled to the ground. . . . [Then, after] I understand where the cliché comes from, [I ask] what is it when it is fresh and new?"[3]

Willa Cather (1873–1947)

Larsen feels that this same problem was faced by writers such as Willa Cather who were brought up in the tradition of British English and had to open their ears to the new sounds of formative American English. As mentioned previously, Cather's family had left their Virginia home when Willa was nine years old, and her first impression of Nebraska and the unending, treeless stretch of the reddish prairie grass was both terrifying and exciting—a feeling akin to having come to the end of the world as she knew it.

The adventure of homesteading, however, lasted only eighteen months before Charles Cather moved his family to a somewhat more citified life in the nearby town of Red Cloud. In that year and a half, Willa had roamed freely across the prairie, forming relationships with many of the German, Bohemian, and Scandinavian immigrants who were the majority inhabitants of Nebraska at that time and who would later populate her short stories and novels. During her teenage years in Red Cloud, Willa passed through a "crew-cut, tomboy period"[4] when her ambition was to have a career in medicine, and her high school graduation address was a remarkable defense of scientific inquiry. But while matriculating at the University of Nebraska in Lincoln, Cather's focus of attention was shifted to literature, and a young English instructor just out of Harvard, Herbert Bates, helped her publish her first writing ventures.

A surprising period of sixteen years would now elapse between Cather's graduation from the university in 1895 and her decision to devote full time to the writing career that was rapidly gaining momentum. Although the author had given up mannish clothes as an undergraduate, her biographers conjecture that she continued to harbor the prevalent belief of her era that successful full-time creative artists were invariably men. Accordingly, she continued to support herself with a series of jobs that had a literary connection: editor of newspapers and magazines in Lincoln, Pittsburgh, and eventually New York City; a teaching appointment at Central High School in Pittsburgh; and a translating position in Washington, D.C. Interspersed throughout these years were important friendships: with Isabelle McClung, daughter of a wealthy Pittsburgh family who housed the writer for five years; with Sarah Orne Jewett, a prominent writer who urged her to concentrate on finding her own artistic voice; and with Lincoln native Edith Lewis who would become her lifelong companion.

Finally, in 1911, Cather left her five-year association with *McClure's* magazine in New York and began to devote herself exclusively to her writing. Houghton Mifflin became her publisher through the early successes of *The Song of the Lark* (1915) and *My Ántonia* (1918). From 1920 on, Cather would be represented by Alfred Knopf who published new editions of *April Twilight*s (an early poetry collection) and *My Ántonia* as well as the critically acclaimed *Death Comes to the Archbishop* and all her other works until her death in 1947.

The process of Cather's finding her own voice had indeed begun, as Libby Larsen described it, with the traditions of British English. This is clearly seen in the Victorian language and formal structure of many poems in the *April Twilight* poetry collection of 1903 and in her first major novel, *Alexander's Bridge* (1912) which shows the strong influence of Henry James, a literary idol of her youth. It would take years of living, and traveling in the East and the Southwest, as well as in Europe, to afford Willa Cather the perspective that was needed to mine for her writing the sounds and sights of the prairie and its people. With the publication of the novel *O Pioneers* in 1913, everything had changed as Cather returned to the scenes of her Nebraska youth, placing the first of a series of strong female protagonists in a new format of discrete scenes widely separated in chronological time.[5]

It is interesting to note that for her two major treatments of Willa Cather texts, Libby Larsen selected the first from a very early short story and the second from one of the major novels of the author's maturity. "Eric Hermansson's Soul" was written during Cather's Pittsburgh years and was published in 1900 in *Cosmopolitan*. Along with other stories from that formative period, they were not highly regarded by their author but are now widely seen to demonstrate all of Cather's major literary themes in embryonic form.[6] In 1996, Libby Larsen created a chamber opera from this tale of a Norwegian immigrant, farming on the Divide[7] in Nebraska. Eric Hermansson has forsaken and smashed his violin, since it has been deemed sinful by an evangelist minister, but his joy in life and music is restored to him in the course of the story by a loving encounter with Margaret Elliott, a visitor from the East Coast. Three seminal moments from the opera were gathered into a cycle for soprano and piano that Larsen published in 1998 as the *Margaret Songs*.[8] The composer's mastery of Cather's work is demonstrated in microcosm by the texts of these songs, two of which, the first and third, are based on poems from the *April Twilight*s collection of 1903, while the second is an artistic mélange of the actual lines of the story with considerable fleshing out by Larsen's own poetic prose.

The opening song, "Bright Rails," uses the first two and last nine lines of Cather's first poem in the collection. In writing no longer tied by language or form to Victorian models, the author writes "How smoothly the train runs beyond the Missouri. . . . The wheels turn as if they were glad to go. . . . As if they, too, were going home." One cannot help being struck by the notion that Cather is hereby, perhaps unconsciously, announcing her intention toward a literary "going home" to her own authentic speech and the geography that formed her.

Larsen begins this ABA setting which shows us Margaret coming West with her brother as guide, by establishing a piano ostinato which will pervade the song, in imitation of the wheels of the train.

Example 12.1, mm. 1–4

Larsen rarely uses key signatures but the center is clearly E-flat, and the scale, a transposed Dorian mode. The voice enters in a fairly narrow-range contemplative chant (see Ex. 12.2) but broadens into a lyrical arc as the poem likens the motion of the wheels to "youth running away" (see Ex. 12.3).

Example 12.2, mm. 4–8

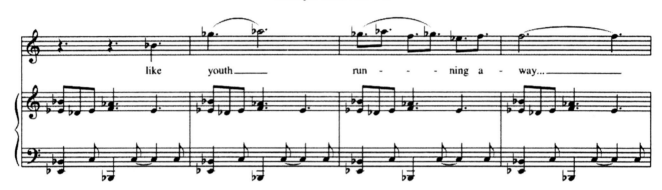

Example 12.3, mm. 25–28

By now, the accompaniment figure has also been developed (see Ex. 12.3) to match the intensity of the text.

The B section of the song shows us the wheels "singing, humming" in a turn to similar rhythmic material in the Mixolydian mode. (Larsen's childhood grounding in the modal scales seems firmly fixed in her harmonic vocabulary). Now the lines "They run remembering, . . . rejoicing, as if they were going home" are set out with vocal recitative and a bridge warm with instrumental thirds which turns back to the musical and textual material of section A.

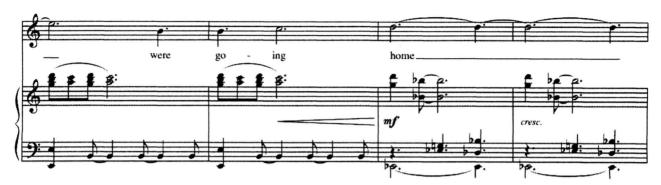

Example 12.4, mm. 41–48

In the second song, "So Little There," Margaret tells her brother Willis that this trip has made her as happy as when "they were children together discovering the ruins of Troy." She contrasts the grand scale of landscape and emotion on the prairie with the smallness and pettiness of "teas and dances . . . gloves and gossip" that constitute life back home where she is engaged to be married to a city sophisticate. In the beginning of this setting, much of the description of the confining life is couched in vocal declamation behind nervous staccato notes and chords in the accompaniment. A piano trill and glissando then usher in "The wind has swept all that away/here at the edge of the world" and with a slow waltz background and increasingly lyric vocal line, the singer describes her longing for authentic experience of nature and emotion. The song ends with vocal recitative for the crucial statement "When everything is so small, why should I expect love to be great?" followed by the piano's closing comment of soft, returning trills in its upper register.

The last of the *Margaret Songs* sets, without alteration, a love poem from *April Twilight* which shows an interesting and innovative structure involving three verses containing six lines each. Lines one, two, and six have three stresses while lines three, four, and five have two, and the rhyme scheme is unusually and elegantly crafted. Moreover, the last verse incorporates two very modern verbal constructs ("What the rose smells/what the stars shine") that seem to prefigure e.e. cummings by several decades.) Again, Larsen has chosen a Cather text from outside the short story to encapsulate the exactly appropriate feeling of this moment in the opera when Margaret tells her brother of last night's encounter with Eric—an experience that will change and enrich each of their future separate lives.

The original poem is called "The Hawthorne Tree" and the composer adds "Beneath" to the title for a greater sense of immediate presence. Larsen keeps much of the piano writing in the treble clef and also repeatedly uses a rapid thirty-second note fluttering figure, both of which devices reinforce the "shimmering" quality of the text.

Example 12.5, mm. 1–5

The continuous, soft sixteenth notes of the accompaniment with all harmonies diffused by the damper pedal (see Ex. 12.5) create the sound world of the "misty marshland" out of which the voice emerges in a broadly arching, ecstatic line.

Example 12.6, mm. 15–19

The final section of the song combines short, a cappella phrases interspersed with the piano's "shimmering" figures, all leading to a climactic high A. The brilliance of the tessitura mirrors the brightness of "what the stars shine," after which the quiet, reflective ending returns to the opening instrumental material as the impassioned present moment fades into the past.

Example 12.7, mm. 33–36

For the seven-song cycle, *My Ántonia*, Larsen has taken lines from Cather's novel and turned them into poetic song texts. This famous literary portrait is of a lively, warm-hearted girl growing up in a Nebraska family of Bohemian immigrants, and to tell her story the writer employs the device of a narrator—a man named Jim Burden who had come to live on the prairie as a child, riding the same train as Ántonia. The book chronicles his memories, many of which center around her unforgettable persona, and his personal focus on their shared past which creates the picture he refers to as "*My* Ántonia."

The composer divides the songs into two thematic groups: landscapes of the countryside and portraits of Ántonia and her friends. Landscapes I ("From the Train") and IV ("Sunset"), as the first and last settings, open and close the cycle with the same pianistic figure that suggests the rhythm of the train which carried the narrator west both in his youth and in later maturity. The text of number two ("Ántonia"), describes many events in the children's lives as they played together, and the vocal line is largely declamatory, except for the octave leaps which underline the emotion behind the words "My Ántonia." In the third song, "Landscape II: Winter," Larsen effectively equates the savage prairie winter with Ántonia's heartbreak over her father's unhappiness and eventual suicide, revealed in arresting moments of dramatic recitative.

Songs four, five, and six form the expressive heart of the cycle as Jim and Ántonia move past childhood. "Tony," in "The Hired Girls," (number four), is Ántonia, who at this point is working in town as a domestic, and enjoying the weekly dances with the other "handsome," lively young women. Larsen calls the 3/4 dance of the accompaniment a "waltz" (see Ex. 12.8) but it is really closer to the middle-European "ländler," the peasant dance with a heavy first-beat accent from which the more refined waltz, with its second-beat stress, probably derived.

Slow waltz (♩ = 108, Valse Anders Sveen)

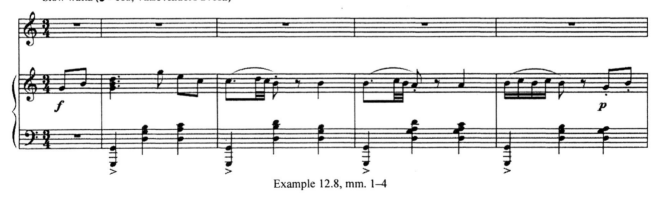

Example 12.8, mm. 1–4

The composer invents dialogue to introduce Ántonia and her companions in this setting as the dance tune continues.

Example 12.9, mm. 9–14

It pauses only for Jim's free recitative as he delivers the line Cather uses to characterize his romantic view of the world after which the enthusiastic dancing resumes with the piano postlude.

Example 12.10, m. 40

The fifth song (Landscape III, "Prairie Spring") is one of those perfect weddings of text and music that create a sense of inevitability in the listener. Using the apparently simple materials of all-black-note chords in the treble register, Larsen creates a rhythmic and dynamic pattern of growing brilliance and excitement to match Cather's ecstatic text: "Spring, the throb of it, in the sky, in the clouds, in the warm, high wind."

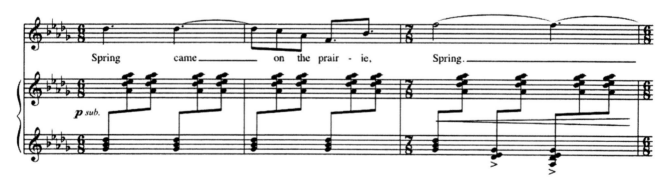

Example 12.11, mm. 10–15

The breathless emotional crescendo culminates with the "larks singing straight at the sun" as Larsen takes the vocal line up a soaring octave and a half to a high A-flat and a confirming melisma.

Example 12.12, mm. 30–38

Number six, "Ántonia in the Field," draws most of its text from Cather's description of Jim's encounter with his friend eight months after her father's death when she is fifteen and beginning to share the field chores with her brother. Larsen sets the stage for this visual memory as the piano follows her "Warmly" indication with a slow, widely ranging melodic line in a 6/4 meter that slides into waltz rhythm with the voice's entrance.

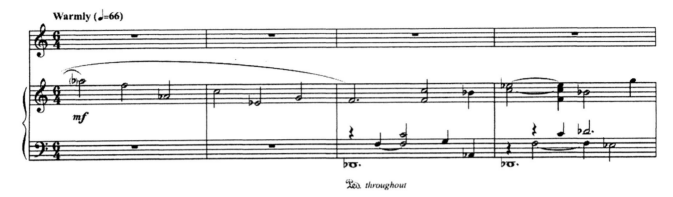

Example 12.13a, mm. 1–4

Example 12.13b, mm. 8–12

It is interesting that into the middle of declamatory vocal material describing their meeting and Ántonia's appearance ("sunburned, with her blouse open at the neck and her throat plastered with dust"), Larsen has inserted a line of her own which she asks to be sung "rapturously." With this line ("Oh, she was beautiful"), the composer has made explicit a depth of feeling which the writer never more than hints at in the novel.

Example 12.14, mm. 25–28

Now the song ends with a restatement of the octave leaps from song number two, this time rendered "lovingly" as "My Ántonia" is held in fond recollection.

Example 12.15, mm. 34–38

Libby Larsen's *My Ántonia* is dedicated to "Clara, Serena, Florence, and Hannah White, my grandmother and her sisters, and for all the daughters of the prairie." One is tempted to add two more names to this list of prairie daughters—those of Willa Cather and Libby Larsen.

John Musto (b. 1954)

John Musto was Brooklyn born and New York trained, and his career represents an amalgam of all the major American musical influences of the twentieth century. He received his earliest musical instruction from his father, a jazz guitarist, so that his boyhood was steeped in the improvisational language and structures of American popular music. As his pianistic talent became evident, he turned to classical music and enrolled at the Manhattan School. Here his principal piano teachers were Seymour Lipkin, who is known for his masterful performances of Beethoven and Schubert, and Paul Jacobs who, before his early death, was an electrifying performer of the Baroque and twentieth-century keyboard repertoire.

Despite all the high-level input of John Musto's mentoring as a pianist, it is noteworthy that he is a self-taught composer, and his biographical sketches imply that his improvisational experiences in jazz gave him the confidence which led naturally into the classical composition process. Musto the pianist has certainly remained in demand through the years, frequently performing his own works that include keyboard chamber music, and two piano concerti premièred in 2005. Musto the pedagogue has also been an active force in the New York musical scene, both as a professor at Brooklyn College and as a frequent guest lecturer at Juilliard and his alma mater, the Manhattan School of Music.

However, on examining his catalog of works, it becomes clear that the first of his musical personae to emerge in response to the inner creative forces was actually Musto, the song composer. It would, of course, be difficult to ignore the probable influence on this development of his marriage in 1984 to Amy Burton, soprano, a prominent member of the New York City and Metropolitan Operas. In the intervening twenty-five years, Musto and Burton have often appeared together in concert, and they have recently recorded his *Collected Songs* on Bridge Records, together with Patrick Mason, baritone. The past decade has also seen Musto moving into a new genre of vocal composition, with the production of three operas: *Volpone* (2004), *Later the Same Evening* (2007), and *Bastianello* (2008). In all of these, Musto has collaborated with Mark Campbell as librettist, and the team is presently working on a fourth for the Wolf Trap Opera Company, which had provided the original commission for *Volpone*.

Most of John Musto's texts for his songs of the 1980s and 1990s were drawn from the writing of American poets. These included Robert Frost, Dorothy Parker, Langston Hughes, e.e. cummings, Carl Sandburg, James Agee, Lawrence Ferlinghetti, Eugene O'Neill, Edna St. Vincent Millay, and Louise Bogan. The last two are found in one of Musto's strongest works, a three song cycle called *Recuerdo*[10]—the Spanish word for his theme of remembrance, which is also the title of the second poem. The first song of his cycle sets "Echo," one of the best-known poems of Christina Rossetti, who as an English writer will not be treated here. Suffice it to say that "Echo" is a romantic Victorian supplication to a deceased love whose presence can only be recaptured in dreams.

Millay's memory in the next song text is light years away from this in mood and setting. "Recuerdo" was the third poem in *A Few Figs from Thistles*, a small collection of poems written during Millay's Greenwich Village years when she was working with the Provincetown Players, meeting many writers and artists, and living a free, "Bohemian" lifestyle. (For a full treatment of Edna St. Vincent Millay's life and work, see chapter 5). In "Recuerdo," we glimpse two elements of the life that the poet celebrated in the oft-quoted line "My candle burns at both ends." The first is the relationship between the two people who are "very tired [and] . . . very merry"—one of many relationships which transpired in those years of her vibrant youthful beauty and personality. The second is the unconventionality of the way of life the Village celebrated, which could readily encompass going "back and forth all night on the ferry."

When John Musto composed the *Recuerdo* cycle in 1988, he had already accomplished a very smooth and workable integration of contemporary concert music with his early jazz improvisational background. Millay's poem is in three verses and each opens with the "tired [and] . . . merry" couple going back and forth all night on the ferry." This gives Musto the material for a refrain that he precedes by a three-measure ragtime piano prelude.

Example 12.16, mm. 1–3

The piano then continues with a variation on the opening material and the voice enters with a counter melody.

Example 12.17, mm. 4–10

This setting will be repeated with some variation for each repetition of this text and on each repetition, the vocal line will end a step lower as the wearying night drags on. The last repetition also calls for a *meno mosso* tempo that has now gone from the jaunty 104 per eighth note of the beginning to a dragging 69.

John Musto, of course, is a skilled pianist, and there are many virtuoso touches in the accompaniment, such as the piano's aural bursting into the poetic vision of a sunrise.

Example 12.18, mm. 49–51

Notable elements of sophisticated contemporary style are the frequently disjunct vocal line, the rhythmic interpolation of 5/8, 3/8, etc., into the basic ragtime duple meter, and the heavy admixture of both chromaticism and "blue" notes to the basically tonal (mostly G major) harmony. Musto has brilliantly succeeded, with this song, in bringing Millay's 1920s jazz-age ambience forward into the turn of the next century.

Louise Bogan (1897–1970)

For the third setting of his cycle, "A Last Song," Musto chooses to use the final six lines of a longer poem by Louise Bogan called "After the Persian" which was published in *The Blue Estuaries* of 1968, a slim but elegant collection of her life's work as a poet. Bogan was born five years after Edna St. Vincent Millay, also in the state of Maine, but instead of the mountains and seashore of Millay's youth, her surroundings were to be various drab mill towns of the Northeastern United States. Louise's father, Daniel Joseph Bogan, was a paper mill superintendent and she, her parents, and her brother followed him every few years to a new but similar job in another unpleasant living situation. The Bogans had a volatile marriage and her mother's affairs haunted Louise Bogan for much of her life.[11] Although she only attended Boston University for one year, the five years she had previously spent at Boston Girls' Latin School (1910–1915) gave her a rigorous classical education, from which she emerged already reading and writing poetry.

In 1906, Bogan married Curt Alexander, a professional soldier, who the following year was stationed in the Panama Canal Zone where Louise gave birth to a daughter. Ironically, Bogan's brother was to die in battle in 1918, while serving in France in the trenches of World War I. The Alexanders' marriage, never a happy one, was ended with Curt's death in 1920, and the widow then took up residence in New York where her life as a working writer began. A second marriage in 1925, to Raymond Holden, was also troubled and was finally terminated twelve years later by a divorce, but despite personal turmoil, the decades of the 1920s and 1930s were the most productive for Bogan's poetic muse. She published three volumes of verse, *Body of this Death* (1924), *Dark Summer* (1929), and *The Sleeping Fury* (1937), as well as establishing a source of steady income by writing literary reviews. (Besides other occasional commissions, Bogan would hold a position as poetry editor for the *New Yorker* for thirty-eight years, from 1931 to the year before her death.) Reviewing had been the suggestion of Edmund Wilson, who was the editor of *Vanity Fair* in the 1920s and an important member of Bogan's New York circle of writers. Others of the group were William Carlos Williams, Marianne Moore, and John Reed who became part of her sustaining artistic community.

Another fellow poet with whom Bogan would maintain a relationship from 1935 until his death in 1963 was Theodore Roethke. The two writers shared a lifelong battle with emotional illness and both were periodically hospitalized when the depressive episodes became overwhelming. Roethke, for many years, held a teaching appointment at the University of Washington, and on two occasions recommended Bogan to replace him during semesters when he was on leave. Teaching having now proved to be another temperamentally compatible means of self-support, Bogan held occasional academic positions during the last several decades of her life at institutions such as New York University, University of Arkansas, University of Arizona, and Hollins College. She also traveled the summer literary circuits, spending time at the Salzburg Seminar in American Studies in 1958 and the coveted artistic colonies of Yaddo in 1926 and MacDowell from 1957 on.

Louise Bogan was a very intense and very private person whose poems, mostly centered around the themes of love and grief, were brief and highly structured. During the second decade of the twentieth century, when modernism in the arts was taking shape, "Bogan was quietly mastering metrics and defining her style."[12] Although many reviewers found her poetry obscure, the verse which John Musto chose for his setting dedicated to the memory of Jeffery French appears extremely direct and simple in its opening: "Goodbye, goodbye / There was so much to love." The next lines, however, are a wonderfully concise comment on the ambiguity of loving relationships: "I could not love it enough / Some things I overlooked and some I could not find."

The poem as it is written is indeed a remarkable example of Bogan's skillful handling of metrics. There are two verses of three lines each, with the following structure of stresses per line: 2/6/3 succeeded by 6/2/3. It is not surprising that this poetic rhythm is completely "assimilated"[13] in Musto's setting that opens up the tight emotional control of the lyric by means of a poignant six-note motif that is first stated by the piano.

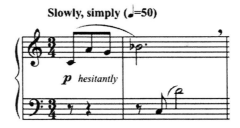

Example 12.19, m. 1

This motif is immediately expanded in the remainder of the instrumental introduction that becomes a concise statement of the expressive contour of the entire song.

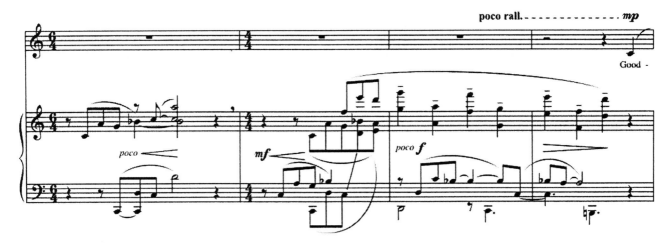

Example 12.20, mm. 2–5

When the voice enters, it is with the interval of a ninth that forms the second half of the opening motif (see Ex. 12.19). All the while, the piano is developing the first half (C, A, G, B-flat).

Example 12.21, mm. 6–9

In fact, Musto's formal control is as tight as Bogan's, as the continuing motivic variation moves to an emotive climax. This occurs when the rather disjunct vocal line gives way to the sweeping canonic contours of the piano as it expresses what the poet hints at in "some I could not find."

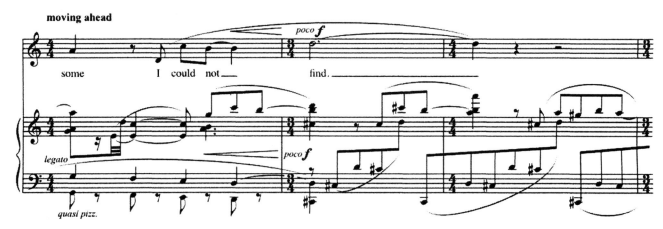

Example 12.22, mm. 15–17

The final line, "Let the crystal clasp them when you drink your wine in autumn" reads poetically like a resignation to the necessary transcending of love's failures. As Musto sets it, with an intense series of rising vocal fourths and "Broadly singing" octaves in the accompaniment, it seems rather like a rejoicing in its successes.

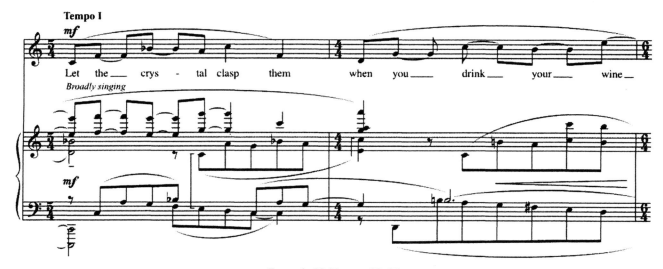

Example 12.23, mm. 23–24

With the composer's closing measures, we remember that "A Last Song" was his title, not the writer's. Here, as the wine is drunk "in autumn," the opening major sixth returns in the piano, now a minor interval and stated twice in inversion. All striving is apparently ended in this elegy to a relationship, but then there is one more sixth, rising upward in persisting memory.

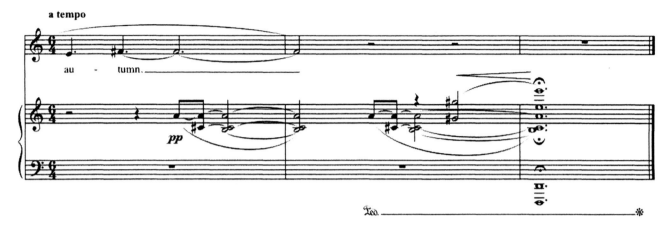

Example 12.24, mm. 28–30

Lori Laitman (b. 1955)

For her "unofficial biography,"[14] Lori Laitman has chosen a title that aptly characterizes her musical career: "The Accidental Art Song Composer." It all began when she was born in Long Beach, New York, into a highly musical family. Her mother was a singer, violinist, and pianist, her two sisters a pianist and violinist respectively, and Lori herself began to study the piano at age five and flute at age seven. The life of a professional flautist remained her goal throughout high school and both undergraduate and graduate years at Yale, where she was also studying composition but writing mostly instrumental pieces.

Laitman had taken a course at Yale from Frank Lewin in writing music for film and theater and this would become a focus of her early composition. After marriage to another musician, Bruce Rosenblum, Laitman taught music with him at Buxton School in Williamstown, Massachusetts, then moved to New York City when he enrolled at Columbia Law School. With the wider opportunities now available, Laitman became the composer for the Dick Roberts industrial film company, and in 1980 also wrote the score to *The Taming of the Shrew* for the Folger Theatre production in Washington, D.C.

During the 1980s, Laitman gave birth to her three children, James, Diana, and Andrew. Since the years of child-raising proved incompatible with the tight scheduling of film score production, Laitman turned to composing chamber music and continued to teach flute at several institutions including the International Conservatory of Music. Here she met koto player Miyuki Yoshikami and to this day, Laitman continues to perform the music for flute and koto that she composed for their duo.

In 1991, a soprano named Lauren Wagner resurfaced in Laitman's life. She had been Lori's roommate at an Interlochen summer session after the composer's sophomore year in high school. Now she had won the Concert Artists Guild competition and wanted Laitman to write her some songs for a debut CD. Responding to this challenge, Laitman first chose to set Sara Teasdale's "The Metropolitan Tower" and found the vocal melody coming to her quite easily, even while involved with the children's activities. This song's performance at Merkin Hall on December 16, 1991, brought Laitman into contact with Paul Sperry, Richard Hundley, and John Musto, all major figures in contemporary American art song, and their praise of her work was the beginning of her finding "[her] voice in writing for voice."[15]

Since that fateful date, Lori Laitman has composed almost 200 songs, and vocal music has become exclusively her genre of choice. The growing reputation of these songs is evidenced in the four solo Laitman CDs that have been released by Albany Records in the past ten years: *The Songs of Lori Laitman* (2000), *Dreaming* (2003), *Becoming a Redwood* (2006), and *Within These Spaces* (2009). Individual songs have appeared on other labels. Laitman's first venture into operatic writing was an adaptation of Hawthorne's *The Scarlet Letter* with librettist David Mason that was commissioned by the University of Central Arkansas and had its debut there in November 2008. A taped performance has been aired and a recording may be in the offing.

Lori Laitman's art songs have been the subject of many journal articles[16] and she has attracted numerous commissions for settings of particular texts. Holocaust poetry has been one of her special interests but the large majority of her songs have set American poets: many contemporary authors such as Dana Gioia, Mary Oliver, and Thomas Lux as well as Emily Dickinson, Sara Teasdale, Elinor Wylie, and others from earlier generations. Among the twentieth century poets who attracted Laitman's notice was William Carlos Williams who has previously been set by very few of our American song writers.

William Carlos Williams (1883–1963)

Williams was born in Rutherford, New Jersey, into a mixed parental heritage that provided richness and complexity to his life as a man and an artist. His father, William George Williams, was an English immigrant to the United States who loved to read Shakespeare and who remained a British citizen all his life. His mother, Elena Hoheb Williams, was born in Puerto Rico and had spent four years in Paris as an art student.[17] After marrying and moving to New Jersey, she continued to prefer French and Spanish over the English language which she learned reluctantly and spoke imperfectly. It was Emily Wellcome, their paternal grandmother, who actually raised William and his brother Ed through their childhood, but as teenagers (1897–1899) the boys were enrolled in schools in Switzerland and France by Elena who took up residence nearby in her beloved and always longed-for Paris.

Back in the United States, William attended Horace Mann School in New York City and by then, having read widely and written his first poem, he had already encountered his lifelong struggle to reconcile art and science. He chose to become a physician in order to support his literary ambitions, and it was at the University of Pennsylvania School of Medicine (1902–1906) that he met Ezra Pound, H.D., and the painter, Charles Demuth.[18] During the next four years, Williams established his pattern of co-existent careers, as he held internships in New York and the University of Leipzig while also beginning to write seriously. In 1909, *Poems* emerged into print informally, through Reid Howell in Rutherford, but his first professional appearance as a poet of note was in the collection *Tempers* that was published in London (1913) by Pound's publisher, Elkin Matthews.

In 1912, Williams had married Florence Herman. Although her sister, Charlotte, would have been his first choice,[19] the relationship grew and flowered through the many years of their life together in the house on Rutherford's Ridge Road which was purchased in 1913. Now with an established medical practice and a family of two young boys who were born in 1914 and 1916, Williams created and maintained for forty years a work schedule of patients in the daytime, and evenings spent in writing or in literary meetings in New York with fellow poets such as Marianne Moore and Wallace Stevens.

Literary historians have associated Williams with Ezra Pound, founder of the Imagist movement, but in the course of time he diverged from Pound and from T. S. Eliot in his dislike of their allusions to foreign languages and classical sources. His proper place is as a representative of the American Modernist movement, whose mission was the renewal of our language from the worn out models of British and European culture.[20] Williams tried to invent a fresh form of American poetry centered on everyday life and ordinary people, and he evolved the concept of the "variable foot" which he felt to be the poetic expression of the rhythms of American speech.[21]

For over fifty years, Williams published a steady stream of poetry, fiction, plays, critical essays, and an autobiography. Probably his best-known poetry is the five-volume collection of *Paterson* that dealt with aspects of life in the larger New Jersey city that was close to Rutherford. Williams was also a valuable mentor for younger poets, especially those involved in literary movements of the fifties such as the Beat Generation and the Black Mountain School.

In 1951, Williams began to suffer over ten years a series of small strokes that became increasingly debilitating. Two years later, he was hospitalized with severe depression, probably as a result of difficulties that his socialist politics caused over a projected consultantship to the Library of Congress. Through all these physical and psychological challenges, Williams continued to write and publish until 1961. He died in Rutherford two years later, and was awarded both the Pulitzer Prize and the Gold Medal for Poetry posthumously.

Hyatt Waggoner makes a convincing case that although William Carlos Williams "thought of himself . . . as a 'naturalist' and a 'realist' . . . the voice we hear in the poetry is almost always wholly romantic."[22] Although the moods are contrasting, romanticism certainly pervades Laitman's two settings of the Williams poems "Full Moon" and "Light Hearted William."[23] In the first (from *Collected Poems* of 1934), the moon is addressed as "blessed" and as "the noon of night . . . that bids love stay." Williams's time-honored thanks to this lovers' moon goes back to Shakespeare and beyond, and Laitman sets it in a melting waltz tempo, a lyrical vocal contour climaxing on "love," and the appropriately bright key of F-sharp major. (Waggoner's theory is borne out by Laitman's opening tempo instruction of "extremely flexible, romantic.")

Example 12.25, mm. 5–10

In the third verse of Williams's brief lyric, nighttime terrors intrude as "curious shapes / awake to plague me." Laitman now uses her always-flexible tonal harmonic contrast to move to A minor and chooses to repeat this disturbing text at a rising dynamic level that equates with increasing anxiety.

Example 12.26, mm. 13–18

The 3/4 time is a unifying factor for the whole setting, and as the poet asks "Is day near, shining girl?," F-sharp major returns briefly, only to blossom into Ċ-major aural warmth and fulfillment—a true harmonic mirroring of the text.

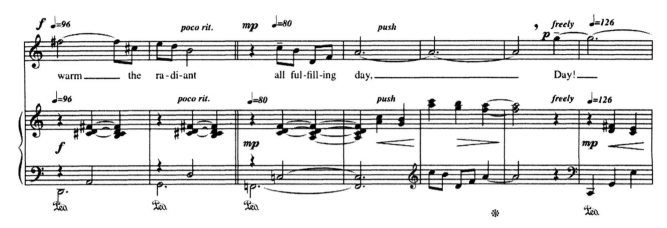

Example 12.27, mm. 26–32

"Light Hearted William" had first appeared in an earlier collection of 1921, called *Sour Grapes*. It is a charming, fantastic, not at all logical portrait of a man who may be the poet's identification of part of his own persona, leaning out of the window in spring and twirling his "November moustaches." Laitman's musical treatment follows the "lightness" of the protagonist's mood. The varied measure lengths and staccato touches in the spare piano accompaniment suggest the subject's quick movements as do the frequently changing key signatures.

Example 12.28, mm. 2–6

The meter settles for a time into a waltz as William sighs "Heigh-ya" and leans out of the window, but soon the variable rhythms and disjunct vocal line return to portray the hero's laughter and final twirling of what have now, possibly in honor of the season, become his "green moustaches."

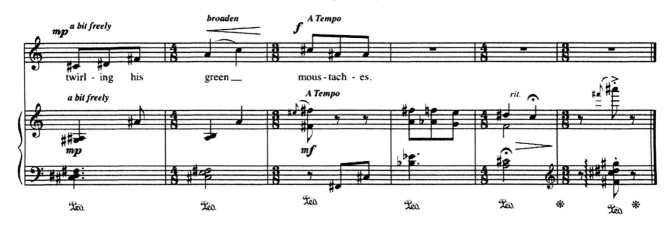

Example 12.29, mm. 54–59

Plums[24] is a pair of songs written by Laitman in 1996 setting Williams poems from the thirties. "To an Old Woman" appeared in *An Early Martyr* (1935) while "This is Just to Say" was published with the *Collected Poems* of 1934. Now we are dealing with Williams the realist, who is reporting the world exactly as he sees it, but we must nevertheless take account of Thomas Whitaker's view that Williams, at one and the same time, always "explores both the external environment and the internal realm of passion, self-knowledge, and ethical values."[25] And indeed, "To an Old Woman" paints a very precise, objective picture of the protagonist, "munching a plum on the street," and lets us know the pleasure she is experiencing by his three repetitions of "They taste good to her." But there is moral comment as well in the fourth verse: "Comforted / a solace of ripe plums." Here we derive Williams's humanity as he empathizes with a creature that has only an occasional bit of fruit in her life for comfort.

Lori Laitman has set "To a Poor Old Woman" in quasi-operatic fashion with the piano participating mostly as harmonic accompaniment. The vocal line is paramount and after the character is introduced in a D centered line, the contour of the three "They taste good to her" statements rise to a fulfilling high A with the Dorian context lightened to D major. Laitman now chooses to repeat "to the one now sucked out in her hand" in a musical sequence featuring a descending leap that suggests her body continually bending down to the fruit.

Example 12.30, mm. 23–27

With "comforted" and "a solace of ripe plums," the harmonies become more expansive and the vocal arch up to "fill the air" is almost ecstatic.

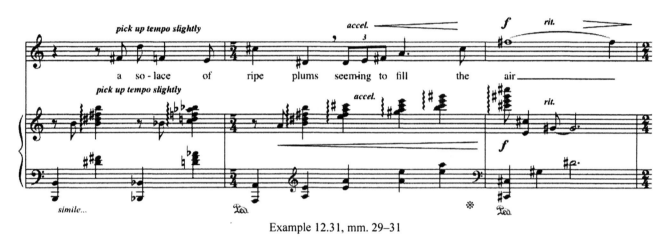

Example 12.31, mm. 29–31

In an interesting final touch, Laitman has everything settle down on a fulfilled A-flat major, while the piano's right hand contributes parallel thirds of chromatic uncertainty.

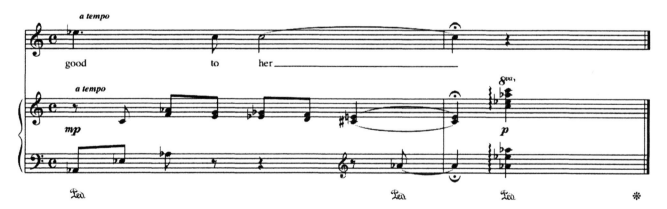

Example 12.32, mm. 33–34

"This is Just to Say" mimics a note left by the poet to a friend or spouse informing them that he has eaten "the plums / that were in / the icebox" which the other person was probably "saving for breakfast." It is a prime example of Williams dealing with the "everyday" and here he does it with a deft, humorous touch. Laitman responds in kind with a one page, mostly narrow range declamatory setting and a "tinkling music box" (her indication) use of the piano in its upper range. She leaves no doubt about the mood of the piece with her tempo annotation in measure twelve and her gratuitous addition to the poetic scene in the final measure.

Example 12.33, mm. 12–17

Ricky Ian Gordon (b. 1956)

Ricky Ian Gordon was born in Oceanside, New York, and raised on Long Island in easy reach of the city that was to nurture his talent and provide much of his artistic inspiration. His father, Sam, had served in World War II and married Eve, his mother, just before going overseas. Eve was a naturally gifted singer and had begun a career entertaining in the hotels of the Catskills.[26] Their first child was already two when Sam returned from the war, so he gave up thoughts of further education and went to work as an electrician, eventually forming his own company. Eve settled down to raise a family of three girls and one boy in one of the new Long Island post-war suburban developments modeled on the Levittown prototype.

Following this conventional beginning, the Gordon family encountered the sixties, and the three sisters, like many of their peers, came under the influence of feminism, sexual liberation, eastern spirituality, the drug culture, and radical politics. Ricky, as the youngest child, grew up in a somewhat different environment, in which his emerging talent consumed all his energy and his major challenge was finding friends who shared his artistic passions.

When he was a small child, Ricky's sisters would often read poetry to him, and the first lines he would remember were from the "Ballad of the Harp Weaver" by Edna St. Vincent Millay, whose poems he would later set to music. In those early years, Gordon would often pick out melodies by ear on his mother's piano, and when, at the age of seven, he played the first movement of the Moonlight Sonata after one hearing, a local teacher named Mrs. Fox was engaged to begin his serious study of the instrument. *The Victor Book of the Opera*, owned by Mrs. Fox, began to open up for Gordon the world of musical drama, and at summer camp in 1965 he auditioned for and received a role in *The King and I*.

By his early teens, Ricky Gordon was making up his own songs, and in the next few years set about absorbing musical experiences of all varieties, becoming an ardent fan of both Joni Mitchell and the Metropolitan Opera. By a fortunate coincidence, he was able to enroll at the "free school" program which had recently begun at West Hempstead High School, under the acronym SAFE (i.e., for students and faculty education). With the approval of his SAFE advisor, Ricky now foraged all of the New York cultural scene, and was encouraged to attend foreign film festivals, a course in film criticism, a dance class at the Alvin Ailey School, and many of the current opera and musical theater productions. In later years, the composer "would always consider himself saved by SAFE. The program made a home for him . . . [and] he now realized that he wanted a great deal for the future. . . . He wanted art, fame, and the same heady life he was now experiencing."[27]

In 1974, Gordon passed the entrance auditions to the Carnegie Mellon College of Fine Arts. Having begun his studies as a piano major, he soon realized that the necessary grueling practice schedule was not for him, and transferred to a concentration in composition. Following his junior year, the composer joined a small summer stock company in Paines

ville, Ohio, and after this experience made the decision to leave college and move to New York to begin the life of a professional musician. He shared an apartment on West 70th Street with an actor and a novelist, and began by cleaning other people's apartments to earn money for living expenses, but by 1979 he was firmly established in the New York musical theater world as the accompanist to singer and comedian Phyllis Newman (the wife of the well-known lyricist, Adolph Green).

The ensuing years brought ever-increasing levels of professional involvement. In 1982, Gordon wrote a score for a production of Brecht's *A Man's a Man*; in 1984 he was performing in the Grand Casino in Monaco where he sang and played his own settings of Yeats and May Sarton; and in 1986 his second musical, *Toby Tyler*, was composed for the Milwaukee Children's Theater (the first had been *Dr. Faustus*, written at Carnegie Mellon). From 1990 on, the flow of composition has never stopped, and with the exception of a *Piano Collection for Solo Piano and Piano Four Hands* (Carl Fischer, 2005), Ricky Ian Gordon's works have been vocally centered in both conventional and innovative forms.

Major operatic milestones have been *The Tibetan Book of the Dead* (premièred at the Houston Opera in 1996), *Orpheus and Euridice* (2002), *Morning Star* (written with William Hoffman for the Chicago Lyric Opera), and most recently, *The Grapes of Wrath* (premièred in 2007 by the Minnesota Opera). During much the same period, Gordon has composed an impressive number of seven art song collections as well as theater pieces such as *My Life with Albertine* (2003) and a mixed media production called *Green Sneakers* (2008) that is scored for baritone, string quartet, empty chair, and pianist.

On examining the art song collections, one finds two prevalent text sources. The first is American poets of the last century and a half, beginning with Emily Dickinson and moving through Edna St. Vincent Millay, Dorothy Parker, Langston Hughes, James Agee, Sylvia Plath, Howard Moss, Delmore Schwartz and John Ashbery, to name only the most prominent of his wide-ranging choices. The second source is Ricky Ian Gordon himself and it is particularly in this group, when the composer serves as his own lyricist, that his early and strong musical theater influence seems most pronounced.

Langston Hughes (1902–1967)

Of all the American poets he has set, Gordon seems to have the greatest affinity for Langston Hughes, whose poetry he has used in thirty solo art songs and three choral arrangements. Ten of these settings are grouped into a cycle called *Genius Child*, written for the African American singer Harolyn Blackwell, who premièred it at the Bermuda Festival in 1993. "Langston Hughes," says Gordon, "seemed a natural choice . . . [as] I think he is the most terse, economical, and wise American poet. . . . [I chose] poems which reflected how I was feeling at that time . . . [and] began with 'Kid in the Park' because I had such a searing identification with the line 'lonely little question mark.'"[28]

In the opening two songs of the cycle, "Kid in the Park" and "Genius Child," the composer leaves no doubt about the feelings of alienation and compassion for the disaffected that he shared so strongly with Langston Hughes. (For extensive material on the life and works of this poet, see chapter 3). Interestingly, the poem "Kid in the Park" had been written by Hughes in 1950, almost thirty years after the author's "black pride" period, and was originally published under the title "Waif" in the spring issue of the *Minnesota Quarterly*. Here the loneliness of the central figure seems more a universal statement, not specifically related to black separation from white society, and Gordon lets us know what it feels like to be any child whose home is "just around the corner but not really anywhere."

He describes his tempo as "Slow, Desolate" (58 to the quarter note) and opens with a desultory little hum in nervously changing meters as the "kid" looks for comfort in the sound of his own voice.

Example 12.34, mm. 2–6

Then the composer begins the body of the song which will maintain a 4/4 meter and a syncopated accompaniment motive that rises up to meet a wistfully descending vocal line.

Example 12.35, mm. 8–12

The harmonic language is tonal but replete with jazz chords and the key scheme rising in half-steps (A minor, B-flat minor, B minor) is also a familiar one from the popular scene. One is reminded of Stephen Holden's apt characterization in the *New York Times* that Gordon's songs "blithely blur the lines between art song and the high-end Broadway music of . . . Bernstein and . . . Sondheim." The composer ends his moving portrait of a child whose world holds no certainty by setting the last line of the poem back in the uneasily changing meters. Then the piano makes its final comment, repeating its unrelenting motive once again in the opening key, as if to say the outer world goes on despite the inner struggles of its inhabitants.

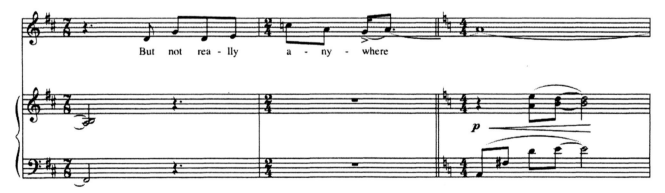

Example 12.36, mm. 29–35

The title song of the cycle, *Genius Child,* sets a poem that was first published in *Opportunity* (August 1937) and was slightly altered by Langston Hughes for its inclusion in the collection *Fields of Wonder* (1947). The setting incorporates Gordon's signature harmonies (tonal, jazz-inflected) and gently syncopated rhythmic patterns, but the mood is quite different from the sadness of "Kid in the Park." Now the composer musically reveals the poetic despair of the "genius child" whom "nobody loves." He also makes musically explicit the violence that threatens him both internally and from the outside world that sees him as a "monster of frightening name." Gordon accomplishes this with a rapid, driving tempo (120 to the quarter note), and an almost frantic rate of key change and meter signatures, as a metaphor for the line "lest the song get out of hand."

Example 12.37, mm. 8–14

The climax of the poem is a shockingly concise poetic summary by Langston Hughes of a desperate solution to the genius child's suffering: "Kill him, and let his soul run wild." Gordon sets this line with unaccompanied vocal declamation, punctuated at the beginning with an aggressive, accented attack on "Kill him!" The piano answers with a bullet-like arpeggiated descent, and then both join together at "wild" with a joyfully running piano figure behind the release of a high G-flat for the singer.

Example 12.38, mm. 31–35

Toward the end of the cycle, Gordon sets the Hughes poem "My People" which was first published as "Poem" in *Crisis* of August, 1923, and also in *The Weary Blues* collected in 1926. The title "My People" first appeared in *The Dream Keeper* (1932) and was retained in *Selected Poems* of 1957. It was written in Langston Hughes's early period of literary identification with the struggles and sorrows of his race, as well as with their strength and beauty. It is the latter that he portrays in "My People" and for its setting, Gordon has abandoned his syncopated rhythms for a flowing, unchanging 3/4 meter in a tempo indicated as "slow and dreamy."

The original poem is a brief six lines of uneven poetic feet in which the beauty of the night, the stars, and the sun are respectively aligned with the beauty of the faces, eyes, and souls of "my people." Gordon has expanded the poetic material first of all by repeating "of my people" after each couplet.

Example 12.39, mm. 5–12

His second strategy for expansion is to set the entire text twice, the second time beginning with a chordal staccato figuration in the piano that serves to intensify the poetic meaning.

Example 12.40, mm. 33–36

The key scheme remains the same in the second "verse" but there is further lyrical expansion of the accompaniment, and the vocal line rises in its most expressive arc to a high A-flat.

Example 12.41, mm. 53–56

In this setting, Gordon has made no attempt to link the "people" of Langston Hughes to any racial musical stereotypes. This is not even "Broadway" music but a generic, universal tribute to human ethnic pride of identification.

Jake Heggie (b. 1961)

In his early years, Jake Heggie covered the United States from coast to coast, having been born in West Palm Beach, Florida, moving to Ohio at the age of two, and ending up in the state of California. He had begun piano lessons at five, and by the time he was sixteen his interest in composition came under the tutelage of Ernst Bacon, who was fortuitously living in Orinda, California. This mentorship lasted for two important years of exposure to Bacon's strong predilection for vocal composition, after which Heggie continued his self-guided course of musical training with two years in Paris. Returning to the United States at the age of twenty, he enrolled at UCLA, where he studied piano with Johana Harris and composition with Roger Bourland, Paul Des Marais, and David Raksin. Apparently, the West Coast has continued to nurture the creative sensibilities of this composer, and although he travels widely giving concerts and workshops, San Francisco has been his home since 1993.

Jake Heggie has composed a cello concerto and other orchestral and chamber works, but over the last two decades his emphasis has been primarily vocal composition. In 1998, he was appointed composer in residence to the San Francisco Opera, where his first opera, *Dead Man Walking*, was performed to the great acclaim of critics and audiences. Other operas followed in close succession: *The End of the Affair* in 2004; *At the Statue of Venus* in 2005; *To Hell and Back*, 2006; and most recently, *Last Acts*, which premièred at the Houston Grand Opera in 2008.

Concurrently with his operatic commissions, Jake Heggie has composed over 200 art songs, which have been performed, often with the composer at the piano, by some of the brightest stars in the American vocal scene, such as Frederica von Stade, Renée Fleming, and Susan Graham. When questioned about his strong commitment to American art song, Heggie replies that it has a twofold source. First of all, he says "the voice still takes my breath away . . . [as] the most magical instrument," and secondly, "it is thrilling to sit in a concert hall and hear American performers sing songs in their own language." He goes on to say "and I love American English [which] is a very expressive language," thus clearly defining his preference for American poets, in pursuit of the most authentic joining of words and music.[29]

The list of American poets that Heggie has set in individual songs and cycles with piano, in choral arrangements, and in works with orchestra, chamber orchestra, and chamber group accompaniment is long and varied. It ranges from Emily Dickinson, Hart Crane, Amy Lowell, Edna St. Vincent Millay, and Anne Sexton to Frederica von Stade and Jake Heggie himself. One of his most favored American poets has been Vachel Lindsay, a writer whose legacy has been distorted by the early concentration of literary historians on only one aspect of his work. (See chapter 2 for a discussion of Lindsay's "General William Booth Enters Into Heaven.")

Vachel Lindsay (1879–1931)

Lindsay was born in Springfield, Illinois, to a father who was a successful but uncultivated physician and a mother who had graduated in 1869 at the top of her class from Glendale Female College, Ohio, "in an early American assertion of female potential."[30] Having great confidence in her son's abilities, Mrs. Lindsay educated him at home until the age of eleven. Thereafter, he attended Springfield secondary schools and from 1897 to 1900 studied medicine unsuccessfully at Hiram College, Ohio. Having failed to become a physician, he now enrolled successively at Chicago Institute of Art (1901–1903) and the New York School of Art (1903–1908) but again, did not graduate from either institution.

Paradoxically, Lindsay had spent most of his time during the unproductive academic years writing poetry, which enterprise was strongly encouraged by the painter Robert Henri who was one of his art instructors. In 1908 he returned to his parents' home in Springfield and began serious writing, both of poetry, often accompanied by intricate drawings, and prose commentaries on American history, politics, and socio-religious theory.

In the summers of 1906, 1908, and 1912, Lindsay undertook walking tours across the country during which he would recite his own poetry in exchange for food and lodging. It was these declamations that formed the basis of his later dismissal as a kind of "prairie troubadour" by those who knew little of his writing except for "The Congo" and "General William Booth." Publication of his poems in Harriet Monroe's *Poetry* magazine[31] in 1913 brought considerable fame but little happiness, since his courtship of Sara Teasdale was rejected in 1914 in favor of a St. Louis businessman whose financial profile won over that of a struggling poet. (See chapter 5 of this volume for an extended treatment of Sara Teasdale.)

Except for one year, 1923–1924, when he taught poetry at Gulfport Junior College for Girls in Mississippi, Lindsay would earn a meager living for the rest of his life by traveling the country and giving recitations of his work. Besides the collected volumes of his poetry (*Collected Poems* of 1925 was dedicated to Sara Teasdale), other works were constantly coming to publication beginning with *The Art of the Moving Picture* in 1915, and including the far-ranging *Golden Book of Springfield* in 1920 which was a prediction of the nature of urban society in the year 2018. After a move out of Illinois to Spokane, Washington, in 1924, he was married at the age of forty-five to Elizabeth Conner, who was twenty-two years younger. The birth of their two children in 1926 and 1927 having increased the financial pressure on Lindsay, and following exhausting walking tours during the last three years of his life, the poet succumbed to overwhelming depression and committed suicide in 1931 by drinking a bottle of Lysol. A year later, Sara Teasdale, who had divorced her husband in 1929, ended her own life with an overdose of sleeping pills.

In 2000, Jake Heggie published settings of Vachel Lindsay's *Moon Poems*, a group of sensitive, delicate, sometimes ironic verses that are a far cry from the rousing rhythms of "The Congo" and "General William Booth." Heggie has titled his cycle *Songs to the Moon*[32] and it was premièred by Frederica von Stade at the Ravinia Festival of August 20, 1998 with Martin Katz at the piano. The work had been commissioned by Music Accord, a consortium of music presenters that included the Library of Congress, Wolf Trap Foundation, the Chamber Music Society of Lincoln Center, and the Boston Symphony Orchestra at Tanglewood.

Heggie uses Lindsay's "To Gloriana," the first of the *Moon Poems*, as the opening of the cycle as well. "Gloriana" was the adoring title that Renaissance Britons applied to their beloved Queen Elizabeth, usually adding "the Virgin Queen" to the term of address, and praising her in extravagant language. So it is entirely appropriate that Vachel Lindsay dedicates his eight-line verse to the "girl with the burning, golden eyes . . . and snowy throat" and offers her "gold and silver moons . . . and diamond stars" among many gifts. One of the other offerings that is especially interesting occurs in the line "I bring you prairie skies," which suggests that the poet cannot completely hide his American Midwestern ethos under the mantle of the Renaissance troubadour.

Jake Heggie titles this opening song "Prologue: Once More to Gloriana," inferring that a long line of dedications to this feminine devotional icon has preceded this one. To his credit, he does not attempt to outdo all the former tributes in grandiose complexity. This is a simple, lovely setting: tonal, diatonic, with a haunting, lyrical line and a regular 3/4 meter broken into a flowing eighth note rhythm by the off-beat accompaniment structures.

Example 12.42, mm. 11–16

Two small but arresting details occur in the piano prelude. The first is in measure one: a forte, accented, dotted note figure that is reminiscent of a trumpet call announcing a royal dedicatory event. The second, beginning in the left hand of measure six, is a polytonal element of E-flat, B-flat, E-flat, appearing as a soft, cloudy comment on the clear opening G major environment.

Example 12.43, mm. 1–7

The E-flat counterpoint will recur at the end of the first verse, now moved to the right hand and revealing its textual derivation from the line it surrounds ("and mists that float").

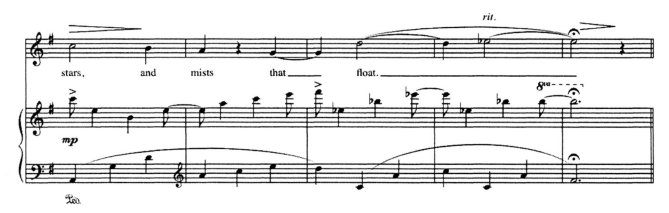

Example 12.44, mm. 29–33

"Euclid" is Lindsay's second *Moon Poem* and Heggie's second setting of the cycle. This is a total about-face in mood, to an ironic juxtaposition of the "solemn graybeards'" academic arguments about the circle and the "silent child's" perception of their drawings as "charming round pictures of the moon." Heggie plays this for its humorous elements, with a rapid tempo, staccato bass line, and jazz rhythms and harmonies in the piano prelude and interludes.

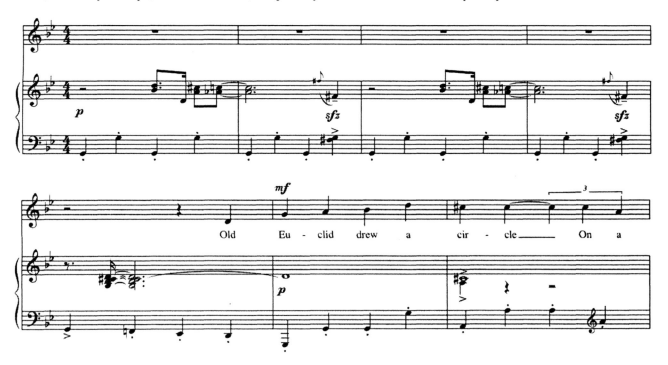

Example 12.45, mm. 1–7

A descending chromatic scale pokes fun at the mathematical language of the savants, after which pianist and singer are instructed to "let 'er rip."

Example 12.46, mm. 20–27

The jazz rhythms are stilled finally as the "silent child" ignores their chatter and gazes at their drawings with an artist's eye.

Example 12.47, mm. 35–39

Of the thirty-two *Moon Poems* in Vachel Lindsay's collection, ten are recountings of what various animals, people, or mythological beings had to say about the moon from their perspective. Heggie's setting of "What the Gray-winged Fairy Said" is a very evocative piece of word-painting, beginning with the delicate bell sounds made by soft, dissonant piano chords surrounding the text line "The moon's a gong, hung in the wild."

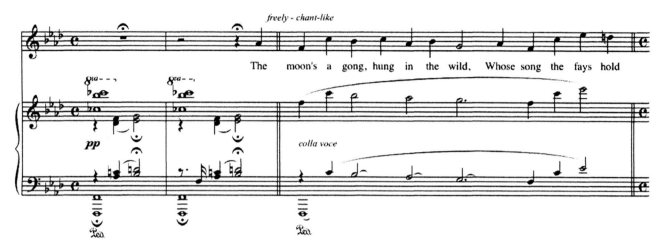

Example 12.48, mm. 1–3

The dynamic level of voice and accompaniment rises as the moon, now full, becomes a "splendid gong," and its beating is portrayed by the piano in mm. 11 and 12.

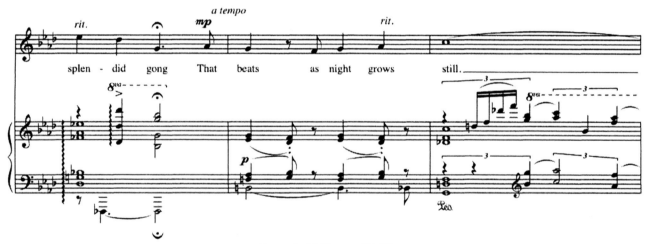

Example 12.49, mm. 10–12

As a final, luminous touch, Heggie lets us hear Lindsay's "evening song" of "dove or whippoorwill" in the last three notes of the vocal line and in the right hand of the piano postlude.

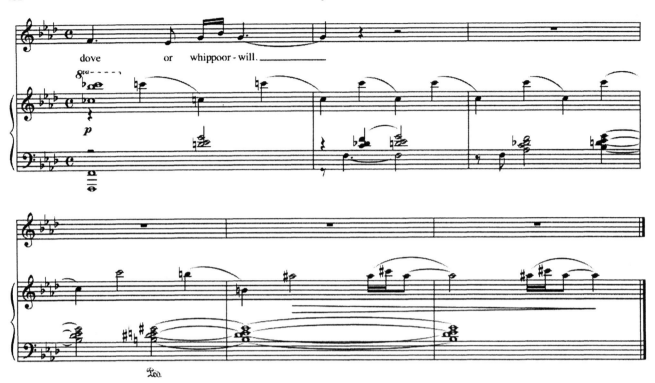

Example 12.50, mm. 16–21

When *Songs to the Moon* was published in 2000, it was included in a volume titled *Faces of Love, Book 2*. In the Foreword to this volume, Jake Heggie tells his performers that "In these songs, the singer encounters the full gamut of the influences I grew up with: folk music, jazz, pop, opera, rock, art song." This statement is a perfect characterization of not only Jake Heggie's songs but those of all the composers we have examined in this chapter who are writing at this exciting and explosive juncture of the twentieth and twenty-first century.

Notes

1. The majority of the following biographical material is derived from a telephone interview with R. Friedberg, 22 September 2009.

2. Mary Ann Feldman, Larsen article in *The New Grove Dictionary of Music and Musicians*, edited by Stanley Sadie (London: Macmillan, 2001).

3. Interview with R. Friedberg, September 2009. Also, see chapter 1 for Ned Rorem's comments on the musical rhythms of spoken language.

4. Philip Gerber, *Willa Cather* (New York: Twayne Publishers, 1995), 9.

5. Gerber, *Willa Cather,* 35.

6. Willa Cather, *Early Stories* (New York: Mead & Co., 1957). Introduction by Mildred R. Bennett.

7. This was a tract of land between the Little Blue and Republican rivers, appearing as "the Divide" in many Cather stories.

8. Libby Larsen, *Margaret Songs* (New York: Oxford University Press, 1998).

9. Libby Larsen, *My Ántonia* (New York: Oxford University Press, 2004).

10. John Musto, *Recuerdo* (New York: Southern Music, 1988).

11. Wendy Hirsch, "Louise Bogan" in *American National Biography* (New York: Oxford University Press, 1999).

12. Hirsch, "Louise Bogan."

13. See Langer on "assimilation" in the Introduction.

14. Lori Laitman, "The Accidental Art Song Composer," *Artsongs.com*, http://www.artsongs.com/meet/chattybio (23 September 2009).

15. Laitman, "The Accidental Art Song Composer."

16. One of the most comprehensive is Carol Lines, "The Songs of Lori Laitman," *Journal of Singing* 64 (September/October 2007): 31–46.

17. For a detailed account of William Carlos Williams's ancestry see Paul Mariani, *William Carlos Williams* (New York: McGraw-Hill, 1981).

18. See material on Ezra Pound in chapter 10 of this volume.

19. William was "double-crossed" by his brother, Ed, who hastened to Charlotte first with his own proposal. She married neither of the Williams brothers.

20. See Libby Larsen's comments earlier in this chapter on Willa Cather's similar mission.

21. It has been suggested that Williams's poetic rhythms were influenced by the percussive quality of the newly invented typewriter on which he composed most of his poetry.

22. Hyatt W. Waggoner, *American Poets from the Puritans to the Present* (New York: Dell Publishing, 1968), 369–86. Waggoner attributed this paradox to the conflicting influences on Williams of the Imagist Ezra Pound, and his exotic mother.

23. Lori Laitman, *Two William Carlos Williams Songs*, "Full Moon" and "Light Hearted William" (Fayetteville, Ark.: Classical Vocal Reprints, 2007). These songs are dedicated "in honor of Richard Miller, tenor and master teacher."

24. Lori Laitman, *Plums* (Fayetteville, Ark.: Classical Vocal Reprints, 1996). This publisher has probably the most extensive catalog in the country of art songs by American composers.

25. Thomas R. Whitaker, *William Carlos Williams* (Boston: Twayne Publishing, 1989).

26. The information about Ricky Ian Gordon's early life is derived from Donald Katz, *Home-Fires: An Intimate Portrait of One Middle-Class Family in Post-War America* (New York: HarperCollins, 1992). This remarkable book is a 600-page compilation of Katz's detailed interviews with the Gordon family, covering their lives from 1945 to 1990.

27. Katz, *Home-Fires,* 330.

28. Ricky Ian Gordon, Foreword to *Genius Child* (New York: Williamson Music, 1996).

29. The foregoing quotations are derived from Meredith Ziegler, "Jake Heggie's 'Paper Wings': Feeding the Genre of American Art Song" in *Journal of Singing* 64 (January/February 2008): 287.

30. Ann Massa, *Vachel Lindsay: Fieldworker for the American Dream* (Bloomington: Indiana University Press, 1970), 5.

31. *Poetry* was founded 100 years ago in 1912 by the young Chicago poet, Harriet Monroe. A bequest of $200 million dollars from Ruth Lilly in 2002 has funded a small, elegant building in Chicago's Gold Coast neighborhood that houses the magazine and the Poetry foundation that publishes it.

32. Jake Heggie, *The Faces of Love, Book 2* (New York: Hal Leonard, 2000).

Epilogue

"The American experience" says Wallace Stegner, "has been the confrontation by old peoples and cultures of a world as new as if it had just risen from the sea."[1] The wonder of this newness was indeed proclaimed by America's nineteenth-century writers[2]—Emerson, Melville, Whitman, and their confrères—but the ties to older musical cultures lingered, and, as we have seen, the American art song began as an offshoot of the European Romantic tradition.

In the course of this study, we have watched it strive self-consciously for the sound and feel of America and then, having achieved this goal, come in full maturity to the realization that (paraphrasing Virgil Thomson) "American art song is art song written by Americans." What this means, of course, is that twentieth and twenty-first century American composers setting American poetry have been subject to all the musical and literary influences of neo-Romanticism versus the avant-garde, and all the psychological influences of post-war despair and intermittent idealism that have produced the infinite variety of their work.

Yet the authors would be remiss if they failed to share with the reader a conviction that three general trends do seem to emerge from the wealth of material that has formed the basis of this study. The first of these has to do with the underlying rhythmic frame of reference in the American art song, which brings us back to Ned Rorem's idea of instrumental as well as vocal music deriving from national speech patterns.[3] Ruth Schonthal develops this suggestion, and with the keen ear of one who is not native-born points out to us the open, deliberate middle-tempo cadences of American, as opposed to European, language.[4] Some of our poets, such as James Purdy, consciously pursue "the American soul [through] the rhythms and accents of American speech,"[5] and others do it unconsciously. It remains for the composers to translate this, as they do, into an amalgam which draws from the crisp authority of New England and its village bandmasters, the gentle flow of the speech and ballads of the South and the West, and the energizingly heavy accent with a syncopated overlay of the African culture and its descendants (spirituals, ragtime, jazz, and Broadway).

The rhythmic schemes which result tend to have a direct, forceful, uncluttered quality which ties in with the second observable trend, i.e., simplicity.[6] Dickinson's and Wylie's bare-bones poetry, Thomson's naked, diatonic chords, Weisgall's breathtakingly brief settings of Crapsey's laments—all these are representative of what seems to be a national artistic urge to cut away the dead wood, as it were, and get to the heart of the matter. Not surprisingly, it is this very quest that brings us to the third characteristic.

Americans, in our origins, are the sons and daughters of rebels, pioneers, and adventurers. With the crossing of the seas, the old order has been abandoned and the struggle becomes a search toward a new order. Although he virtually exterminates the Native American, the new immigrant absorbs his intoxication with the land and the spirit indwelling in the land, and it could almost be said that Transcendentalism is the Indian heritage passed through the New England intellectual tradition.

The new order, then, toward which America's artists are groping in the nineteenth, twentieth, and twenty-first centuries is an inward construct of the mind and spirit. Cut off from the geographical mother country, the American must find his roots in a spiritual grasp of the universal order, and must find a framework that can support the successive horrors of the Civil War and the more recent global catastrophes.

The search for this spiritual order runs through the American art song like a silver thread. Bowles and Tennessee Williams give us a simple, folk-like solution in "Heavenly Grass"; Rorem and Roethke portray the Oriental path of mystic union with the Absolute in "Memory"; and in "Sure On This Shining Night," Barber and Agee define the quest in terms of the Romantic, "wandering far alone" and weeping for wonder at a Beauty which he cannot name. The poetic tradition of pre-occupation with the spiritual order derives from Emerson and is upheld by Whitman, Dickinson, Frost, Stevens, and Roethke, to name only the major protagonists. An impressive number of the composers of this study have been inspired by poetic accounts of this journey, and have added their individual musical perceptions to the lining out of its tortuous but luminous path.

* * *

America has come of age in the art song, it has produced a veritable chorus of voices in its maturity, and the new century continues to advance. We contemplate with gratitude the riches of the past, and eagerly await the future.

Notes

1. Wallace Stegner quoted in Pete Hamil, "All Need What's Left," *San Antonio Express*, 14 October 1981.
2. See Irving Howe, "The American Voice—It Begins on a Note of Wonder," *The New York Times Book Review*, 4 July 1976.
3. See Introduction.
4. See chapter 10.
5. See chapter 11.
6. See remarks by John Corigliano, chapter 11.

Selected Bibliography

Bibliographic Tools

American National Biography. New York: Oxford University Press, 1999.

Anderson, Elliott, and Mary Kinzie. *The Little Magazine in America: A Modern Documentary History.* Yonkers, N.Y.: Pushcart Press, 1978.

Carman, Judith, et al. *Art Song in the United States: An Annotated Bibliography.* Iowa City: University of Iowa: National Association of Teachers of Singing, 1976.

————. *Art Song in the United States: An Annotated Bibliography, First Supplement.* Iowa City, Ia.: University of Iowa: National Association of Teachers of Singing, 1978.

Dictionary Catalog of the Music Collection. New York: New York Public Library.

Dissertation Abstracts International. Ann Arbor, Mich.: University Microfilms, 1938–.

Granger, Edith, ed. *Index to Poetry and Recitations.* Chicago: A. C. McClurg and Co., 1918 (and supplements).

Jackson, Richard. *United States Music, Sources of Bibliography and Collective Bibliography.* Brooklyn, N.Y.: Institute for Studies in American Music, 1976.

Krummel, Donald W., Dyen, Doris J., and Root, Deanne L., eds. *Resources of American Music History.* Urbana: University of Illinois Press, 1981.

Mead, Rita. *Doctoral Dissertations in American Music, A Classified Bibliography.* Brooklyn, N.Y.: Institute for Studies in American Music, 1974.

Music Index. Annual Index to articles on music in various periodicals, 1949–.

Nicely, Tom. *Adam and his Work, a Paul Goodman Bibliography.* Metuchen, N.J.: Scarecrow Press, 1979.

Oja, Carol J., ed. *American Music Recordings: A Discography of 20th-Century U.S. Composers.* Brooklyn, N.Y.: Institute for Studies in American Music, 1982.

Sadie, Stanley, ed. *The New Grove Dictionary of Music and Musicians.* London: Macmillan, 1980 and 2001.

Slonimsky, Nicholas, and Laura Kuhn, eds. *Baker's Biographical Dictionary of Musicians.* New York: Schirmer Books, 2001.

American Music

Anderson, E. Ruth. *Contemporary American Composers.* Boston: G.K. Holland, 1976.

Barber, Samuel. "On Waiting for a Libretto." *Opera News* 20, no. 13 (27 January 1958): 4–6.

Beeson, Jack. "Grand and Not So Grand." *Opera News* 27, no. 9 (5 January 1963): 8–13.

Bloch, Adrienne Fried, and Carol Neuls-Bates, eds. *Women in American Music.* Westport, Conn.: Greenwood Press, 1979.

Chase, Gilbert. *America's Music.* New York: McGraw-Hill, 1966.

Dello Joio, Norman. "The Composer and the American Scene." *Music Journal* 22 (March 1964): 31–32.

———. "The Quality of Music." *Music Educators' Journal* 48, no. 5 (1965): 33–35.

———. "The Contemporary Music Project for Creativity in Music Education." *Music Educators' Journal* 54 (March 1968): 4–72.

Ewen, David. *American Composers*. New York: G.P. Putnam, 1982.

Finney, Ross Lee. "Analysis and the Creative Process." *Scripps College Bulletin* 33, no. 2 (February 1959): 1–17.

———. "Employ the Composer." *American Music Teacher* 11, no. 22 (1961): 8–9.

———. "Theory in a Period of Change." *American Music Teacher* 15, no. 2 (1967): 22–23.

Flanagan, William. "The Riotous Garden of American Opera." *High Fidelity* 8 (November 1958): 42–44.

———. "How to Succeed in Composing without Really Succeeding." *Bulletin of the American Composers' Alliance* 11, no. 1 (1963): 6–8.

Gagne, Cole, and Tracy Caras. *Soundpieces: Interviews with American Composers*. Metuchen, N.J.: Scarecrow Press, 1982.

Gruen, John. *The Party's Over*. New York: Viking, 1972.

Hitchcock, H. Wiley. *Music in the United States: A Historical Introduction*. Englewood Cliffs, N.J.: Prentice-Hall, 1969.

Howard, John Tasker. *Our American Music*. New York: Crowell, 1965.

Ivey, Jean Eichelberger. "The Contemporary Performing Ensemble." *College Music Symposium* 8 (Fall 1968): 120–28.

———. "Electronic Music Workshop for Teachers." *Music Educators' Journal* 55 (November 1968): 91–93.

———. "The Composer as Teacher." *Peabody Conservatory Alumni Bulletin* 14, no. 1 (Fall/Winter 1974).

Kagen, Sergius. "The Teaching of Carl Friedberg." *Juilliard Review* 4 (Winter 1956–57): 28–32.

———. "Training Accompanists at Juilliard." *Juilliard Review* 7, no.1 (1959–60): 5.

———. "Mack Harrell." *Juilliard Review* 7, no. 2 (1960): 15.

Larsen, Arved M. "The Contemporary Woman Composer." *Pan Pipes* 68, no. 1 (November 1975): 2.

Marrocco, W. Thomas, and Harold Gleason. *Music in America*. New York: W. W. Norton, 1964.

Owen, Lynn. "Wife, Mother, Opera Singer." *Music Journal* 25, no. 36 (April 1967).

Page, Tim. "Music-Debuts in Review." *The New York Times*, Sunday, April 8, 1984.

Persichetti, Vincent. *Twentieth Century Harmony*. New York: Norton, 1961.

Rosenfeld, Paul. *An Hour with American Music*. Philadelphia: Lippincott, 1929.

Southgate, Harvey. "Rochester Report: Artistic Climate Revamped." *High Fidelity/Musical America* 16 (March 1966): 133.

Thomson, Virgil. *The Art of Judging Music*. New York: Knopf, 1948.

———. *American Music since 1910*. New York: Holt, Rinehart and Winston, 1971.

Weisgall, Hugo. "The 201st Quarterly." *Perspectives of New Music* 3, no. 2 (1965): 133–36.

American Art Song

Ardoin, John. "Rorem-Flanagan Concert." *Musical America* 82, no. 37 (May 1962).

Bloomquist, Marvin Robert. "The Songs of Ned Rorem." Kansas City: University of Missouri Dissertation, 1970.

Finck, Henry T. *Songs and Song Writers*. New York: Scribner's, 1900.

Flanagan, William. "American Songs: A Thin Crop." *Musical America* 72 (February 1952): 23.

Friedberg, Ruth C. "The Songs of John Duke." *NATS Bulletin* 19, no.4 (May 1963): 8–13.

———. "Six Poems of Emily Dickinson" (review). *NATS Bulletin* 35, no.3 (Jan/Feb 1979): 38–39.

———. "The Recent Songs of John Duke." *NATS Bulletin* 36, no.1 (Sept/Oct 1979): 31–36.

———. *American Art Song and American Poetry, Vols. I, II, and III*. Metuchen, N.J.: Scarecrow Press, 1981, 1984, 1987.

———. "Three Poems by Mark Van Doren" (review). *NATS Bulletin* 39, no.3 (Jan/Feb, 1983): 36–37.

Hall, James Husst. *The Art Song*. Norman: University of Oklahoma Press, 1953.

Kagen, Sergius. "The American Concert Song." *Juilliard Review* 1 (Fall 1954): 11–16.

Middaugh, Bennie. "The Songs of Ned Rorem." *NATS Bulletin* 24 (May 1968): 36–39.

Miller, Phillip L. "The Songs of Ned Rorem." *Tempo* 127 (December 1978): 25–31.

Nathan, Hans. "The Modern Period—United States of America." in *A History of Song*, ed. Denis Stevens. New York: Norton, 1960.

Rorem, Ned. "Music for the Mouth." in *Music from Inside Out*. New York: George Braziller, 1967.
———. "The American Art Song." in *Setting the Tone*. New York: Coward-McCann, 1983.
Upton, William Treat. *Art Song in America*. New York: Ditson, 1930 (Johnson Reprint Corp., 1969).
Woods, Billy Jon. "The Songs of Sergius Kagen." *NATS Bulletin* 27, no. 3: 24–25.
Yerbury, Grace D. *Song in America from Early Times to about 1850*. Metuchen, N.J.: Scarecrow Press, 1971.

Composers

Albee, Edward. "William Flanagan." *Bulletin of the American Composers' Alliance* 9, no. 4 (1961): 12.
Anderson, Donna K. "The Works of Charles Griffes: A Descriptive Catalog." Ann Arbor: University of Michigan Dissertation, 1966.
———. *Charles T. Griffes: An Annotated Bibliography-Discography*. Detroit: College Music Society, 1977.
———. *Charles T. Griffes: A Life in Music*. Washington, D.C.: Smithsonian Institution Press, 1993.
Anderson, E. Ruth, comp. *Contemporary American Composers*. Boston: G. K. Hall, 1976.
Arvey, Verna. *In One Lifetime*. Fayetteville: The University of Arkansas Press, 1984.
Bacon, Ernst. *Words on Music*. Westport, Conn.: Greenwood Press, 1973 (originally published by Syracuse University Press, 1960).
Bauer, Marion. "Charles Griffes as I Remember Him." *Musical Quarterly* 29 (July 1943): 355–80.
Beeson, Jack. "In Memoriam: Douglas Moore." *Perspectives of New Music* 8 (Fall/Winter 1960): 158–60.
———. "Virgil Thomson's Aeneid (The Operas)." *Parnassus* 5, no. 2 (Spring/Summer 1977): 457–78.
Bellaman, Henry. "Charles Ives: The Man and his Music." *Musical Quarterly* 19, no.1 (January 1933): 45–58.
Bischoff, Simon, ed. *Paul Bowles Photographs*. New York: Scalo Publishers, 1994.
Block, Geoffrey. *Charles Ives: A Bio-Bibliography*. Westport, Conn.: Greenwood Press, 1988.
Block, Maxine, ed.. *Current Biography*. New York: H. H. Wilson, 1940.
Boretz, Benjamin, and Edward Cone, eds. *Perspectives on American Composers*. New York: Norton, 1971.
Bowles, Paul. *Without Stopping*. New York: Putnam, 1972.
Broder, Nathan. *Samuel Barber*. New York: G. Schirmer, 1954.
Caponi, Gena Dagel, ed. *Conversations with Paul Bowles*. Jackson: University Press of Mississippi, 1994.
Carter, Elliott. "Ives Today: His Vision and Challenge." *Musical Quarterly* 21, no. 4 (May/June 1944): 199–202.
Chase, Gilbert, ed. *The American Composer Speaks*. Baton Rouge, La: State University Press, 1966.
Cooper, Paul. "The Music of Ross Lee Finney." *The Musical Quarterly* 53, no.1 (January 1967): 1–21.
Copland, Aaron. *The New Music*. New York: Norton, 1968.
———. *Music and the Imagination*. Cambridge, Mass.: Harvard University Press, 1966.
Cowell, Henry, and Sidney Cowell. *Charles Ives and His Music*. New York: Oxford University Press, 1969.
Dabrishus-Quin-Still, contributors. *William Grant Still: A Bio-Bibliography*. Santa Barbara, Calif.: Greenwood Press, 1996.
Diamond, David. "Integrity and Integration in Contemporary Music." in *The Alice and Frederick Slee Lectures*. University of Buffalo, New York, Spring 1961.
———. "From the Notebook of David Diamond." *Music Journal* 22 (April 1964): 24–25.
Downes, Edward. "The Music of Norman Dello Joio." *The Musical Quarterly* 48, no. 2 (April 1962): 149–72.
Eaton, Quaintance. "Beeson on Camera." *Opera News* 24, no. 13 (21 May 1970).
Engel, Carl. "Charles Martin Loeffler." *Musical Quarterly* 2, no.3 (July 1925): 320 ff.
Evett, Robert. "The Music of Vincent Persichetti." *The Juilliard Review* 11, no. 2 (Spring 1955): 15–20.
Ewen, David. *Composers since 1900*. New York: H.W. Wilson, 1969.
———. *Composers since 1900, First Supplement*. New York: H.W. Wilson, 1981.
Finn, Robert. "Richard Hundley, Non-Conformist." *The (Cleveland) Plain Dealer*. June 3, 1983.
———. "Season Finale." *The (Cleveland) Plain Dealer*. May 16, 1985.
Flanagan, William. "American Songs: A Thin Crop." *Musical Quarterly* 72 (February 1952): 23 ff.
———. "My Ten Favorite Composers." *HiFi/Stereo Review* 19 (September 1967): 68–69.
———. "Ten Composers I Hate." *HiFi/Stereo Review*, 19 (October 1967): 89.
Friedberg, Ruth C. and Robin Fisher, eds. *The Selected Writings of John Duke: 1917–1984*. Lanham, Md.: Scarecrow Press, 2007.

Garland, Peter. "Paul Bowles and the Baptism of Solitude." in *Americas: Essays on American Music and Culture (1973–80)*. Santa Fe, N.M.: Soundings Press, 1982.

Gilman, Lawrence. *Edward MacDowell: A Study*. New York: Da Capo Press Reprint Series, 1969.

Glanville-Hicks, Peggy. "Paul Bowles-American Composer." *Music and Letters* 26, no. 2 (April 1945): 88–96.

Goss, Madeleine. *Modern Music-Makers*. New York: Dutton, 1952.

Haas, Robert Bartlett, ed. *William Grant Still and the Fusion of Cultures in American Music*. Los Angeles: Black Sparrow Press, 1972.

Harris, Roy, et al. *The Bases of Artistic Creation*. New Brunswick, N.J.: Rutgers University Press, 1942.

Hill, Edwin Burlingame. "Charles Martin Loeffler." *Modern Music* 13, no.1 (November–December 1935): 26–31.

Hitchcock, H. Wiley. *Ives*. New York: Oxford University Press, 1977.

———. "Editing Ives' 120 Songs." in *Ives Studies*, edited by Philip Lambert. New York: Cambridge University Press, 1997.

Hoffman, William. "John Corigliano on Cracking the Establishment." *The Village Voice*, 21 February 1977.

Holms, James. "Ned Rorem." Vol. 16, *The New Grove Dictionary of Music and Musicians*. London: Macmillan, 1980. 190–91.

Hoover, Kathleen, and John Cage. *Virgil Thomson, His Life and Music*. Freeport, N.Y.: Books for Libraries Press, 1959.

Ives, Charles. "Essays before a Sonata" reprinted in *Three Classics in the Aesthetic of Music*. New York: Dover, 1962.

Kagen, Sergius. *On Studying Singing*. New York: Dover, 1960.

———. *Music for the Voice*. Bloomington: Indiana University Press, 1968.

Kerman, Joseph. "American Music: The Columbia Series (II)." *The Hudson Review* 13 (1961): 408 ff.

Kimberling, Victoria. *David Diamond: a Bio-Bibliography*. Metuchen, N.J.: Scarecrow Press, 1980.

Kirkpatrick, John. *Charles E. Ives—Memos*. New York: Norton, 1972.

Kolodin, Irvin. "Farewell to Capricorn." *Saturday Review/World* 1 (1 June 1974): 44–45.

LePage, Jane Weiner. *Women Composers, Conductors and Musicians of the Twentieth Century*. Metuchen, N.J.: Scarecrow Press,1980.

Levy, Alan. *Edward MacDowell: An American Master*. Lanham, Md: Scarecrow Press,1998.

Livingston, Carolyn Lambeth. *The Songs of Charles T. Griffes*. Master's Thesis, Department of Music, University of North Carolina, 1947.

MacDowell, Edward. *Critical and Historical Essays*, edited by W. J. Baltzell. Boston: Stanhope Publishing, 1912.

Maisel, Edward M. *Charles T. Griffes*. New York: Knopf, 1943.

Mason, Daniel Gregory. *Contemporary Composers*. New York: Macmillan, 1918.

Miller, Jeffrey, ed. *The Letters of Paul Bowles*. New York: Farrar, Straus, and Giroux, 1994.

Neubert, Colleen Gray. "Lee Hoiby: His Life, His Vocal Writing Style and an Annotation of Selected Songs for High Voice with Performance Considerations." Morgantown, University of West Virginia Dissertation, 2003.

Owen, Richard. "Husband, Father, Attorney, Composer." *Music Journal* 25, no. 37 (April 1967).

Page, Robert. "In Quest of Answers—an Interview with Vincent Persichetti." *Choral Journal* 14, no. 3 (November 1973): 5–7.

Peabody News, "Jean Eichelberger Ivey—a Retrospective." July 1983.

Peabody Notes, Obituary: Mary Howe. Vol. 18, no. 2 (Winter, 1965).

Perlis, Vivian. *Charles Ives Remembered (an Oral History)*. New Haven, Conn.: Yale University Press, 1974.

Perry, Rosalie Sandra. *Charles Ives and the American Mind*. Kent, Ohio: Kent State University Press, 1974.

Pollack, Howard. *Aaron Copland: The Life and Work of an Uncommon Man*. New York: Henry Holt, 1999.

Reilly, Peter. "William Flanagan." *Stereo Review* 21, no. 5 (November 1968): 134.

Rorem, Ned. "(William Flanagan) . . . and His Music." *Bulletin of the American Composers' Alliance* 9, no. 4 (1961): 13–19.

———. *The Paris Diary*. New York: George Braziller, 1966.

———. *The New York Diary*. New York: George Braziller, 1967.

———. *Music from Inside Out*. New York: George Braziller, 1967.

———. *Music and People*. New York: George Braziller, 1968.

———. *Critical Affairs*. New York: George Braziller, 1970.

———. *The Final Diary*. New York: Holt, Rinehart and Winston, 1974. Reprinted by North Point Press as *The Later Diaries*.

———. *Pure Contraption*. New York: Holt, Rinehart and Winston, 1974.

———. *An Absolute Gift*. New York: Simon and Schuster, 1978.

———. "Interview." *NATS Bulletin* 29, no. 2 (1982): 5ff.

———. *Setting the Tone*. New York: Coward-McCann, 1983.

———. *Settling the Score*. Orlando, Fl.: Harcourt Brace, 1988.

———. *The Nantucket Diary*. Northpoint Press, 1989.

———. *Knowing When to Stop*. New York: Simon and Schuster, 1994.

———. *Other Entertainment: Collected Pieces*. New York: Simon and Schuster, 1996.

———. *Lies: A Diary*. New York: Counterpoint Press, 2002.

———. *Wings of Friendship: Selected Letters 1944–2003*. New York: Counterpoint Press, 2005.

———. *Facing the Night: A Diary and Musical Writings*. New York: Counterpoint Press, 2006.

Saylor, Bruce. "The Music of Hugo Weisgall." *Musical Quarterly* 59, no. 2 (1973): 239–62.

Scherman, Thomas. "Douglas Moore, the Optimistic Conservative." *Music Journal* 27 (October 1969): 24–25.

Schlegel, Ellen Grolman. *Emma Lou Diemer: A Bio-Bibliography*. Santa Barbara: Greenwood Press, 2001.

Schumann, William. "The Compleat Musician: Vincent Persichetti and Twentieth Century Harmony." *Musical Quarterly* 47, no. 3 (July 1961): 379–85.

Slonimsky, Nicholas, ed. *Baker's Biographical Dictionary of Musicians*. New York: Schirmer Books, 1978.

Thomson, Virgil. *Virgil Thomson*. New York: Knopf, 1967.

Trimble, Lester. "William Flanagan (1923–1969)." *Stereo Review* 23, no. 118 (November 1968).

Waldrop, G. W. "Winter Colonists at the MacDowell Colony." *Musical Courier* 153 (15 January 1956): 26.

Woods, Billy Jon. "Sergius Kagen: His Life and Works." Nashville: George Peabody College for Teachers Dissertation, 1969.

Poets and Poetry

Agee, James. *Permit Me Voyage*. New Haven, Conn.: Yale University Press, 1934.

———. *Letters of James Agee to Father Flye*. Boston: Houghton Mifflin, 1971.

Aiken, Conrad. *Nocturne of Remembered Spring and Other Poems*. Boston: The Four Seas Company, 1917.

Aldrich, Thomas Bailey. *The Poems, Volume I*. Boston and New York: Houghton Mifflin, 1930.

Alexander, Eleanor. *Lyrics of Sunshine and Shadow (the Tragic Courtship and Marriage of Paul Laurence Dunbar and Alice Ruth Moore—A History of Love and Violence among the African American Elite)*. New York: New York University Press, 2001.

Allen, Gay Wilson. *American Prosody*. New York: Octagon Books, 1966.

———. *Carl Sandburg*. Minneapolis: University of Minnesota Press, 1972.

———. *Walt Whitman Handbook*. New York: New York University Press, 1975.

Amacher, Richard E. *Edward Albee*. New York: Twayne, 1969.

Anderson, Charles R., ed. *Sidney Lanier, Poems and Poem Outlines*. Baltimore: Johns Hopkins Press, 1945.

Atkinson, Brooks, ed. *The Writings of Ralph Waldo Emerson*. New York: Modern Library, 1940.

Bassan, Maurice, ed. *Stephen Crane: a Collection of Critical Essays*. Englewood Cliffs, N.J.: Prentice-Hall, 1967.

Beckett, Lucy. *Wallace Stevens*. London: Cambridge University Press, 1974.

Benét, Stephen Vincent. *Selected Works*. New York: Farrar and Rinehart, 1942.

Berryman, John. *Stephen Crane*. New York: Octagon Books, 1975.

Bianchi, Martha Dickinson, and Alfred Leete Hampson, eds. *The Complete Poems of Emily Dickinson*. Boston: Little, Brown, 1937.

Bishop, Elizabeth. "Efforts of Affection: A Memoir of Marianne Moore." *Vanity Fair* 46, no. 4 (June, 1983): 44–61.

Blessing, Richard Allen. *Wallace Stevens' "Whole Harmonium."* Syracuse, N.Y.: Syracuse University Press, 1970.

Bogan, Louise. *The Blue Estuaries: Poems 1923–1968*. New York: Farrar, Straus and Giroux, 1968.

Bogan, Louise, and Ruth Limmer. *Journey Around My Room: The Autobiography of Louise Bogan*. New York: Viking Press, 1980.

Bontemps, Arna, ed. *American Negro Poetry*. New York: Hill and Wang, 1963.

Bowers, Neil. *Theodore Roethke*. Columbia: University of Missouri Press, 1982.

Brittin, Norman A. *Edna St. Vincent Millay*. New York: Twayne, 1967.

Butscher, Edward. *Adelaide Crapsey*. Boston: Twayne, 1979.

Buttel, Robert. *Wallace Stevens: The Making of Harmonium*. Princeton, N.J.: Princeton University Press, 1967.

Cady, Edwin H. *Stephen Crane*. Boston: Twayne, 1962.

Capouya, Emile. "The Poet as Prophet." *Parnassus* 3, no. 1 (1974): 23–30.

Cather, Willa. *April Twilights, 1903*. Lincoln: University of Nebraska Press, 1962.

———. *Early Stories*. New York: Dodd, Mead and Co., 1957. Introduction by Mildred R. Bennett.

———. *My Ántonia*. New York: Oxford University Press, 2006. Introduction by Janet Sharistanian.

Chase, Richard, ed. *Melville—A Collection of Critical Essays*. Englewood Cliffs, N.J.: Prentice-Hall, 1963.

Chénetier, Marc, ed. *Letters of Vachel Lindsay*. New York: B. Franklin, 1978.

Colum, Mary. *Life and the Dream*. Garden City, N.Y.: Doubleday, 1947.

Cooper, James Fenimore, Jr. *Afterglow*. New Haven, Conn.: Yale University Press, 1918.

Cowley, Malcolm. "The Case against Mr. Frost." in *Robert Frost, A Collection of Critical Essays*, edited by James M. Cox. Englewood Cliffs, N.J.: Prentice-Hall, 1962.

Crapsey, Adelaide. *Verse*. New York: Knopf, 1922.

Crawley, Thomas. *The Structure of "Leaves of Grass."* Austin: The University of Texas Press, 1970.

Cullen, Countee. *On These I Stand (An Anthology of the Best Poems)*. New York: Harper and Row, 1947.

cummings, e.e. *Complete Poems*. New York: Harcourt, Brace, Jovanovich, 1972.

Deutsch, Babette. *Poetry in Our Time*. Garden City, N.Y.: Doubleday, 1963.

Dickinson, Emily. *The Complete Poems*, edited by Thomas H. Johnson. Boston: Little, Brown, 1960.

Doty, Mark A. *Tell Me Who I Am*. Baton Rouge: Louisiana State University Press, 1981.

Drake, William. *Sara Teasdale, Woman and Poet*. San Francisco: Harper and Row, 1979.

Dunbar, Paul Laurence. *Complete Poems, with the Introduction to "Lyrics of Lowly Life" by W. D. Howells*. New York: Dodd, Mead, 1970.

Eliot, T. S. *The Music of Poetry*. Glasgow: Jackson, Son and Co., 1942.

Ellmann, Richard, and Robert O'Clair, eds. *The Norton Anthology of Modern Poetry*. New York: W. W. Norton, 1973.

Emerson, Ralph Waldo. *Poems*. Cambridge, Mass.: Riverside Press, 1895.

Engel, Bernard F. *Marianne Moore*. New York: Twayne, 1964.

Falk, Signi. *Tennessee Williams*. Boston: Twayne, 1978.

Fitzgerald, Robert, ed. *The Collected Short Prose of James Agee*. Boston: Houghton Mifflin, 1958.

Franchere, Hoyt C. *Edwin Arlington Robinson*. New York: Twayne, 1968.

Franklin, Benjamin. *The Sayings of Poor Richard,* collected and edited by Paul Leicester Ford. New York: The Knickerbocker Press, 1890.

Friedman, Norman. *e.e. cummings: The Art of His Poetry*. Baltimore: Johns Hopkins Press, 1960.

———. *e.e. cummings, The Growth of a Writer*. Carbondale: Southern Illinois University Press, 1964.

Frost, Robert. *Complete Poems*. New York: Holt, Rinehart and Winston, 1962.

Funnell, Bertha H. *Walt Whitman on Long Island*. Port Washington, N.Y.: Kennikat Press, 1971.

Fussell, Paul, Jr. *Poetic Meter and Poetic Form*. New York: Random House, 1907.

Gerber, Philip L. *Robert Frost*. Boston: Twayne, 1966.

———. *Willa Cather*. New York: Twayne Publishers, 1995.

Goodman, Paul. *Collected Poems*. New York: Random House, 1973.

Gould, Jean. *The Poet and Her Book: A Biography of Edna St. Vincent Millay*. New York: Dodd, Mead, 1969.

———. *Amy—The World of Amy Lowell and the Imagist Movement*. New York: Dodd, Mead, 1975.

Gray, Thomas. *Elinor Wylie*. New York: Twayne, 1969.

Gregory, Horace, and Marya Zaturenska. *A History of American Poetry, 1900–1940*. New York: Harcourt, Brace, 1942.

Hadas, Pamela White. *Marianne Moore*. Syracuse, N.Y.: Syracuse University Press, 1977.

Hart, James D. *The Oxford Companion to American Literature*. New York: Oxford University Press, 1948.

Hénault, Marie. *Peter Viereck*. New York: Twayne, 1969.

Herschberg, Max J. *The Reader's Encyclopedia of American Literature*. New York: Crowell, 1962.

Heyen, William, comp. *Profile of Theodore Roethke*. Columbus, Ohio: Charles Merrill, 1971.

Hine, Daryl and Joseph Parisi, eds. *The "Poetry" Anthology*. Boston: Houghton Mifflin, 1978.

Hoffman, Daniel. *The Poetry of Stephen Crane*. New York: Columbia University Press, 1956.

Hoffman, Frederick J., Charles Allen, and Carolyn F. Ulrich. *The Little Magazine*. Princeton, N.J.: Princeton University Press, 1947.

Hoffman, Frederick J. *Conrad Aiken*. New York: Twayne, 1962.

Holland, Lawrence B., ed. *The Norton Anthology of American Literature,* Vol. 2. New York: W. W. Norton, 1979.

Holmes, Oliver Wendell. *The Complete Poetical Works.* Boston: Houghton, Mifflin, 1895.

Howells, William Dean. *Poems.* Boston: Ticknor, 1886.

Hughes, Langston. *Collected Poems.* New York: Knopf, 1969.

Johnson, Thomas H., ed. *The Poems of Emily Dickinson.* Cambridge, Mass.: Belknap Press of Harvard University Press, 1958.

———. *Complete Poems of Emily Dickinson.* Boston: Little, Brown, 1960.

Kalem, T. E. "The Laureate of the Out cast." *Time,* 7 March 1983: 88.

Katz, Joseph, ed. *The Poems of Stephen Crane.* New York: Cooper Square Publishers, 1971.

Kennedy, Richard S. *Dreams in the Mirror: A Biography of e.e. cummings.* New York: Liveright, 1980.

Kunitz, Stanley, and Howard Haycraft, eds. *Twentieth Century Authors.* New York: H. W. Wilson, 1942.

Kunitz, Stanley, ed. *Twentieth Century Authors, First Supplement.* New York: H. W. Wilson, 1961.

Lanier, Sidney. *The Science of English Verse.* New York: Scribner's, 1893.

Lawson, Victor. *Dunbar Critically Examined.* Washington, D.C.: Associated Publishers, 1941.

Lazarus, Emma. *Selected Poems.* New York: Library of America, 2005.

Lindsay, Nicholas Vachel. *Collected Poems.* New York: Macmillan, 1925.

Litz, A. Walton. *Introspective Voyager.* New York: Oxford University Press, 1972.

Londré, Felicia Hardison. *Tennessee Williams.* New York: Frederick Ungar, 1979.

Longfellow, Henry Wadsworth. *Poems, Volume III.* Boston: Houghton Mifflin, 1910.

Lowell, Amy. *The Complete Poetical Works.* Boston: Houghton, Mifflin, 1955.

Macdonald, Dwight. "Death of a Poet." *New Yorker* 33 (16 November 1957): 38.

Mariani, Paul. *William Carlos Williams.* New York: McGraw-Hill, 1981.

Marks, Barry. *A. e.e. cummings.* New York: Twayne, 1964.

Martin, Jay. *Conrad Aiken: A Life of His Art.* Princeton, N.J.: Princeton University Press, 1962.

Massa, Ann. *Vachel Lindsay: Fieldworker for the American Dream.* Bloomington: Indiana University Press, 1970.

Melville, Herman. *Billy Budd, Benito Cereno and The Enchanted Isles,* foreword by Carl Van Doren. New York: Readers' Club, 1942.

———. *Works* (Vol. 16, *Poems*). New York: Russell and Russell, 1963.

Meredith, Robert. "Everywhere a Single Voice." *Poetry* 128, no. 2 (1976): 100–105.

Merton, Thomas. *The Seven Storey Mountain.* New York: Harcourt, Brace, 1948.

Millay, Edna St. Vincent. *Collected Poems.* New York: Harper and Row, 1956.

Miller Jr., James E. *Walt Whitman.* New York: Twayne, 1962.

Millett, Fred B. *Contemporary American Authors: A Critical Survey.* New York: AMS Press, 1970 (Reprinted from 1940 edition: Harcourt, Brace and World).

Moore, Marianne. *Tell Me, Tell Me.* New York: Viking, 1966.

Moreau, Genevieve. *The Restless Journey of James Agee.* New York: William Morrow, 1977.

Morgan, Richard G., ed. *Kenneth Patchen: A Collection of Essays.* New York: AMS Press, 1977.

Moritz, Charles, ed. *Current Biography.* New York: H. W. Wilson, 1968.

Moss, Howard. *Writing Against Time, Critical Essays and Reviews.* New York: William Morrow, 1969.

Murphy, Frances and Hershel Parker, eds. *The Norton Anthology of American Literature,* Volume 1. New York: Norton, 1979.

Nasso, Christine, ed. *Contemporary Authors.* Detroit: Gale, 1978.

Nitchie, George W. *Marianne Moore: An Introduction to the Poetry.* New York: Columbia University Press, 1969.

Norman, Charles. *e.e. cummings, The Magic Maker.* New York: Duell, Sloan and Pearce, 1964.

Ohlin, Peter H. *Agee.* New York: Ivan Obolensky, 1966.

Olson, Stanley. *Elinor Wylie: A Life Apart.* New York: Dial, 1979.

Ostriker, Alicia. "Paul Goodman." *Partisan Review* 43, no. 2 (1976): 286ff.

Parker, Dorothy. *The Portable Dorothy Parker.* New York: Viking Press, 1944.

Patchen, Kenneth. *When We Were Here Together.* New York: New Directions, 1957.

———. *The Love Poems.* San Francisco: City Lights, 1966.

———. *Collected Poems.* New York: New Directions, 1968.

Perry, Margaret. *A Bio-Bibliography of Countee P. Cullen.* Westport, Conn.: Greenwood, 1971.

Pound, Ezra. *Collected Early Poems.* Introduction by Louis L. Mortz. New York: New Directions, 1976.

Prokosch, Frederic. *Chosen Poems*. Garden City, N.Y.: Doubleday, 1948.

Purdy, James. *An Oyster Is a Wealthy Beast*. Los Angeles: Black Sparrow Press, 1967.

———. *Mr. Evening and Nine Poems*. Los Angeles: Black Sparrow Press, 1968.

———. *The Running Sun*. New York: Paul Waner Press, 1971.

———. *Collected Poems*. Amsterdam: Athenaeum-Polak and Van Genned, 1992.

Revell, Peter. *Paul Laurence Dunbar*. Boston: Twayne, 1979.

Riddel, Joseph N. *The Clairvoyant Eye*. Baton Rouge: Louisiana State University Press, 1965.

Ridgeway, Jaqueline. *Louise Bogan*. Boston: Twayne Publishers, 1984.

Robinson, Edwin Arlington. *Collected Poems*. New York: Macmillan, 1922.

Robinson, W. R. *Edwin Arlington Robinson. A Poetry of the Act*. Cleveland: Press of Western Reserve University, 1967.

Roethke, Theodore. *Collected Poems*. Garden City, N.Y.: Doubleday, 1966.

Sandburg, Carl. *Chicago Poems*. New York: Holt, 1916.

———. *Good Morning, America*. New York: Harcourt, Brace, 1928.

Sanders, G. D., and J. H. Nelson, eds. *Chief Modern Poets of England and America*. New York: Macmillan, 1929.

Schor, Esther. *Emma Lazarus*. New York: Schocken, 2006.

Schreiber, Ron, ed. *31 New American Poets*. New York: Hill and Wang, 1969.

Seaver, Edwin, ed. *Cross-Section, 1945–1948*. Nendeln, Liechtenstein: Kraus Reprint, 1969.

Sewall, Richard B., ed. *Emily Dickinson, A Collection of Critical Essays*. Englewood Cliffs, N.J.: Prentice-Hall, 1963.

———. *The Lyman Letters—New Light on Emily Dickinson and her Family*. Amherst: University of Massachusetts Press, 1965.

———. *The Life of Emily Dickinson*. New York: Farrar, Straus and Giroux, 1974.

Smith, Susan Sutton, ed. *The Complete Poems and Collected Letters of Adelaide Crapsey,* Albany: State University of New York Press, 1977.

Spiller, Robert E., Willard Thorpe, Thomas J. Johnson, Henry Seidel Canby, and Richard M. Ludwig, eds. *Literary History of the United States*. New York: Macmillan, 1963.

Sprague, Charles. *The Poetical and Prose Writings*. Boston: A. Williams, 1876.

Squires, Radcliffe. *Frederic Prokosch*. New York: Twayne, 1964.

Stein, William Bysshe. *The Poetry of Melville's Later Years*. Albany: State University of New York Press, 1970.

Stephenson, Nathaniel Wright, comp. *An Autobiography of Abraham Lincoln*. Indianapolis, Ind. Bobbs-Merrill, 1926.

Stevens, Wallace. *The Collected Poems*. New York: Knopf, 1955.

Stovall, Floyd, ed. *The Poems of Edgar Allan Poe*. Charlottesville: University Press of Virginia, 1965.

Tabb, John Bannister. *The Poetry of Father Tabb* (ed. Francis A. Litz). New York: Dodd, Mead, 1928.

Tanner, Tony. "Bird Song." Partisan Review 39 (Fall 1972).

Teasdale, Sara. *Collected Poems*. New York: Macmillan, 1966.

Thoreau, Henry David. *Walden*. New York: Harper and Row, 1965.

Untermeyer, Louis. "The Swimmers." *The Yale Review* 4, no. 4 (July 1915): 786–87.

———, ed. *Modern American Poetry*. New York: Harcourt, Brace and World, 1969.

Valéry, Paul. *The Art of Poetry*. New York: Vintage, 1961.

Van Doren, Carl. *Benjamin Franklin*. New York: Viking, 1938.

Van Doren, Mark. *The Autobiography of Mark Van Doren*. New York: Harcourt, Brace, 1958.

———. *Collected and New Poems*. New York: Hill and Wang, 1963.

———. *That Shining Place*. New York: Hill and Wang, 1969.

Viereck, Peter. *New and Selected Poems, 1932–1967*. New York: Bobbs-Merrill, 1967.

Vincent, Howard P. *Collected Poems of Herman Melville*. Chicago: Packard, 1947.

Vinson, James, ed. *Contemporary Novelists*, 2nd edition. New York: St. Martin's, 1976.

———, ed. *Great Writers of the English Language: Novelists*. New York: St. Martin's, 1979.

———, ed. *Great Writers of the English Language: Poets*. New York: St. Martin's, 1979.

Waggoner, Hyatt H. *American Poets from the Puritans to the Present*. New York: Dell Publishing, 1968.

Wakeman, John. *World Authors, 1950–1970*. New York: H.W. Wilson, 1975.

Warren, Austin. "Emily Dickinson." in *A Collection of Critical Essays*, edited by Richard B. Sewall. Englewood Cliffs, N.J.: Prentice-Hall, 1963.

West, Rebecca, ed. *Selected Poems of Carl Sandburg*. New York: Harcourt, Brace and World, 1926.

Whitman, Walt. *Leaves of Grass: the First Edition*, edited by Malcolm Cowley. New York: Viking Press, 1960.

———. *Complete Poetry and Selected Prose and Letters*. London: Nonesuch Press, 1967.

Whittier, John Greenleaf. *The Complete Poetical Works*. Boston: Houghton Mifflin, 1894.

Widmer, Kingsley. *Paul Goodman*. Boston: Twayne, 1980.

Wiggin, Kate Douglas, and Nora Archibald Smith, eds. *Golden Numbers*. New York: Doubleday, Doran, 1902.

Williams, Tennessee. *In the Winter of Cities*. Norfolk, Conn.: New Directions Books, 1956.

———. *Androgyne, Mon Amour*. New York: New Directions, 1977.

———. *Letters to Donald Windham, 1940–1965*, ed. Donald Windham. New York: Holt, Rinehart and Winston, 1977.

Williams, William Carlos. *Collected Poems*. New York: New Directions, 1962.

Wylie, Elinor. *Collected Poems*. New York: Knopf, 1932.

Young, B. R. *Emma Lazarus in Her World: Life and Letters*. Philadelphia: Jewish Publication Society of America, 1995.

Young, Stark. *The Pavilion*. New York: Scribner's, 1951.

Poetry and Song

Brown, Calvin S. *Music and Literature*. Athens: University of Georgia Press, 1948.

Castelnuovo-Tedesco, Mario. "Music and Poetry: Problems of a Songwriter." *The Musical Quarterly* 30, no. 1 (1944): 102–11.

Cooke, Deryck. *The Language of Music*. London: Oxford University Press, 1959.

Day-Lewis, C. *The Lyric Impulse*. Cambridge, Mass.: Harvard University Press, 1965.

Duke, John. "Some Reflections on the Art Song in English." *The American Music Teacher* 25, no. 4 (February/March 1976): 26.

———. "The Significance of Song." *Ars Lyrica* 1, no.1 (1981): 11–21.

Ferguson, Donald. *Music as Metaphor*. Minneapolis: University of Minnesota Press, 1960.

Friedberg, Ruth C. *American Art Song and American Poetry*, Vols. 1, 2, and 3. Metuchen, N.J.: Scarecrow Press, 1981, 1984, 1987.

Ivey, Donald. *Song: Anatomy, Imagery, and Style*. New York: Free Press, 1960.

Langer, Susanne. *Philosophy in a New Key*. Cambridge, Mass.: Harvard University Press, 1951.

———. *Feeling and Form*. New York: Scribner's, 1953.

———. *Problems of Art*. New York: Scribner's, 1957.

Perrins, Laurence. *Literature—Structure, Sound and Sense*. New York: Harcourt, Brace, and World, 1970.

Index

About the Authors

Ruth C. Friedberg has had a richly varied career as a performer, teacher, and writer. She was a member of the Duke University music faculty for twelve years and has also taught at the New School of Music in Philadelphia, the University of Texas at Austin and San Antonio, San Antonio College, and the University of the Incarnate Word. Friedberg has performed in concerts of chamber music and the vocal literature all over the United States as well as in Canada, Latin America, and Asia. During her tenure at Duke University, she recorded a two-volume series of LPs with tenor John Hanks called *Art Song in America*, which was originally published by Duke University Press and reissued by them on CD in 1998. After moving to Texas, she began a ten-year term as keyboard artist for the San Antonio Symphony.

In the 1980s, Friedberg completed the first edition of *American Art Song and American Poetry* (a three-volume work). She has also written many journal articles, reviews of new music publications, and entries in the Grove's dictionaries and *American National Biography*. Other recent publications are a collection of poetry titled *Coasts*; *The Complete Pianist: Body, Mind, Synthesis*; and the fifteen-volume series of *Art Songs by American Women Composers*, which Friedberg has collected and edited. Ruth Friedberg is widely in demand for her lecture recitals that combine her performing and academic interests. She has presented at the University of Michigan, University of Arkansas, Duke University, University of Calgary, Albright Institute in Jerusalem, Hong Kong Baptist College, and throughout Latin America.

An alumna of Smith College where she was elected to Phi Beta Kappa, **Robin Fisher** received both the Fulbright-Hayes scholarship and a Rotary Foundation Grant for studies abroad in music and European history. During the nine years she spent in Germany and Austria, she performed to critical acclaim in both concert and opera in such cities as Paris, Vienna, and Prague, and under contract with the Wuppertal Opera. Her teaching career began at Baylor University in 1994 where she was awarded several grants for research in the history of American art song. She completed doctoral studies at the University of Texas at Austin in 2001 with a dissertation about the writings and songs of John Duke. She is currently on faculty at California State University, Sacramento, as professor of voice, and she is an active performer in opera and concert.

This new edition of *American Art Song and American Poetry* is the second collaboration for the two authors. The first was *The Selected Writings of John Duke: 1917–1984*, published by Scarecrow Press in 2007.

CPSIA information can be obtained at www.ICGtesting.com
Printed in the USA
BVOW052310100612

292079BV00002B/5/P